Evolutionary Psychology

Evolutionary Psychology

Hans van de Braak

Erasmus University, Rotterdam

PEARSON

Harlow, England • London • New York • Boston • San Francisco • Toronto • Sydney
Auckland • Singapore • Hong Kong • Tokyo • Seoul • Taipei • New Delhi
Cape Town • São Paulo • Mexico City • Madrid • Amsterdam • Munich • Paris • Milan

Pearson Education Limited
Edinburgh Gate
Harlow
Essex CM20 2JE
England

and Associated Companies throughout the world

Visit us on the World Wide Web at:
www.pearson.com/uk

First published 2013 (print and electronic)

© Pearson Education Limited 2013 (print and electronic)

ISBN 978-0-273-73794-0 (print)
ISBN 978-0-273-73797-1 (ebook)
ISBN 978-0-273-78686-3 (cse text)

British Library Cataloging-in-Publication Data
A catalogue record for this book is available from the British Library

Library of Congress Cataloging-in-Publication Data
Braak, Hans van de, 1936-
  Evolutionary psychology / Hans van de Braak, Erasmus University, Rotterdam.
    pages cm
  Includes bibliographical references and index.
  ISBN 978-0-273-73794-0
  1. Evolutionary psychology.   I. Title.
  BF698.95.B73 2013
  155.7–dc23

                                                    2013000414

ARP Impression 98
Printed in Great Britain by Clays Ltd, St Ives plc
Typeset in 10/12 by 71

Brief contents

List of figures xi
Acknowledgements xv
Publisher's acknowledgements xvi
Introduction xxi
Timeline of evolutionary psychology xxv

Part 1 BASICS 1

1 The history of evolutionary psychology 2

2 Problems and solutions in evolution 34

3 The place of humans in evolution 55

Part 2 PROBLEMS 87

4 Males and females 88

5 Fathers, mothers and others 118

6 The evolution of social life 148

7 The origin and expression of emotions 175

8 Brain and cognition 205

9 The origins of language 234

10 Culture in evolution 261

Part 3 SPECIALS 287

11 The evolutionary paradox of mental illness 288

12 Evolution through development 315

Glossary 338
References 347
Index 379

Contents

List of figures   xi

Acknowledgements   xv

Publisher's acknowledgements   xvi

Introduction   xxi

Timeline of evolutionary psychology   xxv

Part 1 BASICS   1

1 The history of evolutionary psychology   2

Learning outcomes   2

1.1 Introduction   3

1.2 Emergence from three sciences   4

1.3 Biology   6

1.4 Psychology   16

1.5 Neuroscience   24

1.6 Summary   30

Study questions   31

Suggested reading   31

2 Problems and solutions in evolution   34

Learning outcomes   34

2.1 Introduction   35

2.2 Evolutionary approaches to problems   35

2.3 Genome, nervous system and culture as solutions   43

2.4 Levels of complexity   48

2.5 Replaying the tape of life   51

2.6 Summary   52

Study questions   53

Suggested reading   53

3 The place of humans in evolution   55

Learning outcomes   55

3.1 Introduction   56

3.2 The geological timescale   56

3.3 From the ladder of life to the tree of life   59

3.4 We are primates   66

3.5 What makes us human?   74

3.6 Summary   84

Study questions   84

Suggested reading   85

Part 2 PROBLEMS   87

4 Males and females   88

Learning outcomes   88

4.1 Introduction   89

4.2 The origin of sexual reproduction   89

4.3 The theory of sexual selection   91

4.4 Mating systems in human evolution   96

4.5 Mate preferences of men and women   102

4.6 Summary   115

Study questions   115

Suggested reading   116

5 Fathers, mothers and others   118

Learning outcomes   118

5.1 Introduction   119

5.2 Inbreeding avoidance   119

5.3 Origin of the human family   125

5.4 When mothers needed assistance   128

5.5 Parent–offspring conflict   138

5.6 Summary   144

Study questions   145

Suggested reading   146

6 The evolution of social life   148

Learning outcomes   148

6.1 Introduction   149

6.2 Why live socially?   149

6.3 The social evolution of primates   153

6.4 Solutions to the problem of cooperation   158

6.5 Cognitive capacities for cooperation   165

6.6 Summary   172

Study questions   173

Suggested reading   173

7 The origin and expression of emotions   175

Learning outcomes   175

7.1 Introduction   176

7.2 Why did emotions evolve?   176

7.3 Facial expressions in primates   184

7.4 The neural basis of emotions   187

7.5 The emergence of social emotions   195

7.6 Summary   202

Study questions   202

Suggested reading   203

8 Brain and cognition   205

Learning outcomes   205

8.1 Introduction   206

8.2 Evolution of the brain   206

8.3 Cognitive capacities in apes and corvids   216

8.4 Selection pressures for great ape cognition   221

8.5 Social cognition in chimpanzees and humans   226

8.6 Summary   230

Study questions   231

Suggested reading   231

9 The origins of language   234

Learning outcomes   234

9.1 Introduction   235

9.2 The origin of flexible communication   235

9.3 The gestural origin of language   240

9.4 The vocal origin of language   246

9.5 The cognitive origin of language   251

9.6 Summary   257

Study questions   258

Suggested reading   258

10 Culture in evolution   261

Learning outcomes   261

10.1 Introduction   262

10.2 What is culture?   262
10.3 Cultural inheritance   268
10.4 How culture is incorporated in evolutionary theory   273
10.5 Cumulative cultural evolution   280
10.6 Summary   283
Study questions   283
Suggested reading   284

Part 3 SPECIALS   **287**

11 The evolutionary paradox of mental illness   288
Learning outcomes   288
11.1 Introduction   289
11.2 Defining mental illness   289
11.3 Distinguishing normal responses from mental disorders   293
11.4 Explaining the adaptive function of mental illness   297
11.5 Summary   312
Study questions   312
Suggested reading   313

12 Evolution through development   315
Learning outcomes   315
12.1 Introduction   316
12.2 The rise of evo-devo   316
12.3 Types of developmental reorganisation   322
12.4 Why mammals play   327
12.5 How play evolved through development   332
12.6 Summary   335
Study questions   336
Suggested reading   336

Glossary   338
References   347
Index   379

Figures

1.1	Route of Darwin's five-year voyage	8
1.2	The components of evolutionary theory	10
1.3	The emergence, divergence and convergence of three sciences	16
1.4	The short and long pathways to the amygdala	27
1.5	Anomalocaris	30
2.1	Two parts of the human genome	44
2.2	The history of the human genome	45
2.3	Upward and downward causation	46
3.1	The geological timescale	57
3.2	(a) Darwin's sketch of a tree of life; (b) Darwin's tree diagram in *On the Origin of Species*	62
3.3	The largest tree of life	63
3.4	The tree of multi-cellular life	64
3.5	The tree of primates	65
3.6	Geographic distribution of the living non-human primates	68
3.7	Branching diagram of relationships between some groups of vertebrates	69
3.8	Changing positions of the continents	71
3.9	A provisional phylogeny linking fossils to living primates	73
3.10	The hominid tree	76
3.11	Modes of advanced tool-making in hominin evolution	78
3.12	Behavioural innovations in the Middle Stone Age in Africa	81
4.1	Mating systems in primates	99
4.2	Hypothetical stages in the evolution of the mating systems in humans and African apes	100
4.3	Body size sexual dimorphism in three primate mating systems	102
4.4	Modified images of the same person with four different waist–hip ratios	107
4.5	Statue of the Hindu goddess Parvati	108
4.6	The Venus of Willendorf	108
4.7	Hormonal changes across the ovulatory cycle	113
5.1	Co-residence duration and sexual aversion	124
5.2	A pathway to family formation in birds	127
5.3	Development of reproductive strategies	129
5.4	The great ape reproductive problem and the human solution	131
5.5	Marriage types in hunter-gatherer societies	143
5.6	Ranking of mate traits by parents and their children	145
6.1	A simplified view of complexity in levels of sociality	151
6.2	Significant association between female mortality/wounding rates with number of male neighbours: (a) Female reproductive success versus number of adult neighbours, and (b) average adult female monthly mortality and wounding rates versus number of male neighbours	154

6.3	Ring-tailed lemur	155
6.4	Affinity between two interbreeding groups	158
6.5	Allogrooming between adult female impalas	162
6.6	Temporal discounting in pigeons, rats, and humans	166
6.7	Investor and trustee reputation in two economies	168
6.8	Cooperation between two partners, sharing goals and intentions, as well as complementary roles	169
7.1	Darwin's pictures of anger in different species	180
7.2	Facial expressions of emotions	183
7.3	Chimpanzee and human facial expressions characterised by the chimpanzee and human FACS systems	186
7.4	Paul MacLean's triune brain (a) artistic version; (b) scientific version	189
7.5	Organisation of behaviour with respect to potential for neuromodulation and action specificity	194
7.6	Development of emotions over the first three years	196
7.7	Pride expression in response to victory by a sighted (left) and congenitally blind (right) athlete	198
7.8	The phylogeny of hominid social organisation	200
8.1	A bacterium E. coli swimming in sugar	207
8.2	The nerve net of a contracted hydra	208
8.3	Symmetry of animal bodies	209
8.4	The central nervous system of a crayfish	210
8.5	Mammalian brain size as a percentage of body size	211
8.6	Maps of the areas of the human neocortex	213
8.7	Lateral prefrontal cortex scaling in primates	214
8.8	Increase of human brain size	215
8.9	Social complexity and cognitive capacities	225
8.10	The Sally–Anne test of understanding false belief	229
8.11	False belief test by Hare and his colleagues (2001)	230
9.1	Presenting (a) nest material and (b) play bows	237
9.2	Mirror neurons in human and macaque monkey brains	244
9.3	Vocal tracts of chimpanzee and human, scaled to look the same size	248
9.4	Possible evolutionary relationships between language and music	250
9.5	Components of a theory of mind (Baron-Cohen's model)	252
9.6	In primates, mean group size increases with relative neocortex volume (ratio of neocortex volume to volume of the rest of the brain)	255
9.7	Grooming time and group size in individual primate species	256
10.1	History of the hammer and knife: (a) from the first crudely shaped pounding stone to the steam hammer (b) from the chopper to the modern knife	266
10.2	A culture pyramid	267
10.3	Explosion of oxygen and animal evolution	275
10.4	Standard evolutionary theory	275
10.5	Standard evolutionary theory with niche construction and ecological inheritance	276
10.6	Standard evolutionary theory with cultural inheritance	277
10.7	Multiple independent inventions of farming	278
10.8	Gene–culture coevolution with ecological inheritance	279
11.1	A model for the development of psychopathology	290

11.2 Origin and spread of humans   298
11.3 Four dopamine pathways in the brain   300
11.4 The dopaminergic exploration of distant space in mammals   302
11.5 Shared vulnerability model of creativity associated with psychopathology   307
11.6 A model of the aetiology of a specific phobia   310
12.1 The four gill arches from an embryo to an adult   318
12.2 The timeline of evo-devo   320
12.3 (a) Broad heredity; (b) Narrow heredity   321
12.4 Attributes and consequences of three types of play   331

Acknowledgements

In preparing this textbook, I am grateful to a number of people. To start with, I thank Janey Webb, Jane Lawes, Neha Sharma and Joy Cash from the Pearson editorial staff for their guidance, feedback and dedication. I also thank freelance copy-editor Jill Birch for her part in the editing process. Further, I am grateful to the anonymous reviewers who gave me many helpful comments to improve the manuscript. Next I would like to thank my colleagues at the Institute of Psychology of the Erasmus University Rotterdam for answering my questions, reading a chapter or helping me otherwise. Henk Schmidt encouraged me to keep writing books. Liselotte Gootjes and Jan van Strien answered my questions about the human brain. Jorg Huijding helped me with the interpretation of experimental results. Ingmar Franken and Elke Geraerts read the chapter about mental illness. Eveline Osseweijer helped me in composing the list of figures. My final thanks go to my wife Elly for her love, wisdom and encouragement.

Publisher's acknowledgements

We are grateful to the following for permission to reproduce copyright material:

Figures

Figure 1.2 after *Principles of Human Evolution*, 2nd ed., Wiley-Blackwell (Lewin, R. A. & Foley, R. 2004) Fig.2.5, p.34; Figure 1.4 from *The Emotional Brain: The Mysterious Underpinnings of Emotional Life*, Simon & Schuster (LeDoux, J. 1996) Fig. 6.13, p.164; Figure 1.4 from *The Emotional Brain: The Mysterious Underpinnings of Emotional Life*, Simon & Schuster (LeDoux, J. 1996) Fig. 6.13, p.164, With the permission of The Free Press, a Division of Simon & Schuster, Inc., Orion Publishing, and Brockman Inc. Copyright © 1996 by J. LeDoux. All rights reserved.; Figure 2.1 from *Genomes 3*, Garland Science (Brown, T. 2007); Figure 2.2 from *Evolution*, 3rd ed., Blackwell Publishing (Ridley, M. 2005) Fig. 19.1, p.559; Figure 2.3 adapted from *The Music of Life: Biology Beyond Genes*, Oxford University Press (Noble, D. 2006) Figs. 1 & 2, p.5, p.51; Figure 3.1 from *The Human Career: Human Biological and Cultural Origins*, University of Chicago Press (Klein, R. 2009), Copyright © 2009 The University of Chicago, reproduced by permission of the publisher.; Figures 3.5, 3.6, 3.8, 3.9 from *The Human Career: Human Biological and Cultural Origins*, The University of Chicago Press (Klein, R. 2009), Copyright © 2009 The University of Chicago, reproduced by permission of the publisher.; Figure 3.7 from *Evolution: What the Fossils Say and Why It Matters*, Columbia University Press (Prothero, D. 2007) Fig.5.3, p.130, Copyright © 2007 Columbia University Press. Reprinted with permission of the publisher; Figure 3.10 from Genetics and the making of Human sapiens, *Nature*, 422, pp.849-857 (Carroll, S. 2003), Reprinted by permission from Macmillan Publishers Ltd; Figure 3.11 from *The Dawn of Human Culture*, John Wiley & Sons Inc. (Klein, R. & Blake, E. 2002) Fig.7.7, p.232, ; Figure 3.12 from The revolution that wasn't: a new interpretation of the origin of modern human behavior, *Journal of Human Evolution*, 39(5), pp.453-563 (McBrearty, S. & Brooks, A. 2000), with permission from Elsevier.; Figure 4.1 from *Principles of Human Evolution*, Blackwell Publishing (Lewin, R. & Foley, R. 2004) Fig.7.1, p.166; Figure 4.2 from *Sexual Selection and the Origins of Human Mating Systems*, Oxford University Press (Dixson, A. 2009) Fig.9.1, p.179; Figure 4.3 adapted from *Primate Sexuality: Comparative Studies of the Prosimians, Monkeys, Apes, and Human Beings*, 2nd ed., Oxford University Press (Dixson, A.F. 2012) Fig.7.1(a) p.232, ; Figure 4.5 adapted from Universal allure of the hourglass figure: An evolutionary theory of female physical attractiveness, *Clinics in Plastic Surgery*, 33(3), pp.359-370 (Singh, D. 2006), with permission from Elsevier.; Figure 5.1 from Rethinking the Taiwanese minor marriages data: evidence the mind uses multiple kinship cues to regulate inbreeding avoidance, *Evolution and Human Behavior*, 30, pp.153-160 (Lieberman, D. 2009), with permission from Elsevier.; Figure 5.2 from Life history and the evolution of family living in birds, *Proceedings of the*

Royal Society of London B, 274(1616), pp.1349-1357 (Covas, R. & Griesser, M. 2007), Copyright © 2007, The Royal Society, used by permission.; Figure 5.3 from Sex, attachment, and the development of reproductive strategies, *Behavioral and Brain Sciences*, 32, pp.1-67 (Del Giudice, M. 2009), reproduced with permission from Cambridge University Press.; Figure 5.4 from *The Evolution of Language*, Cambridge University Press (Fitch, W. 2010) Fig.6.1, p.242, ; Figure 5.5 from Sexual selection under parental choice: the role of parents in the evolution of human mating, *Evolution and Human Behavior*, 28, pp.403-409 (Apostolou, M. 2007), with permission from Elsevier.; Figure 5.6 from Meet the parents: Parent-offspring convergence and divergence in mate preferences, *Personality and Individual Differences*, 50(2), pp.253-258 (Perilloux, C., Fleischman, D. & Buss, D. 2011), with permission from Elsevier.; Figure 6.1 from *Relationships: A Dialectical Perspective*, Psychology Press (Hinde, R. 1997) p.xv; Figure 6.2 from Group territoriality and the benefits of sociality in the African lion, Panthera leo, *Animal Behaviour*, 78, pp.359-370 (Mosser, A. & Packer, C. 2009), with permission from Elsevier.; Figure 6.4 from *Primeval Kinship: How Pair-Bonding Gave Birth to Human Society*, Harvard University Press (Chapais, B. 2008) Fig.14.1, p.221, Copyright (c) by the President and Fellows of Harvard College; Figure 6.5 from Reciprocal allogrooming in impala, *Animal Behaviour*, 44, pp.1073-1083 (Hart, B. & Hart, L. 1992), with permission from Elsevier.; Figure 6.6 from Why be nice? Psychological constraints on the evolution of cooperation, *Trends in Cognitive Sciences*, 8, pp.60-65 (Stevens, J. & Hauser, M. 2004), with permission from Elsevier.; Figure 6.7 from *Cooperation in Primates and Humans: Mechanisms and Evolution*, Springer (Kappeler, P. & van Schaik, C. (Eds) 2006) Fig.8.3, p,.148, With kind permission from Springer Science+Business Media and the author; Figure 6.7 from Recordkeeping alters economic history by promoting reciprocity, *Proceedings of the National Academy of Sciences of the USA*, 106, Fig.3(E-F) pp.1009-1014 (Basu, S. et al.), Copyright (2009) National Academy of Sciences, USA; Figure 6.8 from Reliance on head versus eyes in the gaze following of great apes and human infants: the cooperative eye hypothesis, *Journal of Human Evolution*, 52, pp.314-320 (Tomasello, M. et al. 2007), with permission from Elsevier.; Figure 7.4b from *The Triune Brain in Evolution: Role of Paleocerebral Functions*, Plenum Press (MacLean, P. 1990) Fig.2.1, p.9; Figure 7.5 from Emotions: From brain to robot, *Trends in Cognitive Sciences*, 8, pp.554-561 (Arbib, M. & Fellous, J. 2004), with permission from Elsevier; Figure 7.6 from *Handbook of Emotions*, 3rd ed., Guilford Press (Lewis, M, Havilland-Jones, J. & Barrett, L (Eds) 2010) p.316; Figure 7.8 from *Principles of Human Evolution*, Blackwell Publishing (Lewin, R. & Foley, R. 2004) Fig.7.9, p.180; Figure 8.2 from *The Evolution of Culture in Animals*, Princeton University Press (Bonner, J. 1980) Fig.4, p.39, © 1980 by Princeton University Press. Reprinted by permission of Princeton University Press.; Figure 8.3 from *Where Do We Come From? The Molecular Evidence for Human Descent*, Springer Verlag (Klein, J. & Takahata, N. 2002) Fig.7.3, p.159, ; Figure 8.4 adapted from *The Evolution of Culture in Animals*, Princeton University Press (Bonner, J. 1980) Fig.5, p.41, © 1980 by Princeton University Press. Reprinted by permission of Princeton University Press.; Figure 8.5 from Evolution of the brain and intelligence, *Trends in Cognitive Sciences*, 9(5), pp.250-257 (Roth, G. & Dicke, U. 2005); Figure 8.6 from Ecological dominance, social competition and coalitionary arms races: Why humans evolved extraordinary intelligence, *Evolution and Human Behavior*, 26, pp.10-46 (Flinn, M., Geary, D. & Ward, C. 2005), with permission from Elsevier.; Figures 8.7, 8.8 from Précis of Principles of Brain

Evolution, *Behavioral and Brain Sciences*, 29(1), pp.1-36 (Striedter, G. 2006), Reproduced by permission of the publisher.; Figure 8.9 from Primate cognition: from 'what now?' to 'what if'?, *Trends in Cognitive Sciences*, 7, pp.494-497 (Barrett, L., Henzi, P. & Dunbar, R. 2003), with permission from Elsevier; Figure 8.10 from *Mindblindness: An Essay on Autism and Theory of Mind*, The MIT Press (Baron-Cohen, S. 1995) Fig.5.4, p.70, © 2008 Massachusetts Institute of Technology, by permission of The MIT Press.; Figure 8.11 from Do chimpanzees know what conspecifics know?, *Animal Behaviour*, 61(1), pp.139-151 (Hare, B., Call, J., Tomasello, M. 2011); Figure 9.2 from *The Evolution of Language*, Cambridge University Press (Fitch, W. 2010) Fig.13.1, p.453, Reproduced by permission of the publisher.; Figure 9.3 from *From Hand to Mouth: The Origins of Language*, Princeton University Press (Corballis, M 2002) p.140, © 2002 by Princeton University Press. Reprinted by permission of Princeton University Press.; Figure 9.4 from *The Prehistory of Language*, Oxford University Press (Botha, R. & Knight, C (eds) 2009) Fig.4.1, p.61, after: Brown, S. (2000). The 'musilanguage' model of human evolution. In N. L. Wallin, B. Merker, and S. Brown (eds), The origins of music. Cambridge, MA: MIT Press, 271–300; Figure 9.5 adapted from *Mindblindness: An Essay on Autism and Theory of Mind*, The MIT Press (Baron-Cohen, S. 1995) Fig.4.1, p.31, © 1995 Massachusetts Institute of Technology, by permission of The MIT Press; Figure 9.6 from Evolution in the social brain, *Science*, 317, pp.1344-1347 (Dunbar, R. & Shultz, S. 2007); Figure 9.7 from Group size, grooming and social cohesion in primates, *Animal Behaviour*, pp. 1617-1629 (Lehmann, J., Korstjens, A.K., & Dunbar, R. I. M. 2007), Reprinted with permission from Elsevier; Figure 10.1b from *Préhistoire de l' Art Occidental*, Éditions d' Art Lucien Mazenod (Leroi-Gourhan, A. 1971) André Leroi-Gourhan; Figure 10.2 from *The Question of Animal Culture*, Harvard University Press (Laland, K. & Galef, B. 2009) pp.99-124, Reprinted by permission of the publisher. Copyright © 2009 by the President and Fellows of Harvard College.; Figure 10.3 from *Our Cosmic Origins: From the Big Bang to the Emergence of Life and Intelligence*, Cambridge University Press (Delsemme, A. 1998) Fig.6.2, p.170, Reproduced by permission of the publisher.; Figure 10.4 from Niche construction, biological evolution and cultural change, *Behavioral & Brain Sciences*, 23, Fig.1a, p.134 (Laland, K.N., Odling-Smee, F.J. & Feldman, M.W. 2000), Reproduced by permission of the publisher and the author; Figure 10.5 from Niche construction, biological evolution and cultural change, *Behavioral and Brain Sciences*, 23, Fig.1b, p.134 (Laland. K. Odling-Smee, J. & Feldman, M. 2000), Reproduced by permission of the publisher and the author; Figures 10.6 from Niche construction, biological evolution, and cultural change, *Behavioral and Brain Sciences*, 23, Fig.2a, p.136 (Laland. K. Odling-Smee, J. & Feldman, M. 2000), Reproduced by permission of the publisher and the authors; Figure 10.7 from *Human Web: A Bird's-Eye View of World History*, W.W. Norton & Company (McNeill, J. & McNeill, W. 2003) p.27, Copyright (c) 2003 by J.R. McNeil and William H. McNeill. Used by permission of W.W. Norton & company, Inc.; Figure 10.8 from Niche construction, biological evolution, and cultural change, *Behavioral and Brain Sciences*, 23, Fig 2c, p.136 (Laland. K. Odling-Smee, J. & Feldman, M. 2000), Reproduced by permission of the publisher and the author; Figure 11.1 from *Brave New Brain: Conquering Mental Illness in the Era of the Genome*, Oxford University Press (Andreasen, N. 2001) Fig.3.1, p.36, Reproduce by permission of the author: Nancy C. Andreasen, M.D., PH.D., Andrew H. Woods Chair of Psychiatry, Director, Psychiatry Iowa Neuroimaging Consortium (PINC), Associate Director for

Translational Technologies, Iowa Institute for Clinical and Translational Science, The University of Iowa Carver College of Medicine; Figure 11.2 from *Where Do We Come From? The Molecular Evidence for Human Descent*, Springer Verlag (Klein, J. & Takahata, N. 2002) Fig.10.10, p.267, With kind permission from Springer Science+Business Media; Figure 11.3 from *Essential Psychopharmacology: Neuroscientific Basis and Practical Applications*, 2nd ed., Cambridge University Press (Stahl, S. 2004) Fig.9.24, p.272, Reproduced by permission of the publisher.; Figure 11.4 from Why your "head is in the clouds" during thinking: The relationship between cognition and upper space, *Acta Psychological*, 118, pp.7-24 (Previc, F., Declerck, C. and de Brabander, B 2009), with permission from Elsevier; Figure 11.5 from Creativity and psychopathology: A shared vulnerability model, *Canadian Journal of Psychiatry*, 56, pp.144-153 (Carson, S. 2011); Figure 11.6 adapted from *Anxiety and its Disorders: The Nature and Treatment of Anxiety and Panic*, The Guilford Press (Barlow, D. 2002) Fig.10.2, p.340; Figure 12.1 from *Your Inner Fish: A journey into the 3.5 billion-year history of the human body*, Penguin (Shubin, N. 2008) p.88, and Penguin UK and © Kalliopi Monoyios; http://kalliopimonoyios. com; Figure 12.2 from Knowing your ancestors: themes in the history of evo-devo, *Evolution & Development*, 5, pp.327-330 (Love, A. & Raff, R. 2003); Figure 12.3 from *The Changing Role of the Embryo in Evolutionary Thought: Roots of Evo-Devo*, Cambridge University Press (Amundson, R. 2005) Fig.5, p.156, Reproduced by permission of the publisher.; Figure 12.4 from *The Genesis of Animal Play: testing the limits*, MIT Press (Burghardt, G. 2005) Figure 5.1, Burghardt, Gordon M. foreword by Brian Sutton-Smith., The Genesis of Animal Play: Testing the Limits, figure 5.1, © 2005 Massachusetts Institute of Technology, by permission of The MIT Press.

Tables

Table 4.1 from *Foundations of Evolutionary Psychology* Lawrence Erlbaum Associates (Crawford, C & Krebs, D. (Eds.) 2008) Fig.4.1, p.72, Foundations of evolutionary psychology by CRAWFORD, CHARLES Copyright 2008 Reproduced with permission of TAYLOR & FRANCIS GROUP LLC - BOOKS in the format Textbook and Other Book via Copyright Clearance Center. Order Details IDs 63204997 63204998; Table 4.1 from *Sexual Selection*, Princeton University Press (Andersson, M. 1994) Table1.1.1, p.10, © 1994 by Princeton University Press. Reprinted by permission of Princeton University Press.; Table 4.2 from Attractive women want it all: Good genes, economic investment, parenting proclivities, and emotional commitment, *Evolutionary Psychology*, 6(1), pp.134-146 (Buss, D. & Shackelford, T. 2008); Table 5.1 from *Inbreeding, Incest, and the Incest Taboo*, Stanford University Press (A. Wolf & W. Durham (Eds) 2004) Table 2.1, p.39, Copyright (c) 2004 by the Board of Trustees of the Leland Stanford Jr. University; Table 5.2 from Parent-offspring conflict in mate preferences, *Review of General Psychology*, 12(1), pp.47-62 (Buunk, A., Park, J., Dubbs, S. 2008); Table 7.1 from Emotional endophenotypes in evolutionary psychiatry, *Progress in Neuro-Psychopharmacology & Biological Psychiatry*, 30, pp.774-784 (Panksepp, J. 2006), with permission from Elsevier.; Table 9.1 adapted from *The Evolution of Communication*, The MIT Press (Hauser, M. 1996) p.48, ; Table 9.2 from *Origins of Human Communication*, The MIT Press (Tomasello, M. 2008) Table 2.1, p.24, © 2008 Massachusetts Institute of Technology, by permission of The MIT Press

Text

General Displayed Text on page 105 adapted from *Monogamy: Mating Strategies and Partnerships in Birds, Humans and Other Mammals*, Cambridge University Press (Reichard, U. & Boesch, C. (Eds) 2003) p.4, Reproduced by permission of the publisher.

In some instances we have been unable to trace the owners of copyright material, and we would appreciate any information that would enable us to do so.

Picture Credits

The publisher would like to thank the following for their kind permission to reproduce their photographs:

(Key: b-bottom; c-centre; l-left; r-right; t-top)

Alamy Images: Classic Image 180tl, 180tc, Top-Pet-Pics 237cr; **Bob Willingham:** 198; **© David M. Buss, all rights reserved.:** 36; **Cambridge University Library, Reproduced by kind permission of the Syndics of:** 62; **FLPA Images of Nature:** Danny Ellinger / FN / Minden Pictures 237cl; **Getty Images** 182cr; **Gordon Burghardt:** 330; **Jerome Wakefield:** 293; **Joy Cash:** 108bl; **Robert Trivers:** 95; **Robin Dunbar:** 225; **Science Photo Library Ltd:** Jim Cartier 108br, Paul D Stewart 7, Richard Bizley 30; **Shutterstock. com:** 155

All other images © Pearson Education

In some instances we have been unable to trace the owners of copyright material, and we would appreciate any information that would enable us to do so.

Introduction

To introduce this textbook, we focus on a few questions which you may have in mind.

- What is evolutionary psychology?
- What is the ambition of this evolutionary science?
- What kind of questions does evolutionary psychology pose?
- How does this textbook cover evolutionary insights?
- What specific questions does this textbook discuss?
- How can you learn more about evolutionary psychology?

We will now consider each of these in turn.

What is evolutionary psychology?

It is not a branch of psychology such as personality psychology or social psychology, but an evolutionary approach to the entire field of psychology. The central claim of evolutionary psychology is that mental functions (perception, emotion) and behavioural patterns (reproduction, sociality) are products of evolutionary history, just like anatomical structures (hands, legs) and physiological functions (respiration, digestion). In order to arrive at better, more profound insights, evolutionary psychology applies evolutionary biology to psychological topics such as perception, cognition, emotion, motivation, learning abilities, personality, psychopathology, sexuality and sociality.

What is the ambition of this evolutionary science?

It wants to integrate biological insights about evolution in psychology. Evolutionary insights have revolutionised biology and the same could happen in psychology. The impact of evolutionary thought in biology is huge, witness the famous statement of biologist Theodosius Dobzhanski in 1973 that 'nothing in biology makes sense except in the light of evolution'. Systematic attempts to import biological insights about evolution in psychological science have been made since the 1990s. Thus, the ambition of evolutionary psychology is to revolutionise psychology to the extent that nothing in psychology makes sense except through the lens of evolution. Evolutionary psychology is a fast-growing science in terms of publications, and has over the past decades gained influence and acceptance within the field of psychology (Cornwell 2005; Fitzgerald and Whitaker 2010).

What kind of questions does evolutionary psychology pose?

In a classic paper, the ethologist (i.e. behavioural biologist) Niko Tinbergen (1963) identified four questions which any evolutionary scientist should pose when explaining a behavioural pattern, emotional response or mental function. Each question tackles a different level of explanation which should not be confused with one another. Consider, for example, this question: why are we afraid of snakes? This question can be answered in terms of: (a) causation or causal mechanism – how do stimuli like snakes elicit the response of fear in the brain?; (b) development or ontogeny – how does fear depend on early experiences of the individual?; (c) phylogeny, or evolutionary history of a species or group of species – why did fear evolve both in humans and monkeys?; and (d) adaptive function – why did the response of fear for snakes acquire greater fitness value than alternatives? As a rule of thumb: how-questions are proximate questions about causation and development, why-questions are ultimate questions about phylogeny and function. To summarise, WHY something evolves or has fitness value is quite different, although complementary, to HOW something works or develops:

Ultimate question: WHY?	Proximate question: HOW?
Phylogenetic history	Ontogenetic history
Adaptive function	Causal mechanism

Note that the time domain is important to these questions: (a) causal questions deal with real time, from moment to moment in which cause and effect are close; (b) developmental questions deal with the time of lifespan of individuals, from childhood to adulthood; (c) phylogenetic questions deal with 'deep time', that is, thousands or millions of years of evolutionary history in which animals descended from ancestors; and (d) functional questions deal with 'deep time' as well because the functions of emotion or behaviour are the product of a selection history. Thus with the help of Tinbergen's four questions evolutionary psychology attempts to explain how and why emotions, behaviours and cognitions evolved as solutions to problems that our ancestors recurrently faced. For more literature about the proximate–ultimate distinction and Tinbergen's questions, see Alessi (1992), Beatty (1994), Mayr (1961, 1997), Dewsbury (1999), Zeifman (2001), Bolhuis and Verhulst (2009) and Laland et al. (2011).

How does this textbook cover evolutionary insights?

We follow some of the recommendations to improve evolutionary coverage in evolutionary textbooks, as proposed by David Hillis (2007):

1. It makes clear that Charles Darwin had important insights about evolution, but it makes equally clear that scientists have learned a great deal about evolution since his time.

2. It shows how evolution is relevant to human lives. Although other animal species may pass in review, the main focus is on humans and their close relatives (i.e. monkeys, apes).

3. It will emphasise 'tree of life' thinking. Many students come into biology courses with 'ladder of life' thinking. They think that animal species form a static hierarchy with humans on top and bacteria at the bottom. They need to be exposed early and often to phylogeny, the tree of life which represents the evolutionary history of a species or group of species. They need to learn that all extant species are equally distant in evolutionary time from the common ancestor of all life.

4. It will emphasise that biological terminology is an integral part of learning about evolution. Students should know that humans, together with monkeys and apes, are 'primates' who share traits such as grasping extremities (hands and feet), large brains and social life. They should also know what is meant by terms like adaptation, homology or inclusive fitness as well as understand the Latinised names for animals such as *Eukaryota* (organisms consisting of cells in which the genetic material is contained with a distinct nucleus) or *Homo sapiens* (the living human species). When key terms and names arise, they will immediately be explained. At the end of this textbook you will find a glossary, or alphabetical list of terms in the domain of evolutionary science with the definitions of these terms.

5. It emphasises the great magnitude of evolutionary time. Many students readily understand that evolution may occur across short time spans, for example, when bacteria rapidly evolve resistance to antibiotics. But many have a hard time thinking about evolution over the four-billion-year history of life. Humans entered the scene only a few million years ago. The scale of evolution is immense, so students need to 'enlarge their mind' to deal with this. Consequently, large-scale thinking is necessary for a deeper understanding of the everyday world and the usual subjects studied as part of a psychology course.

What specific questions does this textbook discuss?

Chapter 1 answers the question how evolutionary psychology emerged from three sciences: psychology, biology and neuroscience. Along the way you are made familiar with evolutionary theory and basic biological concepts.

Chapter 2 deals with the question how we can identify problems that our ancestors faced repeatedly such as avoiding predators, finding mates, raising offspring and cooperating with one another. This chapter deals also with different approaches within evolutionary psychology about how the problems can be studied. A case study about a current problem (obesity) demonstrates how the approaches work and differ from one another.

Chapter 3 makes clear what our place is among other species. One way to put ourselves in the right place is to use a long timescale; a second way is to use tree-of-life thinking, and a third is to look at how we originated from other primates, and what characteristics we share with them.

Chapter 4 deals with the transition from asexual to sexual reproduction. It explains why sexuality emerged which made males and females dependent on one another for the production of offspring. Note that the word 'sexual' originally means: belonging to the female or male sex. So asking why sexuality arose, is asking why sexes emerged.

Chapter 5 analyses the subsequent transition to parental care. This includes a discussion of why families are rare in nature, how fathers became involved in child care, and why parents and offspring have conflicting interests.

Chapter 6 is about the evolutionary transition from living solitarily to living socially. Why and how did this happen? Another topic is social cooperation because in many animals, cooperative behaviour is restricted to genetic relatives. But humans are quite willing to cooperate with unrelated individuals which raises the question of how special human cooperation is, and how it is maintained by cognitive capacities.

Chapter 7 deals with another transition when new emotions such as pride and guilt evolved from basic emotions like joy and fear. This chapter will discuss why and how emotions originated, how they are expressed and processed in the brain, and what happened in the distant past that we needed new emotions.

Chapter 8 is focused on the transition from fixed responses towards flexible responses. While many animals can make do with reflexes and basic emotions, humans evolved large brains and advanced cognition such as a mind-reading capacity. An important question will be why the human brain evolved to be large and our cognition to be advanced.

Chapter 9 is about the evolutionary transition from animal communication with a limited repertoire of fixed calls to human language with many words that can be flexibly arranged into sentences. This chapter focuses on the question why and how this flexible form of communication arose.

Chapter 10 considers culture as a set of transmitted beliefs and behavioural traditions that we learn from parents, teachers, peers and even celebrities we never meet. Important issues will be why cultural transmission or inheritance became important in human evolution, and how it can be incorporated in evolutionary theory.

Chapter 11 explores the evolutionary paradox of mental illness which should have been eliminated if natural selection works well. But because mental illness (e.g. schizophrenia, depression) still exists, we examine whether it has some adaptive significance.

Chapter 12 examines why development of the individual is important for the evolution of species. Whereas many organisms simply develop from larvae into adults, humans pass through intermediate stages like childhood and adolescence. How does such a developmental reorganisation take place? Why and how did we become a playful species?

How can you learn more about evolutionary psychology?

This textbook has been written to guide you in studying evolutionary psychology. To help you in learning more about this science, each chapter ends with sections of Suggested reading. If you want to engage in further study and find the most recent publications in the field, online research is the best approach, using search engines (e.g. Google scholar, Medline/PubMed, PsycINFO, Scopus, Scirus). Using key words in the textbook and the names of authors as search terms, you can find articles and scan the table of contents of recent issues of the main journals in the field.

The main journals in the field are *Evolutionary Psychology* (http://www.epjournal.net/) and *Evolution and Human Behavior* (http://www.sciencedirect.com/science/journal/10905138). You are also encouraged to search in a wider field, scanning journals as they appear in the Suggested reading and References sections of this textbook, for example: *Animal Behaviour, Behavioural and Brain Sciences, Brain and Cognition, Current Anthropology, Emotion, Evolution and Development, Evolutionary Anthropology, Journal of Evolutionary Biology, Human Nature, Journal of Human Evolution, Journal of Personality and Social Psychology, Nature* and *Science*.

Timeline of evolutionary psychology

1859

Charles Darwin (1809–1882) anticipated the emergence of psychology as an evolutionary science in the concluding chapter of his book *On the Origin of Species* (**1859**). Darwin's evolutionary theory implied that every human attribute, from bodily organ to physiology, behaviour and mental function, is subject to natural selection. His theory also suggested bodily and mental continuity between humans and their ancestors: no trait could be absolutely new.

1886

George Romanes (1848–1894) was a friend and colleague of Darwin who argued that the instincts of animals could provide evidence for the heritability of mental faculties. In emphasising, like Darwin, the mental continuity between animals and humans, Romanes laid the foundations for comparative psychology with works like *Animal Intelligence* (**1881**) and *Mental Evolution in Man* (**1888**).

1963

Niko Tinbergen (1907–1988) received the Nobel prize in 1973, with Karl von Frisch and Konrad Lorenz, for 'discoveries concerning organization and elicitation of individual and social behavior patterns'. He placed evolution centre-stage in the science of animal behaviour (ethology) with what we now know as Tinbergen's four questions about causation, development, phylogeny and adaptive function in his paper On aims and methods of ethology, *Zeitschrift für Tierpsychologie*, 20, 410–429 (**1963**).

1964

William Hamilton (1936–2000) is best known for his classic paper on The genetical evolution of social behavior, *Journal of Theoretical Behavior*, 7, 1–52 (**1964**), reprinted in *Narrow Roads of Gene Land: Volume I Evolution of Social Behavior* (**1996**). He expanded the concept of fitness into inclusive fitness, defined as a measure that combines (a) an individual's direct genetic contribution to future generations through its own offspring, with (b) the indirect contribution made by aiding the reproduction of relatives.

1971

Robert Trivers (b. 1943) built on Darwin's sexual selection theory and Hamilton's work on inclusive fitness. He is most well known for his classic papers on The evolution of reciprocal altruism, *The Quarterly Review of Biology*, 46, 35–57 (**1971**), Parental investment and sexual selection, in B. Campbell (Ed.), *Sexual Selection:*

and the Descent of Man (pp. 136–179) (1972), and Parent–offspring conflict, *American Zoologist, 14*, 249–264 (1974). These and other papers are reprinted in his book *Natural Selection and Social Theory* (2002).

1975

Edward Wilson (b. 1929) published a book about *Sociobiology* (1975) which was intended as a synthetic study about the biological explanation of animal social behaviour. It provoked heated debates about 'genetic determinism', the misguided belief that social behaviours are genetically fixed; about 'reductionism', the imperialist claim that a particular domain (e.g. the social, the mental) is reducible to another (e.g. the biological, the neural); and about its ignorance of mind and culture as indispensable ingredients for the explanation of human behaviour. He made up for this last omission with the book *Genes, Mind, and Culture* (1981) which he wrote with Charles Lumsden. While sociobiology became taboo in the social sciences, many people regarded evolutionary psychology as its successor.

1980

Paul Ekman (b. 1934), inspired by Darwin's study about *The Expression of Emotions in Man and Animals* (1872), pioneered in the cross-cultural study of how emotions are expressed – e.g. *The Face of Man: Expressions of Universal Emotions in a New Guinea Village* (1980) – and developed an instrument to objectively measure facial expressions (Ekman and Friesen 1978).

1982

Frans de Waal (b. 1948) published in 1982 his book *Chimpanzee Politics* in which he compared the power struggles in chimpanzees with those of human politicians. Since then, all his works draw parallels between these closely related primates, from sex and violence to social life and kindness. His work has been translated into over a dozen languages.

1992

Leda Cosmides (b. 1957) and **John Tooby** (b. 1952) launched an influential approach in evolutionary psychology with the proposal that recurrent problems faced by our hunting and gathering ancestors have selected for psychological adaptations. Our brain and mind are proposed to contain cognitive mechanisms being specialised for solving problems such as avoiding predators, recognising relatives or detecting cheaters. Reasoning about social exchange and its associated risk of non-reciprocation serves as an important test case in their research programme. The approach and its programme are explained in Barkow, Cosmides and Tooby (eds), *The Adapted Mind* (1992).

1996

Joseph LeDoux (b. 1949) is best known for his studies of fear. In his book *The Emotional Brain* (1996), he explains how the response of fear is elicited in the brain. During experiments he discovered two brain pathways for emotional responses to danger. Both paths start at the thalamus, a brain area which is involved in the selection of external stimuli. The short pathway generates an automatic response (freezing, increased blood pressure, release of stress hormones in the blood stream), while the long pathway allows cognitive mediation of emotional responses.

1998

Jaak Panksepp (b. 1943) developed an evolutionary theory of emotions which emphasises that emotions are older than cognitions, with the implication that much of the human mind was laid down in ancient emotions that we share with many other animals. He published *Affective Neuroscience: The Foundation of Animal and Human Emotions* (1998) and criticised the cognitive bias in evolutionary psychology in Panksepp and Panksepp (2000), The seven sins of evolutionary psychology, *Evolution and Cognition*, 6, 108–131.

1999

David Buss (b. 1953) is committed to the mental mechanism approach in evolutionary psychology as introduced by Cosmides et al. (1992). He is best known for his papers about sex differences in mate preferences, as well as his influential textbook *Evolutionary Psychology* (first published 1999, with new edition in 2004, 2008 and 2012) in which mating, parenting and kinship problems are prevalent.

2005

Peter Richerson (b. 1943) and **Robert Boyd** (b. 1948) focus in their research on cultural evolution and the mechanisms that produce and shape human culture. These mechanisms include psychological biases in how people learn from one another. In the frequency-based bias people use the most common behaviour or belief as the most advantageous one. But in the model-based bias they imitate successful or prestigious individuals. Richerson and Boyd published their influential theory in *Not by Genes Alone: How Culture Transformed Human Evolution* (2005).

2005

Michael Tomasello (b. 1950) is particularly known for his publications on social cognition, shared intentionality, and communication in great apes and human children. In Understanding and sharing intentions, a paper he published in 2005 with colleagues (*Behavioral and Brain Sciences*, 28, 675–735), it is proposed that the crucial difference between cognition in humans and other primates is the capacity to share goals and intentions in cooperative activities.

2007

Robin Dunbar (b. 1947) is best known for the social brain hypothesis which holds that selection pressures for primate cognition come from the demands of living in complex societies. In Evolution in the social brain, which he published with Susanne Schultz in 2007 (*Science*, 317, 1344–1347), it is suggested that particularly the demands for intense pair bonding may have selected for our large brains.

2012

David Buss, in the most recent edition of his textbook (2012), makes a plea for a unified psychology in which disciplinary boundaries between personality, social, developmental and cognitive psychology dissolve. He considers the boundaries not merely arbitrary but misleading and detrimental to scientific progress. Studying human psychology through evolutionary problems and their solutions is a more natural way of making progress and thereby crossing disciplinary boundaries.

Unifying psychology is one thing, another thing is integrating psychology with other life sciences (e.g. developmental biology) as well as with other social sciences (e.g. sociology). Integration may benefit from the growing insight that there is a multiple inheritance system between successive generations of individuals – genetic, epigenetic, cultural, ecological – that can produce evolution (e.g. Odling-Smee et al. 2003; Jablonka and Lamb 2005; Distin 2011; Piersma and Van Gils 2011). The author of the textbook you are reading, shares this view. Note that the multiple inheritance issue is a matter of debate.

Part 1 BASICS

1 The history of evolutionary psychology

This chapter will cover:

1.1 Introduction

1.2 Emergence from three sciences

1.3 Biology

1.4 Psychology

1.5 Neuroscience

1.6 Summary

Learning outcomes

By the end of this chapter, you should be able to explain how:

- evolutionary psychology poses new questions that expand the timescale of its subject-matter
- evolution by natural selection works
- biological concepts are defined
- evolutionary psychology emerged from three sciences
- the use of evolutionary thought in psychology triggers discussion.

1.1 Introduction

Darwin anticipated the emergence of evolutionary psychology

Psychology has a long tradition of recognising a set of sub-disciplines which include cognitive, personality and biological psychology. Accordingly, evolutionary psychology is often represented as a new branch of psychology which studies how natural selection over vast periods of time, has shaped the mind and behaviour. However, it should not be considered as a specialism within psychology but more as a lens through which we view all areas of psychology. It uses evolutionary thinking to formulate and answer new questions about learning, emotions, cognition, social life and so on (e.g. Gaulin and McBurney 2004). In the concluding chapter of his book *On the Origin of Species* (1859), Charles Darwin anticipated the emergence of psychology as an evolutionary science. His theory implies that mental functions of the brain (memory, intelligence), emotions (fear, pride) and behavioural patterns (mating, social interaction) are products of evolutionary history, just like anatomical structures (limbs, organs) and physiological functions (respiration, digestion).

In this chapter we first focus briefly on the art of asking new questions which is important for the advancement of science. Then, we give an example of how evolutionary psychology attempts to formulate new questions. The main part of this chapter is devoted to the history of evolutionary psychology. Along the way, you will learn how evolutionary theory works, how biological concepts are defined, and how the use of evolutionary thought in psychology triggers discussion.

The art of asking new questions

Science owes its advancement to the art of asking new questions. Philosophers in ancient Greece already practised this art. For example: what is the material origin of things? Interestingly, the answers they gave – e.g. water, air, fire, earth – were different from before because they didn't invoke the gods as being part of the story. The reflections of philosophy, such as these, marked the beginning of a quest that is still going on. Philosophers who specialised in science, became 'natural philosophers' and studied the nature of things. In the nineteenth century the term 'natural philosopher' was abandoned and replaced by 'scientist'.

Scientists are engaged in a systematic enterprise that accumulates knowledge about the world, which is compressed into testable laws and principles. Today, this enterprise has grown into a huge tree with the major branches of natural science (e.g. physics, chemistry, biology) and social science (e.g. economics, sociology, history). Psychology is partly natural science, partly social science. For example, biological psychology studies how behaviour is based on neural and endocrine processes, while social psychology studies how an individual's thoughts, feelings and actions are influenced by other people.

Why do we have so many emotions?

Evolutionary psychology attempts to formulate new questions that expand the scales of time and space of psychology's subject-matter. Consider emotions, as an example. Psychologists know a lot about what emotions are, how we recognise them from facial expressions, how they are caused, and how they may develop into

species

the largest natural population of organisms that can potentially interbreed to produce fertile offspring.

character

any distinguishable characteristic, feature, trait or property of an organism that enables it to survive and reproduce in its local environment.

savanna

usually semi-arid plain covered with grasses and occasional scattered trees.

bipedalism

ability to walk and run on two feet in an upright position, as in humans and birds. The most important adaptation to erect posture and bipedalism in humans was a positional change of the *foramen magnum*. Great apes and bears also engage in short periods of bipedal locomotion when carrying food or looking for food.

disorders. Far less is known about the evolutionary question why the human **species** is so emotional (Turner 1997, 2000). Humans have, when compared with other primates such as monkeys and apes, many emotions. Not only basic emotions like fear, anger, sadness, disgust and joy, but also new emotions such as pride, love, guilt, shame, remorse, contempt, and so on. Why do we have so many emotions?

An answer may be found in the evolutionary past when our African ancestors faced a major problem. About eight million years ago, global climate was growing colder and drier which encouraged the expansion of grasses and the contraction of trees and bush at lower latitudes. Among the adversely affected animals were various ape species who either became extinct or adapted to the change by spending more time on the ground. We know from fossil records that living on the ground favoured a shift in locomotion from quadrupedal to bipedal (Klein 2009). The suggestion that the **characteristic** of humans to walk upright began in grassland with scattered trees, is better known as the **savanna** hypothesis. 'Adaptation to open terrain was the spark that initiated the human lineage' (Potts 1996: 82). The hypothesis predicts that natural selection favours anatomical and behavioural changes that will increase the chances of survival in a grassier environment.

The physical traits that distinguish humans from other great apes, include our greatly enlarged brains and upright style of walking. Change in brain size and walking style involve alterations of skeletal features. Although ancient skulls have been found that document the enlarged brain of our ancestors, no one has yet found bones that indicate clearly when and where **bipedalism** began. This lack of information has made it difficult to determine why walking on two legs became advantageous. Among the contenders are carrying food items and children, reducing the amount of skin surface exposed to sunlight, improved sight, wading through water, intimidation among males and showing off to females.

Another characteristic of humans is their extended emotional repertoire, which is thought to originate from the time when they changed from living in the forest to a life on the ground. To survive in the open country where food was patchy and predators close by, group organisation required higher standards. Positive emotions such as pride and friendliness were better able to regulate relationships in a group than negative emotions like fear and anger. The old, negative emotions would easily destabilise social structures, while new, positive emotions enabled early humans to forge social bonds and fine-tune solidarity. For example, pride comes when social expectations are met, and pushes individuals to meet them in the future. Generally, positive emotions help to broaden the individual's thought and action (Fredrickson 1998). The question why we have so many emotions will be discussed further in section 7.5 (The emergence of social emotions).

1.2   Emergence from three sciences

Evolutionary psychology emerged from evolutionary biology, psychology and neuroscience. These three sciences all evolved in parallel, but in different directions. This divergence has two reasons: first, each science developed its own focus and 'specialisation' and so as a consequence the three fields grew apart. Second, philosophical issues at the heart of scientific investigation served to separate them further. Let's have a closer look at these issues that are relevant to all three sciences.

Neuroscience, evolutionary biology and psychology spring from a philosophical tradition that has struggled with old and what we now know as false dichotomies of mind–body, nature–nurture and animal–human. We shall briefly examine each of these central 'problems' that remain at the heart of philosophy.

Mind-body

mind-body problem
ancient issue of how to account for and describe the relationship between mental and physical processes.

At the centre of philosophy was the distinction between **mind and body**. This is known as 'dualism' and is mostly associated with the French philosopher René Descartes (1596–1650). He is also known as Renatus Cartesius as Latin was the language that scholars used in those times. He saw the body as a non-thinking substance occupying space, and the mind as a thinking substance that does not need space. He explored questions of how mind and body interact. If the mind is totally different from the body, how could something material (the body or brain) interact with something immaterial (the soul or mind)? He argued that the interaction could not be like ordinary physical interactions, since minds were not even located in space. A consequence of this argument was that the mind–brain problem separated psychology from neuroscience. In due time however, Cartesian dualism has been replaced by the monist view that every mental state is identical with a particular brain state but that there may be no general laws relating the two (Valentine 1997).

Since the 1980s, the fields of psychology and neuroscience have become increasingly allied, as may be seen from the rise of cognitive neuroscience. The driving forces for this new science were advances in brain imaging technology and information-processing models of psychologists. However, not everybody is happy with the claim that minds are brains. Some philosophers (e.g. Bennett and Hacker 2003) criticise the assumption in neuroscience that the brain has the capacity to believe, think, reason, and so on. The question would then be: does it make sense to ascribe these capacities to the brain? The authors argue that it is not the brain that thinks but the person that uses his or her brain. In other words, we should not mistake the part for the whole. They call this error the mereological fallacy (from the Greek mereo = part).

Nature-nurture

nature-nurture controversy
the dispute over the relative contributions of hereditary and constitutional factors (nature) and environmental factors (nurture) to the development of the individual.

The **nature–nurture** dichotomy became notorious when Francis Galton (1822–1911) argued that human beings display large, heritable differences in 'natural ability', that is, intelligence, combined with eagerness and power to work. He strongly believed that the environment had virtually no role to play and that high natural ability or genius should run in families. That is why his book *Hereditary Genius* (1869) was a study about the genealogies of statesmen, men of science, and other eminent personalities. To counter Galton's claim about the predominant role of nature, the French botanist Alphonse de Candolle (1806–1893) showed that Galton had underestimated the impact of environmental forces. He gathered a large amount of data about the socio-cultural circumstances that supported the emergence of eminent scientists (1873). Candolle's book inspired Galton to study prominent British scientists which he reported in *English Men of Science: Their Nature and Nurture* (1874). Because psychology mostly inclined to the environmental side, the nature–nurture issue estranged it from evolutionary biology that tended towards the nature side. Nowadays, the relationship between nature and nurture is no longer a question of which side or how much of each side explains differences between individuals, but how both sides interact.

Animal–human

The animal–human problem was concerned with man's place in nature. Until the eighteenth century, this question was answered in terms of an ascending scale of nature from bugs at the bottom to humans and gods at the top (Lovejoy 1964). Thus, humans were considered as having immortal souls, being semi-divine creatures and above ordinary animals. It was unclear that human beings were actually part of Nature and therefore a study-object for science. Theologians considered the soul of humans as their monopoly, but at the end of the eighteenth century this changed. New ideas of progress and a growing awareness of historical time gave the static, divinely ordered world a dynamic dimension. In the nineteenth century, evolutionary thought undermined the dichotomy between human beings as the possessors of a reason and an immortal soul, and other animals whose behaviour was merely guided by instincts. From now on, the human mind could become an appropriate subject-matter for scientific investigation (Richards 2002).

1.3   Biology

We will now take a closer look at evolutionary biology, the first science from which evolutionary psychology emerged. Before Darwin conceived his theory of evolution, natural philosophers thought about the origin and order of living beings. Empedocles (fifth century BC), a natural philosopher from ancient Greece, proposed the idea that floating body parts – heads or limbs without trunks, heads without eyes or mouth and so on – were attracted to each other until a perfect combination was achieved. Imperfect combinations, such as human bodies with animal heads, or humans which were half-man half-woman, would perish. He was perhaps inspired by the birth of monstrosities such as two-headed calves.

Aristotle, in the fourth century BC, had a different idea of perfection which he took from his teacher Plato. He came up with the suggestion that all animals could be arranged in a hierarchy according to their degree of perfection. As a criterion of rank in his scale he took the degree of development reached by the offspring at birth. Thus, he conceived eleven grades of perfection, with man at the top and zoophytes (i.e. animals that look like plants, such as sea anemones), at the bottom (Lovejoy 1964). In Christianity this scale of being or ladder of perfection (*scala naturae*) was considered a living proof of divine creation. Until the eighteenth century, many natural philosophers accepted without question this notion of a static hierarchy.

William Paley's designer fallacy

William Paley was a theologian in the eighteenth century who held the idea that if living things are very complicated, they could only be the product of an intelligent designer, not evolution. He advanced his argument of intelligent design in his book *Natural Theology* (1802) and presented the example that, if we were to find a watch by chance, the fine structure of its parts would convince us that a watchmaker had made it. By analogy, if we look at the complex structure of living things, we should accept that there is a supernatural designer. Paley points out that living things have all kinds of instruments designed to accomplish specific purposes. They have instruments for eating, for digesting, for breathing, for running, for reproducing, and so on. Paley emphasises the remarkable match between these instruments and the environment, such as wings that enable birds to travel through the air.

Most people at the time believed the argument for supernatural design to be true, including Darwin when he studied theology in Cambridge from 1828 to 1831 (see Box 1.1 How Charles Darwin became a natural scientist). But after his five-year voyage around the world Darwin became increasingly sceptical about Paley's argument and developed an evidence-based theory.

There are two problems with Paley's **designer fallacy** or wrong reasoning (Nettle 2009). The first problem is that Paley's explanation is not parsimonious. Parsimony is the principle of economy in science which holds that we should use the explanation which assumes the fewest unknown forces. An explanation should make the smallest number of unsupported assumptions and invoke the fewest unobservable constructs. However, the designer hypothesis outlined above suggests the existence of a being whom we have never been able to observe, and who must have powers of some unknown kind to work on such complicated matter as living things.

The second problem is that the designer-hypothesis is not explanatory. Explanation in science shows how complex things that we don't understand arise from simpler things that we do understand. Any agent that can design something as complex as an animal must be more complex than that animal. So, where does the complexity from the designer come from? Therefore, in essence, the problem with Paley's argument is that we end up with an infinite series of increasingly powerful designers. More specifically, we go from something we understand moderately well (an animal) to something we understand not at all (an infinite designer). This procedure doesn't conform with good scientific practice.

In his book *On the Origin of Species* (1859) Darwin explained how natural forces of selection, acting upon inherited features, could gradually shape the evolution of organic structures. He argued that organisms have indeed design-like features as they match the requirements of the environment. But these features are not the result of supernatural design but the cumulative outcome of natural selection. The idea of natural selection is parsimonious because it does not invoke things we do not already know, and it is explanatory because it shows convincingly how complex things arise from simple forces.

designer fallacy

mistaken idea that if living things are very complicated, they could only be the product of an intelligent designer, not evolution.

KEY FIGURE Charles Darwin

Selected works

On the Origin of Species (1859).

Descent of Man and Selection in Relation to Sex (1871).

The Expression of Emotions in Man and Animals (1872).

The complete works of Charles Darwin are accessible online: http://darwin-online.org.uk.

Photo source: Science Photo Library / Paul D. Stewart

BOX 1.1 How Charles Darwin became a natural scientist

Charles Darwin (1809–1882) was the son of a country physician. His formal education began at the age of eight when he joined a grammar school. Darwin disliked learning by rote and often ran home to play. His performance at school gave no hint of his later talent. In *Autobiographies* (2002) he wrote about his unhappiness:

> Nothing could have been worse for the development of my mind than Dr Butler's school, as it was strictly classical, nothing else being taught except a little ancient geography and history. The school as a means of education to me was simply a blank . . . When I left the school I was for my age neither high nor low in it; and I believe that I was considered by all my masters and by my Father as a very ordinary boy, rather below the common standard in intellect. To my deep mortification my father once said to me, 'You care for nothing but shooting, dogs, rat-catching, and you will be a disgrace to yourself and all your family'. But my father, who was the kindest man I ever knew, and whose memory I love with all my heart, must have been angry and somewhat unjust when he used such words. (2002: 10, 11).

Darwin left school at sixteen and joined the University of Edinburgh to study medicine. However, he considered most lectures boring and was disgusted by the dissection of corpses and surgical operations without anaesthetic.

After two years Darwin's father realised that his son had no talent for medicine and encouraged him to study for the clergy at the University of Cambridge. He spent three years there but preferred hunting, collecting beetles, studying rocks and taking long walks with Professor John Steven Henslow, a botanist who stimulated his interest in natural history. In 1831, the same year that Darwin took his final exams at Cambridge, he was invited to join HMS *Beagle* on a surveying trip around the globe. The captain, Robert Fitzroy, wanted a suitable traveling companion. During the five-year voyage (see Figure 1.1), Darwin transformed himself from an amateur to a dedicated geologist and biologist. He recorded his observations in his journal and assembled a huge collection of fossil animals, plants, and rocks which he sent back to Henslow and other scholars. Following his return in 1836, Darwin published books on his voyage and the geology of coral atolls, of volcanic islands and of South America. Meanwhile, Darwin's father understood that his son had become a promising and respectable scientist and supported his work financially. When Darwin married Emma Wedgwood in 1840, they received £18,000 as wedding gifts from their parents and a further £45,000 inheritance with the death of Charles' father in 1848. By 1882, smart investment had more than quadrupled the estate to £282,000. This wealth allowed Darwin to devote himself to a life in science and raise a large family. Emma

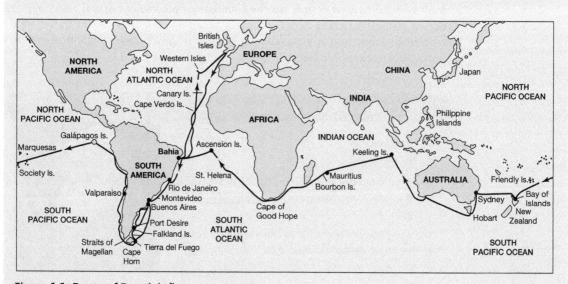

Figure 1.1 Route of Darwin's five-year voyage

gave birth to ten children, seven of whom survived to adulthood.

Some biographies of Charles Darwin

Berra, T. (2009). *Charles Darwin: The Concise Story of an Extraordinary Man.* Baltimore: The Johns Hopkins University Press.

Brown, J. (1995). *Charles Darwin: Voyaging. Volume I.* Princeton, NJ: Princeton University Press.

Brown, J. (2002). *Charles Darwin: The Power of Place. Volume II.* New York: Alfred Knopf.

Brown, J. (2007). *Darwin's Origin of Species: A Biography.* New York: Atlantic Monthly Press.

Desmond, A. and Moore, J. (1992). *Darwin.* London: Penguin Books.

Desmond, A., Moore, J. and Brown, J. (2007). *Charles Darwin.* Oxford: Oxford University Press.

Evolution as the non-random selection of random events

evolution

(1) the change in appearance, or gene frequencies, of populations and species over generations; (2) the origins and extinctions of species.

variation

phenotypic and/or genotypic differences between individuals of a population.

genetic recombination

the production of offspring with combinations of traits that differ from those found in either parent.

mutation

any permanent change in the genetic material of an organism that is not the result of the recombination of the male and female genome. Mutation is mostly the result of exposure to radiation or chemicals.

natural selection

the causal mechanism that accounts for the evolutionary change in populations of organisms; or, the process by which the forms of organisms in a population that are best adapted to the environment increase in frequency relative to those less well adapted forms over a number of generations.

What does Darwin's theory of **evolution** involve? To understand the accomplishment of his theory, we should compare biology with physics and chemistry because there is a substantial difference between these sciences (Kutschera and Niklas 2004). In physics and chemistry one investigates the properties and interactions of objects, such as atoms and electrons, which are physically uniform and invariant in their traits and behaviour. Thus, a single experiment with one entity (e.g. electron or photon) is sufficient to extrapolate the properties of all comparable entities in the universe.

In biology the situation is different. The organisms that biologists investigate show an amazing **variation**. The differences between individuals, such as different eye colour, face structure, hair colour, and body height, are a consequence of **genetic recombination** and random genomic change. Genetic recombination is the term for the production of offspring with combinations of traits that differ from those found in either parent. And random genomic change (or **mutation**) is any change of the genetic material of an organism that is not the result of the recombination of the male and female genome. Genome is the term for the total genetic material within the cell of an organism. Cells house their genome in a dedicated intracellular compartment, the nucleus. As a result of genetic recombination and random genomic change, no two members of the same species look exactly alike, with the exception of identical twins and cloned individuals.

Evolution may, in essence, be regarded as the non-random selection of random events. Random events are the mixing of male and female genome, and mutations. Both are the major sources of variation in a population. The non-random process of **natural selection** evaluates organisms systematically for fitness, that is, the difference in reproductive success of an individual relative to another. This selection mechanism lies at the heart of the evolution theory. It is a process that sorts out the individuals in each generation and determines the direction of evolutionary change. (Another form of selection, viz. sexual selection will be discussed in Part 2 Chapter 4, males and females.)

The components of evolutionary theory

Natural selection – the central component of evolutionary theory – is the causal mechanism that accounts for the evolutionary change in populations of organisms.

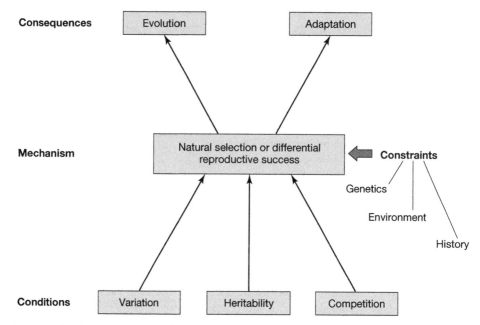

Figure 1.2 The components of evolutionary theory
Source: Lewin and Foley (2004)

Other components act either as the conditions required for natural selection to work, or as constraints on how it operates, or as consequences of its work (Foley 1968; Lewin and Foley 2004; see Figure 1.2).

Four conditions are required:

- *Reproduction.* Organisms must reproduce to form new generations. If they do not reproduce, the cycle of life would have to start again with each deceased generation.

- *Inheritance.* There should be a mode of inheritance resulting in offspring that resemble their parents more than the other individuals in the population. If there was no mode of **inheritance**, the advantageous characteristics of parents would be lost in the next generation. (This condition refers to the field of genetics which Darwin least understood.)

- *Variation.* Individual organisms must have heritable variations in their characteristics which are the result of sexual recombination and mutation. For example, natural selection can only work on body height if different individuals in the population have different body heights.

- *Competition.* If the resources needed to support all populations were infinite, then there would be no differential reproduction. Individuals would have as many offspring as they wanted, a situation which does not correspond with the world we know. In fact, the reality is that resources such as food, energy and water are limited.

inheritance

the transmission of genetic information from one generation (parents) to another (offspring).

When the four conditions are met for any property of a species, natural selection results. If any condition is not fulfilled, selection does not work. Entities such as rocks or planets that do not reproduce, cannot evolve by natural selection. Entities that reproduce but do not vary in any property, cannot evolve because natural selection can only work on differences. So natural selection is defined as the process by which the form and behaviour of organisms in a population that are best adapted to the environment increase in frequency relative to those less well adapted forms over a number of generations (Ridley 2005). Thus natural selection determines the 'fitness', or difference in reproductive success of an individual relative to another.

Two consequences of natural selection are adaptation and evolution, which we will discuss in the next sections. Constraints may influence how natural selection works. For example, genetic inheritance is not only a necessary condition for natural selection but also a constraint. Genetic inheritance systems can be found in all organisms and are mostly confined to parents and their offspring. Here, we explain what is meant by inheritance from parents to offspring. In a later section you will learn that micro-organisms may inherit genes from unrelated organisms, a phenomenon which is known as 'horizontal gene transfer'.

Inheritance

genes
particulate units of inheritance that are passed from parents to offspring.

Today we know that individuals that survive and produce offspring, pass their **genes** on to the next generation. Without this mode of inheritance the advantageous features of parents would simply be lost in each generation. Darwin's book *On The Origin of Species* (1859) was ignorant about how inheritance exactly works (Schwartz 2008). An influential hypothesis at his time, propagated by the French biologist Jean-Baptiste Lamarck (1809, trans. 1914, 2011), suggested that an individual inherits characteristics that its parents acquired during their lifetimes (e.g. muscular strength). A central feature of his hypothesis was that, when confronted with new environments, organisms learn new habits and can change appropriately through an unknown, inner property of life. The origin of new characteristics and their transmission to further generations was believed to be aided by two principles. First, the principle of use and disuse which implies that continuous use of any organ strengthens its power while permanent disuse reduces its capacity until it disappears. Second, the principle of inheritance of acquired characteristics which implies that all acquisitions and losses due to permanent (dis)use of organs are passed on to the new individuals.

germ line
the germ cells that contribute cells to the next generation of individuals. Other cells of the individual constitute the soma, or all somatic cells.

somatic cell
any body cell of multi-cellular organism other than gamete.

Weismann barrier
the principle named after August Weismann (1834-1914) that hereditary information moves only from reproductive cells to somatic cells, and not vice versa. Thus, it rules out any possibility of the inheritance of acquired characteristics.

To prove that inheritance of acquired characteristics was an erroneous idea, the German biologist August Weismann (1834–1914) repeatedly chopped off the tails of mice and showed that the offspring still grew them. Weismann introduced a distinction between **germ line** and soma (or body) which rendered inheritance of acquired characteristics a logical impossibility (1893). He proposed that multi-cellular organisms possess two types of cells, the germ cells which convey heritable information from one generation to the next (the germ line), and **somatic cells**, which are used to build the body. Although environmental effects during the life of an individual may influence somatic cells, the germ cells are considered immune to these influences. The soma–germ line distinction is known as the **Weismann barrier**, or the principle that genetic information moves only from germ line to the soma, and never from somatic to germ cells. Germ cells are initially separate from somatic cells in the developing embryo; later they migrate into the **gonads** (ovaries, testes) of the embryo. For example, during the sixth week of the human embryo the germ cells are incorporated in the gonads (Moore and Persaud 2008: 263).

gonads
collective term for ovaries and testes.

The Weismann barrier ruled out any possibility of the inheritance of acquired characteristics, but we know now that it is possible (Jablonka and Lamb 2005, 2007a, 2007b, 2010; Jablonka 2011). Weismann's claim that somatic changes could not influence the germ line served as a rationale for evolutionary biologists to study heredity without taking notice of development. However, embryologists and developmental biologists who believed that heredity involves more than the inheritance of genes from parents, did not share this view. They had a broad conception of heredity, to be understood as the passing of developmental processes, not traits, from parent to offspring (Amundson 2005). Offspring inherit their modes of development which in turn produce the traits. Due to the discovery of genes, this broad conception of heredity was drastically narrowed in the early twentieth century. Heredity was now considered the transmission of traits, or representatives of traits such as genes, between generations. The narrow conception of heredity excluded the developmental process which requires the individual to pass through a trajectory from fertilised egg to adult. This subject-matter will be discussed extensively in Chapter 12 (Evolution through development).

Heredity normally takes place through the transmission of germ line genes. Jablonka and Lamb (2010) argue that body-to-body (or soma-to-soma) routes of transmission which bypass the germ line, are no less important for understanding the hereditary basis of evolution. **Body-to-body transmission** (in a broad sense also known as '**epigenetic inheritance**') is an umbrella term for the many processes through which developmentally acquired or learned characteristics are reconstructed in successive generations. Body-to-body transmission can take place through developmental interactions between mother and offspring. For example, evidence shows that maternal antibodies transmitted through the placenta and milk, enhance the effectiveness of the neonate's immune system and some effects can be passed on to grandchildren (Lemke et al. 2004, as discussed by Jablonka 2011). Body-to-body transmission can also take place through **social learning** (e.g. patterns of feeding, mating) or through symbolic communication (e.g. language, music). It should be noted that this subject matter is under discussion (see, for example, Jablonka and Lamb 2007a, 2007b), We will take up this issue in Chapter 10 (Culture in evolution).

In Darwin's time, people believed that the inherited material was a fluid (e.g. sperm, blood) and children were a blend of their parents. They were supposed to be averages of their parents with the implication that the mating of tall and small adults would result in children of average height. The problem with this theory of blending inheritance was that a fluid would be diluted in a matter of a few generations. Without a new source of variation, evolution would then soon grind to a halt. In his later book *The Variation of Animals and Plants under Domestication* (1868), Darwin came up with the idea that acquired characteristics of parents would be transmitted to their offspring via microscopic particles. Each cell was supposed to shed constantly particles that circulated throughout the body and eventually found their way to the reproductive cells, where they could be assembled into germ and egg cells, capable of giving rise to new organisms.

The theory that inheritance is not blending but particulate, came from Gregor Mendel (1822–1884) who carried out experiments with garden peas and bees. Mendel read a German translation of Darwin's *On The Origin of Species* before publishing his seminal paper in 1865, but he did not see any connection between his work and Darwin's. Darwin possessed two books that briefly referred to Mendel's work, but there is no evidence that he read the relevant sections. Mendel carried out

---

body-to-body transmission

umbrella term for the many processes through which developmentally acquired or learned characteristics are reconstructed in successive generations. Also known, in a broad sense, as epigenetic inheritance.

epigenetic inheritance

in a broad sense, a type of inheritance that bypasses the germ line and includes body-to-body information transfer between generations of individuals. It can take place through developmental interactions between mother and offspring, social learning, or symbolic communication. Also known as body-to-body transmission.

social learning

a change of behaviour that is the result of social interactions with other individuals, usually of the same species.

many experiments and discovered that: (1) the stuff of heredity consists of particles (now called genes), not fluids; (2) each normal adult carries a pair of genes for each trait; (3) when breeding, each parent gives only one of its pair of genes for each trait; and (4) pairs of genes cannot dilute, but nevertheless influence each other's expression through interactions such as dominance. In 1900, Mendel's insights were rediscovered independently by three botanists: Hugo de Vries, Carl Correns and Erich Tschermak.

In 1953, James Watson and Francis Crick discovered that genes consist of a long spiral-formed molecule, called Deoxyribo Nucleic Acid (**DNA**). This molecule is made of two strands of four distinct bases: adenine, cytosine, guanine and thymine. These chemical building blocks are abbreviated by the single letters A, C, G and T. The strands are held together by strong chemical bonds between pairs of bases on opposite strands: A always pairs with T, and C always pairs with G. If we know the sequence of one strand of DNA, we know also the sequence of the other one. Owing to the complementary structure of bases, the DNA molecule has two unique properties. First, it has the ability to make copies of itself, which is called molecular replication. When the two strands are unzipped, each strand attracts the missing bases which are available in a loose form in the cell nucleus. Unzipping occurs when cells divide during the growth of the body. As the structure of DNA lends itself to replication, each new cell is a copy or replicate of the original DNA molecule.

However, there is a problem because DNA which carries the instructions (in code) for building proteins, cannot leave the cell nucleus. Proteins are the molecules that do all of the work in every organism, such as carrying oxygen, building tissues and breaking down food. Proteins themselves are made up of building blocks, called amino acids, each of which are encoded as a combination of three bases (ACT, GAA etc.) in the DNA molecule. Now, a second property of DNA comes in useful, namely its ability to produce proteins with the help of Ribo Nucleic Acid (RNA). Because RNA is small and mobile, it can move out of the cell nucleus. If there is a need for a specific protein, a RNA-copy is made of the DNA that codes for the needed protein. Outside the cell nucleus, this RNA passes on the instructions about the amino acid sequence of the protein. In molecular genetics this process is summarised as: 'DNA makes RNA which makes protein'.

DNA
deoxyribonucleid acid is the hereditary material – the substance of genes – in all organisms.

Adaptation in the Galápagos finches

The conditions under which natural selection works, have all been tested in the laboratory and in the field. A famous case is about the Galápagos finches. During his five-year voyage around the world, Darwin spent 19 days on the Galápagos Islands. He was impressed by the diversity of wildlife, particularly the variety of finches. His observation that each island appeared to have its own group of species raised the question what could account for this distribution of organisms. Back home, it was John Gould, a prominent English ornithologist, who analysed the finches as they had been collected by Darwin and other members of the *Beagle* crew. He showed that many of these finch species which strongly varied in body size and beak shape, were confined to different islands. This observation influenced Darwin's thinking because it suggested that these birds must have colonised the islands after their volcanic origin from the ocean floor and then evolved into different forms on separate islands.

The importance of the Galápagos finches to our understanding of how evolution works, has been increased by the investigations of Peter and Rosemary Grant. They have studied these finches since 1973 by relating the degree of variation in important environmental factors (e.g. hardness of seeds or scarcity of insects) to the amount of variation in beak size and morphology. During their study a dramatic event enabled them to show natural selection in action. In 1977 a severe drought killed off 85 per cent of the medium ground finches. The deaths were not random because the survivors had larger beaks than the dead individuals who had been unable to crack open their staple food, the seeds of dry fruits. Since beak size is heritable, the evolutionary outcome of the selection event could be observed in the next generation. The offspring of the survivors had a significantly larger beak size than that of the population finches before the drought (Grant and Estes 2009).

adaptation

any structural, behavioural, or cognitive feature of an organism that improves its survival and reproduction in its local environment.

The Galápagos case shows that if the necessary conditions are present – reproduction, variation, inheritance and competition – the consequent evolution may be observed from changes in the appearance and behaviour of populations over generations. Evolution means change in the form and behaviour of organisms between generations within a population of a species. The case also demonstrates **adaptation**, the second consequence of natural selection, which is defined as any distinguishable characteristic, feature, trait, or property of an organism that enables it to survive and reproduce in its local environment. Some authors distinguish adaptations from exaptations if they originated for one purpose but are now used for another purpose (Gould 1991, mentioned by Grant and Estes, 2009: 145; Buss and Haselton 1998). For example, feathers originated probably as insulation devices and were only later exapted, that is, co-opted for flight (Caroll et al. 2005).

homology

similar character resulting from common ancestry. For example, humans and chimpanzees have forward-projecting eyes and grasping hands due to descent from a common ancestor.

The theory of evolution predicts that animals which have common ancestors, also have similar adaptations. For example, the hands of humans look like the paws of rats because both descend from a common ancestor. Similar adaptations which are the result of shared ancestry, are called '**homologies**'. They are useful for reconstructing the tree of life. (This topic will be discussed in Chapter 3.) The theory of evolution further predicts that unrelated organisms which have been subjected to common living conditions, also have similar adaptations. For example, birds and insects have no common ancestors but both have wings because they have undergone similar **selection pressures** (e.g. climate, predation). Similar adaptations which result from common selection pressures are referred to as '**analogies**'.

selection pressures

forces that over a long evolutionary time and in a consistent manner shape the organism's traits which cause it to be successful in survival and reproduction.

To identify an adaptation it is necessary to determine the selection pressures responsible for the origin and maintenance of a trait. Selection pressures are defined as forces that over a long evolutionary time and in a consistent manner shape the organism's traits which cause it to be successful in survival and reproduction. To say that there is 'selection for' or 'selection pressure for' given traits – grasping hands, large brains, cognitive capacities – means that having these traits causes differences in survival and reproductive success (Sober 1993). Selection pressures may come from the physical environment – climate change, limited resources, intensity of predation – and the social environment – social competition, need for cooperation, social learning (e.g. Byrne 2000; Geary 2009, 2010).

analogy

similar characteristic resulting from common selection pressures. For example, bats, birds and (extinct) pterosaurs, developed independently the capacity to fly.

Horizontal gene transfer

Apart from conditions and consequences, the theory of evolution also considers constraints. Recall that genetic inheritance systems are mostly confined to parents and their offspring. Genetic inheritance from parents to offspring is, however, not an ironclad rule because it has recently been discovered that micro-organisms may inherit genes from unrelated organisms, a phenomenon which is called horizontal gene transfer. For example, our cells contain **mitochondria**, being structures for cellular respiration that convert sugars and fats into energy with the help of oxygen. Long ago, mitochondria evolved from independent, free-living bacteria that were incorporated by the ancestors of plants and animals. Without this genome fusion there would be no animals as mitochondria provide our bodies and brains with energy. Similarly, chloroplasts are structures found in the cells of green plants and some algae where photosynthesis takes place which puts oxygen into the air. Like mitochondria, chloroplasts began their life as independent, free-living bacteria but were swallowed by a common ancestor of all plants and algae. Without this gene transfer between photo-synthetic bacteria and a common ancestor of plants and algae, there would be no oxygen to convert sugars and fats into the energy we need (Doolittle 1999).

What is more, inheritance need not be confined to genes but may include culture, being all knowledge and beliefs we learn from each other. For example, human parents transmit not only genes but also language, table manners and hygienic practices to their offspring. Furthermore, culture may also be transmitted horizontally among persons of the same generation. For example, opinion-leaders in politics or fashion successfully spread ideas and bring about rapid cultural change. Thus, we may even learn from people we have never met face to face. Another example is science where peer pressure may encourage a person to accept an idea (Stone et al. 2007).

To summarise, the theory of evolution originally considered the vertical transmission of only genes as a constraint. However, more recently, this has turned into a new opportunity. The incorporation of horizontal gene transfer makes the theory more complicated, but it promises a better understanding of the evolutionary process. The same applies to cultural transmission. Culture needs also to be integrated in the theory of evolution (e.g. Durham 1991). If we want to understand more about ourselves, we should take into consideration that human evolution is increasingly a matter of cultural evolution. The question how culture should be integrated in the evolutionary theory is under discussion. This issue will be discussed in Chapter 10.

Expanded evolutionary synthesis

The theory of evolution was substantially elaborated upon in the early part of the twentieth century with the rediscovery of Mendelian genetics and advances in population genetics. In the 1930s and 1940s a synthesis took place between evolutionary biology, population genetics, systematic biology and paleobiology (Huxley 1942). This synthesis also discarded a number of misconceptions in biology, such as the theory of blending inheritance. Population genetics uses mathematical theory and empirical studies to understand genetic variation and mutation. Systematic biology studies the diversity of life and the phylogenetic (or genealogical) relationships between species. Palaeobiology uses the fossil record to study the history of organisms and their environments. In the last six decades, the evolutionary synthesis expanded as more sciences, such as plant science (botany), cell biology, molecular biology, **ethology** (or behavioural biology), and sociobiology joined forces with evolutionary biology (Kutschera and Niklas 2004). More recently, evolutionary thinking has also influenced disciplines like psychology, neuroscience, computer science and economics.

---

mitochondria

intracellular organelles, derived from bacterial ancestors with their genomes which are the energy factories of the cell.

modern synthesis

integration of population genetics, systematic biology and palaeobiology in evolutionary biology in the 1940s.

ethology

a branch of biology dedicated to the study of behaviour and behavioural traditions.

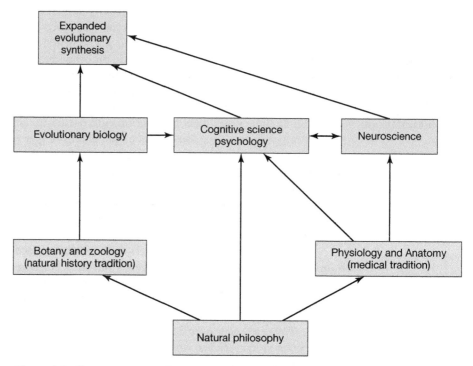

Figure 1.3 The emergence, divergence and convergence of three sciences

To sum up, science has grown enormously through specialisation which is based on the practice of dividing problems into smaller ones that then become the subject-matter of new disciplines. But analysis of separate problems is not all that scientists do. The expanded evolutionary synthesis shows that the integration of specialised bodies of knowledge is also crucial (Figure 1.3).

At the bottom of Figure 1.3 we see the three sciences starting as branches of natural philosophy. As we have argued in section 1.2, these sciences diverged, first, because they specialised and grew apart and, second, because they struggled with the old issues of mind–brain, nature–nurture and animal–human. Next we see the emergence of two traditions: natural history and medicine (Mayr 1997). The natural history tradition which refers to the study of plants and animals, eventually gave rise to evolutionary biology, while the medical tradition, referring to the study of physiology and anatomy, gave birth to neuroscience. In the middle is psychology as it originated from philosophy as well as physiology. How did psychology emerge as a science? And how did it respond to Darwin's theory?

1.4   Psychology

Psychology started long ago as part of philosophy which reflected about matters of the mind, such as the relations between the immortal soul and the body, the nature of consciousness, the innateness of ideas, the mastery of one's passions, and so forth.

In the nineteenth century, psychology turned into a science when it experienced the influence of physiology which made serious advances. The experimental study of the senses paved the way for psychological experimentation. But a method was not enough for doing science; it also needed a theory which provides potential answers to questions.

Evolutionary thought and the birth of modern psychology

Many consider Wilhelm Wundt (1832–1920) as the founding father of psychological science because he started the first laboratory of experimental psychology in 1879. His laboratory in Leipzig was soon to become the centre for anyone interested in the new psychology. Wundt was trained in physiology and medicine and gradually became interested in psychology. He investigated sensation and perception topics, using the methods of physiology, but did not believe that higher mental functions such as cognition or consciousness could be studied experimentally. Social factors played a key role in the establishment of experimental psychology in Germany (Ben-David 1991; Kusch 1995). The first psychologists found themselves in an inconvenient situation because physiology enjoyed a higher academic standing than philosophy, while employment conditions were better in philosophy. Working in the philosophy department, they maintained their scientific standing by applying experimental methods to philosophical subjects.

Not all philosophers could appreciate the ambition of psychology as a natural science. They considered the new science as a rude intrusion on their traditional concerns and banded together to oppose its growth. Some philosophers condemned psychologists as 'experimental fanatics' who confused their 'cult of facts' with a genuine analysis of consciousness. Others agreed with younger psychologists that they should be grouped with chemists and physicists, not with philosophers. However, efforts to move psychology to medicine with physiology, were unsuccessful (Leahey 2000).

Wundt appears to have read a translation of Darwin's *On the Origin of Species* while he prepared the second volume of his lectures about the mind (or soul) of man and animal. He interpreted natural selection mistakenly as dependent on the inheritance of purposeful acquired characteristics. He would never abandon his belief that individual intention and habit were important instruments of behavioural and mental evolution (Richards 1987).

The establishment of psychology as a natural science is mainly associated with Wundt's laboratory. Evolutionary thought was nevertheless crucial to the birth of modern psychology, but mostly underplayed by earlier historians who emphasised the experimental methodology derived from physiology. Evolutionary thinking was essential for the founding of psychology because it supplied a unified theoretical framework that the new science needed. Central evolutionary ideas at the time can be identified which supplied the unified theoretical framework psychology needed (Richards 2002). For example, the idea that humans were not semi-divine beings but rather descendants from primates. Or the idea of spontaneous variation that provided the raw material for natural selection. And the idea of recapitulation, popularised by the German biologist Ernst Haeckel, which held that each individual recapitulates in its development from conception to maturity, the evolutionary stages through which its species has passed. (This matter will be discussed in Chapter 12.) Such notions stimulated interest in human nature on a wide range of fronts. How far were human characteristics present in rudimentary form in other animals? The idea that the diversity of the human stock was the raw material from which future generations would be selected, inspired Francis Galton to start his psychometric studies of individual differences and the development of statistical procedures for analysing them.

Darwin's evolutionary theory implied that every human attribute, from bodily organ to physiology, behaviour and mental function, is subject to natural selection. His theory also suggested bodily and mental continuity between humans and their ancestors: no trait could be absolutely new. Darwin's idea about the mental continuity between humans and their ancestors, stimulated the comparative study of animal minds. For example, George Romanes (1848–1894), a disciple of Darwin, argued that the instincts of animals could provide evidence for the heritability of mental faculties. The empirical proofs of his instinct theory amounted to a collection of anecdotes about animals that transmitted acquired habits to their offspring. For instance, a friend's cat had been taught to beg for food and had borne kittens which adopted the same habit (Richards 1987).

The shift from mind to behaviour

Because the insights of comparative psychology were too speculative and anecdotal, researchers began to shift their attention from mental states to behaviour (Richards 1987). Under the influence of John Watson (1878–1958), this shift in psychology's study object led to what is known as behaviourism. This approach was an attempt to build psychology on observable behaviour, and move away from speculations about the 'invisible' mind. Watson rejected the experimental method of introspection that Wundt and his American disciples such as Edward Titchener used. He argued that psychology should be based on the objective observation of behaviour and not on the subjective introspection of experience.

Watson was also unhappy with the hereditarian bias in psychology as a legacy of its commitment to evolutionary thought. His unease with evolutionary thought was based on the old nature–nurture fallacy which even today causes confusion. This fallacy implies that if you say a behaviour evolved, then it cannot change. This is a mistaken idea because evolution is the gradual change of organisms through their interaction with the environment. Watson, therefore, started from the wrong assumption that an animal comes to a learning situation as a blank slate. Watson's dissatisfaction with heredity originated from his belief that science should provide practical knowledge. A classic statement in his book *Behaviorism* (1924:104) reads:

> Give me a dozen healthy infants, well-informed and my own specified world to bring them up in and I'll guarantee to take any one at random and train them to become any type of specialist I might select – doctor, lawyer, artist, merchant-chief and, yes, even beggar-man and thief, regardless of his talents, penchants, tendencies, abilities, vocations and race of his ancestors.

The democratic message implied by Watson's statement struck a resonant cord in the hearts of American readers. The mind of children had no inherited grooves that determined its course in life, but was malleable through behaviourist principles. Watson's wish to change and control behaviour would therefore downplay the importance of heredity as an ingredient of evolutionary thought.

Watson's conceptual move consisted of three parts. First, the rejection of all speculations on inner mental states as the basis of psychology. Second, the study of animals should be transferable to the understanding of humans. Third, his emphasis on learning as the association between stimuli and responses (see Box 1.2 Learning by association).

BOX 1.2 Learning by association

This idea came from the British philosopher David Hume (1711–1776) who argued that all knowledge is based on experience and that thought is the association of ideas. He mentioned three principles that would enable the association of ideas. The principle of resemblance holds that our thoughts run easily from one idea to other similar ideas, such as when thinking of one friend stimulates the recollection of other friends. The principle of contiguity states that when one thinks of an object there is a tendency to recall other objects that one experienced at the same time and place, such as when thinking about your living room may stimulate thoughts about your partner, piano and bookcase. The principle of causality means that when we think of an outcome we tend also to think of the events that preceded the outcome, for instance when seeing someone wounded will stimulate thoughts about accidents.

The idea of learning by association fitted with Pavlov's conditioning experiments that became known in the United States in the 1920s. Ivan Pavlov (1849–1936), a Russian physiologist, discovered the conditioned reflex during his work on digestion. His research method involved a surgical arrangement that allowed the dog's gastric juices to flow out of the body and to be collected. While studying the secretion in response to substances such as meat powder, Pavlov noticed that objects or events associated with meat powder also caused secretions, for example, the mere sight of the experimenter or the sound of his footsteps.

Conditioning or learning by association is an experimental procedure that makes behaviour dependent on certain conditions. In Pavlov's classical version of conditioning, an animal detects associations between external events, one of which is reinforcing (or aversive), and modifies its behaviour in such a way that the appropriate response is elicited. For example, the unconditional stimulus (e.g. the sight or smell of food) is presented in association with a conditional, that is, arbitrary stimulus (e.g. ringing a bell or flashing a light). After a number of presentations, the response (e.g. salivation) that depended on the unconditional stimulus, is elicited even when only the conditional stimulus is presented.

The instrumental or operant version of conditioning differs from classical conditioning in that instead of bringing a new stimulus into association with a given behaviour pattern, a new pattern is brought into association with reduction of a need (e.g. satisfying hunger). The behaviour of the animal (e.g. pressing a lever, pecking at a target) should first occur spontaneously or by accident. When reinforcement (e.g. food) follows this behaviour, the animal forms or strengthens an association between the behaviour and the need (e.g. hunger). The difference between both forms of conditioning is that in classical conditioning the animal learns passively to associate the stimulus with the consequence, while in operant conditioning it actively performs the behaviour that becomes conditioned. Both forms of conditioning as they are practised in laboratory, have parallels in nature. Free-living animals have frequently been observed to try out some new behaviour when foraging or building a nest. If some behaviours prove to be effective, they are reinforced and become associated with the situation.

The behaviourist approach found fertile soil in American society because it promised to deliver understanding in practical issues, such as education and psychotherapy (Plotkin 2004). At the same time, the triumph of behaviourist thinking signalled the decline of evolutionary theorising in psychology which spread to other social sciences, such as cultural anthropology and sociology (Richards 1987). Psychologists, followed by anthropologists and sociologists downplayed the influence of evolutionary history and insisted that human behaviour could be understood only through culture and principles of learning theory. In this context, evolutionary thought became irrelevant and almost disappeared from psychology. The revival of evolutionary thinking in psychology had to wait until the 1990s.

The limits of behaviourist thinking

In due time the limits of behaviourist thinking became clear. For example, the work of Marian and Keller Breland (1961) undermined an important assumption of behaviourism. They had a business called *Animal Behavior Enterprises*, that used operant conditioning principles to teach animals to do various tricks. The animals were then put on display at fairs and amusement parks. The animals seemed conditionable but as time passed, instinctive behaviour overruled learned behaviour. As an example, pigs had learnt to carry wooden coins to a 'piggy bank' and deposit them, usually four or five coins for one reinforcement. At first, pigs were eager to run over for each dollar, but after a few weeks they would drop the coin, root it, toss it up in the air, and so on.

The observations of Breland and Breland undermined Watson's assumption that an animal comes to a learning situation as a blank slate, that is, without genetic predispositions. Later research by Martin Seligman (1970) found that animals are evolutionary prepared to form certain associations and counter-prepared to form others. Conditioning a pigeon's pecking response in order to obtain food by pecking a button is easy, but conditioning its wing-preening to get food is impossible because they are counter-prepared.

Today, it is easy to brush behaviourism aside because pigs, rats, let alone humans, are a lot more complicated than behaviourists anticipated. The weak point of behaviourism was indeed that it did not provide a theoretical framework which could explain a large range of subjects. The strong point of behaviourism, however, was its conditioning methodology that has influenced experimental study in psychology and neuroscience. For example, much of the research on the neural mechanisms of emotion has focused on fear conditioning in rats (Pinel 2003). Watson would probably applaud these experiments because it involves careful measurements of behaviour and neurobiological variables (Thompson 1994). In this sense, we may regard neuroscience as the continuation of behaviourism. More about neuroscience in section 1.5.

Behaviourism was a systematic attempt to make psychology as empirical as the natural sciences. In doing so, behaviourists changed psychology into a science of behaviour, banning any reference to mental processes, such as reasoning and imagination, but also categories like emotion, belief and desire (Plotkin 2004). The problem with behaviourism was that it pleaded for an atheoretical approach that was quite unlike what happened in the natural sciences.

The revival of evolutionary psychology

The revival of evolutionary psychology owes much of its prestige to cognitive science which arose in opposition to behaviourism. It allowed psychologists to develop theories about mental processes that are supposed to cause behaviour and solve problems. During the reign of behaviourism, psychologists were forbidden to postulate mental entities that could not be perceived with the senses. Thus, they were trapped in an absurd position, comparable to that of geneticists not allowed to postulate the existence of genes, neuroscientists not allowed to speculate about neurons and transmitters, evolutionary biologists unable to invoke natural selection as a non-random process, or chemists without the ability to assume atoms and subatomic particles (Plotkin 2004).

With the rise of cognitive science, psychology became a science again, allowed to claim the existence of mental mechanisms not immediately visible to the eyes.

Mental mechanisms became 'visible' when the study of human cognition made use of brain imaging technology in the 1980s (Raichle 2009). The experimental designs for analysing mental processes by using information-processing theory fit well with emerging brain scanning techniques, such as functional Magnetic Resonance Imaging (fMRI). Since then, the collaboration between cognitive scientists and neuroscientists has resulted into a wealth of knowledge. It should be noted that fMRI records are closely associated with the **oxygenation** level of the blood rather than the neural activity directly. Magnetic resonance images respond to the metabolic, not the informational, aspects of neural activity. So there is no simple, direct step between an fMRI image and a thought (Uttal 2009).

oxygenation
the process by which concentrations of oxygen increase within a tissue.

Three influences account for the development of cognitive psychology (Anderson 2005). First was the research on human performance, which was stimulated during the Second World War by governments who needed information on how to train soldiers to use sophisticated equipment and how to deal with diminished attention under stress. We can trace three main influences underlying the emergence of cognitive psychology. First and of particular influence were ideas to treat cognition (e.g. perceiving, remembering, reasoning and problem-solving) as the processing of information. Second were developments in computer science, especially artificial intelligence that tried to get computers to behave intelligently. The third influence on cognitive psychology was linguistics. The work of linguists showed that language was much more complicated than expected and that behaviourism was incapable of explaining its complexity. In the 1970s, a related new science called cognitive science emerged that integrated research efforts from psychology, artificial intelligence, linguistics, philosophy and neuroscience.

The new theorising in evolutionary biology was another stimulus for the revival of evolutionary thought in psychology. For the first half of the twentieth century, the major task in evolutionary biology was to synthesise Darwin's evolutionary theory with Mendel's genetics. The science of genetics indeed made great progress, but evolutionary biologists had not developed theories of how selection might have shaped phenotypes, that is, the observable characteristics of organism, including how they evolved to interact with one another and their physical environment. When evolutionary biologists turned their attention to these questions, they began to generate new theories, for example, about behavioural strategies of animals to find food, parental investment into offspring, conflicts between parents and offspring, and altruism between related and unrelated individuals.

An overview of these new theories appeared in 1975, written by Edward Wilson, under the title: *Sociobiology*. It was meant as a synthetic study about the biological explanation of animal social behaviour. Its second mission was to introduce evolutionary thinking into the social sciences (e.g. sociology, psychology, anthropology). Particularly the last chapter, which applied evolutionary thinking to humans, triggered the hostility of social scientists, caused by Wilson's announcement that evolutionary biology in due time would cannibalise psychology and sociology.

Wilson's book provoked fierce responses among social scientists as well as biologists (e.g. Sahlins 1977; Lewontin et al. 1984; for a review about the sociobiology debate which also affected evolutionary psychology, see Segerstråle 2000). Looking back, three issues were involved. First, '**genetic determinism**', the misguided belief that social behaviours are genetically fixed. Second, 'reductionism', the imperialist claim that a particular domain (e.g. the social, the mental) is reducible to another (e.g. the biological, the neural). And third, its discussion about ignorance of mind

genetic determinism
the doctrine that animal behaviour and mental activity are largely, or completely, controlled by the genetic constitution of the individual.

and culture as indispensable ingredients for the explanation of human behaviour. Wilson made up for this last omission with his later book *Genes, Mind, and Culture* (1981) which he wrote with Charles Lumsden.

Evolutionary approaches in psychology

modularity
the notion that the brain/mind is composed of a number of modules that can solve specific problems. An example is the module for face recognition.

computationalism
the idea that the human mind is an information-processing system that resembles a computer made out of organic components rather than silicon chips.

nativism
1) doctrine that the mind has certain innate structures and mental behavioural tracts are largely determined by hereditary rather than environmental factors; 2) the theory that babies are born with a fundamental knowledge of the world.

adaptationism
the assumption that any trait of interest is biological in origin and that it must have evolved to solve a particular environmental problem.

The hostility towards sociobiology had mixed effects. A long-lasting negative effect is probably that many psychologists and sociologists still associate sociobiology with a biological take-over. A positive effect is that sociobiology has opened up new evolutionary approaches in psychology (Gangestad and Simpson 2007). There are three evolutionary approaches which focus on the **modularity** of mind, on behavioural strategies, and on the coevolution of genes and culture, respectively.

The first, and most influential approach in evolutionary psychology proposes that recurrent problems of our hunting and gathering ancestors selected for a mind adapted to the environment in which they were living, termed the 'environment of evolutionary adaptedness', or EEA (Tooby and Cosmides 1992, 2005). This approach is based on four assumptions: (1) *computationalism*, the assumption that the human mind is an information-processing system that resembles a computer, specifically in its capacity to form representations of events and objects and to carry out complex sequences of operations on these representations; (2) **nativism**, the assumption that much of the human mind is taken to be innate; (3) **adaptationism**, the assumption that the human mind resulted from selection pressures for solving particular problems faced by our ancestors (e.g. avoiding predators, exchanging resources); and (4) **modularity**, the assumption that the human mind consists of a number of cognitive modules, each equipped to perform a discrete task (see, for a review Callebaut 2005).

Neuroscientists have indeed discovered cognitive modules. The human capacity to recognise faces is an example of a highly heritable module with a well-defined neural structure and computational function (Kanwisher et al. 1997; Kanwisher and Yovel 2006; Barrett 2008; Wilmer et al. 2010). Psychophysical studies suggest that the cognitive representation of faces relies on different computational processes from other stimuli. And neuroimaging has identified brain areas in humans and other primates that respond much more strongly to faces than to other stimuli. Other findings suggest that face recognition is heritable as developmental deficits of this capacity run in families.

This approach is critical about the standard view in the social sciences that humans are endowed with a strong, general cognitive capacity (intelligence, reasoning) that allows them to solve a range of problems. If it could be demonstrated that human reasoning is based on a set of adaptive specialisations, this would be an argument in favour of the modular conception. Consider the social exchange of goods and services where there is a time lapse. This type of exchange poses a problem: one party can take the benefits and run. How could this problem be solved? The hypothesis is that human reasoning about social exchange and the associated risk that the other party will not reciprocate, is a module. It serves as an important test case in the research programme of the modular approach (Cosmides and Tooby 2005) and will be discussed in Chapter 6 (The evolution of social life). However, the assumption that the human mind is entirely composed of innate, special-purpose modules – 'the massive modularity hypothesis' – has been criticised (see Box 1.3 The contested modularity of mind).

BOX 1.3 The contested modularity of mind

The conception of a modular mind, proposed by philosopher Jerry Fodor (1983, 1985, 1998, 2000) and adopted by evolutionary psychologists John Tooby and Leda Cosmides (1992, 2005), implies that the mind consists of evolved cognitive modules. Fodor argues that input systems such as auditory and visual perception operate separately from one another. Cosmides and Tooby presume that modularity involves the whole mind. Natural selection would then have favoured specialised modules for solving problems that our ancestors repeatedly faced such as finding food, attracting a mate or detecting predators and cheaters. Critics argue that there is a qualitative difference between lower- and higher-level processes in the mind. Lower-level input processes like perception and output processes like motor performance may be considered modular unlike higher-level processes like thought or language. For example, Johan Bolhuis and Euan Macphail (2001) suggest that there is no evidence for modularity in central systems such as those involved in learning and memory. The idea of massive modularity was inspired by artificial intelligence research which has, however, abandoned the emphasis on modular organisation because intelligent machines require decision-making across modules. So, it would make sense if evolutionary psychologists as well shifted away from the emphasis on the modular organisation of mind (Bolhuis et al. 2011). For more critical studies about the limits of localising cognitive processes in the mind–brain, see Uttal (2001, 2009, 2011) and Shallice and Cooper (2011: Chapter 2).

Critics have further remarked that the modular approach ignores the evidence that basic emotional circuits emerged much earlier in brain evolution than the higher cognitive capacities (Panksepp and Panksepp 2000). Though emotions and cognitions interact, they should be distinguished, particularly in older brain areas where the power of affect is strongest. The essential character of the mind was laid down within very ancient emotional and motivational neurochemical systems in the brain that we share with many other animals. Most modules are, then, to be found within these homologous brain areas, while the neocortex – the part of the brain that most recently evolved as the source of our cognitive, linguistic and cultural capacities – serves as a general computer.

Pleistocene

geological epoch spanning 1.6 million to 10,000 years ago, characterised by repeated cycles of glaciation and warming.

Another issue concerns the idea that the human mind is adapted to the recurrent problems of our hunter-gatherer ancestors. They lived in the **Pleistocene** epoch spanning 1.6 million to 10,000 years ago, characterised by repeated cycles of glaciation and warming. The question is whether evolutionary psychology should confine itself to this epoch. It makes more sense to expand the timescale to the Cenozoic, spanning 65 million years ago to the present because archaeologists consider this era the most relevant one in the study of primate evolution (e.g. Klein 2009). After all, we are primates which include apes, monkeys and lemurs whose first common ancestor appeared 65 million years ago (mya), after the disappearance of the dinosaurs. Consequently, the mind and behaviour of humans can best be explained by comparing it with our close relatives. The primate background of human species will be discussed in Chapter 3 (The place of humans in evolution).

A final issue concerns adaptationism, the assumption that the mind resulted from selection pressures for solving particular problems faced by our ancestors. Adaptationism, derived from the term adaptation, is defined as any trait of an organism that enables it to survive and reproduce in its local environment. To identify an adaptation it is necessary to determine the selection pressures responsible for the origin and maintenance of a trait. This requires understanding of the relationship between the organism and its environment. To this end, one can use two methods for generating hypotheses: reverse engineering – inferring the adaptive origin of traits through analysis of its structure, function and operation – and adaptive thinking – inferring what adaptations will be produced in a particular environment.

Miocene

a geological period, extending from around 23-5 mya.

Reverse engineering starts with a trait such as face recognition as it involves specific brain areas (especially the fusiform gyrus in the temporal lobe). This analysis should lead to the history of selection for this trait which may reveal that pressures for identifying conspecifics were especially at work in social species like sheep, monkeys and humans (e.g. Kendrick et al. 2001). Adaptive reasoning starts with a particular environment like the African savanna during the **Miocene** (about 23–5 mya) when human-like creatures abandoned living in the trees. Archaeological findings show that the grassy environment attracted herds of herbivores (primitive antelopes, buffaloes) as well as predators (primitive lions, hyenas). The question is then what kind of problems our ancestors faced and which adaptive traits were required to solve them. For example, intense sociality might be a defence against predation pressure. An alternative would be not to work with hypothesised adaptive traits that are uniquely human, but rather with problems and traits such as social cognition and social emotions we share with our close primate relatives (see, for a critical review about reverse engineering, Richardson 2007: Chapter 2; and for a critical review about testing adaptive hypotheses in evolutionary psychology Pigliucci and Kaplan 2006: Chapter 7).

fitness

the reproductive success of an organism relative to another which is determined by natural selection.

The second evolutionary approach in psychology is commonly labelled as 'human behavioural ecology' which inherited from sociobiology a concern with the ultimate function of behaviour, that is, **fitness** (e.g. Smith and Winterhalten 1992). Recall that this term describes the difference in reproductive success of an individual relative to another. For example, evolutionary theory predicts that parents will maximise the production of children. But in practice they may trade-off between the quantity and quality of offspring. Birth spacing and anti-conception devices are means to achieve this goal.

gene–culture coevolution

theory that human populations share learned traditions that are expressed in cultural practices, and transmitted socially between individuals in the form of cultural inheritance. The theory presumes that human cultural practices modify natural selection processes in human environments, so that cultural transmission affects some selected human genes.

The third evolutionary approach is known as '**gene–culture coevolution**' and based on the argument that evolution does not only work by genes but also by culture. The approach differs from other approaches in its conviction that humans rely heavily on learning capacities. Individuals acquire ideas, beliefs, values and tools (in short: culture) by learning from other individuals (Richerson and Boyd 2005; Henrich and McElreath 2007). The advantage is that the time required for learning from each other is much shorter than the time it takes to pass genes from one generation to the next. Furthermore, the ability of humans to learn from one another, allows them to live in almost any environment (Sear et al. 2007). In Chapter 2 we will see how the three evolutionary approaches identify problems in evolution.

1.5   Neuroscience

Evolutionary psychology owes its revival also to neuroscience. For, psychologists cannot formulate hypotheses about the evolution of the mind without knowledge of the brain. Consider brain size, for example. Humans have disproportionately large brains, compared with other primates, such as monkeys and apes. We live in large groups and need a large amount of computational power to keep track of our own relationships and those of others. In addition, groups are not static but subject to permanent change, due to marriages, births, separations, new friendships, migrations, and so on. One part of our brain, the neocortex, is particularly larger and supposed to have evolved for solving complex social problems. Comparative analyses of primates show that relative neocortex size correlates with social group size (Joffe and Dunbar 1997). The larger the group, the larger the neocortex. Living in groups means that the neocortex serves, first, as a social input device for visual stimuli such as facial expressions, bodily gestures and status markers, and, second, as a processing device whereby social information is encoded, interpreted and associated with stored information.

Comparative neuroanatomy

Neuroscience originated from neuroanatomy (see Box 1.4 The origin of neuro-anatomy) and became an evolutionary science in the second half of the nineteenth century when a famous discussion took place among comparative neuroanatomists about the question whether or not animals had a common body plan (Northcutt 2001). A body plan is the blueprint according to which an organism develops a pre-determined number, arrangement and size of body components. Today, we know that the body plan is implemented by the organism's genes, but can be influenced by environmental factors, such as malnutrition or exposure to toxic agents.

One of the debaters was Étienne Geoffrey Saint-Hilaire (1722–1844), who searched for homologies between organisms. Recall, homologies are similar adaptations resulting from shared ancestry. For example, when we compare the bodies of animals with an exoskeleton such as insects and those with an endoskeleton such as vertebrates, there appears to be an inversion of the dorsal and ventral bodyside. Both insects and humans have their brain at the front side, but while the remaining part of the insect nervous system is at the ventral side, it lies at the dorsal side of the

BOX 1.4 The origin of neuroanatomy

Neuroscience consists of various sub-disciplines, such as neuroanatomy, neurophysiology and neurochemistry. Since the end of the twentieth century, new branches of neuroscience have developed, such as cognitive neuroscience. Neuroanatomy had its provisional start in ancient Egypt with the introduction of vivisection on condemned criminals (Von Staden 1989, 1992). About 300 BC, two Greek physicians in Alexandria, Herophilus and Erasistratus, managed to break through the age-old taboo on opening the human body for the mere sake of getting better knowledge. Cutting through the body was taboo because the skin symbolised the integrity of the individual and community. Transgression of the skin would result in moral and physical dangers. However, various circumstances allowed the Greek physicians to dissect body and brain. The early, Ptolemaic rulers who had the ambition to make Alexandria a famous centre of art and science, extended their patronage from eminent scholars such as Euclides (geometry), and Aristarchos (astronomy) to Herophilus (anatomy) and Erasistratus (physiology). It was the rulers who handed condemned criminals to them. Because criminals were regarded as objects who only spoke the truth under torture, vivisection was considered hardly different from torture.

In addition, the eager scientists seized upon the ancient practice of embalming as a legitimating precedent. An external circumstance was the secularisation of the body. Stoic and Epicurean philosophers agreed that animate and inanimate things were nothing but matter. Even the soul was considered as being nothing but matter of a certain kind. Moreover, Aristotle's success in developing biology as a major branch of science by dissecting and vivisecting various animals, helped to pave the way for the Alexandrian practice. Herophilus separated the nerves from the tendons and blood vessels which was a considerable source of confusion before his time. He studied also many cranial nerves, and made a distinction between motor and sensory nerves. He described the anatomy of two parts of the brain, the cerebral cortex that is essential for cognition, memory and voluntary movements, as well as the cerebellum which is responsible for planning motor programmes and preserving equilibrium. After Herophilus' death, the taboo on opening body and brain ruled again. It would take centuries before dissection became an acceptable practice. When Andreas Vesalius published his anatomical atlas *De humani corporis fabrica* in 1543, the taboo on dissection ended definitively.

human body. In 1822, Geoffrey argued that the dorsal and ventral side were reversed, but similar, that is, homologous. Critics ridiculed his inversion hypothesis but in 1996 molecular findings on the comparative development of the nervous system of both groups of animals provided evidence that he had been correct and that the dorsal and ventral body surfaces are reversed between the groups (Butler and Hodos 2005). On one thing Geoffrey was mistaken. He believed that homologous organs in different animals were evidence of a grand unity of plan pervading the whole organic world. However, when Darwin published his theory in 1859, it became clear that homologous structures were not due to a plan but to common ancestry.

In those times, neuroanatomists held erroneous assumptions about evolution. For example, they assumed that evolution was a progressive process, from simple to complex organisms and brains. But evolution is not a linear, progressive process from 'low' to 'high' species such as humans, showing an increasing complexity of the brain. Complexity, including neuroanatomic complexity, happens to occur among many species. Another mistaken assumption among neuroanatomists was anthropocentrism, the belief that humans are the smartest creatures on the planet having the largest and most complex brains. But other species such as dolphins, chimpanzees and ravens are also very smart with their large and complex brains. Modern comparative neuroanatomists consider most of these assumptions wrong (Butler and Hodos 2005). In Chapter 8 (Brain and cognition) we will take up the matter of intelligence and brain size in humans and other species.

Evolution and development of the brain

Today, neuroanatomists have placed their hope in the new science of evolutionary developmental biology that seeks to generate a synthesis of evolutionary biology and developmental biology (known as evo-devo). This science is based on the principle that changes in the development of individuals create the evolution of species (Garstang 1922; Hall 1999). Comparative neurobiologists always viewed brain evolution as the transformation of adult brains over time, but this is clearly not what happened. In order to understand how brains evolved, it is necessary to analyse in different species the stages of the developing brain, from baby to adult. It has been found, for example, that embryonic tissues gave rise to many new features of vertebrates, including endocrine organs, large parts of the skull, jaws and nerves.

How should we understand this interaction between evolution and development? According to the evolutionary theory, the production of variation between individuals is assumed to be random. This assumption has been challenged in the 1980s by authors who insist that the variants available to natural selection are not really random (Striedter 2007). The idea is that random mutations are channelled through mechanisms of development that favour the emergence of some phenotypes, while others may be impossible for embryos to develop. If that is true, then natural selection chooses not among a random selection of phenotypes but from a set that is biased by the mechanisms of development. This idea is important because development seems then to constrain the power of natural selection. The interaction between evolution and development will be discussed in Chapter 12 (Evolution through development).

A life-threatening problem

Now that neuroscience has turned into an evolutionary science, we would like to know how it explains life-threatening problems. It is true that evolution is, in essence, a matter of reproductive success, but first we have to survive, otherwise we cannot reproduce. How would evolutionary neuroscience explain the emotion of fear when a predator is nearby? When and why did fear actually originate in the evolutionary history of animals?

The emotion of fear is based on evolved neural programs in the brain which come immediately and unconsciously into action when we encounter survival problems. The most important feature of this emotional response is that it is involuntary. Thinking what to do when we meet a dangerous predator, would be too slow for matters of life-or-death. That is the reason why the brain may be considered as an adapted organ that helps us to survive, even when we are not aware of it.

How can we study fear in the brain? We know from the section about behaviourism that animals learn by association. The strong point of behaviourism was its conditioning methodology that has influenced experimental study in psychology and neuroscience. For example, much of the research on the neural mechanisms of emotion has focused on fear conditioning in rats (Pinel 2003). Fear conditioning is the establishment of fear in response to a neutral stimulus (the conditional stimulus) that is presented before an aversive stimulus (the unconditional stimulus). In the usual fear conditioning experiment, the rat hears a tone and then receives a mild electric shock to its feet. After several pairings of the tone and the shock, the rat responds to the tone with defensive behaviour (e.g. freezing) and nervous system responses (e.g. increased heart rate and blood pressure). Study of fear conditioning reveals how evolved mechanisms in the brain serve as a protection against dangers.

The neural circuitry of fear

thalamus

large paired masses of grey matter lying between the brainstem and the cerebrum, the key relay station for sensory information flowing into the brain.

In his book *The Emotional Brain* (1996), Joseph LeDoux explains the neural circuitry of fear. During experiments he discovered two brain pathways for emotional responses to danger. Both paths start at the **thalamus**, a brain area which is involved in the selection of external stimuli. The short pathway generates an automatic response (freezing, increased blood pressure, release of stress hormones in the blood stream), while the long pathway allows cognitive mediation of emotional responses (Figure 1.4). Why is the brain organised this way?

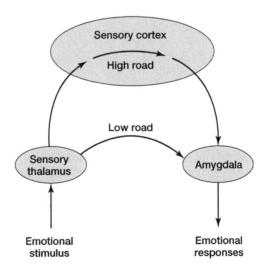

Figure 1.4 The short and long pathways to the amygdala
Source: LeDoux (1996)

The advantage of the short pathway is that it provides a fast signal that warns us about danger. The disadvantage is that it cannot immediately tell the amygdala, a brain area involved in emotional behaviour, what the dangerous thing exactly is. That is why the short pathway is a quick but dirty processing system. To illustrate, when we mistake the garden hose for a dangerous snake, our brain responds within 100 milliseconds, which is an adequate reaction time from the point of view of survival. Within a second the danger signal has also passed along the long pathway so that we know whether the danger is real or not. The advantage of the long path is that it works accurately but the disadvantage is that it works slowly. The parallel transmission of the danger signal is based on the principle 'better safe than sorry'. In situations where rapid responses are required, speed is more important than accuracy.

Why would we mistake the garden hose for a dangerous snake? Most humans no longer live in jungles but rather in urban environments. We should be more afraid of fast cars and fire weapons than of dangerous animals. The reason is that over the course of evolution we have become highly prepared for dangerous beings, such as predators. Because this evolutionary preparedness has great survival value, it became hardwired into our brain.

An evolved fear mechanism

There is ample evidence from experiments with monkeys and humans for an evolved fear mechanism with four characteristics: selectivity with regard to input, automaticity, encapsulation and a specialised neural circuitry (Öhmann and Mineka 2001). Each of these characteristics is assumed to be shaped by evolutionary conditions. The selectivity results from the evolutionary history of deadly threats that have plagued mammals. The automaticity means that the mechanism originates from animals with primitive brains and therefore not under voluntary control but only elicited by stimuli whether we want it or not. Encapsulation has to do with the need to rely on time-proven solutions that are immune to recently evolved cognitions. Finally, the fear mechanism is based on specific neural circuitry that has been shaped by evolution and is located in sub-cortical or even brainstem areas.

It is important to make a distinction between the input- and output-side of emotion. At the input-side is the problem, that is, the fearsome thing. At the output-side is the solution, namely the bodily response of people when they see dangerous things. Experiments reveal that the faces of people in all cultures respond in a similar way to frightening things (Griffiths 1997). They show raised and drawn-together brows, short horizontal and/or vertical forehead wrinkles, opened and staring eyes, and either tightly pressed lips or open mouth with lips raised. If emotional responses to frightening things are indeed universal, an evolutionary explanation is obvious.

The experiments do not show, however, that people in all cultures are frightened by the same things, meaning that at the input- or problem-side, fear may be largely a matter of learning which things are dangerous. Still, an evolutionary explanation is possible because there is experimental evidence for learning preparedness in the case of fear. Seligman (1971) has argued that phobias are best understood as cases of highly prepared learning of fear. Prepared learning is a species-specific and innate tendency to learn a certain type of knowledge. Some associations between stimuli and responses may be more easily formed than other ones. For example, animals may be prepared to associate new foods with illness. Seligman suggested that humans learn certain fears more readily due to preparedness. For example, we are predisposed to acquire fear for predators because they were prevalent sources of danger in our evolution.

Two hypotheses about the origin of fear

When and why did fear actually arise in the evolution of animals? The first hypothesis proposes that fear evolved in the first placental mammals 100 mya in response to predators which include venomous snakes, raptors and carnivores (Isbell 2006). Most mammals responded by evolving physiological resistance to snake venoms. But monkeys, apes and humans responded by enhancing the ability to detect snakes visually before the strike. Thus, predation would be a strong selection pressure for neural structures involved in predator detection and avoidance. The implication is that an animal whose amygdala doesn't work well, is in a disadvantageous situation which reduces its chances of survival and reproduction. If we understand fear as originally stemming from having to deal with predation, we might suppose that it could arguably be much older than 100 mya. For example, there is fairly good evidence for a similar structure of the **amygdala** in the brains of amphibians, reptiles, birds, and mammals (Martinez-Garcia et al. 2007). When groups of animals share a similar feature, in this case a structure in the brain, it indicates descent from common ancestors.

A second hypothesis implies that fear originated in the Cambrian period (542–488 mya), when marine animals adopted active predation as a new feeding strategy (Budd 2001). The feeding strategies at that time were mainly passive, such as filtering algae and free-living bacteria from the surrounding water (Brusca and Brusca 2003). The impetus for the evolution of large, apparently predatory creatures was most likely the rising level of oxygen in the air and sea. Much oxygen is needed for large size and predation because nothing else can provide the necessary energy (Lane 2009).

Anomalocaris: a fearsome predator

As an example, *Anomalocaris* was a fearsome predator whose name may be translated as 'strange crab' because it is difficult to classify. According to palaeobiologist Simon Conway Morris (1999), this marine creature belongs to the arthropods, a highly diverse group of animals that includes shrimps, crabs, spiders and centipedes. Arthropods are invertebrate animals with an articulated exoskeleton covering a segmented body. *Anomalocaris* had an armoured body between two and five feet long (60–150 cm). At the front of its head were two appendages for grabbing prey and manoeuvring it into its circular mouth that was lined by tooth-like structures that could crush through the armour of prey. All species of *Anomalocaris* propelled themselves through the water by means of lateral flaps that moved up and down in a wavelike fashion, as with modern rays. The presence of eyes on stalks would have helped to locate prey (Figure 1.5).

Active predation was perhaps triggered by an evolutionary innovation, namely eyes (Parker 2003). In the sea where sunlight could not penetrate farther than a few

amygdala
an almond-shaped structure – part of the limbic system – located in the medial part of the temporal lobe of the brain, involved in emotion.

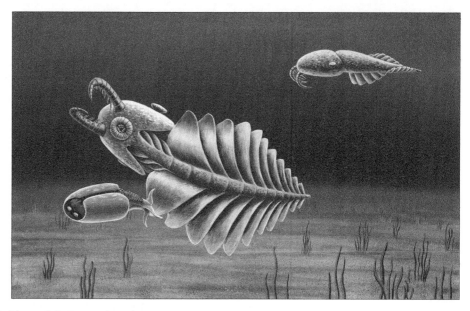

Figure 1.5 Anomalocaris

Sources: Conway Morris (1999)/Science Photo Library / Richard Bisley

hundred metres below the surface, eyes were a real boon. The first fossil evidence of animals with eyes dates back to the early Cambrian, roughly 550 mya (Nilsson and Pelger 1994).

1.6 Summary

- Evolutionary psychology attempts to formulate new questions, expanding the scales of time and space of psychology's subject-matter.

- Psychology started as a science in the 1880s by adopting the experimental method from physiology. But method is not enough for doing science; it also needs theory. From evolutionary biology, it took an influential theory with the potential to explain the behaviour and mind of humans and other animals. Unfortunately, the application of evolutionary thought produced too much speculation and too few empirical results. Psychology, then, dropped evolutionary theorising and switched towards the atheoretical approach of behaviourism with its animal experiments.

- The price for this conversion was twofold. First, behaviourists considered the mind as a black box, and second, psychology still needed a unified theory that could explain a wide range of phenomena over wide scales of time and space. A solution for the first problem was the rise of cognitive science in the 1950s, which made psychology again a real science. A solution for the second problem was the extended evolutionary theory which attracts, since the 1930s, one science after the other.

- Wilson's sociobiology opened up new evolutionary approaches in psychology. The most influential apfproach dates from the 1990s which is focused on mental mechanisms as adaptations to problems which our ancestors recurrently faced. The second approach is commonly labelled as 'human behavioural ecology' which inherited from sociobiology a concern with the ultimate function of behaviour, that is, fitness. The third approach is known as 'gene-culture coevolution' and based on the argument that evolution does not only work by genes but also by culture.

Study questions

1. Why did the histories of evolutionary biology, psychology and neuroscience diverge and converge respectively?

2. Which problems are connected with the designer fallacy?

3. Which components are necessary for evolution to work?

4. How did evolutionary thought in psychology revive?

5. What is meant by 'the modularity of mind' and why is it contested?

Suggested reading

Biology

Hall, B. and Hallgrimsson, B. (2008). *Strickberger's Evolution: The Integration of Genes, Organisms, and Populations.* Boston: Jones and Bartlett Publishers.

Jablonka, E. and Lamb, M. (2005). *Evolution in Four Dimensions: Genetic, Epigenetic, Behavioral, and Symbolic Variation in the History of Life.* Cambridge, MA: The MIT Press.

Jablonka, E. and Lamb, M. (2007a). The expanded evolutionary synthesis – a response to Godfrey-Smith, Haig, and West-Eberhard. *Biology and Philosophy.* 22, 453–472 (three reviews of *Evolution in Four Dimensions* on pp. 415–451).

Jablonka, E. and Lamb, M. (2007b). Precis *of Evolution in Four Dimensions. Behavioral and Brain Sciences, 30,* 353–92.

Kutschera, U. and Niklas, K. (2004). The modern theory of biological evolution: an expanded synthesis. *Naturwissenschaften, 91,* 255–276.

Pigliucci, M. and Müller, G. (Eds) (2010). *Evolution – The Extended Synthesis.* Cambridge, MA: The MIT Press.

Ridley, M. (2005). *Evolution. Third Edition.* Oxford: Blackwell Publishing.

Stearns, S. and Hoekstra, R. (2005). *Evolution: an introduction. Second Edition.* Oxford: Oxford University Press.

Psychology

Bolhuis, J., Brown, G., Richardson, R. and Laland, K. (2011). Darwin in mind: New opportunities for evolutionary psychology. *PLoS Biology, 9 (7),* 1–8.

Burghardt, G. (2009). Darwin's legacy to comparative psychology and ethology, *American Psychologist, 64,* 102–110.

Carey, F. and Whitaker, M. (2010). Examining the acceptance of and resistance to evolutionary psychology. *Evolutionary Psychology, 8*, 284–296.

Confer, J., Easton, D. Fleischman, D. et al. (2010). Evolutionary psychology: Controversies, questions, prospects, and limitations. *American Psychologist, 65*, 110–126.

Cornwell, E. (2005). Introductory psychology texts as a view of sociobiology/evolutionary psychology's role in psychology. *Evolutionary Psychology, 3*, 355–374.

Dewsbury, D. (2009). Charles Darwin and psychology at the bicentennial and sesquicentennial: An introduction. *American Psychologist, 64*, 67–74.

Fitzgerald, C. and Whitaker, M. (2010). Examining the acceptance of and resistance to evolutionary psychology. *Evolutionary Psychology, 8*, 284–296.

Holcomb, H. (2005). Buller does to Evolutionary Psychology what Kitcher did to Sociobiology. *Evolutionary Psychology, 3*, 392–401.

Kurzban, R. (2002). Essay Review. Alas poor evolutionary psychology: Unfairly accused, unjustly condemned. *Human Nature Review, 2*, 99–109.

Laland, K., Sterelny, K., Odling-Smee, J. et al. (2011). Cause and effect in biology revisited: Is Mayr's proximate–ultimate dichotomy still useful? *Science, 334*, 1512–1516.

Panksepp, J. and Panksepp, J. (2000). The seven sins of evolutionary psychology. *Evolution and Cognition, 6*, 108–131.

Saad, G. (2011). Futures of evolutionary psychology. *Futures, 43*, 725–728.

Sear, R., Lawson, D. and Dickins, T. (2007). Synthesis in the human evolutionary behavioural sciences. *Journal of Evolutionary Psychology, 5*, 3–28.

Smith, E., Borgerhoff Mulder, M. and Hill, K. (2001). Controversies in the evolutionary social sciences: A guide for the perplexed. *Trends in Ecology and Evolution, 16*, 128–135.

Webster, G. (2007a). What's in a name? Is 'Evolutionary psychology' eclipsing 'sociobiology' in the scientific literature? *Evolutionary Psychology, 5*, 683–695.

Webster, G., Jonason, P. and Orozco, T. (2009). Hot topics in evolutionary psychology: Analysis of title words and citation counts in *Evolution and Human Behaviour, 1979–2008*. *Evolutionary Psychology, 7*, 348–362.

Neuroscience

LeDoux J. (1996) *The Emotional Brain: The Mysterious Underpinnings of Emotional Life*. New York: Simon & Schuster.

Northcutt, R. (2001). Evolution of the nervous system: Changing views of brain evolution. *Brain Research Bulletin, 55*, 663–674.

Öhmann, A. and Mineka, S. (2001). Fears, phobias, and preparedness: Toward an evolved module of fear and fear learning. *Psychological Review, 108*, 483–522.

Platek, S., Hasicic, A. and Krill, A. (2011). Boldly going where no brain has gone: Futures of evolutionary cognitive neuroscience. *Futures, 43*, 771–776.

Webster, G. (2007b). Evolutionary theory in cognitive neuroscience: A 20–year quantitative review of publication trends. *Evolutionary Psychology, 5*, 520–530.

Reference books

Barkow, J., Cosmides, L. and Tooby, J. (Eds (1992). *The Adapted Mind: Evolutionary Psychology and the Generation of Culture*. New York: Oxford University Press.

Buss, D. (Ed.) (2007). *The Handbook of Evolutionary Psychology*. Hoboken, NJ: John Wiley and Sons, Inc.

Crawford, C. and Krebs, D. (Eds) (2008). *Foundations of Evolutionary Psychology*. New York: Lawrence Erlbaum Associates.

Dixon, D., Henkins, I., Moody, R. and Zhuravlev, A. (2001). *Cassell's Atlas of Evolution: The Earth, Its Landscape, and Life Forms*. London: Cassell and Co.

Dunbar, R. and Barrett, L. (Eds) (2007). *Oxford Handbook of Evolutionary Psychology*. Oxford: Oxford University Press.

Kaas, J. (Ed.) (2007). *Evolution of Nervous Systems: A Comprehensive Reference, Four Volumes*. Amsterdam: Academic Press.

Keller, E. and Lloyd, E. (1992). *Keywords in Evolutionary Biology*. Cambridge, MA: Harvard University Press.

Laland, K. and Brown, G. (2002). *Sense and Nonsense: Evolutionary Perspectives on Human Behaviour*. Oxford: Oxford University Press.

Mayr, E. (1985). *The Growth of Biological Thought: Diversity, Evolution, and Inheritance*. Cambridge, MA: The Belknap Press of Harvard University Press.

Palmer, D. and Barrett, P. (2009). *Evolution: The Story of Life*. London: Octopus Publishing Group.x

Platek, S. and Shackleford, T. (Eds) (2009). *Foundations in Evolutionary Cognitive Neuroscience*. Cambridge: Cambridge University Press.

Reece, J. Urry, L., Cain, M. et al. (Eds) (2011). *Campbell Biology, Ninth Edition*. San Francisco: Pearson Education.

Richards, G. (2002). *Putting Psychology in its Place: A Critical Historical Review*. Hove: Routledge.

Thain. M. and Hickman, M. (2001). *The Penguin Dictionary of Biology*. London: Penguin Books.

Toates, F. (2011). *Biological Psychology, Third Edition*. Harlow England: Pearson.

2 Problems and solutions in evolution

This chapter will cover:

2.1 Introduction

2.2 Evolutionary approaches to problems

2.3 Genome, nervous system and culture as solutions

2.4 Levels of complexity

2.5 Replaying the tape of life

2.6 Summary

Learning outcomes

By the end of this chapter, you should be able to explain how:

- evolutionary problems can be defined
- evolutionary approaches in psychology suggest problems of our ancestors
- genome, nervous system and culture may be considered adaptive systems for solving problems
- during a number of times new evolutionary entities learned to cooperate, forming higher levels of organisation
- rerunning the tape of life may show which solutions in evolution are most adaptive.

2.1 Introduction

Evolutionary psychology requires thinking on a wide timescale, asking questions which go deep into the history of evolution. Why do we live in groups and societies while many animals live solitarily and only meet to reproduce? Why do we have culture while most animals haven't? These questions suggest that living socially and sharing culture served as solutions to problems with which our ancestors were confronted.

The aim of this chapter is to provide criteria for identifying problems for which our ancestors had to find solutions. Criteria may come from different approaches in evolutionary psychology, focusing on mental mechanisms, behavioural strategies, and learning capacities which are thought to have solved ancestral problems.

Criteria may also come from the genome, the nervous system, and culture, to be considered adaptive systems that evolved one after another as solutions. Organisms need a genome to run their lives but it cannot solve all our problems because it works slowly. Otherwise we would not have a more rapid working nervous system and cultural inheritance system.

We will further look at the increasing complexity of life in the course of evolution as individuals needed to cooperate, forming higher levels of social organisation such as families, colonies and societies. We presume that each new level of social living had to solve new problems.

Finally, you are invited to participate in a thought experiment about 'replaying the tape of life'. Imagine that a comet or radical climate change would wipe out all life on Earth. If evolution can start all over again, we may envision different options. Evolution yields the same outcomes each time, it generates a different outcome each time, or it shows a recurrent pattern. We focus on which option is most likely.

2.2 Evolutionary approaches to problems

What is meant by a problem?

If organisms are hungry, they look for food. The behaviour of plants and animals shows that they are geared to regularities. They expect that somewhere something edible should be found. If that expectation proves to be wrong, they have a problem that needs to be solved. Trees may find much-needed water by pushing their roots into deeper layers of the earth. Like all plants, they 'know' how to run their life with the help of genes and some hormones (Tudge 2005).

Consider flowering plants. How do they know when warmer days are about to arrive, and when to open their flowers? They are able to 'remember' a long period of cold and will only flower in spring. This adaptation, with the technical term vernalisation, prevents premature flowering after a short period of cold in autumn. It is understood that a particular protein represses flowering during prolonged cold exposure (Marx 2004). Flowering plants are said to be vernalised. The stems of vernalised plants elongate in response to light, followed by the appearance of flowers.

Humans have a long tradition of gathering plants and hunting prey. How did they adapt to declining food in the wild or food that could not keep pace with growing populations? They relied on their learning capacity to grow food, breed animals and pass these innovations on to their offspring. This transition from food collection to food production took place independently on different continents between 3,000 and 10,000 years ago. It is considered as one of the landmark shifts in human history (Diamond 1997; McNeill and McNeill 2003).

Organisms are driven by two biological imperatives: the urge to survive and to reproduce. Survival is necessary otherwise we would be unable to reproduce. Evolutionary psychology presumes that humans have managed to solve various problems in their evolutionary history. These problems are referred to as **adaptive problems,** that is, problems which have an impact on reproductive success. But how can we identify which all of these problems are? A number of scientists addressed this question. Consider evolutionary psychologist David Buss who puts it like this (2012: 65):

> No amount of conceptual work can definitively yield a complete list of all the adaptive problems our ancestors have faced. This indeterminacy is caused by several factors. First, we cannot rewind the tape of life and see all the things our ancestors confronted in the past. Second, each new adaptation creates a problem of its own, such as becoming coordinated with other adaptive mechanisms. Identifying the full set of human adaptive problems is an enormous task that will occupy scientists for decades to come.

The argument that problems in evolution must by definition have an impact on reproductive success, leads Buss (2012) to identify five classes of problems which include problems of survival (finding food and a place to live, avoiding predators), problems of mating (finding and retaining a mate), problems of parenting (helping offspring to survive and grow), problems of kinship (helping offspring of genetic relatives), and problems of group living (detecting cheaters, negotiating social hierarchies).

adaptive problem

a problem recurrently faced by our ancestors which had an impact on their reproductive success.

KEY FIGURE   David Buss

David Buss is an evolutionary psychologist at the University of Texas at Austin. His research interests include human sexuality, mating strategies, conflict between the sexes, homicide, stalking and sexual victimisation.

Photo source: © David M. Buss, all rights reserved.

Selected works

Evolutionary Psychology: The New Science of the Mind (1999, 2004, 2008, 2012).

The Handbook of Evolutionary Psychology, Editor (2007).

Why Women Have Sex: Understanding Sex Motivation from Adventure to Revenge (and Everything in Between) (2009), with Cindy Weston.

The Evolution of Personality and Individual Differences (2011), Editor with Patricia Hawley.

Modular evolutionary psychology

The three evolutionary approaches in psychology we discussed in Chapter 1 suggest various problems and solutions. The modular approach considers mental modules for the evolved solutions for problems. If people in current societies suffer from phobias of snakes (or strange food, strangers, heights), these automatic responses are exaggerated forms of fear that would otherwise be adaptive. Such responses reveal information about ancestral problems. We learned in Chapter 1 that the fear mechanism in our brain originated from the problem of predation. Not only fear but the whole human repertoire of emotions may reveal problems that our ancestors faced repeatedly. Disgust could protect us against toxic food and shame against behaviours that other group members consider anti-social. This matter is the subject of Chapter 7 (The origin and expression of emotions).

Human characteristics may also indicate problems (Buss 2012). We prefer to aid close relatives, but why exactly are we more generous towards relatives than to strangers? This question suggests the problem of altruism which will be the subject of Chapter 5 (Fathers, mothers and others). We prefer to mate with strangers rather than relatives, but why? And how do we know which individuals should be avoided? This suggests the problem of incest-avoidance which we discuss in Chapter 5 as well. Or consider the social exchange of costly resources in trade which often involve considerable time delays. This kind of sociality requires cognitive capacities to establish each other's intentions and expectations. The issue of why humans evolved to live socially will be discussed in Chapter 6 (The evolution of social life).

Further characteristics may come from traditional human societies, such as hunters-gatherers which are still to be found in some regions of the world (e.g. Aboriginals in Australia, Indians in Amazonia, Bushmen in South Africa). The hunting and gathering lifestyle is a long tradition which goes back to extinct human species. A characteristic of these societies is that they are explicitly egalitarian. They deviate in this regard from modern societies which have mostly explicit differences of income, status and power between groups of people.

A typical characteristic of hunter-gatherers is that they resist authoritarian leadership and social hierarchies (e.g. Boehm 1993, 2001). Presumably, one way to restrain dominating individuals was using tools as weapons. Tools such as wooden spears were invented for hunting prey but could also be used for deterring predators and against despotic individuals. The invention of tools-turned-into-weapons made men more dangerous to one another and thereby reduced differences of body size or strength in fighting. Christopher Boehm (2001) estimates that weapons would have had equalising effects by 500,000 years ago. The use of weapons may also have influenced the relationship between the sexes. Weapons for killing prey could be used against alpha males who monopolised access to females. This would have levelled the uneven distribution of females and lowered the costs of competition for females. The issue of how monogamous relationships may have originated will be dealt with in Chapter 4 (Males and females).

Human behavioural ecology

Human behavioural ecology is another approach which has been developed by evolutionary ecologists who were attracted by the idea of adaptation in evolutionary biology. They were fascinated by the variation of behaviour across cultures as people in different cultures eat different foods, spend different amounts of time hunting, gathering or fishing, have different marriage customs, divide tasks between males and females differently, and decide differently about the optimal family size. Because they felt that Wilson's sociobiology failed to offer sufficient explanations for this variation, human behavioural ecologists developed mathematical models in order to better understand which behaviours were optimal for increasing their chances of survival and reproduction within the current environment (Smith and Winterhalten 1992).

Many studies which use this approach have been conducted in environments that are thought to have remained stable for thousands of years. One reason for picking these environments for their studies is that tribes in Southern Africa or Amazonia have not been heavily influenced by western culture. The approach of human behavioural ecology assumes that adaptive behaviours in current environments were also adaptive in ancient environments. For example, it has been suggested that both modern working couples and hunter-gatherer couples practise birth spacing as an adaptive behavioural strategy (Barrett et al. 2002). In theory, parents are able to produce children with an interbirth interval of 12 to 18 months. But in practice, the time intervals are a few years. If evolution is about reproductive success, that is, maximising your fitness, why do parents limit their reproduction?

The answer would be that in modern societies, parents may reduce offspring production in favour of increasing wealth. In tribal societies, it is particularly the need of women to gather loads of food and carry them over long distances that limits their ability to produce offspring. As women during their foraging travels also carry offspring who are under four years of age, a short interval between births means that having more than one small child at a time, enlarges their backload. Thus, if intervals are too short, women will have an unacceptable workload which may compromise the health of mother and offspring. The issue of how ancestral women practised birth spacing and engaged help from relatives and fathers will be discussed in Chapter 5 (Fathers, mothers and others).

Gene–culture coevolution

A third evolutionary approach in psychology which may provide criteria for problems, is gene–culture coevolution (Richerson and Boyd 2005). This approach is based on the argument that evolution does not only work by genes but also by learning and creative capacities. Humans acquire knowledge, beliefs and tools (in short: culture) mostly by learning from significant others. We can learn from parents, teachers, peers, and even from media-personalities we have never met in person. The advantage is that the time required for learning from one another is much less than the time it takes to learn all things by yourself. In other words, the emergence of culture and the resulting need to learn from other individuals, suggests that individual learning was a problem.

Social learning may, for example, be based on a prestige bias. This is a preference which assumes that learning by yourself is costly, and that we do better when paying attention to, and learning from individuals who are highly successful, skilled and respected. Some non-human primates may also use social learning to acquire new habits. A famous example is about macaque monkeys on Kishima Island (Japan) who learned from a young female to wash potatoes instead of brushing the sand off with their hands. The first individuals who learned this new habit were her mother and peers, but nowadays transmission is mostly from mother to offspring. Experts consider potato-washing as the first documented case of an animal innovation that became a tradition (Hirata et al. 2008; De Waal and Bonnie 2009). Social learning and culture are the subject of Chapter 10 (Culture in evolution).

Humans excel in learning as well as creative capacities. They modify the acquired cultural items, and even invent new things. A classic example of social learning and creating is Henry Ford's invention of the assembly line in 1908 which allowed him to produce automobiles at lower costs than his competitors. An assembly line is a type of industrial production in which prefabricated, interchangeable parts are used to assemble a finished product. A conveyor belt carries the product through a series of work stations until it is finished. Ford (1922) learned the idea from the overhead rail systems in the slaughter houses of Cincinnati.

The track, high above head level, carried small wheeled trolleys which rolled by their own weight down an incline. After catching, killing and scraping, the hogs were hung from the overhead rail and moved continuously past a series of workers. Each man performed a single operation. One opened the animal, the next took out the entrails, the third removed heart, liver etc., and the hose man washed it out. An anonymous Cincinnatian invented this system in 1869 (Giedion 1969). Ford turned this 'disassembly line' into an assembly line.

Why do we excel in creative capacities? One reason may be that our ancestors became increasingly able to master the selection pressures from traditional 'hostile forces of nature' (e.g. predators, diseases, food shortages). Since then, the human species has become its own selection pressure because the competition among con-specifics became more important (Flinn et al. 2005; Striedter 2005). According to this hypothesis, the increasing social competition improved the cognitive capacities of our ancestors and increased their brain size disproportionately in a few million years. As a result, human minds created impressive products, such as technology, language, teaching and writing. Thus improved cognition and increased brain size indicate the problem of social competition. The issue of selection pressures for social cognition will be discussed in Chapter 8 (Brain and cognition).

To sum up, the different approaches suggest the following criteria for identifying significant problems:

- requirements for reproduction: e.g. survival, mating, parenting, kinship, social living.
- mental mechanisms: e.g. phobias that reveal information about ancestral dangers.
- human characteristics: e.g. the preference to help close relatives suggests the problem of altruism; the preference to mate with non-relatives indicates the problem of incest-avoidance.
- characteristics of traditional human societies: e.g. egalitarian characteristics suggest the problem of abuse of power.
- human behavioural strategies: e.g. birth spacing indicates the problem of fitness limitation.
- learning capacities: e.g. social learning suggests the problem of individual learning overload.
- creative capacities: e.g. improved cognition and increased brain size indicate the problem of social competition.

The evolutionary psychology of obesity

obesity

nutritional disorder developing chronically when energy intake exceeds energy expenditure.

In this section we use the case of **obesity** to see how different evolutionary approaches in psychology would explain the problem of obesity (Nettle 2009). Obesity is a major risk for cardiovascular diseases, hypertension, stroke and cancer. Among the non-fatal, but debilitating health problems is infertility. That is why obesity may be considered a critical problem because it has an impact on reproductive success. Obesity and overweight are both labels for ranges of weight that are greater than what is generally considered healthy for a given height. For adults the ranges are determined by using weight and height to calculate a number that is called the 'body mass index' which correlates with one's amount of body fat. An adult with a BMI between 25 and 29.9 may be considered overweight; an adult who has a BMI higher than 30 may be considered obese. Obesity which results from long-term intake of energy exceeding energy expenditure, is the most common nutritional disorder worldwide. Globally, there are more than 1 billion overweight adults, at least 300 million of them are obese whose fat storage level compromises their health. It is the prevalence, or total number of cases in a population or during a specified period, that counts (Power and Schulkin 2009).

Normally, storing fat on the body is an efficient way of conserving energy which can be used at later times when food is scarce. Most fat is stored in adipose tissue throughout the body: under the skin, around inner organs (e.g. heart, lungs, stomach, liver), and in muscle tissue. It is thought to perform different adaptive functions, such as being a source of stored energy, insulation to reduce heat loss, and protection for the internal organs. Among animals, fat seems also to serve as a predictor of individual quality. It is important in assessing fighting quality and mate choice. In sum, fat in moderate amounts is a good thing in our diets and bodies. But obesity is excess adipose tissue in large numbers of cells called adipocytes which are specialised for storage of fat.

Obesity as a mismatch between mind and modern environment

How would the modularity approach in evolutionary psychology deal with obesity? It would argue that there is a mismatch between ancient modules in our mind and contemporary environment. The reason is that evolution cannot look into the future. It does not strive towards a goal, but only keeps all the things that in the past have proven to be valuable for reproduction. The human taste for fat foods was adaptive in the past environment of hunters and gatherers because meat was scarce, that is, not easy to catch. Compared to other primates, they had larger brains and brain tissue is 'expensive' in that it needs more energy than other tissue (Aiello and Wheeler 1995). At rest, the brain **metabolism** accounts for 20–25 per cent of an adult human's energy needs, which is far more than the 8–10 per cent observed in other primates. No matter what selected for relatively large brains in humans, the increased energy need could not be achieved without a shift to a high-quality diet. This shift involved high-quality foods such as animal products (meat, milk), nuts, or underground tubers.

metabolism

the totality of enzyme-mediated biochemical pathways occurring within the body, both anabolic (build up) and catabolic (break down).

In this approach, the past environment is mostly associated with the geological epoch of the Pleistocene from 1.6 mya to the emergence of agriculture 10,000 years ago. The implication is that the human mind has undergone the selection pressures of past environments, but not those of modern ones ('a Stone Age-mind in a modern world'). While a preference for fat food was adaptive in past environments, this taste has become maladaptive in the modern world because wealth may lead to overconsumption. The obesity problem is in full swing in the rich nations such as the United States and most of Europe. It is also beginning to develop in many Asian and African countries. Populations shift from being rural to urban, jobs require less physical activity, average incomes rise, and diets are becoming higher in fat and lower in fibre (Power and Schulkin 2009).

According to this approach there is a mismatch between evolved modules and the modern world. As the modules in our mind are no more in tune with the modern environment, this would explain why people have a tendency to eat more than is necessary. What module or mechanism might be relevant in the case of obesity? Many critical variables within the body such as blood pressure, blood sugar and water balance, are tightly controlled by automatic mechanisms. But whether body weight is similarly regulated has long been a matter of discussion. Recent studies of humans and other animals suggest that the body has mechanisms which monitor the amount of stored energy and regulate this resource to remain at a particular level. These mechanisms are slightly biased in favour of preserving fat rather than eliminating it. This tendency makes evolutionary sense when we know that fat has survival value.

arcuate nucleus (ARC)
a small region at the base of the brain that plays a central role in energy regulation.

Research to identify weight control mechanisms in the brain started from the knowledge that the **arcuate nucleus (ARC)** of the thalamus, a small region at the base of the brain, plays a central role in energy regulation (Power and Schulkin 2009). Certain parts of the hypothalamus have been labelled as appetite respectively satiety centres. A critical regulator of how much energy is maintained in storage, appears to be the protein leptin (from the Greek root *leptos*, meaning 'thin'). Fat cells give rise to this protein leptin which produces a hormonal signal that reflects the cells' state of energy storage. Obesity seems to be caused by the absence of this substance. When the energy-status signal is absent, the brain acts as if the body is starving and behaves accordingly by stimulating hunger and conserving energy. The bodies of most patients with obesity are thought to have leptin resistance as the energy-regulating system does not respond to the leptin's signal that fat stores are abundant (Flier and Maratos-Flier 2007). It should be noted that the weight control mechanism does not work on its own but is part of neurohormonal systems that stimulate and inhibit feeding behaviour (Lovejoy 2009).

Obesity as a low-income problem

How would human behavioural ecology deal with obesity? For much of the human history, meals were a matter of catch-as-catch-can. For our gathering and hunting ancestors, food was only available now and then. Survival required that they had the capacity to store energy in the form of fat tissue for times when scarcity was the rule. Our ability to store fat remains essential to life, but in recent history the amount of energy packed away as fat, has increased. Fat storage compromises a person's health, owing to technological advances in food production as well as the reduced need for physical activity.

This approach would reveal that poor diet and obesity is common among people with low incomes. They have little to spend and have no better strategy available to them than getting their calories from the cheapest sources which are fats, sugar – as found in fast food, biscuits etc. The prediction is that as the budget gets smaller, greater proportions of the calories come from cheap fats as well as sweets, and less from expensive fruits, lean meat and vegetables. High fat and sugar consumption might have been adaptive in past environments but not in current ones where it causes health problems in the long run. Note that the presumed selection pressure for fat storage – food shortage in the Pleistocene – cannot so easily be translated into a trait that explains contemporary shopping behaviour.

Explaining obesity as a mismatch and a low-income issue are both based on the assumption that humans evolved in conditions of relative food shortage. Now that food is easily acquired, many people cannot regulate their appetite to healthy levels. Is the assumption of food shortage correct? Knowledge about the diets of living hunter-gatherers may shed light on the alleged food shortage of our ancestors. David Waynforth (2010) points out that living hunter-gatherer adults consume around 2580 calories per day while the average consumption in the US is 2248 calories per day. Higher levels of physical activity in hunter-gatherers cancel out their higher caloric intake. This suggests that the modern sedentary way of life with its low levels of physical activity is a critical factor. From what is known about hunter-gatherer diets we cannot conclude that we are evolutionarily adapted to limited food. What is more, we aren't all fat. Overeating is not the norm in a food abundant world because we have evolved mechanisms that regulate food intake.

We may, alternatively, address obesity through the proximate question of how children come to overvalue food. The proposal of Waynforth (2010) is to apply the concept of marginal value to eating. This concept implies that the utility of food to the child will change depending on how much food has already been consumed. As the elapsed time between eating moments will influence how attractive the food is, children will eat more of a food when it is less frequently available. If this logic is applied to parents attempting to control the diet of their children, increasing the time between feeding moments will lead to an increased food intake in the next session. To put it briefly, treating some foods as rare items results into a wrong perception of a food's marginal utility.

Obesity as a social learning problem

Since not everyone is susceptible to the problem of obesity, there must also be cultural influences at work which may explain differences between groups of individuals. While the preceding approaches focus on mental mechanisms and behavioural strategies, the approach of gene–culture coevolution would argue that obesity is a learning problem. People learn initially from parents and peers what to eat (e.g. Benton 2004). But later on they may improve their diet, modelling themselves on influential individuals with better food preferences. Recall that in social learning, people use characteristics of individuals in their social world to find out who has the best ideas, beliefs or preferences that may be adopted (Richerson and Boyd 2005). Consistent with this approach, programmes for improving diets might use media-personalities as role models.

We conclude our case study by summarising the differences between approaches (Table 2.1), and a brief comment. The approaches have in common that they are concerned with explaining the function of adaptive traits for reproductive success. They are different in what their special focus is, which criteria indicate problems, for which environment behaviour is supposed to be adaptive, and how quickly behaviour can respond to unprecedented environmental changes. For example, the modular approach has a focus on mechanisms in the brain, while human behavioural ecology is focused on behavioural strategies, and gene–culture coevolution on learning as well as creative capacities.

Table 2.1 Differences between evolutionary approaches

Approach	Criteria for problems	For which environment is behaviour adaptive?	How quickly can adaptive behaviour respond, if the environment changes in an unprecedented way?
Modular evolutionary psychology	human characteristics, mental modules	past environment	at the speed of genetic change
Human behavioural ecology	human behavioural strategies	current environment	at the speed of individual learning
Gene–culture coevolution	learning and creative capacities	any environment	at the speed of cultural change

Source: Adapted from Nettle (2009)

Another difference is that human behavioural ecology assumes that behaviours are adapted to current environments whereas modular evolutionary psychology assumes that the mental mechanisms underlying behaviours are adapted to past environments. The gene–culture coevolution approach differs from the other approaches in its conviction that the human capacity to create artefacts (e.g. tools, symbols) and learn from each other, allows us to be successfully adaptive in any environment.

It seems that these differences have been overemphasised in debates between the approaches. Actually, the approaches have considerable scope for complementing each other. For example, human behavioural ecology assumes that humans are capable of using behavioural strategies to achieve their goals, but are not concerned with the mental modules on which this capacity is based. Thus the evolutionary approach which focuses on these mechanisms, may enrich the human behavioural ecological explanations. As the cultural evolution approach is focused on capacities to learn from each other, it may also enrich the explanations of human behavioural ecology. Although agreement on a common framework does not yet exist, proposals have been presented (e.g. White et al. 2007).

2.3 Genome, nervous system and culture as solutions

genome
the total genetic material within the cell of an organism.

Additional criteria for identifying problems may come from three adaptive systems: **genome**, nervous system and culture. These systems have stored information about the past in such a way that they can improve chances of survival and reproduction. The genome is composed of all the genes that 'know' how to build a body. A genome will do for plants, but not for animals. Plants are self-feeders, making their own carbohydrates, fats and proteins from raw materials. The energy to do this comes from the sun. But animals are not self-supporting as they depend on scattered food sources which explains why they are mobile organisms. They need therefore an additional system, allowing them to adapt more rapidly to changing environments. For example, the nervous system 'knows' how to respond to dangerous predators and potential partners. As humans live in ever-more dynamic environments, they need culture as another additional system. Culture 'knows' all the things an individual could never learn by itself. Thus, we may presume that each

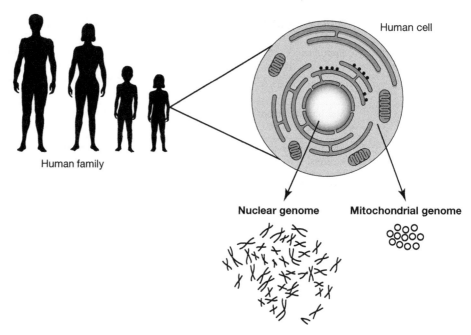

Figure 2.1 Two parts of the human genome
Source: Brown (2007)

new system evolved to solve problems. Evolutionary scientists consider the genome, the nervous system, and culture indeed as adaptive systems which evolved one after the other (Bonner 1980; Lumsden and Wilson 1981; Plotkin 1994; Dawkins 2009). Let's look at each of these systems and consider their problem-solving capacity.

The genomic system

Each living being has a genome which contains all the genes that are needed to build the organism, ensure that it works satisfactorily and protects against diseases. What exactly is a genome? Most genomes, including the human genome and those of all other cellular life forms, are made of DNA (Brown 2007; Barnes and Dupré 2008). The human genome consists of two distinct parts: the **nuclear genome** which contains about 25,000 genes, and the **mitochondrial genome**, an energy-generating organelle in each cell, which contains just 37 genes (Figure 2.1).

Almost every somatic cell of the human body has a genome of each parent while human reproductive cells (egg cells and sperm cells) have just one genome. Reproductive cells have one genome because each parent contributes its own genome to its offspring. Genomes are complicated things, studied by the science of **genomics** (see Box 2.1 Genomics).

Recall from Chapter 1 that the German biologist August Weissman introduced a distinction between germ line and soma which rendered inheritance of acquired characteristics a logical impossibility. He proposed that multi-cellular organisms such as humans, possessed two types of cells, the germ cells which conveyed heritable information from one generation to the next (the germ line), and somatic cells, which were used to build the body (or soma). Although environmental effects during the life of an individual may influence somatic cells, the germ cells are immune

nuclear genome
the total genetic material within the cell containing about 25,000 genes.

mitochondrial genome
an energy-generating organelle in each cell, containing 37 genes.

genomics
the branch of genetics concerned with the study of genomes.

to these influences. The so-called Weismann barrier amounts to the principle that information moves only from germ line to the soma, and never from somatic to germ cells. Remember that this principle is under discussion.

In the longer term, sexual reproduction means that in each generation individual genomes are reshuffled from body to body. While individual genomes are reshuffled, the collective database of survival instructions forms the '**gene pool**' of a species. This is the sum total of all genes in an interbreeding population at a particular time and can be described by the frequencies of different genes it contains. So, each individual's genome is a sample from the gene pool – a kind of species 'database'.

gene pool
the sum total of all genes in an interbreeding population at a particular time that can be described by the frequencies of different genes it contains.

BOX 2.1 Genomics

Genomics is the branch of genetics concerned with the study of genomes. This science has developed since the 1980s, using computer-based technologies and systems to collect and analyse vast amounts of data on DNA of various organisms. These data are generated by projects such as the Human Genome Project (HGP), a truly international endeavour, begun in 1988, to map the entire human genome, and finished in 2003 (Strachan and Read 2004). For many scientists, this was biology's equivalent of a periodic table of genes. The major rationale of HGP was to acquire fundamental information about our genetic make-up which would further the scientific understanding of human genetics and of the role of various genes in health and disease. There are several distinct but overlapping areas of

genomics. Structural genomics is about mapping the genomes of any organism. Functional genomics deals, for example, with how gene products such as proteins work and how gene functions change under different conditions, such as disease states. Comparative genomics identifies similarities between genomes of different species. Phylogenomics is the field of bioinformatics that integrates knowledge about the evolutionary history of organisms (i.e. phylogeny) with analysis of their genomes (i.e. genomics) and proteins (i.e. proteomics). Its basic hypothesis is that well-characterised genes in one organism provide valuable insights into the homologous genes of related organisms. The human genome reflects the history of the human gene set since early life. Figure 2.2 shows the percentage of human genes that

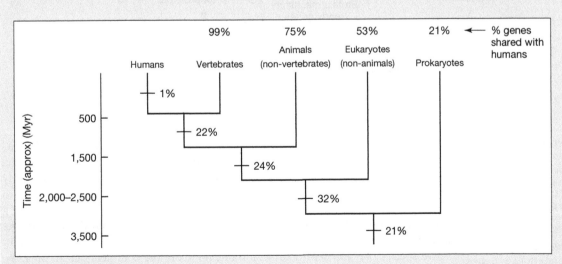

Figure 2.2 The history of the human genome
Source: Ridley (2005)

are homologous with genes of other organisms (Ridley 2005). For example, we share 99 per cent of our genes with **vertebrates** (animals with a skeleton, such as fishes and humans). Only 1 per cent of our genes are 'unique', and have no homologues with other vertebrates. The history of human genes is very incomplete as it is based on comparisons with a small number of species, and uncertain because methods to identify genes are subject to error.

The career of genomics began with identifying genes and continued with sequencing and mapping entire genomes. Meanwhile, issues concerning the status of knowledge in genomics are frequently discussed (O'Malley and Dupré 2005). The first issue is that early genomics shared the reductionist aspirations of genetics which led to the mistaken belief of genetic determinism. This belief considers causation in life to be entirely one-way: the genes cause the proteins, the proteins cause the cells, and so on. However, for many biologists (e.g. Noble 2006) the real future is going beyond reductionism, meaning that life is two-way: bottom-up causation from parts to the organism, as well as top-down causation from the organism to the parts (Figure 2.3).

The second issue is about the decline of hypothesis-driven research in biology and the growing influence of the data-driven approach of genomics. The answer to these issues would come from the emerging, post-genomic science of systems biology which aims to obtain a fundamental, comprehensive and systematic understanding of life.

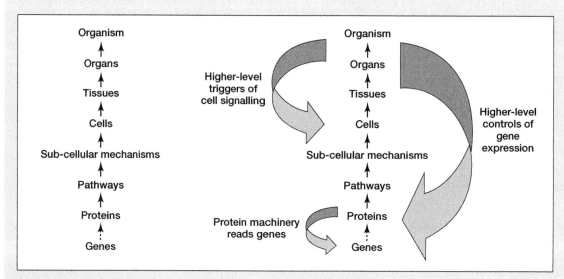

Figure 2.3 Upward and downward causation
Source: Noble (2006)

vertebrates
animals that possess a spinal cord protected by a segmented vertebral column of cartilage and/or bone.

invertebrate
animals that lack an internal skeleton. All animals other than fish, amphibians, reptiles, birds and mammals are invertebrates .

A convenient assumption would be that every species is perfectly suited to its environment. Genomes are indeed active adapting systems for the organism, being remodelled over the course of evolutionary time. But humans are an incredibly young and rapidly evolved species, so that their genome has not been allowed to make fine adjustments that protect people from diseases. Human beings share a common ancestor with chimpanzees just six million years ago and the current species *Homo sapiens* has been here only for 200,000 years. We are a young and very active species that learned to walk upright, populate the continents at an amazing speed, and re-create the planet with the help of science and technology.

Thus, Greg Gibson (2009) argues that recent human evolution has changed and disrupted our genetic make-up that evolved over millions of years. Rapid evolutionary changes have made us susceptible to diseases like cancer, diabetes and depression. That is why Gibson compares humans with adolescents:

> Like an adolescent still growing up and trying to come to terms with a constantly changing world, we're just a little uncomfortable with who we are. Presumably we'll get to a more comfortable genetic place, but not for a few more hundred thousand generations. (2009: 13)

Thus we may conclude that the human genome cannot keep up with a fast moving species like humans. Increased susceptibility to diseases indicates the problem of a slow working system.

The nervous system

After the slow genome, over millions of years, the rapid nervous system emerged. While plants have a fixed place and can suffice with a genome, animals have a nervous system which adapted them to a mobile way of life. Moving around means that animals often encounter fast changing environments, and have many interactions with enemies which require quick responses. The origin of this rapid-response system may be dated to about 560 million years ago with the emergence of active marine animals.

Mapping the genomes of various species has demonstrated that the evolution of genes related to the nervous system is much faster in primates than in other mammals, such as rodents (Dorus et al. 2004). Moreover, within primates, the evolutionary acceleration is most prominent in apes with whom we share a more recent common ancestor than with monkeys. The selection pressure for a change of the nervous system is presumed to be intense.

Change of the nervous system enables an expansion of the learning repertoire: from learning by trial and error to learning from one another. At its simplest, the nervous system works by trial and error when animals search for food, and try various actions such as digging for roots, robbing a conspecific (member of the same species) of its catch, or moving into new habitats. They will learn from their experiences and keep them in mind. Memory is indeed a vast archive with lists of opportunities, potential problems and alternative solutions.

As we saw with the genome, evolution does not provide perfect solutions. So, neither was the nervous system a perfect adaptive system. Consider the evolution of human social life. While hunter-gatherers lived in small groups, today's families and working groups are engulfed by large corporations and complex societies. Living satisfactorily in such structures requires that people pass through a long process of socialisation, and are able to keep up with the pace of knowledge. The rapid evolution of social complexity appears not to be in tune with the rate of neural maturation. Prefrontal structures in the brain which are involved in impulse control and making judgements, are not fully mature until after 25 years of age. We may consider this mismatch as a problem that plays a role in teenage depression, acting-out behaviour, drug abuse and suicide (Gluckman et al. 2009).

The cultural system

We have argued that a genome will suffice for plants, but that animals need a nervous system as a result of their mobile lifestyle. Among animals are humans who depend heavily on a third system, culture. Culture emerged when the human brain's database not only recorded personal experiences but also collective experiences, handed down from past generations by behaviour, word of mouth, books, and today by internet. Human culture operates even faster than the individual's nervous system as we may learn to solve problems from people whom we have never met.

The cultural system contains collective experiences which are passed down from one generation to another. In the earlier section about the evolutionary approach of gene–culture coevolution, we have seen that culture is about all the things we learn from each other. Thus culture depends on the nervous system because the ideas and beliefs we share with other people, are present in our brain as mental representations.

The genomic and nervous system aren't perfect problem-solvers, but culture isn't either. According to the evolutionary approach of gene–culture coevolution, social learning from prestigious peers has the advantage of saving time and costs of learning all by ourselves. Social learning may also be based on a conformist bias, meaning that it depends on the commonness of the behaviour, not on its characteristics. For example, we may buy a car because most people use this means of transport. This is a frequency-dependent bias which tells us nothing about the advantages or disadvantages of the car.

To be sure, social learning has the advantage of saving time and information costs over individual learning. However, learning from others has a serious drawback. Studies show that if the social learning system comes to lack sufficient individual learning, behaviour ceases to track environmental variation. When the environment does change, fitness declines and the population may collapse or even vanish (Whitehead and Richerson 2009). Applied to our example, this argument implies that we cannot do without social learning, but still need to learn by ourselves. To conclude, environmental changes may indicate the problem of insufficient individual learning.

To summarise, the three adaptive systems which we have examined provide the following criteria for identifying problems:

- the genomic system: e.g. increased susceptibility to diseases indicates the problem of a slow adapting genome.
- the nervous system: e.g. slow maturation of the brain indicates the problem of rapid evolution of social complexity.
- cultural system: e.g. environmental changes may indicate the problem of insufficient individual learning.

Now we are ready to examine how the complexity of life has increased over evolutionary time. Individuals needed to cooperate, forming higher levels of social organisation. These levels should lead us to problems.

2.4   Levels of complexity

A simple conception of evolution holds that individual organisms are engaged in a competitive struggle for food, mates and other precious things. But competition is only part of the story. Cooperation among genetically similar individuals produces coalitions whose power to compete can be great. Societies of cooperating individuals show that ants, termites, bees, hunting dogs and humans have enormous competitive advantage over solitary animals (Vermeij 2004). For example, cooperative hunting dogs succeed in more than 80 per cent of attempts to catch prey animals in Africa, a figure which is much higher than in solitary hunters. In human societies, the power of cooperation to compete is to be seen in all kinds of organisation, such as professions, corporations and political parties.

Evolutionary trends towards increasing complexity

Cooperative structures make life more complex. A further approach to identify problems, would then be to look for cases in which the complexity of organisms has increased over evolutionary time. There is indeed a long history of support for the general idea of overall evolutionary trends towards increases in size, complexity and diversity (Carroll 2001). Two fundamental mechanisms are supposed to explain these trends. First, a random, passive tendency to evolve away from the initial minimal size and simple structure of organisms, through an increase in variance. And second, a non-random, active process that biases evolution towards increased size and complex structure (see Box 2.2 Are some organisms more complex than others?).

BOX 2.2 Are some organisms more complex than others?

The evolution from unicellular to multi-cellular organisms raises the difficult issue of complexity. It seems evident that elephants are more complex than bacteria. Elephants have a large repertoire of behaviours – walking, bathing, nursing, uprooting trees, trumpeting etc. – whereas bacteria have not. This may be true, but it is hard to find agreed-upon criteria to measure complexity. Although evolutionary biologists tend to avoid the question of increasing complexity, criteria used to measure the complexity of organisms include number of genes in genome, number of organs or tissues in an organism, number of cell types possessed by an organism, number of interactions between the parts of an organism, number of statements required to describe the organism, or part – whole structure of the organism (McShea 2001; Hall and Hallgrimsson 2008). The most commonly used metric of complexity is the number of different types of cells that an organism has. James Valentine and his colleagues (1994) have found a marked increase of cell types in multi-cellular organisms.

Sponges (*Porifera*) and jelly-fishes (*Cnidaria*) have between 6 and 12 cell types, flatworms (*Annelids*) about 200, and humans (*Hominidae*) about 400. One may conclude that the complexity of organisms increased during at least part of the evolutionary history of life on Earth. The increasing complexity of multi-cellular animals (or metazoans) is associated with changes in lifestyle. Early marine animals swam above the sea bottom, feeding on accumulated debris. The scattered distribution of food might give a selective advantage to animals that could eat more food more rapidly, leading to the evolution of a mouth and gut that enabled selective digestion. The increased success of these animals would create a niche for predatory animals, such as *Anomalocaris*, with a grasping mouth, appendage-driven propulsion, and eyes on stalks to locate prey (see Figure 1.5). Selection for more efficient predation would generate selection for better defence and escape in prey animals, resulting into an arms race between predator and prey.

A case in point are human organisms whose complexity, measured by their number of cell types, has increased over evolutionary time. This does not imply that humans are especially complex because they have very complicated brains, sophisticated societies or exceptional mental capacities. The mistaken idea that there is a

Great Chain of Being with humans at the top, was abandoned long ago in biology (McShea 1996). It is not at all obvious that humans are more complex than other species. Great complexity may be expected in specialised structure of organisms. We may think, for example, of the ingenious echolocation system which bats and dolphins use. They emit series of high-pitched sounds that echo back from the object and are detected by ear.

What exactly do we mean by complexity? The word complexity has been applied to various objects and processes, or more generally called, systems. The weather, a computer, and the world economy are supposed to be complex systems. In biology, rain forests, genomes, human brains and cultures, are usually considered complex. We have different dimensions to measure the complexity of an object or process. How hard is it to describe? How hard is it to create? How high is its degree of organisation, or hierarchy? (Mitchell 2009). Considering the last mentioned dimension, we may take the view that complex systems have many different types of parts with strong interactions. As an example, humans are multi-cellular organisms with many different types of parts, such as genes, cells, tissues and organ systems with strong interactions

Hierarchy of organisms

Daniel McShea (2001) has long been trying to make sense of the idea that the complexity of some organisms increases over evolutionary time. He proposed a scale that can be used to measure the degree of hierarchy of organisms. This scale is defined in terms of levels of nestedness, meaning that a higher-level entity contains as parts entities from the next lower level. He proposes the following scale of nestedness:

- Level 1: prokaryotic cells: the simplest cells, such as bacteria.
- Level 2: aggregates of level 1 organisms, such as eukaryotic cells, i.e., more complex, nucleated cells whose evolutionary ancestors originated from the fusion of prokaryotic cells.
- Level 3: aggregates of level-2 organisms: all multi-cellular organisms, such as fishes, reptiles and mammals.
- Level 4: aggregates of level-3 organisms: insect colonies and animal and human societies.

Each level is supposed to be more complex than the previous level. McShea points out that nestedness only describes the part–whole structure of an organism, not any of its functions, such as reproduction by egg and sperm cells, or internal communication by hormones or nerves. This scale of nestedness covers changes which involve lower-level entities joining to form higher-level entities.

prokaryotes

single-celled organisms lacking a nucleus and organelles.

eukaryotes

organisms with a cell nucleus, and organelles such as mitochondria with their own genome.

Maynard Smith and Szathmáry (1995, 1999) have developed a similar scheme which describes explicitly the function of parts and wholes. Their scheme includes the unique and important origin of sex, that is, the change from asexual to sexual reproduction. In **prokaryotes** – the simplest cells without a cell nucleus – new individuals emerge by dividing a single cell into two. But in **eukaryotes** a new individual only arises by the fusion of two sex cells which are produced by different individuals. Since then most organisms can reproduce only as part of a sexual population in which males and females depend on one another. In McShea's scheme, the change from asexual to sexual reproduction would be a new level between 2 and 3.

The argument of Maynard Smith and Szathmáry (1995) is that many changes from lower-level to higher-level entities have the common feature that lower-level organisms have lost their ability to reproduce. Recall from Chapter 1 that our cells contain mitochondria, being structures that convert sugars and fats into energy with the help of oxygen. Originally, mitochondria were independent, free-living organisms, but the ancestors of plants and animals incorporated them so that they could only reproduce within their host (level 2). A subsequent change occurred when unicellular organisms turned into multi-cellular organisms. Consider human bodies which are composed of somatic and reproductive cells. The ancestors of somatic cells were once able to reproduce independently, but with the emergence of reproductive cells they lost this ability (level 3).

Another transition to a higher level of complexity occurred when groups of individuals relinquished their reproductive capacity to one or a few individuals. Animals like ants, bees, termites and wasps live in colonies in which the queen has the capacity to reproduce while the other individuals are non-reproductive and engaged in brood care (workers) or protection of the colony (soldiers). The typical cooperative brood care in these insects is the reason why they are called 'eusocial' (true social) species. Humans did not give up their ability to reproduce, but evolved in such a manner that they were only able to reproduce as part of a complex society. We may call them 'ultrasocial' because raising children requires much investment not only from parents but also from societal institutions like marriage, medical care and education (level 4).

To summarise, the argument of increasing complexity implies that there have been a number of times when new evolutionary entities learned to cooperate, forming higher levels of organisation. The transition from solitary to social living indicates the problem of cooperation which will be dealt with in Chapter 6 (The evolution of social life). Now that we have examined how evolutionary trends towards increasingly complex life may furnish criteria for identifying problems, you are invited to participate in a thought experiment. What does it teach us about problems and solutions in evolution?

2.5   Replaying the tape of life

A thought experiment

Animals are defined by characteristics, such as sexuality, living in groups, walking on all fours, and so on. When animal species have similar characteristics, the theory of evolution can explain them by two principles: shared ancestry and shared selection pressure. Humans and apes are alike because they descend from common ancestors who lived in groups, had large brains, and so on. Recall from Chapter 1 that these characteristics are termed homologies. Birds and insects, however, have no common ancestors but are alike in having wings because they have been subjected to the influence of similar living conditions. Such properties are referred to as analogies.

If two species have similar characteristics, it may be difficult to decide whether they are homologies or analogies. Stephen Gould (1991b) proposed that analogies can be identified by conducting thought experiments or computer simulations. Consider *Replaying the tape of life*. Imagine that a comet or radical climate change would wipe out all life on Earth. This is not far-fetched, because many experts claim that we are in the thick of a climate change, which will eradicate numerous animal species. Once the disaster has run its course, evolution will start over again. The question is whether the same plant and animal species, including *Homo sapiens*, would once again make their appearance. This would not be the first mass extinction among life forms, followed by the emergence of new ones. Some 65 million years ago, a comet impact terminated the life of many animals, including the dinosaurs. The catastrophe that took place 250 million years ago was even more dramatic: it resulted in the extinction of 80 per cent of all marine animals and 70 per cent of all vertebrate terrestrials.

Three options when evolution starts again

If evolution can start all over again, there are three options. First: evolution yields the same outcomes each time. Second: evolution yields a different outcome each time. Third: evolution shows a recurrent pattern. Which option is most likely? The first option is unlikely because we have defined evolution as the non-random selection of random events. Gould prefers the second option because he emphasises the random component. Simon Conway Morris (2003) chooses the third option that each evolutionary restart results in a number of recurring solutions for problems. One reason is that evolution operates within constraints because the materials of life allow only a limited range of solutions to a particular problem. Recurring solutions are, for example, senses, intelligence and large brains. These characteristics are analogies which resulted from shared selection pressures. The fact that they evolved many times independently, is perhaps the best evidence for adaptation (Foley 1999).

Conway Morris supports his argument with evidence that sensory organs, intelligence, social life, parental care, large brains, tool-use and culture evolved several times independently in different species. For example, eusociality (or true sociality) refers to a colonial system whereby only one female is reproductive while the other animals gather food and care for the young. Eusociality has evolved several times independently: in naked mole-rats, ants, bees, wasps, voles and crustaceans. Large brains evolved several times: in humans, dolphins, parrots and ravens.

Richard Dawkins (2004) adds more evidence to this argument. It has, for example, been estimated that eyes evolved independently between 40 and 60 times in the animal kingdom. Echolocation has evolved at least four times: in bats, toothed whales, oilbirds and cave swiftlets. Furthermore, true flapping flight has evolved four times: in insects, pterosaurs, bats and birds. The venomous sting has evolved at least ten times independently, for example in jellyfish, spiders, scorpions, centipedes, insects, snakes and stingrays.

Summing up, a remarkable number of adaptations evolved many times independently in different species. This fact ensures that analogies are strong solutions to problems.

2.6 Summary

- Evolutionary psychology requires that we think on a wide timescale, and ask why-questions which go far into the history of evolution. These questions are about problems which have an impact on reproductive success. However, we don't know all of the problems that our ancestors experienced as we cannot rerun the tape of life. The aim of this chapter was therefore to provide criteria for identifying problems for which our ancestors had to find solutions.

- Different approaches in evolutionary psychology provide criteria, such as requirements for reproduction, mental mechanisms, human characteristics, behavioural strategies, and learning as well as creative capacities.

- Adaptive systems, such as the genome, the nervous system and culture, provide additional criteria because each new system evolved to solve problems which the previous system couldn't.

- Evolutionary trends towards increasing complexity of life provide criteria, such as the need of individuals to cooperate, forming higher levels of organisation like sexual populations, groups and societies. Each higher level emerged because the lower level was unable to solve all problems.

- By 'replaying the tape of life' we may learn which biological properties evolved many times independently, and may therefore be considered strong adaptations.

Study questions

1. How can evolutionary problems be defined?

2. How do mental mechanisms, behavioural strategies and learning capacities indicate ancestral problems?

3. How can genome, nervous system and culture be regarded as problem-solving systems?

4. How did evolutionary entities learn to cooperate, forming higher levels of organisation?

5. Which solutions would be most adaptive if we could rerun the tape of life?

Suggested reading

Evolutionary approaches to problems

Buss, D. (2009). The great struggles of life: Darwin and the emergence of evolutionary psychology. *American Psychologist, 64,* 140–148.

Richerson, P. and Boyd, R. (2005). *Not by Genes Alone: How Culture Transformed Human Evolution.* Chicago: The University of Chicago Press.

Smith, E. and Winterhalten, B. (Eds) (2009). *Evolutionary Ecology and Human Behaviour.* New Brunswick: Aldine Transaction.

White, D., Dill, L. and Crawford, C. (2007). A common, conceptual framework for behavioural ecology and evolutionary psychology. *Evolutionary Psychology, 5,* 275–288.

Genome, nervous system and culture as solutions

Dorus, S., Vallender, E., Evans, P. et al. (2004). Accelerated evolution of nervous system genes in the origin of *Homo sapiens. Cell, 119,* 1027–1040.

Gibson, G. (2009). *It Takes a Genome: How a Clash Between Our Genes and Modern Life Is Making Us Sick.* Upper Saddle River, NJ: Pearson Education.

Plotkin, H. (1994). *Darwin Machines and the Nature of Knowledge: Concerning Adaptations, Instinct and the Evolution of Intelligence.* London: Penguin Books.

Whitehead, H. and Richerson, P. (2009). The evolution of conformist social learning can cause populations collapse in realistically variable environments. *Evolution and Human Behaviour, 30,* 261–273.

Levels of complexity

Maynard Smith, J. and Szathmáry, E. (1999). *The Origins of Life: From the Birth of Life to the Origins of Language.* Oxford: Oxford University Press.

McShea, D. (1996). Metazoan complexity and evolution: is there a trend? *Evolution: International Journal of Organic Evolution, 50,* 477–492.

McShea, D. (2001). The hierarchical structure of organisms: a scale and documentation of a trend in the maximum. *Paleobiology, 27,* 405–423.

Replaying the tape of life

Conway Morris, S. (2003). *Life's Solution: Inevitable Humans in a Lonely Universe.* Cambridge: Cambridge University Press.

Dawkins, R. (2004). *The Ancestor's Tale: A Pilgrimage to the Dawn of Life.* London: Weidenfeld and Nicolson.

Gould, S. (1991b). *Wonderful Life; The Burgess Shale and the Nature of History.* London: Penguin Books.

3 The place of humans in evolution

This chapter will cover:

3.1 Introduction

3.2 The geological timescale

3.3 From the ladder of life to the tree of life

3.4 We are primates

3.5 What makes us human?

3.6 Summary

Learning outcomes

By the end of this chapter, you should be able to understand:

- what is meant by anthropocentrism and how it originated
- how a large timescale puts humans in a proper perspective
- how the tree of life helps to relate humans to other species
- how primates originated and differ from other mammals
- how humans originated and what characteristics make them different from other primates.

3.1   Introduction

We share planet Earth with numerous living beings. The aim of this chapter is to make clear what our place is among other species. To this end we use different approaches. We may easily understand that evolution occurs across short time spans when bacteria rapidly evolve resistance to antibiotics. But to put the evolution of human life in a proper perspective we need a larger timescale.

There is a long misguided tradition in Western thought of regarding the universe as ordered in a hierarchy with 'lower organisms' at the bottom and humans at the top. Darwin's theory replaced this ladder-of-life thinking with tree-of-life thinking. According to this approach, evolution can be understood as a branching process, representing the separate forms of life.

Another approach to putting ourselves in the right place is to look at the origin of primates. Any zookeeper can tell you that the primate house is the most popular exhibit. It is easy to see why. Because monkeys and apes are curious, playful, agile, and social, they are fun to watch. The fascinating thing is that we see ourselves reflected in them. What characteristics do we share with them? Where, when and how did primates originate?

Humans are curious, social and playful, just like monkeys and apes. But we also differ in a number of respects from other primates. So, what makes us human? In this approach we focus on the origin of humans and discuss three important characteristics that are associated with them. Other distinct characteristics will be reviewed in later chapters.

3.2   The geological timescale

Making sense of time

In nature, animals keep track of time over an impressive range of scales: from tens of microseconds used for sound localisation to yearly seasonal changes (Buonomano 2007). For humans, the capacity to keep track of and tell time is critical across scales ranging from the nanosecond accuracy of atomic clocks used for global positioning systems to the billions of years needed for studying the evolution of the universe. In between these extremes we track the minutes and hours that govern our daily activities as well as the years in which significant events mark our personal life.

A broader timescale divides the history of mankind into periods such as Antiquity, Middle Ages, Renaissance and Modernity. This scale helps us to remember that the Greek philosopher Aristotle lived more than two millennia ago; that Michelangelo Buonarotti was an Italian artist living at the time of the Renaissance; and that Charles Darwin published his evolution theory in 1859. To put humans in a proper evolutionary perspective we need a timescale that includes the history of life (Figure 3.1).

The geological timescale is a scheme spanning the entire history of the Earth, from roughly 4.6 billion years ago to the present (Klein 2009). It divides the history into named units (eras, periods, epochs) and is marked by first events such as the emergence of first life forms about 3.5 billion years ago (prokaryotes, e.g. bacteria), vertebrate animals (fish), birds, mammals, primates and modern humans (between

Era	Period	Epoch	Ma	Some proposed firsts
CENOZOIC	Quaternary	Holocene	0	
				0.006 First cities
				0.011 First farmers
			0.01	0.012 First people in the Americas
		Pleistocene		0.05 First fully modern humans
				0.20 Oldest firm evidence for fire
			1.6	1.6–1.4 First hominins in Eurasia
				2.6 Oldest stone artifacts and *Homo*
	Tertiary	Pliocene		4.1 Oldest known *Australopithecus*
			5.2	7.5 First hominins (humans *sensu lato*)
		Miocene		20–17 Oldest known monkeys and apes
			23.3	
		Oligocene		
			34	35–30 Oldest known higher primates
		Eocene		50 Oldest known primates of modern aspect
			56.5	
		Paleocene		
MESOZOIC	Cretaceous		65.5	65.5 First primates
			145.5	120 First placental mammals
	Jurassic			160 First birds
			199.5	
	Triassic			220 First mammals and dinosaurs
			251	
PALEOZOIC	Permian		299	300 First reptiles
	Carboniferous			
			359.2	370 First amphibians
	Devonian		416	
	Silurian		443.7	
	Ordovician			475 First vertebrates (fish)
			488.3	
	Cambrian			550 First chordates
			542	
PRECAMBRIAN (= PROTEROZOIC and before)				800 First multicellular life (sponges, algae)
				1400 First nucleated cells (eukaryotes)
				3500 First unicellular life (prokaryotes)
				4000 First complex organic molecules
			4600	4600 Origin of solar system and Earth
				15,000 Origin of the Universe

Figure 3.1 The geological timescale

Source: Klein (2009)

200,000 and 150,000 years ago). Without the geological timescale, the vast abyss of time between the old age of planet Earth and the young age of humans is hard to comprehend. Working without such a scale would be like studying history without a calendar. A popular way to convey the vastness of geological time is to use the analogy of a 24-hour clock. If the Earth was formed at midnight, then life did not appear until 06.00, the first animals and plants only made it on to land as late as 22.00, and humans made their appearance about 23.59, less than one minute before midnight.

Fossils help divide the geological timescale

geological timescale

a scheme spanning the entire history of the Earth, from roughly 4.6 billion years ago to the present. It divides the history into named units (eras, periods, epochs) and is marked by first events such as the emergence of new life forms.

The **geological timescale** is an essential tool for scientists to construct an accurate chronology of the evolution of life and other events. It organises the evolutionary history into blocks of time during which important events occurred such as the formation of an early supercontinent, mountain building and eruption of volcanoes. The geological timescale derives from successive rock layers and fossils extracted from them. It allows scientists to go anywhere in the world and examine rock layers, identify fossils and give them an appropriate age.

Fossils are mostly associated with the remains of organisms that lived long ago and are preserved in rock, ice, amber, peat or volcanic ash. Body remains refer to the hard parts of animals (shells, bones, skulls) because soft tissues (guts, brains) do not fossilise. Fossils also include other material indicators of past life like footprints, wormholes, feeding trails and chemical traces (Klein and Takahata 2002). Since layers of sediment pile up in chronological order and fossil species also are expected to appear in chronological order, the two orders are expected to correlate. Thus, lower layers should contain older species and younger species should be found in higher layers. Concentrating on fossil species with a worldwide distribution, scientists developed a timescale with a number of intervals, defined by the presence of a particular set of fossils in rocks.

Cenozoic

the geological period spanning 65 millions of years ago to the present when the first primates appeared.

primates

term referring to prosimians (lemurs, tarsiers, lorises), monkeys, apes and humans which have in common a set of derived morphological characteristics (traits) that include binocular vision, shortened snout, grasping hands and feet, and considerably larger brains relative to their body size than other mammals.

The scale in Figure 3.1 is divided into four intervals of time (Klein 2009). The Precambrian was a time when early bacteria, algae and multi-cellular organisms emerged. The Palaeozoic ('ancient life') was a time when corals, fish, amphibians, insects and reptiles emerged. The Mesozoic ('middle life') was a time when mammals and birds made their appearance. And the **Cenozoic** ('recent life') was a time when **primates** and humans entered the scene. The intervals of time are demarcated by dramatic changes in the fossil record. For example, at the end of the Mesozoic the collision of a large celestial body with the Earth led to a mass extinction of animals which included the dinosaurs. This was only one of five mass extinctions that occurred over the past half-billion years (Wilson 1992; Ridley 2005). Mass extinctions may be caused by meteorite impacts, major volcanic eruptions, ice ages, large changes in ocean chemistry, but also by human activity. Living at the end of the Cenozoic, we are in the midst of a mass extinction resulting from human overpopulation, damaged ecosystems and human-induced climate change.

While mass extinction may mark the end of an interval, new intervals of geological time may start with a recovery and emergence of new species. The most spectacular, large-scale expansion of life-forms occurred at the dawning of the Palaeozoic era. It happened so rapidly and was so extensive that palaeontologists named it the 'Cambrian Explosion' (Klein and Takahata 2002). In Chapter 12 we have more to say about this remarkable expansion of life forms (Box 12.2 The Cambrian Explosion).

3.3   From the ladder of life to the tree of life

A look at the geological timescale (Figure 3.1) makes clear that it is less detailed for intervals before the Cenozoic. The reason is that the study from which the figure derives – *The Human Career* (Klein 2009) – addresses the evolution of primates which began only in the early Cenozoic. In this geological interval, the Miocene, Pliocene and Pleistocene epochs are considered the most relevant ones in the study of primate evolution. The increasing brevity of the intervals at the top of the geological column reflects the fact that younger rocks are more abundant than older ones. It also reflects the fact that early geologists underestimated the amount of time that passed before *Homo sapiens* appeared on the scene. This underestimation originated from an older, anthropocentric view than the evolutionary one (Cartmill amd Smith 2009). People who believed that all things were created for man's benefit could not understand that the Earth was devoid of human beings throughout more than 99.9 per cent of the history of life.

The ladder of life

viviparity
reproduction in animals such as mammals whose embryos develop within the female parent.

oviparity
laying eggs in which embryos have developed little. Birds and many invertibrates are oviparous.

Where does the anthropocentric view come from? You may recall from Section 1.3 (Biology) that the Greek philosopher Aristotle, in the fourth century BC, proposed that living beings can be arranged in a hierarchy according to their degree of perfection (Barnes 1995). In his text *Generation of Animals*, Aristotle took as a criterion of rank the degree of development reached by the offspring at birth. For example, he considered **viviparous** animals like mammals whose embryos develop within the female parent and give birth to live young, to be more perfect than **oviparous** animals that lay eggs with little embryonic development within the mother. In his text *On the Soul* he suggested another hierarchical arrangement based on the 'powers of the soul'. He proposed three types of souls. Plants have a vegetative, or nutritive soul which allows them to grow and reproduce. Animals have, in addition, a sensitive soul which enables them to respond to the environment, experience pleasure and pain, and have a memory. Humans have also a rational soul which provides all the functions of the other two souls but also the capacity to think. Thus, Aristotle conceived eleven grades of perfection, with sea anemones at the bottom and humans at the top.

In Antiquity, scholars had already identified several kinds of animals that were more or less human-like in their appearance. For example, the unavailability of human cadavers led Galen, a Greek physician, to dissect monkeys as proxies when teaching anatomy to his students. While the anatomical similarity to humans remained a topic of discussion, many authors were particularly interested in the psychology of monkeys and their presumed lack of rational thinking. As only humans had immortal souls, non-human primates such as monkeys and apes were placed in an inferior category (Gundling 2005).

Following the Middle Ages when newly discovered animals arrived in Europe, scholars made the first reliable descriptions of non-human primates. In 1641 Nicolas Tulp, a Dutch physician and anatomist, provided a detailed description of an ape and included a drawing of the specimen. He called the primate *Homo sylvestrus*, referring to the Indonesian name orangutan, or 'wild man of the woods'. In 1699 Edward Tyson, an English physician and anatomist, published a description of a young chimpanzee. He placed his study within the prevailing conception of the ladder of life. In Christianity this conception became known as the *Great Chain of Being* and served as a living proof of divine creation (Lovejoy 1964). Until the eighteenth century, many natural philosophers accepted without question this notion of a static hierarchy in which people were superior to all other creatures.

From the ladder to the escalator of life

In the nineteenth century naturalists proposed the idea that organisms were not part of a static, immutable hierarchy. The French naturalist Georges-Louis Leclerc Comte de Buffon developed a theory in his *Histoire naturelle* (1749–1788: 36 volumes) that ancestral species could give rise to new species under the influence of climatic conditions. In England, Erasmus Darwin, the grandfather of Charles Darwin, published in 1794 his study *Zoonomia* in which he argued that all living beings were derived from a single common ancestor. In his mind, nature was constantly changing and progressing towards perfection as organisms became better adapted to their environment.

scala naturae

mistaken idea that all animals can be arranged in a hierarchy according to the degree of perfection.

In France, Jean-Baptiste Lamarck (1809) published his book *Philosophie Zoologique* in which he explained why species change. Recall from section 1.3 (Biology) his hypothesis that, when confronted with new environments, organisms learn new habits and can change appropriately through an unknown force within the organism. This force would cause organisms to produce offspring different from itself, such that the changes would cumulate over many generations until new species emerged. The origin of new characteristics and their transmission to further generations was believed to be aided by the principle of use and disuse, and the principle of inheritance of acquired characteristics.

anthropocentrism

the tendency to place ourselves at the centre of evolution.

Georges-Louis Leclerc Comte de Buffon, Erasmus Darwin and Jean-Baptiste Lamarck opposed the notion of a static hierarchy of species but they still believed that organisms strove towards perfection along a more or less predetermined pathway. The ladder of life was now viewed as more of an escalator than a fixed arrangement of species, with humans at the top, and change in one direction. Darwin's evolutionary theory put an end to the ladder-of-life and escalator-of-life thinking but common presentations of evolution may still mirror the Great Chain of Being by viewing it, inadvertently, as a progressive process.

lineage

line of descent of a population from its ancestral population. When the members of a population breed and produce the next generation, we can imagine a series of populations over time. Each population of a species is ancestral to the descendant population in the next generation. So a lineage is a series of ancestor-descendant populations, and evolution is then change between generations within a population lineage.

For example, in their book *The Major Transitions in Evolution*, John Maynard Smith and Eors Szathmáry (1999) take the reader from the origin of life to the first multi-cellular organisms, to animal and human societies, and, finally, to language. In this textbook we have adopted an **anthropocentric** focus as well, not because we believe that humans are the measure of all things but because we want to know more about ourselves. The question remains why we seem to have some psychological need to place ourselves at the centre of evolution (Nee 2005).

The tree of life

Darwin used the word 'evolve' just once in the final sentence of his book *On the Origin of Species*. He considered evolution as 'descent with modification', and the word 'descent' refers to the way evolutionary modification takes place in a series of populations that are descended from one another. When the members of a population breed and produce the next generation, we can imagine a **lineage** of populations, consisting of a series of populations over time. Each population of a species is ancestral to the descendant population in the next generation. So, a lineage is a series of ancestor–descendant populations, and evolution is then change between generations within a population lineage (Ridley 2005).

Darwin wrote about 'descent with modification' but there is only one illustration in *Origin of Species* that shows evolution as a branching, or tree-like, process in which the different branches of the tree represent the various forms of life. In a single stroke this tree dismissed the idea of progress in evolution with the implication that all life is equally evolved. Darwin hit upon the metaphor of 'the tree of life' while thinking about the origination and extinction of species (Eldredge 2005). Species may be said to have lifetimes, more or less like individual organisms, as well as a sort of birth (origination), histories, and deaths (extinction). The origination, lifespan and extinction of species can be mapped on a branching tree. Figure 3.2 shows (a) Darwin's sketch of a tree of life in one of his notebooks, and (b) the tree diagram he included in *On the Origin of Species*.

The diagram was meant to illustrate that the modified descendants of any one species will succeed better the more they become diversified in structure so that natural selection can do its work. It shows Darwin's conception of evolution as a branching, or tree-like process (Pagel 2009). Lines that reach to the top of the diagram represent extant, or surviving species. Lines that end farther down are lineages that have become extinct, revealing his hunch that extinction rates are high. The two large groups of branching species coming from common ancestors A and I are so-called monophyletic groups. That is, each of these groups derives from a common ancestor that is not shared with any other species. Within these groups, common ancestors are indicated by letters with superscript numerals where lineages converge.

All living organisms today are the terminal twigs of the crown of the tree of life, and all the organisms that ever lived are on the branches within the tree. Most branches end before they reach the crown so that the animals alive today are only a small fraction of all the types of animals that have lived in the past. In the nineteenth century the only evidence that one could use to relate living groups of organisms with one another was the morphology of their hard tissues (shells, bones, skulls). But in the twentieth century new kinds of evidence became available such as genetic and genomic evidence. Molecular methods allowed scientists to reconstruct the major branches of the tree of life (Stearns and Hoekstra 2005; Ridley 2005; Hall and Hallgrimsson 2008). Any branch of the tree of life is considered a natural group of related organisms that all share a most recent common ancestor.

The largest tree of life

At its largest, the tree of life has three main branches. The first branch is the *Bacteria,* or common prokaryotes which are simple unicellular organisms living in almost all environments (e.g. *Escherichia coli* in the human gut). The second branch is the *Archea,* or simple unicellular organisms inhabiting extreme, that is, hot or salty environments (e.g. *Methanobacterium*). The third branch is the *Eukaryota,* or multi-cellular organisms such as fungi, plants and animals whose cells have a nuclear genome and mitochondria with their own genome. According to molecular evidence, the tree of life on planet Earth began about 3.7 billion years ago (Figure 3.3).

Figure 3.2 (a) Darwin's sketch of a tree of life; (b) Darwin's tree diagram in *On the Origin of Species*

Sources: (a) Notebook B 1837; Darwin Archive Cambridge University Library Syndicate; (b) Darwin (1859)

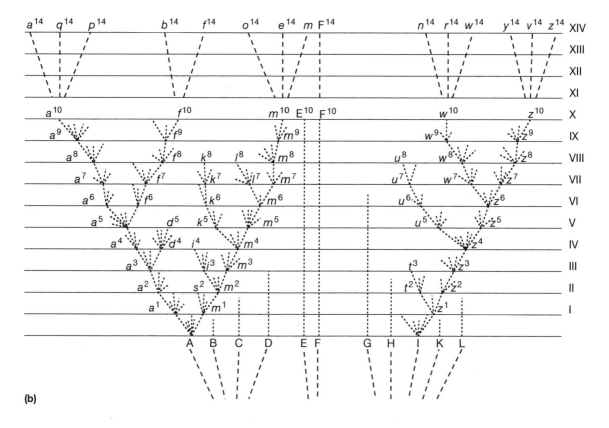

(b)

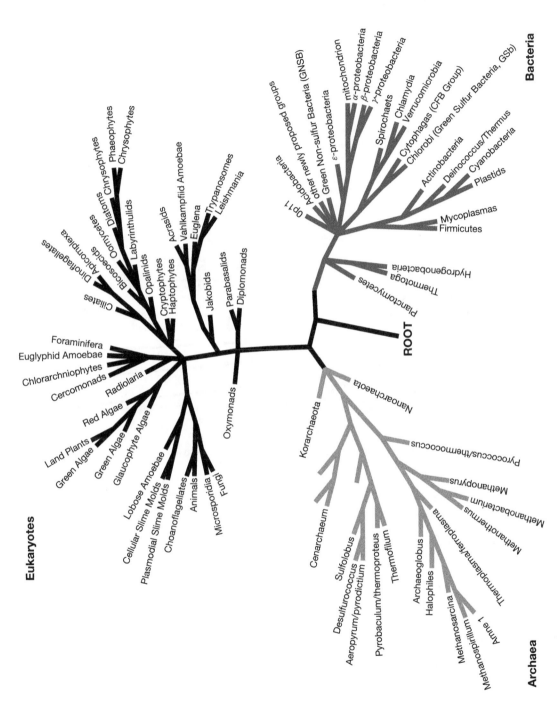

Figure 3.3 The largest tree of life

Source: Stearns and Hoekstra (2005)

Without the reconstructed tree of life we cannot make much sense of the pattern of life, and the origin of humans. With ladder-of-life thinking in mind it is difficult to understand that all extant species are equally evolved, in the sense that the lineages to which they belong have existed over the same evolutionary time. Tree-of-life thinking makes clear that all extant species are equally distant in evolutionary time from the common ancestor of all life.

The tree of multi-cellular life

If you look at the left side of the *Eukaryota* branch, you can see the minor branch of animals. Now look at Figure 3.4 which shows all multi-cellular organisms, divided into three major groups: fungi, plants and animals which share a common ancestor at about 800–1000 million years ago.

Figure 3.4 The tree of multi-cellular life

Source: Stearns and Hoekstra (2005)

The tree of primates

Focusing on the branch 'animals', you may discern the tiny branch 'mammals' from which primates like humans and chimpanzees descend. Figure 3.5 represents the tree of primates with divergence rates between representative apes, monkeys and prosimians, based on fossil and genomic data. The term 'K–T boundary' refers to the mass extinction that took place at the transition from the Cretaceous to the Tertiary. The 'K' represents the Greek word *Kreta*, or chalk.

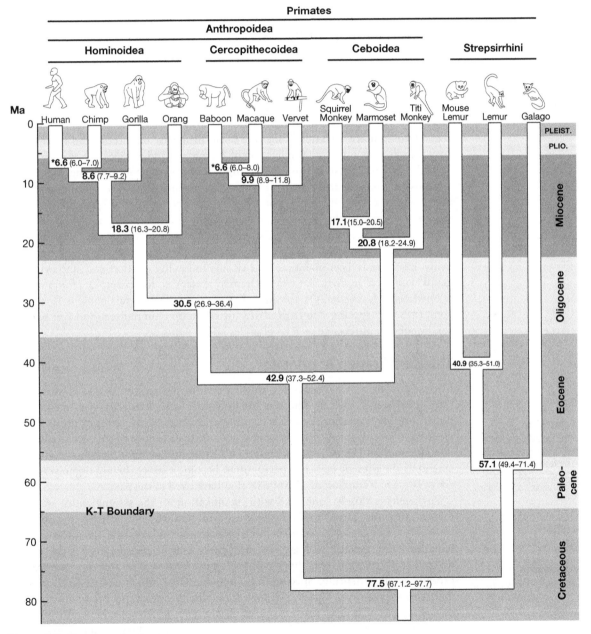

Figure 3.5 The tree of primates

Source: Klein (2009)

A frequently occurring misconception is that humans evolved directly from chimpanzees. The tree of primates shows, however, that they merely shared a most recent ancestor about 6.6 million years ago. We don't know the identity of their most recent ancestor. What we do know is that humans and chimpanzees are the two different tips of a branched twig.

3.4   We are primates

Origin of the term 'primates'

We are more closely related to apes and monkeys than to any other animal species. The anatomical similarities among monkeys, apes and humans led the Swedish naturalist Carolus Linnaeus (1707–1778) to group them in the order Primates (literally: the first). He believed that humans were superior to all other creatures and stood at the top of the ladder of life. Mammals and birds were called 'secundates', and the remaining animals 'tertiates'. Only the term 'primates' has stuck, and most people have forgotten its mistaken implication of hierarchy (Tudge 1996).

Today, all biologists adhere to a single naming scheme after the practice of Carolus Linnaeus. In this scheme, groups of organisms are always given Latin names which are meant to be a label, not a definition. The name of a species always consists of two words: the genus name followed by the species name. The name of a genus is always capitalised and italicised and the name of the species is always italicised but not capitalised. For example: *Homo sapiens* (literally: knowing man). If a genus has already been mentioned, a closely following citation may abbreviate the genus name: *H. sapiens*. An extinct human species is, for example, *Homo erectus*; abbreviated: *H. erectus*. Or consider chimpanzees. Their genus name is *Pan*, which comprises two species: *Pan troglodytes* (or common chimpanzee) and *Pan paniscus* (or, bonobo); abbreviated as *P. troglodytes* and *P. paniscus*.

The classification of primates

The tree of life as we discussed it in the previous paragraph, is also known by the term '**phylogeny**' and its adjective 'phylogenetic'. A phylogeny is a tree diagram illustrating the evolutionary history and relationships of a species or group of species. A phylogeny is to a species what a genealogy or family tree is to an individual. As suggested by Darwin's tree diagram, a phylogeny includes branches that do not extend to the present because species often become extinct. Living organisms today are only a small fraction of all animals that have lived in the past.

phylogeny
the genealogical history of a group of organisms, represented by its hypothesised ancestor-descendant relationships.

Phylogeny is closely connected with classification, or the assignment of species to higher categories based on their presumed evolutionary relationships. The scientific study of classification and determining phylogenetic relationships is known as systematics, or systematic biology. The most basic unit of classification is the species, defined as a group of individuals that look more or less alike and can interbreed to produce fertile offspring. **Speciation** is the process by which new species originate and thereafter remain separate. It may start when populations become isolated by exploiting different resources or by geological events which split them into subpopulations becoming so different that they cannot exchange genetic material anymore.

speciation
the process by which new species originate and thereafter remain separate.

More inclusive categories than species are genus, tribe, subfamily, family, superfamily, infraorder, suborder, semiorder, order, class, phylum and kingdom. A genus comprises species that share a more recent common ancestor with each other than they do with species in other genera (the plural of genus). A family is made up of genera sharing a more recent common ancestor with one another than with genera in other families; and so on. The classification of organisms is based on principles of grouping them together on the basis of shared characteristics such as having a nervous system, a spinal cord, mammary glands and grasping hands. Living humans belong to the following groups: *Animalia*, the kingdom that includes most organisms sharing a nervous system; *Chordata*, the phylum that includes animals sharing a spinal cord; *Mammalia*, the class that includes animals giving birth to live young who suckle; and *Primates*, the order that includes lemurs, tarsiers, galagos, monkeys, apes and humans sharing an enlarged brain, enhanced vision and grasping hands.

There are presently about 300 primate species which have been classified into different groups. Table 3.1 classifies living groups of primates, with special reference

Table 3.1 Classification of extant groups of primates

Order Primates

    Semiorder: *Haplorhini* (i.e. dry-nosed primates)

        Suborder: *Anthropoidea* ('higher primates')

            Infraorder: *Catarrhini* (i.e. flat-nosed, Old World higher primates)

                Superfamily: *Cercopithecoidea* (Old World monkeys)

                    Family: *Cercopithecidea* (macaques, baboons, vervet monkeys)

                Superfamily: *Hominoidea* (apes, humans)

                    Family: *Hylobatidae*

                        Genus: *Hylobates* (gibbons, siamangs)

                    Family: *Hominidae* (great apes, humans)

                  Subfamily: *Ponginae*

                    Genus: *Pongo* (orangutan)

                  Subfamily: *Gorillinae*

                    Genus: *gorilla* (gorilla)

                  Subfamily: *Homininae*

                    Tribe: *Panini*

                      Genus: *Pan* (chimpanzees)

                    Tribe: *Hominini* (humans)

                    Genus: *Homo*

                      Species: *sapiens*

            Infraorder: *Platyrhini* (i.e. downward-nosed, New World higher primates)

                Superfamily: *Ceboidea* (New World monkeys)

                    Family: *Cebidae* (capuchins, squirrel monkeys, marmosets, tamarins)

                    Family: *Pithecidae* (sakis, titis, uakaris)

                    Family: *Atelidae* (spider, howler, and woolly monkeys)

        Suborder: *Tarsiiformes* (tarsiers)

    Semiorder: *Strepsirrhini* (i.e. moist-nosed primates)

        Suborder: *Lemuriformes* (lemurs)

        Suborder: *Lorisiformes* (lorises, galagos)

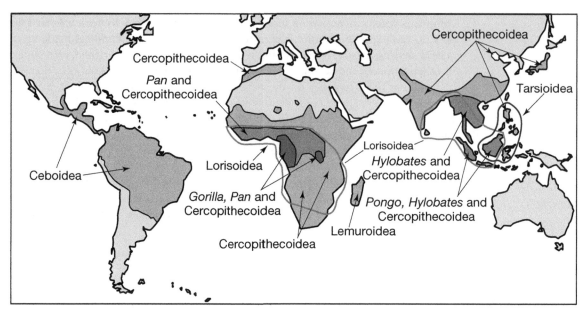

Figure 3.6 Geographic distribution of the living non-human primates

Source: Klein (2009)

to the superfamily of apes and humans (Klein 2009). As there are many primate species, only one species is mentioned: *Homo sapiens*. This table should be read in combination with Figure 3.5 (The tree of primates) and Figure 3.6 (Geographic distribution of the living non-human primates).

The defining characters of primates

Fossil and molecular evidence have made it increasingly clear that humans and African apes, particularly chimpanzees, are closely related (Sibley and Ahlquist 1984; Enard and Pääbo 2004; Perelman et al. 2011). We share 97.6 per cent of our genome with chimpanzees, 96 per cent with gorillas, 94.7 per cent with gibbons, 91.1 per cent with rhesus monkeys, and only 58 per cent with galagos. Many palaeontologists, therefore, consider the traditional classification of humans and their closest ape relatives inadequate and inconsistent with our place in evolution. In the traditional classification, **great apes** and humans were assigned to different families, but in modern classification they are collectively referred to as '**hominids**' that belong to the family *Hominidae*. Living humans (*H. sapiens*) and the fossil species most closely related to us (e.g. *Australopithecus*, *H. erectus*) are called '**hominins**' and belong to the tribe *Hominini*.

This is not a matter of just naming but it reflects a changing view on how we classify life forms and put humans in the right place. The difference between the traditional and modern way of biological classification is that the anatomical characters that we use to name and describe organisms, are not all the same. Every organism has a combination of ancestral characters inherited from distant ancestors, and derived characteristics inherited from a very recent common ancestor. For example, we have grasping hands which we inherited from our ape ancestors, but also hair

great apes

the gorillas, common chimpanzees, and bonobos of Africa and the orangutans of Southeast Asia. These species are referred to as great apes because they are the largest apes.

hominids

the humans and great apes (chimpanzees, gorillas, orangutans).

hominins

living humans (H. sapiens) and the fossil species most closely related to us (e.g. Australopithecus, H. erectus).

lesser apes

the gibbons and siamangs of Southeast Asia. These species are known as lesser apes because they are the smallest apes.

which we inherited from our distant mammalian ancestors. All mammals have hair which makes this characteristic unsuitable for distinguishing primates from other mammals like rodents and cats. The traditional classification schemes often mixed together ancestral and derived characters, but with the advent of modern classification – known as cladistic, or phylogenetic systematics (Hennig 1966) – ancestral characteristics were discarded as irrelevant to the determination of phylogeny.

So, what are the defining characteristics of primates? Primates can be distinguished from mammals by certain evolutionary trends (Klein and Takahata 2002). Primates have gradually become less dependent on their sense of smell (olfaction); their snout length has been reduced, their skull shortened, and their face flattened accordingly. At the same time, they became increasingly dependent on three-dimensional (stereoscopic) vision as an adaptation to active life in tree canopies where the judgement of distances and depth is essential for survival. This lifestyle resulted into the development of forward-projecting eyes and, concurrently, of grasping hands and feet, improved mobility of digits, an opposable thumb and the replacement of claws by flat nails.

Thus, forward-projecting eyes and grasping limbs are characteristics which help to distinguish primates from other mammals. They are limited to primates and should not be confused with ancestral characteristics (Klein 2009). The characteristics we share with other animals must therefore be divided into 'shared ancestral characteristics' that developed early in the history of a species or a group of species, and 'shared derived characteristics' that developed much later in another group. By using only the shared derived characteristics, we can construct a branching diagram of relationships between organisms. This kind of diagram is called a '**cladogram**' which makes a statement about who is related to whom and provides evidence by showing the shared derived characteristics at branching points (Figure 3.7). What is more, a cladogram is testable, because anyone can propose a better hypothesis and look for evidence that falsifies the branching diagram.

At the point where primates branch off from other mammals, two shared derived characteristics are shown: opposable thumb and stereovision. More shared derived characteristics of primates are listed in Box 3.1.

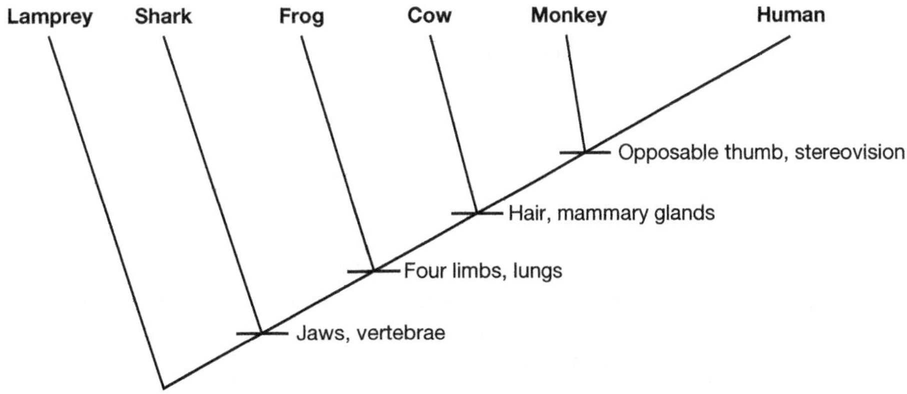

cladogram
branching diagram of relationships between organisms by listing shared derived characters at the branching points.

Figure 3.7 Branching diagram of relationships between some groups of vertebrates
(Shared derived characters are shown at the branching points.)
Source: Prothero (2007)

BOX 3.1 Shared derived characteristics of primates

1. Grasping hands and feet with five highly mobile digits, including a big toe, and an opposable thumb.

2. Flat nails on the hands and feet which replaced the mammalian sharp claws, and sensitive pads on fingers and toes.

3. Highly developed visual sense. Eyes tend to be closely spaced and to face in the same direction, thereby producing substantial overlap between the fields of vision and thus a high degree of stereoscopic three-dimensional vision (depth perception). This feature is associated with a unique neural apparatus for processing visual signals and with enlarged visual centres in the occipital and temporal lobes of the brain.

4. Shortened snout, and flattened face compared with most other mammals, generally associated with a limited sense of smell and small olfactory bulbs in the brain.

5. Reduced number of incisors and premolars compared with those in the earlier mammals and many living ones, combined with a relatively simple cusp pattern on the molars.

6. Locomotion is hind-limb dominated, meaning that hind-limbs do most of the work, and the centre of gravity is nearer the hind-limbs than the forelimbs.

7. Females have small litters, and gestation and juvenile periods are longer than in other mammals of similar size.

8. Unique fissure pattern on the surface of the cerebral cortex of the brain, associated with the larger brain of primates, compared with other mammals.

9. Social life, meaning that they interact regularly with other members of their species. The composition of primate groups may vary considerably from species to species. Some live in monogamous families, others in female-bonded group, or in fission–fusion societies.

These characteristics are compiled from Fleagle (1999), Klein and Takahata (2002), Boyd and Silk (2003), and Klein (2009).

The origin of primates

To understand why the defining characters of primates evolved, requires that we know where, when and how they originated. From the late Triassic, about 200 mya, to the middle Eocene about 44 mya, the position of continents changed as can be seen in Figure 3.8. In the late Triassic, the continents were joined in a single super-continent, Pangea. Fragmentation divided it into a northern continent, Laurasia, and a southern content, Gondwana. Further fragmentation led to the modern continents. The lower part of Figure 3.8 indicates where and when early primates lived (Klein 2009).

KEY FIGURE   Richard Klein

Richard Klein is an anthropologist at the Stanford University, Stanford, California. His primary interest is in the coevolution of anatomy and behaviour in human evolution. His research is mainly on ancient animal remains as indicators of early human ability to make a living.

Selected works

The Human Career (2009)

The Dawn of Human Culture (2002) with Blake Edgar

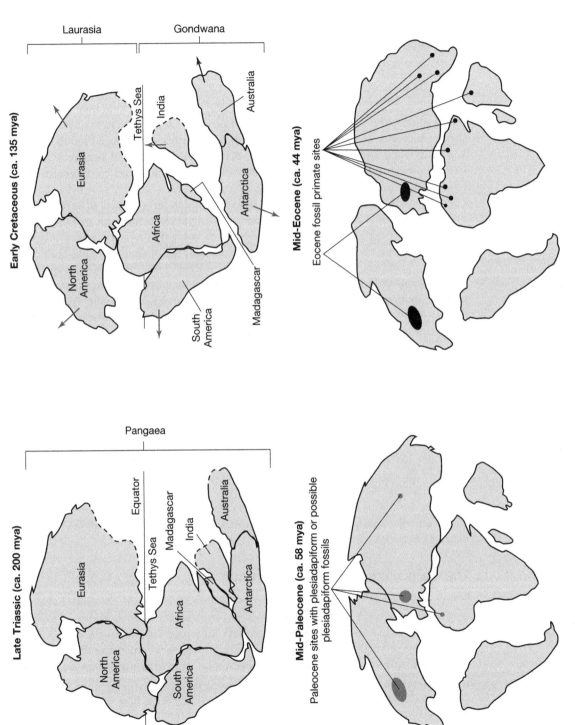

Figure 3.8 Changing positions of the continents

Source: Klein (2009)

Primates originated from insectivores which are small, nocturnal animals with a sensitive snout and an acute sense of hearing. Several hypotheses have been proposed to explain the origin of primates (Klein 2003; Cartmill and Smith 2009). According to the arboreal hypothesis, flowering plants and trees dominated in the Palaeocene, creating a niche for organisms that could feed on nectar, nuts and fruits. Plants underwent a process of radiation, which amounted to a diversification and divergence of species. This radiation of plants resulted in an explosion in pollinating insects as well as birds and mammals that could live on them. Although the earliest primates probably continued to feed on insects, the development of their molars suggest they also fed on fruits and seeds. As the first primates specialised in insects and fruits, they were supposed to be arboreal. Living in trees could explain characteristic primate adaptations such as grasping hands and feet and convergent front-facing eyes required for safe clambering.

Critics noted, however, that many mammals living in trees such as squirrels, manage quite well in the arboreal world despite having eyes on the sides of their head. This led to the visual predation hypothesis which holds that frontal eyes are adaptations for preying on animals. Predators have stereoscopic vision, enabling both eyes to see the same scene and allowing an accurate hand grab. Primates have the best stereo vision with 50 per cent overlap. The importance of predation in explaining primate anatomy and behaviour is still a matter of discussion. Foraging for fruit and flowers which are available in the far ends of tree branches, may have been equally important in the selection for primate grasping hands and feet.

Both hypotheses demonstrate that it makes sense to ask why the defining features of primates evolved (Preuss 2007). Consider another derived characteristic which primates share with one another: large brain size (Box 3.1, item 8). Encephalisation, or expansion of brain size relative to body size was an early feature of primate evolution, particularly referring to an enlarged visual cortex. High-acuity vision became more important when early primates shifted from a nocturnal to a diurnal lifestyle.

While the visual cortex underwent early expansion, the frontal cortex experienced only later expansion in primate evolution. Primate studies indicate that different parts of the expanded frontal cortex are involved in attention, working memory, and planning of behaviour. Working memory is the short-term memory which holds briefly in mind a particular task that has to be accomplished. Apparently, primates faced recurrent cognitive tasks which required such a memory. We will take up this issue in Chapter 8 (Brain and cognition).

The main stages in primate evolution

Living primates are for the most part tropical animals. Most of them are living in trees, and only some baboons and humans have successfully abandoned forested areas for a life in open savanna. Climate plays an important role in the distribution and diversity of primates. Change of climate as well as competition for resources are thought to be major forces in the extinction of many primate groups during the Cenozoic (Fleagle 1999). Actually, the fossil record contains many more potential ancestors than the living primates require. This underlines the idea that a lot of fossil primates have no living descendants. Though it is impossible to reconstruct a complete and compelling phylogeny of extinct and extant primates, a provisional phylogeny is feasible with the well-established order in which major groups diverged and the disputed times when major groups diverged (Martin 1990; Klein 2009; Figure 3.9).

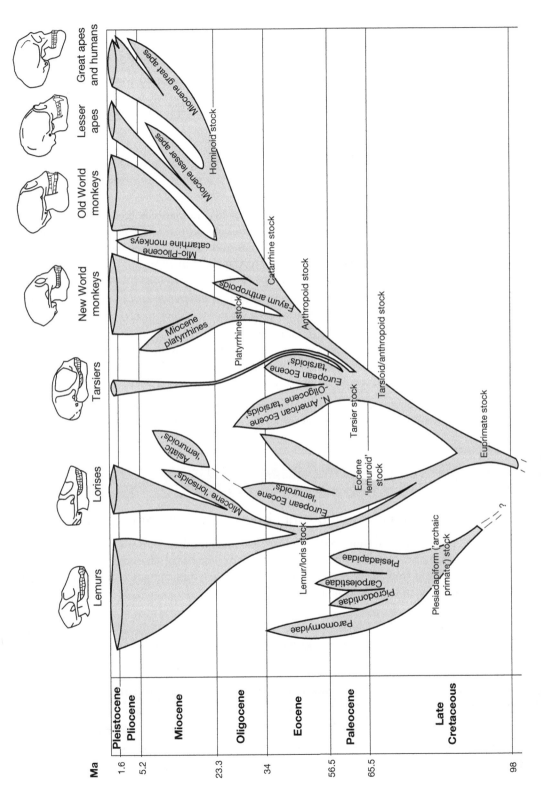

Figure 3.9 A provisional phylogeny linking fossils to living primates

Source: Klein (2009)

At the left side of Figure 3.9 we see the geological intervals of the Cenozoic which correspond roughly with the main stages of primate evolution (Klein 2009). The stages may be viewed as a series of radiations, or increases in the size of populations spreading out from the original centre to exploit new habitats and food sources:

- *Late Cretaceous.* In the first radiation, primates could hardly be distinguished from insectivores with regard to brains, special senses or locomotion. The main differences were in the morphology of their teeth, and perhaps the addition of seeds and fruits to the insectivorous diet.

- *Paleocene.* In the second radiation, lemur-like and tarsier-like animals originated which differed from their ancestors by their grasping hands and feet, with flattened nails instead of claws, as well as a reorganised brain and face due to a shift from olfaction to vision.

- *Eocene.* In the third radiation, monkey-like animals emerged which were mainly arboreal and quadrupedal, mainly walking on top of branches and less leaping between them. They fed less on insects and more on leaves and fruits. Their brain became larger because of the shift to visual dominance.

- *Oligocene.* In the fourth radiation, a difference emerged between what we now recognise as monkeys and apes. The main difference was in dental morphology because monkey-like primates had a greater tendency to eat leaves.

- *Miocene.* In the fifth radiation, apes developed large bodies and upright locomotion. That is, monkeys have a tendency to walk with their limbs swinging in parallel to one another, but apes (like humans) swing their limbs in opposition to one another for balance (unlike monkeys, apes and humans lack a tail to use for balance).

The next section focuses on the late Miocene, Pliocene and Pleistocene in which humans and our evolutionary ancestors made their appearance in evolution.

3.5 What makes us human?

Characteristics that distinguish humans from other primates

The previous section made it clear that humans share various characteristics with other primates. But what makes us human? The list of characteristics that make us different from them is extensive (see Box 3.2 Selected characteristics that distinguish humans from other primates).

BOX 3.2 Selected characteristics that distinguish humans from other primates

- largely reduced hair cover
- skull balanced upright on vertebral column
- chin
- S-shaped spine column
- **bipedalism**
- large brain

- intense sociality
- strong capacity for social cognition
- small canine teeth
- parabolic shape of dentary arch
- short and wide pelvis
- much eyewhite

- buttocks
- no grasping big toe
- long penis
- penis contains no bone
- low sperm density
- female breasts are permanently enlarged

- long gestation, childhood and lifespan
- elongated thumb
- protruding nose
- **advanced tool-making**
- imagination
- **symbolism**

- trade
- fire control
- cooking
- creativity
- wide geographic distribution
- large repertoire of emotions
- sense of morality

- strong capacity for cultural transmission

The characteristics in bold type will be discussed below. The list is based on Klein and Takahata (2002), Carroll (2003), Flinn et al. (2005), Striedter (2005), Lecointre and Le Guayder (2006), Pasternak (2007) and Stringer (2011).

When looking for characteristics that make humans different, we should keep two things in mind. The first is that morphological characteristics (e.g. bipedalism) and behavioural characteristics (e.g. language) are not easily quantifiable. By contrast, molecular differences can be quantified and compared quite well. Recall that comparisons of DNA sequences for chimpanzees and humans show more than 96 per cent identity, indicating that there are a large number of molecular similarities. The second thing is that we should avoid anthropocentrism, the tendency to place ourselves at the centre of evolution. One can equally find characteristics that make non-human species different. Different species excel in different ways: cheetahs are the fastest runners, dolphins the fastest swimmers, eagles have the keenest eyesight, moths have the most sensitive sense of smell, and so on (Klein and Takahata 2002).

The hominid tree

To answer the question 'What makes us human?' we will first look at the origin of humans and then discuss three characteristics that are associated with them: bipedalism, advanced tool-making, and symbolism. Other characteristics such as intense sociality, large emotional repertoire, and language will be discussed in Part 2. With regard to the origin of humans, we need a framework that represents our history back to the separation of the human and ape lineages (Carroll 2003). The tree in Figure 3.10 shows the phylogenetic relationships among hominids (i.e. great apes and humans). The phylogenetic relationships among hominins (i.e. extant and extinct humans) are uncertain and the identity of the last common ancestor of chimpanzees and humans is not known. The shaded area represents the evolution of living hominins as a series of radiations in which many branches of our lineage were formed, but died out.

The earliest representative of the genus *Homo* is usually regarded as being *Homo habilis* and dates possibly from 2.3 mya. *H. erectus* dates from 1.9 mya, evolving by 600,000 years ago into *H. Heidelbergensis*. Between 200,000 and 150,000 years ago, the African descendants of *H. Heidelbergensis* had become distinct as *H. sapiens*, also known as 'anatomically modern humans'. They are distinguished from 'archaic' *H. sapiens*, or *H. Heidelbergensis* by a less robust skeleton, smaller or absent brow ridges, shorter jaws, larger forehead, developed chin, and smaller teeth. The hominin tribe includes the *Australopithecines* and extinct members of the genus *Homo*. One of the main criteria for inclusion in the tribe *Hominini* is the presence of features that indicate bipedalism, for example, a platform foot with the enlarged great toe brought in line with the other toes.

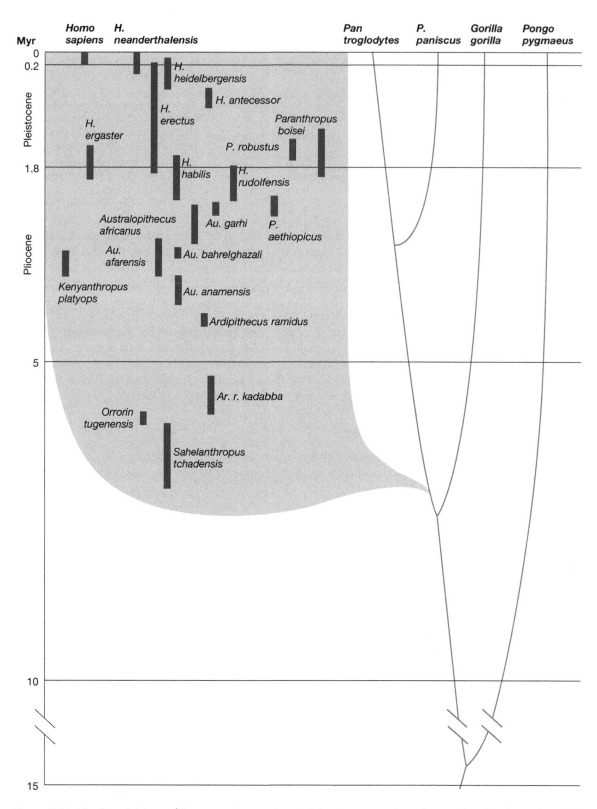

Figure 3.10 The hominid tree (The approximate times of divergence are based on molecular data. The solid bars refer to the time span of the fossil species.)

Source: Carroll (2003)

Bipedalism

Bipedalism which involves using just the hind legs for support during locomotion, emerged very early in hominin evolution. It represents a key innovation leading to a suite of characteristics that make us different from our primate relatives. *Orrorin tugenensis* (shaded area, Figure 3.10) is a serious candidate for being the first hominin that walked upright because its femurs resemble that of later bipedal species. Fossils of *O. tugenensis* were found near Lake Baringo in Kenya. They have pushed back the origins of hominins into the late Miocene, about 6 – 7 mya (Richmond and Jungers 2008). *Orrorin* means 'original man' in the dialect of the tribe in the region of northwestern Kenya. The species name *Tugenensis* refers to the Tugen Hills were the remains were found. All *Orrorin* fossils are housed in the National Museum of Kenya, Nairobi (Sawyer and Deak 2007).

The emergence of bipedalism required many adaptations of the bones and muscles of the hind legs, the pelvis and the hip joints, but also other parts of the skeleton and the skull. The most important adaptation to erect posture and bipedalism was a positional change of the *foramen magnum*, the large opening in the inferior part of the occipital bone of the skull through which the spinal cord, accessory vessels, and vertebral arteries enter the skull to connect with the brain. In quadrupedal primates, the opening lies at the back of the skull but in bipedal humans it is at the base of the skull. That is why the skull came to be on top of the spinal column 'like a ball on a scepter' (Klein and Takahata 2002: 252). Thus, the position of the opening is used as a measure of the degree of bipedalism in hominin evolution.

Why did bipedalism, considered as a defining characteristic of hominins, emerge? The factors that selected for bipedalism are difficult to reconstruct, though we know that bipedalism emerged in a time when global climate became cooler and drier. This climate change favoured the expansion of grasses and the contraction of trees and bushes. Recall from section 1.1 (Introduction) that this change of vegetation which supposedly selected for bipedalism is known as 'the savanna hypothesis'. This hypothesis only predicts that natural selection favours certain anatomical and behavioural changes that enhance fitness in grassland with scattered trees and bushes (Klein 2009). It does not explain why bipedalism would be more advantageous in open vegetation.

Potential benefits of bipedalism include the use of our forelimbs for jobs that have nothing to do with walking, such as making tools, throwing projectiles and carrying food items or babies. Walking upright also enables one to see further away and detect danger and facilitates certain forms of behaviour such as threat and sexual displays. By exposing less skin surface to direct sunlight at midday, bipedalism also reduces the danger of heat stress, particularly for the brain.

foramen magnum
the large opening in the inferior part of the occipital bone of the skull through which the spinal cord, accessory vessels and vertebral arteries enter the skull to connect with the brain.

Advanced tool-making

The genus *Homo* first appeared in the fossil record in East Africa around 2.3 mya. Its appearance is associated with material artefacts, or man-made objects indicating that the new hominins were engaged in making sophisticated tools. Anthropologists characterise several modes of advanced tool-making in hominin evolution (Clarke 1968; Foley and Lahr 1997; Klein and Edgar 2002; Taylor 2010). These modes, represented in Figure 3.11, cover the late Pliocene (2.5–1.6 mya) and the Pleistocene (1.6 mya to 10,000 years ago).

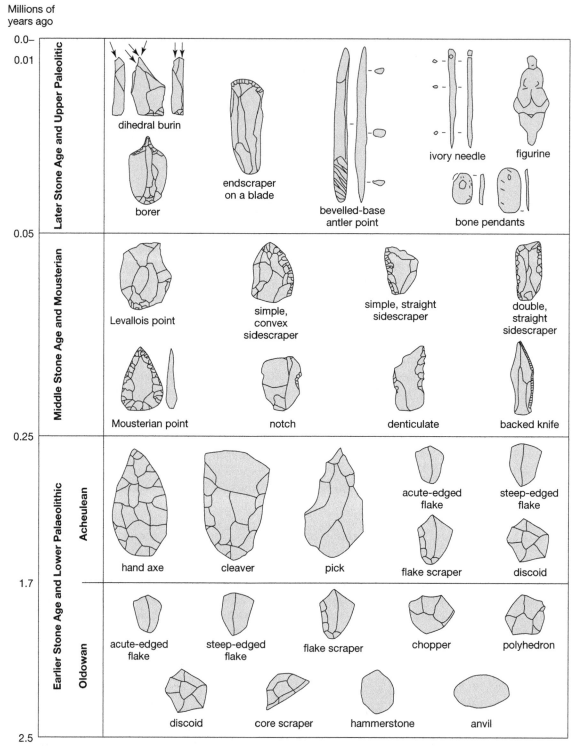

Millions of years ago

Figure 3.11 Modes of advanced tool-making in hominin evolution

Source: Klein and Edgar (2002)

1. *Oldowan tools.* Named after the Olduvai Gorge sites in Tanzania where they were found, are associated with fossils of *Homo habilis*. These tools first appeared around 2.5 mya and are characterised by chipping stones to make a cutting edge which can be used to break open animal carcasses or strip fibres from plants.

2. *Acheulean tools.* Named after the town of St Acheul in northern France where they were found, are associated with fossils of *Homo ergaster* and *Homo erectus*. These tools first appeared around 1.5 mya and are characterised by chipping from both sides with multiple strikes to make a two-sided cutting edge. These hand axes were used for cutting meat, woodwork and digging.

3. *Mousterian tools.* Named after Le Mousterier, a cave site in the Dordogne province, France, where they were found, are associated with *Homo neanderthalensis* and *Homo sapiens*. These tools first appeared around 200,000 years ago and are characterised by several phases of manufacturing and reworking. They include spear points for hunting and scrapers for cleaning animal hides.

4. *Upper Palaeolithic tools.* Named after the Palaeolithic period that lasted from 45,000 to 10,000 years ago, are associated with *Homo sapiens*. These sophisticated tools include knives, arrow heads, sewing needles, harpoons and fishhooks.

5. *Mesolithic tools.* Named after the Mesolithic period that lasted from 8,500 to 5,000 years ago, are associated with hunters using microliths (from the Greek *micros*-small, and *lithos*-stone). These tools were made by striking small blades of a wedge-shaped core. By their small size, microliths were designed to be mounted on spears and arrows or they were set in rows to make a continuous cutting edge, each element being replaced as it wore out.

> **Palaeolithic**
>
> a period distinguished by the development of first stone tools. It extends from 2.5 mya to the introduction of agriculture around 10,000 years ago.

Homo sapiens share tool-making with some other animals such as chimpanzees and ravens that routinely make simple tools. Chimpanzees, for example, use stems of plants as probes to insert into a nest of ants who stream up the tool. Or they use stones as hammer and anvil for cracking nuts. The cognitive capacity of animals to manufacture and use tools will be discussed in section 8.3 (Cognitive capacities in apes and corvids). What distinguishes us from other tool-making animals is that we use a wide range of tools and have a capacity to invent new tools consciously and persistently. As we push the frontiers of technology, creating intelligent machines, implants and artificially modified genes, we build on a process that began in the Pliocene when *H. habilis* managed to make the first stone tools. The use of tools set up a positive feedback loop – the first of many that we may find in the history of technology. The better the tools that were used, the more dependent we became on them, and thus the more tools became a criterion for survival (Lipsey et al. 2005).

Symbolism

Bipedalism made our hands free for jobs like advanced tool-making, building shelters and mining minerals. As a result of our technological inventiveness, we differ from our primate relatives in the extent to which we modify the physical world. Beyond that, we also create imaginary worlds through the words of language, works of art and scientific theories. To understand imaginary worlds we need to focus on **symbolism** (or, symbolisation) which many people consider to be the key to what made us different from other primates (Stringer 2011). Symbolisation refers to the capacity to represent objects, people, events or concepts by arbitrary but meaningful symbols and use them in cultural practices. As an example, for our ancestors incised bones could represent traded objects or phases of the moon. For us banknotes with

> **symbolism**
>
> the capacity to represent objects, people, events or concepts by arbitrary but meaningful symbols and use them in cultural practices.

printed numbers on them represent money referring to gold bars in the Central Bank. Money has no value in itself, but by virtue of a socially accepted fiction, it has become as real as the tangible commodities it can buy.

Symbols like incisions in animal bones and numbers on banknotes may be regarded as social inventions. The making and using of symbols that stand for something else is essentially a matter of social agreement. They only work if people trust one another and attach the same meaning to them. In this way symbols enable us to reach other people across time and place. While apes can only interact face-to-face, the rise of symbolism liberated humans from here-and-now encounters. We have learned to communicate with people who are not physically present using interfaces like incised bones, rock paintings, books and cell-phones. The importance of this liberation has been aptly described as a 'release from proximity' (Rodseth et al. 1991; Gamble 1998). Today, we could hardly function without all the symbols that are part of daily life. Symbolic representation – the cognitive capacity to communicate by using symbols that stand for other things – is therefore an important characteristic that makes us human.

When did symbolism emerge? There is growing evidence that 'anatomically modern humans' originated in Africa between 200,000 and 150,000 years ago. But there is no agreement over exactly when and how people became 'behaviourally modern humans' as indicated by the use of symbols. In the 1980s, anthropologists launched the concept of a 'human revolution', suggesting that modern behaviour emerged abruptly between 60,000 and 40,000 years ago (Mellars and Stringer 1989). This revolution was associated with a set of human behaviours such as complex language, art and specialised technologies, enabling *Homo sapiens* to replace the behaviourally inferior *Homo neanderthalensis*. Evidence for behavioural modernity was found in the form of cave paintings, personal decorations, burials of human dead suggesting belief in supernatural beings, specialised tools such as needles and fishhooks, ropes for making snares and nets permitting people to capture birds and fish, sewn clothing, elaborate housing, and boats or watercraft (e.g. Diamond 1994).

The gap between anatomy and symbolism

For many researchers, this amazing evidence supported the idea that behavioural modernity had suddenly appeared between 40,000 and 60,000 years ago (Pfeiffer 1982; Diamond 1994; Mithen 1998; Klein 2009). This raised, however, the question why there was such a large gap between the rise of anatomically modern humans between 200,000 and 150,000 years ago and the advent of behaviourally modern humans. Archaeologist Richard Klein (2009) proposed that the abrupt change in human behaviour resulted from a genetic mutation in early modern Africans, improving brain functions that produced changes in cognition. These changes, in turn, provided new opportunities for behavioural changes and innovations like art and language which we recognise today as modern behaviour.

Opponents to the idea that behavioural modernity was an abrupt change, argued that the change was rather a slow and gradual process (McBrearty and Brooks 2000; McBrearty 2007; Hapgood and Franklin 2008). New behaviours and technical inventions appeared little by little over a long period of time and have been found at sites that are widely separated in space and time. Why did we need these innovations? One hypothesis is that humans are a 'restless species' that left the African continent and populated the whole world while other primates are confined to the tropics and subtropics. In their long journey through the other continents humans evolved to cope with a wide range of habitats, from arctic to tropic, as they presently tolerate.

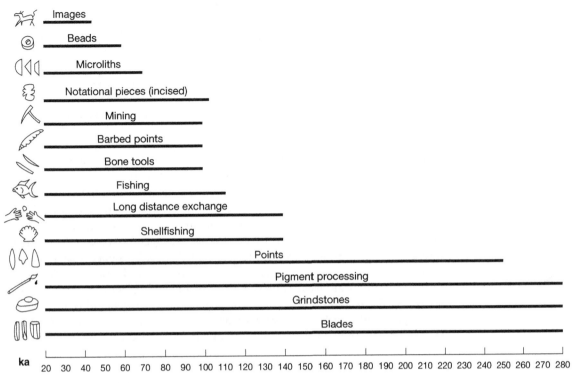

Behavioural Innovations of the Middle Stone Age in Africa

Figure 3.12 Behavioural innovations in the Middle Stone Age in Africa
Source: McBrearty and Brooks (2000)

Exploiting arctic regions, for example, requires behavioural flexibility as they are relatively unproductive habitats with short growing seasons and few plant and animal species (Elton 2008). Nomadic life was a behavioural response to extreme environments. Equally important was a sophisticated material culture which included the manufacture of shelters, harpoons for hunting marine animals, and the control of fire. Thus, living above the Arctic Circle required that people were able to learn from one another and create innovations which added to the existing pool of cultural items (e.g. tools, beliefs, knowledge). Figure 3.12 is a display of behavioural innovations which are part of a gradual and cumulative change over the past 300,000 years, making the concept of a sudden appearance unlikely.

At present, the literature converges on a number of common ingredients thought to characterise modern human behaviour. These ingredients include increasing diversity and standardisation of man-made objects (tools, clothing), personal ornaments (tattoos, beads), art objects (carved Venus figurines), art images (rock paintings), structured living spaces, rituals (burials with grave goods and red ochre, a pigment that was also used to decorate bodies), economic intensification (exploitation of food resources requiring specialised technology), enlarged geographic range, and expanded exchange networks.

A common proxy for the process of attaining behavioural modernity is the occurrence of personal ornaments which many authors consider as tangible manifestations of symbolic, or symbol-mediated behaviour. Accordingly, it is important to establish when and where these symbolic objects first appeared in the archaeological record. Until recently, the first perforated shell beads were found in Blombos Cave, South Africa, with a record of about 70,000 years ago (d'Errico et al. 2005). Recent finds in Morocco pushed the emergence of intentionally perforated shell beads to 82,000 years ago. Wear patterns on the shells imply that some of them were suspended, as in Blombos, and were covered in red ochre (Bouzouggar et al. 2007). Other finds in Israel and Algeria have pushed the emergence even further back to 100,000–135,000 years ago (Vanhaeren et al. 2006). Thus, archaeological evidence narrows the gap between the origin of our modern anatomy and behaviour.

How did symbolism emerge?

The previous section suggested that symbolism is a typical manifestation of modern human behaviour that emerged gradually since 135,000 years ago. How did the making and using of symbols emerge? Symbols are arbitrary and meaningful things that stand for objects, events or concepts. It is the arbitrary nature of symbols that makes them not easy to acquire by non-human animals. Consider the following example. If a monkey produces a 'leopard call', her fellow monkeys run away on hearing that call. In contrast, when humans hear the word 'leopard' they know that this does not necessarily refer to danger, unless we are on the savanna. So, we use words to communicate what is present ('this is a leopard') but also what is absent ('let us visit the zoo to see a leopard') or even abstract ('the leopard is a predator'). The 'leopard call' is a fixed signal whereas the word 'leopard' is an arbitrary symbol because the animal's name could be otherwise (Striedter 2005). This flexible relationship between a symbol and the object it represents, will be discussed in section 9.2 (The origin of flexible communication).

Matt Rossano (2010) proposed that in explaining the emergence of symbolism, we should adopt an important distinction, introduced by the American philosopher Charles Peirce (1931). In his text about signs and symbols Peirce defined three levels of reference: iconic, indexical and symbolic. Iconic signs are ones that bear a perceptual or physical resemblance to their referents such as the photograph of a person or the stylised figure of a female on the ladies' room door. Indexical signs are defined by having a temporal or spatial association with their referents. The footprints that we find in the wild, point to the animal that produced it. Thus a part of the animal may represent the whole animal. Both iconic and indexical signs look like symbols because they stand for something else. But Peirce reserves the term 'symbol' for those cases where the relationship between the signifier and the signified is purely arbitrary. For instance, the dollar sign on a banknote is symbolic because its relation to money is not based on resemblance or association but on social agreement.

From iconic to indexical to symbolic representations

Peirce suggests that the first signs were iconic and then progressed to indexical and symbolic representations. This progression implied that a higher level of reference was built on a lower one. Given the hierarchical nature of referential thinking, Rossano (2010) expects evidence of iconic artefacts in the fossil record, followed by indexical and symbolic artefacts. Iconic artefacts have indeed been found in the form of red ochre which date back to 300,000 years ago (Barham 2002; Hovers et al. 2003). Use of pigments was a consistent feature in the African Pleistocene and part of the behavioural repertoire of *Homo heidelbergensis* and *Homo sapiens* (McBrearty and Brooks 2000). Red ochre could be used for practical reasons (hide preparation, treatment of wounds) but also for symbolic reasons (body painting, ritual burials, decoration of beads). Using pigments for decoration and intimidation is not uncommon in contemporary traditional societies. Some authors have proposed that red ochre would refer to menstrual blood and the fertility that is associated with it (Knight et al. 1995; Watts 1999). As red ochre resembled blood, it may be regarded as an iconic sign.

Beads in the fossil record may serve as evidence of indexical artefacts. In traditional as well as modern societies people often use ornaments as social signals about group identity, wealth or status. Fashions in clothing, hairstyles, tattoos, cosmetics and necklaces are used to communicate signals to other individuals. In the previous section we saw that finds of intentionally perforated and decorated shell beads date back to 100,000–135,000 years ago (Vanhaeren et al. 2006). In contemporary hunter-gatherers beads are commonly used as gifts to reinforce reciprocal relations between groups. What makes shell beads particularly valuable is what they represent when they are worn as necklaces or bracelets. Wearing beads was an important change in the social marking of one's identity, status or wealth. Body painting can communicate social signals, but its use is limited because pigments are less durable and transferable than beads. Shell beads can overcome these limitations and are therefore more effective means of communicating social information. An abundance of beads may demonstrate that one has a network of generous friends, a signal that would be difficult to transmit with pigments.

The capacity to create arbitrary and meaningful relationships between signs and their referents is considered the hallmark of *Homo sapiens*. Unlike pigments and shell beads, oral language did not leave traces in the archaeological record. What we do know from studies of apes learning language is that the step from indexical to symbolic communication is not easy (Deacon 1997). In ape language research visual signs are used instead of acoustic ones because ape vocal cords cannot close fully. Apes have limited control of the tongue and lower jaw, but they have the manual dexterity required for working with a computer keyboard.

Since symbolic communication is considered cognitively demanding, attempts have been made to analyse the capacities required for using symbols. For example, the laboratory-reared bonobo Kanzi learned linguistic skills with the help of a computer keyboard but remained at the level of a two-and-a-half-year old child because his working memory capacity appeared to be a major limiting factor (Savage-Rumbaugh et al. 1998). In humans, word learning may start with indexical signs based on word–object associations but language actually takes off with the capacity to make associations between symbols as it happens in constructing sentences. Enhanced working memory capacity for making many arbitrary symbol–object and symbol–symbol associations must, therefore, have been critical in the transition from indexical representations (beads) to symbolic representations (words) (Coolidge and Wynn 2005).

What were the driving forces behind symbolic representation? And what were the consequences for our cognitive functioning? Rossano (2010) proposed that the forces were particularly social in nature. Fossil evidence indicates that early members of *Homo sapiens* led a complex social life. Groups and campsites became larger, longevity increased resulting in groups with more older than younger adults, interactions between groups became more frequent, and exchange networks of raw materials (pigments, stones, shell beads) expanded. Thus, more social complexity would not only require enhanced working memory but also more empathising and theorising about the mental states of other individuals.

A recent study provided evidence that social interactions have causal effects on boosting cognitive performance (Ybarra et al. 2008). This finding is consistent with other studies, suggesting that social interaction demands a requisite level of cognitive functioning (e.g. Dunbar 2007). In section 9.5 (The cognitive origin of language) we will return to this subject.

3.6 Summary

- There is a long misguided tradition in Western thought – known as 'anthropocentrism' – regarding the universe as ordered in a hierarchy with 'lower organisms' at the bottom and humans at the top. To make clear what our place is among other species, we can use different approaches.

- First, to make sense of the huge gap between the old age of planet Earth (4.6 billion years) and the young age of modern humans (between 200,000 and 150,000 years) we can use the geological timescale. This tool, developed by geologists and palaeontologists, is divided into intervals marking important changes in the fossil record. One of these intervals is the Cenozoic, the era in which humans and other primates made their appearance on the planet.

- Second, biologists have replaced the ladder of life by a tree of life which considers evolution as a branching process. Thus, the origination, lifespan and extinction of species can be mapped on a branching tree. The tree of life shows, for example, that fungi, plants and animals share a common ancestor at about 800–1000 mya.

- Third, to put humans in the right place, organisms can be classified into groups on the basis of sharing characteristics due to common ancestry. While shared ancestral characters like hair and milk glands make clear that we are mammals, shared derived characters like forward-projecting eyes and grasping hands identify us as primates.

- Fourth, we can search for characteristics that make us human, that is, different from our primate relatives. These characteristics include bipedalism, advanced tool-making and symbolism. Language, the symbolic speciality of humans, will be discussed extensively in Chapter 9 (The origins of language).

Study questions

1. What is the origin and history of anthropocentrism?

2. How did Darwin hit upon the metaphor of a 'tree of life'?

3. How are characters used in constructing a phylogeny?

4. Why are forward-projecting eyes a defining characteristic of primates?

5. How are iconic, indexical and symbolic representations thought to build on one another?

Suggested reading

The geological timescale

Klein, R. (2009). *The Human Career: Human Biological and Cultural Origins*. Chicago: The University of Chicago Press.

Klein, J. and Takahata, N. (2002). *Where Do We Come From? The Molecular Evidence for Human Descent*. Berlin: Springer-Verlag.

Prothero, D. (2007). *Evolution: What the Fossils Say and Why It Matters*. New York: Columbia University Press.

From the ladder of life to the tree of life

Eldredge, N. (2005). *Darwin: Discovering the Tree of Life*. New York: W.W. Norton & Company.

Nee, S. (2005). The great chain of being. *Nature, 435*, 429.

Pagel, M. (2009). Natural selection 150 years on, *Nature, 457*, 808–811.

We are primates

Fleagle, J. (1999). *Primate Adaptation and Evolution*. San Diego: Academic Press.

Klein, R. (2009). *The Human Career: Human Biological and Cultural Origins*. Chicago: The University of Chicago Press.

Klein, J. and Takahata. N. (2002). *Where Do We Come From? The Molecular Evidence for Human Descent*. Berlin: Springer-Verlag.

Martin, R. (1990). *Primate Origins and Evolution: A Phylogenetic Reconstruction*. Princeton, NJ: Princeton University Press.

Perelman, P., Johnson, W., Roos, L. et al. (2011). A molecular phylogeny of living primates. *PLoS Genetics, 7*, 1–17.

Wood, B. and Harrison, T. (2011). The evolutionary context of the first hominins. *Nature, 470*, 347–352.

What makes us human?

Bouzouggar, A., Barton, N., Vanhaeren, M. et al. (2007). 82,000-year-old shell beads from North Africa and implications for the origins of modern human behavior. *Proceedings of the National Academy of the United States of America, 104*, 9964–9969.

Bradley, B. (2008). Reconstructing phylogenies and phenotypes: a molecular view of human evolution. *Journal of Anatomy, 212*, 337–353.

Carroll, S. (2003). Genetics and the making of *Human sapiens. Nature, 422*, 849–857.

Coolidge, F. and Wynn, T. (2005). Working memory, its executive functions, and the emergence of modern thinking. *Cambridge Archeological Journal, 15*, 5–26.

D 'Errico, F., Henshilwood, C., Vanhaeren, M. and Van Niekerk, K. (2005). *Nassarius kraussianus* shell beads from Blombos Cave: evidence for symbolic behavior in the Middle Stone Age. *Journal of Human Evolution, 48*, 3–24.

Hapgood, P. and Franklin, N. (2008). The revolution that didn't arrive: A review of Pleistocene Sahul. *Journal of Human Evolution, 55*, 187–222.

Henshilwood, C., d'Errico, F., Van Niekerk, K. et al. (2011). A 100,000-year-old ochre-processing workshop at Blombos cave, South Africa. *Science, 334*, 219–222.

McBrearty, S. and Brooks, A. (2000). The revolution that wasn't: a new interpretation of the origin of modern human behavior. *Journal of Human Evolution, 39*, 453–563.

Richmond, B. and Jungers, W. (2008). *Orrorin Tugenensis* femoral morphology and the evolution of hominin bipedalism. *Science*, *319*, 1662–1665.

Rossano, M. (2010). Making friends, making tools, and making symbols. *Current Anthropology*, *51*, S89–S98.

Reference books

Christian, D. (2004). *Maps of Time: An Introduction to Big History*. Berkeley: University of California Press.

Fagan, B. (1999). *World Prehistory: A Brief Introduction*. New York: Longman.

Henshilwood, C. and D'Errico, F. (Eds) (2011). *Homo Symbolicus: The Dawn of Language, Imagination and Spirituality*. Amsterdam: John Benjamins Publishing Company.

Lecointre, G. and Le Guyader, H. (2006). *The Tree of Life: A Phylogenetic Classification*. Cambridge, MA: The Belknap Press of Harvard University Press.

Roberts, A. (2011). *Evolution: The Human History*. London: Dorling Kindersley.

Thain, M. (2009). *Penguin Dictionary of Human Biology*. London: Penguin Books.

Tudge, C. (2000). *The Variety of Life: A Survey and a Celebration of all the Creatures that Have Ever Lived*. Oxford: Oxford University Press.

White, R. (2003). *Prehistoric Art: The symbolic journey of mankind*. New York: Harry N. Abrams.

Part 2   PROBLEMS

4 Males and females

This chapter will cover:

4.1 Introduction

4.2 The origin of sexual reproduction

4.3 The theory of sexual selection

4.4 Mating systems in human evolution

4.5 Mate preferences of men and women

4.6 Summary

Learning outcomes

By the end of this chapter, you should be able to explain:

- why sexual reproduction originated
- how sexual selection works
- how mating systems influence sexual selection
- why monogamy in humans emerged
- why female attractiveness in humans is an evolutionary anomaly
- what mating men and women prefer in one another.

4.1   Introduction

We may take for granted that males and females need one another for sexual reproduction. But evolutionary biologists consider sex an enigma because it is a costly endeavour. In order to reproduce an individual has to find a potential partner, attract it, and risk contracting sexually transmitted diseases. So why did sexual reproduction originate?

Males and females differ in body size, body form, beauty and voice pitch. Darwin was puzzled by birds such as peacocks in which the males are more beautiful than the females. Why did exuberant coloration and extravagant plumage originate? He also noted that in humans it is the female sex that uses ornamentation. Why this reversal?

In many human cultures, men are allowed to have several women, but for the vast majority of people monogamous relationships are the norm. Did our human ancestors have a harem system like gorillas or did we live like chimpanzees having sex with multiple partners? Why did men and women come to live in pairs?

An important issue for men and women is to assess one another's mate value when deciding to produce offspring. Mate value may be affected by multiple variables like health, age and command of resources. What are the mate preferences of men and women?

4.2   The origin of sexual reproduction

The paradox of sex

Reproduction, being the production of new individuals, can occur in two forms. Unicellular organisms such as bacteria reproduce asexually by dividing themselves into two daughter cells. But in multi-cellular organisms like plants or animals, reproduction is sexual, meaning that two different individuals create a new individual by fusing their genomes. Evolutionary scientists consider sexual reproduction as more costly and complicated than asexual reproduction. It is more costly because each sex contributes only half of its genetic material to the new individual. While the asexual parent transmits all of its genes to future generations, sexual organisms need to produce twice as many per individual, otherwise they suffer from a transmission disadvantage. This problem is so acute that it is labelled *the* cost of sex (Bell 1982).

Sexual reproduction is more complicated because an asexual organism can reproduce by itself while a sexual organism has to find a partner to mate. This can be a big problem, for example for flowering plants, because they are attached to a fixed place and therefore dependent on insects for pollination, being the transfer of pollen from the male to the female reproductive organ. Or consider humans who may need intermediaries like parents, friends, personal ads, or dating agencies to find a fitting partner. Despite its disadvantages, sexual reproduction is very common among large multi-cellular organisms. That is why evolutionary scientists are intrigued by this manner of reproduction. Moreover, if evolutionary theory is unable to explain a common thing like sexual reproduction, it is based on a weak foundation.

Given the costs of sex and the widespread potential for asexual reproduction, why do so many species reproduce sexually? This question has been called the paradox of sex (Otto 2009). Many biologists would answer that sex and recombination have evolved because they generate variation which is needed for natural selection to work upon. But sex and recombination do not always produce more variable offspring. And even when sex acts to increase variation, this variation need not improve fitness. Given these problems, Sarah Otto (2009) argues that recent models have identified some conditions under which sexual recombination could evolve.

Selection varies over time. When the environment changes rapidly over time, genetic associations built up by past selection can become disadvantageous. In this case, sexual recombination can break apart these associations, improving the fitness of offspring. A highly likely mechanism promoting rapid changes in the fitness of gene associations is interactions between hosts and parasites (Hamilton 1990; Bell 1982; Wilkinson 2000; Leung et al. 2012). This mechanism was named the 'Red Queen hypothesis' after Lewis Carroll's character from *Through the Looking Glass* (Carroll 1960) who had the opinion that one must run as fast as one can in order to stay in the same place.

When applied to sexual reproduction, this statement implies that species must evolve as fast as they can to remain in place with respect to other species. That is, if individuals are exposed to parasites carried by their parents, sexual reproduction can promptly evolve because families infected with parasites benefit from producing genetically diverse offspring who may resist diseases. As an example, in *The Red Queen: Sex and the Evolution of Human Nature*, Matt Ridley (1994) examines the reasons why sexual reproduction is the rule rather than the exception. He concludes that sex evolved as a line of defence against invaders of the body. With the re-arrangement of the genome from generation to generation, organisms attempt to remain one step ahead of their adversaries in what looks like an 'evolutionary arms race'.

Selection also varies among individuals. Most models of sexual evolution are based on the assumption that individuals are equally likely to engage in sexual reproduction, aside from their condition in the current environment. However, asexually reproducing organisms such as yeast, aphids, water fleas and dandelions are most likely to engage in sex when they face poor conditions. This is the case when an organism's genotype does not match the requirements of its current environment. So the answer to why so many species reproduce sexually, is that it may have reintroduced variation. But sex may also have evolved to eliminate genetic associations that arose at other times or locations and that are not favourable in the current environment.

Anisogamy

isogamy
fusion of gametes that do not differ in size and/or motility.

anisogamy
fusion of gametes that differ in size and/or motility.

The evolution of sexual reproduction started when two **gametes** of equal size evolved into reproductive cells of unequal size. The original mating type, called **isogamy**, or fusion of gametes that do not differ in size and/or motility, is nowadays common among unicellular organisms such as algae and fungi. The latter mating type, called **anisogamy**, is virtually universal. Any species that has males and females has anisogamy by definition because females are defined as the sex with the larger gametes.

Anisogamy is a remarkable event in evolution because it is the different size of reproductive cells which made us male or female. Models that study what might have selected for anisogamy imply that individuals either produced a few large gametes or many small ones (Bulmer and Parker 2002; Stearns and Hoekstra 2005). Gametes that were larger than average, are supposed to have the advantage of more nutrients, surviving longer and producing more viable offspring. Gametes that were smaller than average, are supposed to have low survival prospects, and having by their greater number an increased probability of fertilisation. Once this process of specialisation had been established, it was difficult to reverse. Since then, males make many, small gametes while females make few, large gametes. Due to this difference in the production of gametes, males need to compete for fertilising females.

gamete

Reproductive cell. In anisogamous organisms an egg or sperm cell. Gametes produced by different sexes fuse to form Zygotes.

4.3 The theory of sexual selection

Differences between males and females

Males and females have different characteristics which are directly involved in reproduction (penis and testes in males, vagina and ovaries in females). Other characteristics (e.g. body size, body hair, body shape, face) also differ between the sexes but tend to be differences of degree rather than of kind. Consider body size. Males are bigger than females in most primates, and the same is true for mammals and birds in general. However, among other animals like crustaceans (i.e. crabs, lobsters, shrimps), orb-weaving spiders, deep-sea fishes and birds of prey, females tend to be larger. In some insect species, females are even five times larger than males (Held 2009).

Why this disparity in body size? This question is mostly answered by referring to the fighting ability of males. They are supposed to compete for a female so that having a large body is advantageous in combat. When females have a larger body size, this would be an advantage for their fecundity. However, selection actually favours smaller females, because larger females have a slower reproductive rate. This question about sexual differences in body size is still unanswered. Nowadays the general idea is that the difference in body size of males and females is a balanced equilibrium between three major forces: selection favouring large male size as an advantage against rivals; selection favouring large female size as an advantage for fecundity; and selection for smaller size as an advantage for overall viability (Fairbairn et al. 2007).

sexual dimorphism

males and females have different phenotypes.

sexual selection

the component or subset of natural selection that is associated with mating success.

Differences between males and females – in body size, body form, beauty, voice, and so on – are a matter of **sexual dimorphism**. Why did sexual dimorphism arise? In his book *Descent of Man and Selection in Relation to Sex* (1871), Darwin proposed that differences between males and females could originate through what he called 'sexual selection'. He was puzzled by a range of male traits such as exuberant coloration, extravagant feathers and elaborate vocalisations in birds which seemed to reduce their chances of survival. Paradise birds, peacocks and song birds may impress the females with their ornaments, but they are at the same time an easy target for predators.

The solution to this puzzle was Darwin's theory of sexual selection that male ornaments might have evolved because females prefer to mate with the best-ornamented males. While natural selection produces adaptive traits that enable organisms to survive and achieve reproductive success, sexual selection produces ornaments like elaborate plumage or vocalisation to acquire mates and armaments such

BOX 4.1 The classic but unfortunate case of the peacock

The peacock is the classic, textbook example of an extravagant male characteristic that is thought to be sexually selected. Darwin (1871) suggested that the evolution of such elaborate plumage in polygynous avian species was a result of female choice. Later empirical studies of mating success supported this suggestion. Peacocks defend small display sites and aggregate to form 'leks', that is, communal mating areas within which males hold small territories, used solely for courtship and copulation. Females are attracted to a lek by the displays of the males and then choose mating partners from among them (Immelman and Beer 1992). Observations of one lek showed that over 50 per cent of the variance in mating success could be attributed to variance in train morphology (Petrie et al. 1991). There was a significant positive correlation between the number of eye-spots a male had in his train and the number of females he mated with. These data supported Darwin's hypothesis that the peacock's train has evolved, at least in part, as a result of a female preference.

However, recent studies in a feral population of Indian peafowl in Japan over a 7-year period did not provide evidence that peahens express any preference for peacocks with more elaborate trains, that is, trains having more ocelli, or eye-spots, a more symmetric arrangement or a greater length (Takahashi et al. 2008). Findings indicate that: (1) the peacock's train is not a universal target of female choice, (2) shows small variance among males across populations, (3) does not appear to reliably reflect the male condition, and (4) is perhaps an obsolete signal for which female preference has already been lost or weakened. Other studies (Dakin and Montgomerie 2011), using observation and experiment, found like Takahashi et al. (2008), no effect of natural variation in train morphology, including displayed eye-spot number and train length, on male mating success. Thus, female mating preferences in feral peafowl populations are more complex than previously thought: females may use some other cue to choose among males.

---

lek

communal mating areas for birds such as peacocks, bowerbirds and wild turkeys within which males hold small territories, used solely for courtship and copulation. Females are attracted to a lek by the displays of the males and then choose mating partners from among them.

intrasexual selection

a form of sexual selection driven by competition within the same sex for suitable mating partners.

intersexual selection

a form of sexual selection driven by female choice of suitable mating partners.

as horns or antlers to deter competitors. Thus the basic idea of sexual selection is that reproductive success can be improved by competing for mates. Males who are larger or more showy than their rivals have better chances of acquiring females. It should be emphasised that sexual selection is generally viewed as a subset of natural selection these days rather than a distinct type of selection.

According to Darwin, sexual selection covered any characteristic that affected reproductive advantage over members of the same sex. Unfortunately, recent empirical studies in feral populations of peafowl do not support Darwin's hypothesis (Box 4.1 The classic but unfortunate case of the peacock).

Intrasexual and intersexual selection

Darwin related sexual selection primarily to males who take the initiative when looking for a mate. He suggested that competition between males is the rule and that females are the choosing sex. That is why he identified two forms of sexual selection: (1) **intrasexual selection**, meaning that males usually compete with one another for a mate, and (2) **intersexual selection**, implying that females choose a member of the opposite sex. Thus, the sex with the greater reproductive potential (mostly the male sex) is considered as the competing sex, and the sex with the lesser reproductive potential (mostly the female sex) as the choosing sex.

It is possible, however, that females compete for a male and that males choose a female. The exception to the rule is known as sex-role reversal: a form of animal behaviour in which each sex behaves in a manner typical of the other sex. For example, in some insect and fish species, males take full responsibility for care of the offspring, and in some polyandrous birds females are aggressive and defend territories (Stearns and Hoekstra 2005). **Polyandry** is a mating system where a female mates with more than one male to produce a brood of young bearing genes from each male.

polyandry
one-female, multi-male mating system in which multiple males mate with a single female.

Although Darwin had gathered much evidence of female mate choice in animal species such as insects, birds and spiders, he was unsure why exactly females choose and why males usually don't. He provided no satisfactory solution to the question why the females generally are the choosiest, and why there is choosiness at all (Cronin 1991). Almost a century passed before Darwin's ideas about sexual selection gained ground. One reason for this delay was that critics accepted male–male competition but rejected female choice. They could understand why animals compete by claws, antlers and horns, but not by feathers, colours or melodies.

Another reason was Darwin's argument that males take the initiative while females choose: in nineteenth-century, Victorian England the idea of female choice conflicted with the established conviction that women are passive. The sexual prudery and male bias among most biologists other than Darwin, would have marginalised sexual selection theory (Miller 2002). The sexual revolution of the 1960s and the rise of feminism contributed to a new appreciation of female choice in human social, sexual and political life.

Forms of mating competition

Sexual selection is about competition for mates. Competition occurs when an individual makes a resource, in this case a mate, less available to others. When a female accepts to mate with a male and fertilise her eggs, she becomes unavailable for others, at least temporarily. Competition for mates can take various forms and may favour characteristics to be selected in the competing sex (Andersson 1994). The forms of competition over mates as well as the traits that may be selected in the competing sex, are listed in Table 4.1.

Scramble competition to be first to find a mate may favour large eyes in the competing sex. Male anglerfishes, for example, have huge eyes to find a mate and a small, streamlined body which is adapted for efficient searching (Andersson 1994). Scramble competition is important for many animals where females are receptive for brief periods (e.g. frogs, toads). Another form of competition is the endurance to stay for longer at the breeding site and mate with females that otherwise would mate with other males. Endurance competition may favour the ability to be reproductive during a major part of the season. For example, elephant seals weigh more than three times as much as females. The reasons for this should be found in the mating system and the form of sexual competition. Female elephant seals gather on the beach during the three-month reproductive season to produce offspring. They form dense clusters on the beach which can only be defended by a dominant male. In this one-male, many-female mating system, only large males achieve high mating success by male–male contests and endurance rivalry.

A further form of mating competition is contest competition where rivals display to or fight each other over mates. Fights over mates select for strength which is often achieved by large body size, and for weapons such as antlers and horns. Sperm competition as a form of mating competition, occurs in species where fertile females are subject to multiple matings with different males. The sperm of each male 'competes' with that of the others in fertilising the eggs. Competing by means of sperm favours mate

Table 4.1 Forms of competition over mates, and traits likely to be selected in the competing sex

Mechanism	Characteristics favoured in the competing sex
I. Scrambles	Early search and swift location of mates; well-developed sensory and locomotory organs
II. Endurance rivalry	Ability to remain reproductively active during a large part of the season
III. Contests	1. Traits that improve success in fights, such as large size, strength, weaponry, agility, or threat signals
	2. Alternative mating tactics of inferior competitors, avoiding contests with superior rivals
IV. Mate choice	1. Behavioural and morphological traits that attract and stimulate mates
	2. Offering of nutrition, territories, nest sites, or other resources needed by the mate for breeding
	3. Alternative mating tactics, such as forced copulation
V. Sperm competition	1. Mate guarding, sequestering, frequent copulation, production of mating plugs, or other means of preventing rivals from copulating with the mate
	2. Ability of displacing rival sperm; production of abundant sperm to outcompete those of rivals

Source: Andersson (1994)

guarding, frequent copulation, production of mating plugs which prevent rivals from copulating with the mate (e.g. moths and butterflies), the ability to remove rival sperm (e.g. rodents), or the production of abundant sperm to outcompete those of rivals.

Males compete also when females choose their mate, even if rivals never meet. Mate choice as a form of competition favours characteristics that attract and stimulate mates. Males can be chosen because they provide immediate benefits, such as a superior foraging area to feed the offspring. Or because the mate has a large body which offers a better protection against predators. Another reason for mate choice may be good genes. Females should then prefer partners who display signals that suggest genes for better survival and reproduction. Male ornaments like the peacock's tail or the red belly of the male stickleback, may advertise their superior fitness and resistance to disease. Female preferences for males with better resistance have been demonstrated in guppies, sticklebacks and pheasants (Stearns and Hoekstra 2005).

What problem did sexual selection solve in evolution?

Males have many, small sex cells while females have few, large ones. For males it is not very costly to produce more extra sperm and thus generate many offspring. Males have the potential to increase their reproductive success by mating with many females. On the other hand, for females it is not feasible to produce more eggs because they can only make a limited number in their lifetime. Thus females have no need to mate with many males to fertilise their limited number of eggs. This difference between the sexes is known as Bateman's principle: males increase their reproductive success more with each additional partner than females.

Angus Bateman (1948) studied fruit flies under laboratory conditions which revealed three important sexual differences. First, male reproductive success varies much more widely than female reproductive success. Many more males failed to produce surviving offspring than females. Second, female reproductive success did not appear to be limited by ability to attract males. Few females failed to copulate but were courted as vigorously as those who did copulate. Males were severely limited by the ability to attract or arouse females. They were certainly interested but not accepted by the females. Third, a female's reproductive success hardly increased after the first copulation. Most females were not interested in more copulations.

Bateman argued that these results could be explained by referring to the energy investment of each sex in their sex cells. Since male fruit flies invest very little metabolic energy in the production of a given sex cell, and females invest considerably, a male's reproductive success is not limited by his ability to produce sex cells but by his ability to fertilise eggs. A female's reproductive success is not limited by her ability to let her eggs be fertilised but by her ability to produce eggs. We can now answer our question: sexual selection solved the problem of the limiting female resource. As a rule, this limiting resource is the driving force behind male–male competition and female choice.

The theory of parental investment

Bateman, on the basis of his experiments with fruit flies, stated that male reproductive success depends on the number of females a male can mate with, while female reproductive success depends on the number of offspring she can produce. He attributed the greater intensity of reproductive competition among males to the smaller size of male gametes and by implication to the faster rate of gamete production by males. When neither sex cares for eggs or young, as in fruit flies, differences in gamete size may explain sex differences in reproductive rate or in competition for members of the opposite sex.

However, involvement of one or two sexes in parental care, will change the differences (Clutton-Brock 1991). The essential role of a male may end with copulation, but the situation is very different for the female who has the prolonged burden of caring for the young. That is the reason why Robert Trivers (1972) began thinking about the evolutionary consequences of parental care. He considered the contribution of parents to the fitness of their offspring in terms of **parental investment**, defined as any investment by the parent in an individual offspring that increases the offspring's chance of surviving (and hence reproductive success) at the cost of the parent's ability to invest in other offspring.

parental investment

any investment by a parent in an individual offspring that increases the offspring's chance to survive but imposes a cost in terms of the parent's ability to invest in other offspring.

KEY FIGURE   Robert Trivers

Robert Trivers is a biologist, working at Rutgers University. He is best known for papers he published about altruism, parental investment and parent-offspring conflict.

Selected works

Social Evolution (1985)

Natural Selection and Social Theory (2002)

Genes in Conflict: The Biology of Selfish Genetic Elements (2008), with Austin Burt

Deceit and Self-Deception: Fooling Yourself the Better to Fool Others (2011)

Photo source: Robert Trivers

Trivers argued that it is the relative parental investment of the sexes in their offspring that controls the operation of sexual selection. The sex which invests the most will be selective about whom they accept as a mate, and the sex which invests the least will compete among themselves for a mate. The greater parental investment by females represents the limiting resource with the result that the competition for mates of the limiting sex increases. But animals live in different circumstances: in some species both parents provide parental care (e.g. swans, modern humans), while in other species only females care for their offspring (e.g. elephant seals, gorillas). How much would the strength of sexual selection differ in these situations? How can the difference be explained?

The different strength of sexual selection

The ability of males to control the access of rivals to potential mates is an important factor that accounts for the different strength of sexual selection (Emlen and Oring 1977). This control can be direct by the physical herding of potential mates. In many ungulates, such as antilopes and gazelles, females and young aggregate into small herds which enables a better detection and avoidance of predators. The reasons for herding are unrelated to reproduction, but one result is that it increases the male potential for control of multiple mates. Control can also be indirect by managing the resources that are needed for successful reproduction. For example, humming birds depend on nectar feeding. When nectar production by flowers is high, territorial defence becomes feasible. Females rear the young alone but need a reliable source of nectar. That is why males allow females to nest within their territory, but aggressively exclude all rivals.

Control is largest when a polygynous male monopolises multiple females, as in elephant seals. His monopoly implies that he will prevent other males from reproduction. In this one-male, multi-female mating system, the male defends the herd and mates with females who care for the offspring. In this kind of mating system, sexual selection is strongest because the more females a male can control, the more intense the fights with rivals, and the greater the differences in the body sizes of the sexes. The strength of sexual selection is weakest in the monogamous mating system. In this system, each sex has one mate for life. Small or absent differences in body sizes of the sexes indicate the lesser strength of sexual selection. In monogamous species, such as albatrosses, swans, gibbons or modern humans, the males are not excluded from reproduction as in one-male, multi-female mating systems.

To summarise, females differ from males, first, because they have few, large gametes and, second, because they invest heavily in offspring. This explains why the female sex is the limiting resource for reproduction in the male sex, and why this sex competes strongly over mates. Thus, sexual selection solved the problem of the limiting female resource. This process of sexual selection is stronger in one-male, multi-female mating systems than in one-male, one-female mating systems because the polygynous male has a greater degree of control over the access to females.

4.4 Mating systems in human evolution

We have seen above that the strength of sexual selection depends on the kind of mating system. We will now focus on the origins of human mating systems. What kind of mating systems do primates have? And which mating systems were relevant in the evolution of humans? Modern humans tend to live in pairs, but how did we end up in this mating system? Did early *Homo sapiens* have a one-male, multi-female system as did gorillas? Or a multi-male, multi-female system like chimpanzees who are promiscuous, that is, have sex with different partners?

What is a mating system?

Mating systems can be defined according to the number of mates that sexes have. Other criteria might be the duration of the bonds between sexes, the ability to control access to mates, and the means through which such control may be achieved. Stephen Emlen and Lewis Oring (1977) proposed an influential classification of mating systems, based on the degree of monopolisation of mates. Their classification was predictive, based on the following logic as summarised by Shuster and Wade (2003):

- Males compete with one another for access to mates.
- Like competition for scarce resources, male reproduction is limited by the spatial and temporal availability of sexually receptive females.
- The strength of sexual selection depends on the rarity of receptive females in relation to the abundance of competing males (so-called 'operational sex ratio').
- Sexual selection favours male traits that allow them to find and monopolise mates.
- Ecological constraints on male monopolisation attempts lead to a species-specific pattern of male–female associations, called a 'mating system'.

polygyny
one male-male, multi-female mating system in which multiple females mate with a single male.

serial monogamy
pairs that mate and raise offspring cooperatively, but then choose to mate with new partners.

Emlen and Oring (1977) made predictions about the kinds of mating systems that resulted from the reproduction and ecology of females. For example, we may predict that the one-male, multi-female mating system is likely to evolve when females form dense clusters and their offspring don't need male parental care. On the other hand, when females are scattered due to widely dispersed food resources, or when young need care from both parents, one may expect that a one-male, one-female mating system will evolve. Now that we know what mating systems are and how they allow us to make predictions, we need to know what kind of mating systems primates have (Box 4.2 Mating systems in primates).

BOX 4.2 Mating systems in primates

- The term **monogamy** (Greek *monos* = one; *gammos* = marriage) refers to a one-male, one-female mating system in which each sex has a single mate for life. Among primates, monogamy occurs in gibbons, lemurs, tamarins, marmosets and humans. Humans tend to be monogamous, but the pattern of marriage, divorce and remarriage suggests **serial monogamy** whereby men and women have successive partners over their lifespans (Fisher 1993).

- The term **polygyny** (*polus* = many; *gunē* = female) refers to a one-male, multi-female mating system in which multiple females mate with a single male. This system is common in baboons, gorillas, orangutans, and occasionally in humans. In orangutans, single males defend a group of females and their offspring, distributed over a large area. This variant is known as 'exploded' polygyny.

- The term **polygynandry** (*polus* = many; *gunē* = female; *andro* = male) refers to a multi-male, multi-female mating system in which both sexes are variable in their mate numbers. In this system, sexual relationships are promiscuous, that is, short-term and indiscriminate with different mates. This mating system is common among macaques, many baboons and chimpanzees. In chimpanzees, several related males cooperate to defend a group of widely distributed females and their offspring. This system of polygynandry is also known as multi-male polygyny.

● The term *polyandry* (*polus* = many; *andro* = male) refers to a mating system in which multiple males mate with a single female. Polyandry is a rare mating system among mammals. It has, for example, been recorded that people in Northern India and tamarins sometimes engage in polyandry. Figure 4.1 depicts the mating systems that prevail in primates.

How did human mating systems evolve?

polygynandry

multi-male, multi-female mating system in which both sexes have a variable number of mates.

polyandry

one female, multi-male mating system in which multiple males mate with a single female.

polygynamy

mating system in which the home range of one male overlaps those of several females.

Many human cultures allow polygyny, but for the vast majority of people, monogamous relationships are the norm. Only a minority of wealthy, powerful men have the means to acquire and maintain multiple wives. How did human mating systems evolve? As humans are primates, we assume that primate models provide important insights about the origins of human sexuality. In order to reconstruct how human mating systems evolved, we focus on the phylogeny of humans and other primates. Recall, a phylogeny is the genealogical history of a group of organisms, represented by its hypothesised ancestor–descendant relationships. The diagram in Figure 4.2 shows the hypothetical stages in the evolution of the mating systems in humans and African apes, based on a reconstruction by Bernard Chapais (2008).

Chapais (2008, 2010) argues that the common ancestor of chimpanzees and humans probably formed large multi-male, multi-female groups where males stayed in the group after puberty, and females emigrated to other groups at sexual maturity. Polygyny, or one-male, multi-female mating groups emerged later due to males who monopolised a small number of females within large multi-male, multi-female groups. Instead of spatially separate one-male, multi-female units as in gorillas, it is more parsimonious to suppose a group structure with members of both sexes. In several monkey species (e.g. baboons, proboscis monkeys), polygynous units are also nested within larger multi-male, multi-female groups.

Precursors of the genus *Homo* had a mating system which consisted of males living with a small number of females within a large multi-male, multi-female group. The transition from polygynous units to monogamous pairs would require a reduced number of females associated with each male and gradually replace the prevailing mating system of polygyny. The tendency of men and women to form long-lasting relationships for the production of offspring would then be present in the earliest members of the genus *Homo* (around 2–2.5 mya). Since then, most humans lived in monogamous families while a minority lived in polygynous families.

Two hypotheses about the emergence of monogamy

In polygynous species, the maximum reproductive success of males is larger than in monogamous species. The question is: why would males switch to a lower level of sexual competition and a lower rate of reproduction? That is, for most males the switch meant a higher rate of reproduction because most had zero success in a polygynous system as opposed to at least some success with monogamy.

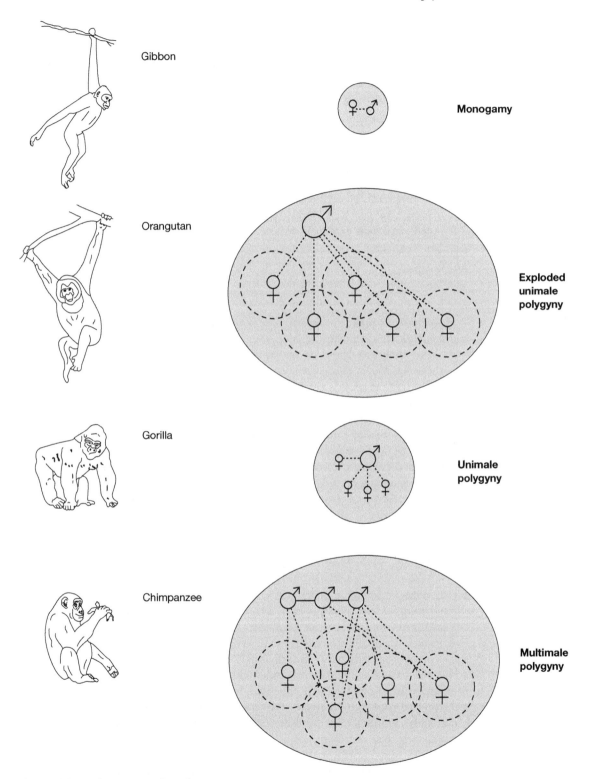

Figure 4.1 Mating systems in primates

Source: Lewin and Foley (2004)

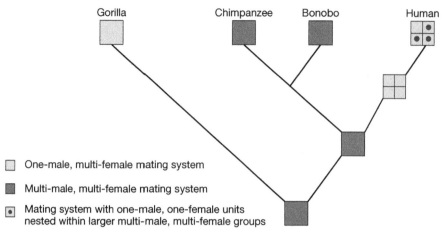

Figure 4.2 Hypothetical stages in the evolution of the mating systems in humans and African apes

Source: Dixson (2009)

How do we explain the emergence of monogamous relationships between males and females? This is mostly explained as a matter of parental cooperation: both sexes form a breeding unit based on sexual division of labour. This parental cooperation hypothesis has two major correlates which receive empirical support (Aiello and Key 2002). The first correlate is that the costs of maternal care are disproportionately high in the human species compared with other primates. The costs of gestation and **lactation** are not very different, but what differs substantially is the cost of provisioning food. Whereas weaned chimpanzees are largely self-sufficient in acquiring food, human babies grow over a longer period and need longer care before they are independent.

The second correlate is that the helping father reduces the maternal costs significantly. Patterns of food provisioning in hunter-gatherers confirm that mother's relatives, older offspring as well as the father may help with provisioning food. Thus, the bond between mother and father would be a parental partnership. However, the idea that women gathered plants and fruits while men hunted for meat to provision their wives and offspring, came under attack. Behavioural ecologists pointed out that hunters did not necessarily favour their wives and children but frequently gave away a large part of their catch. Successful hunters enjoyed high prestige from their generosity among allies and females which made hunting part of a male's mating effort rather than a parental effort (Hawkes 1991, 2002). So, male help in raising the offspring does not necessarily imply that monogamy emerged for reasons of paternal care.

A general principle derived from the comparative analysis of primates is that stable breeding bonds between individuals, whether monogamous or polygynous, are in the first place mating arrangements rather than parenting partnerships. Brotherton and Komers (2003) conclude that in most species which mate monogamously, paternal care evolved after pair-bonding was developed. This would explain why paternal care is absent in many mammals that mate monogamously. Paternal care was therefore not a necessary condition for the evolution of pair-bonding. In other words, male care originated as a mating strategy to monopolise one female, the same strategy that harem-holding primates practise with regard to multiple females.

lactation
the synthesis and secretion of milk by a mother's mammary glands.

The parental cooperation hypothesis implies that monogamy emerged as males refrained from monopolising females and shifted to assisting in maternal care for the offspring. An alternative explanation would be that monogamous pairs replaced the prevailing one-male, multi-female mating system because the costs of polygyny became too high. Most primate species, including our closest ancestors, indeed show intense competition for females. In particular polygynous males, in monopolising the reproductive capacity of females, leave the other males no mating opportunities. This is in sharp contrast to extant human hunter-gatherer societies, which have an egalitarian structure. How can we explain this shift towards a lower level of sexual competition?

Chapais (2008) advanced the hypothesis that any tool made of wood, bone or stone whose original function was to dig up roots or kill animals, could be used as an effective weapon against monopolising males. The capacity to throw weapons from a distance would equalise the distribution of females among males and lower the costs of competition for females. When armed males formed coalitions, it would be very costly to a dominant male to monopolise several females. According to this reasoning, polygyny would give way eventually to monogamy. Thus monogamous relationships were not the product of selection pressures favouring paternal care and pair-bonding but the byproduct of too costly polygyny and the rise of projectile technology. The costly polygyny hypothesis is therefore a more parsimonious explanation than the parental cooperation hypothesis. Monogamy did not evolve as a result of specific selection pressures but by the constraining of polygyny.

Humans are indeed better at throwing projectiles (e.g. stones, spears) than other primates, an ability that required whole-body anatomical changes and evolved in early *Homo* (Bingham 1999, 2000). Although this novel remote-killing capability may have arisen for other reasons such as deterring predators or hunting prey, it could also be used against bullying and dominating behaviour within groups. This hypothesis about the suppression of monopolising males is a specific version of a more general hypothesis which explains the egalitarian character of hunter-gatherer societies as a response to intimidating individuals and too much hierarchy (Boehm 1993).

Human sexual dimorphism

It is very likely that *Homo sapiens* evolved from a polygynous hominid ancestor who shifted from a one-male, multi-female to a one-male, one-female mating system about 2–2.5 mya. As monogamous males have a lower reproductive rate than polygynous ones, we may expect a marked reduction of sexual dimorphism, reflecting the change in mating system. Sexual dimorphism refers to systematic differences in body-form between individuals of different sex but of the same species. In monogamous species, males and females have more or less the same body size, but in polygynous species the difference is greater because males need to fight off competitors.

Dixson (2009) suggests several sexually dimorphic traits which indicate that our human ancestors were polygynous, such as body weight, body composition and body height. Sexual difference in body weight is mostly present in primates which have a polygynous mating system in which male competition for access to females is intense (e.g. gorillas). Selection for a larger male body size has also occurred among some monkey species which have a multi-male, multi-female mating system (e.g. macaques). In monogamous primates, the body size of males and females is almost equal (e.g. gibbons). Humans are sexually dimorphic in body size with an adult

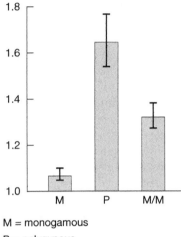

Body size dimorphism

M = monogamous
P = polygynous
M/M = multi-male, multi-female

Figure 4.3 Body size sexual dimorphism in three primate mating systems (adult male body weight divided by adult female body weight)
Source: Dixson (2009)

male-to-female body weight ratio of about 1.1–1.2. Figure 4.3 shows the amount of body size sexual dimorphism in three primate mating systems.

Another indication that human ancestors were polygynous is the sexual difference in body composition. About 40 per cent of the body mass in men is composed of muscle tissue, but only 28 per cent in women. Presumably, selection favoured the increased development of muscular strength in males who out-perform females in tests which assess the strength of hand-grip, arm-pull and arm-thrust. Muscular strength was an asset in the polygynous system in which harem-holders deterred sexual contenders.

A further indication for the polygynous past of human mating may be the sexual difference in body height. Men are on average taller than women, and women have a preference for taller partners. Sexual selection may have favoured female preferences for taller men who were more successful in competing with other males and in hunting for prey. Studies in contemporary humans show indeed that tall men are reproductively more successful than shorter men due to their greater ability to secure resources, intimidate potential rivals, and therefore attract mates (Pawlowski et al. 2000; Nettle 2002; Swami et al. 2008). This outcome suggests that there is indeed selection for tall stature in male partners by female mate choice.

4.5   Mate preferences of men and women

How Darwin considered the pros and cons of marriage

In childhood, males and females grow up apart in a same-sex world, but in adulthood they come together in the other-sex world (Maccoby 1998). From puberty

BOX 4.3 How Darwin considered the pros and cons of marriage

Marry

Children – Constant companion (& friend in old age) who will feel interested in one – object to be loved & played with – Home & someone to take care of house – Charms of music & female chit-chat – These things good for one's health – Intolerable to think of spending one's whole life, like a neuter bee, working, working & nothing after all – Imagine living all one's days solitarily in smoky dirty London House – Only picture to yourself a nice soft wife on a sofa with good fire & books music perhaps – Marry – Marry – Marry QED (*quod erat demonstrandum* = which was to be demonstrated).

Not Marry

Freedom to go where one liked – Conversation of clever men at clubs – not forced to visit relatives & to bend in every trifle – to have the expense & anxiety of children – perhaps quarrelling – Loss of time – cannot read in the evenings – fatness & idleness – Anxiety & responsibility – less money for books &c – if many children forced to gain one's bread – (But then it is very bad for one's health to work too much) – Perhaps my wife won't like London; then the sentence is banishment & degradation into indolent, idle fool.

onwards, the opposite sex is an important subject of attention. Many questions bombard the mating mind. What does the other sex want? Whom shall I date? How to deal with rivals? A question which logically – but mostly not actually – precedes such questions, is whether one should live single or look for a mate. Famous scholars like Galileo Galilei, Isaac Newton and Immanuel Kant preferred to live unmarried. Let us focus, for a start, on how Darwin considered the pros and cons of marriage (Box 4.3). In 1838, at the age of 29, he was torn between his scientific work and the prospect of a married life. In line with his rational nature, he made a list of the advantages and disadvantages of marriage. He concluded in favour of it and married Emma Wedgwood in 1840. We know this from a pencil note, entitled 'This is the Question' (Burkhardt and Smith 1987).

The anomaly of women's attractiveness

anomaly
anything that is irregular or deviates from the norm.

Darwin reflected about a nice soft wife on the sofa and perhaps took beauty for granted. Female attractiveness is, from an evolutionary point view, an **anomaly**. An anomaly is any strange, unusual or unique phenomenon which deviates from an established rule. Why is female attractiveness an anomalous phenomenon? And from which rule are attractive females deviating? We know that for any sexually reproducing animal species, finding a mate is very important because one needs the other sex to pass one's own genes to the next generation. As females are the limiting reproductive resource, the theory of sexual selection predicts that males should compete over access to females. That is why males need to attract females by means of their sexy ornaments and why females are unattractive because they don't need to compete for males and can afford to be choosy.

However, humans are an exception to this evolutionary rule, as observed by evolutionary scientists. In *The Selfish Gene* (1976: Chapter 9), Richard Dawkins puts the emphasis on female attractiveness this way:

> One feature of our own society which seems decidedly anomalous is the matter of sexual advertisement . . . It is of course true that some men dress flamboyantly and some women dress drably but, on average, there can be no doubt that in our society the equivalent of the peacock's tail is exhibited by the female, not by the male. . . . What

has happened in modern western society? Has the male really become the sought-after sex, the one that is in demand, the sex that can afford to be choosy? If so, why?

In *The Descent of Man and Selection in Relation to Sex* (1871: 371, 372) Darwin noted that humans are an exception to the rule that males use physical attractiveness to charm and allure the opposite sex. He put it this way:

> There are, however, exceptional cases in which the males, instead of being the selected, have been the selectors. We recognize such cases by the female having been rendered more highly ornamented than the males . . . Women are everywhere conscious of the value of their beauty; and when they have the means, they take more delight in decorating themselves with all sorts of ornaments than do men.

Darwin did not connect the peculiarity of greater emphasis on female attractiveness in *Homo sapiens* with men's higher investment in parental care. He suggested that human females were more attractive because male choice, not female choice, would dominate sexual selection in humans.

Modern evolutionary scientists who have been drawn to the anomaly of female attractiveness in humans, began to consider sexual selection mainly in terms of parental investment. Recall that according to Trivers' parental investment theory, the most investing sex is more selective about a mate, and the least investing sex more competitive with one another over a mate. Following this theory, it has been argued that humans may be considered as a partially sex-role reversed species (Gottschall 2007). Recall, **sex-role reversal** is a form of animal behaviour in which each sex behaves in a manner typical of the other sex. In many partially reversed species – mainly fish, insects and other invertebrates – males discriminate mainly on physical attractiveness, while females compete aggressively with one another for the best male (e.g. Bonduriansky 2001). However, it is not realistic to say that humans are partially sex-role reversed since men are still larger and more aggressive, and women are more involved in child care. We are partially biparental rather than partially sex-role reversed.

Parental investment is an important factor that influences mating choosiness. As human males have a much larger part in parental investment compared to most other species, we may expect that they are more choosy. The evolutionary riddle of greater emphasis on female attractiveness in male mate choice is then resolved. In general, it is the amount of parental investment that causes choosiness and competitiveness over mates. Substantial investment in offspring may explain why human males became choosy which, in turn, may explain the emphasis on female attractiveness. But we should be aware that, originally, paternal investment in offspring had nothing to do with parenting. In our discussion of mating systems in human evolution, we have seen that pair-bonds in primates are in the first place mating arrangements rather than parenting partnerships. In most species which mate monogamously, paternal care evolved after pair-bonding was developed (Chapais 2008). So, monogamy is another factor, preceding paternal investment, which has an influence on male choosiness and female attractiveness.

sex-role reversal
a form of animal behaviour in which each sex behaves in a manner typical of the other sex.

The shift to monogamous mating

Women spend much more time and money in making themselves attractive than men. It is easy to imagine that without the continuing interest of females in their personal appearance, beauty industries would collapse: cosmetics (nail polish, lipstick, eyeliner, hair care products), clothing and accessories (fashionable dresses,

BOX 4.4 Different forms of 'monogamy'

The simple term 'monogamy' usually refers to relationships of pair-living species such as humans, gibbons, swallows or swans. However, this term does not cover the complexity of one-male, one-female relationships. 'Monogamy' turns out to be a diverse phenomenon which acquired different terms in the literature (e.g. Reichard and Boesch 2003):

- 'Sexual monogamy' refers to an exclusive sexual relationship between a male and a female.

- 'Genetic monogamy' is used when DNA analyses can confirm that a male–female pair reproduce exclusively with each other. All offspring produced are from the pair.

- 'Social monogamy' refers to a male and female's social living arrangement (e.g. shared use of a territory, shared care of offspring). This arrangement

does not imply that male and female have an exclusive sexual and reproductive relationship. In humans, social monogamy is mostly identical with monogamous marriage. In many cultures, most human sexual relationships are socially monogamous.

- 'Serial monogamy' refers to pairs that mate and raise offspring cooperatively, but then choose to mate with new partners.

- 'Monogamous mating system' is synonymous with sexual and genetic relationships, whereas 'monogamous social system' is a synonym for social monogamy.

In this book, the term 'monogamy' refers to 'social monogamy' and we use the term 'monogamous mating system' synonymously with 'monogamous social system', unless otherwise indicated.

---

sexual monogamy
an exclusive sexual relationship between a male and a female.

shoes, handbags, jewellery), and cosmetic surgery (face and breast lift, lip and breast enhancement, liposuction). This female–male difference with regard to beauty and body adornment is clearly under the influence of a long cultural tradition. We know, for example, that females in hunter-gatherer societies employ decoration to create a sexually attractive body. Practices of body decoration include filed teeth, body paintings, tattoos and piercings (Brain 1979). But culture is only part of the story.

An evolutionary perspective suggests that the modern cosmetic and aesthetic industries did not create a demand for female ornamentation, but rather responded to it (Barash and Lipton 2009). The underlying biology responsible for this demand of female attractiveness should be found in the evolution of human mating systems. Recall from the previous section that *Homo sapiens* around 2–2.5 mya changed from a one-male, multi-female to a one-male, one-female mating system which is not identical with an exclusive sexual relationship between a male and a female (Box 4.4 Different forms of 'monogamy'). The shift to a monogamous mating system reduced the intense competition between men but generated a new problem for women as they could no longer afford to wait until the right mate arrived. They needed to compete with each other for the desirable bachelors. Women also competed in the polygynous system but with their husband's other wives. For men the shift to monogamous mating meant that they were restricted to one wife – at least one at a time – which may explain why they became choosy when it came to marriage and parental care (Geary 2010).

social monogamy
one-male, one-female's social living arrangement (e.g. shared use of a territory, shared care of offspring).

What men want

A recurring problem of human ancestral males was to assess women's mate value in terms of enhancing his reproductive success (Symons 1995). As women's value in reproduction is affected by multiple variables like health, hormonal status, and age which cannot be directly observed, physical attractiveness was a suitable fitness indicator. Since humans shifted to monogamous mating, women weren't merely choosy but also actively sought to be chosen by men. Investing in 'good looks' was the answer to men's preference.

Men's preference for female beauty is part of a biological heritage. If female attractiveness indicates a woman's reproductive value, sexual selection would therefore have shaped mate preferences in men for women's beauty. Femininity in female faces – fuller lips, larger eyes, smaller chin, higher cheekbones, smaller lower face area – is a good candidate for a biologically based preference. Overall, femininity is strongly attractive and may signal fertility which is associated with high levels of oestrogen (Rhodes 2006). Oestrogen is the hormone that promotes the division and growth of cells responsible for female secondary sexual characteristics such as deposition of fat in breasts, thighs and buttocks, producing the characteristic female figure.

Male preferences for female beauty are also part of a cultural heritage. Consider standards of female beauty which are subject to cultural conventions. For instance, in the early twentieth century feminine curves became unfashionable. The ideal shape for women de-emphasised their reproductive characteristics – nourishing breasts and wide, childbearing hips. Waistlines were lowered to hip level and 'flatteners', made of cotton and elastic, pressed the breasts tightly against the body in order to give the wearer a flat-chested look that was popular at the time. The cultural climate changed halfway through that century when Marilyn Monroe and Jayne Mansfield made curvaceous women popular again. But at the end of that century the thin-is-beautiful idea led to a fascination with underweight fashion models. Today, in the early twenty-first century, the ideal body shape seems to be a combination of male desire and waifish androgyny; thin, no hips, big bust.

Cultural influences on mate preferences include unprecedented levels of exposure to attractive individuals through various mass media (Roberts et al. 2010). Films, television and magazines present unrealistic distributions of desirable others, and may lead to problems for people and their romantic relationships. Exposure to mass media presents men with a biased view of attractive women. By increasing the upper limit for attractiveness, media may produce a decrease in attractiveness ratings of average women. Kenrick et al. (1989) used exposure to female nude models from *Playboy* and *Penthouse* to study whether full-body attractiveness is more affected than facial attractiveness. Findings suggest that the increased upper limit for facial attractiveness may be corrected more easily than for full-body attractiveness. In another study, men exposed to highly attractive nude models rated their partners as less sexually attractive and less lovable.

Men prefer women with a low waist–hip ratio

Another feature of female attractiveness which reliably signals women's reproductive value is the sexually dimorphic fat distribution of the female body. Women have more gluteofemoral fat (buttocks and thighs) and less abdominal and visceral fat (tummy) than men. Females need large body fat stores for ovulation, probably to provide resources for a long pregnancy and lactation as well as for the development of the foetal and infant brain (Lassek and Gaulin 2008).

The characteristic distribution of fat in buttocks, thighs and breasts which makes the female figure curvaceous, may have evolved to advertise fecundity. Fat

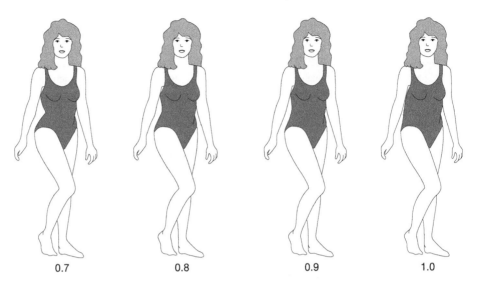

0.7   0.8   0.9   1.0

Figure 4.4 Modified images of the same person with four different waist–hip ratios
Source: Barash and Lipton (2009)

deposits serve as women's ornaments which were probably selected in the context of long-term mating and pair-bonding. In long-term pair-bonding, men preferably mated with women who were able to reproduce repeatedly and produce high-quality offspring. Selection would have favoured female signals that promise high reproductive potential, and that males easily can assess (Thornhill and Gangestadt 2008).

Most men all over the world prefer women who have a low waist–hip ratio (WHR), that is, a relatively narrow waist and relatively broad hips. This ratio is a simple measure of the difference in body shape between women and men. The circumference of the waist is divided by the circumference of the hips. In healthy, premenopausal women the WHR may range from 0.67 to 0.80 and in men from 0.85 to 0.95. In short, the higher the WHR the larger the waist circumference compared to the hips (Figure 4.4; Box 4.5 women's fat distribution in two works of art).

BOX 4.5 Women's fat distribution in two works of art

The ideal fat distribution may be seen from an Indian work of art. David Barash and Judith Lipton (2009), writing about the question of how women got their curves, recall a lecture presented for the BBC by neuroscientist V.S. Ramachandran. In response to a question whether there are such things as artistic universals, he referred to a famous bronze of the Hindu goddess Parvati, dating back to the twelfth century (Figure 4.5).

For Indian eyes, Ramachandran said, Parvati is supposed to be the perfect example of feminine sensuality, grace, poise, dignity; in short: everything that's good about being a woman. For Victorian Englishmen, however, who first encountered this sculpture, the goddess was too voluptuous, her breasts and hips were too big, and her waist was too narrow. Parvati's exaggerated shape is indeed unreal, as we may expect from a supernatural creature.

The male preference for women with a low waist–hip ratio may not be universal. This is indicated by the Venus of Willendorf (Figure 4.6). In 1908 an archaeologist found this small (11 cm) portable, female figure sculpted in limestone (Leroi-Gourhan 1971) in Austria, dating from 20,000 years ago. Small female figurines like the Venus of Willendorf have been unearthed at multiple sites across Europe. The faces are mostly missing or lacking detail, but the breasts, thighs, buttocks and abdomen tend to be very large. Whether pregnant or obese, they do not appear to have a low WHR. The Venus of Willendorf originates from the Palaeolithic (from Palaeo – old, and lithos – stone), a period distinguished by the development of the first stone tools. This period extends from 2.5 million years ago to the introduction of agriculture around 10,000 years ago. During the Palaeolithic, humans lived in small societies such as bands and subsisted by gathering plants and hunting or scavenging animals.

Images of women dominate in Palaeolithic art. Cave paintings and stone or ivory figurines allow us to look at how our ancestors saw themselves, or how they wanted to be seen. Were all Palaeolithic women really fat? We know that hunter-gatherers appreciate fat (Guthrie 2005).

Among traditional Bushmen there was not such a thing as being too fat. Couples at marriages were symbolically anointed with fat. We also know that men are attracted to women who go through periods of fertility. They look at the right curves at the right places. So, fat is not a matter of absolute amounts but rather of specific locations. But where are the right locations? Increasing oestrogen in women of reproductive age promotes fat deposits around two centres: the pelvic girdle and the mammary tissue. Guthrie (2005) argues that these centres of fat resulted, presumably, from two kinds of selection: one has sorted fat into particular deposits, and the other has sorted male attention to these particular locations.

Was the Venus of Willendorf a true representation of an individual? The images of voluptuous women in Palaeolithic art suggest that female obesity was not unknown. We can imagine that men would be sexually attracted to curvaceous women, but the images are probably exaggerations of reality. They may have symbolised the wish for a well-nourished and reproductively successful life. For, the period in which these figurines were sculpted, was one of cold and harsh climate conditions in Europe (Dixson 2009).

Figure 4.5 Statue of the Hindu goddess Parvati

Source: Terry Cash

Figure 4.6 The Venus of Willendorf

Sources: Power and Schulkin (2009) / Science Photo Library Ltd / Jim Cartier

Devendra Singh (2002, 2006) has proposed, on the basis of a series of studies, that a low female WHR reliably indicates a healthy distribution of body fat, greater success in pregnancy and smaller risk for major diseases (e.g. diabetes, hypertension). Sexual selection during human evolution would then have produced male preferences for females with an hourglass figure.

body mass index (BMI)

a measure of weight, scaled for height (body weight in kilograms divided by height in metres squared).

WHR is positively correlated with **body mass index (BMI)** which is a measure of weight, scaled for height (body weight in kilograms divided by height in metres squared). To rule out the effect of BMI on WHR, Singh et al. (2010) controlled BMI by using photographs of women who went through micrograft surgery for cosmetic reasons. Micrograft surgery involves liposuction of the circumference of the waist and transplantation of fat cells into the buttocks. This surgical technique both narrows the waist and enlarges the buttocks which has an effect on WHR without altering BMI.

Subjects from various cultures were asked to view pre- and postoperative photographs and choose the image that they judged most attractive. Subjects had no knowledge of the rationale of the study, or that the photographs they viewed were of the same individuals. Results showed that despite pronounced ethnic and socioeconomic differences between the people who participated in this study, they judged postoperative micrograft surgery photographs of women who had lower WHR as more attractive than preoperative counterparts. According to the authors, this cross-cultural consensus suggests that the link between WHR and female attractiveness is due to adaptation shaped by the selection process.

To conclude, many studies reveal that men prefer women with the following traits: a WHR of about 0.7, facial features indicating sexual maturity but relative youth, symmetric body and face, proportionately longer legs, larger than average breast size and symmetry, small abdomen and waist, and youth. Age is important because the evolved mate preferences of men were sensitive to indications of women's age as it is linked with fertility. Women's fertility peaks at about age 25, and declines by age 45. Men prefer women younger than themselves because they have more reproductive years ahead of them than older ones (e.g. Buss 1989; Sprecher et al. 1994; Dunn et al. 2010; Geary 2010).

What women want

Studies using a budgeted approach in which participants are asked to design a desired mate – reflecting the real world constraint that the prevalence of the highest-quality mates is low – show a sex difference. Men focus on physical attractiveness, women on resources (Edlund and Sagarin 2010). This outcome is consistent with many of the findings in the evolutionary psychology literature (e.g. Buss 2012). Women, like all female primates, prefer dominant men who are able to protect them and their offspring and may provide better access to high-quality resources. It should be emphasised, however, that male dominance does not only provide advantages but may also impose substantial costs on women.

Competition and mate choice by both sexes make human mating a complex process because competing and choosing rarely act independently, but mostly simultaneously or sequentially. A new area of sexual selection research is therefore focused on how and why male and female interests diverge and may result in sexual conflict (Hunt et al. 2009; Arnqvist and Rowe 2005). For example, male–male competition tends to select for dominance in males because this trait is advantageous. However, this same trait may impose substantial costs on females (e.g. aggression, harassment, injuries), as a result of which they will avoid mating with dominant males.

Men possess traits that appear to function mainly in threatening rivals (Puts 2006, 2010). For example, a deep, low-pitched voice indicates dominance and is associated with a high testosterone level, while low-pitch vocalisation, across animals, is a signal of submissiveness. Although men lack antlers or horns, they have a long tradition in manufacturing weapons which serve as extensions of their bodies. Men are also more aggressive than women and in childhood engage in more play-fighting which positively correlates with peer-ranked dominance. Traits that improve the threatening and fighting ability of men are probably not generally preferred by women and are better designed for male–male contests than for the attraction of mates. They reveal an evolutionary history of intense competition for females.

There are circumstances, however, in which women prefer aggressive and formidable mates. In environments characterised by substantial levels of within- and between-group violence it may pay off for men to use aggression in the competition for resources. In these same environments, women and their children will often face more risk of violence. Evidence suggests that in the past sexual assault would have been a source of selection pressure on the psychology of women's mate choice (e.g. Daly and Wilson 1988b). As rape decreases female fitness, women would prefer men who could provide protection from violence. The costs that aggressive-formidable men would also use violence against their long-term partners, outweighed the benefits of protection. Recent internet-based studies of US women found that women's fear of crime predicted the extent to which they valued aggressive-formidable long-term mates (Snyder et al. 2011). Although the studies did not provide evidence that all these men are quicker to resort to coercion within their romantic relationships, at least some men are.

Women, generally, don't possess physical traits to threaten or harm rivals. For that reason, it is unlikely that they will physically threaten same-sex competitors and monopolise mates of the opposite sex. Another reason for women's restraint in using sexual aggression results from their higher parental investment and the consequent greater reproductive cost of injury or death. Competition between females for a mate is typically more subtle than male–male competition. Women usually compete for mates by advertising qualities valued by men (beauty and sexual exclusiveness), by denigrating competitors or by spreading lies about their sexual fidelity (Buss and Dedden 1990).

When there is a shortage of men, female–female competition may intensify and lead to physical aggression (Campbell 2004). Fights are usually between young similarly aged women (15–24 years) who know each other. The fights may occur in bars or in streets and involve hand-to-hand tactics, such as pushing, grabbing, slapping, kicking, and punching. The fights are mostly about an attack on a girl's integrity which include allegations about promiscuity, false accusations, or gossip. Another common reason refers to loyalty in which a girl defends the name of a friend.

Women with high mate value raise their standards

Women prefer successful men as marriage partners. Success can be achieved in different ways across cultures, but the bottom line is that it indicates command over more reproductively useful resources (Geary 2010). In a classic cross-cultural study conducted on women's and men's preferences, Buss (1989) found that women rated 'good financial prospects' higher than did men in all cultures. In a recent study, Buss and Shackelford (2008) emphasise that a woman's physical attractiveness is a cardinal component of women's mate value as it will influence the quality of the man she is able to engage as a long-term partner. Mate value is a construct that broadly describes one's value as a mate to a potential or actual partner. The authors hypothesise that women high in mate value are expected to impose higher standards for a set of desirable characteristics, including indicators for good genes (e.g. masculinity), good investment (e.g. earning capacity), good parenting (e.g. fondness of children), and good partner (e.g. emotional commitment). In other words, the authors hypothesise that women have an evolved self-assessment mechanism that calibrates their standards to their mate value. Having a high mate value leads them to raise their standards. Conversely, having a lower mate value results in relaxing the standards.

Participating couples engaged in separate episodes of assessment. They completed at home a battery of instruments, were tested in a laboratory, and were interviewed and observed to provide independent assessment of each participant's physical attractiveness. Table 4.2 shows the correlations between the three measures of physical attractiveness as they were derived from the interviewers and the expressed mate preferences of the interviewed women. Physically attractive women expressed significantly stronger preferences for five of the six good genes indicators (except intelligence); four of the six good investment indicators (except ambition and status); five of the six good parenting indicators (except kind and understanding), and one of the three good partner indicators (except devotion and loyalty).

Table 4.2 Correlations between women's attractiveness and desired mate characteristics

Face	Body	Overall attractiveness	Mate characteristic
Hypothesised good gene indicators			
.22*	.14	.20*	More masculine
.26**	.26**	.28**	Physically attractive
.18	.17	.20*	Good looking
.28**	.30**	.30**	Sex appeal
.18	.27**	.23*	Physically fit
.00	–.02	.10	Intelligent
Good investment ability indicators			
.19*	.21*	.19*	Potential income (expressed in dollars)
.06	–.09	.22*	Good earning capacity
.18	.21*	.22*	College graduate
.14	.14	.13	Ambition and industriousness
.13	.11	.14	Favourable social status or rating

Face	Body	Overall attractiveness	Mate characteristic
.28**	.22*	.25*	Older than self (expressed in years)
Hypothesised good parenting indicators			
.37**	.39**	.40**	Desire for home and children
.18	.20*	.23*	Fond of children
.22*	.21*	.24*	Likes children
.30**	.26**	.28**	Raising children well (goal priority)
.28**	.31**	.30**	Emotional stability and maturity
.11	.10	.12	Kind and understanding
Hypothesised good partner indicators			
.21*	.25**	.24*	Being a loving partner (goal priority)
.11	.14	.14	Devoted to you
.10	.12	.11	Loyal

*$p < .05$, two-tailed; **$p < .01$, two-tailed. This table includes only hypothesised indicators specified in the text; complete statistical analyses may be obtained from the authors.

Source: Buss and Shackleford (2008)

The results support the hypothesis that women with high mate value, indicated by physical attractiveness, raise their standards for all four clusters of indicators that are considered critical to women's reproductive success. They are consistent with previous studies about what attractive women want. For example, Waynforth and Dunbar (1995) in their study of lonely hearts advertisements, found that self-rated attractive women listed a large number of preferred traits. This outcome corresponds with the findings of Buss and Shackleford's study (2008) in which observer-judged attractiveness in women is connected with raised preferences across four clusters of traits.

Women near ovulation prefer more attractive men

Buss and Shackleford's investigation (2008) shows that women's preferences include good genes as indicated by physical attractiveness, good looks, sex appeal and physical fitness. Women's ratings of men's attractiveness change when they approach the 6-day window of high fertility. The reader will be aware that women's reproduction-related hormones vary across the 28-day cycle as shown in Figure 4.7 (Geary 2010). During this window, normally ovulating women show increased attraction to men taller than average but not too tall, with a 0.8 to 0.9 waist–hip ratio (Singh 1995), men with more masculine faces (Penton-Voak et al. 1999), the scent of men who are more socially dominant or intrasexually competitive, men who have relatively symmetrical body features, masculine or muscular bodies, deeper voices, and talent as opposed to wealth (Gangestad et al. 2010).

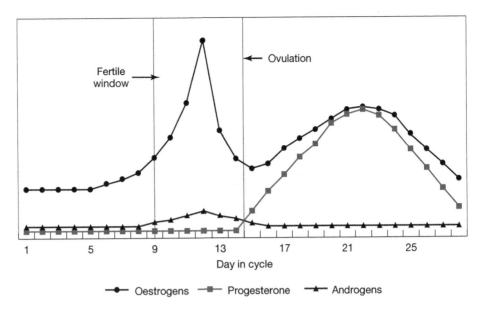

Figure 4.7 Hormonal changes across the ovulatory cycle (Oestrogens (e.g. estradiol) increase at about Day 9 and contribute to ovulation. Androgens (e.g. testosterone) may increase woman's desire for sex. Progesteron increase contributes to preparing the uterus for implantation of a fertilised egg.

Source: Geary (2010)

Attractive features in men, such as prominent cheek bones and chin, as well as facial symmetry, are thought to indicate genetic quality because they are markers of higher testosterone concentrations. High testosterone in turn is only sustainable by healthier men (Roney and Simmons 2008). According to the ovulatory shift hypothesis, ancestral women benefited from mating with multiple men to obtain good genes. That would explain why preferences of women near ovulation shift to the 'sexy' features of potential partners. Studies demonstrate that changes in women's estradiol concentrations predict shifts in attraction to facial cues of men's testosterone (Roney et al. 2011). Other studies show that during the window of high fertility, women engage in more self-grooming and self-ornamentation through attractive choice of dress, and wear more revealing clothing when they are not with their partner (Haselton et al. 2007; Durante and Haselton 2008).

Many studies tend to interpret cyclic shifts in women's preferences for masculinity as evidence for an evolved dual-mating strategy in women to increase offspring health through high parental investment from a long-term partner while benefiting during a highly fertile window from short-term partners who display masculine cues that promise good genes (for a review, see Little et al. 2011). This interpretation has been criticised for several reasons. First, not all women are biased to have an affair around the time of ovulation. As an example, women are less likely to cheat high-status men because they and their offspring would risk losing men's investment (Geary 2010). Second, the interpretation implies that extra-pair copulation in humans must have evolved in the context of something like 'one-night stands'.

However, in the literature there is no discussion of whether this scenario is consistent with mating systems and strategies in preliterate societies (Harris 2011). Third, the ovulatory shifts in women's mate preferences may have less to do with special design for infidelity and more with adaptive allocation of attention to mate value during parts of the life cycle in which women experience higher fertility (Roney 2009). Fourth, the notion that women may be predisposed by hormonal shifts to alter their sexual behaviour, suggests the continued existence of oestrus in human beings. The term 'oestrus' refers to a restricted period of heightened sexual activity in female mammals associated with near ovulation and mating that will result in conception. However, in human beings copulations are not restricted to short periods but may take place throughout the monthly menstrual cycle. Oestrus was lost in the early monkeys and not present in our human ancestors (Dixson 2009).

A new line of mate choice research

Mate choice is one of the most important decision-making tasks that humans face. Through mate choice, they influence the quality of genes and culture that are passed on to the offspring as well as the quality of parental care it will receive. Apart from physical attractiveness, mates also seek psychological attractiveness in one another such as kindness and generosity. In his cross-cultural study about sex differences in human mate preferences, Buss (1989) provided evidence that both men and women favour traits like intelligence and kindness. Recent studies show that women rate personal attributes like intelligence, stability and conscientiousness significantly higher than men (Lie et al. 2002; Furnham 2009; Edlund and Sagarin 2010). Other research findings support the idea that greater verbal intelligence is an important trait in women's mate preferences (Prokosch et al. 2009).

mating intelligence
construct referring to the capacity to understand the beliefs and desires of opposite-sex partners as well as same-sex rivals.

Recently, a new strand of mate choice research has emerged, based on the construct of 'mating intelligence' which refers to the capacity to understand the beliefs and desires of opposite-sex partners as well as same-sex rivals (Miller and Todd 1998; Geher and Miller 2007). This construct has some affinity with social intelligence, being the capacity to understand the beliefs and desires of others in non-sexual relationships (e.g. parents, siblings, friends, pupils). This capacity is important because it may improve stable relationships that are needed for successful parenting. Mating intelligence also has affinity with emotional intelligence which comprises the capacities to understand, manage and modulate emotions adaptively. They are important for human mating which involves a whole range of emotions from lust and love to jealousy and happiness.

The idea of mating intelligence is important for evolutionary psychology because it may be considered an evolved cognitive capacity that helps humans to solve problems. These problems include the need to acquire and retain a mate, to anticipate a mate's dissatisfaction and infidelity, to assess one's own attractiveness and commitment, and to read one another's mind. Mating intelligence is also important from the point of view of psychometrics and behaviour genetics because, like general intelligence, mating intelligence may display heritable differences between individuals. And we know that without differences there would be nothing to be selected in evolution. Moreover, psychological traits such as intelligence have heritabilities between 0.3 and 0.8 (Miller and Todd 1998). In short, more cooperation between researchers in psychometrics, behaviour genetics and evolutionary psychology is needed to improve our understanding of mate choice.

4.6 Summary

- The first question in this chapter was why, given the costs of sex and the widespread potential for asexual reproduction, sexual reproduction originated. Recent models have identified some conditions under which sexual recombination could evolve. For example, when the environment changes rapidly over time, genetic associations built up by past selection can become disadvantageous. Sexual recombination can, then, break apart these associations, improving the fitness of offspring.

- Another question referred to why ornaments such as the peacock's tail originated. Darwin's answer was the theory of sexual selection which holds that male ornaments evolved because females prefer to mate with the best-ornamented males. Subsequently, Trivers made it clear that it is the relative parental investment of the sexes in their offspring that controls sexual selection. The most investing sex will discriminate more about a mate while the least investing sex competes more strongly for a mate.

- The third question was why humans came to live in pairs. The parental cooperation hypothesis proposes that monogamy emerged as males refrained from monopolising females and made contributions to the care for offspring. The costly polygyny hypothesis argues that monogamous mating replaced the prevailing one-male, multi-female mating system because its costs became too high.

- The fourth question focused on why it is the female sex in humans that uses ornamentation to charm and lure the male sex. The answer may be found in the shift to monogamous mating which reduced the intense competition between men, and generated a new problem for women. Instead of waiting until the right mate arrived, good looks became important to be chosen by men.

- The last question concerned what mating men and women prefer in one another. Men focus primarily on physical attractiveness, women on resources. Ample research findings show that men prefer physical attractiveness in women as it indicates health, youth and fertility. Women prefer successful and attractive men because success indicates command over resources while physical attractiveness indicates good genes.

Study questions

1. What is meant by The Red Queen hypothesis?

2. Why does the textbook example of the peacock fail to provide evidence for sexual selection?

3. Why is the strength of sexual selection weakest in the monogamous mating system?

4. How did mating systems evolve in humans?

5. Why has the ovulatory shift hypothesis been criticised?

Suggested reading

The origin of sexual reproduction

Otto, S. (2009). The evolutionary enigma of sex. *The American Naturalist*, *174*, S1–S14.

The theory of sexual selection

Andersson, M. (1994). *Sexual Selection*. Princeton, NJ: Princeton University Press.

Gould, J. and Gould, C. (1997). *Sexual Selection: Mate Choice and Courtship in Nature*. New York: Scientific American Library.

Trivers, R. (1972). Parental investment and sexual selection. In B. Campbell (Ed.), *Sexual Selection: and the Descent of Man* (pp. 136–179). London: Heinemann.

Mating systems in human evolution

Dixson, A. (2009). *Sexual Selection and the Origins of Human Mating Systems*. Oxford: Oxford University Press.

Moorad, J., Promislow, D., Smith, K. and Wade, M. (2011). Mating system change reduces the strength of sexual selection in an American frontier population of the 19th century. *Evolution and Human Behavior*, *32*, 147–155.

Shuster, S. and Wade, M. (2003). *Mating Systems and Strategies*. Princeton, NJ: Princeton University Press.

Mate preferences of men and women

Buss, D. (1989). Sex differences in human mate preferences: Evolutionary hypotheses tested in 37 cultures. *Behavioral and Brain Sciences*, *12*, 1–49.

Buss, D. and Shackelford, T. (2008). Attractive women want it all: Good genes, economic investment, parenting proclivities, and emotional commitment. *Evolutionary Psychology*, *6*, 134–146.

Dixson, B., Grimshaw, G., Linklater, W. and Dixson, A. (2010). Watching the hourglass: Eye tracking reveals men's appreciation of the female form. *Human Nature*, *21*, 355–370.

Edlund, J. and Sagarin, B. (2010). Mate value and mate preferences: An investigation into decisions made with and without constraints. *Personality and Individual Differences*, *49*, 835–839.

Little, A., Jones, B. and DeBruine, L. (2011). Facial attractiveness: evolutionary based research. *Philosophical Transactions of the Royal Society B*, *366*, 1638–1659.

Puts, D. (2010). Beauty and the beast: mechanisms of sexual selection in humans. *Evolution and Human Behavior*, *31*, 157–175.

Roberts, S., Miner, E. and Shackelford, T. (2010). The future of applied evolutionary psychology for human partnerships. *Review of General Psychology*, *14*, 318–329.

Roney, J., Simmons, Z. and Gray, P. (2011). Changes in estradiol predict within women shifts in attraction to facial cues of men's testosterone. *Psychoneuroendocrinology*, *36*, 742–749.

Snyder, J., Fessler, D., Tiokhin, L. et al. (2011). Trade-offs in a dangerous world: women's fear of crime predicts preferences for aggressive and formidable mates. *Evolution and Human Behavior*, *32*, 127–137.

Zietsch, B., Verweij, K. Heath, A. and Martin, N. (2011). Variation in human mate choice: Simultaneous investigating heritability, parental influence, sexual imprinting, and assortative mating. *The American Naturalist*, *177*, 605–616.

Reference books

Dixson, A. (1998). *Primate Sexuality: Comparative Studies of the Prosimians: Monkeys, Apes, and Human Beings.* Oxford: Oxford University Press.

Geary, D. (2010). *Male, Female: The Evolution of Human Sex Differences.* Washington: American Psychological Association.

Kauth, B. (Ed.) (2006). *Handbook of the Evolution of Human Sexuality.* New York: The Haworth Press, Inc.

Ridley, M. (2005). *Evolution, Third Edition.* Oxford: Blackwell Publishing.

Stearns, S. and Hoekstra, R. (2005). *Evolution: an introduction. Second Edition.* Oxford: Oxford University Press.

5 Fathers, mothers and others

This chapter will cover:

5.1 Introduction

5.2 Inbreeding avoidance

5.3 Origin of the human family

5.4 When mothers needed assistance

5.5 Parent–offspring conflict

5.6 Summary

Learning outcomes

By the end of this chapter, you should be able to explain:

- why and how primates avoid incest
- why the human family originated
- how childhood affects reproduction in later life
- why group members other than the parents, help to raise offspring
- why paternal child care emerged
- why parents and offspring have conflicting interests.

5.1 Introduction

In the nineteenth century, scientists and medical practitioners in Europe and the USA were involved in a heated debate over the biological effects of close kin marriage. Charles Darwin, who had married his first cousin Emma Wedgwood, was a leading participant in the discussion. What happens when fathers and mothers are close relatives? How injurious is inbreeding really? How do human and other species avoid inbreeding?

When fathers, mothers and offspring form groups, we call them families. We cannot take these groups for granted because they are rare in mammalian species. Why are families rare? Where do we find species living in family groups, similar to those of humans? How did animal and human families arise?

inbreeding

breeding between two close genetic relatives. The fitness of offspring is sometimes reduced by inbreeding depression.

Mothers are the primary caregivers of infants but raising children is a demanding task, the more since children go through a long period of dependence. While intense care is essential for child survival, most primate fathers provide little or no care. Why not? Where would mothers initially look for assistance? How did paternal child care eventually emerge in human evolution?

inbreeding depression

the phenomenon that descendants of individuals who mated with close relatives tend to have lower fitness due, for example, to lowered genetic variety.

Families are understood as groups that provide warmth, protection, and resources for youngsters. But family harmony is only one side of the coin. Although parents and children share common genes and experiences, their interests may conflict when offspring want more care than parents want to give. Which factors influence parent–offspring conflict?

5.2 Inbreeding avoidance

incest

sexual activity or relationship between first-degree relatives (e.g. brother–sister, parent–child), associated with very high risks of abnormality in offspring.

When two breeding partners are more closely related than two randomly chosen individuals, it is called 'inbreeding'. This may increase the chances of genetic defects and decrease the fitness of offspring ('**inbreeding depression**'). The most extreme form of human inbreeding is **incest**. Incestuous relationships are those between first-degree relatives (e.g. brother–sister, parent–child) and associated with very high risk of abnormality in offspring. Marriages between such relatives are forbidden in almost every culture on religious or legal grounds. Today, inbreeding is rare in Western societies but in many parts of the world – Africa, Central Asia, India, Middle East – marriages between relatives are preferred (Box 5.1 Types of genetic relationships between relatives).

BOX 5.1 Types of genetic relationships between relatives

In all unions between relatives the partners share genes which they inherited from one or more common ancestors. In first-degree relatives, the couple has 50 per cent of their genes in common, while in first-cousin marriages the spouses are predicted to have 12.5 per cent of their genes in common. In kinship terminology, a first cousin is a relative with whom one shares a common ancestor, that is, a grandparent. A second cousin is a relative with whom one shares a great-grandparent. Regardless of the level of inbreeding, if an individual inherits the same mutant gene from both parents, the disorder will contribute to inbreeding depression, that is, a decrease in the fitness of offspring (Table 5.1).

A remarkable case of inbreeding is the marriage of Charles Darwin with his first cousin, Emma Wedgwood. Ironically, Darwin was one of the first experimentalists who demonstrated the negative effects of inbreeding in plant species. These experiments made him worry about the health of his own children because three of his ten children died at age ten or younger. Charles Darwin was a leading participant in the nineteenth-century discussion about the biological effects of close kin marriage. He attempted to convince the parliament that the prevalence of first-cousin marriages should be determined in the 1871 census. His proposal was refused on the grounds that any formal inquiry would be unacceptably intrusive (Bittles 2004).

Berra et al. (2010) have investigated the Darwin/Wedgwood families in which several marriages occurred between close relatives. They conclude from their findings that Darwin's children were subject to a moderate level of inbreeding.

Table 5.1 Types of genetic relationships between relatives

Family relationship	Genetic relationship	Fraction of genes in common	Coefficient of inbreeding (F) in progeny
Incestuous	First degree	1/2	0.25
Uncle–niece	Second degree	1/4	0.125
Double first cousin		1/4	0.125
First cousin	Third degree	1/8	0.0625
First cousin once removed	Fourth degree	1/16	0.0313
Double second cousin		1/16	0.0313
Second cousin	Fifth degree	1/32	0.0156

Source: Bittles (2004)

The genetic disadvantages of preferential marriages between relatives are held to be offset by the social and economic advantages. The advantages consist in strengthening family relationships and keeping property in the family, including landholdings. People consider marrying a partner whose family background is known as favourable for successful and stable unions. High rates of first-cousin marriages are reported in rural areas among the poorest and least-educated parts of society (Bittles 2004). Historic examples of brother–sister marriages have been reported in the royal dynasties of prehistoric Egypt. It was believed that the royal bloodline would be strengthened by brother–sister marriages. But we are not sure whether these marriages were sexual relationships. What we know is that 'some Ptolemies (that is, Greek rulers remaining in Egypt after the death of Alexander the Great) followed Pharaonic custom and married their own sisters, beginning with the marriage of Ptolemy II ('Sister Lover') to his older sister Arsinoe II in about 276 BC' (Von Staden 1989: 29).

In discussions about the dangers of reproductive relationships between close relatives, two terms are often used: incest avoidance and incest taboo. This may cause confusion. Many animals recognise and rule out close kin, despite the need of individuals to mate with their own species. If incest avoidance were completely effective, taboos would be superfluous. So, avoidance and taboo are two different things (Konner 2010). First, cultures contain religious and legal rules, prohibiting things that people tend to do. Second, cultures share some forbidden mating relationships (e.g. parent–offspring) while others are variable (e.g. first cousins). As degree of relatedness cannot explain this cross-cultural variation, we should conclude that cultures may reinforce as well as relax basic avoidance tendencies between close relatives.

Inbreeding avoidance and dispersal

dispersal
the tendency of an organism to move away, either from its birth site (natal dispersal) or breeding site (breeding dispersal).

Inbred animals show lower survival and are subject to deleterious consequences such as sterility. As inbreeding is costly, it follows that natural selection would favour mechanisms of inbreeding avoidance which put physical distance between close relatives or prevent mating between relatives who live together. How do animals avoid inbreeding? Almost all species vulnerable to inbreeding depression use different ways to avoid incest (Pusey and Wolf 1996). **Dispersal** of individuals from their natal group or site is widespread among mammals and birds, and has also been documented in fish, amphibians, reptiles and insects. Dispersal patterns separate close relatives and thus prevent them becoming breeding partners.

In all primate species, individuals disperse away from the group in which they were born and emigrate to another group to breed. Thus dispersal generates outbreeding and prevents inbreeding among close relatives. Dispersal did evolve as a response to inbreeding but it is also a means to reduce competition for food, territory and sexual partners. Nevertheless, inbreeding avoidance is its main function. If males stay in their natal group, they are in the position to commit incest with their mother. If females stay in their original group, incestuous contacts may occur between father and daughter. Primate dispersal patterns constrain incest opportunities.

philopatry
the tendency of individuals to return to or stay in its home area (e.g. male birds and female mammals tend to be more philopatric than the opposite sex).

Which sex disperses? Ultimately, dispersal patterns depend on the relative costs and benefits of dispersal. Generally, females are likely to suffer higher costs from inbreeding depression than males because of their larger investment in offspring and their limited breeding potential. There are also costs other than those of inbreeding, which make it better for females to stay at home. Females and their offspring benefit more than males from familiarity with food resources and nesting sites in their natal environment. This would favour female **philopatry**, that is, the tendency of the female sex to stay in their home area (Pusey 1987).

Young individuals, in all primate species, leave their natal group before they reach their adult size and join another group. Dispersal patterns are sex-biased. In the lemurs of Madagascar, and in most monkey species, the males emigrate. In red colobus monkeys, hamadryas baboons, gorillas and chimpanzees, it is the females who leave and join other groups for breeding. In howler monkeys of Central and South America, both sexes depart (Wilson 1998; Pusey 2004).

Inbreeding avoidance and kin recognition

Kin recognition is another way to avoid inbreeding. Recognition of close relatives may use different mechanisms (Pusey 2004). One mechanism is phenotype matching in which individuals match cues such as odour from other individuals to cues from themselves or their relatives, using the degree of similarity to determine the degree of kinship. Experiments in various species demonstrate that animals match the odours in the urine to odours of their parents and choose mates that differ from their parents.

Olfactory cues for recognising kin may also be at work in humans. In one study (Weisfeld et al. 2003), family members were asked to wear T-shirts on two consecutive nights, and avoid using perfumes or scented soaps. Later on, they were asked to smell the shirts and identify who had worn each shirt, and whether they found the odour aversive. Most family members were able to identify the shirts worn by genetic relatives. The patterns of aversion were interesting from the point of view of incest avoidance. Mothers did not show any aversion. Fathers and daughters considered each other's odours aversive. Brothers and sisters showed aversions to each other's odors as well, but same-sex siblings displayed no aversions. The only cases in which aversions were mutual (father–daughter and brother–sister) represent the greatest danger of incest.

Another mechanism for recognising kin is association or familiarity in which individuals treat others as relatives with whom they had a close association when growing up. The core of kinship is the mother–offspring bond which generates kin recognition. Familiarity between siblings (brothers, sisters) and others is acquired after birth and in relation to the mother (Chapais 2008). For example, a daughter will recognise her sister as that particular individual she meets on a daily basis near her mother and with whom she becomes familiar. And when the mother has close contact with other individuals, the daughter treats them as close relatives, whether or not they actually are. The implication is that mating among these individuals is inhibited.

Edward Westermarck (1891), in his study about the history of human marriage, first proposed to explain incest avoidance by the mechanism of familiarity. Experiments in which the degree of familiarity was manipulated, show that association often has a stronger effect than real kinship. Anne Pusey (2004) refers to experiments in rodent species in which relatives are raised apart and non-relatives raised together. The findings show that individuals raised apart prefer each other as mates over those that are reared together, regardless of relatedness.

Inbreeding avoidance in a natural experiment

The power of familiarity to inhibit sexual attraction has also been demonstrated by a natural experiment in humans. Arthur Wolf (1995) studied marriage practices in Taiwan which provided a natural experiment, testing Westermarck's hypothesis. During the late nineteenth and early twentieth centuries, Taiwanese parents practised two forms of arranged marriage for their children: 'major marriage' and 'minor marriage'. In the major form of marriage, the parents of both bride and groom arranged the union and the two did not meet until the day of marriage. In the minor form of marriage, the bride as a young girl was adopted into the family of her future husband. This practice was meant to let the daughter-in-law adjust and more readily subordinate to her future mother-in-law. Because the future husband and wife were unrelated, their relationship was not incestuous, even though the boy and his future bride grew up as brother and sister in the family.

Wolf studied the records from over 14,000 women between the years 1905 and 1945 and compared marriage in the major and minor fashion. The results of his study favoured Westermarck's original hypothesis that familiarity in childhood weakens sexual attraction in adulthood. Wolf (1995) found that when the future wife was adopted before her third birthday, she resisted later marriage with her intended husband. The parents often had to coerce the couple to consummate the marriage. The minor marriages ended three times more often than major marriages in divorce, and generated 40 per cent fewer children. Women in minor marriages more often committed adultery than in major marriages. And men were more often reported to resort to prostitutes and have extramarital affairs.

Wolf's findings about the impact of childhood association on sexual attraction, suggest that in minor marriages the age of the younger partner at the time of adoption predicts sexual inhibition. His explanation is that the younger partner forms an attachment to the older partner, as well as other caregivers in the family, while at the same time developing anti-sexual feelings towards them. In a recent publication, Wolf (2004) takes a more evolutionary point of view towards inbreeding avoidance. The question is, then, why natural selection produces the opposite effects of association and aversion. He concludes that the dispositions underlying attachment and aversion had to evolve together: 'The fact that attachments and sexual aversions both form more readily before age three than after is not coincidental. They are the same thing' (2004: 90).

Mechanisms to regulate sibling sexual aversions

In rethinking the Taiwanese minor marriages from an evolutionary point of view, Debra Lieberman (2009) proposes a model of human inbreeding avoidance that takes into account the social environments of our ancestors and the kinds of kinship cues that natural selection may have shaped for inbreeding avoidance. Her suggestion is that the mind uses two mechanisms to regulate sibling sexual aversions.

The first mechanism is childhood co-residence duration, referring to the period in which young siblings share parental care with older siblings. This mechanism can be used by younger siblings in recognising older siblings. The second mechanism is maternal–neonatal association which refers to a sibling's exposure to one's mother caring for a newborn (e.g. breastfeeding a baby). Older siblings can use this mechanism for recognising younger siblings. It is not available to younger siblings because the arrow of time makes it impossible for them to see their older siblings being breastfed and cared for when they were young. For that reason, the mind should fall back on co-residence duration to assess probable relatedness when the stronger cue of exposure to maternal care is not present.

Considering exposure to maternal care as the stronger cue, Lieberman et al. (2007) predict that the effects of the two mechanisms on sexual aversion differ for younger siblings detecting older siblings and older siblings recognising younger siblings. A series of studies on college students support this prediction. For individuals exposed to their mother caring for their older sibling, there was no correlation between childhood co-residence duration and aversion to sibling incest. However, for individuals who were not exposed to their mother caring for a younger sibling, childhood co-residence duration did predict the intensity of aversion with sibling incest. In as far as the intensity of aversion is concerned, older siblings exposed to their mother caring for a younger sibling, reported intense levels of disgust towards sibling sex across all durations of co-residence. However, for individuals for whom this cue of exposure was unavailable, disgust towards sex with their older siblings started low and increased gradually, reaching at the age of 15 the level of aversion reported by older siblings who were exposed to mother's care for a baby.

What are the implications for the Taiwanese minor marriages? Lieberman (2009) points out that, as indicated by Wolf, most girls were adopted before the age of four and were likely nursed by their adoptive mother. Adoptive mothers considered nursing of their future daughter-in-law as very important because it affected the quality of their later relationship. When older husbands were exposed to the stronger cue of exposure to one's mother caring for a newborn, their aversions should have been intense, regardless of their age at the time of adoption. In Figure 5.1 the fertility index was calculated as the number of births for women between the ages of 15 and 45 years divided by the number of years the women were married during this time.

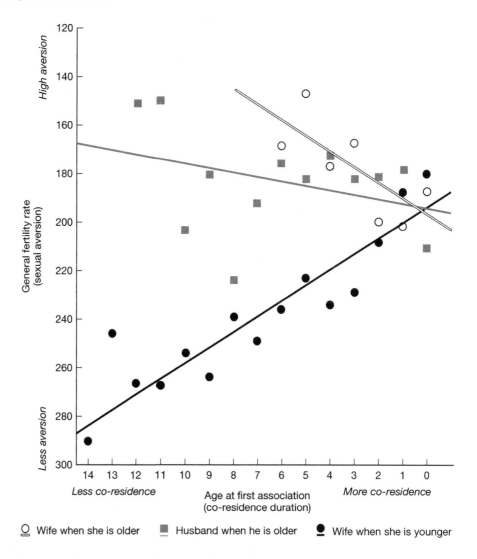

Figure 5.1 Co-residence duration and sexual aversion
Source: Lieberman (2009)

These data support the prediction that the younger and older members of a pair raised as siblings rely on different mechanisms to assess relatedness and regulate the development of sexual aversion.

When females were the older partners, the same pattern applies. As most adopted girls were breastfed by their adoptive mothers, it is likely that young brides would regard them as their real, biological mothers. After a female's future husband was born, she would see that her mother nursed him. Thus, the exposure to maternal–neonatal association indicated that the newborn was a close genetic relative for whom she would develop feelings of sexual aversion. When females were the younger marriage partners, longer co-residence predicts decreased fertility, indicating that each year of living with her future husband made her more certain about their relatedness and would increase her sexual aversion.

5.3 Origin of the human family

In Chapter 4 we pointed out that precursors of the genus *Homo* had a mating system which consisted of males living with a small number of females within a large multi-male, multi-female group. The transition from polygynous units to monogamous pairs would require a reduced number of females associated with each male and gradually replace the prevailing mating system of polygyny. The tendency of men and women to form long-lasting relationships for the production of offspring would then be present in the earliest members of the genus *Homo* (around 2–2.5 mya). Since then, most humans now live in monogamous families while a minority can afford to live in polygynous families. Why precisely did the human family originate? Let us first define what we mean by families.

Defining families

In order to explore parallels between human and non-human families, Stephen Emlen (1995, 1997) defines families as those cases where offspring continue to interact regularly, into adulthood, with their parents. This, typically, occurs when offspring delay dispersal and continue to reside with one or both parents past the age of sexual maturity. Emlen further distinguishes between 'simple' families in which only a single female breeds, and 'extended' families in which two or more females or pairs reproduce. So the presence of a breeding male is not considered to be essential to the definition of a family. When the male is present, the family is called 'biparental' as both mother and father share parental care. When the male is absent, the family is called 'matrilineal' because only the female provides parental care.

Where do we find family-living species?

Early humans lived in groups consisting of multiple generations of family members. Sexually mature offspring continued to live at home and reproduce in their natal family groups, which contained their parents and siblings (Emlen 1995, 1997). Humans are often compared to other primates, especially great apes such as chimpanzees, but the majority of them don't live in extended family groups. Males and females do not form pair-bonds, same-sex young emigrate to another group, and males provide minimal child care, if any. So, non-human primates aren't necessarily the best model of early familial organisation in humans.

Where do we find animals living in family groups, similar to those of early humans, providing insight into the origin of family formation? Such animals are rare as only 3 per cent of bird and mammalian (including human) species are known to live in family groups (Emlen 1995). Various species of mammals and birds live in families which combine long-term pair-bonds with prolonged parental care for offspring. Mammal species with a family life include canids (e.g. wolves, wild dogs, jackals), viverids (mongooses), and some rodents (e.g. naked mole-rats). Among the bird species that live in families, are jays, swans and geese (Emlen 1997).

Better comparisons may thus be found in bird and mammal species which form extended family groups. In these groups, breeders are likely to form pair-bonds, males contribute substantially to child care, and multiple generations – parents, offspring, and even grandparents — live together (Solomon and Hayes 2009). We will focus on parallels between long-lived bird and human species.

Delayed reproduction and family formation

life-history theory
a branch of evolutionary biology, dealing with trade-offs in the allocation of time and resources over the lifespan of an organism.

The key to explaining the origin of families is understanding the causes of delayed dispersal and reproduction (Emlen 1995; Davis and Daly 1997). We saw in the previous section that in most species, individuals at the onset of sexual maturity disperse away from their natal group and emigrate to another group to breed. Dispersal evolved as a solution to avoid inbreeding as well as to reduce competition for food, territory and sexual partners. The point in this section is that families originate when offspring postpone reproduction and remain for longer with their parents (Covas and Griesser 2007). Thus, delay of dispersal and independent reproduction is an exception to the rule. Studies reveal that family living occurs more frequently among long-lived bird species. This finding provides an important link to **life-history theory** which predicts that long-lived species should benefit from a delayed onset of reproduction.

Life-history theory is a branch of evolutionary biology, dealing with trade-offs in the allocation of time and resources over the lifespan of an organism (e.g. Kaplan and Gangestad 2005). Organisms are supposed to maximise their lifetime reproductive success but in doing so they face trade-offs. As an example, in daily life we have a finite budget and should therefore balance the purchase of luxury items against necessary items. When producing offspring, parents face similar trade-offs between quantity and quality, or between present and future reproduction. The life histories of animals show that some species develop slowly and are long-lived, while other species develop fast and are short-lived. In short-lived species, reproduction starts early in life and offspring disperse quickly to breed independently. By contrast, long-lived species may benefit from delaying dispersal and independent reproduction.

Covas and Grieser (2007) argue that slow life histories predispose animals to family living, given the intrinsic tendency to favour future over present reproduction, and the possibility of long-lived parents to prolong investment in offspring. This has been supported by studies that demonstrate a positive effect of reproductive delay on reproductive success. Consequently, delayed onset of independent reproduction combined with extended parental investment can select for the maintenance of family living. A proposed pathway towards family formation in birds, and possibly in humans, can be seen in Figure 5.2. Species with slow life histories tend to start breeding later in life and can invest more in offspring. These two factors can cause offspring to delay dispersal leading to family formation. Resource availability allows parents to extend their investment in offspring.

How childhood affects reproduction in later life

Humans are long-lived species, postponing dispersal and independent reproduction after they have reached sexual maturity, and therefore predisposed to live in families. The lengthy childhood and adolescence of children that delays reproduction is much longer than for other primates. An extended childhood appears to be useful for acquiring the knowledge and skills that intense social species like humans need for a successful adulthood. How does childhood influence reproductive behaviour in later life?

In life-history theory, much depends on the attachment between child and parents (e.g. Chisholm 1999). Attachment is considered an innate motivation system with the evolved function of protecting the child from danger and stimulating the

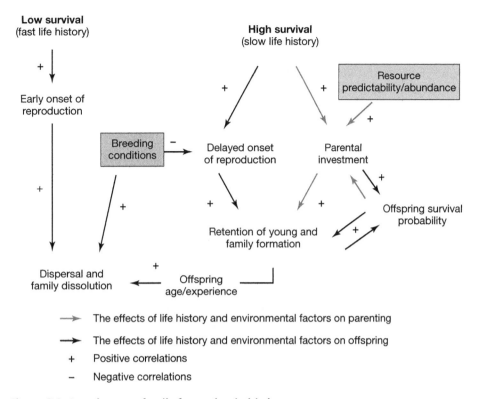

Figure 5.2 A pathway to family formation in birds

Source: Covas and Griesser (2007)

caregiver to provide care. Secure attachment should lead to reproductive strategies based on late maturation and high parental investment; insecure attachment should lead to strategies based on early maturation and low parental investment. Children who stay longer with their parents use the family environment as a cue to guide their later reproductive decisions in adulthood. When they grow up in stressful environments – e.g. lower-income family, single-parent family, poor relationship with parent(s) – they don't delay dispersal and reproduction but reproduce early.

Children who experience a rejecting caregiver, develop an insecure and avoidant attachment, meaning that they avoid physical contact and don't ask for help or comfort (Weinfield et al. 1999). They adopt a minimising strategy because any signal of need would result in further rejection. As adults, these children make shorter estimates of their own life expectancy and are focused on current reproduction (e.g. teenage mothers). About 25 per cent of infants in Western samples are classified as insecure. If children have a caregiver who empathises with their needs, they develop a secure attachment. They use their caregiver as a stable base when they need help or comfort. As adults, they prefer future instead of current reproduction, and tend to invest highly in parenting. In European and North American samples, the proportion of secure infants is about 65 per cent (Del Giudice 2009).

If the caregiver alternates between acceptance and rejection, children are expected to develop an ambivalent attachment. They are easily distressed and may ask strongly for help and comfort, but at the same time protesting to maintain a close relationship with the caregiver. They adopt a maximising strategy by exaggerating their signals of need which are meant to control the caregiver's behaviour. The proportion of ambivalent infants is about 10 per cent.

Humans reproduce late and go through a prolonged period of reproductive immaturity which is lacking in other primates. Del Giudice (2009) argues that in the lengthy childhood of humans, it is the middle childhood (approx. age 7 to 11 years) which shows a sex-specific reorganisation of reproductive strategies. In this period, the peer group becomes the child's primary social world, and same-sex encounters rise to high levels. The main influence on this period comes from intrasexual competition in the peer group.

Empirical studies in middle childhood show that insecure children aged 10 to 11 years, were more likely to violate gender boundaries by flirting, physical contact and sexual gestures. Insecure boys adopted an avoidant strategy which is associated with aggression, self-reliance, and inflated self-esteem. These traits characterise a male, high-risk strategy which favours current reproduction and high mating effort. Insecure girls adopted an anxious/ambivalent strategy which is focused on maximising investment from parents and potential mates. This strategy favours current reproduction and high mating effort as well (Figure 5.3). In Figure 5.3 the term 'adrenarche' refers to the beginning of the developmental phase known as adrenal puberty. Adrenal androgens are hormones which are secreted in the bloodstream at about 6 years of age. They can drive development along sex-specific pathways.

5.4   When mothers needed assistance

Female care is the rule

monotremes

egg-laying mammals comprising the duck-billed platypus and the echidnas, or spiny ant-eaters.

Most animals provide no parental care, other than nutrients in the egg. Among the ones that do, female care is often the rule and male care the exception (Box 5.2 Definition of parental care, investment and effort). In birds, biparental care is the most common form of care. In mammals, care is mostly provided by females. Sometimes males provide additional care in the form of carrying, protecting or feeding the young. Humans belong to the class of mammals which emerged around 225 mya. Being a mammal (from 'mammae' or breasts) implies nourishing young from milk glands. In **monotremes** – a subclass of egg-laying mammals – breasts are dispersed over the chest and abdomen rather than in pairs of distinctive organs, enabling the young to feed simply by licking the mother's skin. Thus, milk glands are modified sweat glands. Specific physiological adaptations for feeding in mammals preceded live birth in placental mammals (Konner 2010).

As indicated above, parental care in mammals is mainly female care but a minority of males provide additional care. It doesn't follow from this that human males only give additional care. Early humans probably fitted this pattern, but over time males have evolved into child-caring partners. In this regard, humans are more like most birds in which biparental care prevails.

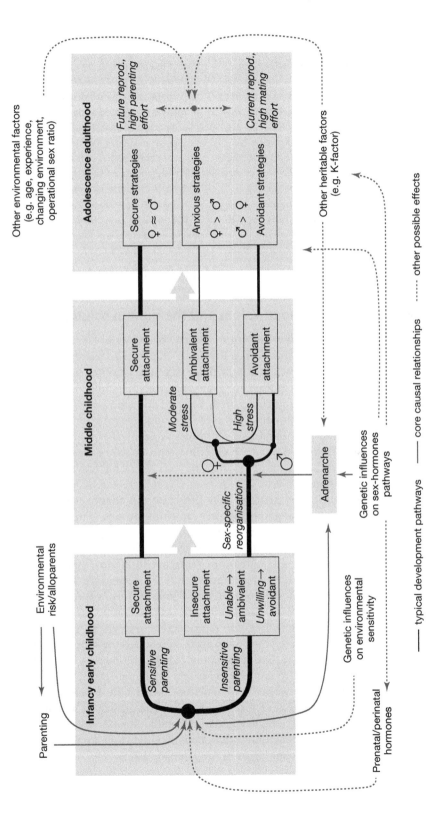

Figure 5.3 Development of reproductive strategies

Source: Del Giudice (2009)

BOX 5.2 Definition of parental care, investment and effort

Studies of parental care evolution use different terms. **Parental care** refers commonly to any form of parental behaviour that is likely to increase the fitness of a parent's offspring. In a broad sense, and applied to humans, this care includes buying or renting a house, producing eggs and sperm, feeding milk, providing school materials, and so on. The term parental care is descriptive and has no implications about costs in terms of required energy or missed mating opportunities. Recall that there is another term which does carry these implications, that is, **parental investment**, referring since Trivers' original definition (1972) to any characteristics or actions of parents that increase the fitness of their offspring at the cost of the parent's ability to invest in other offspring (Clutton-Brock 1991). Parental investment usually refers to parental care of individual offspring, while care for all progeny is designated as **parental effort**. Parental effort plus mating effort are the organism's **reproductive effort**. In general, males are focused on mating effort, females on parental effort. Recall Bateman's principle which holds that males increase their reproductive success more with each additional partner than females. Finally, what remains after reproductive effort is **somatic effort**, that is, the resources (e.g. calories) devoted to physical growth and to maintenance of the physical system during childhood and adulthood.

The great ape problem and the human solution

From a reproductive point of view, primates are exceptional mammals. While pigs and cats have large litters of piglets and kittens, most primate mothers produce just one child at a time. A young chimpanzee, for example, completely depends on its mother for transportation and milk during its first four years of life. The characteristic birth interval for chimpanzees is between five and six years. The combination of a low reproductive rate, long birth interval, and a long childhood puts them at a reproductive disadvantage, compared with other mammals. As the chimpanzee's lifetime reproductive success is constrained, the only solution that remains is offspring survival. This may explain why they are very careful parents.

A mechanical analogy may illustrate the adaptive problem facing long-lived, slow-reproducing species such as chimpanzees (Fitch 2010). Lengthening the interval between births, the **gestation** period, the period of sexual maturity, or the period of infant dependency, decreases reproductive potential. Such changes must be balanced by a compensatory increase in lifetime (Figure 5.4). Humans achieve a higher reproductive capacity mainly by decreasing the birth interval (i.e. shifting the birth interval to the left in Figure 5.4) from 5–6 years (chimpanzees) to 2–3 years.

Early humans solved the reproductive problem of great apes by having babies every two to three years. Why don't chimpanzee mothers wean earlier? (Box 5.3 The weaning conflict). Earlier **weaning** reduces the chances of child survival and makes young less able to compete with other chimpanzees. The big difference is that the human mother weans her child from breast milk much earlier. The reason is that the unique pattern of prolonged early brain growth in humans cannot be sustained much beyond one year by a mother's milk alone. Early weaning – when accommodated by more nutritious adult foods, derived from animal protein – was vital to the development of our larger brain (Kennedy 2005).

gestation
the development of the embryo and foetus in the uterus until birth.

weaning
the process of reducing an offspring's dependence on its mother or parents, particularly with respect to feeding.

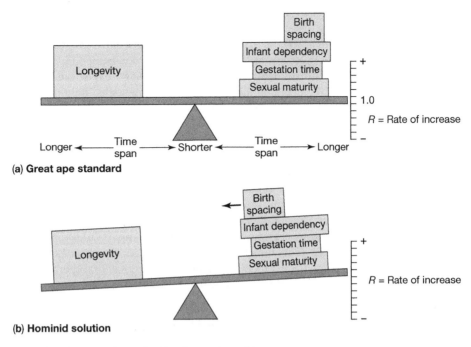

*Hominid = humans plus extinct fossil ancestors of humans

Figure 5.4 The great ape reproductive problem and the human solution
Source: Fitch (2010)

BOX 5.3 The weaning conflict

Weaning is the breaking of an offspring's dependence on its mother or parents, particularly with respect to feeding. In mammals, lactation is an energetically expensive form of parental care. For primate females, energy requirements are raised somewhere between 20 to 50 per cent during lactation. Nursing is one of the clearest forms of parental investment, as defined by Trivers (1972) because it increases the chance of the offspring's survival and decreases the parent's ability to produce and care for future offspring. It often occurs that the young persist in attempting to be get fed when the parent begins to hold back. For example, during weaning, infant macaques can no longer elicit maternal responses and produce hundreds of diverse and ongoing sounds even when ignored for only a few minutes. Weaning is not the absolute denial of milk but the gradual shifting of the conditions under which the infant is granted the nipple. To the extent that nursing does not satisfy the demands

of the child, conflict arises between mother and child. The mother may simply deny access to the breast by blocking the chest with an arm or by running away. The child may respond by whimpering, moaning or tantrums (Nicolson 1987).

In evolutionary biology, the weaning conflict is an example of the parent–offspring conflict which holds that there is a confrontation between the interests of young animals and their parent(s). The young are supposed to obtain the greatest possible parental investment while the parent must restrict such investment in order to maximise further reproductive effort. Thus, maternal rejection and weaning conflict are directly related to mating opportunities and the timing of the mother's next conception. In the higher mammals (e.g. chimpanzees, humans), weaning is sometimes a lengthy process involving behavioural changes on both sides, with the parent taking the active part as a rule.

When meat was in short supply, humans probably also obtained protein from nuts, insect grubs and shellfish. The omega-3 fatty acids in these foods would be critical for the fast-growing brains of women's foetuses (Hrdy 2009). In many traditional cultures, mothers offer their weaned children premasticated food, a mode of nourishment, known as 'kiss-feeding', which facilitated early weaning (Konner 2010). The availability of cow's milk in settled hunter-gatherer societies enabled the decline of weaning age as well. Finally, the control of fire and the invention of cooking would also allow much earlier weaning as cooked food, being soft, is easier to digest by infants (Wrangham 2009).

When the early human mother had weaned her child from breast milk, she gave birth to another child, and was raising two or more children at the same time. In a situation of abundant, reliable food, and help with child care, this works well. But it doesn't apply to the situation of chimpanzees. Fruiting trees are not continuously abundant, and access to alternative sources of food requires mastery of advanced skills, such as nut-cracking or ant-fishing. In addition, chimpanzee mothers cannot count on males who may hunt for meat, but mainly keep it for themselves. In short, chimpanzee foraging practices don't provide mothers with abundant food, making early weaning not an option (Fitch 2010).

Alloparental care and the theory of inclusive fitness

In most primates, males provide little or no child care because they have no exclusive, sexual relationships. The implication is that a male doesn't know who his offspring is. Given paternity uncertainty, he has no incentive to provide additional child care. As early human mothers could not feed and raise offspring alone, their need for assistance was typically resolved by alternative caregivers. This form of assistance is known as **alloparental care** (alternative terms are: allomaternal care, allocare, allomothering, aunting). An alloparent (from the Greek 'allo' for 'other than') may be defined as any member of the group, other than the genetic parent(s), who helps rear the young. Alloparents are mostly close relatives (e.g. sisters, older siblings, aunts, grandmothers) and sometimes unrelated individuals (e.g. female and male friends).

alloparental care

a form of assistance in care for offspring by any member of the group, other than the genetic parent(s), who helps rear the young (e.g. sisters, older siblings, aunts, grandmothers).

Alloparental care appears to be paradoxical because care of offspring that is not your own, is costly. This cost may reduce an individual's ability to produce or rear its own offspring. That is why biologists are interested in species where members of a group assist in raising young which they did not produce. Darwin (1859) was already intrigued by the assistance which sterile workers in ants, bees and wasps provide to offspring. In these insect species, the queen monopolises reproduction while workers are unable to reproduce themselves.

William Hamilton (1964) inspired the study of alloparental care by suggesting that individuals may engage in seemingly unselfish behaviour because they can gain fitness benefits by helping kin. Hamilton predicted that the likelihood of helping others should correspond to the degree to which individuals are related. Parents and their children share 50 per cent of their genes as do siblings; grandparents and grandchildren share 25 per cent of their genes as do half-siblings; and stepchildren and stepparents share no genes. His theory explained kin altruism by arguing that individuals contribute genetically to future generations in two ways: directly, through the production of their own offspring, and indirectly, through helping

inclusive fitness

a measure that combines (a) an individual's direct genetic contribution to future generations through its own offspring, with (b) the indirect contribution made by aiding the reproduction of relatives.

the reproduction of their relatives. The sum of direct and indirect fitness is called **inclusive fitness**. That is why Hamilton's theory is called the inclusive fitness theory.

His argument predicts that genetically determined behaviour which benefits another individual – although at some cost to the agent – will spread by natural selection when the relation $rB > C$ is satisfied (Hamilton's rule). This equation implies that the benefit of the recipient should outweigh the cost of the agent; where r = the degree of relatedness between agent and recipient, B = the benefit or improvement of individual fitness of the recipient caused by the behaviour, and C = the cost to the agent's individual fitness as a result of the behaviour. To put it briefly, altruistic helping will evolve whenever the cost to the helper is less than the fitness benefits of the one who receives the help.

Originally, eusocial ('true social') insects, such as ants and bees, were the major focus of study for inclusive fitness since Hamilton was an entomologist. The application of these investigations to the study of alloparental care in vertebrates (e.g. elephants, wild dogs, humans) was limited because insects and vertebrates differ biologically. In social insects, helping workers are sterile and stay in the nest but in vertebrates, the helpers can become rapidly reproductive when removed from their families. In vertebrates, alloparental care occurs only in a small percentage of birds and mammals.

According to the inclusive fitness theory, the degree of genetic relatedness predicts the amount of alloparental care. Consequently, we may expect that close relatives are more prone to give mothers additional child care than unrelated individuals. For example, Ashleigh Griffin and Stuart West (2003) made an analysis of fifteen bird species and three mammal species which showed that helping is biased towards kin: the greater the helping benefit, the greater the kin bias.

Genetic relatedness to mothers doesn't exclude other factors that maintain helping behaviour, such as mating opportunities for helpers or the potential to inherit the territory. This illustrates that it is not always clear where the help ends and exploitation of the young for the benefit of the helper begins (Hrdy 2009).

Among primate species, the amount of help is also associated with faster growth of infants and female reproductive rates. A comparative analysis of monkeys, apes and humans showed great variation among species in alloparental care and female reproductive rates (Ross and MacLarnon 2000). Species with high levels of alloparental care have young that grow faster and are weaned earlier than in species without extensive alloparental care. Assistance allows mothers shorter birth spacing and more rapid reproduction, a pattern that is typical for humans.

Grandmothers are a special class of alloparents

Sarah Blaffer Hrdy (2007, 2009) provides a comprehensive view of alloparental care in primates, particularly humans. Estimating that it takes 10 to 13 million calories of energy expenditure to raise a human child to adulthood, she argues that this cannot come from one person. In hunter-gatherer societies with high rates of mortality, children without alloparents would be significantly less likely to survive. In other words, alloparents were not just helpful; they were essential for maternal reproductive success. Hunter-gatherer mothers would be confronted with similar problems that working mothers face today, with the exception of the high rates of child mortality.

> **KEY FIGURE** Sarah Blaffer Hrdy
>
> Sarah Blaffer Hrdy was trained as an anthropologist and worked at the University of California, Davis. Her field research was focused on reproductive strategies in primates.
>
> **Selected works**
>
> *Infanticide: Comparative and Evolutionary Perspectives*, co-editor with Glenn Hausfater (1984).
>
> *Mother Nature: Natural Selection and the Female of the Species* (1999).
>
> *Mothers and Others: The Evolutionary Origins of Mutual Understanding* (2009).

menopause

progressive failure of the female reproductive organs, usually between 45 and 55 years.

Among the helpers at the nest, grandmothers are a special class of alloparents (Hawkes et al. 1998; Hrdy 2007; Konner 2010). Humans are the only primates where females live for decades beyond their reproductive capacity, and where grandmothers are engaged in child care. Great apes, such as gorillas and orangutans, reproduce until they die. They show no signs of **menopause**. In humans menopause occurs usually between 45 and 55 years. The immediate cause of menopause is that it results from a drastic decrease in woman's endocrine hormones – especially oestrogen – correlating with the fact that her ovaries run out of suitable eggs. Grandmothers may be at the end of their reproductive period but they appear to be almost universally beneficial across societies in improving the fitness of their relatives. Studies show that the help of grandmothers, particularly maternal grandmothers, was beneficial for child survival (Sear and Mace 2008, 2009).

What remains unknown is the evolutionary 'why'. What is the evolutionary cause of menopause? Why would it be advantageous for humans to have an extended lifespan after menopause? Why do women, unlike most other species, lose the ability to reproduce when they still have decades of life to go? We cannot be certain that menopause evolved because of its fitness benefits. Inclusive fitness theory predicts that grandmothers can gain fitness benefits by helping to raise their daughters' offspring. But that doesn't explain why, in the course of human evolution, women were left with a long post-reproductive period. Sear and Mace (2008) conclude that most attempts to build quantitative models, in which women can compensate for lost fertility by improving the fitness of children and grandchildren, have failed to find fitness benefits sufficiently large enough to favour menopause at 50 years.

The emergence of paternal child care

As long as alloparents were wiling to alleviate the burden of mothers, fathers had no incentive to step in. If males provide care, it may even benefit themselves (Hrdy 2009; Konner 2010) (see Box 5.4 When child care is selfish).

In most primates, males provide little or no child care because they have no exclusive, sexual relationships. Consider chimpanzees, living in multi-male, multi-female

BOX 5.4 When child care is selfish

- Male monkeys and apes may associate with the infants of dominant mothers to gain protection or higher rank.

- Male monkeys and apes do not routinely care for infants but may retrieve and guard them as part of group defence.

- Males occasionally 'babysit' or adopt an infant, not necessarily for the offspring's benefit. Caring for infants may be a way of courting their mothers or easing their way into the new troop.

- Males may use infants in 'agonistic buffering'. They protect themselves from aggression by carrying infants, improving their position in large, hierarchical groups.

- Males may guard young females against other males. Once sexually mature, the females become members of the males' breeding harems.

Source: Adapted from *The Evolution of Childhood: Relationships, Emotion, Mind*, Belknap Press (Konner, M. 2010).

groups where females copulate with a large number of males, if not all group males, and at high frequencies. It has been estimated that female chimpanzees copulate between 400 and 3,000 times per conception, and female bonobo's between 1,800 and 12,100 times per conception (Wrangham 1993). What is more, consistent, long-term preferential relationships between males and females have not been observed in either species.

Since mother–offspring recognition is well-established in chimpanzees and bonobos, but father–offspring recognition is not, males don't know who their offspring are (Chapais 2008). How could paternal child care, then, emerge? The emergence of male parenting is associated with three factors: the certainty of paternity, the cost of lost mating opportunities, and the benefits to offspring (Geary 2000, 2005a, 2010).

Paternity certainty

monogamy
one-male, one-female mating system in which each sex has a single mate for life.

The most reliable way to get paternal care for children is when males are confident about their paternity. We may therefore predict that if the certainty of paternity is high, then selection will favour paternal investment. Certainty may be acquired through pair-bonding. In many species **monogamy** indeed overlaps with paternal care (Clutton-Brock 1991). Monogamy, which has evolved several times independently – in some primates, most canids, some rodents and many birds – is a mating system that offers high paternity certainty. This is consistent with the argument in Chapter 4 – about mating systems in human evolution – which holds that in most monogamous species, paternal care evolved after pair-bonding was developed (Chapais 2008). Paternal care was therefore not a necessary condition for the evolution of pair-bonding. Instead, pair-bonding emerged first and then provided paternity certainty. It originated as a mating strategy to monopolise one female, the same strategy that harem-holding primates practise with regard to multiple females.

If pair-bonding initially evolved as a way for a male to monopolise one female, what was in it for the female? Why would they evolve to bond with the male? Primate studies support the claim that long-term breeding bonds enable father–offspring recognition and favour the evolution of paternal care. Chapais (2008) proposes looking at the gorilla, our close relative that exhibits stable breeding bonds. Most gorilla groups include a single male living permanently with multiple females and their

infanticide

the killing of young by conspecifics (members of the same species). This practice occurs mainly in two situations. In adverse environmental circumstances the perpetrators may be the parents, a situation which has been most often reported in birds of prey. In non-human primates, infanticide may create breeding opportunities for males that have limited sexual access to fertile females. Infants are attacked only by strange adult males, never by males who might be their fathers.

genetic monogamy

male–female pair reproducing exclusively with one another. All offspring produced are from the pair.

offspring. To avoid **infanticide** by strange males, females form a lasting bond with a powerful male with whom they reproduce. Father–offspring recognition is evident from altruistic behaviours like defence against predators, protection against strange males, remarkable tolerance towards infants, and interventions in infants' quarrels.

Monogamy promises high paternity certainty, but recall from Chapter 4 (Box 4.4 Different forms of monogamy) that there is a difference between sexual monogamy (an exclusive sexual relationship between a male and a female); **genetic monogamy** (all offspring produced are from the male–female pair, as confirmed by DNA analyses), and social monogamy (a male and female's social living arrangement with shared use of a territory, shared care of offspring, and the like). So, how confident are men about their paternity? Actual paternity – that is, the state of being the genetic father of a child – and paternity confidence – that is, a man's own evaluation of whether he is the genetic father of a child – may not be identical. Some men may be certain that they are the father when they are not, while other men may doubt whether they are when they actually are.

Today, non-paternity is measured through DNA-paternity tests which prove that a man is not the father of a child. How common is non-paternity? In all fairness, we don't know. Neither do we know much about men's own assessment of paternity. When a woman becomes pregnant and a man is informed he is the father, he probably uses cues of her behaviour around the time she would have conceived as a guide to whether he is likely to be the father. He is more likely to have low paternity confidence if the pregnancy was unplanned or if the couple was unmarried.

Several studies found that the mother's relatives are more likely than the father's relatives to say that the new baby looks like the father, probably reinforcing his paternity confidence (Daly and Wilson 1982; McLain et al. 2000). But whether children actually resemble fathers more than mothers is a matter of debate. One study found that men's investment in children is positively correlated with perceived resemblance to children, as a proxy for paternity confidence (Apicella and Marlowe 2004). A recent study found support for the hypothesis that men will be more likely to divorce women if they suspect or are sure that they are not the father of their wife's child (Anderson et al. 2007).

Mating opportunity costs

Paternity certainty is not sufficient to explain the evolution of men's parental investment. Another condition is that men reduce their mating effort in favour of parenting effort. Recall (from Box 5.2 Definition of parental care, investment and effort) that the organism's reproductive effort consists of two parts: mating effort and parenting effort. Men's shift towards parental effort was under the influence of women's reproductive strategies. One of these strategies is that women on average have an aversion to casual sex, given that men on average prefer more sexual partners than women. Thus more paternal effort devoted to offspring implies higher mating opportunity costs, that is, missed additional mating for men (Geary 2010).

The sex difference in casual sex becomes clear when males and females are asked for the meaning of romantic kissing. One study in a large sample of undergraduate students examined kissing in a casual and non-casual context. In a casual context, kissing may be used as a means to have sex. But in a non-casual context, kisses may serve as a means to maintain and assess the relationship between partners. Results showed that females consider kissing as an important device to assess whether a potential mate will be a suitable long-term partner. Males, on the other hand, appear to use kissing to increase the likelihood of having sex (Hughes et al. 2007).

Benefits to offspring

Certainty of paternity and reduced mating opportunities resulting from women's aversion to casual sex are not sufficient to explain the evolution of paternal care. The third condition is that children receive benefits from their father. A recent review of twenty-two studies of traditional societies (e.g. hunter-gatherer societies) examined whether a father's death influenced child mortality. It reveals that in 68 per cent of the studies, fathers had no apparent effect on child survival. The authors also looked at the effect of other relatives on child mortality and found that grandmothers are generally helpful. The presence of maternal grandmothers was associated with improved child survival in 69 per cent of studies, and paternal grandmothers in 53 per cent of the studies. Grandfathers of either side had no effect (Sear and Mace 2008).

Growth, development, maturation and well-being are other traits likely to be influenced by parental investment. For example, divorce results in increased aggressive behaviour of boys, early onset of sexual behaviour in boys and girls, and lowered educational achievement. One idea that has gained increasing support and attention over the past several decades is that paternal investment early in life may influence the timing of sexual maturity in children, as well as their adult reproductive strategies (Gray and Anderson 2010). A large number of studies have examined the relationship between father absence in childhood and earlier sexual maturity.

If fathers have poor relationships with their daughters, this may accelerate their sexual maturity resulting in premature pregnancies. This approach is used in life-history theory which we met above when answering the question how childhood affects later reproduction. Life-history theory may look at the factors that influence the onset of reproductive development. At what age do children reach sexual maturity? Which factors lead them to favour current reproduction over future reproduction? And particularly: what is the role of the father?

puberty
the physiological and mental transition from juvenility to adolescence, lasting about four years and involving the development of the secondary sexual characteristics and adolescent growth spurt.

Authors of the paternal investment theory suppose that girls detect cues about levels of paternal investment during approximately the first five years of life (e.g. Ellis 2004). Based on these cues, the timing of pubertal maturation and sexual behaviour takes place. Important cues include father presence, quality of father–daughter relationship interactions, and mother's attitude to men. Although there is consistent evidence that father absence predicts timing of daughter's timing of pubertal development, little is known whether cohesion and conflict in father–daughter relationship in early childhood predicts subsequent timing of **puberty**. Nor are we certain whether father absence is the real cause of early puberty.

An alternative explanation for the association between absent father and early puberty might be that it is a matter of shared genetics in that the fast maturation, low parental investment strategy runs in the family. As a result, fathers are often absent and daughters hit puberty early, but the former does not cause the latter. In her study *The Nurture Assumption* (1998: 309), Judith Harris argues 'that conflict-prone parents tend to have troublesome kids which may be due to the genes they share rather than the home they share'.

adrenarche
the onset of pre-pubertal development marked by the secretion of adrenal androgens (hormones) in the bloodstream at about 6 years of age. Adrenal puberty is a peculiar feature of human development, absent in most other mammalian species. It has only been documented in chimpanzees and gorillas which also undergo a prolonged juvenile phase before reproduction.

Recent findings show that less marital conflict, as reported by fathers, predicts later **adrenarche**, that is, the onset of adrenal puberty (Ellis and Essex 2007). Adrenarche is 'the awakening of the adrenal glands' when andrenal androgens are secreted in the bloodstream between 6 and 8 years of age. These hormones drive development along sex-specific pathways. The development of pubic hair, increased skeletal maturation, and body odour are thought to represent physiological manifestations of andrenal androgens (see also Figure 5.3).

On the other hand, greater supportiveness of the mother predicts later develop-ment of secondary sexual characteristics. This corresponds with the second phase of pubertal development, called **gonadarche**, at about 9 or 10 years of age, trigger-ing pubertal events such as maturation of primary sexual characteristics (ovaries) and full development of secondary sexual characteristics (pubic hair, breasts and genitals).

5.5 Parent–offspring conflict

gonadarche

the earliest gonadal changes of puberty in which the ovaries of girls and the testes of boys begin to grow and increase the production of the sex stereoids, especially estradiol and testosterone. Gonads are the organs (testes, ovaries) that make gametes, or reproductive cells. Gonadarche indicates true central puberty while adrenarche is an independent maturational process only loosely associated with complete puberty.

We have seen above that humans achieve a higher reproductive capacity mainly by decreasing the birth interval from 5–6 years (chimpanzees) to 2–3 years. This decrease could be realised because the human mother weans her child from breast milk much earlier. In general, weaning may be considered as a process in which off-spring is conditioned to care for itself. But termination of parental care may meet with resistance. Children may use temper tantrums to manipulate parents. When parental care decreases with the birth of a new sibling, children tend to exaggerate their own need, or pretend distress to receive more care (Salmon 2008). In apes, most weaning conflicts are about nursing and mother's resumption of mating. As wean-ing from milk progresses, young may display depression or regression to infantile behaviour such as whimpering. When mothers resume mating, juveniles may show mating harassment by screaming, threatening, or hitting the copulating partners (Maestripieri 2002).

The weaning conflict about nursing is an example of parent–offspring conflict. Nursing is one of the clearest forms of parental investment, as defined by Trivers (1972) because it increases the chance of the offspring's survival and decreases the parent's ability to produce and care for future offspring. Although parents and off-spring share common genes and experiences, weaning shows that their interests are not necessarily identical, and may conflict. That is the reason why Trivers (1974), in a classic paper, has argued that parent and offspring are expected to disagree over the period or amount of parental investment.

In classical evolutionary theory, parent–offspring relations in families were viewed from the standpoint of the parents. They were assumed to invest in a great number of surviving young, while offspring were assumed to be passive vehicles into which parents would put their care. But in the new view, offspring were considered as active individuals who wanted more care than the parents would like to give. For example, Paul Andrews (2006) found support for the hypothesis that dissatisfied adolescents use suicide attempts to leverage investment from their parents. The cur-rent view of the family is even one of conflict between all family members: parents versus offspring, father versus mother, and siblings with one another (Parker et al. 2002; Royle et al. 2004).

We focus on parents versus offspring. As parental protection, support and resources are limited, family dynamics are governed by conflicting interests. Unlike conflict between unrelated individuals, parent–offspring conflict is constrained by the genetic relatedness of parent and offspring. Parent and offspring are genetically related for 50 per cent. Based on the inclusive fitness theory and parental investment theory, parents are expected to continue investment in their young up to the point at which the cost, in terms of reproductive success, outweighs the benefits of increased survival for the current offspring. For, the more parents invest in current offspring, the less they have to invest in future offspring. In short, when the costs exceed the benefits, parents should stop investing in the current offspring and start to work on the next (Salmon 2008).

Factors affecting parental investment in offspring

Age of the child

One factor that influences parental investment in offspring is the age of the child. We may expect that the higher the age of the child, the greater the fitness pay-off from investing in older children. When times in the course of evolution are very tough, and one child must be sacrificed to save others, it is a cross-cultural universal that the youngest is the likeliest victim of infanticide (Box 5.5 Infanticide in animals). For example, Inuit people ('Eskimos'), living in the Arctic, left babies out in the snow, while in the Brazilian jungle undesired infants were left under the trees. In London in the 1860s, dead infants were a common sight in parks and ditches. In nineteenth-century Florence, unwanted children were abandoned or sent to wet nurses who neglected them. In the same period in France, thousands of infants were sent to wet nurses in the countryside, never to return (Scrimshaw 1984). Studies of homicides in the twentieth century indicate that older children are more valued than infants who are at a much higher risk (Daly and Wilson 1984, 1988a).

Offspring quality

A second factor that affects parental investment is offspring quality. Children born with a severe physical deformity or illness are at a higher risk of being killed. Reasons given in the historical and ethnographic literature for the killing of infants include lack of parental care, inadequate resources, gender bias (infants are not of the 'desired'

BOX 5.5 Infanticide in animals

Infanticide, the killing of unweaned young by conspecifics, is widespread among animals. In non-human primates (i.e. monkeys and apes), infanticide may create breeding opportunities for males that, as a consequence of male–male competition, have limited sexual access to fertile females (Palombit 1999). Infants are attacked only by strange adult males, and never by males who might be their fathers. The attacks occur when males from outside the breeding group take over the troop and drive out the resident male. This behaviour appears to be adaptive from the male point of view. By eliminating the offspring of his predecessor, the male induces the mother to ovulate again and sooner than she otherwise would have. The reason for the mother to go along with this behaviour is that postponing ovulation would put her at a disadvantage with other mothers in the group who breed with the infanticidal male (Hrdy 1999). Human mothers are unlikely to mate with an

individual who has killed her child. The big difference is that infanticidal primates living in multi-male, multi-female groups are promiscuous, having only temporary liaisons whereas humans have long-term relationships which are a powerful disincentive for infanticide.

Hrdy (2009) notes that grandmothers are the most active in defending infants attacked by infanticidal males. Systematic observations show that having a grandmother nearby has a significant impact on the childrearing success of younger kin. In a similar vein, pair-bonds in several polygynous primate species such as capuchin monkeys, mountain gorillas and savanna baboons have been explained as a defence against infanticide. An adult male, particularly one who probably has some paternity of an infant, may serve as an important ally for the mother whose young is at risk of being killed (Palombit 1999).

gender), and death of the mother. Evolutionary explanations of infanticide because of poor infant quality focus on the chances of surviving to reproductive maturity. Strategies for maximising reproductive success and minimising wasted parental effort, may then explain why 'poor quality' infants are killed at or around birth.

Daly and Wilson (1988a) examined in which circumstances parents choose not to raise a child. Assuming that parental psychology has been shaped by selection, they proposed three classes of circumstances in which parents are reluctant to invest in a particular child. The three classes refer to doubt (1) whether the child is their own, (2) whether the child will contribute to parental fitness even if carefully nurtured, and (3) whether extrinsic circumstances discourage child-rearing efforts such as food shortage, lack of social support and so on. By examining a sample of 60 societies from a database, infanticide was reported in a majority of them, and in 112 cases the reason was recorded. Eighty-seven per cent of the reasons fit the hypothesis that the child was not fathered by the woman's husband, the infant was deformed or ill, or the infant had bad chances of surviving and producing offspring due to being a twin, born too soon, or an unmarried mother.

Even when children are not of demonstrably poor quality at birth and people dispose of infants due to 'superstitious beliefs' (e.g. babies born feet first, multiple births, albinism, or birth anomalies such as red hair in black-haired populations), it has been proposed that the parents pursue an adaptive strategy in eliminating infants who are poor vehicles for parental investment (Hill and Ball 1996). Although infanticide may be considered an extreme phenomenon, it reveals the importance of a child's future prospects as predictors of parental investment.

Preference for boys or girls

A third factor that affects parental investment in offspring is the preference for boys or girls. To take an extreme example, China's 1990 census revealed that out of a total of 1.2 billion people, millions of girls that should have been counted seemed either not to have been born, or have been reported, or eliminated after birth. Instead of the normal sex ratio of 105 boys to 100 girls in human populations, the ratio was 111 to 100. The most likely reason for this deviation is that girls were eliminated through prenatal sex determination and subsequent abortion or neonaticide (Hrdy 1999). Female infanticide was practised long before China's one-child policy. In other parts of the world, female infanticide prevails as well (e.g. India, South America). Actually, the preference for boys is a widespread and ancient sex-bias. People reason that daughters depart at marriage, making resources devoted to rearing girls a waste of parental effort.

In 1973, Trivers and Willard published a paper that attempts to explain the sex-bias. Their suggestion is that natural selection will favour sex-biases in parental investment, deviating from the normal ratio, when an individual's capacity to raise offspring depends on its physical condition and/or access to resources. To be more specific, they propose that when (a) one sex has greater variance in lifetime reproductive success than the other sex, and (b) parents vary in their physical condition and/or access to resources, different preferences for male or female offspring are likely to evolve. Since males in many species can have more reproductive success by fertilising more females, mothers in good condition will influence their son's reproductive success more than will mothers in poor condition. They should therefore prefer to invest in sons rather than in daughters. In contrast, females have a lower variance in reproductive success because they are limited by their physiology in producing a large number of offspring during their lifetime. Mothers in poor condition should therefore prefer to invest in daughters as a safe bet.

Although many studies in many species have failed to support the Trivers–Willard hypothesis, some do support it. Studies of red deer show that the females form a dominance hierarchy based on their ability to displace other herd members from resources. Dominance rank correlates with physiological condition, meaning that more dominant females have better body condition and calf survival. Sons of high-ranking females had higher lifetime reproductive success than daughters. Researchers found that the higher a female's rank, the greater the proportion of males in her offspring (Clutton-Brock et al. 1986). Recent studies suggest that maternal dominance in mammals is underpinned by testosterone which enables the mother to influence or even control whichever sex it is best suited to raise. Female testosterone levels rise in response to environmental stressors such as shortage of food or den sites which increase the likelihood of the conception of a male (Grant 1998, 2003, 2007).

In humans, studies comparing native Hungarians and Hungarian Gypsies demonstrate sex-biased investment by parents (Bereczkei and Dunbar 1997, 2002). Gypsies have many more daughters than sons, compared to native Hungarians. As Gypsies are low in social status, Gypsy women are much more likely to marry up the social ladder than are men, and out-reproduce their Gypsy brothers. In marrying up with native Hungarians, Gypsy women also have healthier babies than Gypsy women who marry within their own group. In terms of nursing and providing education, they invest much more in their daughters than in their sons.

Degree of genetic relatedness

A fourth factor that influences parent–offspring conflict is the degree of genetic relatedness. We may predict that parents are sensitive to whether or not a child is their genetic child which may influence the amount of investment. A mother with children from both her previous and current marriage, is equally related to her children and may invest equally in them. But conflict may arise when her partner invests more in the children that are the product of their current marriage than in the children of her previous marriage. From the point of view of offspring, genetic children are related to two parents while stepchildren are related to one of the parents. This difference between siblings may lead to conflict over parental care as well.

Studies about step-parenting in humans reveal that the less genetically the parent is related to offspring, the lower the likely investment. In terms of financial resources, stepfathers invest less in their stepchildren than in their genetic children. It has been reported that genetic children were 5.5 times more likely to receive money for college than did stepchildren (Anderson et al. 2007; Hoffert and Anderson 2003). Parental investment in stepchildren may be terminated or, in rare cases, lead to physical abuse and even infanticide. Stepchildren are reported to run a higher risk of being physically abused or even killed than children who live with genetic parents (Daly and Wilson 1988b, 1998). And the risk is highest for children under two years of age. Recent studies support the finding that step-parents are far more likely to abuse and kill children than genetic parents. It should be emphasised that, although stepchildren are at a greater risk of homicide, abuse and reduced investment, the risk is still very low. Infants were at greatest risk of being killed by genetic mothers who had a mental illness and received short sentences, if convicted. Filicide – killing one's own child – by genetic fathers was accompanied by marital conflict, suicide and uxoricide, that is, killing of a wife (Harris et al. 2007).

How can the tendency to kill offspring be explained from an evolutionary psychological point of view? Male reproductive success may be associated with proprietary behaviour towards mates. Ancestral males are supposed to consider a mate as personal property which should be discouraged from making overtures to rivals. The sexually proprietary mind of men may be interpreted as an evolved response to the adaptive problems of mate retention and potential waste of paternal investment in offspring that is not one's own (Wilson et al. 1995; Daly and Wilson 1998). Sexual alienation of a mate would then in extreme cases result into maladaptive behaviour, that is, the killing of wife and children.

Mate preferences

Evolutionary studies often abstract from the fact that mate choice may be heavily influenced by parents, having different preferences than their children. Mate preferences may differ because parents and offspring are genetically related by 50 per cent, and thus do not always have identical genetic interests (Hamilton 1964; Trivers 1974). For example, parents and their children may share a preference for a mate with good genes indicators, but children will get the greatest genetic benefit from good genes traits because they share 50 per cent of their genes with their own children whereas the parents only share 25 per cent with those same children, that is, their grandchildren.

Parents can increase their genetic interests by improving the fitness of their children through influencing their mate choice. For example, Menelaos Apostolou (2007) analysed marriage types across hunter-gatherer societies – the earliest human societies and still persisting to some extent in remote regions – and classified them in four categories on the basis of who made the mating decision: parental arrangement, kin arrangement (e.g. brother, uncle), courtship with parental approval, and courtship (daughters find their own marriage partner). Results show that parents arrange most of the marriages while free choice (courtship) was the primary marriage type in only 4 per cent of the societies (Figure 5.5).

Parent–offspring conflicts about marriage partners are more apparent in societies with more material resources. Agricultural societies which emerged around 10,000 years ago, leading people to have a sedentary rather than a nomadic life, have more material resources than hunter-gatherer societies (e.g. land, cattle, tools). Parents in these societies control more resources which they can divert to their offspring in the form of inheritance. Consistent with this parental control model, studies show that mating patterns between foraging and agricultural societies differ in two ways (Apostolou 2010). Men in agricultural societies have more decision-making power over marriage arrangements than women, and parents exercise more control over the mating decisions of their male offspring. The reason is that wealth is inherited from father to son, and a son would risk losing his inheritance if he did not comply with his father's preferences.

Recent studies have started to examine the content of parental preferences for in-laws. Parents and children often agree about the appropriateness of potential mates. Simply asking children and parents to indicate sought-after characteristics is unlikely to provide information about conflicting mate preferences. Abraham Buunk and his colleagues (2008), therefore, used an approach designed to closely track the mating trade-offs. Students from three countries were asked to rate how unacceptable some undesirable traits would be to themselves or their parents. The authors hypothesised that conflicts would be likely to emerge on mate characteristics that strongly signal either heritable fitness as indicated by physical attractiveness, or

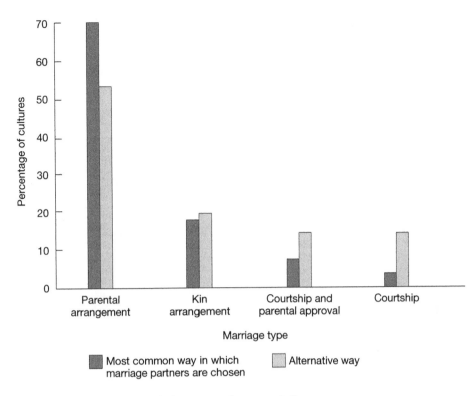

Figure 5.5 Marriage types in hunter-gatherer societies
Source: Apostolou (2007)

parental investment and cooperation as indicated by good family background and similar ethnic background. Children were expected to opt for a partner with good genes who might be a low investing partner whereas parents were expected to choose a high investing partner who might be physically unattractive.

Table 5.2 shows that across all 27 items, the three mate characteristics that were considered most unacceptable to children were: lacking an exciting personality, lacking a sense of humour, and being physically unattractive. The three characteristics that parents considered most unacceptable were: having a different ethnic background and religious belief, and being poor and being divorced.

Table 5.2 Mean levels of unacceptability of characteristics top self versus parents (American students).

Characteristics connoting heritable fitness	Means	Characteristics connoting parental investment and cooperation	Means	Additional characteristics	Means
Physically unattractive	2.93***(1.22)	Lacks good family background	4.49***(1.40)	Unfriendly and unkind	4.53(1.28)
Considerably shorter/ taller than self	3.04***(1.35)	Different ethnic background	4.95***(1.31)	Very different attitudes than self	3.29(1.20)
Physically unfit	3.37***(1.21)	Different religious beliefs	4.67***(1.53)	Physical or mental illness	3.99(1.16)

Characteristics connoting heritable fitness	Means	Characteristics connoting parental investment and cooperation	Means	Additional characteristics	Means
Fat	3.26***(1.29)	Lower social class than self	4.48***(1.21)	Not a virgin	4.44(1.42)
Bad smell	3.07***(1.16)	Divorced	4.62***(1.34)	Had many previous sexual partners	3.85(1.75)
Lacks sense of humor	2.60***(1.29)	Poor	4.62***(1.24)	Much younger/older than self	4.19(1.29)
Lacks artistic abilities	3.55*(1.23)	Not respectful and obedient	4.33***(1.32)	Unable to have children	3.86(1.46)
Lacks creativity	3.23***(1.18)	Low education	4.32**(1.50)		
Unintelligent	3.99(1.51)	Does not like children	3.19(1.64)		
Lacks exciting personality	2.58***(1.19) 3.16	Has children from another relationship	4.32**(1.54) 4.40		

Note: Lower values indicate greater unacceptability to children, and higher values indicate greater unacceptability to parents; asterisks indicate significant differences from the mean score for all 27 items (3.84) in the predicted direction. Values in parentheses are *SDs*.

*$p \leq .05$. **$p \leq .01$. ***$p \leq .001$ (one-tailed).

Source: Buunk et al. (2008)

Another study provided a direct comparison between a sample of college students and their parents (Perilloux et al. 2011). Students ranked traits in an ideal mate while the parents ranked the same traits for the mate that their offspring preferred. The results replicate those of the previous study in that, regardless of offspring sex, parents prefer religious belief more than physical attractiveness, and children prefer physically attractive partners with exciting personality more than parents. A surprising result was that children did not favour traits indicating genetic fitness such as health and good heredity, more than parents. Figure 5.6 is a graphic display of the magnitude of the mean differences between parents and their children.

5.6 Summary

- While Chapter 4 focused on mating, this chapter dealt with parenting. Finding a mate and caring for offspring are essential to sexual reproduction. However, the adaptive problem of inbreeding indicates that potential mates and parents do not include close relatives. To avoid inbreeding, various solutions have evolved. One solution is that sexually mature animals leave the group in which they were born and emigrate to another group to breed. Kin recognition is another way to avoid inbreeding, using different mechanisms such as phenotype matching and familiarity.

- Most animals at the onset of sexual maturity disperse to other groups, but humans remain longer with their parents and postpone independent reproduction. This delay does not necessarily reduce their fitness. Life-history theory predicts that long-lived species such as humans benefit from delayed reproduction. Prolonged parental care enables youngsters to remain longer in the family and favour future over present reproduction.

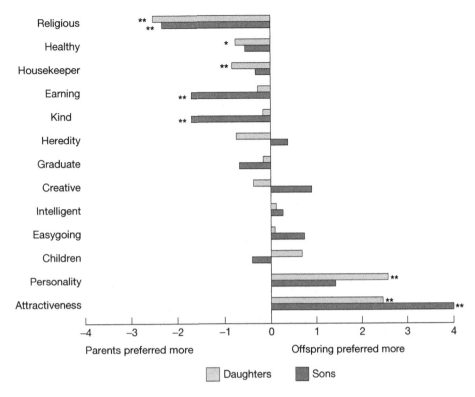

Figure 5.6 Ranking of mate traits by parents and their children
Source: Perilloux et al. 2011

- Parental care is mostly identical with maternal care. But in humans, mothers needed assistance when birth intervals decreased. Help came initially from other group members and later on from fathers who became confident about their paternity through pair-bonding. In addition, women's aversion to casual sex led men to invest more in parenting which had benefits for children.

- Although parents and children share common genes and experiences, their interests may conflict when offspring want more care than parents are willing to give. Different factors influence parental investment in offspring such as age of the child, offspring quality, preference for boys or girls, degree of relatedness, and mate preferences.

Study questions

1. What does the natural experiment in Taiwanese marriages illustrate sexual aversion between siblings?

2. How does childhood affect reproduction in adulthood?

3. How may alloparental care be explained by inclusive fitness theory?

4. How does life-history theory explain the influence of paternal care on the sexual maturity of daughters?

5. How may sex-biased investment in offspring be explained?

Suggested reading

Inbreeding avoidance

Berra, T., Alvarez, G. and Ceballos, F. (2010). Was the Darwin/Wedgwood dynasty adversely affected by consanguinity? *Bioscience*, 60, 376–383.

Lieberman, D. (2009). Rethinking the Taiwanese minor marriages data: evidence the mind uses multiple kinship cues to regulate inbreeding avoidance. *Evolution and Human Behavior*, 30, 153–160.

Lieberman, D., Tooby, J. and Cosmides, L. (2007). The architecture of human kin recognition. *Nature*, 445, 727–731.

Liqun, L. (2011). Is there a sensitive period in human incest avoidance? *Evolutionary Psychology*, 9, 285–295.

Weisfeld, G., Czilli, T., Phillips, K. et al. (2003). Possible olfaction-based mechanisms in human kin recognition and inbreeding avoidance. *Journal of Experimental Child Psychology*, 85, 279–295.

Origin of the human family

Covas, R. and Griesser, M. (2007). Life history and the evolution of family living in birds. *Proceedings of the Royal Society of London B*, 274, 1349–1357.

Davis, J. and Daly, M. (1997). Evolutionary theory and the human family. *The Quarterly Journal of Biology*, 72, 407–435.

Del Giudice, M. (2009). Sex, attachment, and the development of reproductive strategies. *Behavioral and Brain Sciences*, 32, 1–67.

Emlen, S. (1995). An evolutionary theory of the family. *Proceedings of the National Academy of the United States of America*, 92, 8092–8099.

Emlen, S. (1997). The evolutionary study of human family systems. *Social Science Information*, 36, 563–589.

Geary, D. and Flinn, M. (2001). Evolution of human parental behaviour and the human family. *Parenting: Science and Practice*, 1, 5–61.

When mothers needed assistance

Anderson, K. (2006). How well does paternity confidence match actual reality? *Current Anthropology*, 47, 513–520.

Anderson, K., Kaplan, H. and Lancaster, J. (2007). Confidence of paternity, divorce, and investment in children by Albuquerque men. *Evolution and Human Behavior*, 28, 1–10.

Coal, D. and Hertwig, R. (2010). Grandparental investment: Past, present, and future. *Behavioral and Brain Sciences*, 33, 1–59.

Danielsbacka, M., Tanskanen, A., Jokela, M. and Rotkirch, A. (2011). Grandparental child care in Europe: Evidence for preferential investment in more certain kin. *Evolutionary Psychology*, 9, 3–24.

Ellis, B. and Essex, M. (2007). Family environments, adrenarche, and sexual maturation: A longitudinal test of a life history model. *Child Development*, 78, 1799–1817.

Hawkes, K., O'Connell, J., Blurton Jones, N. et al. (1998). Grandmothering, menopause, and the evolution of human life histories. *Proceedings of the National Academy of Science USA*, 95, 1336–1339.

McLain, D., Setters, D., Moulton, M. and Pratt, A. (2000). Ascription of resemblance of newborns by parents and nonrelatives. *Evolution and Human Behavior*, 21, 11–23.

Sear, R. and Mace, R. (2008). Who keeps children alive? A review of the effects of kin on child survival. *Evolution and Human Behavior*, *29*, 1–18.

Strassmann, B. (2011). Cooperation and competition in a cliff-dwelling people. *Proceedings of the National Academy of Science USA*, *108*, 10894–10901.

Parent–offspring conflict

Andrews, P. (2006). Parent–offspring conflict and cost–benefit analysis in adolescent suicidal behavior. *Human Nature*, *17*, 190–211.

Apostolou, M. (2010). Parental choice: What parents want in a son-in-law and a daughter-in-law across 67 pre-industrial societies. *British Journal of Psychology*, *101*, 695–704.

Buunk, A., Park, J. and Dubbs, S. (2008). Parent–offspring conflict in mate preferences. *Review of General Psychology*, *12*, 47–62.

Hill, C. and Ball, H. (1996). Abnormal births and other 'ill omens': The adaptive case for infanticide. *Human Nature*, *4*, 381–401.

Perilloux, C., Fleischman, D. and Buss, D. (2011). Meet the parents: Parent–offspring convergence and divergence in mate preferences. *Personality and Individual Differences*, *50*, 253–258.

Trivers, R. (1974). Parent–offspring conflict. *American Zoologist*, *14*, 249–264.

Reference books

Forbes, S. (2005). *A Natural History of Families*. Princeton, NJ: Princeton University Press.

Hrdy, S. (2009). *Mothers and Others: The Evolutionary Origins of Mutual Understanding*. Cambridge, MA: The Belknap Press of Harvard University Press.

Konner, M. (2010). *The Evolution of Childhood: Relationships, Emotion, Mind*. Cambridge, MA: The Belknap Press of Harvard University Press.

Salmon, C. and Shackelford, T. (Eds) (2008). *Family Relationships: An Evolutionary Perspective*. Oxford: Oxford University Press.

Wolf, A. and Durham, W. (Eds) (2004). *Inbreeding, Incest, and the Incest Taboo*. Stanford, CA: Stanford University Press.

6 The evolution of social life

This chapter will cover:

6.1 Introduction

6.2 Why live socially?

6.3 The social evolution of primates

6.4 Solutions to the problem of cooperation

6.5 Cognitive capacities for cooperation

6.6 Summary

Learning outcomes

By the end of this chapter, you should be able to explain:

- why some species live socially rather than solitarily
- why sociality in primates evolved
- how cooperation between individuals is maintained
- how distinct human cooperation is from animal cooperation
- how cognitive capacities support cooperation.

6.1   Introduction

The previous chapter dealt with relationships between parents and offspring. We also have relationships with individuals who are not our close relatives, such as friends, colleagues and clients. Relationships are further embedded in social structures like groups, corporations and societies. The focus of this chapter is, first, on what we mean by sociality and why we live socially rather then solitarily.

Humans have in common with other primates that they are social species, living in cohesive groups, social networks and complex societies. The social evolution of primates has attracted much attention from primatologists. We discuss three possible explanations for the origin and evolution of social life in primates.

An important aspect of social life is cooperation as it occurs in marriage, work, communities, politics and so on. In many animals cooperation is restricted to genetic relatives and is less likely between unrelated individuals. In human societies, however, individuals are willing to cooperate with many unrelated individuals. We review various solutions to how cooperation between unrelated individuals is maintained.

Social exchange of costly services or valuable resources may be considered a form of cooperation for mutual benefit. However, exchange often involves considerable time delays between giving and receiving, and ample opportunities for cheating. How did our ancestors solve this problem? Another aspect of collaborative activities is that we need to understand and share each other's intentions in order to realise joint goals. What evidence do we have about solving the cheating problem and of understanding one another's intentions in cooperation?

6.2   Why live socially?

Defining sociality

sociality
sustained cooperation between individuals that goes beyond parental care and the continued association of mated pairs.

It is obvious that social life requires interactions and associations between individuals. But defining **sociality** is not easy because modes of living together are varied and complex. For example, some animals, such as baboons, form permanent units in which individuals forage together for most of the time, sleep in close proximity, and care for their offspring. Other animals, such as gazelles, are forced to move over large areas because the availability of food changes, resulting into temporary associations with shifting membership for most activities. In between are animals which form stable associations for some activities, and temporary associations for other activities (Lee 1994).

An essential criterion of sociality is that it should go beyond mating and parenting. A species may then be called 'social' if its members engage, at any point in the life cycle, in sustained cooperation that goes beyond parental care and the continued association of mated pairs (Boorman and Levitt 1980). Activities other than mating and parenting may include foraging, travel, nest-building and nest-defence. In humans, these activities also include commodity production, trade, politics, warfare, education and so on. Thus, social species exhibit stable associations and entertain intersexual social contacts throughout the year. Among the social species are some outstanding groups: colonial invertebrates (e.g. sponges, corals), social insects (e.g. ants, termites), non-human mammals (e.g. lions, elephants), birds (e.g. ravens, jays), and primates (e.g. apes, humans). Solitary species have no social contacts with conspecifics of the opposite sex outside the breeding season and are often intolerant towards members of their own species (Müller and Soligo 2005).

Humans are species in which individuals are engaged in sustained cooperation, and live in groups. But not all species display cooperative behaviours and are group-living. Consider orangutans who could be called a solitary species (Lee 1994). They forage separately, sleep alone, only mix with the opposite sex for mating, and only associate with individuals of the same sex during a couple of hours. Nevertheless, a male's home range covers the foraging areas of two or three females who resist the advances of strange males but only cooperate with familiar males. When food is abundant, orangs often gather in quite large groups. So, even in solitary species who don't interact on a daily basis, a minimum form of sociality can be observed in periods of parental care and in conditions of plentiful resources.

The example of orangutans makes clear that a division of animal species into social and solitary or non-social ones is highly artificial. If we locate animals on a continuum, at one end are eusocial ('true social') species, such as ants and bees who live in colonies of overlapping generations in which one or a few individuals produce all the offspring and the rest serve as sterile helpers (workers, soldiers) who rear juveniles and protect the colony (Lacey and Sherman 2005; Wilson and Hölldobler 2005; Novak et al. 2010). At the other end of the continuum are solitary living species, such as sloths and orangutans, with a minimum of sociality. In between are many species that will be found in association with members of their own or other species at certain times but not always. This is also true of species which live always in groups, such as humans. We are indeed part of groups, but these include many singletons (Krause and Ruxton 2008). As an example, scientists have relationships with their relatives, friends and colleagues. But a major part of their life is spent alone, thinking, reading and writing.

Levels of social complexity

grooming

care of the hair covering and skin by mammals; the mammalian equivalent of preening in birds. An animal's attention to its own body, or 'autogrooming', should be distinguished from 'allogrooming/social grooming' which refers to picking parasites or dirt from the fur as a reward through activation of endogenous opioids in the recipient.

dominance

in ethology referring to a superior position in a rank order or social hierarchy. Dominance is anything but static as lower-ranking animals continually test the ability of higher-ranking animals to maintain their position.

Sociality involves phenomena at different levels of complexity, such as behaviours, mental processes, interactions, relationships and structures (Hinde 1997). Starting with the behavioural level, behaviour is social when individuals engage in actions which influence others and are influenced by them, such as cooperative behaviour. At the psychological level, behaviour may be influenced by social cognition when individuals think about their own social behaviours and those of others. Sociality goes beyond behaviour when two individuals have interactions, for example when **grooming** each other or working on a project. If individuals have a series of interactions, early interactions may affect what happens in subsequent ones. The two individuals can then be said to have a relationship with each other.

If each individual is involved also in others, the relationship is part of social structures. These structures may take the form of a social network through which individuals have regular contacts. In cohesive groups, social structure may take the form of **dominance** hierarchy, with an alpha male or female at the top and others occupying lower ranks. Dominance hierarchies in animals are the result of fights and once established they prevent continuous struggles (e.g. Chase et al. 2002). Ranks can be stable as in baboons or unstable as in chimpanzees where lower ranking animals test the ability of those above them to hold their place. In human societies, hierarchies may take the form of stratification which divides people into layers (strata, classes, castes) according to their relative power, property and prestige.

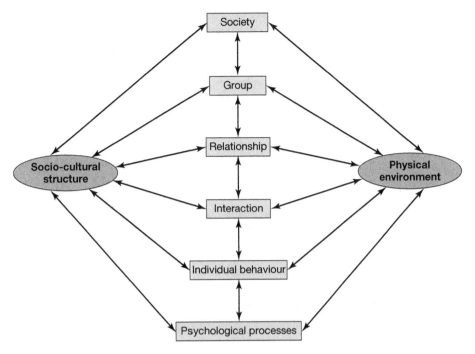

Figure 6.1 A simplified view of complexity in levels of sociality
Source: Hinde (1997)

Jerome Barkow (1992) proposed three psychological traits, enabling humans to generate stratification under favourable conditions. These traits are the tendency to seek a high social rank, to transmit the advantages of a high rank to offspring and close relatives ('nepotism'), and to form alliances with unrelated individuals through exchanges of resources and other favours. Individuals may move from one layer to another, but in some societies this social mobility is impossible. A static stratification is the caste system, still existing in India, which determines a person's worth by birth and lasts a lifetime. There is no moving from one caste to another. In sum, sociality covers phenomena at different levels of complexity, ranging from behaviours to large-scale structures, which influence one another (Figure 6.1).

Costs and benefits of sociality

Most species live solitarily rather than socially. As sociality is an exception to the rule in the animal world, it should have substantial benefits. Living in groups has the benefit that by joining forces, individuals are able to achieve things that isolated individuals can't. On the other hand, the costs of group living are not slight. Direct costs result from competition between group members for food, mates and other resources. In addition, indirect costs arise as group members must coordinate and compromise their activities to maintain the group cohesion (Key and Aiello 1999). As most animals live solitarily rather than socially, group-living could only evolve when the benefits outweighed the costs. The costs will dominate for solitary species while the benefits must be high for social species. In other words, we suppose that important benefits of social life solved problems of solitary living species. We review the benefits of sociality with regard to alloparental child care, predation, foraging and control of territories.

An important benefit of group living is joint care of offspring. Any help a mother can get from alloparents allows her to rear more offspring or to reproduce earlier and thus have more reproductive success over her lifetime. Before the term 'alloparent' entered the vocabulary of biologists, they used the term 'aunt' for any female primate other than the mother who cares for a young animal (Rowell et al. 1964). Their source of inspiration was the British term 'auntie', a close woman friend of the family who helps to care for the young (Wilson 1975). Another form of joint care is to be found in small-bodied primates, such as tamarins, in which previous offspring remain in their natal group to serve as non-reproductive helpers (Lee 1994).

A remarkable form of joint care is the crèche. This invention is a great help for modern working couples, and testifies to the fact that humans are a social species. Yet, the crèche is not uniquely human. Lionesses on the African savanna, belonging to the same pride, bring their cubs from the age of six weeks to two years into a pool. The main benefit of this crèche is that the cubs are protected against infanticidal males. Cubs have more survival chances when more than one female stays behind while the others are hunting for prey (Packer et al. 1990).

Living in groups has the further advantage of reducing the risk of predation ('safety in numbers'). Animals in groups can spend more time in feeding when they share the time costs of vigilance for predators. Larger groups are more effective at detecting the approach of predators. The group-size effect is generally considered to be a consequence of an increased number of individuals scanning for predators. As group size increases, foragers can alternate between periods of feeding and scanning, though studies of bird groups feeding on the ground show that birds can detect predators when they have their head down feeding and when they have their head up in a vigilance pose. This suggests that birds alternate between periods of high and low ability to detect predators (Krause and Ruxton 2008).

kleptoparasitism
food stealing as a foraging strategy in which scavengers improve their hunting success by gaining access to large, high-quality food items.

Group-living also allows animals to join forces in foraging. Patch size, referring to how the food is distributed, is a key factor of whether sociality helps or hinders in joint foraging. If food comes in small, scattered patches, such as grass, leaves or fruits, sociality would be costly for animals (Gaulin and McBurney 2004). For chimpanzees who like fruit, a fruiting tree is not a big patch. Although they live in large groups, the foraging parties are small because the patch size is small. Chimps are social for other reasons, such as the need to defend themselves against the threats posed by other groups. Strange males may kill the offspring of unfamiliar females. If food comes in large patches, such as large prey, then being a social species is beneficial. That is why social carnivores such as wild dogs and lions are often supposed to hunt in packs. But there is an alternative explanation (Box 6.1 Why African lions are social).

BOX 6.1 Why African lions are social

Cooperative hunting was a leading explanation for sociality in female lions, but empirical evidence fails to support this hypothesis. In a recent study, Anna Mosser and Graig Packer (2009) analysed 38 years of data on 46 lion prides in the Serengeti National Park, Tanzania. They found that group-living in lions has no strong associations with increased food intake.

Lions are the only cats who live in large groups, called 'prides'. A lion pride is composed of lionesses (mothers, sisters, cousins), and their cubs, along with a temporary coalition of adult males. The pride has a close bond and is not likely to accept a stranger. Although the pride is a stable unit, it is a fission–fusion group, in which individuals are typically found in a range of subgroup sizes and compositions. Males leave their natal pride by the age of 4 years and remain solitary or form a coalition with other males. Male coalitions challenge one another for residency of the pride. When new males try to join the pride, they have to fight the resident males. The new males are either driven off, or succeed in pushing out the existing males. If the new males succeed, they kill dependent offspring sired by the previous coalition in order to speed up the mothers' return to sexual receptivity (Mosser and Packer 2009). The unrelated males stay a few months or years but the older lionesses stay together for life. Living in a pride makes life easier. Hunting as a group means there is a better chance that the lions will have food, and it is less likely that they will get injured while hunting. Lions live in a matriarchal society. The females work together in hunting and rearing the offspring. Males patrol, mark and guard the pride's territory.

Mosser and Packer's study about the benefits of sociality in African lions shows that success in hunting increases only slightly with increasing size of the hunting group, for example, because not all lions have an active part in the group-hunt. Larger group size is more important in maintaining control of territories than in joint hunting. Larger prides have larger territories and more males to challenge and take over other groups. The grouping patterns for all pride sizes were significantly affected by the number of neighbours. These results are consistent with the hypothesis that grouping patterns reflect the threat of territorial competition rather than the effects of group foraging.

If group-territorial behaviour is subjected to selection pressure, we should expect fitness costs associated with territorial competition. Prides faced with more males in neighbouring groups suffered indeed a reduction of female reproductive success (i.e. fewer surviving cubs), as well as higher mortality and more frequent wounding (Figure 6.2). Mosser and Packer conclude that the primary benefit of group living in lions appears to be numerical advantage in territorial competition and may have been important in the evolution of lion sociality.

6.3 The social evolution of primates

The reader may recall from Chapter 3 that sociality is a defining characteristic of primates (Box 3.1 Shared derived characteristics of primates). All primates are socially organised in networks, cohesive groups or complex societies. The origin and evolution of social organisation in primates has attracted much attention from primatologists. In this section we focus on three possible explanations for why primates evolved into social-living individuals. The first explanation proposes that ecological factors are mainly responsible for sociality; the second explanation uses the phylogenetic history to account for the evolution of primate sociality; and the third explanation emphasises the extension of relations between kin ('blood relatives') to non-kin (in-laws).

Ecology and social evolution

In the attempt to reconstruct the social evolution of primates, lemurs are of special interest because they approach the ancestral condition most closely (Müller et al. 2007). Take a look at Figure 3.5 (The tree of primates) and you will recall where they are placed in the order of primates. This order also includes monkeys, apes and humans, with a common ancestor about 77 mya (Box 6.2 Lemurs, the early primates).

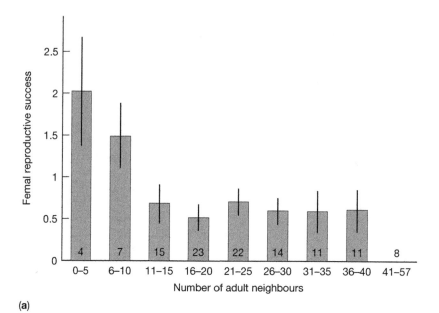

(a)

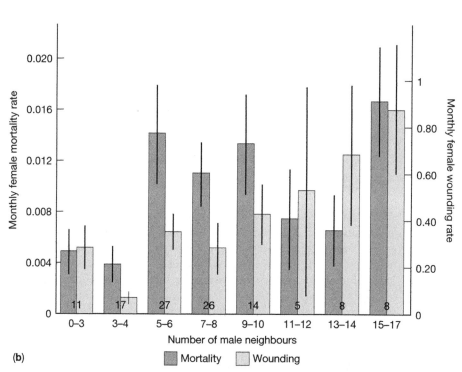

(b)

☐ Mortality   ☐ Wounding

Figure 6.2 Significant association between female mortality/wounding rates with number of male neighbours: (a) Female reproductive success versus number of adult neighbours, and (b) average adult female monthly mortality and wounding rates versus number of male neighbours

Source: Mosser and Packer (2009)

BOX 6.2 Lemurs, the early primates

Lemurs evolved in complete isolation from other primates in the forest ecosystem of Madagascar. Originally, Madagascar lay within the ancient supercontinent Gondwana, with India to its East (see Figure 3.8 Changing positions of the continents). About 160 mya, Gondwana began to fragment, a movement that ceased about 125 mya, leaving Madagascar in its present position. Geological evidence shows that about 88 mya India split from Madagascar, thus completing the islands's isolation (Kappeler 1997; Tattersal 2006). The living lemur species are considered to descend from a single common ancestor that colonised Madagascar from Africa sometime in the early Tertiary period about 60 mya (Karanth et al. 2005). It is thought that the ancestral lemurs arrived in Madagascar by rafting on tangled mats of vegetation such as those that are swept out to sea by the floodwaters of African rivers. Once arrived, they could exploit the vast array of unoccupied niches available which resulted into a huge variety of primates. There are at least 50 species of living lemurs, though some estimates go up to 80 species (Yoder 2007). The primates they left behind in mainland Africa were mostly displaced by more successful monkeys and apes (Redmond 2008).

Lemurs have a body mass, ranging from 50 gram (mouse lemur) to 10 kg (indri) and eyes directed more to the side than in other primates. They are important because they constitute more than 15 per cent of living primate species. Their close phylogenetic proximity to humans makes them highly relevant subjects for comparative studies (Yoder 2007). Lemurs form – together with tarsiers and lorises – the suborder of prosimians (literally: before simians, being monkeys and

Figure 6.3 Ring-tailed lemur
Source: Shutterstock.com

apes) and can be distinguished from other primates by their long muzzles and wet noses much as those seen in dogs that also rely on olfaction. Prosimians belong to the order of primates which includes monkeys, apes and humans (see Table 3.1 Classification of extant groups of primates). Figure 6.3 shows a ring-tailed lemur (*Lemur catta*).

Lemurs are known to have shifted in evolution from nocturnal to diurnal activity which involved a change from solitary foraging to foraging in groups. So the question is which ecological factors may explain their sociality. Living socially provides benefits like protection from predators and sharing information about feeding and sleeping sites. But it remains unclear why other mammals can do without such advantages and primates cannot. That is why Alexandra Müller and her colleagues (2007) compared lemurs with rodents. The aim of their comparative approach was to explore possible determinants for the absence or presence of sociality in rodents and then to apply the findings to the origin of lemur sociality.

Findings indicate that large arboreal rodents who include a substantial amount of fruit in their diet, are more likely to be social than other rodents. The reason is that fruits are patchily distributed in place and time and therefore difficult to find. As a consequence, individuals living in social networks or cohesive groups have the advantage of searching more efficiently for food by sharing information about feeding sites. The authors conclude that, like large arboreal rodents, lemurs have a frugivorous diet which, due to its patchy distribution, should be an important factor behind the origin of social networks in early primates. The consequent evolution of social networks of females is thought to be a prolongation of mother–infant relations.

Phylogeny and social evolution

Answering the why and how of primate sociality is important for understanding the social life of humans. In the previous section we saw that early primates became social as a response to resource availability. In a phylogenetic explanation the emphasis is more on the historic processes that account for sociality. Like morphology and physiology, social behaviour is heritable and subject to historical processes that may constrain social evolution. Susanne Shultz and her colleagues (2011) tested models of social evolution in primates. The models allowed for all kind of transitions between social states but implied that some transitions are less likely than others. For example, the transition from pair-bonding to large multi-male, multi-female groups is less likely than the other way around.

The findings indicate two transitions in primate social evolution, first from solitary living to living in multi-male, multi-female groups about 52 mya), and, second, to either pair-living (about 16 mya) or harems (16 mya). Reconstruction of the evolutionary history of sociality across the primate tree revealed that the first transition was established in monkeys at 52 mya and at 32 mya in lemurs. Harems appeared in monkeys at 16 mya, and pair-living arose in gibbons at 8.6 mya. The authors also examined determinants of social evolution in primates. The transition from solitary to social living is thought to result from increased predation pressure which coincided with the change from nocturnal to diurnal foraging.

The authors conclude that group size is often used as a proxy of social complexity in primates, but group stability appears to be a more important indicator of social complexity (Shultz and Dunbar 2007). There is also strong support for a model of stepwise transitions from solitary living to unstable groups, followed by a second step to stable pairs (one-male, one-female units) and stable harems (one-male, multi-female units). The second transition is considered important as it could facilitate cooperative social behaviour in monkeys, apes and in particular humans.

Kinship and social evolution

Richard Wrangham (1980) has proposed a theory of social evolution that includes food distribution as a key influence. His starting point is that male and female reproductive success is determined by different factors. As offspring require a long period of development and most male primates don't provide child care, reproduction for females is energetically expensive. Access to males is usually not a limiting factor, but access to food certainly is. From this difference comes a basic principle: female reproductive success is determined by access to food, male reproductive success by access to females. This principle has an impact on how females and males are socially organised.

female kin-bonded species
species in which males leave their native group at sexual maturity.

male kin-bonded species
species in which females leave their native group at sexual maturity.

If food is difficult to find, genetically related females are expected to form networks or groups, enabling them to share information about food locations. This kin-based mode of social organisation is known as 'female kin-bonding' and may be found in lemurs and many monkeys. In **female kin-bonded species**, genetically related females constitute the core of a group while males leave the group at sexual maturity to breed in other groups. Apes, in contrast, don't demonstrate female kin-bonding. Social organisation in apes varies greatly, ranging from solitary orangutans and pair-bonded gibbons to one-male harem with son inheritance in gorillas, and male kin-bonded chimpanzees. '**Male kin-bonding**' is a mode of social organisation in which the females leave their natal group at sexual maturity and join another group for breeding. Recall from section 5.2 (Inbreeding avoidance) that dispersal patterns are sex-biased.

Why was female kin-bonding not continued in apes? An answer should start with the divergence of apes and monkeys about 25 mya when early apes probably had the same female kin-bonded groups as monkeys. Things changed, however, when at the end of the Miocene, approximately 10 mya, a cooling climate caused the African forest to shrink and fragment. A drier habitat evolved with small and widely dispersed patches of food, forcing females to forage over large areas. In contrast to monkeys, apes lived more on the ground than in the trees, became less quadrupedal and developed a larger body size. Large females, depending on small, widely dispersed patches of food, were in need of a flexible foraging strategy which was incompatible with tightly kin-bonded groups (Foley 1998).

In apes, ecological change favoured a mode of social organisation in which kin-bonded males defended unrelated females and their offspring against males from neighbouring groups. The emergence of male kin-bonding among the larger apes – the harem system in gorillas and the multi-male, multi-female system in chimpanzees – provided the ancestral condition from which the sociality of later humans would be derived. Humans faced another change which resulted from the consequences of brain enlargement (Lewin and Foley 2004). Producing and raising large-brained offspring requires high energetic costs which required the involvement of fathers in parental care. The tendency of men and women to form long-lasting pair-bonds for raising offspring would be present in the earliest members of the genus *Homo* (around 2–2.5 mya).

affinity
relationship by marriage (or adoption) rather than genetic kinship. Affinity is common in humans but unknown in other primates.

Social organisation in non-human primates is primarily based on kinship: either female kin-bonding or male kin-bonding. Kinship refers to consanguineal bonds ('blood relatives') or genetic relatedness. The breakthrough in human social organisation is affinal kinship, that is, **affinity** *between* groups. Put otherwise, the unique contribution of humans to social organisation is the emergence of in-laws or affines, that is, relatives by marriage (Rodseth et al. 1991). Affinity *within* kin groups is not uniquely human. After transferring into a new group, non-human primates are cut off from their relatives they left in their natal group. Dispersal severs kinship bonds (Chapais 2008). A female who has transferred to a new group, establishes a breeding bond with a particular male and recognises the relatives of her mate as her 'in-laws'. But the male cannot recognise the relatives of the female because she has no contact with her kin after her transfer to the new group. This principle applies to all dispersing individuals in female and male kin-bonded primates. Affinity *between* groups is evidently unknown in non-human primates. But in humans, marriages establish relationships between the spouses' families or kin groups. This is possible because husband and wife maintain long-term relationships with the groups in which they were born.

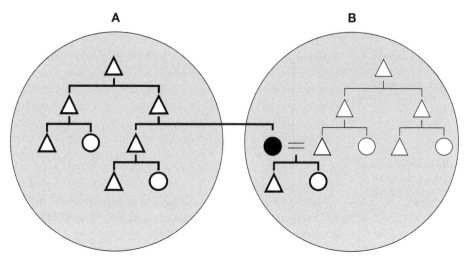

Figure 6.4 Affinity between two interbreeding groups
Source: Chapais (2008)

While relations between groups of non-human primates are dominated by avoidance and hostility, affinity between groups has the potential to reduce aggression (Chapais 2008). The reason is that the evolution of pair-bonding created appeasing bridges between interbreeding groups. Since pair-bonding enabled father and offspring to recognise each other, a transferred female's kin now comprised her father and her uncles, that is, her father's brothers. This extension of kinship is important because it is males who initiate and conduct intergroup conflicts in primates. The fact that male relatives were part of the appeasing bridges meant that they would be inhibited from attacking their female kin, that is to say their daughter or sister (Figure 6.4). In Figure 6.4, we can see that the bridges are created by a single female from group A (solid black circle) after she transferred to group B. Consanguineal kinship connects her to relatives living in A; affinity or affinal kinship connects her 'husband' with her relatives living in A.

6.4 Solutions to the problem of cooperation

Sociality includes a variety of phenomena

In the previous section, sociality referred to modes of group-living such as multi-male, multi-female groups, individuals living in pairs, and harems. You may recall from section 6.2 that sociality also involves phenomena at different levels of complexity, such as behaviours (grooming, helping), cognitive processes (reasoning about the behaviours, mental states of others), interactions (conflict, cooperation), relationships (friendship, marriage) and structures (families, peer groups, societies) (Figure 6.1). Sociality may also range from competitive to cooperative behaviour, or from voluntary (exchange of goods and services) to involuntary (taxation for public services).

Consider social interactions which may be agonistic (aggressive, competitive) and affiliative (friendly, cooperative). Robert Sussman and his colleagues (2004, 2005) in their survey find that agonistic behaviours like fighting, threatening and submissive gesturing in non-human primates are extremely low, normally less than 1 per cent of the activity budget. On the other hand, less than 10 per cent of their activity budget is devoted to active affiliative interactions like grooming, playing, food-sharing, alliance-formation and huddling. Affiliation is a sense of liking and a feeling of social closeness that motivates cooperative behaviour (Bekoff and Pierce 2009). It may arise from familial relationships, pair-bonding or friendship and imply that individuals actually enjoy social contact.

The importance of cooperation

Hamilton's rule
a formula named after William Hamilton (1936-2000) which demonstrates that individuals should be altruistic towards relatives, provided that the benefits exceed the costs as valued by the degree of genetic relatedness between actor and recipient.

In this section we focus on the problem of cooperation which is to explain why an individual should carry out cooperative behaviour that benefits other individuals. Early explanations of cooperative behaviour in animal societies argued that it was maintained by benefits to groups (Wynne-Edwards 1962). Modern explanations of the evolution of cooperation are mostly based on **Hamilton's** theory of inclusive fitness (Hamilton 1964). Recall from section 5.4 (When mothers needed assistance) that inclusive fitness consists of the direct fitness that individuals derive from producing offspring, and the indirect fitness that they derive from assisting relatives. Inclusive fitness implies that selection works by providing benefits to kin so that cooperation will most probably occur among relatives. Inclusive fitness provides a satisfactory explanation of cooperation between kin but cooperation between unrelated individuals remains a problem.

Explaining the problem of cooperation is important because all of the major transitions in evolution rely on solving this problem (Maynard Smith and Szathmáry 1995, 1999; Jablonka and Lamb 2006; Aunger 2007; West et al. 2010; Korb 2010; Bourke 2011). Recall from section 2.4 (Levels of complexity) that cooperative structures make life more complex. The genes that are part of the genome in every cell cooperate with one another. Mitochondria which provide the energy that cells need, were once free-living bacteria but are now cooperative organelles within these cells. Multi-cellular organisms such as animals depend on stable cooperation between the cells that make up their tissue. Many animals live solitarily, but some of them such as primates evolved into social-living animals.

The point is that all of these transitions, from simple to more complex entities, succeeded in solving the problem of cooperation. In each transition, new evolutionary entities learned to cooperate, forming higher levels of organisation. The new entities acquired larger benefits through cooperation than they could expect if acting alone. Explaining the problem of cooperation is therefore fundamental to our understanding of evolution (Box 6.3 An expanded view of social evolution).

BOX 6.3 An expanded view of social evolution

The history of life may be considered the history of biological units forming higher-level units. Once started, this process has been repeated several times leading to a hierarchy of biological systems (Bourke 2011). While social evolution usually refers to different forms of sociality in animals (e.g. groups, colonies, societies), this framework can also be applied to smaller units like genes forming higher-level units like genomes, which in turn form organisms who may cooperate in groups and societies. Applying a hierarchical understanding to the evolution of life results in an expanded view of social evolution. Common principles of social evolution are thought to apply to all levels within the hierarchy. Hamilton's inclusive fitness theory serves as the theoretical tool for analysing social evolution.

Following the proposal of Fred Bourke (2011) in his *Principles of Social Evolution*, we summarise below the timing and frequency of six major transitions in social evolution.

1. From separate replicators (genes) to cell enclosing genome

Life originated when the first self-replicating molecules emerged. The origin of life is estimated to have occurred at 3,500 mya. The first cells were prokaryotes (i.e. single-celled organisms lacking a nucleus and organelles) as they are represented today by the Bacteria and Archaea (see Figure 3.3 The largest tree of life). The first prokaryotic cells appear in the fossil record about 2,500 mya. This was also the time when asexual reproduction originated in the form of cell division.

2. From separate unicells to symbiotic unicell

Eukaryotic cells differ from prokaryotic cells in that they are larger and possess a nucleus, an internal skeleton, and organelles such as mitochondria. Mitochondria were once free-living proteobacteria but became permanently incorporated within other cells (endosymbiosis). The origin of mitochondria is dated at 1,800–2,300 mya and the mitochondrial endosymbiosis occurred between 1,900–1,300 mya and is thought to have occurred once only.

3. From asexual cells to sexual unicell

Although bacteria can transfer genetic material horizontally to one another (see section 1.3 Biology), sexual reproduction involving the fusion of gametes to form a zygote, only occurs in eukaryotes. The origin of eukaryotic sex is believed to have occurred between the origin of eukaryotes between 2,000 and 1,200 mya.

4. From unicells to multi-cellular organism

It is estimated that multi-cellularity evolved from unicellular ancestors at least 25 times independently. Complex multi-cellularity occurred in five eukaryotic lineages (i.e. series of ancestor–descendant populations) which include all the organisms we call animals or plants. In cellular slime moulds the origin of multi-cellularity is estimated to have emerged about 490 mya, and in animals between 761 and 957 mya, or earlier, at 1,450 mya.

5. From multicellular organisms to eusociality

Eusociality, or true sociality refers to colonial systems (e.g. ants, bees, corals, sea anemones) in which only one or a few members of the group reproduce while the other individuals care for the young or defend the colony against predators. Eusocial animals are traditionally defined as multi-cellular organisms with reproductive division of labour, cooperative brood care, and an overlap of parental and offspring generations. Eusocial animals include those without and with reversible workers, that is, individuals being (in-)capable of changing into reproductive form (e.g. eusocial insects vs cooperative breeding birds). Eusociality has arisen at least 24 times, and occurs mainly in eusocial insects but also in social shrimps and mole rats. The earliest date for the origin of eusociality is 170 mya. Across birds eusociality emerged 28 times independently, and disappeared 20 times.

6. From separate species to interspecific mutualism

Interspecific mutualism is a mode of cooperation between members of different species, providing immediate benefits for the partners involved. Mutualistic relationships span a large range of social interactions from facultative to obligate. Mutualism has arisen many times but it is hard to specify how many. An example of interspecific mutualism is the cleaning of client fish by cleaner fish who remove and eat parasites that live on the outside of the client's body. Both parties benefit by exchanging a grooming service for a tasty meal.

eusociality

true sociality, referring to colonial systems (e.g. ants, bees) in which only one female is reproductive while the other animals gather food and care for the young.

reciprocity

a form of cooperation in which benefits are deferred.

Reciprocity

In this section we review various solutions to how cooperation between unrelated individuals is maintained: **reciprocity**, mutualism, punishment and institutions (Clutton-Brock 2009; West et al. 2010; Foley 2001). In social species, individuals often provide resources or services to unrelated individuals who return the benefit at some later point in time. Robert Trivers (1971) proposed calling this mode of

replicator

the mechanism that copies the DNA sequence of the parent and passes it to the offspring.

altruism

an action which does not benefit the actor, but only the beneficiary.

cooperation reciprocal **altruism**, but it is now usually referred to as 'direct reciprocity' or 'cost accounting reciprocity' as no altruism – defined as an action which does not benefit the actor, but only the recipient – is involved. Actually, it is self-interested cooperation which evolves if participants are both actors and recipients, and benefits are greater than costs. A classic example of reciprocity are vampire bats exchanging blood (Wilkinson 1984, 1988). Vampire bats owe their name to the habit of feeding on the blood of mammals such as horses and cattle. During the day they hide, but at night they disperse to suck the blood of their targets. Finding blood is a matter of survival because bats can live without blood only for a few days. So what happens when they fail to find blood? Bats regularly regurgitate a portion of the blood to others in the colony. This blood donation doesn't occur randomly but is directed to their friends from whom they have received blood in the past.

The results of reciprocity studies are not always compelling which is why dissatisfaction with empirical evidence is growing (Clutton-Brock 2009). One reason for discontent is that studies need to demonstrate that the same individuals help one another repeatedly; that they help one another equally; that their help is beneficial to the fitness of their partners; and that their partners are not close relatives or prospective mates. Few of the studies that serve as examples of direct reciprocity, exclude the possibility that cooperation is maintained by other mechanisms such as inclusive fitness, manipulative tactics (e.g. punishment of non-cooperating individuals), or immediate benefits (e.g. joint hunting). As an example, field studies of blood sharing among vampire bats do not provide convincing evidence that the same individuals help each other recurrently and that they are not relatives.

Another example of reciprocity in which animals repeatedly help each other within a narrow timeframe are allogrooming sessions in mammals, such as primates or grazing mammals. In these sessions the partners groom each other in turn. The duration of the turns given by each partner are usually similar. Allogrooming may be found, for example, among impalas where it has the function of reducing parasites on body areas an animal cannot reach with its own mouth (Figure 6.5). Figure 6.5 shows delivered and received bouts (or grooming turns) by one of the partners.

Reciprocity is also important in humans and commonly studied with game-theoretical models. These models take as a starting point a situation in which people – mostly two individuals – can enjoy large benefits if they cooperate with each other, but cannot predict whether the partner will cooperate or not. A classic example are two strangers who together could catch a deer, but each alone could only manage to catch a hare (Hurford 2007). The meat from a deer is worth the meat from three hares. The dilemma facing both parties is the same: is it worth cooperating, not knowing whether the other will cooperate or defect?

	Cooperate	Defect
Cooperate	1.5	0
Defect	1	1

The rows in the table above indicate possible choices for the first person, the columns for the second person. If they cooperate in hunting a deer, each gets half the deer or 1.5 units of meat (top left cell). If the second person defects, the first person gets nothing (top right cell). If both persons don't join in deer-hunting, they only get a hare or one unit of meat (left and right bottom cell).

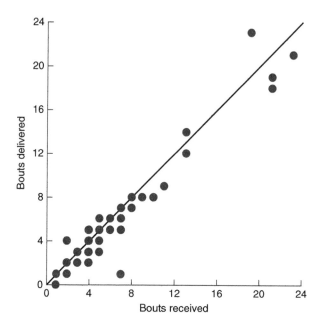

Figure 6.5 Allogrooming between adult female impalas
Source: Hart and Hart (1992)

A whole academic industry has grown around these kind of social dilemmas. These experiments become a bit more realistic when cooperators develop a record of cooperation. In iterated 'prisoner dilemmas', participants meet each other repeatedly in sophisticated versions of the game. None the less, dissatisfaction with Prisoner Dilemma-models has increased because of the gap between reality and the model. For example, partners in real cooperation are not prisoners but often communicate their intentions. And unlike prisoners, they are not constrained to cooperate with particular partners and can develop profitable relationships and stop unproductive ones (Clutton-Brock 2009).

A real-life example of cooperation between unrelated, even antagonistic people in a most unusual situation, concerns the 'live and let live' system in the trenches of the First World War (Ashworth 1980; Axelrod 1984). The first stage of this war began in 1914 and was highly mobile and bloody. But as the frontlines stabilised and neither party could advance, non-aggression between the troops emerged spontaneously in many places along the lines. Early instances of non-aggression were associated with meals, served at the same times on both sides of no-man's land. Later on, soldiers on one side allowed the other side to repair the trenches and collect their casualties, with the other side returning the favour. The unintended consequence of these truces was that each antagonist learned that the other shared similar needs. Truces were arranged either face-to-face or, if the distance between trenches was too far, trench fighters shouted across no-man's-land, promising not to fire.

Thus while both parties were supposed to be in conflict, soldiers in the trenches developed a system of cooperation under suitable circumstances. Among these circumstances were opportunities to make repeated contact across the frontlines and communicate reliable intentions. The headquarters of the British, French and German armies wanted to stop the truces as they were afraid that it would undermine the morale of soldiers. Eventually, the 'live and let live' system collapsed when soldiers were ordered to engage in incessant raids that the headquarters could effectively monitor. Raids were carefully prepared attacks in which enemies had to be killed in their own trenches. Now there was no effective way of pretending that a raid had been undertaken.

Mutualism

mutualism
a form of cooperation between members of different species – interspecific mutualism – or between unrelated members of one species – conspecific mutualism – that provides immediate benefits for the partners involved.

Mutualism is a mode of cooperation between members of different species (interspecific mutualism) or between unrelated members of one species (conspecific mutualism) that provides immediate benefits for the partners involved. Mutualism differs from reciprocity where benefits are deferred. An example of interspecific mutualism is the cleaning of client fish by cleaner fish who remove and eat parasites that live on the surface of the client's body. Both parties benefit by exchanging a grooming service for a tasty meal. How does this exchange work?

A model species in research is the cleaner fish *Labroides dimidiatus* that lives in coral reefs near Australia. It is visited by many other reef fish species who spread their pectoral fins as a signal to the cleaner fish that it wants to be cleaned. Studies demonstrate that cleaner fish have a clear effect on the abundance of parasites. After 12 days, fish on reefs without cleaner fish had on average 3.8 times more parasites than fish on reefs without cleaners (Grutter 1999). Recent studies show that cleaners who enhance their service by touching the customer with their fins, benefit from more cooperative clients. This is particularly helpful if the customer is a predator that could attack the cleaner. The calming effect of the cleaner fish's touch has wider repercussions as it softens the predator so much so that the cleaning station turns into a safe haven for other prey fish (Cheney et al. 2008). Another example of interspecific mutualism refers to ravens that lead wolves to an elk carcass. The wolves tear the carcass apart, a job that ravens are unable to do themselves, so that both parties have a meal (Heinrich 1999).

Conspecific mutualism may be seen in cooperative hunting where each hunter can gain more by acting together than hunting alone. Cooperative hunting is common in social carnivores (e.g. lions, wild dogs, wolves) and primates (e.g. chimpanzees, humans). One of the few well-documented cases of mutualism in primates is cooperative hunting among chimpanzees (Boesch and Boesch-Ackermann 2000; Boesch et al. 2006). All chimpanzee populations have been observed to hunt for arboreal monkey species, preferably red colobus monkeys. Hunting success in chimpanzees is rather high, compared with many other predatory species, such as wolves and lions. One reason may be that chimpanzees depend less on meat and only hunt when success is most likely.

KEY FIGURE   Christophe Boesch

Christophe Boesch is a biologist at the department of primatology of the Max Planck Institute for Evolutionary Anthropology at Leipzig, Germany. His research is focused on the biology of chimpanzees to improve our understanding of human evolution and its cognitive and cultural abilities.

Selected works

The Chimpanzees of the Taï Forest: Behavioural Ecology and Evolution (2000), with Hedwige Boesch-Ackermann

The Real Chimpanzee: Sex Strategies in the Forest (2009)

Mutualism is vulnerable to free riding, where group members can harvest benefits without sharing the costs. This free rider problem is also present in human societies when individuals benefit from public services (e.g. defence, welfare) but resist tax-paying. Free riding is a real problem in chimpanzee hunting. For example, in one population – the chimpanzees of the Taï National Park in Ivory Coast, Africa – free riders constitute 47 per cent of the meat eaters.

How can mutualistic cooperation at Taï then be stable? Hunters rely on individual recognition and identify individual contributions to limit free riding. Active hunters obtain significantly more meat than bystanders and latecomers. According to the mutualistic scenario, we may expect that hunters gain more when hunting in groups than when hunting individually. The success of hunters increases steadily and reaches a maximum when five individuals hunt together. This increase is significant and individual hunters gain significantly less when hunting in groups of three to five.

Punishment and manipulation

In many animal societies, individuals manipulate and punish others to engage in activities that benefit them or to avoid activities that will harm them (Clutton-Brock 2009). For example, manipulators modify their behaviour to take advantage of fixed behaviour patterns of conspecifics, such as grooming. Individuals may regularly associate with alpha males or females, grooming them repeatedly to gain protection from threats by rivals. In many primate species, non-breeding females seek interactions with a mother's infants to gain benefits, such as parenting skills or prospective helpers.

In rhesus monkeys, dominant individuals may punish subordinates that fail to give calls when they find attractive feeding sites (Hauser 1992). In meerkats, the pregnant alpha female suppresses reproduction in subordinate females when they appear to be pregnant as well. The dominant female may then temporarily ban them from the group. This punishment results mostly in abortion of the subordinate's litter (West et al. 2007).

Punishment has also been suggested as an important selective force for cooperation in humans (e.g. Fehr and Gächter 2002; Henrich et al. 2006). In laboratory experiments, group members who were kept anonymous from each other, could choose to contribute money to a common project. As a rule, the result in these economic games is that cooperation gradually declines to the point that no one contributes. But when subjects were given the opportunity to punish others who didn't contribute, cooperation reached high levels.

These experiments suggest that a willingness to punish non-cooperators may be part of human psychology and a key element in understanding our sociality. This suggestion raises the question why people should be willing to punish. The punishers in laboratory experiments such as Fehr and Gächter's (2002) are anonymous. But anonymity is unrealistic among early human groups. Punishers would have to confront free riders which is risky and may lead to commotion in the group, undermining further cooperation. One solution would be that punishing non-cooperators provides the benefit of prestige. Another solution would be that punishment may come from a supernatural punisher (Johnson et al. 2003). Religions often promote cooperation for the common good and threaten defectors with sanctions.

How distinct is human cooperation?

The solutions that evolved to solve the problem of cooperation are used by humans as well as other social species. Research on cooperation in animals and humans demonstrates both similarities and differences. So what makes the social evolution of humans distinct? In their review, West et al. (2011) conclude that humans do not have particularly high levels of altruism. Social insects like ants have higher levels of altruism in that most individuals have given up the capacity to produce offspring. Reproductive altruism is the most extreme form of altruism as it is found in sterile castes of eusocial insects but also in sterile somatic cells in multi-cellular organisms. The genetic basis for reproductive altruism can be traced back to unicellular ancestors in which regulatory genes suppress somatic cells to participate in reproduction (Nedelcu and Michod 2006). Nor are humans different because non-relatives cooperate with one another. Extreme examples of mutualistic cooperation occur between cleaner fish and their clients on the tropical reefs. Neither do humans differ because they use punishment to enforce cooperation. Dominant meerkats are known to attack and evict subordinate individuals who attempt to reproduce.

Human cooperation is distinct because exchange of costly services and resources between non-kin is widespread and often involves long time delays. However, considerable time lapses between assistance or goods given and received, make exchanges susceptible to cheating (Clutton-Brock 2009). The maintenance of long-term exchanges requires therefore the linguistic and cognitive capacity to establish the intentions and goals of both parties. Other animals lack the capacities to make specific agreements about coming events. Reliable exchanges based on mutual obligations and involving time lapses require trust as an instrument of social organisation. That is presumably why social institutions like marriage, economy, law and education arose in humans. Social institutions may be regarded as persistent structures that emerge from the behavioural, emotional and cognitive capacity to maintain cooperation. Social institutions thus 'reside' in both the mind of individuals and their actual interactions with others (Foley 2001; see, for general theories of institutions Turner 2003; Searle 2010).

Consider marriage, as an example. We have seen in section 6.3 (The social evolution of primates) that social organisation in non-human primates is primarily based on female or male kin-bonding. The breakthrough in humans was bonding between groups through in-laws. Marriages establish relationships between the spouses' families or kin groups because husband and wife maintain long-term relationships with the groups in which they were born. Given that kin groups consider pair-bonding and the associated inter-group bonding valuable, marriage could develop into a social institution with the power to regulate issues including prenuptial articles, inbreeding avoidance, authority, dissolution and alimentation.

6.5 Cognitive capacities for cooperation

Human cooperation is special because humans have cognitive capacities, allowing them to make specific agreements about the nature and timing of exchanges. This may explain why cooperation in animals is mostly restricted to close relatives and immediate benefits (Clutton-Brock 2009). The cognitive capacities required for com-

plex cooperation are largely the same as for competition, particularly where deception and manipulation are concerned. Jean Decety and his colleagues (2004) propose
that social cognition, referring to processes of understanding and interaction with
conspecifics, evolved from the interplay between competition and cooperation. Both
forces activate common areas in the brain – the frontoparietal network – which support executive functions such as generating behavioural alternatives, suppressing
inappropriate behaviour, monitoring ongoing action, and anticipating the behaviour
of one's partner. In this section we discuss, first, cognitive constraints that animals
and humans face in social exchanges, and, second, cognitive capacities of humans to
participate in collaborative activities.

Cognitive constraints on social exchange

Social exchange is uncommon in non-human animals because it is thought to be
too cognitively demanding for most of them. They lack cognitive capacities for
making specific agreements about future events. What cognitive constraints do
non-human animals face? We focus on temporal discounting, numerical discrimination and memory decay (Stevens and Hauser 2004). Temporal discounting means
that animals depreciate future rewards which results in a preference for small and
immediate benefits rather than large and delayed benefits. If a monkey, for example,
finds unripe fruit, it may wait for it to ripen. Although waiting may provide a larger
benefit, it runs the risk that another monkey will eat the ripe fruit. This kind of
uncertainty has favoured a strong selection pressure for discounting future benefits.
Temporal discounting may be the rule among animals, but it varies across species.
As an example, while pigeons and rats devalue future food in a matter of seconds,
humans do it on the order of months (Figure 6.6).

Another cognitive constraint on social exchange is numerical discrimination.
Engagement in these transactions implies that parties are able to quantify whether

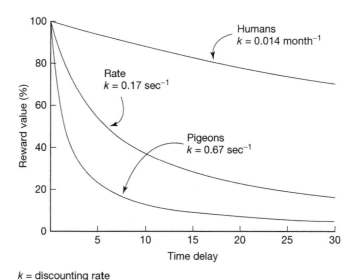

k = discounting rate

Figure 6.6 Temporal discounting in pigeons, rats and humans
Source: Stevens and Hauser (2004)

the exchanged resources and services are equitable. Experiments demonstrate that animals have a number sense which is composed of two systems. One system permits animals to count up to about four with precision; the other system enables them to approximate large numbers. So if animals enter into exchanges, they are limited to small numbers, say two fruits for two fruits, or should accept large margins which makes them susceptible to cheating.

Cognitive constraints also include memory decay. If there are long time intervals between cooperative acts, both parties are likely to forget the debts owed and favours given. The same happens if animals face distractions or reciprocal obligations with multiple partners, increasing the burden on memory. Humans are cognitively constrained in sustaining exchanges that are complex, numerous and heterogeneous. Without external memory devices, the human brain cannot recall all the interactions and transactions which are typical for human societies. About 8,000 years ago, humans in the Middle East invented transactional records which served as memory aids (Schmandt-Besserat 1992). Objects made of clay and modelled into various shapes such as spheres, discs, cones, cylinders, rectangles and animal heads, represented different quantities of goods like grain, wool, oil and animals. This primitive accounting technology played no role in the exchange of goods because this was done face to face and therefore required no bookkeeping. The clay objects rather served as counting devices in a redistributive economy. Individuals had an obligation to surrender surplus goods to the temple. Thus clay objects recorded contributions as today it is done by the national revenue service.

Greater cognitive demands on obligations result in increased use of recordkeeping technology. One may expect that cooperating partners acquire better reputations for trustworthy behaviour when they have a better record of past interactions. Experiments demonstrate that improved memory from recordkeeping promotes the reputation of trading partners such as investors and trustees, and results in greater reciprocity. As reputation is an unobservable construct, an image score served as a proxy to measure the observed interactions. Tests confirmed the hypothesis that the correlation between investor and trustee image scores increased through time and was more pronounced for the recordkeeping economy (Figure 6.7) (Basu et al., 2009).

The role of competitive intentions

It is often difficult to move from the observation that animals appear to cooperate to the conclusion that this behaviour is indeed cooperative. Consider chimpanzees hunting for their favourite meal: red colobus monkey. Boesch and Boesch-Ackermann (2000) describe the 'ideal' hunt as follows. One chimpanzee slowly starts to climb in a tree, usually unnoticed by the monkeys. The others move on the ground, anticipating possible escape routes and ready to join the pursuit. Once the climber is seen by the monkeys, he rushes upwards, moving them in a certain direction while the others on the ground follow and make blocking moves, checking where the climber moves. The climber acts as the driver, following the monkeys without making efforts to capture one on his own.

As the hunt progresses, some chimpanzees take turns in performing the driver movement while others assume a chaser role attempting to catch a monkey by a rapid pursuit. Usually, the chimpanzees select and isolate an individual, often a mother with her baby. Once separated from the main group, the hunt accelerates with chasers coming from different directions. Finally, it is the ambusher who forces

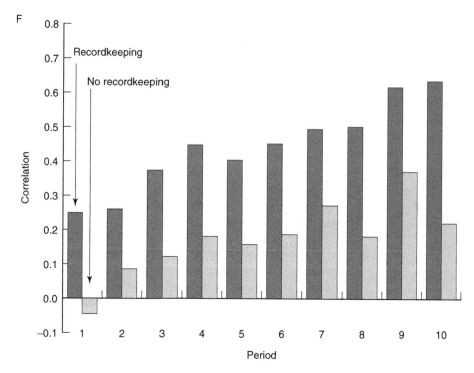

Figure 6.7 Investor and trustee reputation in two economies
Source: Basu et al. (2009)

the prey either backwards towards its pursuers or downwards into the lower canopy where chimpanzees have a good chance of catching it.

The authors call such 'ideal' hunts 'collaborative' hunts because the individuals perform different complementary roles all directed towards the same prey. In Taï chimpanzees, three-quarters of the studied group hunts were collaborative and the most successful.

Do these chimpanzees really cooperate in the hunt? Observation does not immediately lead to explanation. Some scientists argue that chimpanzees are indeed working together with a common goal in mind – finding and catching a prey – and coordinating complementary roles. Others insist that chimpanzees, like wolves and lions, are engaged in similar hunting activities but not having a common goal and taking complementary roles. The reason would be that chimpanzees are more motivated to act competitively than to act cooperatively. They can figure out each other's intentions, but because of their competitive nature they expect that others have competitive rather than cooperative intentions. In this respect, chimpanzees differ importantly from humans (Tomasello 2008).

An experiment by Brian Hare and Michael Tomasello (2004) may show how chimpanzees are more competitive than cooperative. The chimpanzees were made familiar with two human experimenters: a cooperative person willing to share food with the animal, and a competitive person keeping food for himself. In the experiment, the task of chimpanzees was to choose the right container with hidden food. In the competitive condition the experimenter made a reaching gesture for the container with hidden food. The chimpanzee subjects interpreted this gesture correctly and tended to grab the food in anticipation of the competitor. In the cooperative condition, the experimenter made a pointing gesture for the container with hidden food. The chimpanzee subjects were less successful at interpreting this gesture correctly, almost at a near-chance level. The researchers concluded that chimpanzees can read the intentions of others, but that they are more skilful in competitive tasks than in cooperative cognitive tasks.

Sharing goals and intentions

Tomasello and his colleagues (2005) propose that the crucial difference between human cognition and that of other species is the ability to participate in collaborative activities, sharing goals and intentions with others. They call this cognitive capacity 'shared intentionality'. When group-living individuals such as humans share intentions and goals with one another repeatedly, this enables them not only to engage in complex cooperation, but also to invent things like marriage, money, science and government. These social inventions may indeed be considered unique for humans.

Aspects of the cognitive capacity to share goals and intentions, may be seen in a diagram that depicts each participant's understanding of the interaction (Figure 6.8). Tomasello et al. emphasise that the cognitive representation of the goal contains both self and other. In addition, the cognitive representation of the intention also contains both self and other, making it a joint intention.

The proposal to consider shared intentionality as a crucial difference between humans and other primates, has generated various comments. For example, Christophe Boesch (2005) whose field studies of chimpanzees we reviewed, points out that the group hunting behaviour of chimpanzees fulfils the criteria for shared

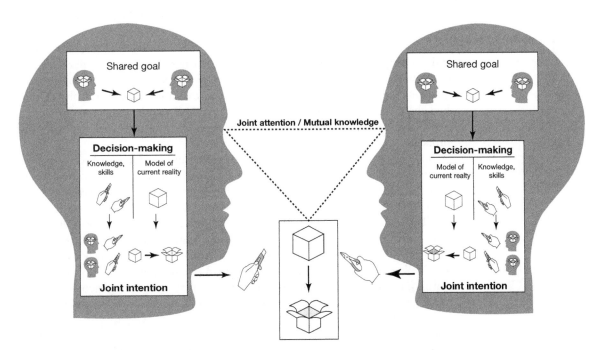

Figure 6.8 Cooperation between two partners, sharing goals and intentions, as well as complementary roles

Source: Tomasello et al. (2005)

goals and intentions, set by Tomasello and his colleagues. It is true, he argues, that chimpanzees don't perform exactly like humans but sharing goals and intentions is not a distinct human capacity. One possible difference might be that human team players plan strategies before they come into action, something which has not been observed in chimpanzees. In addition, Boesch doesn't understand why Tomasello and his colleagues ignore the published evidence in wild chimpanzee group hunting. If we want to understand the cognitive capacities in humans and chimpanzees, both laboratory and field studies are necessary.

Much implementation of shared intentionality in humans is probably learned and culturally transmitted (Tomasello 2009a). We all have to be taught how to cooperate with others. For that reason, we should consider the difference between humans and non-humans not as a black-or-white matter, but rather as a matter of degree (Hurford 2007). To conclude, the jury is still out on the question of whether chimpanzees lack the cognitive capacities necessary for complex forms of cooperation, and what these cognitive capacities exactly are.

Social exchange and cheating

Social exchange is based on the agreement that one person delivers something on the condition that the other person will reciprocate. When people are involved in social exchange, they are concerned with receiving as much as they give. Notions of equity or fairness play a role as they refer to the relative rewards and costs for both partners. Since exchanges often involve long time delays, they are susceptible to cheating. In the course of their social evolution our ancestors are thought to have faced the problem of cheating repeatedly which raises the question of how they solved it.

You may recall from section 1.4 (Psychology) that the modular approach in evolutionary psychology is critical of the view that we have a general cognitive capacity for solving all kinds of problems. This includes the problem of reasoning about social exchange and the associated risk of cheating. Evolutionary psychologists Tooby and Cosmides (1992, 2005) do not believe that a general reasoning capacity can solve all problems. They argue that social exchange only can evolve if individuals have a cognitive adaptation for detecting and avoiding cheaters. Reasoning about exchange serves as a test case in the research programme of their modular approach.

To solve the cheating problem, our ancestors are supposed to have evolved various cognitive capacities. One of these supposed capacities is, for example, the capacity to recognise many different individuals. Recall from section 1.4 (Psychology) that there is, indeed, good neuroscientific evidence for a cognitive capacity to recognise faces. This capacity is considered a highly heritable module with a well-defined neural structure and computational function (e.g. Wilmer et al. 2010). Social exchanges with considerable time delays require also a good memory for transactions. We have seen above, however, that humans are cognitively constrained in sustaining exchanges that are complex, numerous and heterogeneous. Without external memory devices, the human brain cannot recall all the interactions and transactions which are typical for human societies. That is why they invented transactional records which served as memory aids. Greater cognitive demands on obligations result in increased use of recordkeeping technology. In addition, experiments demonstrate that improved memory from recordkeeping promotes the reputation of trading partners, resulting in more social exchanges (Basu et al. 2009).

What is the evidence for a capacity to detect cheaters? In order to test their social exchange theory, Cosmides and Tooby conducted many experiments. One approach is to represent social exchange reasoning as a matter of deontic reasoning. This type of reasoning refers to deontic rules, involving obligations, that are often phrased in terms of 'may' or 'must'. To illustrate, the rule '*if* you are driving on the highway *then* you must keep your speed below 70 mph' cannot be true or false. It may or may not be in force, and it may or may not be obeyed. Put otherwise, deontic reasoning concerns a conditional rule: if–then. Reasoning about social exchange is indeed reasoning about a conditional rule because one person delivers something on the condition that the other person will reciprocate.

This kind of reasoning can be tested with the Wason selection task, developed by Peter Wason (1966). An example of this task is the drinking problem in which participants are told to imagine that they are police officers observing people drinking in a bar to make sure that they comply with the following rule: 'if a person is drinking in a bar, then s/he must be over 16 years of age'. They are also told that each card represents a drinker, having on one side the kind of drink and on the other side the age of the person. The visible sides of the four cards show:

COKE   BEER   16   21

Subjects need to check that the 16-year-old is not drinking beer and to check the age of the beer drinker. They are instructed to choose those cards showing that the rule is being violated. The correct choice is 'drinking beer' and '16 years of age', which most subjects choose. The other two cards don't matter because any one can drink coke and 21-year-olds can drink what they like. This deontic selection task has been used to demonstrate that humans have a specialised capacity for reasoning about social exchange leading to cheater detection. The results are conclusive but other authors have questioned the findings of Cosmides (1989; Cosmides and Tooby 1992). For example, one criticism is that the predicted responses are of those who would be adaptive in contemporary society and therefore could be explained by social learning in the lifetime of the individual. Another criticism is that the effects to which the theory is applied can be accounted for by more general cognitive processes. For instance, the selection task can be treated as a decision task in which individuals choose according to expected utility (Evans 2005).

In a recent experiment on social exchange as a form of cooperation for mutual benefit, Elsa Ermer et al. (2006) focus on strategic social interactions. That is, the exchanging partners require a **theory of mind** for making inferences about the contents of one another's mental states, in particular, desires, goals and intentions. What is a theory of mind? Simon Baron-Cohen (1995) proposed that a theory of mind (ToM) is an inference system evolved to promote strategic social interaction. It is called a theory because in daily life we have no direct evidence to support our assumption that others have mental states. There is more about theory of mind in section 8.5 (Social cognition in chimpanzees and humans).

Ermer et al. (2006) argue that reasoning about social exchange is regulated by a neuro-computational system designed for inferring mental states that cannot be seen, heard, touched, smelled or tasted. They hypothesise that this system is only

Theory of Mind

the ability to understand another individual's mental states such as knowledge, intentions, desires, goals, beliefs; also known as 'mind-reading' or 'mentalising'. It is called a theory because we have no direct evidence to support our assumption that others have mental states.

triggered by intentional violations of social contracts, involving the mental states of both partners (e.g. goals, intentions). But the system is not triggered by innocent mistakes or unintentional accidents. For example, if a person wants to borrow someone's car, the exchange might be: 'if you borrow my car, then you must fill the tank with fuel'. So if the tank could not be filled due to an (unintended) accident, the exchange reasoning is about precautionary rules rather than contractual rules.

An fMRI study using the Wason selection task, supported the hypothesis that reasoning about social exchange activates brain areas implicated in reasoning about precautionary rules, and vice versa. Consistent with the prediction, neural correlates of ToM (the anterior and posterior temporal cortex) were activated when subjects reasoned about contractual rules, but not precautionary rules where a theory of mind is not required.

6.6 Summary

- The emergence of sociality was an important event in evolution as it allowed individuals to achieve more than they could do alone. Species may be defined as social if their members engage in sustained cooperation, going beyond mating and parenting. Sociality has substantial benefits over solitary life when it comes to alloparental care, protection against predation, foraging, control of territories and so on.

- The sociality of primates can be explained by several hypotheses. First, early primates had a high level of fruits in their diet which were patchily distributed and difficult to find. Social networks enabled them to share information about feeding sites. Second, findings from phylogenetic models indicate that primates evolved from solitary living to living in multi-male, multi-female groups and, then, either to pair-living or harems. The transition from solitary to social life was probably due to increased predation pressure. Third, while social organisation in non-human primates is based on female or male kin-bonding, the breakthrough in humans was bonding between groups through in-laws.

- While Hamilton's inclusive fitness theory provides a satisfactory explanation of cooperation between kin, cooperation between unrelated individuals remains a problem. Various answers to the question how cooperation between unrelated individuals in animal and human species is maintained, have been studied: from reciprocity and mutualism to punishment and institutions.

- Human cooperation is distinct because exchanges of services and resources between non-kin are widespread. Since such exchanges often involve long time delays, they are vulnerable to cheating.

- If human exchanges are vulnerable to cheating, they require special cognitive capacities. One proposal is that humans have a unique capacity to establish the intentions and goals of one another. Another proposal is that they have a neuro-computational system for reasoning about social contracts and detecting intentional violations.

Study questions

1. Why do some species live socially rather than solitarily?
2. Why and how did primate sociality evolve?
3. How is cooperation between unrelated individuals maintained?
4. How does human cooperation differ from animal cooperation?
5. How can cognitive capacities maintain cooperation?

Suggested reading

Why live socially?

Lacey, E. and Sherman, P. (2005). Redefining eusociality: concepts, goals, and levels of analysis. *Annales Zoologic Fennici*, *42*, 573–577.

Müller, A. and Soligo, C. (2005). Primate sociality in evolutionary context. *Journal of Physical Anthropology*, *128*, 399–414.

Novak, M., Tarnita, C. and Wilson, E. (2010). The evolution of eusociality. *Nature*, *466*, 1057–1062.

The social evolution of primates

Müller, A. and Soligo, C. (2005). Primate sociality in evolutionary context. *Journal of Physical Anthropology*, *128*, 399–414.

Rodseth, L., Wrangham, R., Harrigon, A. and Smuts, B. (1991). The human community as a primate society. *Current Anthropology*, *32*, 221–254.

Shultz, S., Opie, C. and Atkinson, Q. (2011). Stepwise evolution of stable sociality in primates. *Nature*, *479*, 219–222.

Solutions to the problem of cooperation

Clutton-Brock, T. (2009). Cooperation between non-kin in animal societies. *Nature*, *462*, 51–57.

Fehr, E. and Gächter, S. (2002). Altruistic punishment in humans. *Nature*, *415*, 137–140.

Fehr, E. and Gächter, S. (2003). The nature of human altruism. *Nature*, *425*, 785–791.

Fehr, E. and Gächter, S. (2004). Third-party punishment and social norms. *Evolution and Human Behaviour*, *25*, 63–87.

Hare, B. and Tomasello, M. (2004). Chimpanzees are more skilful in competitive than in cooperative tasks. *Animal Behaviour*, *68*, 571–581.

Marlowe, F. (2009). Hadza cooperation: Second-party punishment, Yes; third-party punishment, No. *Human Nature*, *20*, 417–430.

Marlowe, F., Berbesque, J., Barr, A. et al. (2008). More 'altruistic' punishment in larger societies. *Proceedings of the Royal Society B*, *275*, 587–590.

Novak, M. (2006). Five rules for the evolution of cooperation. *Science*, *314*, 1560–1563.

West, S., El Mouden, C. and Gardner, A. (2011). Sixteen common misconceptions about the evolution of cooperation in humans. *Evolution and Human Behaviour*, *32*, 231–262.

Cognitive capacities for cooperation

Basu, S., Dickhaut, J., Hecht, G. et al. (2009). Recordkeeping alters economic history by promoting reciprocity. *Proceedings of the National Academy of Sciences of the USA, 106*, 1009–1014.

Boyd, R., Gintis, H., Bowles, S. and Richerson, P. (2003). The evolution of altruistic punishment. *Proceedings of the National Academy of the United States of America, 100*, 3531–3535.

Decety, J., Jackson, P., Sommerville, J. et al. (2004). The neural basis of cooperation and competition: an fMRI investigation. *NeuroImage, 23*, 744–751.

Ermer, E., Guerin, S. and Cosmides, L. (2006). Theory of mind broad and narrow: Reasoning about social exchange engages ToM areas, precautionary reasoning does not. *Social Neuroscience, 1*, 196–219.

Rilling, J., Gutman, D., Zeh, T. et al. (2002). A neural basis for social cooperation. *Neuron, 35*, 395–405.

Stevens, J. and Hauser, M. (2004). Why be nice? Psychological constraints on the evolution of cooperation. *Trends in Cognitive Sciences, 8*, 60–65.

Tomasello, M., Carpenter, M., Call, J. et al. (2005). Understanding and sharing intentions: The origins of cultural cognition. *Behavioural and Brain Sciences, 28*, 675–735.

Reference books

Bourke, A. (2011). *Principles of Social Evolution*. Oxford: Oxford University Press.

Fleagle, J. (1999). *Primate Adaptation and Evolution*. San Diego: Academic Press.

Hammerstein, P. (Ed.) (2003). *Genetic and Cultural Evolution of Cooperation*. Cambridge, MA: The MIT Press.

Krause, J. and Ruxton, G. (2008). *Living in Groups*. Oxford: Oxford University Press.

Lewin, R. and Fley, R. (2004). *Principles of Human Evolution*. Oxford: Blackwell Publishing.

Rowe, N. (1996). *The Pictorial Guide to Living Primates*. Charlestown: Pogonias Press.

Sober, E. and Wilson, D. (1998). *Unto Others: The Evolution and Psychology of Unselfish Behavior*. Cambridge, MA: Harvard University Press.

Trivers, R. (1985). *Social Evolution*. Reading, MA: The Benjamin/Cummings Publishing Company.

7 The origin and expression of emotions

This chapter will cover:

7.1 Introduction

7.2 Why did emotions evolve?

7.3 Facial expressions in primates

7.4 The neural basis of emotions

7.5 The emergence of social emotions

7.6 Summary

Learning outcomes

By the end of this chapter, you should be able to explain:

- what emotions are and why they evolved
- how Darwin and later scientists explained facial expressions
- how neuroscientists theorise about the evolution of emotions
- how the brain supports emotions
- why and how social emotions emerged.

7.1 Introduction

Emotions are an integral part of our life. We know how they feel, but when asked what emotions really are or why they evolved, many of us have no satisfactory answer. Psychologists have difficulty as well in defining emotions unanimously and explaining their evolutionary origins. In this chapter we focus first on what emotions are, what kind of emotions there are, and why they evolved.

Emotions can be recognised from changes in the face, voice and behaviour of individuals. Being a keen observer of animals, infants and adults, Darwin published a book about *The Expression of Emotions in Man and Animals* (1872). He was interested in the universality, and by implication the innateness of facial expressions. His book was a bestseller but its claims were contested. We examine, therefore, what went wrong and how recent evolutionary scientists explain emotional expressions.

Darwin emphasised the evolutionary continuity between animal and human emotions. To reveal cross-species similarities, he compared countless sketches and photographs of humans and other animals in different emotional states. Primates are indeed expected to share emotions. We focus here on the question: how similar are the facial expressions of humans and our closest relatives, the chimpanzees?

Emotions may disturb the body. When frightened by someone's outburst of anger, your heart is beating faster and your brain is in a state of emergency as well as when we run into dangerous situations. The involvement of the brain in emotions raises the questions of how neuroscientists theorise about the evolution of emotions, and how brain areas process emotions?

Basic emotions like fear and anger are associated with life-threatening situations. But what about pride, shame and guilt which are involved in social interactions and group-living? What is the function of such emotions? Why did they evolve? What happened in the distant past that we needed them?

7.2 Why did emotions evolve?

There is a long tradition of studying emotions, dating back to the early Greek philosophers. For example, Plato considered emotions as wild, uncontrollable forces that undermined the power of reason. This theme, that still resonates today, considers emotions as making us vulnerable and irrational. Fear and anger that overwhelm us, are experienced as raw and disorganising. The negative side of emotions dominated early theorising in philosophy and psychology. Later theorising by psychologists emphasised the constructive role of emotions in human life. As an example, the ability to monitor one's own and others' emotions in guiding one's thinking and behaviour, appears to be an important determinant of life success.

Theorising by evolutionary scientists also emphasised the useful, adaptive side of emotions. The evolutionary perspective considers emotions as products of natural selection, providing good solutions to recurrent problems that faced our ancestors (e.g. Tooby and Cosmides 1990, 2008; Ekman 1992). This perspective leads to questions about how emotions work. For example, how are they recognised from facial expression, and how are they processed in the brain? It also leads to questions about why emotions exist at all and are passed down from generation to generation. For instance, why do we have negative emotions like fear and anger, and why did positive emotions like pride and gratitude evolve? But first we want to know what emotions are.

What are emotions?

emotion

a relatively brief episode of coordinated brain, autonomic, and behavioural changes that facilitate a response to an external or internal event of significance for the organism.

In the history of psychology, numerous definitions of **emotion** have been proposed (Kleinginna and Kleinginna 1981; Denton 2006). One reason is that different kinds of emotion may be distinguished. For example, if the word 'emotion' is represented by a pyramid, then at the base are the primitive, or primordial emotions which include thirst, hunger for air, hunger for food, pain, hunger for specific minerals, sexual arousal and orgasm (Denton et al. 2009). These emotions are in most cases driven by sensors detecting deviation from normal within the body. In the middle of the pyramid are the primary, or basic emotions of fear, anger, disgust, sadness, joy and surprise, which are hard-wired into the brain and in humans associated with specific facial expressions and recognised across cultures (Ekman 1992). At the apex of the pyramid are the emotions such as those experienced with aesthetic delight of great art, as well as the social emotions of pride, gratitude, shame and guilt which are based on self-consciousness (e.g. Turner 2000; Tracy et al. 2007). In this book we focus on basic and social emotions.

Emotions are brief responses to significant events. They are states, not traits. That is why they are hard to define and hard to measure. In textbooks, articles and other sources, one may find many definitions of emotion, each based on different criteria. Although psychologists do not agree on a precise definition of emotion, they do agree about the general characteristics. Thus, emotion refers to a relatively brief episode of coordinated brain, autonomic and behavioural changes that facilitate a response to an external or internal event of significance for the organism (e.g. Davidson et al. 2009).

The brain change refers to the activation of neural circuits and circulation of neural transmitters (e.g. dopamine, serotonin). The autonomic change refers to involuntary processes in the viscera, being the large organs housed in the thorax (heart) and the abdomen (stomach). For example, a profound, involuntary change in the body is increased heart rate or blood pressure. The behavioural change refers to an impulse to act such as fleeing or attacking, whether or not it is expressed overtly in body posture, vocalisation, or face. In the definition, emotion is conceived as a response to a significant event but from an evolutionary point of view, emotional responses must be considered as evolved solutions for problems having an impact on an organism's reproductive success (Box 7.1).

Finally, emotion should be distinguished from other affective phenomena:

negative emotion

emotion associated with diverse forms of threat, or obstruction of a goal, including anger, fright-anxiety, guilt-shame, sadness, envy-jealousy and disgust.

- *feelings*: the subjective representations of emotions
- *mood*: a diffuse affective state that is often of lower intensity than emotions but considerably longer in duration
- *attitudes*: relatively enduring affectively coloured beliefs, preferences, and predispositions towards objects or persons
- *affective style*: relatively stable dispositions that bias an individual towards perceiving and responding to people and objects with a particular emotional quality, dimension or mood
- *temperament*: particular affective styles that are apparent early in life, and partially determined by genetic factors.

BOX 7.1 The negativity bias in emotions

Humans and other animals recurrently face significant stimuli such as objects ('can I eat it?'), individuals ('is he friendly?'), or events ('is it dangerous?'). To determine which response is most adaptive, we use appraisals to evaluate these stimuli. Appraisals are rapid evaluations about the significance of an object, individual or event which may differ depending on one's history or present condition. Appraisal theorists have established lists of criteria which are supposed to be used in evaluating stimuli (Scherer 2000). Such criteria may refer to the novelty of objects, the kindness of other individuals, or the familiarity of events. As an example, imagine that you are alone at a bus station and a man with an angry face is approaching. You rapidly evaluate the significance of this event for your own well-being. What is his intention? Why is he angry? Is it wise to avoid him? Is it better to put on a brave face? Or should you look for help? The result of this event appraisal will determine your emotional response.

From an evolutionary point of view, individuals should have invested more in defensive, negative responses than in appetitive, positive responses. The bottom-line is that individuals who are unable to deal with life-threatening situations, run the risk not to survive and reproduce. Because it is more difficult to reverse the consequences of dangerous events than those of missed opportunities, it is likely that the process of natural selection has resulted in our propensity to act more strongly to negative than to positive information (Cacioppo and Gardner 1999).

This heightened sensitivity to information about things that may have a negative impact on survival and reproduction, is called the **negativity bias**. This bias is also present in emotions (Rozin 2009). **Negative emotions** such as fear and anger are more powerful than positive emotions like joy or pride because they are crucial in life-threatening situations. Negative emotions which refer to diverse forms of threat, or obstruction of a goal, include anger, fright-anxiety, guilt-shame, sadness, envy-jealousy and disgust. Positive emotions which refer to diverse forms of goal attainment or the movement towards it, include happiness/joy, love/affection, pride and relief (Lazarus 1991).

The negativity bias has been demonstrated in experiments. Our senses may have been selected to be especially sensitive to stimuli that represent potential threats to our survival and reproductive success. As a social species, humans are particularly attuned to threatening facial expressions. Experiments in which subjects were instructed to search for an angry face within a group of happy faces, found that an angry face appears to exert a powerful attraction. Once detected, we seem to pay attention to the face for an extended amount of time (Hansen and Hansen 1988; Fox et al. 2000). These studies indicate that the capacity to detect angry faces has adaptive significance.

A recent study investigated whether the *anger superiority* effect could be found in children with Williams Syndrome (WS), who show clinically reduced social fear of strangers and increased sociability (Santos et al. 2010). To this end, researchers used a 'face-in-the-crowd' task and compared their performance to that of normal children. Findings reveal that WS children failed to show the *anger superiority* effect; rather, they processed angry faces as they did happy faces. It appears that the differences between WS and normal subjects cannot be explained by lower IQ levels or differences in perceptive functioning. A better candidate would be dysregulation of brain systems involved in social fear detection (amygdala, prefrontal cortex).

Emotion decouples stimulus and response

negativity bias

in emotions like fear and anger, a heightened sensitivity to information about things that may have a negative impact on survival and reproduction.

An important theme in the evolutionary study of emotion is that it results from a gradual decoupling of adaptive behaviour from hard-wired **reflex** actions (Scherer 1994, 2000). Outstanding characteristics of a sensorimotor reflex are its stimulus specificity and the rigidity of the response. Stimuli trigger fixed action patterns, ensuring that the adaptive problem indicated by the stimulus is solved. That is why animals who depend heavily on reflexes for survival, interact within their environment in stereotyped ways. A classic example from experiments by the behavioural biologist Niko Tinbergen (1951) is the built-in tendency of birds to respond with fear when they are confronted with a cardboard silhouette that looks like a hawk. When the cardboard doesn't look like a predator, the bird is not threatened and reacts calmly.

reflex
an automatic, unlearned, relatively fixed response to stimuli that does not require conscious effort and often involves a faster response than might be possible if a conscious evaluation of the input was required.

In evolution, sensorimotor reflexes were not sufficient for the demands of more complex species like primates. We have a large repertoire of responses, ranging from reflexes and physiological drives to emotions and cognitions. To be sure, we still have reflexes such as the papillary reflex which widens the pupil of the eye in dim light, or the startle reflex which responds to a sudden, unexpected stimulus such as a loud noise. Physiological drives are considered as context-sensitive responses which are more advanced than reflexes. They enable animals to meet cyclical homeostatic needs crucial to survival, such as nutrition. Hunger motivates an animal to look for food, but unlike a reflex, it does not determine all the behaviours which are necessary to find and consume food.

Emotions may be regarded as a further step in the evolution of adaptive responses which in simpler species were accomplished by reflexes and drives. In emotion, stimulus and response are decoupled which has the advantage that some latency time intervenes between stimulus evaluation and response (Scherer 1994, 2000). In other words, there is some time to choose from different actions. For example, when we see a man coming out of the bushes with a knife, we are prepared to flee or fight. But after a split second we discover that he is a father having just carved a stick for his child. The latency time allows for evaluation of the situation and appraisal of the chances of success and the consequences of an action. This flexibility is an important advance over the stimulus–response reflex. Another advantage of decoupling is that the action readiness in emotion preserves the necessary speed associated with older, automatic responses.

Cognitions represent a further, evolutionary step in adaptive problem-solving over emotions as they are unspecific with respect to stimuli. Although stimulus and response are decoupled in emotions, they are still reflex-like as they may lead to more or less automatic actions. Cognitive capacities such as memory storage and information sharing provide more flexibility in adapting to changes in the environment. For example, abundant evidence supports the conclusion that primates are cognitively advanced animals with large brains. One hypothesis holds that foraging for widely dispersed food favoured the evolution of complex cognitions in primates. A diet that is rich in ripe fruit, requires that individuals need to remember when and where this food can be harvested (e.g. Purves et al. 2008). This hypothesis also has a social dimension as we learned from section 6.3 (The social evolution of primates) that social networks in early primates originated from the need to share information about the locations of ripe fruit.

To conclude, evolution reveals different adaptive responses to significant events in the life of animals. Emotional responses emerged supposedly because new adaptive problems could not be solved by built-in reflexes or drives. Therefore, adaptive solutions became increasingly dependent on more flexible responses such as emotions, learning processes and cognitions (Lazarus 1991).

Changes in body posture, vocalisation or facial expression indicate emotional responses to significant situations. We focus now on studies about the expression of emotions.

Darwin and the expression of emotions

In 1872, Darwin published his book *The Expression of the Emotions in Man and Animals*. As the title suggests, Darwin's book is mainly about expression and not about the underlying emotions. This work was originally intended as a single chapter in his *Descent of Man* (1871) but Darwin's reflections on the nature and origin

Figure 7.1 Darwin's pictures of anger in different species

Sources: Darwin (1872) and Dalgleish (2004)

Photo sources Alamy Images / Classic Image

of emotional expressions expanded into a full-length study. His interest in studying emotions began when he started to make notes of his first child, William, and his other children. Later on, his study included the expression of emotion in adults as well as animals. For example, he sent dozens of questionnaires around Britain and other parts of the British Empire, asking missionaries, zookeepers and colonialists to observe the expressions of 'savages' and animals.

Darwin emphasised the evolutionary continuity between animal and human emotions. To reveal cross-species similarities, he compared and analysed countless sketches and photographs of humans and other animals in different emotional states. He describes how birds ruffle their feathers when angry or frightened. For example, swans, when angered, raise their wings and tail, and erect their feathers. They open their beaks, and make rapid, paddling movements forwards, against anyone who approaches the water's edge too closely. A dog that is on the point of attacking an antagonist, utters a savage growl while his ears are pressed backwards, and the upper lip bares his canines. Something similar happens when humans retract their upper lip, showing the canine tooth on one side of the face. Their face is half averted from the person causing the offence (Figure 7.1).

In his *Expression*, Darwin emphasised two important points. The first point was that emotions in humans and other animals have an adaptive function. This followed logically from his work on evolution. He also argued that the expression of emotions such as grimaces, bared teeth, or tears were functionless remnants of actions from the evolutionary past. His second point was that a limited repertoire of basic emotions is present across species as well as across cultures.

How did current ideas influence Darwin's thinking about emotional expression? How did he explain emotional expression? How did he respond to current theological accounts of human nature (Dixon 2003)? When Darwin started to think about emotions in the late 1830s, he read influential books on moral philosophy and natural theology. One of his conclusions from studying these works was that all actions are determined by habits, by hereditary character, by education or by chance. Thus Darwin began to speculate on how habits that individuals developed during their life, could be inherited. This was a central idea in nineteenth-century evolutionary psychology which implied that mental capacities could be both innate and learned; innate to individuals, but initially learned and transmitted to them by their evolutionary ancestors. Recall from section 1.3 (Biology) that the inheritance of acquired characteristics was a current idea in those times, today mostly associated with the French biologist Jean-Baptiste Lamarck (1744–1829).

The novelty of Darwin's evolutionary psychology was that he shifted the focus away from the experience of the individual to the individual's ancestors (Dixon 2003). He reasoned that if emotions were innate in lower animals, one could assume that they were also innate in humans. The implication was that the current psychology, based on the idea that individuals start life with a blank slate, needed an explanation of innate, inherited capacities. An important influence on Darwin's thought about expression was an essay on the physiology of laughter by philosopher Herbert Spencer (1863, as described by Dixon 2003). Darwin adopted his idea that facial expressions are the product of the involuntary action of the nervous system. But he was particularly struck by a sentence which said that the muscular actions producing emotional expressions are purposeless. Thomas Dixon (2003) notes that Darwin underlined the word 'purposeless' in his copy, and added the phrase: 'so for frantic gestures of rage or intense grief'.

Darwin did not believe that the primary function of expression was to communicate the inner feelings of an individual to his or her fellow man through outer messages. This communicative function was only a byproduct of facial and bodily movements that had other functions. He explained these movements as inherited habits that in the past were connected with emotions but now regarded as 'expressions'. Thus Darwin did not develop a theory about the origin or function of emotions. He was mainly interested in the physiology and expressions associated with emotions.

The most surprising thing about Darwin's *Expression* was that it lacked an explanation in terms of natural selection. The phrase 'natural selection' occurs four times while it is used over one hundred times in the *Descent*. How can we explain the non-Darwinian character of this book (Richards 1987; Dixon 2003)? To understand why Darwin gave hardly any attention to the communicative role and evolutionary benefit of emotional expression, we need to know that he read an influential book about the anatomy and philosophy of expression by Charles Bell (1844, as described by Dixon 2003). Through this book, he became familiar with the muscles and innervations of the human face. But he objected to Bell's claim that emotional expressions such as grimaces, smiles, frowns and blushes were a kind of natural language, invented by a divine being.

In attacking Bell's theory that a supernatural inventor created nerves and muscles, allowing humans to communicate emotions to one another, Darwin denied that expressions had any use at all. He regarded them as habits that were once useful but were rendered useless by changing environmental conditions. As the universality of many expressions in humans and other animals indicated common evolutionary origins, Darwin proposed three explanatory principles:

- *The principle of serviceable associated habits*. This principle holds that expressions begin as voluntary responses, become habitual, and as a result of their adaptive utility, are passed on to the next generation. For example, the bare-teeth expression of an animal, used to threaten an opponent, was originally a part of the action of biting another animal. The facial expression that humans make to express disgust was originally associated with the action of actually spitting out harmful food.

- *The principle of antithesis*. This principle implies that when one emotion is the opposite of another emotion that has an associated expression, the first emotion can lead to an opposite expression. For example, feelings of indignation cause us to move our arms forwards as if to attack somebody. The opposite feelings of apology lead us to retract our arms and hunch our shoulders.

● *The principle of direct action of the nervous system.* This principle stipulates that certain expressions result from an excess of nervous energy, spilling over into other pathways. An example would be the trembling produced by fear.

To conclude, Darwin emphasised the universality and implied innateness of emotional expressions in humans and other animals. But in his zeal to criticise mistaken ideas, he argued that emotional expressions would be functionless. Instead of explaining expressions as naturally selected responses, he got things wrong.

The universality of emotional expressions

Almost one hundred years after Darwin's *Expression*, Paul Ekman and his colleague Wallace Friesen (1971) provided more evidence about the universality of emotional expressions. This evidence came from cross-cultural studies and the development of an instrument to objectively measure facial expression. Their cross-cultural studies were particularly interesting because they focused on the South Fore, a preliterate tribe in New Guinea that existed in isolation from Western culture. The tribe was supposed to associate the same emotion concepts with the same facial expressions as do members of literate cultures.

KEY FIGURE   Paul Ekman

Paul Ekman is a clinical psychologist. He is currently the manager of a company that produces training devices relevant to emotional skills, and initiates research relevant to national security and law enforcement.

Selected works

Facial Action Coding System (1978), with Wallace Friesen

The Face of Man: Expressions of Universal Emotions in a New Guinea Village (1980)

Emotions Revealed: Understanding Faces and Feelings (2003)

What the Face Reveals (2005), with E. Rosenberg

Photo source: Getty Images

Ekman and Friesen (1971) read stories to members of the tribe, describing emotional events such as the death of a child, the meeting of a friend, or the smelling of rotten food. The researchers also showed photographs of the corresponding facial expressions: a frowning face, a smile and a wrinkled nose. When subjects were asked to match each facial expression with a story, they answered in a similar way as Western subjects would do. Ekman and Friesen studied expressions which corresponded with happiness, anger, surprise, disgust, fear and sadness. This evidence supported the hypothesis that certain facial expressions of emotions are universal. The possibility that an isolated tribe used the same expressions one generation after another by chance, was small.

Later studies, based on behavioural and physiological analyses of expressions, provided more support for the universalist claim (Levenson et al. 1992). The relationship between emotional state and its expression has been hotly debated. One view suggests that human facial expression reflects the emotional state of the subjects (Levenson et al. 1992) while the opposing view argues that facial expressions may manipulate the behaviour and emotional state of others, spoiling the evidence for universality (Fridlund 1994; Russell 1994). Specifically, the opposing view argues that universal expressions should show no variation while Ekman and his colleagues insist that some variation is to be expected and cannot injure the claim for universality.

An important source of variation is culture. Facial expressions may differ from one culture to another due to display rules. These are socially learned rules about the management of facial expression. Ekman (2003) tested the influence of display rules and showed that Japanese and Americans had the same facial expressions when watching films of surgery and accidents. But when researchers were also present, the Japanese more than the Americans concealed negative expressions with a smile. This concealment is supposed to be the result of Japanese culture to control negative emotional expressions in public and promote communal harmony.

In sum, the debate about reflection versus manipulation appears to confuse levels of analysis which are both important and do not exclude one another (Hauser 1996). Ekman's work is focused on the mechanisms underlying facial expressions such as changes in physiology (e.g. heart rate). His critics consider the function of facial expression which may be involuntary responses to certain events or voluntary signals that do not reflect true emotional states.

The evidence for universal expressions may come from cross-cultural studies but also from objectively measured facial expressions. That is why Ekman and Friesen (1978) developed the Facial Acting Coding System (FACS) that identifies specific groups of facial muscles – called Action Units (AU) – in emotional expressions. Descriptions have been made about which facial muscles are involved in expressing the basic emotions of happiness, sadness, anger, fear, disgust and surprise which are recognised universally. As an example, for anger, eyebrows are raised and drawn together, lips are stretched and the chin raised. Various studies have validated the usefulness of the FACS system for identifying universal facial emotions and the unique involvement of individual Action Units. Although different expressions may share AUs, each expression has unique AUs. For example, unique for anger are AU9 (nose wrinkler) and AU16 (lower lip depressor) (Figure 7.2).

   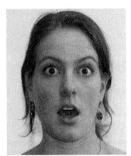

Happy: raised cheek, lip corner pull and mouth open

Sad: Raised inner brow, brow lower, eye lid tight, lip stretch and raised chin

Anger: raised outer brow, brow lower, lid tight, nose wrinkler, raised upper lip, depressed lower lip, lip stretch, jaw drop

Fear: raised upper eye lid, jaw drop

Figure 7.2 Facial expressions of emotions

Source: Kohler et al. (2004)

7.3 Facial expressions in primates

Darwin (1872) emphasised the evolutionary continuity between animal and human emotions. To reveal cross-species similarities, he compared sketches and photographs of humans and other animals in different emotional states. One hundred years later, facial expressions have been found cross-culturally for six basic emotions: fear, anger, surprise, happiness/joy, sadness and disgust (Ekman and Friesen 1971). Can these facial expressions also be found in non-human primates? For example, when full of joy we laugh with our mouth open, making sounds like ha-ha-ha. Humans seem to share this expression with chimpanzees. How similar are facial expressions in humans and chimpanzees, our closest relatives?

Facial expression musculature and sociality

The musculature for facial expression is present in all vertebrates. In the course of evolution, this musculature has been conserved throughout all vertebrate animals. Facial musculature has primarily a function in feeding and respiration. It is only in social mammals that facial musculature has taken an additional function in communication. Studies on non-primate mammals indicate that they are able to recognise individual faces and respond to emotion cues in faces (e.g. stress, anxiety). Sheep are able to discriminate between different breeds of sheep, between sheep sexes, and between sheep faces and human faces (Tate et al. 2006).

Facial expressions are important in primates because they are highly social animals. Although some mammalian species such as lions, wolves and elephants are highly social, all primate species are highly social for at least part of their life. As primates live in complex social networks, they rely on the production and processing of facial expressions to communicate with conspecifics. Facial expressions are rooted in the ancestral communicative displays of primates. A large body of research suggests that humans and chimpanzees use facial expressions in their interactions with conspecifics. Studies of chimpanzees have demonstrated that they are able to recognise the faces of close relatives as well as to accurately classify facial expressions of conspecifics (Burrows 2008). There is evidence that a facial expression like laughing is similar in humans and chimpanzees (Box 7.2 Laughing in humans and chimpanzees).

BOX 7.2 Laughing in humans and chimpanzees

Much research has been done on negative emotions such as fear and anger. In recent times, the attention has been widened to positive emotions like pride and joy. Both negative and positive emotions have their roots in limbic structures that we share with other mammals. All these animals experience joy when playing socially, greeting friends, or grooming one another (Bekoff 2007). The joy experienced during social play connects individuals and relaxes interactions. We can discern social play from serious activities by its exuberant behaviours, excited vocalisations and facial expressions. In humans, we see similar things. When people spontaneously dance, jump, sing or laugh, we infer that they are enjoying themselves. In young children, laughing is easily evoked by playful tickling. The question of why being tickled by someone else is more exciting than tickling oneself, has much to do with social cues that control the underlying neural systems (Panksepp 2000). Thus laughter is a social phenomenon because individuals share joy and playfulness.

How similar is laughter in humans and other primates? Darwin (1872) suggested that monkeys make similar laughing sounds and jaw movements as humans do. He supposed that we may share laughter with close primate relatives because it was present in our common ancestors. Modern research demonstrates that a comparison between chimpanzees and humans produces similarities as well as differences. We first consider vocalisations and then facial expressions. A study among students showed that they could not recognise audio recordings of chimpanzee laughter as being laughlike (Provine 2000). The most common association was 'panting' while other associations described the sounds as 'asthma attack', 'hyperventilation', or 'having sex'. The most conspicuous similarity between human and chimpanzee laughing is its rhythmic structure. The chimp's panting and the human's laughing are bursts of sounds occurring at regular intervals. Though the chimp's rhythm is faster because they vocalise during inhalation as well as exhalation. If we only consider the exhalation, the chimp's rhythm is half the human's. Typically, human laughter is produced by interrupting a single exhalation (ha-ha-ha). In contrast, chimpanzee laughter is produced during each inhalation (ah) and exhalation (ah). The human exhale-only version of laughter is a recent evolutionary development since the inhale–exhale version is shared by other primates (Provine 2000).

Chimpanzees laugh with panting sounds which may originate from playful chasing of one another. Humans laugh as they speak, by modulating an exhalation. The close coupling between breathing and vocalisation in chimps may help to explain why they can't talk.

Laughing may be inferred from vocalisations as well as from facial expressions. In all primates social play is accompanied by the play face or relaxed open mouth display (ROM). This display would originate from the intention to play-bite on one another's body parts (Van Hooff and Preuschoft 2003). In non-human primates, the ROM is considered as a homologue or precursor of human laughter. Another facial expression in non-human primates, the silent bared-teeth display (SBT), is regarded as a homologue or precursor of human smiling.

Jan van Hooff (1972) found that ROM and SBT are displayed in different behavioural contexts: ROM associated with play, SBT related to non-hostility and friendliness. Later research by Bridget Waller and Robin Dunbar (2005) confirmed that ROM was mainly observed during social play whereas SBT signalled friendliness. Both displays may have the ultimate or original function of social bonding.

How similar are facial expressions in humans and chimpanzees?

Similarity in facial expressions of primates is partly due to the general conservation of facial muscles, supporting these expressions. It is also partly the result of ritualisation by which an adaptive facial movement takes on a new function. For example, the facial expression of disgust originated from the rejection of bad-tasting food to protect the body. But later on, it expanded in humans into a stereotypic expression of anything one's culture considers offensive, such as poor hygiene or eating cockroaches (Rozin 1996). The result of this ritualisation is that facial expressions are easy to recognise and understand by conspecifcs.

Determining similarity in terms of homology is not easy. Recall from section 1.3 (Biology) that homology refers to similarity of function in different species resulting from common ancestry. For example, humans have forward-projecting eyes and grasping hands in common with chimpanzees due to descent from a common ancestor. Determining homology in facial expressions is hard because one can make comparisons on many levels. Expressions can be similar due to a common genetic basis, musculature, neural basis or function. For example, in the course of primate evolution, the muscles involved in the production of facial expressions have changed

Chimpanzee			Equivalent human facial expression?		
Facial expression		Prototype AUs	**Facial expression**		Prototype AUs
	Bulging-lip display	**AU17** **AU24**		Angry face	AU4 AU5 AU7 **AU17** **AU24**
	Silent bared-teeth display	AU10 **AU12** AU16 **AU25**		Smile	AU6 **AU12** **AU25**
	Scream	**AU10** **AU12** **AU16** **AU25** **AU27**		Scream	AU4 AU6 AU7 **AU10** **AU12** **AU16** **AU25** **AU27**
	Pant-hoot	AU22 AU25 AU26			
	Relaxed open mouth	**AU12** **AU25** **AU26**		Laughter	AU6 **AU12** **AU25** **AU26**

Figure 7.3 Chimpanzee and human facial expressions characterised by the chimpanzee and human FACS systems

Source: Parr and Waller (2007)

little. Lisa Parr and Bridget Waller (2007), in their study about facial expressions, conclude that primates share similar displays in appearance (expression), physiological structure (musculature), social context (function), and capacity to communicate with conspecifics (meaning).

The question is then how similarity in the facial expressions of humans and chimpanzees can be assessed. The reader will recall from section 7.2 that Ekman and Friesen (1978) developed a Facial Action Coding System (FACS) that identifies specific groups of facial muscles – called Action Units (AUs) – in emotional expressions. Descriptions have been made about which facial muscles are involved in expressing the basic emotions of happiness, sadness, anger, fear, disgust and surprise which are recognised universally. Various studies have validated the usefulness of the FACS system for identifying universal facial emotions and the involvement of AUs. Because of its anatomical basis to facial movements, the FACS is suited for modification and application to non-human primates.

Sarah Vick and her colleagues (2007) have developed a chimpanzee version of the FACS which enables comparison between chimpanzees and humans, based on homologous musculature of the expressions. Facial displays came primarily from a large database of chimpanzee facial expressions at the Yerkes National Primate Research Center (USA). All facial displays occurred naturally during social interactions and were not evoked by experiments. Figure 7.3 shows several chimpanzee facial expressions listed with their AU codes derived from this study, and comparable human facial expressions with their AU codes.

Nine chimpanzee facial expressions are thought to have equivalents in humans. For example, both chimpanzees and humans use the same groups of facial muscles when angry, laughing or smiling. One chimpanzee expression – the pant-hoot – has no human equivalent. In pant-hoots, lips are pursed with rounded mouth and forward pursed lips. The mouth can be slightly open as louder, rhythmic breathing hoot vocalisations 'hoo-hoo' occur. Low-pitched calls may become gradually louder and end with a scream. Pant-hoots are used in situations of general excitement, as a response to noise at a distance, distress, bluff display, play or during piloerection (Parr 2007).

The comparisons between chimpanzees and humans should be interpreted only in terms of the structure of the expression, not their meaning or function. An important question in future research is therefore whether non-human primates attribute an emotional disposition to individuals who produce facial expressions (Parr et al. 2007).

7.4 The neural basis of emotions

Emotions are shaped by natural selection to prepare the organism for threats or opportunities. For example, fear prepares the organism for dangerous situations. Recall from section 1.5 (Neuroscience) that this emotion activates an old and specialised area in the brain – the amygdala – when we run into dangerous situations. If parts of the brain are involved in the processing of emotions, then this hard-wired organ may provide evidence that emotions are adaptive responses. The involvement of the brain in emotions raises different questions. How have neuroscientists theorised about the evolution of emotions? How are brain areas engaged in the processing of emotions?

Early evolutionary theorising regarded the human brain as an organ with a hierarchical structure. That is, neuroscientists distinguished lower and higher levels in the brain which corresponded with early and modern periods in the evolutionary history of species. Lower levels in the brain were associated with animal emotions while higher levels represented the rational side of humans. Thinking in terms of higher and lower levels implied the idea of a conflict between wild passions and civilised reason. This idea of 'the beast in man' is an old theme in the history of Western thought, which received a new impulse with the rise of evolutionary thought (Harrington 1991). We will review some early and modern theories about the evolution of the emotional brain.

Evolutionary theories about the emotional brain

John Hughlings Jackson

An early theory by John Hughlings Jackson (1887) assumed that the nervous system had evolved over time into a hierarchy of functions. High-level functions associated with rational thought had the task of controlling the lower animal levels. In various neurological disorders this high-level control was lost, releasing energy from primitive brain levels. Jackson considered this loss of high-level control and release of low-level energy as the reversal of the evolutionary process. In other words, the loss of control was a kind of backward process or involution which he called 'dissolution'. Jackson's hierarchical theory of mind and brain influenced Sigmund Freud's psychoanalytic theory with its concept of regression – a defence mechanism in which the individual reverts to immature behaviour of an earlier stage of development when overwhelmed by problems – and its image of a rational ego struggling to control the passionate id, the component of the personality that contains the biological drives, providing the psyche with energy.

James Papez

In the late 1930s, neuroanatomist James Papez elaborated on Jackson's idea that the seat of emotions was to be found in lower levels of the brain hierarchy. He described a circuit for emotion which French neuroanatomist Paul Broca had earlier called *le grand lobe limbique* (the Latin word *limbus* means 'rim' or 'border'). Structures contained within this great limbic circuit include the hypothalamus, hippocampus and cingulate gyrus. These brain areas were believed at the time to be primarily concerned with olfactory and gustatory functions (smell and taste).

brainstem

the lower part of the brain that becomes the spinal cord.

limbic system

a loosely defined, widespread group of brain nuclei that innervate one another, forming a network that is involved in emotions, memory formation, drive and motivation. It includes parts of the cerebral cortex, and subcortical structures like amygdala and hippocampus.

Paul MacLean

Neuroscientist Paul MacLean (e.g. 1949, 1990) integrated the ideas of Papez and others into an influential, evolutionary theory of emotion. He argued for a triune model of the brain which consisted of three gross layers, corresponding with the emergence of three groups of animals in successive evolutionary periods: the reptilian brain, the old mammalian brain, and the new mammalian or primate brain (Figure 7.4). According to this brain theory, the reptilian layer (the **brainstem**) dominates in the brain of snakes and lizards. It does not achieve well in learning but tends to use instincts and drives. In humans, the reptilian brain controls survival functions like breathing and heart rate. The palaeo-mammalian layer (the **limbic system**) is associated with the emergence of mammals. It has a major role in the adaptive problems of mammals, such as threats from predators

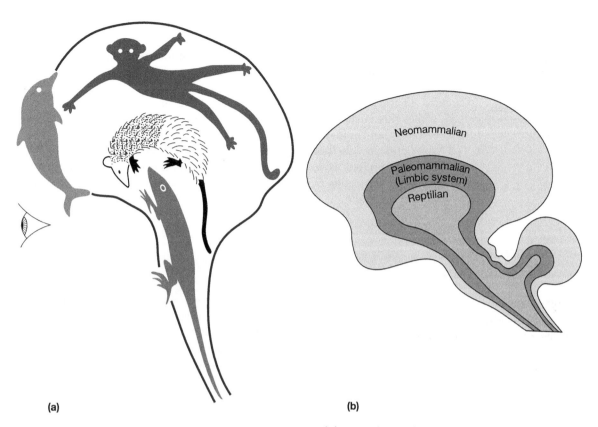

(a)   (b)

Figure 7.4 Paul MacLean's triune brain (a) artistic version; (b) scientific version
Source: Scientific version from MacLean (1990)

and offspring needing parental care. The neo-mammalian or primate layer (the neocortex) is the most recent part of our brain. It consists of two cerebral hemispheres which have expanded in primates in comparison with other mammals. The neocortex is the source of our cognitive, linguistic and cultural capacities. It modulates the expression of emotions that originate from the palaeo-mammalian brain and affords considerable flexibility and creativity in thinking and planning (Baars and Gage 2010).

Joseph LeDoux

An important insight of MacLean was his emphasis on the evolution of the brain as a key to understanding emotions. He regarded emotions as brain functions involved in maintaining the survival of individuals and species. But as pointed out by Joseph LeDoux (1996) in his study *The Emotional Brain*, the drawback of MacLean's theory is that it is not possible to package the emotional brain and its evolutionary history into one, that is, limbic system. As emotions are tightly connected with cognition, memory and motivation, they are involved in many brain areas. In other words, there is nothing wrong with emotional evolution but MacLean's application was too broad.

insula

a small brain area between the temporal and frontal lobes, receiving homoeostatic and emotional information that originates within the body, as well as olfactory and gustatory information (smell and taste).

Emotional responses have an adaptive function by preparing an organism's behaviour for significant events and communicating these events through expressions to other members of the species. But since different emotions are concerned with different adaptive problems – avoiding predators, finding healthy food or caring for offspring – each may need a different brain area. The brain has indeed numerous circuits, supporting different types of emotions. Some may be parallel (e.g. fear and joy), while other circuits process more than one emotion. The circuitry of the amygdala sustains fear, but may also be used to modulate anger (Schulkin et al. 2003).

Despite criticism, the notion of a limbic system or a set of limbic structures in the brain has survived. Neuroscientists distinguish various brain structures that are involved in the processing of emotions (Dalgleish 2004) Box 7.3 Emotion processing structures in the brain).

BOX 7.3 Emotion processing structures in the brain

The amygdala

Research has established that the amygdala is one of the most important brain areas for emotion. It plays a major role in the processing of fear signals. Studies demonstrate that in humans, amygdala lesions can selectively impair the ability to recognise fear. Neuroimaging studies (fMRI) support the involvement of the amygdala in the processing of facial expression. In fear conditioning, rats as well as humans may acquire fear when meaningless stimuli are presented with threatening events (Öhmann 2009). This line of research revealed that two pathways are engaged in the processing of fear. The first one is a fast but crude pathway – the thalamo-amygdala route – while the other one is a slow but accurate pathway – the thalamo-cortico-amygdala route (see Figure 1.4). Direct access to the amygdala, supporting defensive responses on minimal information, makes perfect sense from an evolutionary point of view. There is also evidence that humans with a damaged amygdala have trouble recognising fear as well as anger. Other studies indicate that the amygdala is also engaged in the consolidation of emotional memories.

The prefrontal cortex

Research indicates that the **prefrontal cortex (PFC)**, particularly the orbitofrontal area – lying just above the orbits or eyesockets – is involved in learning emotional and motivational value of stimuli, such as food, drink and sex. It is supposed that the prefrontal cortex works together with the amygdala. Another line of research suggests that prefrontal areas send signals to other areas, guiding behaviour towards the most adaptive goals. This may occur when immediate rewards strongly influence certain behavioural choices, while it is more adaptive to delay gratification. Further research suggests that the left and right sides of the PFC are specialised for negative and positive emotions. The right-sided PFC is specialised in negative emotions which are triggered by threatening or goal obstructing events. The left-sided PFC is specialised in positive emotions which are triggered by attractive, rewarding goals.

The anterior cingulate cortex

The **anterior cingulate cortex (ACC)** is considered as an area where visceral, attentional and emotional information are integrated for the regulation of emotions. This area is thought to monitor conflicts between the actual state of the organism and new information that may have emotional or motivational consequences. When such conflicts are discovered, information about the conflict passes from the ACC to the PFC where differing response options are resolved.

The insula

Like fear, the emotion of disgust has most clearly been shown to have a neural structure (Ward 2010). The **insula** is a small brain area buried within the brain, receiving homoeostatic and emotional information that originates within the body, as well as olfactory and gustatory information (smell and taste). Disgust, meaning literally 'bad taste', is supposed to be evolutionary related to contamination and disease through ingestion of harmful food. Brain imaging studies show that the insula is not only activated when we experience disgusting smells but also when we perceive disgust in the faces of others (Rizzolatti and Sinigaglia 2008; Keysers and Gazzola 2009).

The hypothalamus

Studies indicate that the **hypothalamus** is involved in the processing of rewarding stimuli. It seems to be part of an extensive reward network which includes the PFC and amygdala. Further studies revealed that the hypothalamus has an important role in motivations such as hunger and sex.

hypothalamus

area in the forebrain involved in the control of many autonomic processes (breathing, circulation, temperature, metabolism, sexual function) and in the release of many hormones.

prefrontal cortex (PFC)

the most forward part of the frontal lobe of each cerebral hemisphere, involved in high order functions in cognition such as judgement, prediction, planning, moderating correct social behaviour, and integrating information from outside the body with that from within (e.g. the limbic system).

anterior cingulate cortex (ACC)

an area in the brain where visceral, attentional and emotional information are integrated for the regulation of emotions.

Jaak Panksepp

Neuroscientist Jaak Panksepp (1998a, 2003, 2007) has developed an evolutionary theory of emotions which emphasises several points. The first point is that emotions are older than cognitions, with the implication that much of the human mind was laid down in ancient emotions that we share with many other animals. A second point is that, although emotions and cognitions interact, they should be distinguished. For example, emotions have intrinsic valence, meaning that they are characterised by negative or positive feelings that do not accompany pure cognitions. Furthermore, emotions generate spontaneous facial and bodily expressions which cognitions do not. A third point is that discrete emotions are part of emotional systems in the brain that organise motor programmes and autonomic as well as hormonal changes to respond to adaptive problems faced by animals.

Seven emotional systems in animal brains have been identified by evoking emotional responses through localised electrical stimulation of the brain. The first four systems are pre-mammalian since they are present in all vertebrates. To distinguish emotional systems from emotions they are written in capitals to emphasise that they are not simply psychological concepts. We follow Panksepp's convention of capitalisation. The systems of FEAR, RAGE, SEEKING and LUST appear shortly after vertebrates are born, and are essential ingredients for feelings of anxiety, anger, desire and eroticism in mammals:

- FEAR: this system deals with responses to painful and threatening events, resulting in flight, fight or freeze behaviour.
- RAGE: this system deals with anger as it may be aroused by frustration, bodily irritation or restrained movement.
- SEEKING: this system makes mammals curious about their world and stimulates behaviour towards food, shelter and sex.
- LUST: this system coordinates sexual behaviour and feelings.

When mammals entered the evolutionary scene about 200 mya, the emotional brain expanded because offspring needed sustained parental care. Three additional systems emerged – CARE, PANIC and PLAY – which are fundamental brain substrates for the feelings of nurturance, separation distress/sadness and social joy:

- CARE: this system in mothers and fathers promotes caregiving behaviours as well as social bonding.

Table 7.1(a) Postulated relationships between emotional systems, emotions and emotional disorders

Basic emotional system	Emergent emotions	Related emotional disorders
SEEKING (+ and −)	Interest	Obsessive compulsive
	Frustration	Paranoid schizophrenia
	Craving	Addictive personalities
RAGE (− and +)	Anger	Aggression
	Irritability	Psychopathic tendencies
	Contempt	Personality disorders
	Hatred	
FEAR (−)	Simple anxiety	Generalised anxiety disorders
	Worry	Phobias
	Psychic trauma	PTSD variants
PANIC (−)	Separation distress	Panic attacks
	Sadness	Pathological grief
	Guilt/shame	Depression
	Shyness	Agoraphobia
	Embarrassment	Social phobias, autism
PLAY (+)	Joy and glee	Mania
	Happy playfulness	ADHD
LUST (+ and −)	Erotic feelings	Fetishes
	Jealousy	Sexual addictions
CARE (+)	Nurturance	Dependency disorders
	Love	Autistic aloofness
	Attraction	Attachment disorders

Plus and minus signs indicate affective valence.

Source: Panksepp (2006)

- PANIC: this system responds to separation of young mammals from their (allo-) parents by activating crying and separation calls.
- PLAY: this system organises rough-and-tumble play as it spontaneously occurs in young mammals; it supports laughter as well and may be the neural basis of joy.

What is known about emotional systems, comes mainly from studies of non-human mammals such as rats. Ethical constraints on using invasive technologies to evoke emotional responses limit the study of emotions in humans. The emotional systems – with discrete emotions, related emotional disorders, associated brain areas as well as neurochemicals – are summarised in Tables 7.1(a) and (b).

Table 7.1(b) Postulated relationships between systems, brain areas and neuromodulators

Basic emotional systems	Key brain areas	Key neuromodulators
General pos. motivation	Nucleus accumbens – VTA	Dopamine (+),
		Glutamate (+),
SEEKING/expectancy	Mesolimbic and mesocortical outputs	Opioids (+),
	Lateral hypothalamus – PAG	Neurotensin (+),
		Many other
		Neuropeptides
RAGE/anger	Medial amygdala to Bed Nucleus of Stria Terminalis (BNST)	Substance P (+), ACh (+),
	Medial and glutamate (+) perifornical hypothalamic to PAG	
FEAR/anxiety	Central and lateral amygdala to medial hypothalamus and dorsal PAGCCK, alpha-MSH, NPY	Glutamate (+), DBI, CRH
LUST/sexuality	Cortico-medial amygdala, Bed Nucleus Stria Terminalis (BNST)	Steroids (+), Vasopressin, and Oxytocin, LH-RH, CCK
	Preoptic hypothalamus, VMH, PAG	
CARE/nurturance	Anterior cingulate, BNST	Oxytocin (+),
	Preoptic area, VTA, PAG	Prolactin (+)
		Dopamine (+),
		Opioids (+/−)
PANIC/separation distress	Anterior cingulate, BNST and preoptic area	Opioids (−),
	Dorsomedial thalamus, PAG	Oxytocin (−)
		Prolactin (−),
		CRF (+),
		Glutamate (+)
PLAY/joy	Dorso-medial dienceplalon	Opioids (+/−),
	Parafascicular area, PAG	Glutamate (+)
		Ach (+), TRH?

Plus and minus signs indicate affective valence.

Source: Panksepp (2006)

neuromodulation

the action of endogenous substances or neuromodulators – dopamine, serotonin and opioids – on neurons that are released in certain brain areas and involved at all levels of behaviour from reflexes to cognitions. For example, in primates serotonin has a role in controlling negative emotion or mood, and **opioids** play a role in regulating friendly interactions with conspecifics.

Michael Arbib and Jean-Marc Fellous

The previous theories argue that emotions are based on particular brain structures as they are produced in the course of evolution. But the neural basis of emotions can also be conceived as a matter of **neuromodulation** (Fellous 1999; Arbib and Fellous 2004). What is neuromodulation? To answer this question, we first focus on brain structures involved in emotions. The reader will recall that section 7.2 dealt with emotion as one step in the evolution of adaptive responses from reflexes to

opioids

A class of natural chemical that has similar properties to morphine and heroine, and which modulates behaviour, for example in reducing reactions to tissue damage, and regulating friendly interactions with conspecifics.

cognitions. Each step in this evolution recruits more brain structures. We have seen that various brain structures are involved in emotion processing (Box 7.3 Emotion processing structures in the brain). For example, the experience and expression of fear is impaired when the amygdala is damaged. Decision-making in emotional situations is also impaired in humans with damage to the prefrontal cortex. So these brain structures are engaged in internal and social aspects of emotion, together playing an essential role in the regulation of emotions.

Neuromodulation refers to the action of endogenous substances or neuromodulators on neurons (Fellous 1999; Arbib and Fellous 2004). These substances – dopamine, serotonine and opioids – are released in certain brain areas and involved at all levels of behaviour from reflexes to cognitions. The flexibility of emotional states is achieved by neuromodulators which can change the way single neurons operate. For example, it has been observed that dopamine neurons in monkeys fire to predicted rewards. In primates serotonine has a role in controlling negative emotion or mood, and opioids play a role in regulating friendly interactions with conspecifics. Being groomed increases the concentration of opioids in the brain (Aureli and Whiten 2003).

Emotions evolved to organise an animal's behaviour when it faced significant events as well as to communicate its experience to others by expressions. In the course of evolution, emotions as modes of organising behaviour were preceded by reflexes and drives, and followed by cognitions. They are also in between reflexes and cognitions with respect to their potential for neuromodulation and action specificity (Figure 7.5). Reflexes are sensorimotor responses that are extremely specific to the eliciting stimuli (e.g. knee jerk reflex), the neural basis of which undergoes little neuromodulation. On the other hand, cognitions such as memory and reasoning are highly unspecific with respect to actions and heavily subjected to neuromodulation. In Figure 7.5, the ellipses represent zones of increasing recruitment of brain structures.

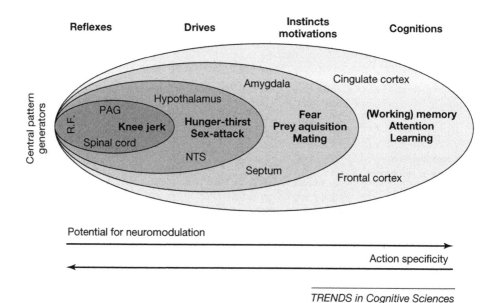

Figure 7.5 Organisation of behaviour with respect to potential for neuromodulation and action specificity

Source: Arbib and Fellous (2004)

7.5   The emergence of social emotions

What makes emotions social?

social emotion

kind of emotion that requires an evaluation of other individuals as well as some degree of self-consciousness. If evaluation implies that individuals may succeed or fail to meet social norms, this may lead to pairs of emotions such as pride–shame and envy–pity.

Since Darwin and Ekman, researchers have studied basic emotions. Some researchers have started to explore emotions such as pride, shame and guilt which are involved in social interactions. Evolutionary studies propose that social emotions resulted from the demands of group living. Climate change and deforestation forced our ape ancestors to switch from tightly organised, female kin-bonded groups to loosely organised male kin-bonded groups (Foley 1998; Lewin and Foley 2004). The problem of our hominid ancestors was to improve group loyalty. As fear and anger are negative emotions and unsuitable for subtle social bonding, emotions like shame and pride arose as better adaptive responses to the pressures of group living. What exactly are social emotions? How did humans come to experience and express a **social emotion** like pride? In general, why and how did social emotions emerge?

There is no agreement as to the number of social emotions. Some theorists consider only pride, shame and guilt, while others include, for example, humiliation, regret, remorse, love, gratitude, contempt and envy. What makes emotions social? Theorists agree that social emotions require an evaluation of other individuals as well as some degree of self-consciousness. The emergence of self-consciousness in individuals is thought to appear between 2 to 3 years of age (Box 7.4 Development of emotions over the first three years of life). If evaluation implies that individuals may succeed or fail to meet social norms, this may lead to pairs of emotions such as pride–shame and envy–pity (Buck 1999). If one succeeds in meeting expectations, one may feel proud; if one fails, one feels ashamed; if the other comparison succeeds, one may feel envious, but if the other one fails, one may experience pity. Thus, social emotions emerge when individuals succeed or fail in meeting group standards. Let us focus on two specific emotions in social life.

BOX 7.4   Development of emotions over the first three years of life

Developmental psychologists think that the child's emotional life at birth is bipolar. The two poles are general distress marked by crying and irritability, and pleasure marked by satiation, attention, interest and responsivity to the environment. Michael Lewis' review (2010) enables us to summarise a model of emotional development (Figure 7.6). By 3 months, joy emerges when the child is seeing familiar faces as well as sadness when positive stimuli are withdrawn. Disgust also appears in the primitive form of spitting out unpleasant food or objects. The child expresses these emotions already in appropriate contexts. Between 4 and 6 months anger emerges when the child is prevented from moving. This emotion is considered a response designed to overcome obstacles. Surprise also emerges

in the first 6 months, for instance when they are confronted with events that violate their expectations. Fear emerges later in the first 7–8 months, for example in stranger fear when a face is unfamiliar and does not correspond with the internal representation or memory of faces.

So in the first 8–9 months children's emotional behaviour reflects the six primary, or basic emotions of joy, sadness, disgust, anger, surprise and fear. In the second year of life the capacity of consciousness or objective self-awareness (self-referential behaviour) arises, resulting in self-conscious emotions which include embarrassment, empathy and envy. These emotions require self-consciousness but not self-evaluation. Between 2 and 3 years the child develops the capacity to evaluate its behaviour against an external (parental) or internal (own) standard. This capacity for self-evaluation gives rise to another set of emotions which include pride, shame and guilt.

The emergence of self-conscious emotions is related to the cognitive capacity to pay attention to the self. Self-conscious emotions differ from basic emotions because they require self-awareness and self-representations. It is true that basic emotions like fear or anger may also involve self-evaluative processes, but they are not required (Tracy and Robins 2007b). Since William James (1890), the term 'self' can refer either to the person as the target of appraisal (for example, when one introspectively evaluates how one is doing), or to the person as a source of agency (for instance, when one attributes the source of perception, thought or behaviour to one's body or mind). Put otherwise, a sense of self refers to an ongoing sense of self-awareness (the 'I') as well as the capacity for complex self-representations (the 'me', or the mental representations that make up one's identity). Both enable self-evaluations and therefore self-conscious emotions.

For evolutionary psychology, the issue of self-conscious emotions raises various questions. For example, can we attribute a self to animals? How is the evolution of self related to the demands of social life? How can self evolution be reconstructed? Recently, Jaak Panksepp and Georg Northoff (2009), drawing on recent literature from both human and animal research, proposed a trans-species core-self based on subcortical–cortical networks. This core-self is thought to be well integrated with basic attentional, emotional and motivational functions that are shared between humans and other mammals. It allows organisms to adapt to and integrate with the physical and social environment.

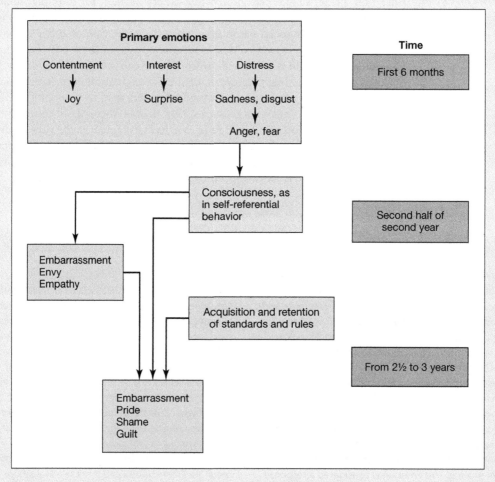

Figure 7.6 Development of emotions over the first three years
Source: Lewis (2010)

Pride and shame

Individuals who succeed at school, work and sport, do not simply show excitement or happiness but particularly pride. As highly social creatures, we are sensitive to our place in status hierarchies which depends on achievement and mastery. Pride is generally regarded as something to be sought out in children and adults, and shame is considered as something to be avoided. While the emotion of pride is associated with status enhancement, shame is associated with status loss. Pride and shame are not included in the set of basic emotions which are thought to be innate, shared with individuals from different cultures and other primates, and recognised by discrete non-verbal expressions. However, recent studies indicate that these emotions have innate, non-verbal expressions. They may, then, be considered as evolved responses to success and failure which resemble the dominance and submission displays in non-human primates (Tracy and Matsumoto 2008).

How are pride and shame expressed? Displays of pride include an expanded posture, head tilted slightly backwards, and arms outstretched from the body. This kind of display may be observed in dominant chimpanzees after defeating a rival as well as in chest-beating displays. The pride display probably originated as a way of appearing larger, more dominant and attracting attention. The expression of shame includes slumped shoulders and narrowed chest. This diminished posture display resembles submission as it may be observed in non-human primates. It probably originated as a signal to accept an aggressor's power, thereby saving energy.

Pride and shame are displays used when individuals experience success and failure. Prototypical situations in which humans show these emotions are sport events (Tracy and Robins 2004a, 2007a; Tracy and Matsumoto 2008). Research findings about sighted and congenitally blind athletes from 37 nations in judo matches in the 2004 Olympic and Paralympic games show that they display the prototypical expressions of pride and shame in response to success and failure (Figure 7.7).

Congenitally blind individuals who could not have learned to show pride and shame from watching other people, none the less displayed the same expressions in the same situation. The authors conclude from this finding that humans have an innate propensity to respond similarly to success and failure. An unexpected finding was that sighted athletes from individualistic cultures (Europe, North America) showed less shame than athletes from other cultures. One explanation would be that they suppressed shame because in their cultures shame is stigmatised and self-assertion emphasised. A further conclusion of the authors is that their findings challenge the idea that only a small set of emotions are basic. Finally, it seems that pride and shame emerged to promote and inhibit social status in evolution.

Why did humans become so emotional?

Most animals appear to display just a few emotional states, whereas humans reveal many such states. Not only can we be fearful, angry, disgusted, sad, surprised or happy, but also more or less intensely fearful, angry and so on. For example, fear can move from concern, through panic, to terror; happiness or joy can move from contentment, through cheerfulness, to elation; and a sad state can vary from a discouraged to a dismayed and despondent state. We have many words for low, moderate and high levels of emotionality.

(a)   (b)

Figure 7.7 Pride expression in response to victory by a sighted (left) and congenitally blind (right) athlete
Source: Tracy and Matsumoto (2008)
Photo source: Bob Willingham

With regard to social emotions, they are relatively new in evolution and may be considered as mixtures of basic emotions. One way to enhance the emotional repertoire of humans would be to generate new emotional states by combining basic emotions. Robert Plutchik (1994) views the combination of emotions analogous to the mixing of colours. For example, the mix of happiness and acceptance would produce friendliness. And pride would be the combination of anger and joy. It is clear that humans possess the capacity to produce new emotions but how this emotional mixing happens on the neural level is unknown. What we know is that social emotions engage the same brain structures as basic emotions (Parr and Waller 2007; Box 7.3).

Why did humans become so emotional? A reflexive response would be that we have no witnesses from ancient times at hand, making any answer speculative. That is why evolutionary scientists are sometimes criticised for telling stories instead of producing testable hypotheses (Box 7.5 Just So Stories). Recent theorising and research findings suggest that a large emotional repertoire is very suitable for facilitating social interactions as well as group organisation (Spoor and Kelly 2004). Emotions like guilt and gratitude, for example, advance cooperation between members of a group and prevent individuals moving on. Sincere emotional expression, in particular facial expression, serves to communicate important information between individuals. And social status can be regulated by pride and shame, resulting in flexible patterns of interaction and organisation. In short, the capacity to use diverse and subtle emotions could help humans to create strong bonds when needed.

BOX 7.5 Just So Stories

Rudyard Kipling (1865–1936) was an English fiction writer, mainly remembered for his tales and poems about British soldiers in India and his tales for children. One of his classics is *Just So Stories* (1994) with tales about the origins of animals. One of his tales 'explains' how the elephant got his trunk. Long ago, when elephants had only bumps for noses, a curious young elephant is determined to find out what crocodiles eat for dinner. When the youngster sticks its nose out too far, a hungry crocodile stretches it into the long trunk that elephants have today.

Kipling's tale about the unfortunate elephant suggests that questioning is a perilous business. Following Darwin's publication of his studies, a lot of journal articles were full of just so stories, that is, speculations and imaginative explanations of why an anatomical structure evolved or how it had survival value in earlier periods.

These studies were not supported by evidence. In one of his articles, the influential and widely read evolutionary scientist Stephen Gould (1978) pointed out that many explanations of adaptive traits are 'just so stories'. In other words, they may tell plausible stories but do not produce testable hypotheses.

Ever since sociobiologists and evolutionary psychologists have studied human beings, they have had to contend with the accusation that their work consists of modern-day just so stories. To call something a Just So Story is to dismiss it as unscientific poppycock. David Barash and Judith Lipton (2009) are right when they argue that it is time to stop this bad habit. Every scientist should know that science does not end up with a story, but generally begins as one. It all starts with questioning: why? how? what if?

How social emotions emerged

As social emotions facilitate interactions and group-living, we should look at how they became part of our life. The reader may recall that we discussed social organisation of primates in section 6.3 (The social evolution of primates). We recapitulate the main points here. Male and female reproductive success is determined by different factors: in females by access to food, in males by access to females. This has an impact on how they are socially organised. Genetically related females form the core of groups, enabling them to share information about food locations. This mode of social organisation, known as 'female kin-bonding', can be found in lemurs and many monkeys. Males leave the group at sexual maturity to breed in other groups. A different mode of social organisation, known as male kin-bonding, evolved in chimpanzees. In this mode of organisation it is the females who leave their natal group at sexual maturity, joining another group for breeding.

Originally, apes probably had the same female kin-bonded groups as monkeys. But things changed at the end of the Miocene, approximately 10–15 mya, when a cooling climate caused the African forest to shrink and fragment (Turner and Antón 2004). A drier and more diverse habitat evolved with small and widely dispersed patches of food, causing females to forage over large areas. This ecological shift required a flexible foraging strategy which was incompatible with tightly kin-bonded female groups. Such a new kind of ecology would favour the evolution of a male kin-bonded social structure in which genetically related males defend females and their offspring against males from neighbouring groups (Foley 1996; Lewin and Foley 2004). The emergence of male kin-bonding among the large African apes (gorillas, chimpanzees) provided the ancestral condition from which the sociality of humans would be derived (Figure 7.8). Figure 7.8 shows that female kin-bonding evolved only in Old World monkeys and male kin-bonding evolved in chimpanzees and humans.

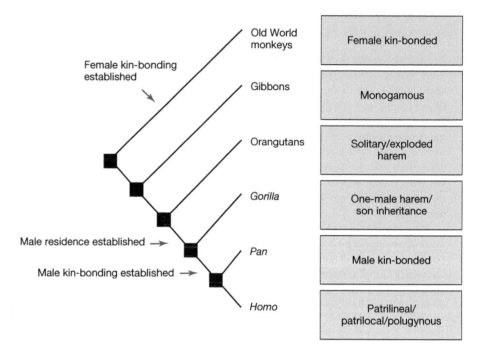

Figure 7.8 The phylogeny of hominid social organisation
Source: Lewin and Foley (2004)

One consequence of the Miocene events was a transition from female to male kin-bonded groups. Another one was that while most monkeys maintained their life in the trees, apes were forced out onto the savanna (Potts 1996; Turner 2007). This habitat was more dangerous than the forest because predators such as primitive tigers and hyenas were present in large numbers, feeding on herbivores like antelopes in the grasslands. Apes are vulnerable on this habitat because they are slower than herding animals. In addition, the high grasses make it difficult to see predators because apes can only stand upright for short periods. This handicap makes clear that walking upright would increase fitness and become one of the first adaptations for humans living on the savanna. Moreover, when danger is present, apes become very noisy and agitated which makes them an easier target for predators. This problem could be solved when neocortical brain areas came to control the vocal expression of emotions.

All this vulnerability would be a minor issue if apes were well organised like monkeys who cross the savanna in military fashion with females and offspring in the centre and males at the flanks. As apes had no core of closely related females, they used male dominance, but on its own this could not sustain tight-knit social structures. What male kin-bonded groups particularly lacked were intergenerational bonds between related females. Thus the problem of apes was that they had no effective social organisation. What could they do? Dominant males could use anger directed at someone's failure to meet expectations. But anger arouses fear in the offending individual and may start a cycle of anger and counter-anger which does not promote solidarity (Turner 2000, 2007).

The function of positive emotions

Negative emotions are adaptive in life-threatening situations that require quick and decisive action in order to survive. That is why they tend to narrow a person's repertoire of thought and action (fight, flight or freeze). For example, studies of eyewitness accounts of crime show that recollections are often limited to the aggressor's weapon. Witnesses can report details about the weapon but little about the aggressive individual. This phenomenon, known as 'weapon focus', has been observed in real-life and laboratory situations (Rossano 2003).

positive emotion
emotion associated with diverse forms of goal attainment or the move towards it, including happiness/joy, love/ affection, pride and relief.

While negative emotions like fear and anger narrow one's attention and are adaptive for facing short-term events, **positive emotions** such as pride and love widen the attention and encourage cognitive flexibility that may enhance long-term survival. Over time, broadening one's focus and repertoire of thought and action may help to build physical, psychological and social resources. This broaden-and-build theory of positive emotions, developed by Barbara Fredrickson (1998), has received empirical support (e.g. Cohn et al. 2009; Garland et al. 2010; Johnson et al. 2010). Positive emotions increase life satisfaction by building resilience, widening people's visual attention, and countering negative emotions in a clinical context. At the interpersonal level, positive emotions increase people's sense of unity with close others, and their trust in acquaintances.

Positive emotions can also improve how members of different groups perceive each other. Consider the following example (Johnson and Fredrickson 2005). When people describe individuals of a different race, they often say: 'They all look the same to me!'. This phenomenon, known as own-race bias (ORB), is present in many races and makes eyewitness identifications highly unreliable. However, no relationship has been found between the ORB and racial attitudes. So what causes the ORB? Research findings suggest that the bias results from how own-race and cross-race faces are perceived. Faces are generally recognised as a whole and not as a collection of parts. But cross-race faces are not perceived as a whole but more like an object. In addition, the brain area involved in face recognition, the **fusiform brain area**, is less active in response to cross-race than own-race faces, suggesting that cross-race faces are less perceived as a whole. Furthermore, when viewing cross-race faces, people focus more on racial cues than on cues of individual identity. Racial differences are detected faster than other differences such as gender, age or emotional expression.

fusiform brain area (FFA)
brain area in the temporal lobe, involved in face recognition.

How can positive emotions reduce the ORB? Positive emotions are supposed to have long-term survival benefits by expanding people's mind. Positive emotion should then be able to significantly reduce the bias. In experiments, Caucasian participants viewed Black and White faces for a recognition task while videos were used to induce joy, fear or neutrality. The results supported the hypothesis. Relative to fear or a neutral state, joy improved recognition of Black faces and significantly reduced the bias. Findings could be generalised to all positive emotions because emotion induction focused on joy and humour. Discussion centred on possible mechanisms for the reduction of the own-race bias. The broadening effect of positive emotions may promote more holistic processing of perception. Another possibility is that positive emotions promote more inclusive social categorisations than races.

7.6 Summary

- Emotions are brief adaptive responses to significant events. Fear, anger and disgust respond to diverse forms of threat, or obstruction of an individual's goal. That is the reason why they are called negative emotions. In the course of evolution, emotions resulted from a gradual decoupling of adaptive behaviour from hard-wired reflex actions. This decoupling represented an advance of flexible responses over fixed action patterns.

- Emotions are inner experiences of individuals and therefore hard to study. One option is to focus on facial expressions as Darwin did in his study about emotional expression. In his study, he shifted the attention from the individual's experience to the individual's ancestors. If facial expressions of basic emotions are universal among humans, we may share them with closely related primates as well. Evidence for universality has indeed come from modern cross-cultural studies as well as from objectively measured facial expressions with the facial action-coding system (FACS).

- Evidence for homology – a trait or behaviour in two related species that is attributable to a common ancestry – comes from the study of facial expressions in humans and chimpanzees. Researchers developed a chimpanzee version of the FACS which enables comparison between chimpanzees and humans. Several chimpanzee facial expressions, for example for anger and joy, are now thought to have equivalents in humans.

- Facial expressions are one option for studying emotions. Another option is to focus on brain structures that are involved in the processing of emotions. Early theorising in neuroscience considered the human brain as a hierarchical organ with different layers. One layer, known as the limbic system, or emotional brain, was associated with the emergence of mammals. This emotional brain had an adaptive role in dealing with predators and caring for offspring. Although the idea of an emotional brain has been abandoned, modern brain-imaging research has identified several emotion-processing structures which we share with other species.

- In the course of primate evolution, basic emotions were insufficient for solving new problems. Climate and ecological change in the Miocene forced our ape ancestors to switch from tightly-knit, female kin-bonded groups to loosely-coupled, male kin-bonded groups. The emergence of social emotions may be considered as a compensation for low sociality. Positive emotions in particular, were adaptive responses to the pressures of group-living.

Study questions

1. What are emotions and why did they evolve?
2. How do we know that humans share basic emotions?
3. How do neuroscientists theorise about the evolution of emotions?
4. How does the brain support emotions?
5. What are social emotions and why did they emerge?

Suggested reading

Why did emotions evolve?

Ekman, P. (1992). An argument for basic emotions. *Cognition and Emotion, 6,* 169–200.

Kohler, C., Turner, T., Stolar, N. et al. (2004). Differences in facial expression of four universal emotions. *Psychiatry Research, 128,* 235–244.

Nesse, R. and Ellsworth, P. (2009). Evolution, emotions, and emotional disorders. *American Psychologist, 64,* 129–139.

Tooby, J. and Cosmides, L. (1990). The past explains the present: Emotional adaptations and the structure of ancestral environments. *Ethology and Sociobiology, 11,* 375–424.

Facial expressions in primates

Burrows, A. (2008). The facial expression musculature in primates and its evolutionary significance. *BioEssays, 30,* 212–225.

Parr, L. (2010). Understanding the expression and classification of chimpanzee facial expressions. In E. Lonsdorf et al. (Eds), *The Mind of the Chimpanzee* (pp. 52–59). Chicago: The University of Chicago Press.

Schmidt, K. and Cohn, J. (2001). Human facial expressions as adaptations: Evolutionary questions in facial expression research. *American Journal of Physical Anthropology, 22,* 3–24.

Schug, J., Matsumoto, D., Horita, Y. et al. (2010). Emotional expressivity as a signal of cooperation. *Evolution and Human Behaviour, 31,* 87–94.

Vick, S., Waller, B., Parr, L. et al. (2007). A cross-species comparison of facial morphology and movement in humans and chimpanzees using the facial action coding system. *Journal of Nonverbal Behaviour, 31,* 1–20.

Waller, B., Cray, Jr, J. and Burrows, A. (2008). Selection for universal facial emotion. *Emotion, 8,* 435–439.

The neural basis of emotions

Arbib, M. and Fellous, J. (2004). Emotions: From brain to robot. *Trends in Cognitive Sciences, 8,* 554–561.

Burgdorf, J. and Panksepp, J. (2006). The neurobiology of positive emotions. *Neuroscience and Biobehavioural Reviews, 30,* 173–187.

Dalgleish, T. 2004). The emotional brain. *Nature Reviews Neuroscience, 5,* 582–589.

Davidson R. (2003). Seven sins in the study of emotions: Correctives from affective neuroscience. *Brain and Cognition, 52,* 129–132.

Panksepp, J. (2003). At the interface of the affective, behavioural, and cognitive neurosciences: Decoding the emotional feelings of the brain. *Brain and Cognition, 52,* 4–14.

Panksepp, J. (2006). Emotional endotypes in evolutionary psychiatry. *Progress in Neuro-Psychopharmacology & Biological Psychiatry, 30,* 774–784.

The emergence of social emotions

Cheng, J., Tracy, J. and Henrich, J. (2010). Pride, personality, and the evolutionary foundations of human social status. *Evolution and Human Behaviour, 31,* 334–347.

Fredrickson, B. (1998). What good are positive emotions? *Review of General Psychology, 2,* 300–319.

Garland, E., Fredrickson, B. Kring, A. et al. (2010). Upwards spirals of positive emotions counter downwards spirals of negativity: Insights from the broaden-and-build theory and affective neuroscience on the treatment of emotion dysfunctions and deficits in psychopathology. *Clinical Psychology Review, 30,* 849–864.

Johnson, K. and Fredrickson, B. (2005). 'We all look the same to me'; Positive emotions eliminate the own-race bias in face recognition. *Psychological Science, 16,* 875–881.

Johnson, K., Waugh, C. and Fredrickson, B. (2010). Smile to see the forest: Facially expressed positive emotions broaden cognition. *Cognition and Emotion, 24,* 299–321.

Spoor, J. and Kelly, J. (2004). The evolutionary significance of affect in groups: communication and group bonding. *Group Processes & Intergroup Relations, 7,* 398–412.

Tracy, J. and Robins, R. (2004a). Show your pride. Evidence for a discrete emotion expression. *Psychological Science, 15,* 194–197.

Tracy, J. and Robins. R. (2006). Appraisal antecedents of shame and guilt: Support for a theoretical model. *Personality and Social Psychology, 32,* 1339–1351.

Tracy, J. and Matsumoto, D. (2008). The spontaneous expression of pride and shame: Evidence for biologically innate nonverbal displays. *Proceedings of the National Academy of Sciences of the USA, 105,* 11655–11660.

Reference books

Carter, R. (2009). *The Brain Book.* London: Dorling Kindersley.

Davidson, R., Scherer, K. and Goldsmith, H. (Eds) (2009). *Handbook of Affective Sciences.* Oxford: Oxford University Press.

Lewin, R. and Foley, R. (2004). *Principles of Human Evolution.* Oxford: Blackwell Publishing.

Lewis, M., Haviland-Jones, J. and Barrett, L. (Eds) (2010), *Handbook of Emotions, Third Edition.* New York: The Guilford Press.

Panksepp, J. (1998a). *Affective Neuroscience: The Foundation of Animal and Human Emotions.* New York: Oxford University Press.

Turner, J. (2000). *On the Origin of Human Emotions: A Sociological Inquiry into the Evolution of Human Affect.* Stanford, CA: Stanford University Press.

8 Brain and cognition

This chapter will cover:

8.1 Introduction

8.2 Evolution of the brain

8.3 Cognitive capacities in apes and corvids

8.4 Selection pressures for great ape cognition

8.5 Social cognition in chimpanzees and humans

8.6 Summary

Learning outcomes

By the end of this chapter, you should be able to explain:

- why animals have brains, unlike plants
- why the nervous system became centralised
- how our brain differs from other brains and why brain size increased
- what cognitive capacities apes share with corvids
- why natural selection favoured complex cognition in great apes
- how we differ from chimps in our capacity for social cognition.

8.1　Introduction

If we view evolution as a series of steps in problem-solving, two major changes have taken place. The first change was the liberation of responses from automatic mechanisms as it occurred in the emergence of emotions. The second change was a shift towards more flexibility when responses became more dependent on learning and cognition. In this chapter we first focus on the physical basis of cognition: the brain. Why do animals have brains, unlike plants? Why did the nervous system become centralised? How does the human brain differ from other brains?

Animals differ in the capacity to use and handle knowledge. Most animals can make do with simple forms of cognition such as memory storage and experience-based learning. But some animals such as corvids (e.g. ravens, crows) and primates show advanced cognition. We will focus on what cognitive capacities they have in common and how they use them for solving problems.

Primates have relatively large brains and demonstrate advanced cognition, compared with other mammals. For example, they learn from observing one another and are competent in using tools. What selection pressures caused their brain to be large and their cognition advanced? Did these pressures come from the physical environment, for example the need to navigate through a large home range and memorise food locations? Did the pressures originate from the social environment, such as living in large groups with the need to remember many individuals and their traits?

Humans have cognitive capacities that they share with close relatives, but they also have capacities that close relatives do not possess. For example, advanced social cognition is necessary for children to acquire language. Without mind-reading capacities for mental states like goals and beliefs, they are unable to understand word meanings and to communicate effectively. We focus on the question of which capacities for social cognition we share with other species and which ones are uniquely developed in humans.

8.2　Evolution of the brain

Why animals have brains

The brain may be considered a problem-solving system, adapted to its environment. You may recall from section 2.3 that the genome, nervous system and culture are systems that in the course of evolution stored information about the past in such a way that they improve our chances of survival and reproduction. A genome, composed of all the genes that 'know' how to build a body, will suffice for plants but not for animals. Plants are **autotrophs**, or food producers as they make their own food from raw materials by photosynthesis. But animals are **heterotrophs**, or food consumers, depending on plants and prey animals to obtain energy. Unlike plants, animals move from place to place which is why they need a brain.

Brains are informed by the senses about the presence of resources and dangers. They evaluate and store this input and generate adaptive responses in the muscles (Allman 1999). If resources for survival vary in space and time, the brain serves as a

autotrophs

food producers such as plants, making their own food from raw materials by photosynthesis.

heterotrophs

food consumers such as animals, depending on plants and particularly prey to obtain energy.

buffer against variability. Thus, in addition to a genome, animals need a brain which allows them to adapt more rapidly to variable environments. The brain 'knows' how to respond to dangerous predators and how to attract potential partners. As humans live in even more dynamic environments, they need culture as a third prob-lem-solving system. In culture, humans have pooled all the know-how, ideas and values that an individual never could learn by itself.

From diffuse to central nervous systems

We can find the basic features of brains in simple organisms, like bacteria, that must solve the problem of locating resources in a variable environment (Allman 1999). Consider the bacterium *Escherichia coli* that has sensory systems to detect nutrients and toxins as well as the capacity to store and evaluate information provided by receptors. The integration of sensory information results into motor action: swim-ming forward ('run') or changing its direction ('tumble'). If the bacterium senses a decreasing concentration of the sugar resource, this causes it to swim forward or change direction by using its flagella. These are long structures that serve as a motor propelling the bacterium along (Figure 8.1). In a similar vein, all brains receive sen-sory stimuli that must be translated into appropriate responses.

The brain is the enlarged anterior part of the vertebrate central nervous system, encased within the skull that serves as a protection. But the first nervous systems were not yet centralised with the brain as a control centre and the spinal cord as a connection between brain and body. Early nervous systems had the shape of nerve nets and evolved about 600 mya in invertebrate animals like jelly fish and hydras (Lichtneckert and Reichert 2007). Nerve nets form loose networks of nerve cells throughout the organism. An important feature of nerve nets is diffuse conduc-tion of the nerve impulse. If we compare nerve nets with a brain, they can contract at any spot that has been stimulated and spread the nerve impulse over the whole body (Figure 8.2).

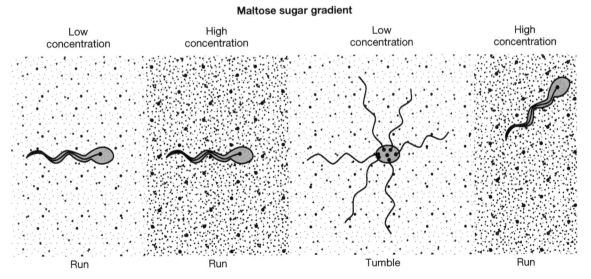

Maltose sugar gradient

Low concentration	High concentration	Low concentration	High concentration
Run	Run	Tumble	Run

Figure 8.1 A bacterium *E. coli* swimming in sugar

Source: Allman (1999)

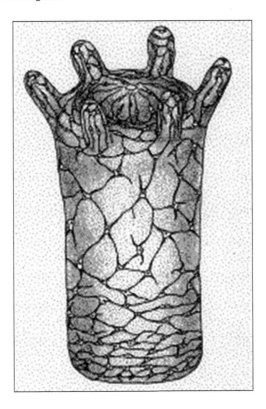

Figure 8.2 The nerve net of a contracted hydra
Source: Bonner (1980)

The evolution of the vertebrate central nervous system may have begun with free-living flatworms which have a bilateral body plan and an aggregate of neural cells in the head that forms the brain (Sarnat and Netsky 2002). The defining features of the brain include its location in the head serving the whole body, and a bilateral body plan. What is a bilateral body plan? One characteristic that differentiates animal bodies is symmetry, the arrangement of body parts in relation to an imaginary axis or plane (Klein and Takahata 2002). Two principal types of body symmetry are distinguished: radial symmetry, referring to rays that emanate from a centre, and bilateral symmetry, implying that the body has two sides. The body of a hydra has radial symmetry, while the body of a fish has bilateral symmetry. The body of the fish has anterior and posterior, as well as ventral and dorsal sides. Only the plane in the antero–posterior direction divides the body into two halves that mirror each other (Figure 8.3).

Body symmetry reflects the lifestyle of animals. If animals spend their life attached to a rock or on the seabed, they tend to be asymmetrical (e.g. sponges) or radially symmetrical (e.g. hydras). In some cases, animals may even lose their brain when permanently attached to a substrate (Box 8.1 The animal that lost its brain). Animals which are mostly on the move are bilaterally symmetrical (e.g. fishes). Their sense and feeding organs are concentrated in the anterior part while the posterior part is specialised in propulsion and steering.

Centralised nervous systems integrate sensory information from the periphery and initiate body-wide responses by the secretion of neurohormones or stimulation

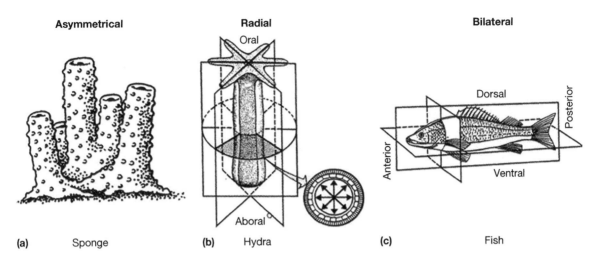

Figure 8.3 Symmetry of animal bodies

Source: Klein and Takahata (2002)

of the body musculature. Why was centralisation of the nervous system and the formation of a brain selectively advantageous to some invertebrate animals? One advantage may be mechanical efficiency. When animals develop a larger body size, they need more neurons to control its body parts. Centralisation permits responses to be quicker as they travel shorter routes. This becomes clear if we compare the central nervous system with the diffuse nervous system in which the whole body responds to a stimulus.

Consider the centralised nervous system of segmented animals like arthropods (Bonner 1980). A crayfish has swimmerettes whose muscles have to be contracted in a sequential fashion. Swimmerettes are body appendages in crabs, lobsters and the like that are modified to increase their resistance to water (Figure 8.4).

BOX 8.1 The animal that lost its brain

Plants may move their leaves towards the sun, but that does not require a brain. Only animals that move from one place to another, have a brain. An exception to the rule that mobility requires a brain, is the seasquirt or tunicate. This small animal starts its life as a larva, has a brain and nerve cord to control its movements, and swims like other marine animals. In its larval stage, the seasquirt is related to our evolutionary branch of the vertebrate animals. The larva resembles a tadpole which has a trunk and tail. The tail is stiffened with a rod that supports the body, and is replaced by a vertebral column in adult vertebrates. However, the seasquirt does not develop into a vertebrate animal. Once mature, it attaches itself permanently to a rock, adopting a primitive feeding strategy of filtering nutrients from the surroundings by drawing in water through the gaping mouth and ejecting the surplus water. The common name, 'seasquirt', refers to this manner of forcing out water. The most remarkable change in the mature seasquirt is that it digests its brain gradually, leaving only some structures needed for filter feeding. Its brain has become superfluous (Greenfield 1996; Tudge 2000; Levinton 2009).

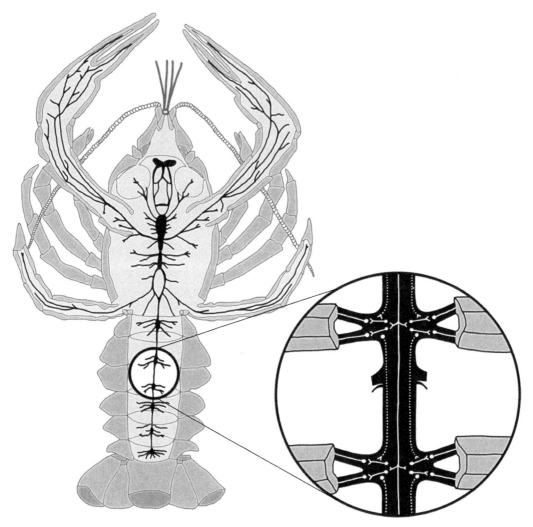

·········· Ganglia with coordinating fibres control the proper sequence of swimmerretes

——— Brain with command fibres control the rate of movement

Figure 8.4 The central nervous system of a crayfish
Source: Bonner (1980)

In each side of each segment is a ganglion, or collection of neurons, and every ganglion is connected to its posterior neighbour. A ganglion will only give instructions to move when it receives a signal via the coordination fibres from the ganglion of its anterior neighbour which has already contracted. Thus, the proper sequential contraction of swimmerettes is due to the coordinating fibres connecting the ganglia. The brain of the crayfish has command fibres extending to every ganglion which control the rate of movement, that is, the time interval between successive contractions. In sum, the ganglia regulate the proper sequence of swimmerettes and the brain controls how fast the animal moves.

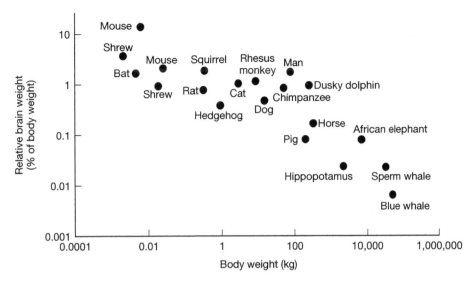

Figure 8.5 Mammalian brain size as a percentage of body size
Source: Roth and Dicke (2005)

Central nervous systems evolved because they had the advantage of quicker responses to significant events. But why would animals need to respond more rapidly? An important factor driving the centralisation of nervous systems was probably active predation. The reader may recall from section 1.5 that in the Cambrian period (ca 542–488 mya), marine animals adopted active predation as a new feeding strategy. Current feeding strategies at the time were based on passive predation such as filtering algae and free-living bacteria from the surrounding water. The shift from filter feeding to active predation implied that animals were moving around, bumping into one another, encountering rapidly changing environments, and therefore needing better senses and faster responses which centralised nervous systems could provide.

How distinct is the human brain?

Absolute size is the most general of all brain properties. Assuming that animals with larger brains are more intelligent than those with smaller ones is misleading. The brain of an adult blue whale is roughly five times the size of an adult human brain (7 kg versus 1.3 kg). However, this does not make the whale more intelligent than humans because whales have simpler brains than humans as well as larger bodies to be controlled. To be more precise, the blue whale's brain is 0.01 per cent of its body weight, whereas the brain–body ratio in humans is about 2 per cent (Striedter 2005). Many small mammals have a body–brain ratio of more than 2 per cent. As an example, the brain of pocket mice and harvest mice is roughly 10 per cent of their body mass (Figure 8.5).

What makes the human brain distinct from other brains? As the absolute brain size is misleading in cross-species comparisons, it would be better to use relative brain size.

encephalisation

enlargement of the brain, relative to body size, over the course of evolution.

encephalisation quotient (EQ)

the ratio between the actual brain size relative to the expected brain size of an average animal of the same body weight.

mosaic evolution

the evolution of different parts of an organism at different rates. For example, many aspects of the human phenotype have evolved relatively slowly since we diverged from our primate ancestors. A notable example is our nervous system which gave us a huge selective advantage. An example within the human brain is the disproportionate increase of the prefrontal cortex.

cerebellum

the 'small brain' behind the **cerebrum** that helps regulate posture, balance, and coordination.

cerebrum

the major part of the brain, excluding the cerebellum and the brainstem.

pons

a key link between the cerebellum and the brainstem.

neocortex

the part of the cerebral cortex that most recently evolved, and the source of our cognitive, linguistic and cultural capacities. It modulates the expression of emotions that originate from the limbic system and affords considerable flexibility and creativity in thinking and planning.

One measure to control for the confounding role of body size is the **encephalisation quotient**. Encephalisation is the enlargement of the brain, relative to body size, over the course of evolution. This enlargement can be quantified in the **encephalisation quotient (EQ)**: the ratio between the actual brain size relative to the expected brain size of an average animal of the same body weight (Jerison 1973). For example, it has been estimated that the EQ of chimpanzees is 2.0, which means that the brain volume of chimpanzees is twice that of an average mammal of the same body weight. The human brain is 3.5 times larger than expected for an ape of our size (Passingham 2008).

Despite the EQ, there is no general agreement on whether one should focus on absolute or relative brain size (Gibson et al. 2001; Striedter 2005). Major increases in relative brain size occurred early on in the evolution of mammals and birds. However, we don't know why increased relative brain size should result in increased intelligence. For, increases in brain size provide more neurons that can be used for intelligence but also for somatic functions like walking or digestion. Is it possible to separate somatic and cognitive functions? On the other hand, absolute brain size appears to correlate with aspects of brain structure such as neuron size and connectivity, as well as with some measures of social complexity such as group size (Kudo and Dunbar 2001).

The prefrontal cortex

Human brains may be larger, not because they expanded as a whole but because a particular part was selectively increased. Animals tend to evolve in a coordinated manner. If their body size increases, the size of limbs and internal organs increases as well because this is necessary to function efficiently as a whole. To a large extent, the variance in the size of individual body parts can therefore be explained by body size. On the other hand, body parts may vary independently of body size when organs evolve in different ways to meet varying selection pressures. This phenomenon is known as '**mosaic evolution**' (Striedter 2005; Barton 2007).

Consider testes. Generally, the size of the testes correlates closely with the size of other organs and the body size. But the testes of animal species which mate promiscuously, are large relative to their body size as an adaptation for sperm competition. You may recall from section 4.3 (The theory of sexual selection) that sperm competition is a form of mating competition in which the sperm of each male 'competes' with that of the others in fertilising the eggs, for example, by removing rival sperm from the female's sex organ.

Similarly, brain structures that are part of specialised neural systems for particular functions, may vary independently of other neural systems and the total brain size as a result of different selection pressures. As an example, the visuomotor system includes various structures (e.g. thalamus, **pons**, **cerebellum** and **neocortex**), so natural selection of visuomotor abilities – important when we need to coordinate hand and eye movements as in drawing and writing – may have caused a coordinated evolution of the relevant brain structures. Support for the idea of mosaic brain evolution can be found in primates. Apart from being large-brained, primates are visually specialised which includes stereoscopic vision, an expanded visual cortex, and a distinctive pattern of connections between eye and brain. This visual specialisation was part of an adaptive change in the evolution of early primates. So, the evolution of relative brain size was associated with a disproportionate expansion of the visual system (Barton 2007).

Of all the human brain areas, it is the prefrontal cortex that is most frequently considered to be disproportionately enlarged (Fuster 2001; Striedter 2005; Smaers

orbitofrontal cortex

brain region above the orbits, or eyesockets, which responds to external stimuli that are likely to be rewarding or otherwise significant. It is involved in learning the emotional and motivational value of stimuli, such as food, drink and sex.

et al. 2011). The prefrontal cortex is associated with cognitive capacities related to purposeful action and complex decision-making. In non-primate mammals, it has two regions whereas in primates it has three regions:

- The first region that primates share with other mammals, is the **orbitofrontal cortex** which responds to external stimuli that are likely to be rewarding or otherwise significant. It is involved in learning the emotional and motivational value of stimuli, such as food, drink and sex. Subjects with lesions of the orbitofrontal region are impulsive and disinhibited in a host of instinctual behaviours.

- The second region that primates share with other mammals, is the anterior cingulate cortex. This region is mainly involved in processing internal body states, including emotions. You may recall from Box 7.3 (Emotion processing structures in the brain) that it has a role in the regulation of emotions. In sum, these two regions are involved in the emotional side of decision-making. Subjects with lesions of the cingulate cortex may lose spontaneity and have difficulty in the initiation of movements and speech.

dorsolateral prefrontal cortex

a brain region, involved in the rational side of decision making such as reasoning and planning. It helps primates to make alternative scenarios of how to deal with objects (e.g. how to extract seeds from hard-shelled food) or with members of the same species (e.g. how to avoid conflict with a rival).

cerebral cortex

the layer of grey matter that covers the outside of the brain. It consists mainly of the neocortex.

- The third region that primates don't share with other mammals, is the **dorsolateral prefrontal cortex**. This region is involved in the rational side of decision-making such as reasoning and planning. It helps primates to make alternative scenarios of how to deal with objects (e.g. how to extract seeds from hard-shelled food) or with members of the same species (e.g. how to avoid conflict with a rival). The dorsolateral prefrontal cortex is in fact one of the distinctive features of the primate brain (Preuss 2007). Subjects with lesions of the lateral region are unable to formulate and carry out plans and sequences of actions.

The size of the prefrontal cortex relative to the neocortex – i.e. the latest part of the **cerebral cortex** – is five times larger in the human brain than in the chimpanzee brain (Passingham 2008). Where exactly in the brain should the prefrontal cortex be located? Figure 8.6 shows a map of the human neocortex, made by

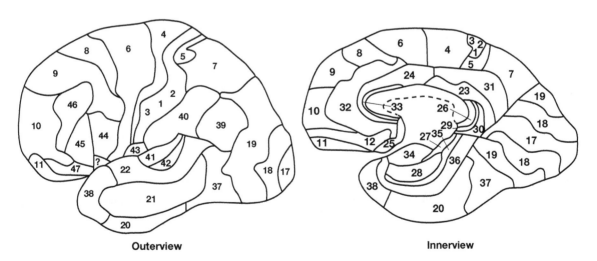

Outerview   Innerview

Figure 8.6 Maps of the areas of the human neocortex

Source: Flinn et al. (2005)

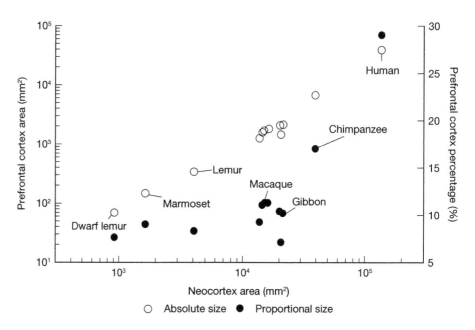

Figure 8.7 Lateral prefrontal cortex scaling in primates
Source: Striedter (2006)

Brodmann's map

map of the cerebral cortex devised by Korbinian Brodmann. Based on cytoarchitectonic structure, anatomical areas are identified by number.

Korbinian Brodmann (1909), and recently updated (2006). The numbered brain areas (Brodmann's Areas or BA) are based on tissue differences. The left section is an outer view of the cortex whereas the right section is an inner view, between the two hemispheres. The prefrontal cortex in humans includes, for example, areas 10 and 46 which support reasoning and planning; areas 44 and 45 are involved in language; areas 11, 13 and 47 are implicated in emotional processing and sociality (Teffer and Semendiferi, 2012).

The lateral prefrontal cortex became disproportionately large in *Homo sapiens*, compared with other primates (Figure 8.7). Georg Striedter (2006, 2005) proposed that its expansion probably increased the ability of humans to consider alternative scenarios of how to interact with external objects. The unusually large lateral prefrontal cortex enabled humans to perform 'unconventional' behaviours, such as suppressing reflexive responses in favour of unconventional ones. For example, given that our eyes have a **sclera** that is white rather than brown as in other primates, humans can make eye movements unconventional. 'Rolling your eyes' can communicate exasperation, and looking away from stimuli objects of interest can mislead competitors.

sclera

the tough external layer of the vertebrate eye.

Humans excel in imagining future events, as well. Brain scanning studies reveal that thinking about the future results in activity in the **frontopolar cortex** (BA 10), the most anterior part of the prefrontal cortex. The relative size of the human frontopolar cortex is two times that of a bonobo or pygmy chimpanzee (Semendeferi et al. 2001) which indicates that prospective thinking also makes humans distinct from other primates.

frontopolar cortex

the most anterior part of the prefrontal cortex, involved in prospective thinking.

Why human brain size increased

Six million years ago, early human-like primates who are generally referred to as australopithecines, diverged from chimpanzees. Since then, absolute brain size has increased roughly fourfold. According to Striedter (2005, 2006) this increase was not gradual but happened in two major growth spurts. The first growth spurt occurred when early humans entered the scene about 2 million years ago (Figure 8.8).

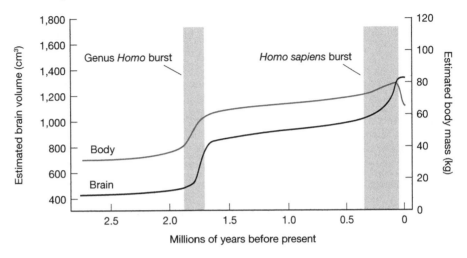

Figure 8.8 Increase of human brain size
Source: Striedter (2005)

This spurt is thought to be related to increased diet quality. Early humans were better able than australopithecines to acquire high-energy meat and tubers. This achievement is important because brains are metabolically expensive organs. The brain accounts for around 2 per cent of total body weight, but requires a disproportionate 20 per cent of its total glucose supplies to support its activities. Once humans had larger brains, it allowed them to invent new tools and raise their diet with other high-energy foods such as shellfish. Moreover, the invention of making fire and cooking improved the digestion of food.

The second spurt in absolute brain size has occurred since *Homo sapiens* emerged 200,000 years ago. This burst is supposed to be driven by increased social struggle for access to resources and mates. An influential hypothesis holds that humans had in some unique fashion become so ecologically dominant that they became their own principal hostile force of nature (Alexander 1990; Striedter 2005; Geary 2005b). Instead of struggling with natural forces – predators, climate change, limited resources – humans were increasingly involved in competing with one another over access to mates and other resources. Since they used **cooperation** as a means of social competition, they not only competed as individuals but also in coalitions of every imaginable size and variety.

Note that comparative analysis of brains and their evolution is a much researched and discussed subject in evolutionary neuroscience. See, in the Suggested reading for this section, for example Healy and Rowe (2007) for a critique of comparative studies of brain size.

cooperation
association between individuals which provides larger benefits than they could expect if acting alone.

8.3 Cognitive capacities in apes and corvids

cognition

all forms of knowing and awareness, such as perceiving, conceiving, remembering, reasoning, judging, imagining and problem solving.

The brain is the physical basis of **cognition**, which refers to the mechanisms or processes by which animals act on mental representations of the world. These processes range from perceiving to imagining. An important change in evolution was, indeed, the transition from more or less automatic responses to stimuli (reflexes, emotions) to more or less flexible responses (learning, cognition). What these responses have in common is that they enable animals to solve problems. Animals that don't distinguish between nutritious and poisonous food, or behave in a friendly way to predators, have been weeded out by natural selection. The reason is that they leave fewer copies of their genes than do individuals whose cognition works appropriately.

Cognition has an immediate impact on behaviours such as eating nutritious food, avoiding predators and finding a suitable mate. In the long run, these behaviours have a positive impact on the individual's fitness – that is, its reproductive success – as well as on the composition of the gene pool – that is, the frequencies of genes as they are present in an interbreeding population (Shettleworth 2010).

corvids (*Corvidae*)

a family of black, black and white, or brightly coloured birds with large heavy bills which include rooks, crows, magpies, ravens and jays.

In this section we examine how apes and **corvids** use **cognitive capacities** to solve problems, and why they have these capacities in common. Corvids (*Corvidae*) are a family of black, black and white, or brightly coloured birds with large heavy bills, which include rooks, crows, magpies, ravens and jays. In the next section we discuss why evolution selected for advanced cognition in great apes.

cognitive capacity

the skill of, or aptitude for perception, concept formation, memory, understanding, awareness, reasoning, judgement, intuition and language.

Convergent evolution of cognition

In the past, studies of complex cognition were mostly restricted to primates. There is, however, increasing evidence that birds (e.g. corvids, parrots) and cetaceans (e.g. dolphins) demonstrate similar levels of cognitive capacity. Corvids, like apes, have evolved large brains relative to their body size, and share a number of cognitive capacities that have arisen independently (Emery and Clayton 2004; Seed et al. 2009). When evolutionary change in unrelated organisms results in the independent development of similar characteristics, it is called 'convergent evolution'. The evolutionary lines leading to birds and mammals separated around 280 mya but resulted in similar cognitive capacities. Thus convergence may be the strongest evidence for adaptation (Foley 1999).

convergent evolution

evolutionary change in two or more unrelated species that results in the independent development of similar adaptations to similar environmental conditions.

Similar cognition in both corvids and apes is thought to be caused by the exposure to similar selection pressures in their evolutionary histories (Seed et al. 2009). Pressures for complex cognition may have come from the physical environment which required corvids and apes to make and use tools for acquiring food. Pressures would also come from the social environment which required group-living animals to learn from one another, use strategies for maximising personal gain, and pursue mutually beneficial cooperation.

caudolateral nidopallium

a brain area in birds that is structurally different but functionally equivalent to the mammalian prefrontal cortex.

Corvids have a brain area that is structurally different but functionally equivalent to the mammalian prefrontal cortex, called the **caudolateral nidopallium**. Mammals have a layered cortex whereas birds have a nucleated structure with pockets of **grey matter** (Emery and Clayton 2005). If the brains of mammals and birds have come up with similar solutions to similar problems, this would be a matter of both neural and cognitive convergent evolution. Laboratory experiments indicate that corvids and apes have cognitive capacities in common, going beyond basic associative

grey matter

the darker tissue of the brain, made up of densely packed cell bodies, as seen in the cerebral cortex.

and reinforcement processes in which responses are simply strengthened through rewards. Emery and Clayton (2004) propose a 'tool kit' of four capacities in corvids and apes that are the basis of complex cognition: causal reasoning, flexibility, imagination and prospection. Each capacity will now be discussed.

How apes and corvids use cognition

Causal reasoning

Corvids and apes are able to use and manufacture tools which implies that they understand the cause–effect relationships by which these tools operate or are effective. For example, chimpanzees use nest perforating tools and ant-dipping probes. Ant-dipping probes are the most commonly observed method of catching ants. The chimpanzee inserts a probe into a nest of ants and gathers the individuals who stream up the tool. The perforating tools are used to open nests so the chimpanzee can gather the ants within.

A recent example shows that apes can make tools for hunting. Chimpanzees in Fongoli (Senegal), have been observed to fashion sharp stick tools before trying to catch galagos or bushbabies. A chimpanzee breaks off a living branch, removes the leaves and side-branches, and sharpens the stick with one or more bites. This stick is designed to probe into tree cavities that are too narrow for its finger or hand. In the case of galago hunting, the cavities are wide enough to admit a whole arm and a tool to spear the resting animal. The point of tool-using is clearly to prevent escape by first killing or injuring the animal (Byrne 2007).

Corvids also use and manufacture tools. Crows, for example, make tools that are used to probe for prey under leaf detritus, and spear the animal onto the sharpened end or the barbs of the leaf, if the prey is located in a hole. The tools are made according to a standard pattern and are carried around in foraging expeditions. The complexity of tool-making consists in the number of steps required to make a tool, comparable to small innovations in human tools. In an experiment with New Caledonian crows, Gavin Hunt et al. (2006) wanted to know what cognitive strategy they use to solve the problem: immediate causal inference (or insight) before attempting to solve the problem, or delayed causal inference with success after a failed attempt. The results showed that their manufacturing skills in the wild may be based on good understanding of what characteristics a tool should have to do the job. In making tools (e.g. twigs) to extract food from vertical holes, the crows used a two-stage strategy to solve the problem. While the first tools were of a similar length but not matched to the hole depth, the second tools were consistently longer than the unsuccessful, first tools. The findings suggest the crows' use of delayed causal inference but did not produce a significant positive correlation between the lengths of first and second tools.

Flexibility

Corvids are able to act on information flexibly. For example, ravens and jays cache food over wide areas for future consumption. Recovery of a cache may require more than remembering where the food is hidden. These animals also have to process information about the type of cached items and how perishable they are. When scrub jays, in experiments, were permitted to hide perishable and non-perishable food items, they were able to recall which foods they cached where and how long ago they had cached them. After caching but before recovering, the jays received new information that the crickets would perish quickly. When tested, they used this new information and shifted to the recovery of peanuts. So, these corvids have a flexible memory for degraded and fresh food items.

Apes demonstrate flexibility by using tactical deception in which behaviours can be switched from honest to deceptive usage (Whiten and Byrne 1988). A classic example is the observation of a female hamadryas baboon grooming a subordinate male behind a rock out of view of the dominant male. In hamadryas society, dominant males mate and control a harem of females which is why subordinate males and their consorts copulate clandestinely. Most tactics direct the focus of attention of another individual towards or away from a particular place or subject. A great majority of tactics can be understood as the result of simple associative learning as individuals associate a behavioural tactic with effective acquisition of a reward in the past. But when animals use a novel tactic, this is strong evidence against explanation by reinforcement learning (Byrne 1995).

Flexibility may be seen in situations where apes have learnt to suppress signals. Consider suppression of vocal signals (Byrne 2003). Vocal inhibition has been reported in apes as a means of deception, but they have difficulty in suppressing sounds. When copulating with consorts, meeting old friends or finding delicious food they are excited and make sounds. Voluntary control of vocalisation has to be learnt. In the mountain gorilla, suppression of calls is often combined with hiding to mate secretly, out of sight of the dominant male. Vocal suppression occurs often in hunting chimpanzees because screams or calls inform the prey of the hunters' intention and may spoil the outcome of the hunt. As chimpanzees are famous for their noisiness, their vocal silence during the hunt is striking. They avoid walking on dry leaves and if youngsters make a sound, they are reprimanded. Adults appreciate the need for silence but the skill to suppress sounds requires prolonged learning.

Imagination

imagination
the cognitive capacity to produce alternative scenarios and situations that are not currently available to perception but formed in the mind.

Imagination refers to the capacity to produce alternative scenarios and situations that are not currently available to perception but formed in the mind. One advantage of imagination is that when facing new problems, different behaviours can be simulated mentally before they are actually executed. The capacity to form mental representations of external objects (e.g. food), or subjects (e.g. conspecifics) may be considered as a precursor of imagination (Emery and Clayton 2004). When corvids cache food, object-permanence – that is, knowledge of the continued existence of objects even when they are not directly perceived – is important for the successful recovery of hidden food items.

insightful learning
a cognitive form of learning involving the mental rearrangement or restructuring of the elements in a problem to achieve an understanding of a problem and to arrive at a solution.

Insightful learning indicates the use of imagination. In a classic study of insight, chimpanzees were presented with a novel problem, a banana hanging on a string out of reach, as well as sticks and boxes which they seemingly used spontaneously to catch the banana (Köhler 1925 [1957]). In one study, a male chimpanzee solved the problem by stacking boxes and climbing on it. Chimpanzees were also observed fitting two sticks together to extend their reach, or untying a rope to let down a basket of bananas. The implication of these experiments would be that the chimpanzees imagined possible solutions to the problem before coming into action. However, the 'suddenness' of insight begs the question of what sort of information processing is necessary or sufficient for this kind of problem-solving.

One answer has been suggested by Paul Schiller (1957) who worked at a primate facility on chimpanzees that had been reared in captivity under impoverished social

play

a kind of behaviour mainly to be found in mammals and birds. Criteria to define and recognise play imply that it (1) is incompletely functional in the context in which it appears; (2) is spontaneous, pleasurable, rewarding or voluntary; (3) differs from other more serious behaviours in form (e.g. exaggerated) or timing (e.g. occurring early in life); (4) is repeated, but not in an abnormal and stereotypic form (e.g. distressed rocking); and (5) is initiated in the absence of stress.

and physical conditions. Schiller was able to show that letting chimpanzees have time to **play** with the boxes and sticks was essential for later success. The animals needed first to understand the possibilities of the various objects. As chimps are playful and driven to experiment with novel objects, no reward was necessary. Chimpanzees had been playfully stacking and climbing on boxes before Schiller suspended any food.

Object play may have augmented the chimpanzees' repertoire of potential solutions. What happened is that the boxes and sticks served initially as toys, but later on as tools for catching a banana. Play and work for food were separate spheres of activity but became associated through repeated experiences. The drive to play with objects is probably an important factor in solving novel problems. Species that show signs of insight are those who indulge in playful activities (Gould and Gould 2007).

Corvids are also supposed to solve novel problems with insight after simulating potential solutions in their mind. A famous problem in experiments is the meat on a string problem in which ravens are expected to access meat suspended from a perch by pulling a string (Heinrich 1995; Heinrich and Bugnyar 2005).

Pulling the food into reach implies that the ravens understand the cause–effect relationship between string, food and certain body parts. The only successful method to pull food up, requires not only fine-tuned motor skills, such as beak–foot coordination, but also the execution of a precise sequence of at least five different steps (reach down, grab string, pull up, hold with foot, release with beak), repeated in the same sequence several times before the food is reached.

Like chimpanzees, ravens are playful species. Can playfulness help to explain the insightful problem solving of ravens? (Box 8.2 Is play necessary for survival?).

BOX 8.2 Is play necessary for survival?

Play is an important part of our life. As children we play with one another and with objects; as adults we play mentally with ideas that sometimes may turn into innovations. In the past, claims have been made about the positive role of play in the mental life of humans and other animals. Play would facilitate learning, imagination, mental flexibility and creativity. But these claims were unsupported by empirical studies. If we compare play with serious activities such as laboratory work or foraging for food, it seems idle and functionless. From an evolutionary point view, play is an enigma. Play is at odds with the central argument of evolutionary theory that behaviour should have survival value, otherwise it will be weeded out by natural selection. Thus, play is an intriguing phenomenon that raises multiple questions. We focus on three questions as they are examined in Gordon Burghardt's study about *The Genesis of Animal Play* (2005).

What exactly is play?

Burghardt proposes five criteria for defining behaviour as playful:

- Play is a kind of behaviour that is not fully functional. It does not immediately contribute to survival and reproductive fitness. For example, when young animals are running around without being chased by a predator, it is not fully functional.

- Play behaviour is spontaneous, voluntary, pleasurable or autotelic behaviour (done for its own sake). Play is thus intrinsically motivated, not done because it is extrinsically rewarding or because it has been ordered.

- Play differs from serious behaviour because it is incomplete, exaggerated, awkward or precocious. Play is incomplete when young animals engage in nipping behaviour without really biting and hurting their playmates. Play may be exaggerated in duration when youngsters chase one another far longer than in serious situations. It is awkward when the animals make mistakes, and precocious when behaviour patterns appear earlier in development than when the behaviour is performed seriously (e.g. fighting, chasing).

- Play behavior is performed repeatedly during a predictable period in the animal's life. An aspect related to repetition is that the animal may repeat an action, as in object play, until it has mastered this action ('master play').

- Play is initiated when an animal is adequately fed, healthy and free from stress. Animals will not play when they are threatened by predators, experience harsh climate conditions, or are subject to intense social competition for food, shelter or mates.

Is play necessary for survival?

Play may have an immediate function for individuals in that it provides physical exercise, thus improving endurance, control of body movements, and integration of sensory and motor coordination. But play may not have any direct function in improving survival or reproductive fitness. We should distinguish between the origin of play and its later functions. The surplus resource theory of play holds that play originated as a means of getting rid of excess metabolic energy. Play was then the byproduct of a process in which young individuals became dependent for longer on their parents. Put otherwise, play used energy that could be devoted to more serious activities. Once it occurred, play may have been selected for diverse functions like motor development, physical fitness, learning capacity, neural processing, cognitive capacities, novel behavioural responses or social skills.

Which animals play?

Play is mainly to be found in mammals because they are associated with factors that favour play, such as high activity levels, extended parental care, and complex behavioural repertoire. Playful mammals include elephants, rodents (rats, mice, squirrels), primates, carnivores (lions, wolves, bears), sea mammals (seals, dolphins), horses and pigs. Play may also be found in some birds which include corvids, woodpeckers, parrots, songbirds, raptors and pelicans.

Bernd Heinrich and Thomas Bugnyar (2007) argue that playful behaviour provides experiences that can be transferred to novel contexts like pulling up food on a string. In the scientific literature play is defined as behaviour that has no immediate survival function but is rewarding in itself (Burghardt 2005). Young ravens play by engaging in aerial acrobatics – for example, tossing rocks for others to catch – or manipulating all sorts of objects with their bills. These objects serve as toys. What may playfulness contribute to solving a new problem like pulling meat up? The solution was not based on trial-and-error learning nor on instinctive behaviour. It is likely that the ravens started from an innate framework of playfulness which they have in common with other mammals and birds. Many play experiences may then strengthen learning processes as well as the capacity to simulate or play mentally with potential solutions.

The cognitive capacity to generate multiple solutions for a problem may further be seen in role taking, in which an individual simulates another's experiences and perspective. This capacity implies that individuals may form mental representations of another's experiences that may be similar or different from their own. In experiments, chimpanzees were expected to reverse roles in a cooperative task, thereby taking the perspective of the partner and simulating its experience. In one experiment, they were trained in pulling a heavy box and to cooperate in doing so, each one pulling on one of the two ropes that were attached to the box. The test was to see whether a trained chimpanzee would gesture to a naïve chimpanzee, encouraging it to help. But this was not what happened because the trained ape looked time and again at the naïve one (Povinelli and O'Neil 2000).

Prospection

Imagination refers to the capacity to simulate scenarios and situations that are currently unavailable to perception but formed in the mind. Another function of simulation may be to imagine possible future events, called prospection. Consider prospective thinking in chimpanzees. We know that they can handle tools and understand cause–effect relationships between body parts, tools and objects. We should add that it is hard to establish how deeply tool users understand what they are doing (Byrne 2004).

Let us have a look at nut-cracking which is a common, tool-using practice in chimpanzees. For example, cracking nuts in the Taï forest (Ivory Coast, Africa) is an important part of the chimpanzees' diet (Boesch and Boesch-Achermann 2000). To crack nuts, the chimpanzees bring together a hard tool to pound the nuts, the nuts, a hard substrate that serves as an anvil, on which the nuts are placed, and sometimes a wedge stone to stabilise the anvil. Wooden clubs serve as hammers for soft nuts and stones for hard nuts. Cracking nuts is mainly a female business because males prefer to remain with other members in the group. The female superiority in nut-cracking mirrors the male superiority in hunting. Infant chimpanzees who remain in close contact with their mothers, are very interested in cracking nuts. Mothers share nuts with them for many years, while the infants learn the practice by observing their mothers' behaviour. Mothers reduce their nut-sharing when infants are aged about six years.

Evidence shows that chimpanzee tool use is not only a matter of learning how to coordinate eye and hand movements, but also of anticipating future needs. A cognitively demanding aspect of nut-cracking is when nuts, stones suitable as hammers, and anvils are not found at the same site, and have to be transported. Selection or manufacture of tools before transport to the site of use, requires specification of future needs, mentally representing the elements that are out of sight, and making a plan of action. Chimpanzees as well as capuchin monkeys manage all of these challenges (Visalberghi et al. 2009). This raises the question of why most animal species possess only a limited tool-use repertoire.

Evidence for prospection in corvids may be found in caching which provides a natural example of anticipating future situations (Emery and Clayton 2004). In a previous section we saw that ravens and jays hide food over wide areas for future consumption. The social context of caching behaviour is important because there is an arms race between storers and pilferers. As pilfering birds may see where storers cache food items, storers use strategies to protect their caches. They wait until the pilferer is distracted or make false caches with inedible items such as stones. Recaching in new sites because an observer saw the hiding of food but not when an observer was present, suggests that the jays use a strategy to protect the items from future pilfering. Recaching behaviour may provide the best evidence for prospection.

8.4   Selection pressures for great ape cognition

Great ape cognition

Complex cognition depends on large brains which are metabolically costly organs. The only sort of environment that will favour such an expensive solution is a complex and unpredictable one. When the environment changes rapidly, rigid stimulus–response behaviour patterns become less adaptive or even maladaptive.

Animals then need more flexible behaviours based on learning and cognitive capacities. In this section we focus on the cognitive evolution of great apes: chimpanzees, gorillas and orangutans (gibbons are the lesser apes).

Evolutionary hypotheses regarding great ape cognition attempt to identify problems that these primates solved through the evolution of cognitive capacities. These problems may range from foraging and food extraction to arboreal travel and social interaction. Although the cognitive capacities unique to great apes, compared with other primates are matters of dispute, they are thought to include: self-recognition (e.g. in a mirror), some comprehension of others' mental states (e.g. intentions), intentional deception, causal reasoning, planning, imitation, demonstration teaching (e.g. how to crack nuts), and using tools.

The accomplishments of great apes in solving technical and social problems are thought to depend on abstract problem representation (Potts 2004b). In the previous section we reviewed this cognitive capacity under the heading of 'imagination': producing alternative scenarios and situations that are not currently available to perception but formed in the mind. In other words, imagination is the capacity to represent a problem as well as its potential solutions abstractly. The question is, then: why did complex cognition evolve in great apes? That is, what are the selection pressures for cognition in great apes?

Selection pressures

You may recall from section 1.3 (Biology) that selection pressures are forces that, over a long evolutionary time and in a consistent manner, shape the organism's traits which cause it to be successful in survival and reproduction. To say that there is 'selection for' or 'selection pressure for' given traits – grasping hands, large brains, cognitive capacities – means that having these traits causes differences in survival and reproductive success (Sober 1993). Selection pressures may come from the physical environment – climate change, limited resources, intensity of predation – and the social environment – social competition, need for cooperation, social learning (e.g. Byrne 2000; Geary 2005b, 2009). Although we focus here on great apes, selection pressures for cognition may also apply to some species of birds and non-primate mammals.

The selection pressures for great ape cognition in which we are interested, are to be found in the Miocene, a period in which the environmental conditions of these animals began to deteriorate around 10 mya. Recall from section 3.2 (The geological timescale) that the Miocene is a geological period, extending from around 23 to 5 mya. The reader may also recall from section 7.5 (The emergence of social emotions) that in the late Miocene, apes and monkeys faced a crisis as the climates began to cool and the environments became drier (Lewin and Foley 2004). The cooling climate reduced and fragmented forest cover, causing a patchy distribution of food resources. While monkeys managed to broaden their diet and maintain their tightly organised groups, great apes could not expand their diet or maintain female kin-bonded groups. We concluded in section 7.5 that apes lacked a cohesive group organisation which is why social emotions probably emerged. The problem was converting great apes with a relatively low degree of sociality into more cohesively organised species, based on elaboration of emotional capacities (Turner 2000).

If we want to know what are the selection pressures for great ape cognition, a reconstruction of the evolutionary history of great apes, past environments and adaptive responses is needed. Richard Potts (2004a) has described the environment

BOX 8.3 Hypotheses about selection pressures for great ape cognition

Ecological hypotheses

- *Forest habitat:* great apes favour forest habitats which are associated with life-history traits (e.g. slower reproductive rate) that select for enhanced cognition.

- *Extractive foraging:* mental and manual capacities are required to remove hard shells from food items.

- *Arboreal travel:* travelling between tree branches and particularly bridging gaps between trees is supposed to be solved cognitively.

- *Dependence on dispersed foods:* dependence on food from isolated areas creates location and foraging problems that favour enhanced memory and mental representation.

- *Seasonal resource availability:* increased seasonality of some foods such as fruits intensifies selection pressure for predicting food availability.

- *Long-term resource variability:* because of ecological and climatic disturbances, resource uncertainty was often a major problem that favoured imagination and group flexibility.

- *Commitment to ripe fruit:* apes' dietary bias towards ripe fruit scattered over the habitat creates prediction and foraging problems favouring enhanced memory and mental representation.

Life-history hypotheses

- *Large body size:* apes have large bodies which pose problems in acquiring food from fragile branches.

- *Long lifespan:* apes have a long lifespan which implies that they face a range of problems that can be solved by enhanced memories and passing information to relatives and offspring.

- *Large brain size:* apes' offspring grow and maintain large brains that are metabolically expensive.

Social hypotheses

- *Complex sociality:* solving social problems of interaction, deception, and cooperation are driving forces of primate cognitive evolution.

- *Flexible grouping:* fission–fusion grouping in apes – i.e. forming subgroups and larger groups for foraging – creates social complexity favouring cognitive problem-solving.

- *Social cohesion:* maintaining coherent groups is important for minimising predation risk, imposing cognitive demands on the brain.

- *Social cohesion:* maintaining cohesion is important when individuals live in dispersed groups, imposing cognitive demands on the brain.

in which great apes evolved, and the consequences this would have had for the evolution of cognition. His studies made use of information about the habitats and environment of great apes; about fossil ape diets based on the analysis of molar morphology and dental microwear; and about the geographic distribution of great apes, including the geographic pattern of extinction.

Various hypotheses about selection pressures have been proposed to explain the cognitive evolution of great apes (Potts 2004a; Dunbar 2010; Box 8.3 Hypotheses about selection pressures for great ape cognition). It is not easy to reconstruct any behaviour that relates convincingly to causes of cognitive evolution in apes. Consider the hypothesis that the extraction of hard-shelled foods such as hard nuts or shellfish, was a selection pressure for the evolution of great ape cognition (e.g. Byrne 1997). As all great apes apply complex cognitive and manual capacities in acquiring high energy from hard-shelled foods, extraction might explain the evolution of planning and mental representation capacities. But removal of hard shells from food items has only been determined in extant apes. It is true that bodily capacities can be inferred from fossil remains but the fossil record is silent about the questions when, where and why the cognitive capacities for insight or cause–effect reasoning emerged. Hypotheses that connect cognitive capacities with problems are in essence not testable with regard to the time and place in which the capacities are supposed to have evolved. However, a common theme in all hypotheses is the importance of foraging success which depends on how animals respond to the availability of food which in turn is sensitive to environmental changes. So information about physical environments in which great apes lived, may shed light on how foraging shaped great ape cognition.

The fruit-habitat hypothesis

Studies about the past environments of great apes reveal that they faced significant climatic transitions in the Miocene, in particular towards drier conditions (Potts 2004b). Great apes in Europe and Southwest Asia had become extinct by the end of this period. In Africa and Southeast Asia, they experienced a diminished range and displacement towards the equator. Studies about the dietary habits of great apes make clear that they focused on ripe fruit which is patchily distributed and susceptible to seasonality. Since the Miocene they have retained their molar design which is associated with frugivory, or fruit eating. Apes have molars with less shearing surface than monkeys who expanded their fruit diet by consuming mature and immature leaves, and other plant parts. The molar design of apes led them to rely exclusively on fruit-producing environments.

All relevant findings have led Potts (2004b) to the fruit-habitat hypothesis which proposes three main phases of selection pressure for great ape cognition. In the first phase, great apes were from the outset constrained by their dental and metabolic bias towards ripe fruit. This made them dependent on wooded habitats in which high-quality fruit could be found. As this fruit was dispersed in time and place, the fruit bias created the problem of fruit predictability. This problem would then strongly favour cognitive capacities of enhanced memory and mental representation of fruiting trees in their foraging range. In the second phase, the great apes' commitment to ripe fruit could be satisfied in dense, fruit-producing environments. But it was precisely these environments that diminished in size, confining great apes to lower latitudes and reducing their populations. In the third phase, the instability of great ape habitats increased, making the uncertainty of locating ripe fruit more intense. Recurrent periods of forest expansion and contraction would favour the cognitive capacity to assess the presence and ripeness of fruit in distant places.

The social brain hypothesis

Selection pressures for great ape cognition not only come from the physical environment (e.g. uncertainty about food availability) but from the social environment as well. The social brain hypothesis implies that the dispersed social groups characteristic of great apes was an important selection pressure for their cognition. In general, this hypothesis has focused on the idea that social complexity, often indexed by group size, was a driving force in the evolution of large brains and complex cognition. One version of the social brain hypothesis is consistent with the fruit-habitat hypothesis in its proposal that a critical selection pressure for great ape cognition was the need to maintain social cohesion when individuals live in dispersed social groups (Barrett et al. 2003; Dunbar 2007). This may be demonstrated by comparing monkeys with great apes.

KEY FIGURE   Robin Dunbar

Robin Dunbar is an evolutionary anthropologist at Oxford University. His research is focused on the evolution of sociality.

Selected works

Primate Social Systems (1988)

Human Reproductive Decisions: Biological and Social Perspectives (1995)

Grooming, Gossip, and the Evolution of Language (1996)

Human Evolutionary Psychology (2002), with Louise Barrett and John Lycett

Photo source: Robin Dunbar

Great apes and monkeys rely extensively on fruits. They differ in that apes are ripe fruit specialists whereas monkeys are generalists, feeding on (un)ripe fruit, and being tolerant of toxins in unripe fruits. Ripening of fruit is associated with the leaching out of toxins, making fruit edible (Wrangham et al. 1998; Dunbar 2007). Monkeys can thus exploit fruits long before apes can, a competitive advantage that may partially explain why great ape populations declined and monkey populations expanded during the Miocene (Dunbar 2007).

The monkeys' diet allows them to live in small foraging areas and in cohesive groups where they encounter each other daily. In contrast, the great apes' diet forces them to forage in large areas with widely dispersed fruit and dispersed groups where individuals meet each other only infrequently. Although the composition of the dispersed groups varies all the time, all individuals recognise each other and maintain long-term relationships. In such complex social systems, individuals must be capable of mentally representing not only distant fruits but also absent group members. Evidence for the increased cognitive capacities of great apes (and humans) may be indicated by the relative brain size (e.g. the ratio of neocortex volume to the volume of the rest of the brain) (Figure 8.9).

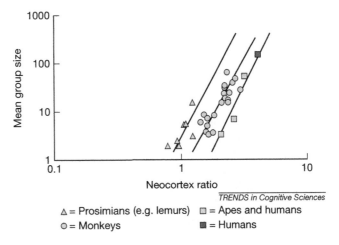

Figure 8.9 Social complexity and cognitive capacities (measured by group size and relative brain size)

Source: Barrett et al. (2003)

8.5   Social cognition in chimpanzees and humans

The real difference between chimpanzees and humans

The reader may recall from section 8.2 (Evolution of the brain) that six million years ago, early human-like primates diverged from chimpanzees. Thus human species share a long evolutionary history with them (Figure 3.5). We have many things in common such as genes, social behaviours, and large brains. At the same time, humans are very different from chimpanzees as we walk upright, depend on culture and maintain pair-bonds. As Dunbar says, 'The real difference lies in a much more intangible set of competences – the ability to live in the virtual world of the mind' (2008: 404).

This capacity is essential for understanding other people. Other persons are physically different from ourselves, but also mentally. They have other minds and mental states – intentions, thoughts, beliefs – that are not directly visible. If we were unable to understand their mental states, human social life would collapse or at least degrade to a lower level of sociality. How did the idea of mind-reading originate and influence the study of human social cognition?

Social intelligence and social brain

Humans may be regarded as natural psychologists in that they are uniquely skilful in their ability to deal with one another. Humans know better than any other animal how to anticipate and work upon the behaviour of fellow members of their species. In particular, they are able to make sense of 'the ghost in the machine': the mind. In other words, since humans diverged from chimpanzees six million year ago, they evolved into *Homo psychologicus*. This is how Nicholas Humphrey (1983) introduced his book about the development of mind. As highly social beings, we must be able to assess the consequences of our behaviour as well as the likely behaviours of others. Humphrey compares social living with playing chess. Like chess, social interactions are often typically transactions between social partners. As the game proceeds, each player must be ready to change his or her tactics, responding to the opponent. Apart from the cognitive skills required for perceiving the current state of play, the chess-player/social partner must be capable of forward thinking.

In essence, Humphrey proposed that living in groups and predicting the behaviour of others requires high levels of cognitive processing. This 'social intelligence hypothesis' as it later became known, served as an alternative to other hypotheses for explaining the evolution of primate and human intelligence (especially ecological and life-history hypotheses; see Box 8.3). A classic study of social intelligence was Frans de Waal's observations of chimpanzees at the Arnhem Zoo (1982). This study demonstrated that great apes have benefits in understanding others, using this information to predict and manipulate their future behaviour.

Richard Byrne and Andrew Whiten (1988) built on Humphrey's idea, calling it 'Machiavellian intelligence' after Niccolò Machiavelli's book *The Prince* in which politicians manipulate people and rivals, thus retaining their power and prestige. Byrne and White suggest that social intelligence is based on the ability to intentionally manipulate and deceive other individuals. This ability to manipulate and deceive appears to be widespread in primates. Robin Dunbar (1992) built further on the idea of social intelligence with his social brain hypothesis. He found that neocortex size places an upper limit on the size of groups which primates can maintain as cohesive units through time. The social brain hypothesis differs from the social intelligence hypothesis in that it does not only apply to competitive situations (social life as a chess game) but includes all aspects of problem-solving, both deceitful and prosocial.

Empirical tests for the social brain hypothesis focus on social complexity. This complexity may come from the size of groups or social networks in which we live (e.g. Kudo and Dunbar 2001). Memory capacity should then impose an upper limit on the number of individuals one can recognise or relationships one can have. In fact, humans are able to attach names to around 2,000 faces but have a group size of only about 150. Memories are not the issue because it is not so much the storage but rather the manipulation of information about social relationships that counts. Studies indicate that the medial prefrontal, or frontopolar cortex (BA 10) is the brain area for social skills, specifically the capacity to understand the mental states of others (Dunbar 1998; Adolphs 2009).

We should further be aware that humans – as well as other primates – live in groups and other social formations that are highly structured. Humans have even created more levels of sociality that are cognitively demanding. Much social complexity comes from nested grouping levels, ranging from small groups with individuals interacting face-to-face to multinational corporations, large societies and global networks with individuals communicating mostly through interfaces (e.g. telephone, computer). The cohesiveness through time of large societies may then largely depend on the extent to which small groups maintain social bonds (Zhou et al. 2005).

Social cognition

Like other primates, humans can only survive by living socially. Unlike other primates, they lead a social life that is much more cognitively demanding. Humans had to become natural psychologists because they faced the problem of understanding the minds of conspecifics. Reading one another's head orientation, facial expression or behaviour was not enough, so humans evolved into competent mind-readers. It is most likely that the major selection pressures for their mind-reading capacity came from complex social environments. Mind-reading is then thought to have two kinds of selected advantages. First, it can help one anticipate others' future behaviour in cooperative projects, and, second, it can lead one to induce false beliefs in others in competitive situations.

Social cognition refers to the knowledge an individual has about other members of the group, and the capacity to reason about the actions and mental states of others. Social cognition may involve multiple capacities which include gaze following, imitation, teaching, social learning and theory of mind. The latter capacity is considered an important condition for language. In no other species has language emerged than in humans. It requires that we understand the effect of our words on the mental states of the partner. This presumes knowledge of what these mental states are. Theory of mind and language are considered uniquely human which is why Passingham (2008) characterised the six million years, separating humans from apes, as a mental gap (Box 8.4 The mental gap between man and ape).

BOX 8.4 The mental gap between man and ape

Richard Passingham (2008) offers the following list of his findings about the cognitive uniqueness of humans:

- *Inner speech:* humans are unique in that they are aware of 'hearing' themselves think.

- *Mental trial and error:* humans can deliberately engage in planning for the distant future.

- *Speech:* humans are unique in naturally learning to speak; children are hungry for language, quite unlike chimpanzees.

- *Understanding mental states:* humans are unique in sharing intentions when they cooperate.

- *Understanding mental states:* humans are unique in that they can reflect on their own mental states as well as those of others.

- *Understanding the world:* humans are unique in that they can achieve an explicit understanding of the physical and social world. They promote this understanding by formulating theories and teaching them in a language.

Theory of mind and language will be discussed further in Chapter 9. For now, we focus on two capacities for social cognition: gaze following and understanding 'false belief'.

Gaze following

gaze
the orientation of the eyes within the face which can be used by others to interpret where an individual is looking. Gaze direction is an effective way of communicating the location of hidden objects and is functionally similar to pointing. Gaze following is widely considered as a crucial step towards understanding another's mental states such as intentions, thoughts or desires. Apes and monkeys are more sensitive to head direction than to gaze direction.

Suppose you are window shopping for jewellery and a stranger follows your **gaze**, making inferences about the items you are interested in. Experience tells us that we quickly become aware of being looked at. It is likely that two types of gaze responsiveness are relevant from an evolutionary point of view: direct gaze and gaze following (Shepherd 2010). Direct gaze is originally associated with detecting predators and the awareness that someone is looking at you. Detection of direct gaze has enormous adaptive value because its helps to avoid predators and other unwanted individuals. This capacity can be found in many species (Emery 2000) and is based on automatic neural responses (Senju and Hasegawa 2005; Itier and Batty 2009).

While responsiveness to direct gaze is widespread among vertebrates, gaze following has only been described in primates as well as in distantly related mammals, such as dogs, marine mammals and some birds. Gaze following has adaptive value because it helps with inferring others' intention and object of attention. However, most non-human species have difficulty in identifying the target of another individual's gaze (Fitch et al. 2010).

Gaze following is widely considered as a crucial step towards understanding another's mental states such as intentions, thoughts or desires. A newborn human is already responsive to its mother's visual orientation, coordinating with her head and eye orientation, and looking in the same direction (gaze following) or at a specific object (joint visual attention). Infants first look in the direction of gaze by 6 months, towards target objects by 12 months and to objects beyond their immediate view (e.g. behind a barrier) at 18 months. Year-old infants manipulate the attention of others by pointing hand gestures, often together with either eye contact or direct gaze. Gaze following at 10–12 months predicts language acquisition over the next year (Shepherd 2010).

Much less is known about the development of gaze following in non-human animals. Apes and monkeys are more sensitive to head direction than to eyes. While humans follow eye gaze from an early age, apes initially follow only head direction and in adulthood respond to gaze as well. Tomasello and his colleagues (2007) suggest that adaptations promoting joint attention may have evolved in human ancestors as they became more dependent on one another ('the cooperative eye hypothesis').

Understanding 'false belief'

Humans are unique in that they are capable of understanding different kinds of mental states of other people. If they are talking with others, they are influencing their mental states. But that presumes knowledge of what these mental states are. Although humans are unable to observe thoughts or beliefs, they understand the actions of others in terms of their supposed intentions, thoughts or beliefs.

A classic test for children's capacity to reflect on the mental states of others is through the understanding of 'false belief'. In the 'Sally–Anne test' (Figure 8.10) the child knows that Sally puts a marble in one place and that later, while Sally is away, Anne puts the marble somewhere else. The child should know that, since Sally was out of the room when her marble was moved from its original to a new location, she won't

(C = child, E = experimenter)

Figure 8.10 The Sally–Anne test of understanding false belief (C = child, E = experimenter)

Source: Baron-Cohen (1995)

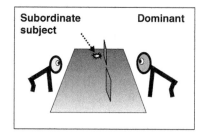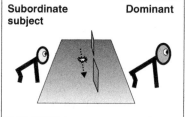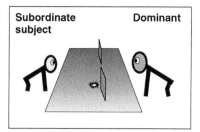

Figure 8.11 False belief test by Hare and his colleagues (2001)
Source: Apperly (2011)

know it was moved, and therefore should still believe that it is in its original location. On the test question 'Where will Sally look for her marble?' the vast majority of normal children pass the test, indicating the original location. Most children with autism indicate the new location. Normal children can pass the test at around the age of three.

How would our closest relatives, the chimpanzees, achieve in such a test? Would they understand false beliefs? There is evidence that they track what others see and use this to determine how they will act in competition for food. Brian Hare and his colleagues (2000) tested whether chimpanzees also track what another individual has seen and thus what the other chimp knows. A subordinate and dominant chimpanzee faced one another across a space that had two barriers and therefore two possible locations to hide food. In the test condition, only the subordinate subject had seen the food being hidden by the experimenter. The results showed that subordinate chimpanzees were more likely to retrieve the food when the competitor had not seen, that is, did not know where the food was hidden.

In another experiment (Hare et al. 2001), the dominant chimpanzee saw food hidden behind a barrier, but did not see that it was then moved and hidden behind a second barrier (Figure 8.11). Thus the dominant chimp, having a false belief about the food's location, would approach the wrong location. In contrast, the subordinate chimp could now retrieve the hidden food with confidence. Yet the outcome was that subordinates were no more likely to approach the food in the false belief condition than in the knowledge condition when the dominant chimp simply did not know where the food was hidden. This result suggests that chimpanzees don't understand false beliefs.

Should we conclude that chimpanzees are not capable of understanding others' minds? The answer of Josep Call and Michael Tomasello (2008) is yes and no. Yes, they can read minds as there is solid evidence that chimpanzees understand the goals and intentions of others. They also understand the perception and knowledge of others. But no, chimpanzees are not competent mind-readers as there is currently no evidence that chimpanzees understand false beliefs.

8.6 Summary

- Unlike plants, animals developed brains because they are mobile and live in varied environments. The transition from diffuse to centralised nervous systems allowed animals to respond faster to significant events.
- The human brain differs from other brains in that the prefrontal cortex expanded disproportionately in the course of evolution.

- Brains enable animals to use cognitive processes like memory storage or stimulus-based learning for solving problems. As some animals like apes and corvids need more complex cognition, it has been proposed that they share a set of four cognitive capacities: causal reasoning, flexibility, imagination and prospective thinking. Experiments have demonstrated evidence for these capacities.

- Great apes require large brains, raising the question about what selection pressures caused their brains to be large and cognition being advanced. Studies reveal that selection pressures for cognition came from the physical and social environment. Climate change and forest fragmentation caused dispersal of food, favouring cognitive capacities for enhanced memory and mental representation of fruiting trees in foraging areas. The consequent dispersal of foraging groups created a selection pressure for social cognition in maintaining cohesive groups.

- Although great apes and humans share social behaviours and cognitions, the real difference is that humans are far more cognitively advanced. With respect to social cognition, humans have the capacity for gaze following in common with many other animals, whereas understanding 'false belief' is considered to be a unique human capacity.

Study questions

1. What is the connection between brain and feeding strategy?

2. Why is the prefrontal cortex an important human brain area?

3. Why did human brain size increase?

4. How are 'selection pressures' defined and what types of hypotheses have been proposed to explain selection for primate cognition?

5. What evidence indicates that chimpanzees don't understand false beliefs?

Suggested reading

Evolution of the brain

Fuster, J. (2001). The prefrontal cortex – an update: Time is of the essence. *Neuron, 30,* 319–333.

Healy, S. and Rowe, C. (2007). A critique of comparative studies of brain size. *Proceedings of the Royal Society B, 274,* 453–464.

Roth, G. and Dicke, U. (2005). Evolution of the brain and intelligence. *Trends in Cognitive Sciences, 9,* 250–257.

Semendeferi, K., Armstrong, E., Scheicher, A. et al. (2001). Prefrontal cortex in humans and apes: A comparative study of area 10. *American Journal of Physical Anthropology, 114,* 224–241.

Smaers, J., Steele, J., Case, C. et al. (2011). Primate prefrontal cortex evolution: Human Brains are the extreme of a lateralized ape trend. *Brain, Behavior and Evolution, 77,* 67–78.

Striedter, G. (2006). Précis of *Principles of Brain Evolution. Behavioral and Brain Sciences, 29,* 1–36.

Cognitive capacities in apes and corvids

Byrne, R. and Bates, L. (2010). Primate social cognition: Uniquely primate, uniquely social, or just unique? *Neuron, 65*, 815–830.

Call, J. and Tomasello, M. (2008). Does the chimpanzee have a theory of mind? 30 years later. *Trends in Cognitive Science, 12*, 187–192.

Emery, N. (2006). Cognitive ornithology: The evolution of avian intelligence. *Philosophical Transactions of the Royal Society B, 361*, 23–43.

Emery, N. and Clayton, N. (2009). Comparative social cognition. *Annual Review of Psychology, 60*, 87–113.

Heinrich, B. and Bugnyar, T. (2005). Testing problem solving in ravens: String-pulling to reach food. *Ethology, 111*, 962–976.

Hunt, G., Rutledge, R. and Gray, R. (2006). The right tool for the job: what strategies do wild New Caledonian crows use? *Animal Cognition, 9*, 307–316.

Seed, A., Emery, N. and Clayton, N. (2009). Intelligence in corvids and apes: A case of convergent evolution? *Ethology, 115*, 401–420.

Shettleworth, S. (2009). The evolution of comparative cognition: Is the snark still a boojum? *Behavioral Processes, 80*, 210–217.

Selection pressures for great ape cognition

Bailey, D and Geary, D. (2009). Hominid brain evolution: Testing climatic, ecological, and social competition models. *Human Nature, 20*, 67–79.

Barton, R. (2006). Primate brain evolution: Integrating comparative neurophysiological, and ethological data. *Evolutionary Anthropology, 15*, 224–236.

Dunbar, R. and Shultz, S. (2007a). Understanding primate brain evolution. *Philosophical Transactions of the Royal Society B, 362*, 649–658.

Dunbar, R. and Shultz, S. (2007b). Evolution in the social brain. *Science, 317*, 1344–1347.

Potts, R. (2004a). Paleoenvironmental basis of cognitive evolution in great apes. *American Journal of Primatology, 62*, 209–228.

Shultz, S. and Dunbar, R. (2007). The evolution of the social brain: anthropoid primates contrast with other vertebrates. *Proceedings of the Royal Society B, 274*, 2429–2436.

Social cognition in chimpanzees and humans

Adolphs, R. (2009). The social brain: Neural basis of social knowledge. *Annual Review of Psychology, 60*, 693–716.

Call, J. and Tomasello, M. (2008). Does the chimpanzee have a theory of mind? 30 years later. *Trends in Cognitive Sciences, 12*, 187–192.

Dunbar, R. (1998). The social brain hypothesis. *Evolutionary Anthropology, 6*, 178–190.

Dunbar, R. (2008). Mind the gap; or why humans are not just great apes. *Proceedings of the British Academy, 154*, 403–423.

Itier, R. and Batty, M. (2009). Neural bases of eye and gaze processing: The core of social cognition. *Neuroscience and Biobehavioral Reviews, 33*, 843–863.

Shepherd, S. (2010). Following gaze: gaze-following behavior as a window into social cognition. *Frontiers in Integrative Neuroscience, 4*, 1–13.

Tomasello, M., Hare, B., Lehmann, H. and Call, J. (2007). Reliance on head versus eyes in the gaze following of great apes and human infants: the cooperative eye hypothesis. *Journal of Human Evolution, 52*, 314–320.

Reference books

Carter, R. (2009). *The Brain Book*. London: Dorling Kindersley.

Decety, J. and Cacioppo, J. (Eds) (2011). *The Oxford Handbook of Social Neuroscience*. Oxford: Oxford University Press.

de Waal, F. and Ferrari, P. (Eds) (2012). *The Primate Mind: Built to Connect with Other Minds*. Cambridge, MA: Harvard University Press.

Easton, A. and Emery, N. (Eds) (2005). *The Cognitive Neuroscience of Social Behavior*. Hove and New York: Psychology Press.

Geary, D. (2005b). *The Origin of Mind: Evolution of Brain, Cognition and General Intelligence*. Washington: American Psychological Association.

Kaas, J. (Ed.) (2007). *Evolution of Nervous Systems: A Comprehensive Reference, Four Volumes*. Amsterdam: Academic Press.

Passingham, R. (2008). *What is Special about the Human Brain?* Oxford: Oxford University Press.

Platek, S., Keenan, J. and Shackleford, T. (Eds) (2007). *Evolutionary Cognitive Neuroscience*. London: The MIT Press.

Purves, D., Brannon, E., Cabeza, R. et al. (2008). *Cognitive Neuroscience*. Sunderland, MA: Sinauer Associates.

Shettleworth, S. (2010). *Cognition, Evolution, and Behavior*. Oxford: Oxford University Press.

Striedter, G. (2005). *Principles of Brain Evolution*. Sunderland, Mass.: Sinauer Ass., Inc.

Ward, J. (2010). *The Student's Guide to Cognitive Neuroscience. Second Edition*. Hove and New York: Psychology Press.

Ward, J. (2012). *The Student's Guide to Social Neuroscience*. Hove and New York: Psychology Press.

9 The origins of language

This chapter will cover:

9.1 Introduction

9.2 The origin of flexible communication

9.3 The gestural origin of language

9.4 The vocal origin of language

9.5 The cognitive origin of language

9.6 Summary

Learning outcomes

By the end of this chapter, you should be able to explain:

- why selection favoured flexible communication in some animals
- how gesturing originated as a precursor of vocal language
- how speech may have originated
- why the evolution of theory of mind spurred language
- why human evolution selected for language.

9.1 Introduction

Language is thought to be the most important trait that distinguishes humans from other animals. It allows us to exchange complex information and influence other people. Without language we could not read texts and our system of education would collapse. Language is even thought to be uniquely human. What exactly makes it unique? Focusing only on uniqueness does not make sense because language evolved from other forms of communication in animals. So this chapter starts with comparing animal and human communication.

Language did not come out of the blue but is supposed to have originated from several sources. Consider gestures which are an important part of our daily communication. Speakers use gestures to underline their message, and even gesticulate when their conversation partner is not present as in phone calls. How did language originate? Did humans start with gesturing with vocalising added later on? What evidence can we find in our closest relatives, the chimpanzees?

The evolution of human language is closely linked with social cognition, the last topic of the previous chapter. When children acquire language they need to understand the meaning of words as well as the effect of words on the mental states of others. Language then, is supposed to rely on theory of mind. In non-human primates a theory of mind is missing. Does that explain why non-human primates have no language? Why did humans actually need language? What was the problem that language solved in the course of evolution? Put another way, what pressures in human evolution selected for language?

9.2 The origin of flexible communication

Language and communication

communication

the transfer of information from sender to receiver by verbal or non-verbal means.

The uniqueness of humans is mostly associated with language. The immediate questions are: why it did evolve, what advantages does it have, and how similar/different it is from other forms of communication? Thus a sensible strategy is to explore what makes language unique and what it has in common with animal **communication**. A range of authors have emphasised the uniqueness of language. Thomas Huxley (1825–1895), a famous supporter of Darwin's theory, wrote that 'the possession of articulate **speech** is the grand distinctive character of man' (1863: 63). A century later, Stephen Pinker (1994), in his book about *The Language Instinct*, wrote that

speech

a sound production system which is specialised in complex articulated vocalisations. Articulation implies tight coordination between the various organs and muscles that play a role in speech, including the vocal tract, lips, jaw, tongue and soft palate.

> Nonhuman communication systems are based on one of three designs: a finite repertoire of calls (one for warnings of predators, one for claims to territory, and so on), a continuous analog signal that registers the magnitude of some state (the livelier the dance of the bee, the richer the food source that it is telling its hivemates about), or a series of random variations on a theme (birdsong repeated with a new twist each time: Charlie Parker with feathers. (1994: 334)

Charles Hockett (1960, 1963), the first linguist to suggest that language evolved gradually over evolutionary time, composed a list of 16 design features, some of which could be found in every communication system but only human language would have all the features (see Table 9.1).

Table 9.1 Hockett's design features of communication

Feature	Definition
1. Auditory–vocal channel	Sound is transmitted from the mouth to the ear.
2. Broadest transmission and directional reception	An auditory signal can be detected by any perceiver within hearing range, and the perceiver's ears are used to localise the signal.
3. Rapid fading	In contrast to some visual and olfactory signals, auditory signals are transitory.
4. Interchangeability	Competent users of as language can produce any signal that they can comprehend.
5. Total feedback	All signals produced by an individual can be reflected upon.
6. Specialisation	The only function of the acoustic waveform of speech is to convey meaning.
7. Semanticity	A signal conveys meaning through its association with the objects and events in the environment.
8. Arbitrariness	The speech signal itself bears no relationship with the object or event that it is associated with.
9. Discreteness	Speech is comprised of a small set of acoustic distinct units or elements.
10. Displacement	Speech signals can refer to objects and events that are removed from the present in both space and time.
11. Productivity	Speech allows for the expression of an infinite variety of meaningful utterances as a result of combining discrete elements into new sentences.
12. Traditional transmission	Language structure and usage is passed on from one generation to the next via pedagogy and learning.
13. Duality of patterning	The particular sound elements of language have no intrinsic meaning, but combine to form structures (e.g. words, phrases) that do have meaning.
14. Prevarication	It is possible to lie.
15. Reflexivity	It is possible to use language to talk about language.
16. Learnabillity	It is possible for a speaker of one language to learn additional languages.

Sources: Hauser (1996: 48); Fitch (2010: 19)

Consider features 7 and 8 – semanticity and arbitrariness – referring to the meaningful and symbolic aspects of human language. You may recall from section 3.5 (What makes us human?) that symbolisation has been defined as the capacity to represent objects, people, events or concepts by arbitrary symbols that only work if people attach the same meaning to them. We may define language, then, as a socially-based symbolic communication system with a vocabulary of many thousands of words (feature 11) that can be flexibly combined and recombined into sentences and narratives, enabling us to reach other people across time and place. While apes can only interact face-to-face, the emergence of language liberated humans from here-and-now interactions (feature 10: displacement). The question whether socially-based symbolism makes language uniquely distinct from other animal communication systems is difficult to answer. We should be aware that the 'shared versus unique distinction' is an issue that pervades the debate on language evolution (Hauser et al. 2002). With this issue in mind we need to answer the question: what is animal communication?

ritualisation

the process by which an action or behaviour takes on a new, communicative function. For example, the facial expression of disgust originated from the rejection of bad-tasting food to protect the body. Or, courtship feeding of mates is taken from feeding young, signalling the readiness to breed.

For all organisms, humans included, communication serves as a vehicle to convey information and express to others what has been perceived. As organisms differ with respect to what things they can convey and express, a variety of communication systems can be found in nature (Hauser 1996). Bats use echolocation, monkeys give alarm calls and food calls, and humans use language. Communication may then be defined as the transfer of information via signals from sender (speaker) to receiver (listener).

A signal is any act or feature that coevolved between sender and receiver. Both partners must on average benefit from the signal, otherwise it would not be naturally selected (Maynard Smith and Harper 2003). For example, if one stag roars and the other stag retreats, it is a signal that conveys information about the future actions of the sender that is of interest to the receiver. The process by which certain behaviours acquire new, communicative functions is called '**ritualisation**' (Box 9.1 Examples of ritualisation).

BOX 9.1 Examples of ritualisation

Figure 9.1 Presenting (a) nest material and (b) play bow

Sources: Lorenz (1991), Allen and Bekoff (1997)
Photo sources: (a) FLPA Images of Nature/Danny Ellinger/FN/Minden Pictures
　　　　　　　(b) Alamy Images/Top-Pet-Pics

In many animals certain movements may become ritualised and stereotyped to serve communicative functions. In his classic study 'The courtship habits of the Great Crested Grebe' (1914), biologist Julian Huxley described how the male grebe courts the female by fetching nest building material from under water, returning to the surface with the material in its beak and executing movements that are identified as those of building a nest. From these movements the message can be read: 'Let us build a nest' (Figure 9.1a).

Ritualised movements not only occur in courtship but also in play. When animals play, they use action patterns that are used in other contexts, such as fighting and mating behaviour. To solve the problems that might arise by mistaking play for mating or fighting, many species have evolved play-soliciting signals that are stereotypical and easy to recognise. For example, the 'play bow' in dogs and other canids such a coyotes and wolves is a highly ritualised and stereotyped movement that stimulates other individuals to engage in social play. The message is: 'Let us play' (Allen and Bekoff 1997). When performing a play bow, an individual crouches on its forelimbs, remains standing on its hind legs, and may wag its tail and bark (Figure 9.1b).

Fetching nest building material in water birds and play bow in canids are kinds of signals that have been phylogenetically ritualised under specific selection pressures (Tinbergen 1951). But some social behaviours that serve as communicative signals, such as the human gesture for greeting one another ('hello!'), have rather been ontogenetically ritualised as individuals created or learned them during their lifetimes (Tomasello and Call 2007).

Signals are thought to evolve from animal traits or actions that begin as cues for certain states of the animal. An animal may produce an involuntary vocal cue associated with a bodily response when perceiving a predator. Such a vocal cue could come from a change of breathing before running away from the danger. If this sound benefits the individual's kin because they associate the sound with danger and develop a retreat response, the sound can be selected to serve as an alarm call. Animal signals such as alarm calls evolved to serve fixed functions. A sound that evolved into an alarm call cannot be used as an aggressive signal to intimidate a rival or as a courtship signal to impress females. Thus in most animals, signal and function are coupled in a one-to-one mapping which is why they are considered as fixed signals (Griebel and Oller 2008).

Selection pressures for flexible communication

While non-human animals have a limited repertoire of relatively fixed calls, humans have an immense vocabulary of flexible words and sentences. Given that vocal signals in human communication are decoupled from functions, Griebel and Oller (2008) suppose that selection pressures for flexibility must have occurred. These pressures would then have favoured variable sounds rather than fixed vocal signals. Increased flexibility in communication takes two forms. When animals are able to increase their repertoire of sounds, they show signal flexibility. When these signals acquire more functions, animal communications display more functional flexibility. Production of more signals is expected to evolve first, followed by the emergence of more functions.

Empirical evidence supports the expectation that a larger repertoire of signals paves the way for functional flexibility (Griebel and Oller 2008). For example, some birds use song as a signal to demarcate their territory. But they can learn to produce elaborate songs which serve other functions. Male songbirds use vocalisations in courting females and when they are in sexual competition with other males. Song may also have a deceptive function when birds imitate other bird species to pretend that the territory is too crowded for further habitation. The only case in which both signal and functional flexibility appear to be highly developed, is in humans. We use large numbers of words and sentences for many functions such as explanation, teaching, advertising, criticism, persuasion, denial, affirmation and acknowledgement.

Several selection pressures are thought to favour flexible communication in animal species. Important pressures include sexual selection and social cohesion. We will give some examples as they are reviewed by Griebel and Oller (2008). You may remember from Chapter 4 that sexual selection refers to competition for mates. Animals use various signals to impress the opposite sex in courtship which results in intersexual selection, as well as to intimidate same sex rivals, resulting in intrasexual selection. Mating songs are used in many species, from frogs and whales to song-birds. Humpback whales produce songs that have a similar structure as in birdsong and human vocal communication. The rhythmic groupings of sounds are called 'songs' in birds and 'phrases' in humpbacks. In both songbirds and humpback whales individuals may learn new song elements by imitation. Many species tend to expand their vocal repertoire while some species produce new song themes replacing old ones. Sometimes intra- and intersexual pressures may select for different songs. For example, some birds such as the European starling differentiate a song into two versions, one used for male–male competition and the other for courting females.

Another pressure that is supposed to select for flexible communication is social cohesion. Signals may sometimes emerge which serve to keep groups of individuals together, demarcate boundaries between groups or strengthen bonds between parents and offspring. Examples can be found in social mammals like killer whales (orcas), dolphins and primates. Killer whales are group-living animals that produce various sounds (e.g. clicks, whistles, calls). Groups of animals may have some sounds in common but each group has its own, identifiable repertoire. Dolphins also live in groups, each with its own repertoire of vocal signals, serving similar social functions as in killer whales. Dolphins differ from killer whales as their groups are less stable and resemble the fission–fusion sociality of chimpanzees in which groups divide into subgroups or fuse with other groups.

Vocal signals may not only keep groups of individuals together and differentiate between groups, but strengthen the bonds between parents and offspring as well. In some monkey species, infants produce variable sequences of sounds – labelled as 'babbling' because they are a version of adult sounds – that seem to elicit parental care. Similar things happen in humans. When parents interpret infant vocalisations as expressing pleasure, these signals may serve as bonding devices. Producing a variety of vocalisations may elicit parental care and provide parents with clues about the fitness of their offspring. Findings indicate that parents use infant vocalisations as fitness indicators, which led John Locke (2006) to propose a parental selection hypothesis. According to this hypothesis, parents in the course of human evolution apportioned care partly on the basis of their infants' vocal behaviour. Persistent crying would then reduce care while cooing and babbling would increase care and social interaction.

language
a system for expressing or communicating thoughts and feelings through speech sounds or written symbols.

To conclude, **language** is a flexible communication system in which words are used to express thoughts and shared with other individuals. Several reasons make the study of language evolution complex (e.g. Christiansen and Kirby 2003; Számadó and Szathmáry 2006; Tallerman and Gibson 2012). One reason is that in language and communication distinct but interacting timescales are involved. When we produce and comprehend vocalisations a short timescale is involved in which causal mechanisms in the brain are at work. When language is transmitted from one generation to another, the longer timescales of individual lifespan and cultural change are involved. When human language appears to derive from gestural communication in primates, the even longer timescale of phylogenetic history is involved. And when we examine why communication and language are adaptive, i.e. confer fitness benefits to its users, we are engaged in long selection histories.

Another reason is that human language is a novel inheritance device that opened up the possibility of cumulative cultural evolution. That is, language allows humans to build on the achievements of their ancestors as this may be seen in the advancement of science. It enabled humans also to create complex societies by introducing written laws about marriage, education and so on. A further reason is that we know little about the first stages of spoken language because speech leaves no traces in the fossil record. So we shall probably never know how or when it exactly originated. Theories suggest that language emerged to coordinate hunting, support thinking, commit mates, or strengthen mother–offspring bonds. At the end of this chapter we have more to say about this topic.

A final reason for the complexity of language evolution is its uniqueness, given that it occurred only in the human lineage, and its similarity to animal communication from which it evolved. So with this 'shared versus unique distinction' in mind, we examine in the next section, first, which parts of human communication are unique and which ones we share with other species. And, then, we focus on gestures which humans share with non-human primates. The question is: how did gesturing pave the way for vocalising?

9.3 The gestural origin of language

Components of human communication

syntax

the set of rules that describes how words and phrases in a language are arranged into grammatical sentences, or the branch of linguistics that studies such rules.

Which parts of human communication are unique and which ones do we share with other species? To answer this question, it makes sense to regard language as a communication system that consists of various components (Hauser et al. 2002; Fitch 2010). Special components include **syntax**, semantics and phonology. Syntax refers to the system of rules that governs the construction of words and sentences; semantics to the meaning we attach to words; and phonology to the sounds – vowels, consonants – we use in speech. General components of human communication include audition, vision, motor control and memory which we have in common with other vertebrates.

Some components are thought to be unique, unless we have good reasons to suppose otherwise. Among these components is a theory of mind because without this cognitive capacity we cannot understand the meaning of words nor the effect that words have on the mental states of others. Another unique component of human communication is the capacity for generalisation (Számado and Szathmáry 2006). Topics of conversation are not necessarily linked to the observable present. While many animals live in the present, we can also talk about the past and make plans for the future. We can make generalisations about the living and non-living worlds, for example by theorising about biological and geological evolution, or invent persons that are not made of flesh and blood such as puppets on a string, characters in novels or legal personalities.

A further unique component is that unlike other animals having a limited repertoire of vocal sounds with fixed meanings, humans can arbitrarily link sounds to an indefinitely large set of meaningful words. A related component in human language is the use of recursive grammar which refers to the capacity to embed clauses meaningfully in sentences and repeat this in a manner that still makes sense. For example, one can embed the sentence 'John knows a lot about history' in a new meaningful sentence 'Robert knows that John knows a lot about history', and again in another new and meaningful sentence 'Henry said that Robert knows that John knows a lot about history', and so on. The claim that this capacity for recursion is uniquely human has been challenged. Research findings demonstrate that certain songbirds – European starlings (*Sturnus vulgarus*) – accurately recognise acoustic patterns with a recursive, self-embedding structure. That is, they produce long songs composed of smaller acoustic units that are the basic elements of individual song recognition (Gentner et al. 2006).

Finally, some components of language stand midway between unique and common. For instance, we share our capacity for vocal learning with songbirds, but not with other primates. What we do share with our closest relatives, the chimpanzees, is using gestures in communication.

Gestural communication in humans

Manual gestures and facial expressions are integral parts of human communication. Humans make faces and gesticulate with their hands, even when the conversation partner is not physically present as it occurs in telephone calls. In fact, it is difficult to suppress manual gestures while speaking. This is a strong indication that one origin of language should be found in gestures (Corballis 2002, 2009; Gentilucci and Corballis 2006). Although we communicate mostly by voice, gestures still play an important role. We use gestures to invite people to join our company or indicate to a foreign shopkeeper how many items we want to have. We can also imagine that a simple gesture – a forefinger crossing the lips – would warn our ancestors on the savanna to be on the alert for predators. In everyday language, the words 'gesture' and 'gesticulation' are used interchangeably for hand movements that accompany speech, but in science 'gesture' has become the accepted term.

Gestural communication is non-verbal communication that confers additional information about the motivation and emotional state of the speaker and can strengthen or explain the meaning of verbal communication. Iconic gestures are used to represent things spatially that words cannot specify. For instance, a person may say that 'the wedding cake was this <gesture> large'. Among the gestures that occur alongside speech are also so-called deictic gestures which point to an object with the extended forefinger. In early development, children use deictic gestures such as pointing to or holding up an object which are acts that distinguish them from chimpanzees. By the time children are using two-word phrases, they are combining vocalisations and gestures, using words for actions and gestures for objects that they desire. Later in development, speech takes a superior role with a supporting role for gesture (Fitch 2010).

A strong argument for the gestural origin of human communication is that living great apes use gestures with relative ease and flexibility. Gestures are volitional and intentional as well as performed with close attention to the other individual's state of attention. The presence of these characteristics in all living great apes suggests that a similar capacity for gestural communication was most probably available to the last common ancestor of chimpanzees and early humans (Fitch 2010).

Gestural communication in apes

gestures
movements of the limbs, head and body used to communicate with conspecifics.

Gestures may be considered as movements of the limbs, head and body used to communicate with conspecifics. There are two basic kinds of great ape gesture: attention-getters and intention-movements (Tomasello 2008). 'Ground-slap' is an example of a gesture to attract the attention of another individual. An individual slaps the ground and looks at another individual. This gesture probably originated in a playful context and is often used to initiate play. A second basic type of gesture is intention-movements such as 'touch back' (by infants to mothers as a request to ride

Table 9.2 Some gestures used by chimpanzees

	Gestural action	Goal/function
Intention-movements		
Arm-raise	C raises arm towards R, beginning hitting	Initiate play
Touch-back	C touches back of R lightly, beginning climbing on	Request ride-on-back
Hand-beg	C places hand under R's mouth, beginning taking food	Request food
Head-bob	C 'bobs and weaves' in bowing position at R, beginning play	Initiate play
Arm-on	C approaches R and places arm on R's back, beginning dragging	Initiate tandem walk
Attention-getters		
Ground-slap	C slaps the ground (or an object) and looks towards R	Often play
Poke-at	C pokes at a body part of R	Various functions
Throw-stuff	C throws something at R	Often play
Hand-clap	C slaps own wrist or hand, as approaches R	Often play
Back-offer	C insistently puts its own back in the face of R	Typically grooming

Notes: C = communicator   R = recipient
Source: Tomasello (2008)

on her back) and 'arm raise' (by youngsters to initiate play with others). Intention-movements occur when an individual performs only the first step of a normal behaviour sequence, enough to elicit a response from another individual. Intention-movements are considered to be ritualised because behaviour sequences are abbreviated and have acquired a communicative function (Tomasello 2008). For example, a youngster may approach another one with the intention in mind to play, raise his arm to playfully hit the other, then hit the other and start to play. After several such instances the other has learned that the arm-raise gesture is an invitation to play.

The gestural repertoires of various ape species range between twenty and forty gestures. Josep Call and Michael Tomasello (2007) report from their studies that 'ground-slap' is the most commonly used gesture, followed by arm-raise, throw-stuff, poke-at, head-bob, and hand-clap (see Table 9.2).

Apes demonstrate that they can dissociate between means and ends in that they use multiple gestures for a particular context or activity. Most gestures serve as requests for play, sex, food, grooming or support in agonistic encounters. In addition, a particular gesture such as 'ground-slap' can be used in multiple contexts. Thus, findings indicate that there is not a one-to-one correspondence between gestures and contexts which argues in favour of gestural communication as a relatively flexible precursor of human communication.

Flexibility appears to be a key feature of gestural communication in great apes (Call 2008). Not only do they use gestures flexibly, they also adjust their gestures to the attentional state of the other individual. For example, laboratory experiments show that chimpanzees use visual gestures when the other individual is looking and can also alter the attentional state of the other one by placing themselves in front of her. When she does not respond, they switch to touching gestures or vocalising. Laboratory experiments further show that chimpanzees can acquire new gestures to solve novel problems. As an example, pointing is not part of their natural repertoire, but chimpanzees can learn pointing gestures to direct the attention of humans. In conclusion, the studies we reviewed above (Call and Tomasello 2007; Tomasello 2008; Call 2008) as well as other ones (e.g. Pollick and de Waal 2007; Pika 2008) support the gestural origin hypothesis of language.

KEY FIGURES   Josep Call and Michael Tomasello

Josep Call is a comparative psychologist at the Max Planck Institute for Evolutionary Anthropology at Leipzig, Germany. His research is focused on identifying the unique cognitive and cultural processes that distinguish humans from their nearest primate relatives, the great apes.

Michael Tomasello is a developmental psychologist at the Max Planck Institute for Evolutionary Anthropology at Leipzig, Germany. His research is focused on processes involved in social cognition, social learning, shared intentionality, and communication in human children and great apes.

Selected, co-authored works

Primate Cognition (1997)

The Gestural Communication of Apes and Monkeys (2007)

Mirror neurons for language?

Another argument for the gestural origin of human communication comes from the discovery of 'mirror neurons' in the brain of macaque monkeys. In a remarkable experiment Vittorio Gallese and his colleagues (1996) found that about 17 per cent of neurons recorded in the ventral premotor area, involved in planning movement, responded both when the macaque grasped food with its hand or mouth and when it observed another individual making the same movement. The relevant brain area, known as F5, corresponds to **Broca's area** in the human brain (Figure 9.2) which is involved in the production of speech.

Because mirror neurons are activated when observing and executing the same hand action, they may be involved in understanding the meaning of action. In the evolutionary history, this understanding would provide the link between actor and observer which also exists between the sender and receiver of messages. For, communication requires that both parties understand each other. Giacomo Rizzolatti and Michael Arbib (1998) therefore proposed that mirror neurons served as the first communication system in language evolution. Since comparable neurons have been found in humans, area F5 is regarded as the homologue of Broca's area in the human brain. Broca's area in humans can be divided into Brodmann areas 44 and 45. Brain imaging shows that area 45 is activated by spoken and **sign language**, whereas area 44 is activated by non-linguistic motor functions which include complex hand movements and sensorimotor learning (Corballis 2010). (Sign language

Broca's area

region of the left frontal lobe which is believed to take part in the production of language (BAs 44 and 45).

sign language

any system of communication based on hand signals, especially one used by deaf people. There are many such systems, and like natural languages they tend to be mutually unintelligible.

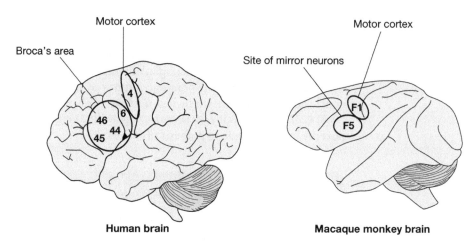

Figure 9.2 Mirror neurons in human and macaque monkey brains
Source: Fitch (2010)

is any system of communication based on hand signals, especially one used by deaf people. There are many such systems, and like natural languages, they tend to be mutually unintelligible.)

Since the discovery of mirror neurons in 1996, many brain imaging studies have been performed in an attempt to identify a human mirror system, homologous to the monkey brain areas. Mirror neurons are very interesting neurons which may support cognitive capacities like understanding actions and mental states as well as imitation and linguistic capacities. But the mirror system hypothesis has been criticised on several points (for critical reviews, see Hickok 2008; Fitch 2010; Uttal 2011). First, one cannot leap from observations of highly specialised neurons to global properties of human psychology such as imitation, mind-reading and speech. Second, macaque monkeys do not exhibit many of the behaviours supposedly encoded by mirror neurons. For example, the function of mirror neurons in macaque brains cannot be for imitation because this capacity in monkeys is very limited. Actually, the puzzle is why imitation appears to be rare in non-human primates. Third, although understanding the mind of others is considered a crucial component of human communication, there is no evidence for mind-reading in monkeys. Thus, the mirror neuron system should change substantially before it might lead to imitation and speech. Put another way, we cannot infer for sure from studying monkey brains how human brains perform (Stamenov 2002; Hurford 2002).

Following a period in which research was criticised for not having produced sufficient evidence for mirror neurons in humans, new studies claim that humans do have them, and that they are not restricted to the premotor cortex (Dinstein et al. 2008; Mukamel et al. 2010; Keysers and Gazzola 2010). Direct recordings in monkeys show that neurons in frontal and parietal areas discharge during execution and perception of action. Indirect recordings of neural activity in humans support the existence of sensorimotor mirroring mechanisms in homologue brain areas. Mukamel and colleagues state:

> The findings suggest that multiple systems in humans may be endowed with neural mechanisms of mirroring for both the integration and differentiation of perceptual and motor aspects of actions performed by self and other. (2010: 750).

Mirror neurons are regarded as a mapping mechanism between observing and executing actions which enables us to simulate the actions of someone else by using our own motor system and, then, attribute the associated intentions, goals and emotions to the other person. This internal simulation only works if the observed action is mapped onto the specific neural circuits supporting the action concerned. If the mapping is not selective enough, we risk attributing wrong intentions and emotions to the other person. Similarly, language is thought to be based on mirror neurons that evolved to map words onto the motor structures that we use to verbalise them. Thus the mapping allows us to attribute social and emotional meanings to spoken words (Dinstein et al. 2008).

The fact that human and monkey brains have a mirror neuron system in common suggests that progression of this system may have played a key role in the evolution of the human capacity to communicate, initially by gestures and later by speech (Rizzolatti and Sinigaglia 2008). Above we mentioned that Broca's area in humans can be divided into Brodmann areas (BA) 44 and 45. Brain imaging demonstrates that BA 45 is activated by spoken and signed language, whereas BA 44 is activated by non-linguistic motor functions such as complex hand movements and sensorimotor learning. As BA 45 is involved in both speaking and signing, Corballis (2010) argues that this may be consistent with the idea that language evolved from manual gestures rather than from vocal calls.

Non-human primates are, indeed, much better adapted to communication by using manual gestures than by **vocalisation**. Attempts to teach language to non-human primates demonstrate that they are unable to develop verbal skills due to their deficient vocal apparatus and cortical control of vocalisations. That is the reason why the bonobo Kanzi learned a vocabulary by pointing to symbols on a keyboard, and using manual gestures (Savage-Rumbaugh et al. 1998). Later studies revealed that during communicative interactions with humans, Kanzi modulated his vocal output. These 'conversations' are considered similar to the close-range, affiliative vocal exchanges that have been studied in monkeys. It is suggested that the variable vocalisations of non-human primates may serve to communicate meaning to conspecifics (Tagliatela et al. 2003; Slocombe and Zuberbühler 2005).

Given that modern human language is primarily vocal with a secondary role for manual gestures, how could vocal control which is lacking in non-human primates emerge? Corballis (2010) argues that facial expressions and mouth movements provided a bridge between manual gestures and speech. Researchers have identified an area in the monkey brain anterior to the premotor area that is engaged in control of the orofacial musculature (Petrides et al. 2005). If facial expressions and oral movements play a role in speech perception, then both facial perception and oral production of speech could be incorporated in the mirror neuron system.

An important clue for the controlled production of vocalisation comes from genetics. It has been discovered that half of the members of a four-generational English family, known as the KE family, have a severe deficit in vocal articulation due to a mutated gene, called *FOXP2* (Vargha-Khadem et al. 1995, 2005). This is the first gene to be discovered of the many genes that are involved in speech and language. *FOXP2* is also present in songbirds and linked with vocal learning. The affected members of the KE family were impaired on verbal and performance IQ tests and tests of mouth movement (oral praxis), including simple movements of clicking the tongue, and making sequences of movements like blowing up the cheeks, licking the lips, and smacking the lips. When their brains were examined,

vocalisation

sound produced by the passage of air, causing vibration of membranes in the respiratory tract, such as the vocal cords in the syrinx of birds and the larynx of mammals. Apart from human speech, the most complex vocalisations are the songs of songbirds, whales and some primates (howler monkeys and gibbons).

they showed no activation in Broca's area while covertly generating verbs. It has been speculated that mutations of the gene *FOXP2* in humans is involved in the origin of spoken language. If that speculation is true, the origin of language would have coincided with the emergence of *Homo sapiens* during the last 200,000 years (Enard et al. 2002).

Recent findings suggest that the date of the *FOXP2* mutations, and therefore the origin of spoken language, should be moved further back in time to 1.8 or 1.9 mya (Krause et al. 2007; Diller and Cann 2012). This was also the time when human brain size began to grow enormously from the 450 cc of australopithecine and chimpanzee brains to the 1,350 cc of modern human brains. You may recall from section 8.2 (Evolution of the brain) that this growth spurt of the human brain is thought to be related to increased diet quality. Early humans were better able than australopithecines to improve their diet with high-energy foods like meat, tubers and shellfish.

9.4 The vocal origin of language

Vocalisations in non-human primates

Scenarios for language evolution suggest that gestural communication preceded speech but in a later stage vocalisations superseded gestures. The term 'vocalisation' may range from simple vocal sounds like food calls and predator alarm calls, to complex vocal sound patterns like speech in humans or songs in songbirds, whales, gibbons and humans. Calls differ from songs in their brevity and scanty syllabic structure. However, the borderline is difficult to draw because call sequences can be lengthy, and songs may consist of only a few elements or even a single repeated syllable type (Immelmann and Beer 1992). Unless otherwise indicated, we use 'call' and 'vocalisation' interchangeably.

Supposedly, the shift from gestures to vocalisations was a slow, gradual process because our primate ancestors had little if any intentional control over the production of vocalisations. The gestural flexibility of living non-human primates is indeed in sharp contrast to the lack of flexibility in their vocal production (Tomasello 2008). The reason is that vocal calls are very much tied to emotions which are often associated with urgent functions like escaping from predators, surviving in fights, or keeping contact with the group. In such situations there is little time for deliberation.

It is true that non-human primates can control whether they produce a vocalisation or remain silent (Seyfarth and Cheney 2010). For instance, after threatening a subordinate a female baboon may or may not give a reconciliatory grunt to her opponent. Similarly, when capuchin monkeys find food, they may call or keep silent. It is also true that primates can make subtle modifications in the acoustic structure of their calls. But overall, the structure of calls in non-human primates is largely innate (Hammerschmidt and Fischer 2008).

Whereas the production and usage of vocalisations is highly constrained, comprehension of vocalisations is more flexible and can be modified by experience. In their natural habitats, primates learn to recognise the alarm calls of other species of primates or birds, even though these calls differ acoustically very much from their own. They also learn to recognise the calls of their predators and during their lives must learn to identify the voices of individuals who are newly born or become members of the group.

BOX 9.2 Voice areas in the human and monkey brain

Recognising species-specific vocalisations is important for the survival and social interaction of vocal animals. Studies provide evidence about a voice region in humans that is sensitive to human voices and vocalisations. In adults, the cerebral processing of vocal sounds involves the 'temporal voice areas' which are located along the middle and anterior parts of the superior temporal sulcus (STS).

At the age of four, infants show well-developed capacities for voice perception. Recent research revealed that seven-month infants whose speech perception is not yet operational, show cerebral voice sensitivity (Belin and Grosbras 2010). Not only does cerebral voice processing develop relatively early, it also has a long evolutionary history going back to macaque monkeys. Studies provide evidence that they have a voice region specialised for the processing of acoustical features that distinguish human vocalisations from those of other species. This voice region is sensitive to the vocalisations of conspecifics as well as to the vocal identity of conspecific individuals. The findings make clear that the temporal regions of both the macaque and human brain are adapted for recognising conspecific signals (Petkov et al. 2008, 2009).

Calls are individually distinctive and can be associated with specific social contexts which allows listeners to extract relevant information from these associations (Seyfarth and Cheney 2010). Consider baboons who throughout the day hear the vocalisations that members of the group give to each other. Higher-ranking individuals may give threat-grunts to lower-ranking ones who respond with submissive screams. A threat-grunt–scream sequence not only provides information about individual identities and who is threatening whom, but also about kin-relationships and ranks in the dominance hierarchy. Baboons are very sensitive to sequences of grunts and screams that appear to threaten harmonious relationships between kin or violate the existing dominance hierarchy. As an example, they listen carefully when hearing that a subordinate individual gives a threat-grunt followed by the scream of a dominant individual. Thus, if baboons cannot see what is precisely taking place elsewhere, flexible understanding of vocalisations enables them to create a mental picture of what happened to whom (Box 9.2 Voice areas in the human and monkey brain).

The remarkable difference between the production and comprehension of vocalisations in non-human primates is puzzling because producers are also perceivers. Why is it that individuals can infer many meanings from the vocalisations of others but are heavily constrained in producing new calls? Seyfarth and Cheney (2010) suggest that the difference may arise because call production depends on mechanisms of **phonation** or 'voicing'. Voicing means that vocal cords can vibrate to produce vocal sounds. Mechanisms of phonation are largely innate whereas comprehension depends on learning mechanisms which are considerably flexible. This raises the crucial question of why natural selection did not favour flexible vocal production.

phonation
the production of voiced sounds by means of vibrations of the vocal cords.

It is probable that after chimpanzees and humans diverged around six million years ago, our ancestors developed much greater control over the physiology of vocal production. Since then, producing vocal sounds became more flexible and more dependent on auditory experience and vocal learning. But what selection pressures may have produced these physiological changes? Seyfarth and Cheney (2010) suggest that the communication of non-human primates lacks three features that are abundantly present in humans: the capacity to understand the mental states of others (or theory of mind), the capacity to generate new words, and a syntax that provides rules for the construction of words and sentences. In particular, the lack of a theory of mind would explain the lack of the other features (new words and syntax). We will take up this issue in the next section (9.5 The cognitive origin of language).

The origin of speech production

The human capacity for speech may be taken for granted but consider what happens in verbal communication (MacNeilage 2008). Humans speak at a rate of about fifteen consonants and vowels per second, and manage to organise these sounds neatly into meaningful syllables, words and sentences. A complex mental organisation is required for speech production. For example, while speaking we draw on a mental dictionary in which concepts are linked with instructions on how to pronounce the relevant sounds. The bodily organisation of speech production is many millions of years old and originally not selected for the delivery of words. For instance, the lungs served initially as a flotation device in fish and evolved into a gas exchange system in terrestrial species. The vocal cords that can vibrate to produce vocal sounds, originated from valves to prevent water from entering the lungs. The vocal tract or airway between the vocal cords and the mouth that shapes the sounds we make, originally served for food ingestion.

The vocal or respiratory tract in humans is unusual compared with other mammals in that the larynx – i.e. the upper part of the windpipe that contains the vocal cords – lies lower in the throat than that of dogs or apes. The lowered or descended **larynx** in humans is thought to be an adaptation for speech, increasing the phonetic range of human vocalisations. However, it has recently been argued that the descended tongue root is the critical factor in speech production, rather than the descent of the larynx (Fitch 2010; Figure 9.3). From Figure 9.3, it can be seen that humans have a lower larynx and longer oral cavity but the air sac is absent.

larynx
the muscular and cartilaginous structure at the top of the trachea (windpipe) and below the tongue that contains the vocal cords.

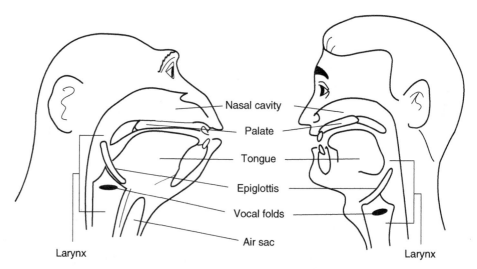

Figure 9.3 Vocal tracts of chimpanzee and human, scaled to look the same size
Source: Corballis (2002)

What is speech? Generally, it refers to making vocal sounds which we have in common with other animals. Many species produce vocal sounds to communicate messages: frogs croak, dogs bark, lions roar and humans speak. Speech may be considered a sound production system which is specialised in complex articulated vocalisations. Articulation implies tight coordination between the various organs and muscles that play a role in speech, including the vocal tract, lips, jaw, tongue and soft palate. A typical feature of speech is that we make rapid movements in opening and closing our mouth which is necessary to produce vowels and consonants respectively. How did this remarkable capacity originate?

Peter MacNeilage (1998, 2008) has proposed a theory of speech evolution – the frame/content theory – based on syllables (frames) that can be filled with vowels and consonants (content). He suggests that syllabic frames originated from the rhythmic jaw movements associated with feeding in mammals. The idea that syllables can be viewed as frames to be filled by different sounds, is strongly supported by findings about a variety of speech-errors. It is indeed widely agreed that analysis of errors in speaking or slips of the tongue may provide insights into the control of speech production. There are several types of speech-errors and the most revealing type are 'exchanges' in which two different units change places. For example, initial consonants of a syllable may exchange places (well made → mell wade), vowels exchange places (ad hoc → odd hack), or final consonants of a syllable may exchange places (top shelf → toff shelp).

Syllabic frames into which sounds can be inserted, are rare among primate vocalisations. That is the reason why MacNeilage attempts to bridge the evolutionary gap between humans and other mammals by his proposal that the motor control of speech movements may have initially borrowed from the motor control of similar movements in feeding behaviour such as biting, chewing, sucking and swallowing. This idea makes sense because the vocal tract in mammals evolved for feeding before it was co-opted for speaking.

MacNeilage further suggests that the lip-smacking, tongue-smacking and teeth-chattering in monkeys may be regarded as precursors to speech. These motor actions were originally associated with chewing, sucking and licking but became ritualised and acquired new, communicative functions. Monkeys use lip-smacking, tongue-smacking and teeth-chattering when submitting to dominant animals and when they are eager to make friends. Lip-smacking often accompanies grooming behaviour which refers to cleaning and removing fleas from the fur of another monkey. As both speaking and ritualised lip-smacking are quiet, close-contact and affiliative vocalisations, this commonality may support the idea that communicative movements of the mouth preceded speech (Fitch 2010).

The capacity for vocal learning

Human speech has to be learned by listening to others. In their early years, children do this without formal training. Exposure to speech is enough. We share the capacity for vocal learning not with monkeys or apes, because their vocalisations are largely innate, but we have this capacity in common with some bird species. Vocal learning is a challenge because the required movements are mostly invisible and must be inferred from the sounds we hear. Despite this difficulty, the capacity to learn complex vocalisations has evolved independently in humans, songbirds, parrots and hummingbirds (Catchpole and Slater 2008; Fitch et al. 2010). Since Darwin (1871), we have known

BOX 9.3 Music and language

Music and language may have a common evolutionary root. The term 'musilanguage' conveys the idea that music and language are branches of the same tree (Brown 2000; Mithen 2005). When we listen to accomplished orators, poets or actors, we can hear that their speech has a certain degree of musicality. The musical quality of speech is a matter of pitch, rhythm, tone and timbre that we normally ascribe to music. In daily discussions we rely on prosodic cues like timing and pitch to interpret the speaker's intention. As words in themselves may not reveal what is really meant, we attend as well to the speaker's intonation and facial expression. Prosody refers to the non-linguistic components of speech such as pitch and tone that help

to convey precise meaning and emotional content. The issue of emotion is important because this topic is often neglected in language studies. Language is usually considered a medium of communication which excels in expressing thoughts while music is a better medium for expressing emotions. There is a special branch of study, dedicated to the relation between music and emotion (e.g. Juslin and Sloboda 2010). We do not know when the 'specialisation' of language and music in human evolution started. The evolutionary relationship between music and language allows different interpretations: first, one derives from the other; second, both are independent; and third, they have a common root (Figure 9.4).

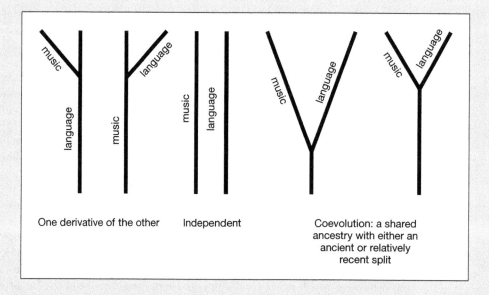

Figure 9.4 Possible evolutionary relationships between language and music
Source: Mithen (2009)

that many songbirds must be exposed to the songs of their conspecifics in order to sing properly. But only since the 1960s have scientists started to investigate the birds' capacity for vocal learning. In fact, birdsong learning is an interesting, analogous trait of human speech and music learning (Marler 2000).

Birdsong, human speech and music have basic similarities (Fitch 2006; Box 9.3 Music and language). The most obvious one is that all three are learned. The capacity to learn vocalisations is innate but learning requires a rich input from the environment and a prolonged period of practice. Another similarity is that birdsong, speech and music go through a 'sensitive period' early in life in which individuals must be exposed to the vocalisations of adult conspecifics. Birds with vocal learning produce in this period highly variable song, termed 'subsong' which develops into normal conspecific song. Subsong in young birds appears to be analogous to babbling in human infants who have a strong tendency to vocalise to themselves. This babbling occurs with hands and mouth. While deaf infants gradually stop vocal babbling, hearing infants decrease manual babbling and turn to vocal babbling. Both babbling and subsong are thought to be necessary for producing adequate vocalisations.

9.5   The cognitive origin of language

Theory of mind and language

Vocalisations in non-human primates are largely innate, but in humans they are largely learned. True, we have some innate calls (e.g. laughter, crying, screaming, moaning), but language has to be learned. This conclusion, drawn from the previous section, indicates a problem. The two sorts of vocal communication – non-human primate vocalisation and human language – are so different that comparison between them reveals little about their common ancestry. We may therefore follow another approach, as proposed by Cheney and Seyfarth (2007), that examines language evolution through its relation with cognition, in particular the evolution of theory of mind.

Recall from the previous section that the vocal communication of non-human primates lacks three features that are abundantly present in humans: the capacity to understand the mental states of others (or theory of mind), the capacity to generate new words, and a syntax that provides rules for the construction of words and sentences. In particular, the lack of a theory of mind may explain the lack of the other features (new words and syntax).

A theory of mind is crucial to language because engaging in conversation with someone requires the speaker to attend closely to the listener. The speaker has to be sure that the message came across. If not, the message has to be rephrased. At the same time, the listener has to attend closely to the speaker in order to be sure what meaning the speaker intends to impart. If not, questions may help to clarify the intended meaning. In short, without a theory of mind human conversation would regress to the level of non-human primates. The essential role that a theory of mind plays in language is also demonstrated by the fact that we often use shortcuts like half-formed sentences or metaphors which are sufficient for the listeners to understand what we mean. This manner of speaking is possible because listeners can use their theory of mind to fill the gaps. 'Language is sketchy, thought is rich', as Lila Gleitman and Anna Papafragou (2005) put it. Limitations of time and patience also explain why we often use shortcuts. A typical example is the waitress who told another that 'The ham sandwich wants his bill'.

A full-blown theory of mind enables us to understand each other's beliefs, knowledge, ignorance and other mental states when we communicate. However, a theory of mind is not a single capacity but consists of components that are thought to have evolved. Figure 9.5 shows three basic components that, according to Baron-Cohen (1995, 2005), underlie the human capacity to represent other's

BOX 9.4 Components of a theory of mind

Simon Baron-Cohen (1995) hypothesised that a fully developed theory of mind consists of four kinds of capacities that develop independently. These capacities are detection of intentions of others, detection of eye direction, shared attention, and understanding the mental states of others. Figure 9.5 is a schematic diagram of Baron-Cohen's model.

The first component (ID) interprets whether a certain movement is produced by natural forces (e.g. a rock falling down) or an agent's self-propelled movement (e.g. a predator approaching you). ID is also sensitive to sound, distinguishing between vocally created sounds, and other sounds like water flowing in a river. This basic component has an ancient heritage and is widely shared among vertebrates (Fitch 2010). The second component (EDD) interprets eye-like stimuli as 'looking at me', or 'looking at something'. This component is widely shared and certainly well-developed in non-human mammals. These two components (ID and EDD) are thought to be present in our non-linguistic primate ancestors. The

third component (SAM) interprets whether the self and the other are perceiving the same event. Whereas ID can build a dyadic representation, 'mother wants the cup', SAM can build a triadic representation, 'mother sees that I see the cup'. SAM allows joint attention behaviours like pointing and gaze following. This component is considered to be present in chimpanzees, with some restrictions on the contexts in which it is used (Fitch 2010). The fourth component (ToMM) allows understanding of the mental states of others such as 'mother thinks this cup contains water'. This capacity is regarded to be uniquely human as it can represent all kinds of mentalising: believing, intending, pretending, and so on. It enables one to know that someone's belief is true or false. The classical test for children's capacity to reflect on the mental states of others is through the understanding of 'false belief'. The reader may recall from section 8.5 (Social cognition in chimpanzees and humans) the 'Sally–Anne test' (Figure 8.10 The Sally–Anne test of understanding false belief).

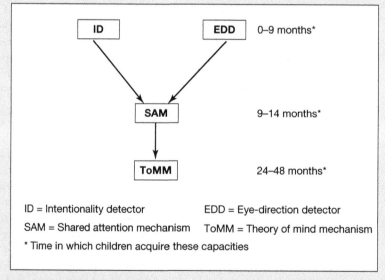

Figure 9.5 Components of a theory of mind (Baron-Cohen's model)
Source: Baron-Cohen (2005)

mental states as they may differ from our own. We should bear in mind that this model, based on developmental data about children, is still debated. The top three – intentionality detector (ID), eye-direction detector (EDD), and shared attention mechanism (SAM) appear to be shared with other species in some form; only the theory of mind mechanism (ToMM) may be uniquely human (Box 9.4 Components of a theory of mind).

The evolution of a theory of mind selected for language

Vocal communication in non-human primates lacks three features that are largely present in humans: a theory of mind, the capacity to generate new words, and syntax. In what sequence did these features evolve? Cheney and Seyfarth (2010) propose that the evolution of a theory of mind created selection pressures for the capacity to generate new words and syntax. Findings indicate that language acquisition in children very much depends on a theory of mind. In the same vein, it is difficult to imagine how our ancestors could have learned new words and learned grammar without a rudimentary theory of mind, providing them with a notion of other individuals' mental states. This proposal that the evolution of mind spurred the evolution of language, is based on empirical and theoretical arguments.

With regard to empirical arguments, there is no evidence for a large vocal repertoire in monkeys or apes that is comparable to young children. Similarly, there are only a few examples of syntax in which chimpanzees combine calls that may carry new meaning, transcending the meaning of the individual calls. Combining words into new words is common practice in human language (e.g. 'doghouse', 'lightning operation'). In as far as a theory of mind is concerned, there is a sharp contrast between primate vocalisations and human language. While human language is based on understanding the mental states of others, the calls that monkeys and apes produce do not take into account the mental states of listeners. The result is that they cannot communicate with the intent to inform conspecifics who are ignorant or need correct information (Cheney and Seyfarth 1999; Seyfarth and Cheney 2003). For example, infant monkeys often give alarm calls for harmless species like pigeons. Adults then look up but give no alarm calls of their own. By contrast, when an infant gives an alarm call for a genuine predator like an eagle, adults look up and give alarm calls themselves. So, adults do not act as if recognising the ignorance of the infant or correcting the false information the infant gave.

With respect to theoretical arguments, Seyfarth and Cheney (2010) suggest that an evolutionary scenario in which a theory of mind served as a prime mover of large vocabularies and syntax, is highly likely if we consider word learning in children. When children acquire the capacity to share attention with others, this skill is essential for early word learning. And in assigning words to objects or events, they make use of gestures and gaze directions of others. Furthermore, studies show that children's earliest skills of joining attention with their mothers correlate highly with their earliest skills of comprehending and producing language (e.g. Tomasello 2008). Equally important and in marked contrast to monkeys and apes, children are intensely motivated to acquire new words and share their knowledge with others.

KEY FIGURES   Richard Seyfarth and Dorothy Cheney

Richard Seyfarth is a psychologist and **Dorothy Cheney** is a biologist at the University of Pennsylvania. Their field research in Africa is focused on the cognition and communication in primates (e.g. vervet monkeys, baboons).

Selected, co-authored works

How Monkeys See the World: Inside the Mind of Another Species (1990)

Baboon Metaphysics: The Evolution of a Social Mind (2007)

The lack of syntax in the vocalisations of non-human primates does not refer to an inability to understand that an event can be described as a sequence of calls. For example, baboons are able to distinguish between a sequence of calls in which individual Alpha apparently threatens Beta and a sequence of calls in which it is Beta who threatens Alpha. Non-human primates seem capable of thinking in simple 'sentences', but unable to distinguish between what they know and what others know. In contrast to humans, they are also unmotivated to make their thoughts explicit. Seyfarth and Cheney (2010) conclude that human-like language could only occur when our ancestors were motivated to share their private thoughts with others. The evolution of a theory of mind would also serve as the selection pressure for the physiology of flexible vocal production (e.g. lowered larynx).

Why humans have language

The evolution of a theory of mind may have served as a strong selection pressure for flexible vocal communication. But why did we need this kind of communication anyway? What was the problem that language solved? Did the pressures that selected for language, like social cognition, come from the social environment? Recall from section 8.4 (Selection pressures for great ape cognition) that selection pressures may be regarded as forces that over a long evolutionary time and in a consistent manner shape the organism's traits which cause it to be successful in survival and reproduction.

The usual answer is that language evolved because it allowed us to exchange technical information: explain where food can be found, teach how to make tools, fire and build shelter. Once generations could build on the know-how that previous generations had acquired, language became an attractive medium. It is also most likely that language evolved because it enabled humans to find their way in a complex social world where knowledge about kinship relationships, dominance hierarchies and alliances was vital. We focus on three hypotheses which have been proposed for the social functions of language.

The problem of social bonding

Terrence Deacon (1997) advanced the social contract hypothesis, supposing that early pair-bonded humans needed a kind of marriage contract to stabilise their bond. You may recall from section 4.5 (Mate preferences of men and women) that producing and raising large-brained offspring requires high energetic costs, necessitating bi-parental care. The tendency of men and women to form long-lasting pair-bonds would be present in the earliest members of the genus *Homo* (around 2–2.5 mya).

The problem was that in traditional hunter-gatherer societies males went hunting, leaving their mates at risk of being mated by other males. At the same time, 'husbands' were exposed to the risk of mating with females from other groups. As this would put considerable strain on their relationships, verbal contracts are thought to be the solution to this problem. Deacon's proposal sounds plausible because human pair-bonds are still notoriously unstable. However, the frequency of adultery in modern humans indicates that language has been unsuccessful in solving the commitment problem. Elaborate courtship rituals and emotional bonding would be better solutions.

As our pair-bonded ancestors lived in large multi-male, multi-female groups, it makes sense to focus on the possibility that language evolved to service social bonds more generally. Robin Dunbar (1993, 1996) proposed the social bonding

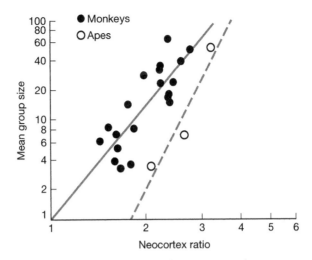

Figure 9.6 In primates, mean group size increases with relative neocortex volume (ratio of neocortex volume to volume of the rest of the brain)

Source: Dunbar and Shultz (2007b)

hypothesis which states that language – especially in the form of gossip or social talk – provided a substitute for grooming in non-human primates. Grooming refers to cleaning and removing parasites from the fur of another member of the group, but it is also an important form of social bonding. Individuals pay careful attention to who grooms whom. Grooming one another is far from random because primates can raise their rank in the social hierarchy if they succeed in grooming high-ranking individuals. In particular, individuals may form grooming cliques which provide mutual support.

Dunbar's hypothesis implies that a social bonding problem arose when the size of the group increased. Among the factors that may influence group size in primates, are food distribution and predation pressure. In addition to this, the social brain hypothesis suggests that in social bonded species like primates, group size can be constrained by cognitive capacities (Dunbar 1992). This hypothesis is based on the finding that group size and neocortex size are highly correlated (Figure 9.6). The size of the neocortex is assumed to limit the number of social relationships that an individual can maintain. If the group size increases too much, individuals cannot maintain close bonds with all group members.

Maintaining relationships does not only require cognitive capacities but also time for grooming one another. Grooming can take up to 20 per cent of the total day for social species (Dunbar 2009). Grooming is a typical one-on-one interaction that will take up an increasing part of each individual's time budget when the number of partners is growing. Thus, as a consequence of the need to maintain social bonds and keep enough time for feeding, moving and resting, there was a selection pressure for the evolution of complex vocalisation as a form of 'vocal grooming'. The spread of vocal sounds replaced the hand-stroking, picking and biting, allowing individuals to serve multiple partners at the same time.

Dunbar has shown that groups of 150 individuals are characteristic of a wide range of contemporary and historical human societies. This number is about three

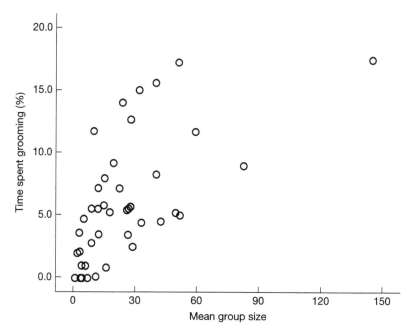

Figure 9.7 Grooming time and group size in individual primate species
Source: Dunbar (2009)

times larger than the average group size for chimpanzees and baboons. The predicted grooming time for this number of individuals would be 36.6 per cent, which is much higher than the average time spent on grooming (17.4 per cent) for any primate species (Dunbar 2009; Figure 9.7).

The absolute upper limit on an individual's grooming time is 20 per cent of total day time. Dunbar argues that this limit creates a ceiling on group size at about eighty individuals. Only a more efficient bonding mechanism such as language could break through this limit. The claim that language is more efficient in maintaining social bonds is indicated by the finding that humans from a wide range of societies are involved in social interactions for an average of 20 per cent of their day. If humans groomed one another like other primates, the required social time would be 36.6 per cent which suggests that language is almost twice as efficient as grooming. It is important to note that social time is not necessarily identical with grooming time. Dunbar argues that the difference is minimal but this may not be factually true. His colleagues note that social time includes other activities such as play or courtship that are not directly related to social bonding (Lehmann et al. 2007).

Other studies on non-human primates support Dunbar's general claim that vocal – to be distinguished from verbal – communication is important for social bonding. They show that over evolutionary time, increases in the size of the vocal repertoire among non-human primates were associated with increases in both group size and time spent on grooming, considered as a measure of social bonding (McComb and Semple 2005). These findings suggest that increasing group size was a pressure that selected for more vocalisations as an addition to grooming. Field studies on vocal communication in birds also support the hypothesis that group size as one basic component of social complexity affects the diversity of calls. The larger the group the larger the vocal complexity (Freeberg 2006).

Dunbar's hypothesis that language replaced grooming as a social bonding device may be challenged by an alternative hypothesis. Dean Falk (2004) proposed the baby talk hypothesis that early language originated from the vocal interactions between mothers and infants. The special language that mothers use to communicate with their infants – known as baby talk or motherese – would have replaced cradling arms as a means for keeping the little ones content. Early hominin mothers needed to put their babies down next to them while foraging which is probably why they developed a vocal manner of monitoring infants. The argument is, then, that selection for vocal language occurred after early hominin mothers engaged in affective vocalisations towards their infants. In many cultures, learning the rhythms of speech is, indeed, facilitated by the way mothers address their infants. This infant-directed speech (or motherese) shows repetitions and rising intonations. The following example, used by Falk (2004: 495), contains the pitched syllables (in capitals) that characterise motherese:

Aren't YOU a nice BABY? Good GIRL, drinking all your MILK. Look, look, that's a giRAFFE. Isn't that a NICE giRAFFE? DOGgie, there's the DOGgie. Ooh, did you see the lovely DOGgie?

When ten months of age, children begin to babble in rhythms that are typical for language. Then, the vocal turn-taking that characterises conversation also develops between mothers and their babbling babies.

9.6 Summary

- In contrast to most animals using fixed signals in communication, some species like songbirds and humans evolved flexible forms of communication. While animal signals such as alarm calls are bound to specific contexts, humans can use words freely in multiple contexts. One important selection pressure for flexible communication is possibly social cohesion. Vocal signals keep groups of individuals together, differentiate between groups, and strengthen the bonds between parents and offspring.

- One argument in favour of the gestural origin of language refers to the fact that living great apes use gestures with relative flexibility. This suggests that a similar capacity would be available to the last common ancestor of chimpanzees and early humans. An additional argument may be that the macaque brain area for grasping food is the homologue of Broca's area for speech production in the human brain. Both areas have a mirror neuron system that would be involved in the evolution of gestures and speech.

- While call production in non-human primates is largely innate, our human ancestors developed much greater control over vocal production. Since then, producing vocal sounds has become more flexible and more dependent on auditory experience and vocal learning. One theory suggests that speech originated from syllables, serving as frames to be filled with vowels and consonants. The rapid movements of opening and closing our mouth in producing vowels and consonants, would have drawn on the rhythmic jaw movements associated with feeding.

- Vocal communication in non-human primates differs so much from human language that comparison between them reveals little about their common ancestry. An alternative approach is to study language evolution through its relation with the evolution of a theory of mind. Similar to language acquisition in children, depending on a theory of mind, we can imagine that our ancestors could only learn new words and grammar after they had developed a theory of mind.

- There are three hypotheses why human evolution selected for language. One hypothesis proposes that verbal contracts served as a solution to the problem of social bonding. A second hypothesis argues that language replaced social grooming as it is used in non-human primates. A third hypothesis proposes that language emerged from mother–infant vocalisations that replaced cradling arms which mothers needed for foraging.

Study questions

1. Which components of human communication are unique and which ones do we share with other species?

2. What selection pressures are thought to have favoured flexible communication?

3. What evidence do we have for the gestural origin of human language?

4. What evidence do we have for the vocal origin of human language?

5. What evidence do we have for the cognitive origin of language?

Suggested reading

The origin of flexible communication

Chater, N., Reali, F. and Christiansen, M. (2009). Restrictions on biological adaptation in language evolution. *Proceedings of the National Academy of the United States of America, 106*, 1015–1020.

Deacon, T. (2010). A role for relaxed selection in the evolution of the language capacity. *Proceedings of the National Academy of the United States of America, 107*, 9000–9006.

Fitch, W. (2005). The evolution of language: a comparative review. *Biology and Philosophy, 20*, 193–230.

Hauser, M., Chomsky, N. and Fitch, W. (2002). The faculty of language: What is it, who has it, and how did it evolve? *Science, 298*, 1569–1579.

Számado, S. and Szathmáry, E. (2006). Selective scenarios for the emergence of natural language. *Trends in Ecology and Evolution, 21*, 555–561.

The gestural origin of language

Corballis, M. (2010). Mirror neurons and the evolution of language. *Brain & Language, 112*, 25–35.

Gallese V., Fadiga, L., Fogassi, L. and Rizzolatti, G. (1996). Action recognition in the premotor cortex. *Brain, 119*, 593–609.

Mukamel, R., Ekstrom, A., Kaplan, J. et al. (2010). Single-neuron responses in humans during execution and observation of actions. *Current Biology, 20*, 750–756.

Pika, S. (2008). Gestures of apes and pre-linguistic human children: Similar or different? *First Language, 28 (2)*, 116–140.

Pollick, A. and de Waal, F. (2007). Ape gestures and language evolution. *Proceedings of the National Academy of Sciences of the USA, 104*, 8184–8189.

Rizzolatti, G. and Arbib, M. (1998). Language within our grasp. *Trends in Neurosciences, 21*, 188–194.

The vocal origin of language

Arbib, M., Liebal, K. and Pika, S. (2008). Primate vocalisation, gesture, and the evolution of language. *Current Anthropology, 49*, 1053–1076.

Belin, P. and Grosbras, M. (2010). Before speech: Cerebral voice processing in infants. *Neuron, 65*, 733–735.

MacNeilage, P. (1998). The frame/content theory of evolution of speech production. *Behavioral and Brain Sciences, 21*, 499–546.

Petkov, C., Kayser, C., Steudel, T. et al. (2008). A voice region in the monkey brain. *Nature Neuroscience, 11*, 367–374.

Seyfarth, R. and Cheney, D. (2010). Production, usage, and comprehension in animal vocalisations. *Brain and Language, 115*, 92–100.

The cognitive origin of language

Dunbar, R. and Shultz, S. (2007a). Evolution in the social brain. *Science, 317*, 1344–1347.

Falk, D. (2004). Prelinguistic evolution in early hominins: whence motherese? *Behavioral and Brain Sciences, 27*, 491–541.

Fitch, W., Huber, L. and Bugnar, T. (2010). Social cognition and the evolution of language: Constructing cognitive phylogenies. *Neuron, 65*, 795–814.

Freeberg, T. (2006). Social complexity can drive vocal complexity: Group size influences vocal information in Carolina chickadees. *Psychological Science, 17*, 557–561.

Lehman, J., Korstjens, A. and Dunbar, R. (2007). Group size, grooming and social cohesion in primates. *Animal Behaviour, 74*, 1617–1629.

Levy, F. (2012). Mirror neurons, birdsong, and human language: a hypothesis. *Frontiers of Psychiatry, 2*, 1–7.

McComb, K. and Semple, S. (2005). Coevolution of vocal communication and sociality in primates. *Biological Letters, 1*, 381–385.

Scott-Philips, T. and Kirby, S. (2010). Language evolution in the laboratory. *Trends in Cognitive Sciences, 14*, 411–417.

Seyfarth, R. and Cheney, D. (2003). Signalers and receivers in animal communication. *Annual Review of Psychology, 54*, 145–173.

Reference books

Cheney, D. and Seyfarth, R. (2007). *Baboon Metaphysics: The Evolution of a Social Mind.* Chicago: The University of Chicago Press.

Fitch, W. (2010). *The Evolution of Language.* Cambridge: Cambridge University Press.

Hauser, M. (1996). *The Evolution of Communication.* Cambridge, MA: The MIT Press.

Oller, K. and Griebel, U. (Eds) (2004). *Evolution of Communication Systems. A Comparative Approach.* Cambridge, MA: The MIT Press.

Oller, K. and Griebel, U. (Eds) (2008). *Evolution of Communicative Flexibility: Complexity, Creativity, and Adaptability in Human and Animal Communication.* Cambridge, MA: The MIT Press.

Rizzolatti, G. and Sinigaglia, C. (2008). *Mirrors in the Mind: How our Minds Share Actions and Emotions.* Oxford: Oxford University Press.

Tallerman, M. and Gibson, K. (Eds) (2012). *The Oxford Handbook of Language Evolution.* Oxford: Oxford University Press.

10 Culture in evolution

This chapter will cover:

10.1   Introduction

10.2   What is culture?

10.3   Cultural inheritance

10.4   How culture is incorporated in evolutionary theory

10.5   Cumulative cultural evolution

10.6   Summary

Learning outcomes

By the end of this chapter, you should be able to explain:

- how culture can be defined
- how animal and human culture differ
- why cultural inheritance became important in evolution
- how culture is incorporated in evolutionary theory
- how humans achieve cumulative cultural evolution.

10.1 Introduction

A leitmotiv in this textbook is the evolution of flexibility. Initially, problems were solved by more or less fixed responses like reflexes and emotions, but later on flexible responses evolved such as learning and cognition. In this chapter we focus on culture considered as beliefs or rules of behaviour that we learn from parents, teachers or celebrities we have never met.

Culture is mostly associated with humans, but field research shows that other animals have cultures as well. For example, chimpanzees have grooming and tool-using traditions, and songbirds have vocalisation traditions. This raises a couple of questions. What is culture? How similar and different are human and animal culture?

Since chimpanzees and humans transmit traditions across generations, we presume that their common ancestors made a significant step towards a cultural inheritance system. As all animals inherit genes but most of them can make do without such a thing as culture, the question is: why did cultural inheritance become important in evolution?

In some social species, culture serves as a new inheritance system that provides individuals with solutions for problems that they can learn from one another. As standard evolutionary theory only recognises genetic inheritance, the question arises as to how culture is incorporated in evolutionary theory.

When the essential ingredients of evolutionary theory are present in culture – variation, selection and inheritance – we have cultural evolution, analogous to genetic evolution. When cultural evolution leads to improvements over generations of learners, it is called 'cumulative cultural evolution'. In which species does this evolution occur? What capacities does it require?

10.2 What is culture?

Culture is a difficult concept to pin down

culture

information that is capable of affecting individuals' behaviour which they acquire from other individuals through teaching, imitation and other forms of social learning.

To laypersons, the term '**culture**' may evoke images of fine art and fashion, but historically anthropologists have characterised culture in terms of traditional beliefs, values and behaviours associated with a particular population. Anthropology, or cultural anthropology originated from nineteenth-century 'ethnology' which studied non-Western societies. Edward Tylor (1832–1917), the founding father of anthropology, defined culture as 'that complex whole which includes knowledge, belief, art, law, morals, custom, and any other capabilities and habits acquired by man as a member of society' (1871: 1). For Tylor and many other anthropologists, culture was by definition human culture.

Culture has proven to be a difficult concept to pin down. Since Tylor's proposal, anthropologists have developed many different definitions of culture. In a classic review of concepts and definitions of culture, Alfred Kroeber and Clyde Kluckhohn (1952) concluded that the term 'culture' had been used in more than 150 different ways in the anthropological literature. Today, different definitions remain, referring to rules of behaviour (e.g. rituals, social norms, law, morals), shared ideas (e.g. myths, beliefs), material artefacts (e.g. pottery and tools in the archaeological record), or ethnic markers (e.g. customs, dialects). Outsiders coming afresh to the anthropological literature, are still struck by the seemingly radically different views that anthropologists have of what 'culture' is (Plotkin 2002).

Geneticists and biological anthropologists who were eager to explore how cultural phenomena interact with genes, chose a pragmatic approach in studying culture. They considered culture as information that is capable of affecting individuals' behaviour which they acquire from other individuals through teaching, imitation and other forms of social learning. 'Information' includes knowledge, beliefs, values and skills. **Cultural change** can then be modelled as an evolutionary process in which favourable cultural variants are selected and socially transmitted. Culture is broken down into specific traits – for example, consumption of starch-rich or starch-poor diet – which allows their frequencies to be tracked mathematically (Laland et al. 2010).

cultural change
an evolutionary process in which favourable cultural variants are selected and socially transmitted.

Defining culture broadly enables one to include culture in other animals. Findings from field research show that non-human primates – especially chimpanzees and some monkey species – have behavioural repertoires that are called 'cultures'. Evolutionary psychologist Andrew Whiten and his colleagues (1999) published an influential article entitled 'Cultures in chimpanzees' which presented a synthesis of long-term studies, revealing 39 different patterns in tool-usage, grooming and courtship behaviours. They defined culture as patterns of behaviour that are transmitted repeatedly through social or observational learning to become a population-wide characteristic.

Since 1999, behavioural traditions have also been reported in other non-human animals like birds and whales (e.g. Enggist and Pfgister 2002; Rendell and Whitehead 2001). Foraging and vocalising traditions are a source of adaptive behaviour because individuals can acquire solutions to problems of what to eat or whom to mate with, by imitating others. The definition of culture that Whiten et al. (1999) proposed is still valid, judging by the fact that recent studies define animal traditions as enduring behaviour patterns that are shared by members of a group and that are acquired in part through social learning (Fragaszy and Perry 2008).

Significant differences between humans and other animals

Typical traditions in chimpanzees that are transmitted across generations are grooming and tool-using behaviours. Behavioural traditions can also be found among humans when they greet and kiss one another, or use hammers and drive cars. These traditions are acquired through individual and social learning. But defining culture in terms of socially transmitted behaviours runs into problems because some behaviours are traditional practices, whereas others deserve a higher cultural status (Premack and Hauser 2006). For example, driving on the right-hand side of the road is a socially transmitted behavioural tradition, but trivial in that it lacks significant social consequences. If the driving practice changes from right to left, culture would not change fundamentally. However, if a nation changes from the English to the Chinese language, this would have severe social consequences. First, because language acquisition requires a long socialisation process, and second, because language is an important source of cultural identity, promoting similarity within a population and dissimilarity between populations. Thus in thinking about culture, we should distinguish trivial behaviours from consequential socially acquired practices. Otherwise we would overlook significant differences between humans and other animals.

Consider another significant difference: the human capacity to share values and beliefs that go beyond the world of our senses. A classic example is about a foreigner visiting Oxford for the first time, who is shown a number of colleges, libraries,

BOX 10.1 Forms of social learning

- **Social learning** is a change of behaviour that is the result of social interactions with other individuals, usually of the same species.

- **Imitation** refers to any form of learning in which individuals can learn a new behaviour by copying the behaviour of another individual, either of its own or another species, and incorporating it into its own action pattern, vocal repertoire, or practical know-how. Imitation is well represented in the higher mammals, particularly in primates and in the vocal learning of many bird species (e.g. songbirds, parrots). Imitation of other species' vocalisations is sometimes called vocal mimicry or mocking. Imitation should be distinguished from 'social facilitation' which refers to the tendency for some behaviours by members of a group to be taken up by others, spreading through the group. Social facilitation is an important means of achieving synchronisation of behaviour in a group. This can be important when a quick reaction is needed in taking flight from a predator. While imitation is learning a new behaviour, social facilitation evokes behaviour that is already part of an individual's repertoire.

- **Teaching** is a one–to–one or one–to–many form of learning in which one knowledgeable individual incurs some costs or at least does not derive any immediate benefit, while the naïve individual(s) acquire(s) knowledge or skills more rapidly or

efficiently than it (they) would in the absence of the knowledgeable individual.

- **Emulation** does not involve learning about the particular behaviours in which other individuals engage; rather, it involves learning about the outcomes. For example, apes learn that a tool can be used to cause some desired effect by watching a demonstrator, but they don't pay close attention to the details of how the tool is used. In the wild and in the laboratory, chimpanzees achieve better in emulation than in imitation.

- **Local enhancement**, like emulation, does not involve learning about the particular behaviours in which others are engaged. It is a type of learning in which the activities of older individuals direct the attention of younger animals towards a particular part of the environment. In foraging, for example, younger individuals will learn to find sources of food more quickly if they see experienced individuals looking for a place. Another example refers to young chimpanzees who are stimulated by their nut-cracking mothers to acquire the technique themselves by trial and error. Through sharing nuts, mothers support the attempts of their offspring.

Sources: Immelmann and Beer (1992), Boesch and Boesch-Ackermann (2000), Danchienne et al. (2008), and Galef (2009)

imitation

any form of learning in which individuals can learn a new behaviour by copying the behaviour of another individual, either of its own or another species, and incorporating it into its own action pattern, vocal repertoire or practical know-how.

emulation

the ability to comprehend the goal of a model and engage in similar behaviour to achieve that goal, without necessarily replicating the specific action of the model.

playing fields and administrative offices. He then asks 'But where is the university?' (Ryle 1963). This anecdote demonstrates that we can think in abstractions and construct our world accordingly. Things that we imagine and share can become powerful components of human culture. Science, religion and money are social inventions that make us very different from other animals. These mental creations are based on social agreement and are transmitted across generations. Thus human culture is for a large part imagination made real (Plotkin 2002, 2010).

Researchers disagree over the question in what ways human cultures and animal cultures are fundamentally different or fundamentally similar (Laland and Galef 2009). For example, one difference is that animals don't use symbols as we do when using letters in language and numbers in mathematics. Another difference is that humans are very competent in imitating one another whereas chimpanzees are far less skilful in this respect (Box 10.1 Forms of social learning). A third difference is that humans are superior in generating innovations, building on the achievements of others which gives their culture a cumulative character.

local enhancement

a form of social learning in which the activities of some individuals direct the attention of other individuals towards a particular part of the environment.

Any comparison between humans and other animals results in differences as well as similarities. Critics who have taken issue with claims of 'animal culture', emphasise the differences. For instance, Bennett Galef (2009) points out that much of human culture in the developed world clearly depends on imitation, teaching and language. In contrast, chimpanzees never teach and have no symbolic language, unless taught by humans. What is more, humans build on previous achievements as may be seen in science and technology, whereas our closest relatives, the chimpanzees, do not. The absence of cumulative culture in them would indicate that there are fundamental differences between animal traditions and human culture.

Michael Tomasello (2009b) is another critic who emphasises that human cultural traditions have at least three different characteristics. The first one, universality, implies that in all human societies there are some traditions that are practised by virtually everyone. Children who do not learn language, social rituals (e.g. greeting), and everyday behaviours such as feeding, dressing, and the like, will not be considered as normal members of the group. The second characteristic, uniformity, refers to the similar methods individuals employ to acquire cultural traditions. The method of social learning prevails particularly in conventional behaviours like linguistic symbols and rituals, whereas individual discovery and idiosyncratic use are not viable options. A third characteristic, the ratchet effect, refers to human cultural traditions that often show an accumulation of modifications over generations (Tomasello 1999). Historians of technology and palaeontologists have shown that tools like the hammer and knife have gradually been modified to meet novel requirements (Basalla 1988; Leroi-Gourhan 1993; Figure 10.1)

Different grades of culture

The implication of both criticisms is that humans differ so much from other animals that we should use different terms: animal traditions versus human culture. However, restricting the definition of culture to humans is of limited use in providing a framework for comparing species or for understanding the evolutionary precursors of human culture. Andrew Whiten (2009) argues therefore that we might distinguish different grades of culture, not only with respect to the transmission mechanisms that are involved (e.g. imitation, teaching, language), but also to the content of cultural traditions (e.g. social, tool-usage) and patterning of cultural traditions (e.g. multiple, diverse traditions), as well as to the cumulative elaboration of culture over time. The perspective of a graded culture can be depicted in terms of a 'culture pyramid' (Figure 10.2)

The base of the pyramid represents social information transfer which is widespread among animals. Social information transfer can be based on cues provided inadvertently by individuals engaged in activities. Individuals who find a location of resources, unintentionally draw the attention of other individuals with similar needs for these resources (Danchin et al. 2004). This occurs, for example, when Egyptian vultures discover a troop of hyenas bringing down a prey animal. Much of this inadvertent social information has temporary effects, serving short-term functions. Only a subset of such socially learned behaviour turns into enduring traditions which represent the second level of the pyramid. When species have multiple diverse traditions (e.g. grooming, tool-using, vocalising), this may be called culture, representing the third level. The fourth level is the smallest set of culture, defined by its cumulative character.

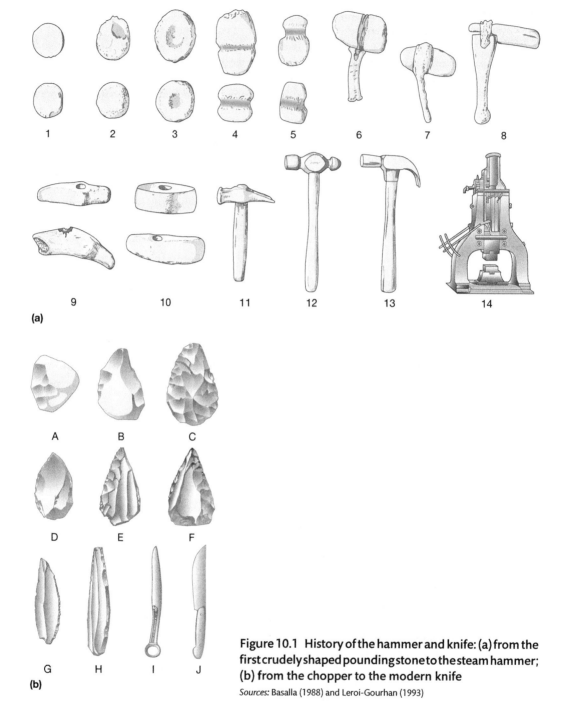

Figure 10.1 History of the hammer and knife: (a) from the first crudely shaped pounding stone to the steam hammer; (b) from the chopper to the modern knife

Sources: Basalla (1988) and Leroi-Gourhan (1993)

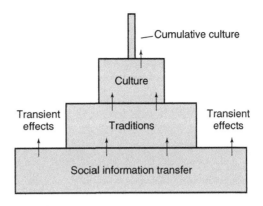

Figure 10.2 A culture pyramid
Source: Whiten (2009)

Table 10.1 Aspects of culture in humans and chimpanzees

	Humans	Chimpanzees
1. Population-level patterning		
Populations differentiated by multiple, diverse traditions?	Yes, countless	Yes
Cumulative traditions?	Yes, extremely elaborate	Minimal, disputed
2. Transmission mechanisms		
Teaching?	Yes, but rare in hunter-gatherers	Disputed
Imitation?	Yes	Yes, limited
Conformity to conventions?	Yes	Controversial
3. Content of traditions		
Social	Yes e.g. language, gestural conventions, moral norms	Yes e.g. tool-use, grooming
Non-social	Yes e.g. tool-construction, hunting, clothing, shelter	Yes e.g. foraging, hygiene

Source: Adapted from Whiten (2009)

With the perspective of a graded culture in mind, Whiten (2009) analysed the findings from chimpanzee fieldwork (Whiten et al. 1999, 2001) by himself and his colleagues. This led to the conclusion that: (1) chimpanzees can sustain multiple traditions that include a diversity of types of behaviour; (2) genetic and environmental explanations for behavioural differences can be ruled out; and (3) different groups may therefore develop unique cultural profiles, consisting of multiple, diverse traditions. The picture provided by the chimpanzee fieldwork community of researchers is summarised in Table 10.1. Aspects of culture are discriminated within three categories, and their manifestations are indicated for two species, humans and chimpanzees (Whiten et al. 2003, 2004).

To conclude, what is culture? It should be clear by now that the concept of culture can be defined in many ways which may overlap and are open to discussion. Broadly speaking, culture can be thought of in two ways: first, as the socially transmitted pool of products – e.g. behavioural traditions, social constructions – that characterise populations of social animals; and second, as the capacity by which individuals produce these outcomes. Both conceptions of culture will be elaborated in the following sections.

10.3 Cultural inheritance

Our primate ancestors made a significant step towards a cultural inheritance system (Whiten 2005). Local chimpanzee communities have traditions of grooming and tool-use which are transmitted across generations. Populations of early humans spread across the globe and developed new behaviours and tools that could be transmitted across generations (see Figure 3.12 Behavioural innovations in the Middle Stone Age in Africa). Since then, the modest pool of human culture has grown into an ocean of cultural items – knowledge, skills, technologies, social constructions – on which modern humans depend. The demand for life-long learning indicates how much culture needs to be transmitted in order to maintain our standard of living. We should therefore expect that human evolution proceeds along two paths – genes and culture.

Behavioural and symbolic inheritance

The cultural inheritance system evolved on top of the genetic inheritance system, providing a rich repertoire of solutions to problems. The concept of cultural inheritance is based on the argument that genes are not the only resource that contributes to heredity. Particularly in social animals, much of an individual's behaviour is the result of skills, beliefs and norms that are inherited from others.

Eva Jablonka and Marion Lamb (2005) emphasise that cultural inheritance includes two different forms: behavioural inheritance and symbolic inheritance. In order for a habit or skill to be transmitted, it has to be displayed. For example, vocal imitation is important for young birds to acquire and reconstruct the appropriate sounds of its species. Similarly, it was crucial for the evolution of language that humans were able to imitate sounds as well as lip and tongue movements. Thus, the acquisition of behavioural culture depends essentially on behaviour display.

Behavioural culture is something that humans and other animals share. What makes us different is that we are able to think and communicate through symbols (e.g. words, numbers). Recall from section 9.2 (The origin of flexible communication) that animal signals such as alarm calls evolved to serve fixed functions. A sound that evolved into an alarm call cannot be used as an aggressive signal to intimidate a rival or as a courtship signal to impress females. Thus in most animals, signal and function are coupled in a one-to-one mapping which is why they are considered as fixed signals. But humans are quite free in decoupling signals from functions because they are capable of representing objects symbolically. Symbols such as words can be used arbitrarily to represent objects or inventions. Grammatical rules (syntax) allow us to combine words flexibly into sentences and stories, and use our imagination to create fictions.

While the transmission of a behavioural pattern requires that it has to be displayed, transmitting symbolic culture is highly dependent on active instruction. The reason is that symbols are organised into complex, rule-governed systems in which the elements refer to one another. For example, words are part of a language system in which their meaning depends on the relations they have to the represented objects and situations, as well as the relations they have to other words. The same applies to other symbolic systems such as mathematics, music, visual arts and science. In conclusion, the uniqueness of human culture is that we are able to represent objects, ideas, beliefs and institutions by arbitrary symbols.

Gene pool and cultural pool

The reader may recall from section 2.3 (Genome, nervous system and culture as solutions) that each living being has a genome which contains all the genes that are needed to build the organism, ensure that it works satisfactorily and protects against diseases. Almost every somatic cell of the human body has a genome of each parent while human reproductive cells (egg cells and sperm cells) have just one genome. Reproductive cells have one genome because in sexual reproduction each parent contributes its own genome to its offspring. In the longer term, sexual reproduction implies that in each generation individual genomes are reshuffled from body to body. The collective database of survival instructions is the gene pool of a species. It is the sum total of all genes in an interbreeding population at a particular time and can be described by the frequencies of different genes it contains. Thus each individual's genome is a sample from the gene pool.

The idea of a gene pool is convenient when we imagine an individual at conception taking a dip into the gene pool and coming up with a handful of genetic instructions (Plotkin 1994). Once the individual has received its instructions, it is cut off from the gene pool, and cannot dip back into the gene pool for further instructions. In a static world this is not an issue but in a fast changing world, it is a serious problem. We can imagine therefore that more rapid problem-solving systems evolved like the immune system and the nervous system, matching the pace of environmental changes.

Culture may be regarded as the most recent system from which individuals, analogous to the gene pool, acquire solutions to problems they face (e.g. how to hunt? how to make fire? how to build a house? how to learn mathematics or a foreign language?). Culture is important because it offers a system of inheritance that works much more rapidly and flexibly than genetic transmission. We are not limited to learning only from parents and teachers, but may also acquire insights from scholars whose works we can read. Learning from anybody whom we consider authoritative shortens the generation time in cultural evolution. While we are stuck with our genes, we can replace outdated items by drawing new ones from the cultural pool.

We can distinguish between two models of cultural transmission from which individuals draw items – behaviours, ideas, beliefs – from the cultural pool. Imitation is the simplest form of cultural transmission, called 'unbiased transmission' which occurs when each individual acquires behaviour by randomly copying another individual within the population (Boyd and Richerson 1985). Consider the taste for popular songs, for example. While individuals tend to copy the choices of those around them, at the same time trends and fashions in popular culture are constantly changing which make the outcomes unpredictable. A model, capturing both seemingly conflicting tendencies of conformity and change, involves the random copying of cultural items with occasional innovation. Using computer simulation, R. Alexander Bentley and his colleagues (2007) show that the random-copying model predicts a continual flow of cultural variants between individuals becoming highly popular by chance alone. Similar to earlier evidence of copying behaviour in downloading music and choosing baby names or dog breeds, the random-copying model offers a simple explanation for the regular turnover of pop music albums in the twentieth century. That is, most people simply and randomly imitate the choices of others.

'Biased transmission' is another model of cultural transmission which implies that people have preferences that influence the likelihood that a cultural item will be transmitted (Richerson and Boyd 2005). There are two kinds of biases at work. 'Content biases' affect the probability that individuals imitate a cultural item because of its content. For example, people may prefer cars because they provide more privacy than buses, or prefer evolutionary theory over creationist stories because it provides evidence. 'Context biases' affect the likelihood that a cultural item will be acquired because of the characteristics of the model. For instance, model-based biases make the behaviours, ideas and beliefs of successful individuals more likely to be transmitted than those of other individuals. Model-based biases may include age, sex, ethnicity, beauty and healthy appearance.

Psychological experiments suggest that we tend to imitate successful, prestigious individuals (e.g. Mesoudi 2008). This tendency is greater when individuals find it difficult to discover the best model on their own. Field studies also report that people often adopt the new practices of knowledgeable individuals (Richerson and Boyd 2005). While model-based biases focus on the quality of a cultural item, frequency-dependent biases are based on the commonality or rarity of an item.

Acquiring knowledge and beliefs from the pool of culture is analogous to acquiring genes from parents. In effect, individuals take samples from the gene pool and the cultural pool that characterise populations of natural parents, and 'cultural' parents like successful individuals. An essential property of culture is further that it can give rise to cultural evolution in which the nature and frequency of socially transmitted practices progressively diversify, analogous to genetic evolution (see Table 10.2).

A unit of cultural inheritance

The concept of cultural evolution is modelled on genetic evolution. If the essential ingredients of evolutionary theory are present – variation (people vary in traits such as language, knowledge and beliefs), selection (some cultural traits are more copied than others), and inheritance (similarity between traits as a result of social transmission) – we have cultural evolution. Both genetic and cultural evolution are considered to have a unit of inheritance (see top row of Table 10.2). In genetic evolution, the unit of inheritance is the gene which has the unusual property of being able to copy itself. The gene is a replicator, a mechanism that copies the DNA sequence of the parent and passes it to the offspring. The property of self-copying, or DNA replication ensures that heritable traits are transmitted correctly from one generation to another.

What unit of inheritance would have an equivalent role in cultural evolution? In his influential book *The Selfish Gene* (orig. 1976; 1989: 192) Richard Dawkins proposed the term 'meme' for a unit of culture that is passed from one individual

---

biased cultural transmission

condition in which people preferentially adopt some cultural variants rather than others. A bias may be based on content, frequency or model.

Table 10.2 Genetic and cultural evolution compared

	Genetic evolution	Cultural evolution
Unit of inheritance	Gene (DNA)	Meme (imitated action, neural replicator)
Mechanism of inheritance	Sexual reproduction	Social transmission (social learning, imitation, teaching)
Direction of transmission	Vertical (from parents to offspring), horizontal (between unrelated micro-organisms)	Vertical (from parents to offspring), horizontal (from siblings and peers), and oblique (usually one-to-many as from teachers or the media)
Rate of evolution	Slow, fast	Fast
(In-)dependence	Genes can exist without culture	Culture cannot exist without genes

to another. (Meme is shorthand for 'mimeme' – meaning: 'something imitated' – originating from the Greek 'mimesis', or imitation.) As examples, he mentions tunes, ideas, catch-phrases, fashions and ways of making pots. Similar to genes that replicate themselves in the gene pool by leaping from body to body via sperms or eggs, memes replicate themselves from brain to brain by imitation. In his later book *The Extended Phenotype* (1983) he answered criticisms of being insufficiently clear about the distinction between the meme itself, as a replicator, on the one hand, and its phenotypic effects on the other. 'A meme should be regarded as a unit of information residing in a brain' (1983: 109), and be distinguished from its outward, visible manifestations in the form of words, songs, gestures, fashions or skills.

Dawkins' proposal inspired a new approach to cultural evolution which, analogous to genetics, became known as 'memetics' (e.g. Blackmore 1999; Distin 2005). The memetic approach assumes that cultural knowledge is stored in brains as discrete packages of information, comparable to how biological information is stored in genes. Once expressed in behaviours (e.g. gestures) or artefacts (e.g. words, tools), these packages of information can be replicated in the heads of other individuals through social learning. It has been proposed that after the emergence of *Homo habilis* who made the first stone tools (2.5 mya), our ancestors developed a larger brain and a sophisticated culture, based on the capacity for imitation (Donald (1991, 1993). When humans acquired imitative capacity, evolution selected for the best imitators. This capacity would have played an important role in acquiring skills for hunting or gestures for communication.

The literature promoting memetics has attracted a number of criticisms. We focus on two points. One criticism comes from Eytan Avital and Eva Jablonka (2000) who understand the meme, as defined by Dawkins, as a representation of a behavioural act stored in the nervous system and transmitted by social learning through generations of communicating individuals. This usage of the term meme neglects the role of learning and development that underlie the regeneration of behavioural practices:

> Because the transmission and expression of a mental representation cannot be separated, the accuracy of transmission depends on the conditions in which the behavior is produced. (2000: 27)

For example, the ease with which students learn music depends on its complexity (melody, rhythm, pitch, measure), kind of teacher, musical instrument, age at which they take lessons, motivation, and so on. Students are not simply copying the teacher but actively reconstructing the required patterns of behaviour, emotion and musical concepts, through learning. This replication is quite unlike that in genes where there is a single mechanism of DNA replication at work which is commonly not influenced by the function of the genes it replicates.

Another criticism emphasises the gap between the detailed understanding of the cellular and molecular bases of genetic inheritance and the global ideas of memetics (Mesoudi et al. 2006; Mesoudi 2011). A more detailed picture of cultural inheritance requires an understanding of how the brain processes relevant information. That is, how can imitative processes, as they are executed in the brain, be studied? Memes may be considered to be units of cultural inheritance but they have been left at the periphery of cognitive neuroscience due to their inexact definition and difficulty, or even impossiblity, of measurement. Even so, Robert Aunger (2002) made an attempt to specify the material basis of memes in the brain, and proposed that memes should be defined as electrochemical states of multiple neurons that can be replicated within the brain.

Aunger emphasises that an exact understanding of how information is replicated through transmission between individuals is missing:

> We need to establish that, in the process of communication, one brain produces speech (for example), and that this speech transforms the hearer's brain. But we also need to know that the communication introduces new information to the hearer's brain which resembles the information in the speaker's brain that caused the speech in the first place. That would be a true relationship of inheritance and would constitute a process of information acquisition from others through a mechanism other than gene replication . . . Hence, models of social learning must be matched to models of memory before we can determine whether units of cultural inheritance . . . exist. (Mesoudi et al. 2006: 347, 348)

Can neuroscientific work support the theory that memes are units of cultural inheritance? A line of research that may turn out to have important implications for cultural evolution involves mirror neurons. Recall from section 9.3 (The gestural origin of language) that the discovery of mirror neurons in the late 1990s led to the proposal that they are involved in human imitation. Initially, these neurons were found in the premotor cortex F5 of the macaque brain. Findings indicated that the monkey appeared to infer the intention of another's actions within its own motor system. Subsequently, Brodmann area 44 was proposed as the human homologue to this region, based on a body of evidence. Experiments demonstrated that BA 44 is activated when humans observe actions or hear words related to actions (e.g. Fadiga et al. 2002).

In a recent paper, Adam McNamara (2011) argues that although memes are difficult to define, neuroimaging technology is now sufficiently advanced to measure the changes to memes over time. Memes are replicants, or copies of something (e.g. a gesture, facial expression, or word) with the three prerequisite properties of any evolutionary system: variance, selection and replication. Memes replicate within the human environment using imitative behaviour as their method for replication. McNamara (2011) argues, then, that for a meme to replicate, it must pass through four stages: assimilation (perception by an individual), retention (within memory), expression (by some movement, speech, or gesture which can be perceived by others), and transmission (to another individual).

But what precisely is a meme? The author uses the example of a chair. If the word 'chair' is a meme, what constitutes the 'chair' meme? Does it include the neural substrate for perceiving a chair? Or the neural substrate for pronouncing the word chair? Or the neural substrate for taking a seat? Or does it refer to the image of the chair as we see it in commercials? Or the chair that has been imitated by a competitor? McNamara proposes distinguishing between memes that are represented either as neural substrates within the nervous system (internal memes) or in some other form within the environment such as imitated actions or copied objects (external memes). Internal memes are considered to be more interesting from a neuroscientific point view than external ones. Internal memes refer, then, to neural networks that enable external memes to be perceived and transmitted through communicative motor actions like manual gestures or spoken words.

According to McNamara (2011), at least two requirements have to be met for memes to evolve within the imitative capacity of humans. Firstly, memes have to be learned so that the brain is required to rapidly connect perceptual related brain areas (sight, audition) with internal state areas (emotion) and motor areas (hand and mouth movements). Secondly, a meme must be able to elicit behaviour from its host which enables its transmission to other hosts. In order to replicate, a meme requires a communicative motor action because to be transmitted, whether by speech, gesture or facial expression, we must move our muscles. Movement is prerequisite to communication. The required motor component is most probably residing within BA 44 which is activated when we observe actions or hear action-related sentences.

In an fMRI study, NcNamara et al. (2008) investigated whether brain regions were involved in making associations between novel sounds and gestures. The study was designed as an exercise to create a new meme and track the brain activity of that process. By viewing videos and imitating novel gestures, the task of participants was to learn the novel sound – action association. The creation of this novel association which was assimilated into the motor cortex, allowed the researchers to track the changes in neural activity and connectivity between brain regions as learning and replicating of the new meme took place. The authors conclude that BA 44 is dynamically involved in linking gesture and sound, providing evidence that one of the mechanisms required for the evolution of human communication is found within this motor area.

10.4 How culture is incorporated in evolutionary theory

The extended synthesis

Culture serves as a new inheritance system that can solve the problems of some social animal species. As standard evolutionary theory only recognises genetic inheritance, the question arises how culture is incorporated in evolutionary theory. The reader may recall from section 1.3 (Biology) that Darwin's theory of evolution was considerably elaborated upon in the early part of the twentieth century with the rediscovery of Mendelian genetics and advances in population genetics. In the 1930s and 1940s a synthesis took place between evolutionary biology, population genetics (the mathematical study of variation and mutation), systematic biology (the study of the diversity of life and the phylogenetic, or genealogical relationships between species), and palaeobiology (the study of the history of organisms and their environments).

niche construction

the practice of countless organisms to modify their local environments by consuming resources, constructing nests, holes, burrows, paths, webs, thus providing protection for their offspring. The human capacity for niche construction (and destruction) has been further amplified by culture as innovation and technology has had an enormous impact on the environment.

This synthesis which became known as 'the Modern Synthesis', expanded in the second half of the twentieth century as more sciences – plant science (botany), cell biology, molecular biology, ethology (behavioural biology), and sociobiology – joined forces with evolutionary biology. More recently, new biological domains have emerged such as evolutionary developmental biology, epigenetic inheritance and evolutionary genomics. As evolutionary thinking has also influenced disciplines such as neuroscience, psychology and economics, this has called for an expansion of the Modern Synthesis.

A recent study about the expansion of the Modern Synthesis therefore refers to 'the extended synthesis' (Pigliucci and Müller 2010). It includes two branches of evolutionary analysis – **niche construction** theory and gene–culture coevolution theory – which help to explain the role of culture in evolution. Niche construction theory investigates how organisms modify environments, and gene – culture coevolution theory explores how genes and culture interact over evolutionary time.

Niche construction theory

According to this theory, organisms have two roles in evolution (Odling-Smee et al. 2003). The first role is surviving, reproducing and thereby passing genes on to the next generation. The second role is interacting with environments, drawing food from environments, shaping habitats by building nests, digging burrows and excreting materials. F. John Odling-Smee and his colleagues (2003) argue that the latter role is far less understood by evolutionary biologists, and can be called 'niche construction'.

Niche construction can be local and global. An example of local niche construction is the beaver's dam which affects many future generations of beavers that inherit the dam, its lodge, and the altered stream, as well as many other species that now have to live with a lake. An example of global niche construction is oxygen production by photosynthetic organisms which demonstrates the extreme effects that niche construction can have on a global scale and over long periods of time. The contribution of these organisms to the Earth's 21 per cent oxygen atmosphere occurred over thousands of millions of years and took many generations of photosynthesising bacteria to achieve. This massive production of oxygen must have changed selection pressures for other organisms who evolved a capacity for aerobic respiration. According to Wilson (1992), two trends in the distant past were probably linked: the explosion of oxygen about 2.5 billion years ago, and then the explosion of animal evolution about 540 million years ago, also known as 'the Cambrian Explosion' (Figure 10.3).

Standard evolutionary theory assumes that individuals survive, reproduce and transmit their genes to the next generation. Figure 10.4 shows standard evolutionary theory in which populations of organisms are considered to transmit genes from one generation to the next, under the direction of natural selection. This theory is only concerned with genetic inheritance.

ecological inheritance

if organisms modify the environment and some of the associated selection pressures, each new generation inherits the changed environment and its modified selection pressures from the previous generation.

The argument of niche construction theory is that organisms not only carry genes to be transmitted to the next generation, but also modify the environment and some of the associated selection pressures. Thus each new generation inherits the changed environment and its modified selection pressures from the previous generation. This legacy has been labelled '**ecological inheritance**'. Figure 10.5 shows the extended standard evolutionary theory with niche construction and ecological inheritance.

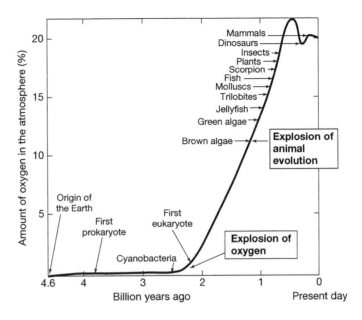

Figure 10.3 Explosion of oxygen and animal evolution
Source: Delsemme (1998)

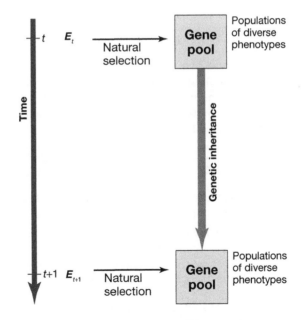

Phenotype = the morphological and behavioural traits displayed by an organism, resulting from the interaction between its genotype and its environment.
(Genotype = the genetic composition of an organism.)
Gene pool = the sum total of all genes in an interbreeding population at a particular time.
E = environment at different times.

Figure 10.4 Standard evolutionary theory
Source: Laland et al. (2000)

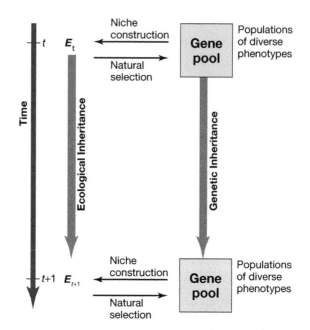

Figure 10.5 Standard evolutionary theory with niche construction and ecological inheritance

Source: Laland et al. (2000)

Gene–culture coevolution theory

phenotype
the observable – morphological and behavioural – characteristics of an organism as a result of the interaction between its genotype and the environment.

genotype
the hidden genetic constitution of an organism.

The reader may recall from section 1.3 (Biology) that we touched upon gene–culture coevolution in Chapter 1. This theory is based on standard evolutionary theory but adds the argument that genes and culture are two interacting forms of inheritance. First attempts to develop this theory date from the 1980s (e.g. Cavalli-Sforza and Feldman 1981; Boyd and Richerson 1985).

KEY FIGURES   Peter Richerson and Robert Boyd

Peter Richerson is an environmental scientist at the University of California, Davis. His research focuses on the processes of cultural evolution.

Robert Boyd is an anthropologist at the University of California, Los Angeles. His research is focused on the evolutionary psychology of the mechanisms that give rise to and shape human culture, and how these mechanisms interact with population dynamic processes to shape human cultural variation.

Selected, co-authored works

Culture and the Evolutionary Process (1985)

Not by Genes Alone: How Culture Transformed Human Evolution (2005)

The Origin and Evolution of Cultures (2005)

The gene–culture coevolution theory holds that human populations share learned traditions that are expressed in cultural practices, and transmitted socially between individuals in the form of cultural inheritance. The novelty of gene–culture coevolution is its presumption that human cultural practices modify natural selection processes in human environments, so that cultural transmission affects some selected human genes.

For example, when our ancestors domesticated cattle by introducing agriculture, they modified natural selection pressures on a gene that enabled the enzyme lactase – needed for the digestion of milk – to be synthesised by human adults (Laland et al. 2010). Babies need milk which contains sugar, called lactose. In most humans, the capacity to digest lactose disappears in childhood, but in some populations the activity of lactase digestion persists in adulthood. This is known as lactose tolerance which occurs frequently in northern European, Middle Eastern and African populations but is absent in other populations. It appears that there is a strong correlation across cultures between the frequency of lactose tolerance and the cultural practice of dairy farming and milk drinking.

Various lines of evidence support a scenario in which early humans exposed themselves to a strong selection pressure for lactose tolerance by drinking fresh milk. Analysis reveals that a high frequency of the tolerance gene depended on the probability that the children of milk drinkers became milk drinkers themselves. It was also found that dairy farming evolved first, which then favoured lactose tolerance. The case of dairy farming, having an effect on lactose tolerance in less than 9,000 years, is the most extensively investigated example to date of gene–culture coevolution (for other topics of gene–culture coevolution, see Laland et al. 2010: 140).

Figure 10.6 presents the model of gene–culture coevolution. A new element in this model, apart from cultural inheritance, is 'development' which refers to the individual's process of learning skills and knowledge. Learning allows individual organisms to

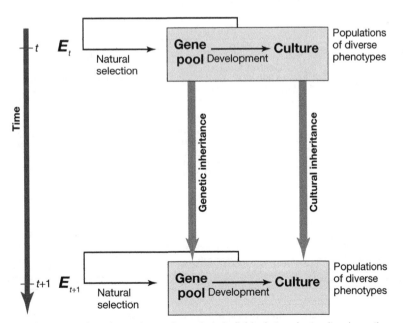

Development = learning and experience help individuals to adopt cultural practices.

Figure 10.6 Standard evolutionary theory with cultural inheritance

Source: Laland et al. (2000)

fine-tune their behaviour to local circumstances in a way that would be impossible by inheriting only a sample from the gene pool (i.e. its individual genome). The developmental aspect of culture is especially significant in humans because they depend much more on culture than any other social species. Thus, the links between genetic and cultural evolution cannot be understood without reference to intermediate, ontogenetic processes of learning and cognition that connect them (Odling-Smee et al. 2003).

Gene–culture coevolution and niche construction

Let us consider the cultural practice of farming from the combined point of view of gene–culture coevolution and niche construction theory. Both theories emphasise the active role of organisms and the inheritance of descendants. When the last ice age ended around 10,000 years ago, the world became warmer and wetter, and the climate became more stable. Our ancestors had spent the most part of their evolution as hunter-gatherers, but climate conditions favoured a new method of subsistence. Humans invented farming several times in widely different places and this practice spread from there in all directions (Figure 10.7; McNeill and McNeill 2003). In some cases it spread by geographic expansion of farmers, in other cases through hunter-gatherers who adopted the practice of domesticating plants (e.g. wheat, barley) and animals (e.g. goats, sheep). Farming was the most important cultural practice since humans migrated out of Africa as it changed diets, exposed humans to animal pathogens, accelerated growth of populations, and changed the social life of many human populations (Richerson and Boyd 2010).

Farming was an important form of human niche construction because new technologies and lifestyles enabled humans to extract more resources from a given area of land. It stimulated population growth and encouraged humans to settle in large,

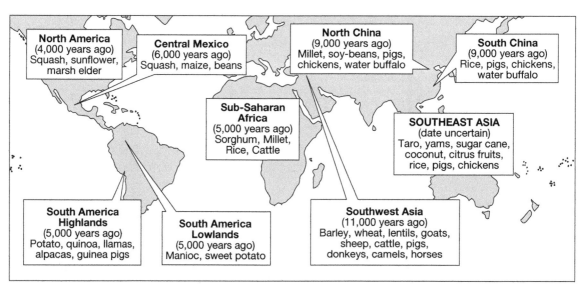

People invented agriculture several times in widely different places. The transition from food collection to food production is one of the landmark shifts in human history. All dates and locations are approximate and subject to revision by further archaeological work.

Figure 10.7 Multiple independent inventions of farming

Source: McNeill and McNeill (2003)

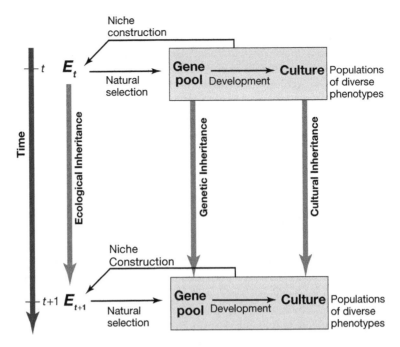

Figure 10.8 Gene–culture coevolution with ecological inheritance

Source: Laland et al. (2000)

concentrated communities, called villages and cities. Denser settlement favoured more exchange of ideas and social learning which accelerated the pace of technological change. This acceleration boosted the growth of population which eventually resulted in a new method of subsistence: the cultural practice of industrial production. The key of industrialisation was the factory system that harnessed new sources of energy to machines, tended by labour in urban settlements. Labour was recruited through emerging labour markets and became appendages to machines to produce commodities sold in markets.

Today, we are aware that industrial production and its associated practice of consumption have a large impact on the biosphere as is evident from human-induced climate change, pollution, overpopulation and overharvesting (Wilson 2006). Technology plays a crucial role in these problems because it has the effect of pushing back the limits to population size, a phenomenon that is non-existent in other species. Thus the cultural inheritance that humans transmit to their descendants is largely for a technological culture. We owe our standard of living to achievements such as the harnessing of fire (500,000 years ago), farming (10,000 years ago), mining of metals (6,000 years ago), and industrial production (250 years ago). Each generation passes this cultural and ecological inheritance on to the next generation. Figure 10.8 shows a model of gene–culture coevolution with the incorporation of ecological inheritance.

Implications of the extended evolutionary theory

The reader may recall from Chapter 1 (section 1.3 Biology) that culture needs to be integrated in the theory of evolution. The argument was that if we want to understand more about humans, we should take into consideration that human evolution is increasingly a matter of cultural evolution. We have seen in the previous section that two theories are helpful in incorporating culture and the associated concept of niche construction in standard evolutionary theory. What are the implications of this incorporative enterprise? We now focus on the implications that the extended evolutionary theory has for the social sciences (Odling-Smee et al. 2003).

In the past, social scientists had several reasons that made it difficult for them to use evolutionary theory. A first reason was that they were horrified by abusive practices inspired by mistaken interpretations of Darwin's theory. Entrepreneurs used natural selection as an alibi for exploiting labourers, and politicians abused it for proposing eugenic policies. Politicians were inspired by the term 'eugenics' (from the Greek word for 'good in stock'), invented by Darwin's nephew Francis Galton. He insisted that analogous to breeding superior cattle, it should be possible to produce a superior race of man by stimulating marriages between families of high rank (Schwartz 2008). In Nazi Germany, the misguided belief of creating a superior human race led to the extermination of many millions of Jews and gypsies.

A second reason for social scientists not using the evolutionary theory relates to the sociobiology controversy. You may recall from section 1.4 (Psychology) that social scientists were shocked by Edward Wilson's book *Sociobiology* (1975) which was meant, among other things, to introduce evolutionary thinking into the social sciences (e.g. sociology, psychology, anthropology). In particular, its final chapter, which applied evolutionary thinking to humans, evoked the anger of social scientists because Wilson announced that evolutionary biology in due time would cannibalise psychology and sociology.

A third reason for social scientists not to use evolutionary theory was that it offered them too little, because most social scientists are interested in human behaviour and culture, not in genes. However, Odling-Smee et al. (2003) are convinced that the gene–culture theory may animate social scientists' interest because it allows culture to play a substantial role in the evolutionary process.

A fourth reason why evolutionary theory was not embraced by social scientists, has to do with the assumption in evolutionary explanations about organisms having a passive role in adaptive processes. The niche construction theory may strengthen the interest of social scientists as it emphasises the active role of humans in evolution. They don't just pass genes on to the next generation but actively adapt the environment to their needs.

ratchet effect

human cultural traditions that are faithfully transmitted to new generations, serving as a ratchet to prevent having to 're-invent the wheel'.

10.5 Cumulative cultural evolution

The ratchet effect

In section 10.2 (What is culture?), we discussed how human cultural traditions differ from animal traditions. An important difference is that human culture is an accumulative process of successive improvements over generations of learners. Tomasello (1999: 5) called it the 'ratchet effect' which he described as:

cumulative cultural evolution

cultural change that requires creation of inventions and faithful social transmission to prevent new generations having to re-invent the wheel.

> the process of **cumulative cultural evolution** that requires not only creative invention but also, and just as importantly, faithful social transmission that can work as a ratchet to prevent slippage backward – so that the newly invented artifact or practice

preserves its new and improved form at least somewhat faithfully until a further modification or improvement comes along. (1999: 5).

Cumulative cultural evolution seems to be rare in non-human animals. There are some examples of chimpanzee behaviours that may have resulted from the accumulation of modified socially learned behaviour. In West African chimpanzee populations, it has been observed that some individuals use not only anvil stones and hammer stones in nut-cracking but also an extra stone to stabilise the anvil stone upon which the nut is placed (Sugiyama 1997). Another case of cumulative culture has been observed by Gavin Hunt and Russell Gray (2002). They propose that the tool-manufacturing skills in New Caledonian crows have been acquired through cumulative cultural evolution. Crows manufacture distinct types of tools to facilitate the capture of invertebrates in trees: one made from twigs, and another made from the long barbed edges of tree leaves. The authors present evidence from the field that crows have diversified and cumulatively modified the design of this tool. Early versions of tools were simpler and less efficient than later ones.

Critics note, however, that it is still unclear whether the techniques in these species are socially learned. They showed from laboratory experiments that hand-raised juvenile New Caledonian crows spontaneously manufacture and use tools without any contact with adults of their species. This suggests that the manufacture and modification of tools is at least partly a genetically inherited capacity and not dependent on social input (Kenward et al. 2005). Other critics have made the point that we have very little data on the behaviour of previous generations of chimpanzees, since long-term studies began about 40 years ago. This makes it difficult to conclude whether a ratcheting effect did occur over generations (Boesch and Tomasello 1998).

Ratcheting in human cultural evolution may be inferred from the historical records of technology which show that new developments build on previous ones (see Figure 10.1). For example, the first wheel as a mechanical device for transportation was invented about 5,000 years ago. It was a simple wooden disk with a hole for the axle, later to be replaced by a spoked wheel. Before the creation of the wheel, heavy objects were transported on sledges – wooden platforms on cylindrical rollers to facilitate movement. It is thought that these rollers inspired the invention of wheels (Basalla 1988).

Cumulative cultural evolution can also be observed in the laboratory. Christine Caldwell and Ailsa Millen (2008a, 2008b, 2009, 2010) simulated a generational succession of improvements through the repeated removal and replacement of human participants within experimental groups. These groups were instructed to build a paper aeroplane that would fly as far as possible, and a tower of spaghetti that was as tall as possible. Participants had a few minutes to build their plane or tower, but they could also observe the accomplishments of previous participants. The experiments showed that information accumulates within the groups such that later generations produced designs that were more successful than earlier ones.

Cumulative cultural evolution can be demonstrated in humans, but the capacities required for ratcheting have still to be established. In the literature, several capacities have been suggested (e.g. Caldwell and Millen 2008a) which we review below (Box 10.2 Human capacities for ratcheting).

neophobia
a persistent and irrational fear of change or of anything new, unfamiliar or strange.

BOX 10.2 Human capacities for ratcheting

A capacity for true imitation

Boyd and Richerson (1996) argue that true imitation is necessary for cumulative cultural evolution. True imitation is any form of learning in which individuals can learn a new behaviour by copying the behaviour of another individual, either of its own or another species, and incorporating it into its own action pattern, vocal repertoire, or practical know-how (see Box 10.1. Types of social learning). True imitation is important because ratcheting requires faithful social transmission.

A capacity for understanding the goals of other individuals

Tomasello (1999) does not only emphasise the importance of faithful social transmission but also the need for understanding the goals of other individuals. He argues that humans have three types of cultural learning: imitative learning, instructed and collaborative learning. These forms of learning require that individuals can put themselves in the shoes of others. Imitators need to understand what goals their models have in mind; students need to understand what the goals of instructors are, and vice versa; and collaborators need to understand each other's goals.

A capacity for adaptive filtering

Enquist and Ghirlanda (2007) suggest that culture can be adaptive and can evolve, if individuals are capable of identifying and discarding maladaptive culture. This suggestion implies that the evolution of 'adaptive filtering' may have been crucial for the origin of human culture. Changes in the social or physical environment may turn a trait from adaptive into maladaptive. For example, among Alaskan natives the value of preserving food by fermentation has been reduced after plastic bags replaced traditional earthen pits as food containers. Plastic bags favour the growth of lethal botulism bacteria. Thus, a capacity to filter out maladaptive traits favours the accumulation of adaptive traits, generating the ratchet effect that is typical of human culture.

A capacity for innovation

Tomasello (1999) argues that the process of cumulative cultural evolution requires creative invention. Reader and Laland (2003) prefer the term innovation, referring to a process that introduces new or modified behavioural variants into a population's repertoire. Innovation is mostly associated with humans but may also occur in other animals. Classic examples are the washing of potatoes by Japanese macaques, novel tool-use in chimpanzees and milk-bottle-top opening by British titmice (for a review, see Reader and Laland 2010). Among the processes underlying innovation is neophilia – attraction towards new things. Whereas most animals display **neophobia** and avoid new things (e.g. unfamiliar food, fire), humans have overcome their fear for new things in the course of evolution. For example, humans learned to control and use fire (Wrangham and Carmody 2010). Compared with other animals which are not as large-brained as the human species, we excel in the capacity to add novel variants to the cultural pool.

A capacity for recursion

The reader may recall from section 9.3 (The gestural origin of language) that syntax is recursive, and allows us to generate meaningful sentences of any length, and of infinite variety. For example, we can embed the sentence 'John knows a lot about history' in a new meaningful sentence: 'Robert knows that John knows a lot about history', and again in another new and meaningful sentence: 'Henry said that Robert knows that John knows a lot about history', and so on. Thus, recursion is a capacity to apply a rule repeatedly with the output of each application being input to the next, in principle indefinitely. Recursion is not only involved in language, but also in theory of mind, and mathematics. Theory of mind – the ability to reflect on and understand another individual's mind – is recursive because concepts such as knowing, thinking and believing describe the mental states of ourselves and of others. The mental states 'I know what you are thinking' and 'I know that you know what I am thinking' demonstrate that we are capable of thinking recursively. In mathematics, recursion helps to generate terms in a sequence. An example is the use of integers for counting. As long as we have rules allowing us to generate a number from the preceding number in a sequence, there is no limit to the number of objects we can count. The basic rule is simply to add 1 to the preceding number. In sum, a capacity for recursive speaking, thinking and counting is important because it allows us to use our mind flexibly and creatively (Corballis 2003).

10.6 Summary

- Culture allows humans and other social animals to learn from one another. As social learning is less costly than individual learning, the emergence of culture suggests that learning all things by yourself was a problem. Taking into account that there are significant differences between humans and other animals, culture can be thought of in two ways: first, as the socially transmitted pool of products that characterise populations of social animals; and second, as the capacity by which individuals produce these outcomes.

- Humans depend on a gene pool as well as a cultural pool. All living beings have a genome which contains all the genes that are needed to build the organism, ensure that it works satisfactorily and protects against diseases. Each individual's genome is a sample from the gene pool which contains all the genes in an inter-breeding population. As humans can take only one dip into the gene pool, they need another more rapid inheritance system, a cultural pool, when living in a fast-changing world.

- Culture serves as a new inheritance system that can solve the problems of humans and some other social species. As standard evolutionary theory only recognises genetic inheritance, culture needs to be incorporated in evolutionary theory. Two theories help to explain the role of culture in evolution. Niche construction theory investigates how organisms modify environments, and gene–culture coevolution theory explores how genes and culture interact over evolutionary time.

- One aspect of culture that is thought to be uniquely human is the accumulative process of successive improvements over generations of learners. This aspect of cultural evolution, also known as the ratchet effect, requires creative invention as well as faithful social transmission, preserving the newly invented artefact or practice.

Study questions

1. What are the differences and similarities between human and animal culture?

2. What is meant by the distinction between the inheritance of behavioural and symbolic culture?

3. What is meant by biased and unbiased cultural transmission?

4. Why is the assumption of passively adapting organisms in evolutionary explanations wrong?

5. Why does cumulative cultural evolution mainly occur in humans?

Suggested reading

What is culture?

Laland, K. (2004). Social learning strategies. *Learning & Behavior*, 32, 4–14.

Lycett, S. (2010). The importance of history in definitions of *culture*: Implications from phylogenetic approaches to the study of social learning in chimpanzees. *Learning & Behavior*, 38, 252–264.

McGrew, W. (1998). Culture in nonhuman primates? *Annual Review of Anthropology*, 27, 301–328.

Mesoudi, A., Whiten, A. and Laland, K. (2004). Is human cultural evolution Darwinian? Evidence reviewed from the perspective of *The Origin of Species*. *Evolution*, 58, 1–11.

Whiten, A., Goodall, J. McGrew, W. et al. (1999). Cultures in chimpanzees. *Nature*, 399, 682–685.

Whiten, A., Horner, V. and Marshall-Pescini, S. (2003). Cultural panthropology. *Evolutionary Anthropology*, 12, 92–105.

Whiten, A., Hinde, R., Laland, K. and Stringer, C. (2011). Culture evolves. *Philosophical Transactions of the Royal Society B*, 366, 938–948.

Cultural inheritance

Bentley, R., Lipo, C. Herzog, H. and Hand, M. (2007). Regular rates of popular culture change reflect random copying. *Evolution and Human Behavior*, 28, 151–158.

Henrich, J. and McElreath, R. (2003). The evolution of cultural evolution. *Evolutionary Anthropology*, 12, 123–135.

Henrich, J., Boyd, R. and Richerson, P. (2008). Five misunderstandings about cultural evolution. *Human Nature*, 19, 119–137.

Jablonka, E. and Lamb, M. (2007b). Précis of *Evolution in Four Dimensions*. *Behavioral and Brain Sciences*, 30, 353–392.

McNamara, A. (2011). Can we measure memes? *Frontiers in Evolutionary Neuroscience*, 3, 1–7.

Mesoudi, A. (2008). An experimental simulation of the 'copy-successful-individuals' cultural learning strategy': adaptive landscapes, producer–scrounger dynamics, and informational access costs. *Evolution and Human Behavior*, 29, 350–363.

Whitehead, H. and Richerson, P. (2009). The evolution of conformist social learning can cause population collapse in realistically variable environments. *Evolution and Human Behavior*, 30, 261–273.

Whiten, A. (2005). The second inheritance system of chimpanzees and humans. *Nature*, 437, 52–55.

How culture is incorporated in evolutionary theory

Laland. K., Odling-Smee, J. and Feldman, M. (2000). Niche construction, biological evolution, and cultural change. *Behavioral and Brain Sciences*, 23, 131–175.

Laland, K., Odling-Smee, J. and Myles, S. (2010). How culture shaped the human genome: bringing genetics and the human sciences together. *Nature Reviews/Genetics*, 11, 137–148.

Mesoudi, A., Whiten, A. and Laland, K. (2006). Towards a unified science of cultural evolution. *Behavioral and Brain Sciences*, 29, 329–383.

Richerson, P., Boyd, R. and Henrich J. (2010). Gene–culture coevolution in the age of genomics. *Proceedings of the National Academy of Sciences of the USA*, 107, 8985–8992.

Cumulative cultural evolution

Boyd, R. and Richerson, P. (1996). Why culture is common, but cultural evolution is rare. *Proceedings of the British Academy, 88,* 77–93.

Caldwell, C. and Millen, A. (2008a). Studying cumulative cultural evolution in the laboratory. *Philosophical Transactions of the Royal Society B, 363,* 3529–3539.

Hill, K. (2010). Experimental studies of animal social learning in the wild: Trying to untangle the mystery of human culture. *Learning & Behavior, 38,* 319–328.

Kirby, S., Cornish, H. and Smith, K. (2008). Cumulative cultural evolution in the laboratory: An experimental approach to the origins of structure in human language. *Proceedings of the National Academy of Sciences of the USA, 31,* 10681–10686.

Ramsey, G., Bastian, M. and van Schaik, C. (2007). Animal innovation defined and operationalized. *Behavioral and Brain Sciences, 30,* 393–437.

Reader, S. and Laland, K. (2002). Social intelligence, innovation, and enhanced brain size in primates. *Proceedings of the National Academy of Sciences of the USA, 99,* 4436–4441.

Reference books

Distin, K. (2011). *Cultural Evolution.* Cambridge: Cambridge University Press (see page xxiii).

Fragaszy, D. and Perry, S. (Eds) (2008), *The Biology of Traditions: Models and Evidence.* Cambridge: Cambridge University Press.

Hurley, S. and Chater, N. (Eds) (2005). *Perspectives on Imitation: From Neuroscience to Social Science, Two Volumes.* Cambridge, MA: The MIT Press.

Jablonka, E. and Lamb, M. (2005). *Evolution in Four Dimensions: Genetic, Epigenetic, Behavioral, and Symbolic Variation in the History of Life.* Cambridge, MA: The MIT Press.

Laland, K. and Galef, B. (Eds) (2009). *The Question of Animal Culture.* Cambridge, MA: Harvard University Press.

Mesoudi, A. (2011). *Cultural Evolution: How Darwinian Theory Can Explain Human Culture and Synthesize the Social Sciences.* Chicago: The University of Chicago Press.

Odling-Smee, F. John et al. (2003). *Niche Construction: The Neglected Process in Evolution.* Princeton, NJ: Princeton University Press.

Pigliucci, M. and Müller, G. (Eds) (2010). *Evolution – The Extended Synthesis.* Cambridge, MA: The MIT Press.

Richerson, P. and Boyd, R. (2005). *Not by Genes Alone: How Culture Transformed Human Evolution.* Chicago: The University of Chicago Press.

Whiten, A., Hinde, R., Stringer, C. and Laland, K. (Eds.) (2012). *Culture Evolves.* Oxford: Oxford University Press.

Part 3 SPECIALS

11 The evolutionary paradox of mental illness

This chapter will cover:

11.1 Introduction

11.2 Defining mental illness

11.3 Distinguishing normal responses from mental illness

11.4 Explaining the adaptive function of mental illness

    11.4.1 The dopamine theory of mental illness

    11.4.2 The byproduct theory of mental illness

    11.4.3 The mismatch theory of mental illness

11.5 Summary

Learning outcomes

By the end of this chapter, you should be able to explain:

- how mental illness can be defined in evolutionary terms
- how an evolutionary approach helps to distinguish normal responses from mental illness
- how the dopamine theory explains the adaptive function of mental illness
- how the byproduct theory explains the adaptive function of mental illness
- how the mismatch theory explains the adaptive function of mental illness.

11.1   Introduction

People may associate mental illness with abnormal mental states such as delusions ('I am Napoleon'), phobias (for spiders, flying) or famous persons who have publicly stated that they suffered from depression (e.g. actor Anthony Hopkins, scientist Stephen Hawking, musician Janet Jackson). The evolutionary paradox of mental illness is that natural selection seems unable to eliminate mental disorders such as schizophrenia, phobias or depression. To resolve this paradox, we first need to know how clinical psychology and psychiatry define mental illness, and how it can be defined in evolutionary terms.

Humans suffering from mental disruptions need the help of clinicians. In order to prevent patients being wrongly diagnosed, clinicians use a classification system of disorders. Although useful to practitioners, a significant objection to the current system is that it fails to distinguish normal responses to adversity from genuine disorders. How can an evolutionary conception of mental disorder be used to distinguish normal from abnormal responses? In answering this question, we focus on sadness versus depressive disorder because this is currently the best studied example of a wider problem.

Given that natural selection is unable to weed out mental disorders, we may suppose that they are somehow adaptive. We discuss three theories to resolve this paradox. The dopamine theory proposes that human migration out of Africa between 100,000 and 50,000 years ago and subsequent colonisation of the world, required adaptive traits that made the human mind vulnerable to mental illness. The byproduct theory implies that mental illness is the maladaptive side-effect of selection for some other adaptive trait. The mismatch theory holds that adaptive traits in our ancestral environment became maladaptive in the current environment.

11.2   Defining mental illness

A note on terminology

'Mental illness' and 'psychopathology' are general terms referring to patterns of behaviour, emotion or thought processes that are considered abnormal or 'maladaptive'. 'Psychopathology' is also used for the scientific study of mental disorders. Two disciplines are involved in the study, diagnosis and treatment of psychopathology: abnormal, or clinical psychology (a branch of psychology), and psychiatry (a branch of medicine). The evolutionary science of psychopathology is known as 'evolutionary psychopathology' (a branch of psychology) and 'evolutionary psychiatry' (a branch of medicine).

Above we used the term 'maladaptive' which is derived from 'adaptation'. It should be emphasised that what evolutionary psychologists mean by adaptation differs from what clinicians mean by this term (McNally 2011). Clinical psychologists refer to behaviour patterns as either 'adaptive' or 'maladaptive', using the standard of psychosocial adjustment of patients. Evolutionary psychologists, on the other hand, use the evolutionary definition of adaptation, being any trait that improves the survival and reproduction of an organism. In other words, a trait is adaptive if it improves fitness and maladaptive if it reduces fitness.

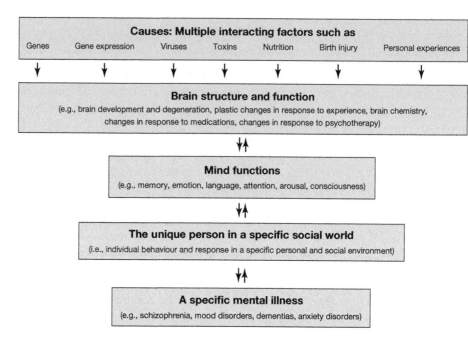

Figure 11.1 A model for the development of psychopathology

Source: Andreasen (2001)

neurotransmitter

a chemical substance that communicates between one neuron to another or between a neuron and a muscle cell. For example, serotonin and dopamine.

Mental illness arises from multiple interacting causes, many of which are not fully understood (Andreasen 2001). Among the many factors are genes predisposing individuals to mental illness, viruses or drugs having an impact on the functioning of brain cells, **neurotransmitters** like dopamine or **serotonin** involved in the transmission or inhibition of nerve signals, mental functions like memory and attention, individual behaviours in a personal and social environment, and specific mental disorders as they result from many interacting factors (Figure 11.1).

serotonin

a neurotransmitter in the brain and other parts of the central nervous system that has roles in bioregulatory processes like emotion, mood, appetite, sleep and pain.

Towards an evolutionary definition of mental illness

Mental disorders are the topic of clinical psychology and psychiatry. Clinicians want to know how an individual's mind became deranged and how it can be treated. Mental disorder is therefore a basic concept in the theory and practice of clinical science. The question is, then, how to define mental disorder, and its counterpart, mental health.

For a start, the *APA Dictionary of Psychology* (VandenBos 2007), defines mental health as:

mental disorder

a set of symptoms indicating that a cognitive or emotional capacity (a) fails to perform its naturally selected function, and (b) causes significant harm to the individual and its environment, judged by the standards of present culture.

> a state of mind characterized by emotional well-being, good behavioral adjustment, relative freedom from anxiety and disabling symptoms, and a capacity to establish constructive relationships and cope with the ordinary demands and stresses of life.

And it defines mental disorder as:

> characterized by psychological symptoms, abnormal behaviors, impaired functioning, or any combination of these. Such disorders may cause clinically significant distress and impairment in a variety of domains of functioning and may be due to organic, social, genetic, chemical, or psychological factors.

This definition of mental disorder assumes a kind of norm from which people deviate. The term 'abnormal' may refer to deviation from a statistical, biological or cultural norm. Mental disorder, or abnormality, has indeed be conceptualised in different ways (Wakefield 1992a; Thambirajah 2005).

Mental disorder as statistical deviance

Mental functions can be considered abnormal if they are exceptional, that is, deviate from a statistical norm. If we regard infrequent mental states or traits as abnormal, then chronic sadness or low intelligence may be considered deviations by these standards. But the same applies to intellectual boldness and creative talent which we cannot call mental disorders. The problem of using the criterion of statistical deviance is that certain moods or traits may mistakenly be labelled as pathologies.

Mental disorder as distress or suffering

Another way of defining abnormality is to consider disorder as the presence of distress or suffering. A hallmark of mental disorder is indeed that individuals experience personal distress and seek relief from their illness with a therapist. This criterion for diagnosing mental disorder has two problems. In some mental disorders such as the antisocial personality disorder, patients do not complain of emotional distress. Persons with this disorder do not show their emotions and are good at manipulating other people's emotions. Another problem with this criterion is that people often experience personal distress and painful emotions but they disappear when the stressful or painful events stop and individuals manage to return to psychological equilibrium. The loss of a loved person or the exclusion from social circles may cause much mental suffering, but that does not mean that one's mind is disordered.

Mental disorder as deviance from societal norms

Abnormality may be considered deviation from societal norms. It is true that in the past violation of social or cultural standards has been regarded as mental disorder. For example, the Victorians were wrong in their belief that masturbation and female orgasm were disorders (Horwitz and Wakefield 2007). And some American slaveholders were also wrong in believing that runaway slaves suffered from the mental disorder 'drapetomania', or the compulsion to flee. A more recent example refers to Soviet psychiatrists, arguing that political dissidents suffered from 'sluggish schizophrenia'. Likewise, homosexuality has long been considered a mental disorder because sexual health implied that people ought to be conventionally heterosexual, and if not, they were mentally ill. In the early 1970s, however, the American Psychiatric Association decided that it is not a mental illness (Murphy 2006). Since social norms about acceptable behaviours, emotions and cognitions show much variation across cultures, this criterion for defining what is mentally normal, is also problematic.

Mental disorder as somatic lesion

Another way of defining abnormality is to consider the mind as disordered if it can be based on the demonstration of somatic lesion, that is, malfunction of a normally occurring process. This criterion is also problematic. Psychiatrist Thomas Szasz (1987) claimed that mental disorder is a fiction, used by institutions as a pretext for repressive acts. He argued that the only respectable concept of disease is that of damage to bodily structures, and that mental disorders do not result from tissue damage. Psychiatrists often agreed with the first point but maintained that mental disorders would eventually be explained by abnormalities in the brain. Szasz responded that if mental derangement is indeed a brain disease, then the disorder is not a mental but a physical one (Murphy 2006).

Mental disorder as whatever mental health professionals treat

Attempts to analyse the concept of mental abnormality often failed which is why disappointment led to the suggestion that a mental disorder is simply any problem or condition that health professionals treat. But many problems that they treat are not disorders. This criterion is questionable because mental health professionals may deal with problems of living such as marital conflicts, parent–offspring conflicts, and employer–employee conflicts, causing some harm but not a serious disorder. In addition, professionals and patients may have wrong conceptions about whether a condition should be considered a disorder. Medical books from the Victorian period reveal, for instance, that people sought out professional treatment because they were believed to suffer from 'masturbatory disease' or 'perverse' clitoral orgasms.

Mental disorder as impaired functioning

Defining disorders has also been based on difficulties that result in impairment of social, occupational and personal functioning. Such dysfunction then has been called maladaptive behaviour. The problem with this criterion is that individuals who suffer, for instance, from agoraphobia and cannot go out, may nevertheless manage to live well with help from relatives. Agoraphobia – literally 'fear of the market place' (Greek) – refers to anxiety and panic symptoms with places or situations where escape may be difficult such as crowds, public places, and travelling alone. As a consequence, individuals suffering from agoraphobia avoid 'dangerous' situations.

Mental disorder as biological disadvantage

If we consider both mental and physical disorder, then a biological point of view appears to be appropriate. Biological science is the foundation of somatic medicine, so the mind/brain can be regarded as on a par with other parts of the organism. A biological approach based on the evolutionary theory may then have the potential to deal with mental and physical disorder. The standard theory of evolution implies that reproductive fitness is the criterion for health. A disorder is then any condition that reduces longevity or fertility. In the past, the argument that organisms tend to maximise fitness may be correct but today, with contraceptive technology, lowered fertility does not indicate disorder. It is rather the failure of a specific mechanism that shows that something has gone wrong.

Mental disorder as harmful dysfunction

Jerome Wakefield (1992a, 1992b, 2005) states that the problems with the previous definitions can be avoided by defining mental disorder as harmful dysfunction. According to this definition, a collection of symptoms indicates a mental disorder if it meets two criteria. The first criterion is dysfunction: a cognitive or emotional capacity fails to perform its natural biological function. For example, a natural, that is, naturally selected function of perception, is to provide correct information about the environment. But hallucinations, or false perceptions indicate dysfunctions. Likewise, emotional capacities to respond adequately to threat or adversity are naturally selected functions. If they fail to accomplish their natural function, they are in disorder. The second criterion is that dysfunction must be harmful. To be considered a disorder, the dysfunction must cause significant harm to the individual as well as the environment, judged by the standards of present culture. For instance, while a disposition to highly aggressive responses in males may have been adaptive in past environments, today it is generally regarded as harmful. So, at present, the loss of aggression's function should not be considered a disorder. (For reviews of Wakefield's conception of mental disorder, see Murphy 2006; McNally 2011.)

KEY FIGURE   Jerome Wakefield

Jerome Wakefield is professor of Social Work, and professor of the Conceptual Foundations of Psychiatry at the New York University. His research interests include the validity of psychiatric diagnostic criteria, psychiatric epidemiology, and integrative clinical theory. His areas of research include validity of psychiatric diagnostic criteria, psychiatric epidemiology, and integrative clinical theory.

Photo source: Jerome Wakefield

Selected work

The Loss of Sadness: How Psychiatry Transformed Normal Sorrow into Depressive Disorder, with Allan Horwitz (2007). Translated into French, Portuguese, Swedish, and Japanese (under contract).

11.3 Distinguishing normal responses from mental disorders

Objections to diagnostic systems

How can Wakefield's evolutionary conception of mental disorder be used in the case of depressive disorder? Since ancient times, clinicians have attempted to classify mental disorders. Classification is meant to offer guidelines for making correct diagnoses, being the first step towards understanding the disorder. At the same time, it has been demonstrated that classification systems enhance agreement among clinicians and researchers. Ultimately, diagnostic systems should lead to identifying the cause of the disease, and developing the means of prevention and cure. Ideally, diagnostic systems should label diseases according to their causes but since causes of most mental disorders are unknown, the current systems are based on common clinical features (symptoms), shared history, and/or common treatment response. Psychiatric symptoms refer to abnormal mental states, to be discovered by exploring the internal experiences of the patient. Abnormal mental states include, for example, delusions, which are fixed false beliefs, and severe anxieties without an apparent stimulus. The current clinical description of mental disorders is atheoretical, and not based on a particular explanation for the cause of an abnormal mental state. However, this is not always true because some causal information may sneak in when clinicians adhere to certain biological or psychological theories (Murphy 2006).

Currently, there are two classification systems in use worldwide, one produced by the World Health Organisation, and the other by the American Psychiatric Association. The two systems are broadly similar and have proved to be useful to practitioners. Critics, however, argue that the current systems fail to distinguish normal responses from genuine disorders (e.g. Nesse and Jackson 2011). For example, another criticism holds that classification is not explicitly based on a theory of human behaviour. In their analysis, Horwitz and Wakefield (2007) make a strong case for distinguishing between normal responses and genuine disorder, as well as for basing clinical diagnosis on an evolutionary explanation of emotions. We focus, therefore, on some important parts of their case study about normal sadness which tends to be treated as a mental disorder. This case is an example of a wider problem that amounts to the mistaken and improper pathologising of normal behaviours, emotions or cognitions. For other cases, see Wakefield et al. (2005) and Hughes (2011).

The link between response and environment

Horwitz and Wakefield (2007) argue that the evolutionary point of view provides clinical science with a compelling criterion for where normality ends and abnormality begins. For, we should regard the mind as disordered if it fails to function as it originally was selected for. The most plausible demarcation point between human normality and abnormality in the medical sense is, then, between naturally selected functioning and dysfunctioning, that is, the mind's capacities that were naturally selected to respond to specific environmental challenges. The link between response and environment is important because responses should be activated in specific contexts and not in others. Fear responses, for example, are expected to arise in dangerous situations such as life-threatening events, not in safe ones. Similarly, sadness should be activated by a specific kind of loss, for example, the loss of loved ones.

Emotional responses like fear and sadness show much variation between individuals because they may be more or less sensitive to the experience of loss. One may further anticipate that individuals vary in their responses because they are influenced by their cultures. So it is no easy task to decide whether a response corresponds with the naturally selected range. However that may be, we expect that most humans are capable of responding with normal emotions to situations of danger and loss. Yet we should be aware that the understanding of how normal emotions work precisely and why exactly they originated and became selected, is incomplete.

Diagnosing depressive disorder

You may recall from Chapter 7 (The origin and expression of emotion) that negative emotions like fear, anger and sadness overwhelm us, and are therefore experienced as disorganising. The negative side of emotions which dominated early theorising, led to questions about their usefulness. Chapter 7 explained that negative emotions respond to life-threatening situations and that without them, we would not survive, let alone produce offspring. Evolution teaches that negative emotions are, in principle, normal and adaptive responses in specific situations. To distinguish between normal and abnormal emotion requires, therefore, close attention to the link between response and context.

Horwitz and Wakefield (2007) built their case on the definition of Major Depressive Disorder as used by the American Psychiatry Association (2000). Diagnosis requires that five out of nine symptoms have been present during the same two-week period and represent a change from previous functioning; at least one of the symptoms is either depressed mood or loss of interest. Diagnostic criteria for Major Depressive Disorder include suffering nearly every day from low mood, reduced interest in activities, psychomotor agitation, substantial weight loss or decreased appetite, sleeping problems, fatigue or loss of energy, feelings of worth-lessness or excessive or inappropriate guilt, diminished capacity to think, concentrate or decide, and recurrent thoughts of death or suicide.

These symptoms serve as criteria for diagnosing Major Depressive Disorder. There is, however, an important clause in the definition which implies that patients are excluded from diagnosis if their symptoms are due to what the manual defines as a normal period of bereavement after the death of a loved one, lasting no more than two months, and not including serious symptoms like psychosis or suicidal thoughts.

The pathologising of sadness

The problem with the *Diagnostic and Statistical Manual of Mental Disorders (DSM)* definition of Major Depressive Disorder is that symptoms like low mood, loss of interest in daily activities, sleeping problems, reduced appetite, and difficulties with concentration, may apply to a wide range of unfortunate events. These events include, for example, being deceived by a romantic partner, passed over for an expected promotion, failed for an important assessment, confronted with a serious illness, and so on. Negative experiences may be considered as an inherent part of normal life; they are normal problems of life, not necessarily disorders. In other words, if *DSM* excludes bereavement from diagnosis, one may argue that it should also exclude other normal responses to significant loss. But *DSM* does not shut out responses other than bereavement. Thus, any sadness response which involves at least five symptoms and lasts for at least two weeks can be mistakenly classified as a disorder.

The point is that the symptoms cannot, in themselves, be used to distinguish normal sadness from depressive disorder. The symptoms are, in essence, no different from natural responses after significant life disruptions. Horwitz and Wakefield (2007) argue, rather, that a disorder is indicated by the absence of an appropriate context. For, contextuality is an inherent aspect of emotions which have the naturally selected function of being aroused in specific situations and not in others. The question is, then, in what kind of situations sadness responses are expected to be normal and not disordered?

Sadness is a normal response to situations of loss such as the death of loved ones and reversals of fortune. The intensity of sadness is a major concern for clinical diagnosis because normal responses need to be distinguished from disorders. According to Horwitz and Wakefield (2007), normal sadness to loss can be characterised by at least three essential components: it is context-specific, proportional to the loss, and ends about when the loss ends.

First, sadness responds to the 'right' kinds of losses, and not outside that range. Such losses, falling within the range, include loss of valued intimate attachment (e.g. parent, spouse, child), loss derived from hierarchical aspects of life (e.g. loss of power, status, resources, respect, prestige), and loss related to the failed achievement of important goals and ideals.

Second, the severity of the sadness response is reasonably proportional to the importance and duration of the loss that has been experienced. In addition, the response is supposed to be based on accurate perceptions of the negative circumstances. For instance, loosing one's romantic partner may cause deep sadness, but if it leads to suicidal thoughts the emotion is not normal.

depression/depressive illness

mental disorder with core symptoms like depressed mood, disturbed sleep, reduced libido, feelings of worthlessness, anhedonia (i.e. significant diminished enjoyment of previously pleasurable activities), recurrent thoughts of suicide.

Third, the sadness terminates when the loss situation ends or gradually ceases, and individuals manage to adjust to the new circumstances. To sum up, if sadness does not occur after a concrete, significant loss, is not proportional to the suffered loss, and does not stop when the loss ends, then we have good reason to presume that it is a disorder.

We noted above that symptoms like low mood, loss of interest in daily activities, sleeping problems, reduced appetite, and difficulties with concentration, may apply to a wide range of unlucky events. These events are an inherent part of normal life. One may therefore share the concern put by Horwitz and Wakefield (2007) that the boundaries of clinical **depression** have been expanded, thereby running the risk of diagnosing sadness as clinical depression, pathologising a normal emotion, and inflating the prevalence of clinical depression – i.e. the total number of cases in a given population. In a recent study, Gordon Parker and his colleagues (2010) find some support for the Horwitz and Wakefield hypothesis (2007: 6) that clinical depression is distinguished from normal sadness by the fact that the patient's symptoms occurred despite there being no appropriate reason for them in the patient's circumstances. However, Parker et al. (2010) conclude that attempts to differentiate clinical depression and normal sadness by symptoms alone may be limited.

Sadness as a naturally selected response to loss

How do we know that sadness is a normal, naturally selected solution to the problem of loss? Horwitz and Wakefield (2007) provide evidence from studies about human and non-human primates, human infants, and different cultures. We know from previous chapters that humans share many traits with other primates, especially with chimpanzees (e.g. section 7.3 Facial expressions in primates). Similarities between humans and non-human primates include loss situations that commonly lead to sadness responses. Infant monkeys, for example, who are separated from their mothers, show physiological responses – higher levels of cortisol – similar to those that correlate with sadness in humans. Similar responses occur in adults who suffer from being separated from partners and peers. If separated individuals are reunited with their intimates, sadness disappears rapidly. The same happens if infants find mother substitutes. Prolonged separation and isolation, however, may result in malfunctioning brains which also happens when humans suffer from depressive disorder.

Findings about human infants provide further evidence relevant to the question of whether sadness is a normal, naturally selected response to loss. Child psychiatrist John Bowlby (1981, 1985, 1991) was the first to argue that human infants need attachment to mothers, and that sadness should be considered as a natural response to attachment loss. Initially, infants who have lost their mother respond by withdrawing and crying but when separation lasts longer, they cease to be active and become apathetic. This kind of work suggests that sadness is a naturally selected response in infants after they lose attachment with loved ones.

Cross-cultural investigations provide a third source of evidence, supporting the idea that sadness was selected for dealing with loss situations. Recall that Chapter 7 discussed Paul Ekman's findings about universal facial expressions. People in different cultures were shown photographs and asked to select from different pictured emotions the one that matched the narrated story about a lost child. Agreement was high among subjects about the expression of sadness – downcast eyes, drooping or tense upper lids, eyebrows drawn together and lower lips drawn down.

Although sadness is a naturally selected response, culture can influence it in different ways (Horwitz and Wakefield 2007). Cultural meanings affect which particular events are considered as losses. In the United States, for example, the failure of a mother to give birth to a baby boy is not a reason for deep sadness. But in Zambia it means a decline in social status and may lead to divorce and depression in women. Thus, natural selection and cultural norms are complementary parts in the explanation of how normal and abnormal sadness should be distinguished.

11.4 Explaining the adaptive function of mental illness

The evolutionary paradox of mental disorders

heritability
the proportion of phenotypic variation that can be attributed to genetic differences between individuals.

The logic of evolutionary theory infers that maladaptive traits reduce fitness and are therefore expected to be ruled out by natural selection. The paradox is that mental disorders still exist and have withstood the power of natural selection (Keller and Miller 2006). On the one hand, evidence confirms that mental disorders are heritable and are passed on through generations. Behavioural geneticists estimate that mental disorder **heritability** ranges from 20 to 80 per cent of the genetic differences between people. In addition, the stronger the genetic relationship between people, the more they tend to develop the same disorder. On the other hand, evidence shows that mental disorders reduce fitness. Most disorders do not arise after the reproductive years but rather in early childhood or during the reproductive years. People suffering from mental disorders have considerably lower fertility rates, in particular because they have difficulty in finding a mate. In other words, reduced fertility results from lower marriage rates rather than fewer offspring once people married.

Given that natural selection is unable to weed out mental disorders, we may suppose that they are somehow adaptive. In this section we discuss three theories to resolve this paradox. The dopamine theory proposes that human migration out of Africa between 100,000 and 50,000 years ago and subsequent colonisation of the world, required adaptive traits that made the human mind vulnerable to mental illness. The byproduct theory implies that mental illness is the maladaptive side-effect of selection for some other adaptive trait such as creativity. The mismatch theory holds that adaptive traits in our ancestral environment became maladaptive in the current environment.

11.4.1   The dopamine theory of mental illness

Human migration out of Africa

dopamine

a neurotransmitter that has an important role in motor behaviour and also involved in mental processes such as reward-driven learning.

As stated above, given that natural selection doesn't eliminate mental disorders, we may suppose that they are somehow adaptive. The **dopamine** theory proposes that human migration out of Africa between 100,000 and 50,000 years ago and subsequent spreading all over the world, required adaptive traits that made the human mind vulnerable to mental illness. You may recall from section 3.5 (What makes us human?) that non-human primates are mostly confined to the continents on which they arose. A quick look at Figure 3.6 (Geographic distribution of the living non-human primates) tells us that they live almost entirely in the tropics and subtropics. In contrast, humans colonised most parts of the world (Figure 11.2).

Why did humans leave Africa? The expansion was presumably the result of a more intense search for resources because the foraging territories would have to increase in size to support the human subsistence strategy (Cartmill and Smith 2009). One scenario holds that the migrants were used to foraging for shellfish on the African shore of the Red Sea, but evaporation caused the sea to become increasingly salty so that plankton, the base of the marine food chain, disappeared (Oppenheimer 2003). Presumably, for groups of individuals to walk over many generations from Ethiopia to the tip of South America, requires strong motivation, far stronger than a daily search for one's meal. The long intercontinental journey of *Homo sapiens* suggests a curiosity and taste for risk which we may recognise in migrant behaviour of our own time (Whybrow 2005).

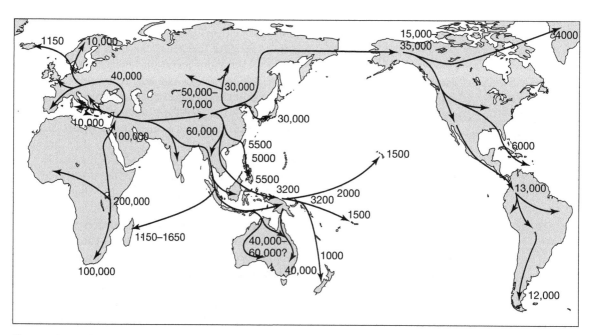

Figure 11.2 Origin and spread of humans

Source: Klein and Takahata (2002)

Research findings from non-human primates about curiosity and impulsivity – defined as the tendency to act quickly in novel circumstances, without restraint and without regard for the consequences – suggest that these characteristics are heritable. Bold individuals rapidly explore new situations while shy individuals avoid such situations. Each individual seems to show a response that is consistent over its lifetime. Lynn Fairbanks (2001) studied variations in curiosity and impulsivity among vervet monkeys. By introducing an 'intruder' into a stable group of monkeys, she discovered that the impulse to investigate novel situations varies among individuals and with age. How quickly an individual approaches the intruder, how close it sits, and whether it sniffs, touches or threatens the stranger, are behaviours that show remarkable consistency over time.

These findings are compatible with those from other studies with various monkey species which show that dopamine – a neurotransmitter, or chemical substance in the brain that is involved in reward-driven learning – plays an important role in the migratory behaviour of males. In a discussion with Peter Whybrow (2005: 69), Fairbanks argues that over generations, curiosity and impulsivity are closely linked with dominance of the dopamine system, as well as associated with migration. In fact, males who show boldness and aggression in their curiosity, have more offspring, control more resources, and dispose of larger territories after dispersal to another group. However, there is always a trade-off in that these individuals are also more likely to be killed in a fight or eaten by a predator.

Are these findings about non-human primates similar to those in humans? Psychiatrist Robert Cloninger (1994) identified in his research behavioural clusters, describing four temperamental styles, from shy to bold. **Temperament**, the biological foundation of personality, is present early in life and includes characteristics such as energy level, emotional responsiveness and willingness to explore. Studies of animals, ranging from fishes to primates, have documented differences in temperament, particularly along the shy–bold continuum, where shyness refers to 'harm avoidance' and boldness to 'novelty seeking'. Combined with 'reward dependence' and 'persistence', being the intermediate factors on the continuum, shyness and boldness represent the styles in which people interact with one another and how they respond to challenges.

The novelty-seeking style of temperament is particularly relevant if we want to understand migratory behaviour. Individuals scoring high on this style are bold and curious. They like to explore new environments and are typically risk-takers. Findings from later research emphasise the role of the dopamine reward system. For example, Chen and his colleagues (1999) discovered that specific dopamine receptors in the brain – located at synapses which are specialised junctions where neurons communicate with one another – associate with the trait of novelty-seeking. Thus, curiosity and risk-taking are essential to migratory behaviour. Without these mental traits our ancestors would not have crossed the Bering Strait 20,000 years ago, and colonised the American continent.

temperament
the biological foundation of personality, present early in life and including characteristics such as energy level, emotional responsiveness and willingness to explore. Studies of animals, ranging from fish to primates, have documented differences in temperament, particularly along the shy–bold continuum.

The rise of dopamine levels in human evolution

We have seen that the novelty-seeking style of temperament is associated with dopamine. This chemical is not only involved in temperament but also in goal-directed behaviour and cognitive capacities. Remarkably, dopamine is involved in clinical disorders as well. That is what Fred Previc (1999, 2009) investigated with his intriguing

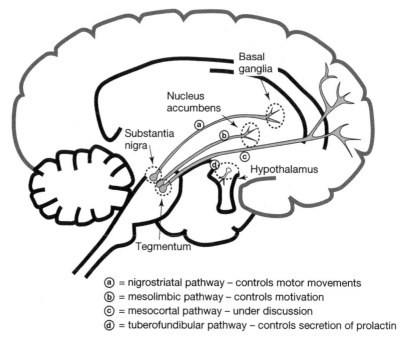

ⓐ = nigrostriatal pathway – controls motor movements
ⓑ = mesolimbic pathway – controls motivation
ⓒ = mesocortal pathway – under discussion
ⓓ = tuberofundibular pathway – controls secretion of prolactin

Figure 11.3 Four dopamine pathways in the brain
Source: Stahl (2004)

theory about the role of dopamine in the evolution of human behaviour and mentality. We now focus on some significant parts of his theory.

First, some words about dopamine in the brain (Previc 2009). High amounts of dopamine have been found in brainy and intelligent non-human species such as parrots and dolphins. But dopamine has particularly expanded throughout primate and human evolution. This transmitter is especially rich in the prefrontal cortex of the human brain because this region is involved in higher mental functions such as planning, reasoning and mathematics. The amount of dopamine that may influence many neurons, is regulated by the **dopaminergic system** in our brain. Dopaminergic neurons are, then, neurons for which dopamine serves as the principal neurotransmitter. Within the dopaminergic system, there are different pathways. Two of them are relevant in our context. The nigrostriatal dopamine pathway is closely involved in most types of motor actions, and the mesolimbic dopamine pathway is heavily implicated in exploratory behaviour, motivational drive and creative impulse (Figure 11.3).

You may recall from section 7.4 (The neural basis of emotions) that we reviewed evolutionary theories about the emotional brain. Among the authors discussed was evolutionary neuroscientist Jaak Panksepp who identified several emotional systems in animal and human brains. The 'seeking system' is one of these systems, making mammals curious about their world and stimulating them to find food, shelter or sex. A very important neurochemical in this system is dopamine and the associated mesolimbic pathway. This dopaminergic circuit tends to energise planning and foresight as well as promote states of eagerness in both humans and animals (Panksepp 1998a).

dopaminergic system

a brain system that regulates the amount of dopamine influencing many neurons. This system consists of different pathways that are involved in physiological, motor, motivational and cognitive functions.

Why did dopamine levels increase during human evolution? In Previc's theory, the dopaminergic expansion is due to a combination of factors. A general, enabling factor is the ability of mothers to pass their high levels of dopamine prenatally to their offspring. It is now widely believed that processes in the womb influence offspring. So apart from genetic and cultural inheritance, there is also epigenetic inheritance. Specific factors that favoured increasing dopamine levels include, for example, physiological adaptation to hot stressful environments which requires dopamine to activate heat-loss mechanisms. Despite the ability of humans to thrive in tropical environments, they still run the risk of **hyperthermia**. That is, thermoregulation may fail when the body produces or absorbs more heat than it can dissipate. The adaptation of early humans to heat stress was particularly important for engaging in persistence hunting and midday scavenging. Persistence hunting implies that an animal is pursued in the heat over long distances until it enters a hyperthermic condition and dies. This kind of hunting is still practised by modern Bushmen in Africa.

Another factor was increased consumption of meat and shellfish which led to greater supplies of dopamine precursors and conversion of them into dopamine. It is generally accepted that consumption of shellfish was widespread along the coast of South Africa <100,000 years ago. Previc (2009) argues that shellfish are rich in iodine and essential fatty acids which increase dopamine activity and stimulate mental functions. Consuming shellfish proved to be a stable factor in the diet, so much so that it promoted longevity. A longer lifespan would, then, have resulted in population pressures, and increased migration to other parts of the world.

Previc believes that levels of dopamine are now much higher in modern industrialised societies than in agrarian and hunter-gatherer societies. For, demographic pressures increased competition for resources and rewarded dopaminergically mediated achievement motivation. It concerns the desire to overcome obstacles and master difficult challenges. High scorers in achievement motivation tend to set higher standards and work with greater perseverance than equally gifted low scorers (e.g. McClelland 1961, 1988).

Dopamine is important for attending to distant space and time

Dopamine enables and stimulates motor behaviours like locomotion, vocalisation, facial movement and exploratory behaviour. Dopamine in the brain is particularly important for attending to distant space and time (Previc 2009). Dopamine is involved if an animal shifts its attention from near to distant space. If a rat finds food, it can either eat it on the spot or take it to the nest as occurs in hoarding behaviour. Hoarding distal food fails if the animal is deprived of dopamine. If a monkey attends to distant space, it shows upward movements and attentional biases produced by dopaminergic activation. Upward biases include rearing its hind legs and raising of the head. This behaviour resembles the upward head and eye movements when humans are engaged in mental activities such as problem-solving, reasoning and making plans which activate the dopaminergic prefrontal cortex (Figure 11.4).

The human concept of space goes beyond the here-and-now, and includes the capacity to imagine more distant and abstract worlds. Presumably, imaginative thinking played an important role when our ancestors travelled through the continents without compass, map or Global Positioning System. The capacity for imagination, used in abstract and creative thinking, is a recently evolved capacity of the human species (e.g.

hyperthermia
failing function of thermoregulation when the body produces or absorbs more heat than it can dissipate.

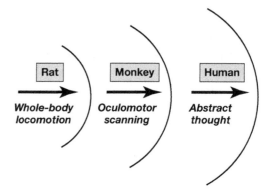

Figure 11.4 The dopaminergic exploration of distant space in mammals
Source: Previc (2009)

Mithen 2007). Dopamine is also involved in distant goals which do not provide immediate rewards. This has been studied, for example, in feeding behaviour. Research findings show that dopamine neurons are much more activated during preparatory behaviours before food consumption than during the actual consumption of foods.

Increased dopamine is further implicated in cognitive skills (Previc 2009). Consider working memory, being the capacity to store, retrieve and operate on items in memory on a short-term basis of a few seconds. Mental operations would be impossible if we could not maintain one piece of information ready while retrieving another piece. In decision-making, for example, which activates dopamine neurons in the prefrontal cortex, we hold some alternatives in mind while weighing what we shall do. And in language, we interpret the sentences a partner spoke and simultaneously prepare a response.

From all of the cognitive skills involving dopamine, the skill to invent new solutions to problems and create original ideas, may be regarded as the most distinguishing capacity of the human species (Box 11.1 Evolutionary ingredients of **creativity**). The mesolimbic dopamine pathway (see Figure 11.1) provides us with an intense motivational drive directed to distant goals, and is thought to promote associations between remote ideas. For example, an architect, combining the notion of 'house' and 'desk', creates a new idea that residents may find appealing: 'apartments as extending drawers'.

creativity

the cognitive capacity to generate new and valuable ideas. This capacity is thought to be not a single capacity, like intelligence, but one that consists of different ingredients, in particular: intrinsic motivation, intelligence, thinking style, personality and expertise.

BOX 11.1 Evolutionary ingredients of creativity

We may consider creativity as a capacity to generate new and valuable ideas. This capacity is thought to be not a single capacity, like intelligence, but one that consists of different ingredients, in particular: intrinsic motivation, intelligence, thinking style, personality, expertise and psychopathology (e.g. Sternberg and Lubart 1995a, 1995b; Amabile 1996; Simonton 2003). Supposedly, the confluence of these ingredients in the course of human evolution explains why we are more creative than other animals. The question is whether and to what extent we share those ingredients with our hominid ancestors.

Intrinsic motivation is apparent when we engage in activities that are rewarding in themselves, rather than through the benefits (income, status) they provide. Extrinsic motivation arising from the expected reward or punishment, tends to undermine creativity. But rewards supporting one's sense of competence – without connoting control – or enabling deeper task involvement, increase intrinsic motivation and enhance creativity (Amabile 1996). The evolutionary precursor of intrinsic motivation is possibly the urge to play which serves no immediate purpose beyond enjoyment (Box 8.2 Is play necessary for survival?).

Intelligence contributes to creative performance to an IQ score of 120, suggesting a threshold score for intelligence that is necessary but not sufficient to explain creativity (Sternberg and O'Hara 1999). Other studies do not show a significant threshold but support the importance of insight, or the clear and often sudden discernment of a solution to a problem by means that are not immediately obvious (Sternberg and Lubart (1995b). Recall from section 8.3 (Cognitive capacities in apes and corvids) that some non-human animals have a capacity for insight.

Thinking style can be any kind of thinking that enhances creative performance. Divergent thinking refers to the capacity to produce novel solutions to a problem (e.g. make a list of the different ways that you can use a brick). Out-of-the-box thinking tends to challenge the established rules in a discipline (Boden 1992). For instance, composer Arnold Schönberg made his own musical scales. Analogical thinking looks for similarities in different phenomena. Analogies like 'the body as a machine', 'the heart as a pump', and 'the brain as a computer' stimulated scientific advance. Chimpanzees may also think analogically. In a test, when shown a closed lock and a key and a closed painted can, chimpanzee Sarah selected the can opener rather than the paint brush as the appropriate completion to make the two relationships 'similar' (Holyoak and Thagard 1995).

Personality can be defined as the configuration of characteristics – e.g. interests, drives, capacities – that constitutes an individual's unique adjustment to life. In creativity research, certain personality dimensions have been proposed to be useful to creative efforts. Personality traits that define creative individuals include openness to experience, adventurousness, rebelliousness, autonomy, playfulness and novelty-seeking (Runco 2007). Studies suggest that non-human primates also have personalities (King et al. 1999; Gosling and Harley 2009). Recall from earlier in this section that some male vervet monkeys, when confronted by a stranger in the group, showed a bold, novelty-seeking style of temperament. And temperament is the biological foundation of personality.

Expertise refers to the characteristics, skills and knowledge that distinguish experts from novices and less experienced people (Weisberg 2006). Evidence shows that the development of expert performance demands about ten years of deliberate practice and study ('the ten-year rule'). What matters is effortful study in which people are continually tackling challenges that lie just beyond their competence.

Psychopathology refers to patterns of behaviour or thought processes that are abnormal or maladaptive. This term is considered to be synonymous with mental illness or mental disorder. In a mild form, psychopathology can contribute to creative work. For example, creative persons may have a relative inability to filter out irrelevant information, known as weakened **'latent inhibition'**. This inability implies that the available store of ideas will enlarge, thereby increasing the odds of novel ideas (Simonton 2003; Carson et al. 2003; Carson 2011). For more explanation, see the main text.

11.4.2 The byproduct theory of mental illness

latent inhibition

the capacity to screen from conscious awareness stimuli previously experienced as irrelevant. Reductions in latent inhibition have been generally associated with the tendency towards psychosis. However, 'failure' to screen out previously irrelevant stimuli might also hypothetically contribute to creativity, particularly in combination with high IQ.

Why did natural selection not eliminate disorder?

The assumption that selection should eliminate mental disorders overlooks an important issue (Brüne 2008). The issue is that most adaptive traits do not function optimally because evolution by selection is a frugal process, resulting in compromises. Consider, for instance, the evolution of human bipedalism. You may recall from section 3.5 (What makes us human?) that global climate around 8–5 mya became cooler and drier, reducing rainforests and expanding grasses so that larger distances between trees had to be traversed on foot. The shift from quadrupedalism to bipedalism required a reorganisation of the vertebral column. In modern humans, the vertebral column is shaped in a double S-curve, allowing them to travel large distances at low energy costs. The raised centre of mass of the body above the hip joints may cause problems when the vertebral discs are squeezed between the verte-brae. Thus disc prolapses are built-in compromises of walking upright.

Mental illness as a byproduct of creativity

Given that natural selection does not work optimally and that genes for mental ill-ness can be inherited, we may infer that it has adaptive benefits. We will discuss, first, the theory that mental illness is a byproduct of selection for another adaptive trait such as creativity. And second, the theory that adaptive traits like fear and sadness may turn maladaptive due to a mismatch between ancestral and current environment.

We have seen in the previous section that, according to Previc's theory, the role of dopamine in creativity comes from a phenomenon, known as 'reduced latent inhibition' (Previc 2009). Normally, we filter out irrelevant information, but creative persons are like highly dopaminergic schizophrenics who demonstrate a reduced tendency to filter out incoming information (Carson et al. 2003; Flaherty 2005). The memory of creative people has, therefore, been compared with a vast attic where all kinds of objects are put away because one can never tell when they will prove to be necessary (Mlodinow 2003). Similarly, lots of ideas, observations, remarks and ques-tions assemble themselves in the creative mind.

Creative people are, indeed, more prone to be flooded by ideas and less likely to censor them. They have brains and minds that function somewhat differently from those of normal persons (Andreasen 2005). While creative individuals experience their mind as producing a constant stream of ideas, the observer may experience such persons as jumping from one topic to another. When associations between remote ideas organise themselves into a new and valuable idea, we consider the result as creative. But if the associations fail to self-organise, the outcome is regarded as erroneous, unusual, bizarre or even insane.

Both things – creativity and psychopathology – may happen in the same person. For example, John Nash, a creative scientist who received the 1994 Nobel prize in Economic Sciences, was also diagnosed as a schizophrenic suffering from delusions. He has been reported as once saying: 'the ideas I have about supernatural beings came to me the same way that my mathematical ideas did, so I took them seriously' (Nasar 1998: p. 11). Delusions, or fixed false beliefs, are a common symptom of schizophren-ics. A person may believe that a colleague is sending messages into his brain or plan-ning to steal his car. In his deluded mind, the associations with a colleague have gone awry, for example, because the colleague is mistaken for an evil character from a story.

The theory of dopamine overactivation in schizophrenia is thought to be one of the longest standing and most widely accepted in neuropsychology (Previc 2009). Elevated levels of dopamine can account for the positive symptoms of schizophre-nia, ranging from delusions and hallucinations to a thinking style characterised by jumping from one idea to another. 'Positive symptoms' of schizophrenia represent an excess or distortion of normal function, as distinct from a deficiency or lack of normal function. Positive symptoms include delusions or hallucinations, disorgan-ised behaviour and conceptual disorganisation. Negative symptoms include apathy, blunted affect, emotional withdrawal, poor rapport and lack of spontaneity.

The empirical evidence for a linkage between mental illness and creativity is quite strong (Nettle 2006a). The evidence comes from biographical and survey studies which found high levels of psychopathology such as depression and schizophrenia in creative people. Evidences also comes from family studies, suggesting that an inherited personality or cognitive trait has effects for both creativity and mental illness. In addition, psychometric studies have found that creative persons and bipolar (manic-depressive) patients share high levels of the personality traits neuroticism – characterised by a chronic level of emotional instability and proneness to psychological distress – and openness to experience.

Daniel Nettle (2006b: 418) emphasises that:

> the crucial finding is not that rates of mental illness are higher in creative groups (though they are cf. Andreasen 1987; Ludwig 1995). Rather, the key finding is that there are measurable cognitive affinities between those successful in the creative professions and those diagnosed with serious mental illness, whether or not the creative individuals show any symptoms of psychopathology.

It is, then, likely that mentally ill patients and healthy creative individuals share a similar style of thought, jumping from one idea to another instead of following the usual lines of associative thinking. The psychological term for this style of thinking is 'loosening of associations' (VandenBos 2007).

Creativity and high moods

In section 11.4.1 (The dopamine theory of mental illness) we proposed that the human vulnerability to mental disorder is associated with the urge to explore and colonise the world. Like our ancestors, we are still exploring unknown worlds such as outer space and deep oceans. We also discussed the importance of dopamine in human evolution for attending to distant space and time. Distant space is not necessarily concrete, but may include the abstract world of science and fiction. And distant time may include the large timescale of evolution that we need to understand animal bodies and minds.

The question is now how dopamine is implicated in mental disorder (Previc 2009). When the brain is flooded by dopamine, so-called **hyperdopaminergic disorders** may occur such as autism, obsessive-compulsive disorder (OCD), **mania** and schizophrenia. Consider OCD, for instance. Recall from section 7.4 (The neural basis of emotions) that Panksepp (1998a) identified the seeking system in animal and human brains that makes one curious and eager to find attractive things like food, shelter and sex. Dopamine and the associated mesolimbic dopaminergic circuit play an important role in the seeking system. If you take a look at Table 7.1 (Postulated relationships between emotional systems, emotions and emotional disorders), you can see that OCD is an emotional disorder related to seeking. Thus, an obsessive, compulsive interest in something is associated with a brain overflowed by dopamine.

In contrast, when the brain is deprived of dopamine, so-called **hypodopaminergic disorders** may emerge such as Parkinson's disease and **phenylketonuria**, a genetic disorder leading to progressive mental retardation (Previc 2009). Let us focus on mania because, from all of the mental disorders, it is most closely associated with heightened creativity and is thought to have been present in our ancestors since they left Africa. Recall from section 3.5 (What makes us human?) that defining

hyperdopaminergic disorder

mental disorder associated with abundance of dopamine (e.g. autism, obsessive-compulsive disorder, mania and schizophrenia).

mania

mental state characterised by overactivity, increased cognitive activity ranging from enhanced creativity to overoptimistic ideation, and inflated self-esteem.

hypodopaminergic disorder

mental disorder associated with deprivation of dopamine (e.g. Parkinson's disease, phenylketonuria).

phenylketonuria

a mental disorder associated with a metabolic imbalance leading to progressive mental retardation.

characteristics of modern humans since their appearance about 200,000 years ago are: abstract thinking, formulating behavioural strategies, symbolic behaviour, and capacity for creating behavioural, economic and technological innovations (e.g. specialised hunting of dangerous animals, exchanging raw materials, making special-purpose tools such as projectiles).

Mania, in everyday life associated with intense enthusiasm, or craze for something, is in clinical terms referred to as bipolar disorder when it fluctuates with depression. In other words, people with this disorder cycle between high and low moods. Characteristics of mania are overactivity, increased cognitive activity ranging from enhanced creativity to overoptimistic ideation, and inflated self-esteem. Mania may often end in hospitalisation, and is regarded as a full-blown mental illness while **hypomania** is a milder version in which people feel creative, energetic and happy.

hypomania
a milder version of mania in which people feel creative, energetic and happy.

Hypomania is important for creative achievement because it provides vast energy for accomplishing a task when immediate rewards are absent. For example, writing and composing are lonely activities without instant feedback, requiring an inordinate enthusiastic mood to carry on (Nettle 2001). In general, hypomania endows pioneering minds – ranging from artists and scientists to discoverers, inventors and entrepreneurs – with unusual energy, creative power, infectious enthusiasm and a taste for adventure (Gartner 2005; Whybrow 2005; Previc 2009).

Although the diagnostic criteria for mania and hypomania are identical according to the *DSM-IV* (APA 2000), the disturbance of hypomania is not sufficiently severe to cause marked impairment in social or occupational functioning or to require hospitalisation. Diagnostic criteria for (hypo)mania include inflated self-esteem or grandiosity, less need for sleep, pressure to keep talking, flight of ideas or racing thoughts, distractibility, increased goal-directed activity, and extreme involvement in pleasurable activities that tend to have painful consequences.

Research findings indicate that the creativity-enhancing effects of high moods were particularly marked for patients with a history of hypomania (Richards and Kinney 1990; Kinney and Richards 2007). By contrast, in most patients diagnosed with full-blown mania, high moods did not facilitate creativity. To make matters worse, extreme mood swings tended to destroy rather than favour creative efforts. These findings support the idea that creativity is an inverted function of increasing levels of (hypo)manic symptoms. With mild mood elevation, creative efforts improve but they are impaired if moods rise too high.

Thus, a likely scenario of human evolution would be that selection pressures for the benefits of creativity came with a dysfunction, called 'mental disorder'. Mental illness may, then, be regarded as the evolutionary byproduct of an adaptive trait. Quirks like reduced latent inhibition and hypomania demonstrate that a touch of madness contributes to creative capacity (e.g. Nettle 2001; Carson et al. 2003; Carson 2011).

Protective factors against the risk of psychopathology

How are creative people protected against the risk of psychopathology? Shelley Carson (2011) has proposed a 'shared vulnerability model' of the association between creativity and psychopathology with factors that are common to creativity and psychopathology (Figure 11.5). According to this model, there are factors that make creative people vulnerable to psychopathology and protective factors that allow them to produce and control uncommon or bizarre thoughts, without

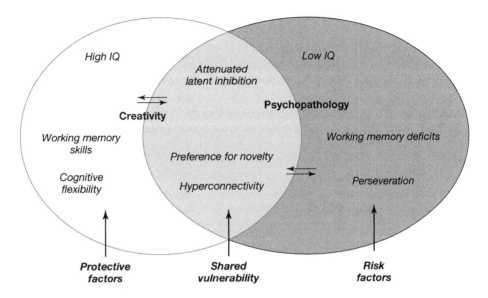

Figure 11.5 Shared vulnerability model of creativity associated with psychopathology
Source: Carson (2011)

becoming mentally disorganised by them. This model is thought to explain why a greater risk of psychopathology is to be found in creative people, and why the rate of mental disorders such as schizophrenia remains stable while it is known that people with schizophrenia reproduce at a lower rate than the general population.

Factors that make individuals vulnerable to psychopathology include reduced latent inhibition, increased sensitivity to novelty seeking and neural hyperconnectivity. Reduced latent inhibition has been observed in schizophrenic people and can also be induced by ingesting psychoactive substances. As we have seen above, reduced latent inhibition increases creativity by adding unfiltered ideas to the available store, thereby increasing the odds that novel ideas will emerge. In addition, creative individuals are inclined through the internal rewards of the dopaminergic system to search for novel stimuli. Because novelty seeking is also associated with alcohol and drug intoxication, it stimulates creative work as well as increases the risk of psychopathology.

Carson (2011) regards neural hyperconnectivity as a third vulnerability factor that is thought to be caused by irregularities in the developing brain. Whereas hypoconnectivity (loss of cortical connections) leads to an inability to perform perceptual, cognitive and motor tasks, hyperconnectivity (the connection of normally unrelated parts of the brain) has been found in schizophrenics and their first-degree relatives and may be responsible for bizarre associations. Hyperconnectivity is also associated with above-normal abilities such as synaesthesia, the tendency to make cross-modal sensory associations (e.g. sounds experienced as colours). Synaesthesia runs in families and is more prevalent in highly creative people than in the general population. Carson suggests that patterns of neural hyperconnectivity may be responsible for both the bizarre ideas of schizophrenics and the unusual ideas of creative people.

Factors that help to protect vulnerable people from psychopathology include high IQ, enhanced working memory and cognitive flexibility. Research findings indicate that IQ is correlated with measures of creativity up to a score of 120 which suggests a threshold that is necessary but not sufficient to explain creativity (Sternberg and O'Hara 1999). You may recall from Box 11.1 (Evolutionary ingredients of creativity) that other studies do not show a significant threshold but support the importance of insight, or the clear and often sudden discernment of a solution to a problem by means that are not immediately obvious (Sternberg and Lubart 1995b).

However, a high IQ is thought to function as a cognitive reserve, helping to protect people against the risk of mental disorders (Barnett et al. 2006). In contrast, a low IQ combined with reduced latent inhibition tends to increase the odds of becoming mentally disordered. In a similar vein, it is suggested that people with higher working memory capacity may also be protected from psychopathology. If creativity is based on the capacity to combine and recombine many ideas, then being able to keep them simultaneously in mind without becoming overwhelmed, is an argument for creative rather than deranged cognition.

A third protective factor is cognitive flexibility which enables people to consider a problem from different points of view. This capacity to think in a flexible manner is important because the lack of it is considered to be a hallmark of schizophrenic thinking. The capacity for flexible cognition is associated with the personality trait of openness to experience which is typically found in creative people.

11.4.3 The mismatch theory of mental illness

Having discussed the theory that mental illness is a byproduct of selection for another adaptive trait like creativity, we will now focus on the mismatch theory. This theory holds that adaptive traits in our ancestral environment may become maladaptive in the current environment. Recall that we came across this type of explanation in section 2.2 (Evolutionary approaches to problems) where we discussed obesity. This problem of overweight can be explained as a mismatch between an adaptive response to the shortage of resources in the environment of our ancestors and the abundance of food in the modern environment. The reason for a mismatch is that evolution cannot look into the future and only retains things that in the past have proven to benefit fitness. Whereas a strong appetite for fat and sugar was adaptive for hunter-gatherers, it is no longer the case today.

Specific phobia

Traits that were adaptive in the environment of our ancestors may be maladaptive in the environment of their descendants. For example, emotional responses function sub-optimally because of the low threshold at which a stimulus can elicit a response. The threshold for fear is usually low because the cost of being injured or killed by not responding is much higher than responses to false alarms ('better safe than sorry'). The mechanism of eliciting fear responses has therefore been likened to the principle of the smoke detector which works at low thresholds to detect small concentrations of smoke (Nesse 2005). The low threshold for fear may help to explain why anxiety disorders are the most common of all psychopathologies. The environment in which humans evolved was full of threats which selected more strongly against false negatives (e.g. failing to run from a predator) than against false positives (e.g. running from one's own shadow). As a consequence, part of our evolutionary heritage is an easily triggered fear response (Pennington 2002).

Consider specific phobia, a persistent and irrational fear of a specific situation, object or activity which is consequently either strenuously avoided or endured with marked distress. Diagnostic criteria for specific phobia also include that people are aware that the fear is unreasonable, that they tend to avoid anxious situations, and that anxiety reduces normal functioning (APA 2000). Phobic people may develop fears of heights, dogs, water, blood, flying, driving, insects, and so on. How can such phobias be explained from an evolutionary point of view?

A sophisticated hypothesis implies that humans have an evolutionary prepared tendency to fear those stimuli that once posed a recurrent threat to our ancestors. Recall from section 1.5 (Neuroscience) that snakes signified recurrent and deadly threats in the environment of early mammals. Most mammals responded by evolving physiological resistance to snake venoms, but monkeys, apes and humans responded by enhancing the ability to detect snakes visually before the strike. Recent observations of contemporary, preliterate hunter-gatherers in the Philippines support the hypothesis that humans and snakes share a long evolutionary history with complex interactions. These people are reported to have pythons on the menu and have been eaten by pythons (Headland and Greene 2011).

You may also recall from section 1.5 (Neuroscience) that neuroscientists revealed a specific fear mechanism with four characteristics: selectivity with regard to input, automaticity, encapsulation, and a specialised neural circuitry (Öhman and Mineka 2001, 2003). Selectivity implies that we learn fear of snakes more easily than fear of most other stimuli. Automaticity means that the mechanism originates from animals with primitive brains and is therefore not under voluntary control whether we want it or not. Encapsulation relates to the need to rely on time-proven solutions that are immune to recently evolved cognitions. Finally, the fear mechanism is based on specific neural circuitry that has been shaped by evolution and is located in subcortical or even brainstem areas.

Therefore, it makes evolutionary sense to fear snakes. Assuming that many people fear spiders as well, can we infer that these insects also presented deadly threats to our ancestors? Probably not because only 0.1 per cent of the 35,000 spider species are potentially harmful to humans (Renner as cited in Merkelbach and De Jong 1997). It is unclear why humans would have developed a fear of spiders because they die at the hands or feet of humans rather than the other way around (McNally 2011). While fear of snakes is a naturally selected response, a phobia for spiders may instead be considered an oversensitivity to threat detection (Murphy 2005, 2006).

This oversensitivity raises other questions. Why are some people more susceptible to phobias than others? Why are phobias more common among women? Research findings show that specific phobias are consistently found more in women than men (Barlow 2002). The differences are strong for fears of animals, lightning, enclosed places and darkness. On the other hand, phobias of heights, flying, injections, dentists and injury do not significantly differ between the sexes. It should be noted that men tend to underreport their fears, probably due to traditional gender roles. It is also possible that men have learned to take more risks and women to be more risk-avoiding. Recent findings indicate that phobias are highly heritable and co-morbid (Czajkowski et al. 2011). In a large community sample it was found that nearly 76 per cent of individuals diagnosed with a lifetime phobia reported one or more co-occurring phobias (e.g. animal phobia, agoraphobia, blood phobia).

To conclude, the aetiology of a specific phobia (aetiology is the study of the causes of illness) involves ultimate as well as proximate factors that make people

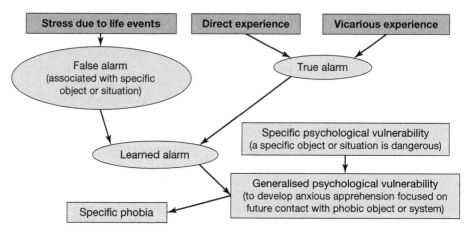

Figure 11.6 A model of the aetiology of a specific phobia
Source: Barlow (2002)

vulnerable. David Barlow (2002) proposed a model with an ultimate factor, called 'generalised biological vulnerability' (Figure 11.6). This factor includes the heritable tendency to associate fear with objects or situations that presented deadly threats to our ancestors as well as a low threshold for dangerous objects and situations. This ultimate factor may interact with proximate factors such as the experience of stress due to negative life events and early learning experiences that make individuals (over-)sensitive to dangers ('generalised psychological vulnerability').

Depression

Consider another adaptive trait that may turn maladaptive due to a mismatch between ancestral and current environment. One theory suggests that depression is associated with unfavourable changes in one's place in the group, or having a perception that one's place is unfavourable (Gilbert 1992). People may, for example, feel depressed when outcompeted by colleagues or just perceive that they have been outsmarted. In general, group-living animals tend to change their behaviour when they change place in the social hierarchy. Recall from section 6.2 (Why live socially?) that in cohesive groups, social structure may take the form of dominance hierarchy, with an alpha male or female at the top and other group members occupying lower ranks. Dominance hierarchies are the result of fights which, once established, prevent continuous struggles. Ranks can be stable as in baboons or unstable as in chimpanzees where lower ranking animals test the ability of those above them to hold their place.

Research findings about vervet monkeys suggest that changes in the hierarchy are associated with changing serotonin levels. Serotonin is a chemical substance, or neural transmitter in the brain and other parts of the central nervous system that has a role in the bioregulatory processes of emotion, mood, appetite, sleep and pain. Serotonin levels in vervet monkeys fall when they lose their higher place, and rise when they acquire a higher status and receive more submissive behaviour from lower ranked individuals (McGuire and Troisi 1998). Humans are also sensitive to changes in their social place. Recall from section 7.5 (The emergence of social emotions) that we are highly social creatures, and sensitive to our place in status hierarchies as this depends on achievement and mastery. Pride is generally regarded as something desirable in children and adults, and shame is considered as something to be avoided. Pride is associated with status enhancement, shame with status loss. Abnormally low levels of serotonin have been found in depressed patients which may explain their severely pessimistic, dysfunctional attitudes. The attitudes are negatively biased views of oneself, the world and the future (Meyer et al. 2003).

The idea is that depression may have evolved as a response to lowered rank in social life, leading the individual to reduce its aspiration level and accept its place. The mismatch explanation of depression implies that we inherited a response from our ancestors that is activated when we feel outsmarted by other people. Dominic Murphy (2005, 2006) expects that the depressive response will fire frequently in the modern world because mass media bombard us with information about those who occupy better places than we have. This issue raises, therefore, further questions. Why aren't we all depressed? If not, how can we distinguish between normal sadness and genuine depression? (See section 11.3 Distinguishing normal responses from mental illness.)

Not every mismatch is a disorder

Mismatches between ancestral and current environment are considered to be important evolutionary causes of psychopathology. They may be explained by cultural evolution overtaking biological evolution such that biology has been unable to keep up with rapidly evolving culture. The mismatch problem is not only involved in mental disorders such as phobias or depression, but also in 'lifestyle diseases' such as hypertension or obesity (Brüne 2008; Gluckman and Hanson 2006).

Here, we focus on a mismatch problem that we met earlier in Chapter 10 (Culture in evolution) under the title of 'gene–culture coevolution'. Our ancestors spent the most part of their evolution as hunter-gatherers. However, from about 10,000 years ago, climate conditions and major changes in the distribution of vegetation and animals led them to adopt the new practices of domesticating cattle and cultivating plants. You will recall from section 10.4 (How culture is incorporated in evolutionary theory) that cultural practices can modify natural selection processes in human environments, thereby affecting some selected human genes.

The dairy culture was initiated some 10,000 years ago with the domestication of sheep, goats, camels and cattle. The herding of animals allowed the collection of milk as a new food source. To absorb milk, our ancestors needed to have the enzyme lactase in the gut which enables digestion of the sugar lactose found in milk. Babies can digest lactose because the enzyme lactase breaks it down into absorbable glucose and galactose. In most human adults the capacity to digest lactose disappears after weaning. But a genetic capacity of adult humans to digest milk sugar evolved independently in populations with a long history of dairy-farming and milk-drinking, and resulted in a condition known as 'lactase persistence' (Ennatah et al. 2008). This condition evolved in northern European, the Middle East, and sub-Saharan African populations, but not in Asian populations.

lactose intolerance
incapacity to digest milk sugar resulting in bloating, gas and diarrhoea.

Lactose intolerance exemplifies a mismatch between an ancestral environment where lactose digestion after weaning was unknown, and a modern environment where dairy-farming people exposed themselves to a strong selection pressure for lactase persistence. The remarkable thing is that Western medical textbooks often define the inability to digest lactose as a metabolic disorder ('adult hypolactasia'). But from an evolutionary point of view, this inability is normal, that is, adaptive, and shared by 70 per cent of the world's population. It only emerges in an environment that differs from the one to which most people are adapted (Gluckman et al. 2009). This example illustrates that by transforming our environment we create mismatches. It also shows that such mismatches make it difficult to define disorder. For, we cannot conclude that the major part of the human race has this disorder because it lacks the enzyme lactase, a lack that has no consequences for their health and fitness.

11.5 Summary

- An evolutionary definition of mental disorder implies, first, failure of an adaptive trait to perform its naturally selected function, and, second, significant harm to the individual as well as the environment, judged by the standards of present culture.

- Evolutionary psychology helps to distinguish normal responses to unfortunate events from genuine disorders. For example, sadness should be considered a naturally selected response to situations of loss such as the death of loved ones, and not to be confused with depressive disorder.

- Natural selection is unable to eliminate mental illness, so we may suppose that it is somehow adaptive. Three theories may explain this issue. The dopamine theory proposes that human migration out of Africa and subsequent colonisation of the world required special adaptive traits that made their mind vulnerable to mental illness. Rising levels of dopamine in human evolution are thought to be implicated in both such traits and mental illness.

- The byproduct theory explains mental illness as a maladaptive side-effect of selection for another adaptive trait like creativity.

- The mismatch theory explains mental illness as an adaptive trait that became maladaptive in the current environment.

Study questions

1. What evidence indicates that mental illness is an evolutionary paradox?

2. Which criteria can be used to distinguish normal sadness from genuine depression?

3. How does the dopamine theory explain mental illness?

4. How does the byproduct theory explain mental illness?

5. How does the mismatch theory explain mental illness?

Suggested reading

Defining mental illness

De Block, A. (2008). Why mental disorders are just mental dysfunctions (and nothing more): some Darwinian arguments. *Studies in History and Philosophy of Biological and Biomedical Sciences, 39*, 338–346.

Ereshefsky, M. (2009). Defining 'health' and 'disease'. *Studies in History and Philosophy of Biological and Biomedical Science, 40*, 221–227.

McNally, R. (2001). On Wakefield's harmful dysfunction analysis of mental disorder. *Behavioral Research and Therapy, 39*, 309–314.

Varga, S. (2011). Defining mental disorder: Exploring the 'natural function' approach. *Philosophy, Ethics, and Humanities in Medicine, 6*, 1–10.

Wakefield, J. (1992a). The concept of mental disorder: On the boundary between biological facts and social values. *American Psychologist, 47*, 373–388.

Wakefield, J. (2001). Evolutionary history versus current causal role in the definition of disorder: reply to McNally. *Behavioral Research and Therapy, 39*, 347–366.

Distinguishing normal responses from mental illness

Allen, N. and Badcock, P. ((2006). Darwinian models of depression: A review of evolutionary accounts of mood and mood disorders. *Progress in Neuro-Psychopharmacology & Biological Psychiatry, 30*, 815–826.

Hughes, V. (2011). Shades of grief: When does mourning become a mental illness that doctors should treat? *Scientific American, 304* (6), 17–18.

Nesse, R. (2000). Is depression an adaptation? *Archives of General Psychiatry, 57*, 14–20.

Nettle, D. (2004). Evolutionary origins of depression: a review and reformulation. *Journal of Affective Disorders, 81*, 91–102.

Parker, G., Fletcher, K. and Hadzi-Pavlovic, D. (2010). Is context everything to the definition of clinical depression? A test of the Horwitz and Wakefield postulate. *Journal of Affective Disorders, 136*, 1034–1038.

Wakefield, J., Horwitz, A. and Schmitz, M. (2005). Are we overpathologizing the socially anxious? Social phobia from a harmful dysfunction perspective. *Canadian Journal of Psychiatry, 50*, 317–319.

Explaining the adaptive function of mental illness

Keller, M. and Miller, G. (2006). Resolving the paradox of common, harmful, heritable mental disorders: Which evolutionary genetic models work best? *Behavioral and Brain Sciences, 29*, 385–452.

The dopamine theory of mental illness

Beyin, A. (2011). Upper Pleistocene human dispersals out of Africa: A review of the current state of the debate. *Published online, Vol. 2011, Article ID 615094, 17 pages.*

Chen, C., Burton, M. Greenberger, E. and Dmitrieva, J. (1999). Population migration and the variation of dopamine D4 receptor (DRD4) allele frequencies around the globe. *Evolution and Human Behavior, 20*, 309–324.

Fairbanks, L. (2001). Individual differences in response to a stranger: Social impulsivity as a dimension of temperament in vervet monkeys. *Journal of Comparative Psychology, 115*, 22–28.

Previc, F. (1999). Dopamine and the origins of human intelligence. *Brain and Cognition, 41*, 299–350.

The byproduct theory of mental illness

Carson, S. (2011). Creativity and psychopathology: A shared vulnerability model. *Canadian Journal of Psychiatry*, 56, 144–153.

Carson, S., Peterson, J. and Higgins, D. (2003). Decreased latent inhibition is associated with increased creative achievement in high-functioning individuals. *Journal of Personality and Social Psychology*, 85, 499–506.

Flaherty, A. (2005). Frontotemporal and dopaminergic control of idea generation and creative drive. *The Journal of Comparative Neurology*, 493, 147–153.

Nettle, D. (2006a). Schizotypy and mental health amongst poets, visual artists, and mathematicians. *Journal of Research in Personality*, 40, 876–890.

Post, F. (1994). Creativity and psychopathology: A study of 291 world-famous men. *British Journal of Psychiatry*, 165, 22–34.

Simeonova, K., Chang, K. and Ketter, T. (2005). Creativity in familial disorder. *Journal of Psychiatric Research*, 39, 623–631.

The mismatch theory of mental illness

Czajkowski, N., Kendler, K., Tambs, K. et al. (2011). The structure of genetic and environmental risk factors for phobias in women. *Psychological Medicine*, 41, 1987–1995.

Ennatah, S., Jensen, T., Nielsen, M. et al. (2011). Independent introduction of two lactase-persistence alleles into human populations reflects different history of adaptation to milk culture. *The American Journal of Human Genetics*, 82, 57–72.

Hagen, E. (1999). The functions of postpartum depression. *Evolution and Human Behavior*, 20, 325–539.

Marks, I. and Nesse, R. (1994). Fear and fitness: An evolutionary analysis of anxiety disorders. *Ethology and Sociobiology*, 15, 247–261.

Meyer, J., McMain, S., Korman, L. et al. (2003). Dysfunctional attitudes and 5-HT2 receptors during depression and self-harm. *American Journal of Psychiatry*, 160, 90–96.

Murphy, D. (2005). Can evolution explain insanity? *Biology and Philosophy*, 20, 745–766.

Nesse, R. (2005). Natural selection and the regulation of defenses. A signal detection analysis of the smoke detector principle. *Evolution and Human Behavior*, 26, 88–105.

Sloman, L., Gilbert, P. and Hasey, G. (2003). Evolved mechanisms in depression: The role and interaction of attachment and social rank in depression. *Journal of Affective Disorders*, 74, 107–121.

Reference books

Adriaens, P. and De Block, A. (Eds) (2011). *Maladapting Minds: Philosophy, Psychiatry, and Evolutionary Theory*. Oxford: Oxford University Press.

APA (2000). *Diagnostic and Statistical Manual of Mental Disorders, Fourth Edition, Text Revision*. Washington, DC: American Psychiatric Association.

Baron-Cohen, S. (Ed.) (1997). *The Maladapted Mind: Classical Readings in Evolutionary Psychopathology*. Erlbaum: Taylor & Francis.

Brüne, M. (2008). *Textbook of Evolutionary Psychiatry: The Origins of Psychopathology*. Oxford: Oxford University Press.

Horwitz, A. and Wakefield, J. (2007). *The Loss of Sadness: How Psychiatry Transformed Normal Sorrow into Depressive Disorder*. Oxford: Oxford University Press.

Runco, M. and Pritzker, S. (Eds) (1999). *Encyclopedia of Creativity. Volumes I and II*. San Diego: Academic Press.

Thain, M. (2009). *Penguin Dictionary of Human Biology*. London: Penguin Books.

12 Evolution through development

This chapter will cover:

12.1 Introduction

12.2 The rise of evo-devo

12.3 Types of developmental reorganisation

12.4 Why mammals play

12.5 How play evolved through development

12.6 Summary

Learning outcomes

By the end of this chapter, you should be able to explain:

- why egg-to-adult development is important for evolution
- how evolutionary developmental studies arose
- how developmental trajectories are reorganised
- why mammals are playful, unlike reptiles
- how play evolved through development.

12.1   Introduction

In this final chapter we focus on the combined study of evolution and development as it occurs in evolutionary developmental biology and psychology (also known as evo-devo). Why precisely is egg-to-adult development important for explaining the evolution of organisms? How did evolutionary developmental studies arise?

The development of any animal can be thought of as a time-sequence of more or less well-defined stages. Many organisms such as insects, for instance, spend most of their lifetime as eggs or larvae before emerging for a short time as an adult. Humans, on the other hand, do not simply change from egg into adult but pass through intermediate stages like childhood and adolescence, spending most of their lifetime as adults. So, developmental trajectories are susceptible to evolutionary change, or reorganisation. The question is then: how are developmental trajectories reorganised?

Sometimes, animals display novel structures like wings (insects, birds) and feathers (birds), or unusual behaviour such as play (mammals, birds). Evo-devo studies attempt to explain these novelties as the result of developmental reorganisation. While biologists are mainly interested in explaining morphological structures, psychologists are more interested in cognition and behaviour. We focus therefore on the novelty of play behaviour. Its novelty refers to the fact that unlike other animals, only mammals and birds play. The evolutionary paradox of playfulness is that it does not benefit fitness, yet acquired a role in the development of individuals. Why did play arise? How did play evolve through development?

Human childhood allows youngsters to play abundantly. In our complex society, however, children are at the same time expected to acquire skills and knowledge which refines into schooling with its connotation of discipline. What makes schooling and playing incompatible? What happens if children are deprived of play?

12.2   The rise of evo-devo

Why is egg-to-adult development important for evolution?

You may recall that we have touched already on the issue of development and evolution in section 1.5 (Neuroscience). Comparative neurobiologists were used to viewing brain evolution as the transformation of adult brains over time, but this is clearly not what happened. In order to understand how brains evolved, it is necessary to analyse in different species the stages of the developing brain, from baby to adult (Northcutt 2001). It has been found, for example, that embryonic tissues gave rise to many new features of vertebrates, including endocrine organs, large parts of the skull, jaws and nerves. The implication is that evolution cannot change one kind of adult brain directly into another. Rather, evolving a new brain can only proceed by changing the egg-to-adult developmental trajectory over a period of generations.

A satisfactory theory of evolution should therefore include, first, an account of how fitness differences cause changes at the level of populations, and, second, an account of how developmental trajectories produce different phenotypes on which natural selection can act (Arthur 2011). The standard evolutionary theory assumes

evo-devo

shorthand for evolutionary developmental biology.

developmental bias

the tendency to constrain or expand the way embryos develop into adults..

that the production of variation, or different individuals, is random. This assumption has been challenged in **evo-devo** because variants available to natural selection are not entirely random. Evolution is, rather, channelled through development that may constrain or expand the production of variant phenotypes. The technical term for this tendency to constrain or expand how embryos develop into adults is '**developmental bias**' (Arthur 2004, 2011). Thus, the direction of evolutionary change may not only be determined by natural selection but rather by the interaction between selection and developmental bias.

An example illustrates how a developmental constraint may influence the direction of evolutionary change. In chimpanzees an infant's skull passes easily through the birth canal, but in *Homo sapiens* the fit became so tight that further increases in relative brain size required changes in development (Striedter 2005). Humans have circumvented this childbirth constraint in part by having their brain grow more after birth than it does in chimpanzees. This constraint in development helps to explain why human neonates are so helpless, why human childhood is unusually long, why children require more parental care than in other species, and why the evolution of human sociality is more advanced than in many other social species. In section 12.3 (Types of developmental reorganisation) we will discuss how developmental bias may influence the trajectory from egg to adult. Let us first focus on the fusion of evolutionary and developmental biology.

The connection between development and evolution

development

the progressive series of changes in structure, function, and behaviour patterns that occur over the lifespan of an organism.

In the history of biology, the term 'evolution' had different meanings (Richards 1992). In the eighteenth century, 'evolution' – literally: unrolling a scroll, or roll of papyrus, parchment, or paper which one used for writing and reading – referred to 'the unfolding of an embryo'. Because 'evolution' was already used in embryology, Darwin preferred the term 'descent with modification'. After a period in which the words **development** and evolution were used interchangeably, 'evolution' began its new life as a term for the change in appearance, or gene frequencies, of populations and species over generations. And the term 'development' referred to the process by which a fertilised egg becomes an adult.

ontogeny

the process of development from fertilised egg to adult.

In the nineteenth century, Ernst Haeckel (1866) proposed a connection between development and evolution, as summarised in his phrase: '**ontogeny** is the brief and rapid **recapitulation** of phylogeny' (1866, Vol. 2: 300). That is, changes over the lifetime of an individual recapitulate changes in the evolutionary history of a species. Whereas Haeckel proposed that descendants recapitulate the *adult* stages of their ancestors, other embryologists insisted that descendants pass through the *embryonic* stages. In the early history of evo-devo, much attention was devoted to recapitulation as it meant a revolutionary blending of evolutionary and developmental themes. However, Haeckel's belief that each animal, in the course of its development, repeats the evolutionary history of its ancestors, has since been corrected on two essential points.

recapitulation

the idea that development of the individual (ontogeny) repeats the evolution of species (phylogeny).

First, it is thought today that the development of the more complex animal recapitulates only some of the features of its less complex relative, and thus, presumably, of their last common ancestor. For example, dog and human embryos look very similar because they show features that derive from their common descent. Both dog and human embryos possess rudimentary gill slits as a result of their shared aquatic ancestry. Gill slits are openings in the gill – the respiratory

terrestrial

referring to animals that spend most of their time on the ground rather than in the air, water or trees.

organ of aquatic animals – through which water flows. Thus, dogs and humans go through an embryonic stage that reflects an important event – the transition from water to land (Box 12.1) – that occurred during the evolution of their marine ancestors. But for the rest, **terrestrial** vertebrates develop along divergent trajectories (Arthur 2011).

BOX 12.1 The transition from water to land

Aspects of the embryonic development of an individual are known to reflect important events that occurred during the evolution of its ancestors. How does human embryonic development reflect the transition from water to land? We focus first on the evolutionary transition and then on human embryonic development. The conquest of land by vertebrates is thought to have taken place in the Devonian and the Carboniferous period between 385 and 318 mya (Laurin 2010). To make sense of these periods, you may wish to take a look at Figure 3.1 (The geological timescale). Why did aquatic animals come on to land? Various hypotheses have been proposed but they are difficult to test. One hypothesis holds that the new environment was a potential food resource which required a set of new features such as limbs instead of fins to capture prey on land. A second hypothesis suggests that our distant ancestors crawled onto land to raise their body temperature by basking in the sun. A third hypothesis proposes that during the Devonian and Carboniferous periods water environments were inhabited by large predators which made land a much safer place.

Life in this new environment would have been difficult for aquatic animals. What kind of adaptations were involved? The change from aquatic to terrestrial life required that fins evolved into limbs. It required also

a new respiratory system for consuming oxygen to be used for metabolism. Oxygen as it is present in water and air, can enter the body surface simply by diffusion (Schmidt-Rhaesa 2007). For example, flatworms have no respiratory system but their body surface allows simple diffusion of oxygen. But large animals depend on the evolution of circulatory systems that distribute oxygen throughout the body with the help of carriers such as haemoglobin. Respiratory systems functioning in water are called 'gills', while those in air are called 'lungs'.

The loss of gills and the acquisition of lungs can be regarded as an adaptation for living on land. How is this reflected in human embryonic development? To answer that question, we follow a small part of Neil Shubin's argument in his exciting study *Your Inner Fish: A journey into the 3.5 billion-year history of the human body* (2008). Human life starts as a fertilised egg and then develops from a single cell into a cluster of cells that looks like a tube. After a few weeks, the front end of the tube becomes thick and folds over the body. This big blob will later turn into a head. Four swellings that develop around the base of the big blob will become the throat. Each swelling, or gill arch will form different tissues (Figure 12.1; for more details, see Moore and Persaud 2008; Schoenwolf et al. 2009).

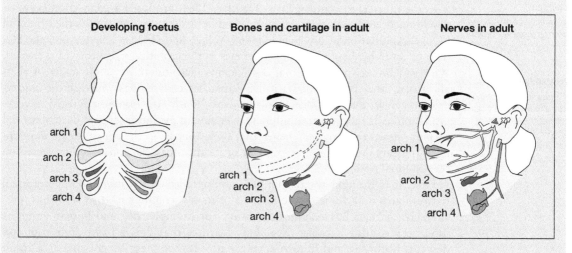

Figure 12.1 The four gill arches from an embryo to an adult

Source: Shubin (2008)

The first arch forms the upper and lower jaws, two ear bones, as well as the supporting blood vessels and muscles. The second arch forms the third ear bone, a throat bone, and muscles that control facial expression. The third arch forms bones, muscles, and nerves lower in the throat which are used to swallow food. The fourth arch forms the lowest parts of the throat which include the larynx and the supporting blood vessels and muscles.

The developing foetus on the left in Figure 12.1 shows four arches as well as four indentations. Shubin argues that fish embryos have the same indentations that will open up to form the spaces between gills where water is flowing. In humans, these indentations normally are sealed. To conclude, each head from a fish to a human shares the four arches in its developmental trajectory.

Second, Haeckel stated not only that 'ontogeny recapitulates phylogeny' but also that 'phylogeny causes ontogeny'. This belief about the direction of causation assumes that development plays a passive role, depending entirely on what happens in evolution. Walter Garstang (1922) was the first to correct this one-way causation, summarised in his phrase: 'ontogeny does not recapitulate phylogeny, it creates it' (1922: 98). The correction implied that the evolution of species could only occur through an embryonic form rather than through changes in considerably different adult forms. As Garstang (1922: 99) put it: 'The first bird was hatched from a reptile's egg'. Since evolution cannot change an adult reptile directly into an adult bird, it can only proceed by changing the egg-to-adult trajectory over a period of generations. This view that evolution results from heritable changes in development was mostly lost in the 1940s when the Modern Synthesis of evolutionary biology and population genetics constituted a new theoretical framework (Gilbert 2010).

The timeline of evo-devo

How did evo-devo studies arise after Haeckel's fusion of evolutionary and developmental themes? Figure 12.2 depicts the timeline of evo-devo as reconstructed by Love and Raff (2003). The central line, coming from Darwin's evolution theory (1859) and Haeckel's recapitulation idea (1866), runs to the Modern Synthesis (1940s) and further down to the ongoing synthesis of evolutionary and developmental studies. You may recall that we discussed the Modern Synthesis in section 1.3 (Biology) and section 10.4 (How culture is incorporated in evolutionary theory).

The left-hand line in Figure 12.2 highlights how nineteenth-century comparative embryology ended up in evo-devo studies. The rediscovery of Mendelian genetics in 1900 drove a wedge between development and evolution. Genes were now what mostly mattered in evolution while embryos were merely regarded as vehicles that carried genes from one generation to another. Thus embryology became separated from evolutionary biology and the Modern Synthesis. The discovery of the role of DNA in 1953 – molecular genetics – did not bring them together. Comparative evolutionary embryology – see bold arrows in Figure 12.2 – is considered as a key source of the current evo-devo research agenda.

Why did embryology become separated from evolutionary biology and the Modern Synthesis? Recall from section 1.3 (Biology) that Weismann introduced a distinction between the germ line and soma (or body) which rendered inheritance of acquired characteristics a logical impossibility. Weismann's claim that somatic changes could not influence the germ line served as a rationale for evolutionary biologists to study heredity in isolation from development. Embryologists who believed

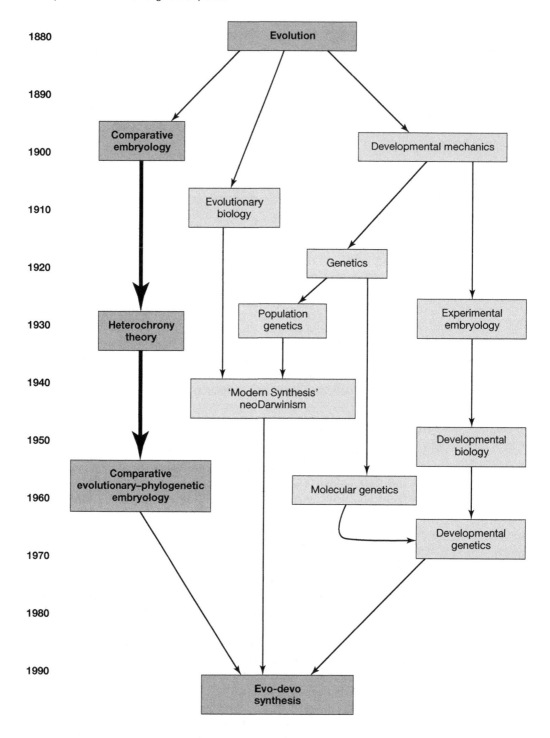

Figure 12.2 The timeline of evo-devo

Source: Love and Raff (2003)

that heredity involves more than the inheritance of genes from parents, did not share this view. That is why a dispute arose about a broad versus narrow conception of heredity (Figure 12.3; Amundson 2005).

The early stages of embryological development reflect heredity that is shared with remote ancestors. That is, early embryological traits like gill slits which we share with all vertebrates, are inherited from our fish ancestors. Other traits like **bipedalism** and reduced hair cover are shared with our human ancestors. The individual differences that we inherit only from our parents appear late in development. Thus the embryological and developmental stages that we pass through, reveal our hereditary ancestry.

This broad conception of heredity was drastically narrowed in the early twentieth century due to the discovery of chromosomes, genes and DNA. Heredity was now considered to be the transmission of traits, or representatives of traits, such as genes, between generations. This narrow conception of heredity excluded both the developmental process and the connection of the organism with its ancestors. It focused on phenotypic traits of succeeding generations as they depend on genes.

bipedalism
ability to walk or run on two feet in an upright position as in humans and birds (see p. 338).

quadrupedalism
having a four footed means of locomotion.

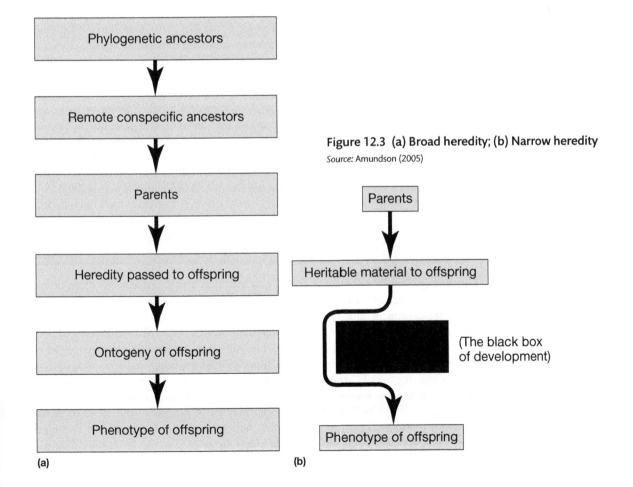

Figure 12.3 (a) Broad heredity; (b) Narrow heredity
Source: Amundson (2005)

In the late 1970s, Stephen Gould's book *Ontogeny and Phylogeny* (1977) renewed the interest in nineteenth-century embryology, particularly in uncovering developmental mechanisms underlying evolution. The major proposed cause was heterochrony or, change in the timing of developmental events. For example, the time when organisms reach sexual maturity may accelerate under certain conditions. We discuss this topic in the next section.

The right line in Figure 12.2 illustrates how developmental mechanics and experimental embryology – being divorced from genetics and the Modern Synthesis – turned into developmental biology. Developmental mechanics was focused on finding the molecules and processes that caused the visible changes in embryos. Experimental embryology added the experimental method to observation in the study of embryos, with the intention of discovering how embryonic cells respond to disruptions. In recent years, it has become customary to speak of developmental biology as the discipline that studies embryonic and other developmental processes (Gilbert 2010).

regulatory gene
a kind of gene that turns another gene or group of genes on or off.

More recently, population genetics of the 1940s has been followed by the emergence of developmental genetics. While population genetics attempts to explain variations within species that enabled certain adult individuals to reproduce more frequently, developmental genetics emphasises the **regulatory genes** that are responsible for determining body patterns. Regulatory genes are genes that switch other genes on or off. One set of these genes are so-called *Hox* genes, discovered in the late 1970s, first found in fruit flies and later on in other animals. These regulatory genes are remarkably stable across species, suggesting deep links of homology among multi-cellular organisms (Papini 2008). The origin of *Hox* genes will be discussed in Box 12.2 (The Cambrian Explosion).

The lines in Figure 12.2 converge in the ongoing evo-devo synthesis with its rapidly growing literature. As evolutionary developmental biology attempts to understand how evolution and development affect one another, it has stimulated evolutionary psychology to incorporate a developmental perspective (for a discussion about evo-devo, see Lickliter and Honeycutt 2003). It is now widely accepted that a major path to evolutionary change is through developmental trajectories. Thus ontogeny plays a central role in shaping cognition and behaviour (Quartz 2003).

12.3 Types of developmental reorganisation

The development of any animal can be considered as a time-sequence of more or less well-defined stages. Many organisms spend most of their lifetime as eggs or larvae and only a short time as adults (e.g. insects). Humans, on the other hand, do not simply change from egg to adult, but pass through intermediate stages like childhood and adolescence. Developmental trajectories are thus subject to evolutionary change. As noted previously, the reason is that evolution cannot change one adult organism directly into another one; it can only achieve this by changing the developmental trajectory. So, evolution through development is a matter of developmental reorganisation.

Wallace Arthur (2004, 2011; see also Gilbert 2010) proposed four types of developmental reorganisation that can occur: changes in time, place, amount and type. The technical terms for these types of changes are:

- **heterochrony** (literally 'other timing') refers to changes in the timing of developmental events;

- **heterotopy** (literally 'other place,) refers to changes in the placement of the organism's body parts;
- **heterometry** (literally 'other amount') refers to changes in the size of the organism's body or body parts; and
- **heterotypy** (literally 'other type') refers to the origin of new phenotypes.

We explain the first three types of developmental reorganisation shortly with examples and, then, discuss heterotypy extensively in section 12.4 (Why mammals play) and 12.5 (How play evolved through development).

The four types of developmental reorganisation

Heterochrony

heterochrony

change in the timing of developmental events. For example, the time when organisms reach sexual maturity may accelerate under certain conditions.

This type of developmental reorganisation – **heterochrony**, referring to changes in the timing of important developmental events – can be demonstrated with two examples, one about centipedes (Arthur 2011) and one about humans (Hochberg 2009). All centipedes have long periods of embryogenesis. It takes some weeks before the hatchling emerges from the egg and a year to reach adulthood. Centipedes are segmented earth worms that may differ remarkably from one another. In some species the hatchling has seven fully developed leg-bearing segments with the adult segment being reached after a year. So there is a temporal relationship between hatching and segmentation. In other species of earth worms, the hatchling has the full adult complement of segments. Why do these species differ in their developmental trajectory in terms of fitness? Why has segmentation accelerated in the latter species? An adaptive hypothesis suggests that the former species are surface-dwellers that inhabit the leaf-litter layer of terrestrial ecosystems. These kind of earth worms can be found under stones and rotting logs. The other species, however, is subterranean and mostly found in the upper layers of the soil. If it hatched with only seven segments, its burrowing capacity would be considerably impaired.

Our second example of heterochrony is about humans. You may recall from section 5.3 (Origin of the human family) that life-history theory attempts to explain and predict life-histories as trade-offs in the allocation of time and resources over the lifespan of an organism. Important trade-offs are, for instance, between mating and parenting or between present and future reproduction. These trade-offs determine the timing of birth, amount of parenting and pace of growth. In life-history theory, phases and transitions between phases such as puberty, have a central place because multiple endocrine mechanisms evolved to activate physiological and behavioural traits at the right time when children pass from one phase to another.

In the course of human evolution, the number of phases has gradually increased (Hochberg 2009). Some 3–4 mya the extinct species *Australopithecus afarensis* (see Figure 3.5 The tree of primates) had only two pre-adult phases: infancy and juvenility. About 1,900,000 years ago *Homo habilis* developed an additional life-history phase: childhood. Another life-history phase with its pubertal growth spurt and rapid sexual maturity emerged some 100,000 years ago: adolescence. So, *Homo sapiens* passes through four prolonged pre-adult phases: (1) infancy, which lasts 30–36 months, with rapid growth of the brain; (2) childhood, lasting 2–6 years, with slowing growth rate; (3) juvenility, lasting 6–11 years, with slowing growth rate, and (4) adolescence, which lasts for 11–15 years, with growth acceleration, culminating in fertility at an average age of 18.

Life-history theory is relevant for evo-devo studies because changes in the timing of important developmental events – that is, heterochrony – may occur in transitions between phases. Consider puberty, the transition from juvenility to adolescence when children first enter the world of mating and reproduction. The original prediction was that early stress in the family would lead to premature onset of puberty, as part of children's strategy directed to current instead of future reproduction. Recall that we discussed life-history theory and particularly the question of how childhood affects later reproduction in section 5.3 (Origin of the human family).

Puberty research focused then on the effects of father absence on the age at menarche – i.e. the first incidence of menstruation in a female, marking the onset of puberty – although the original idea was that children should be sensitive to more than just a present or absent father. Later studies on puberty timing in both sexes show that stressful and negative family relationships tend to accelerate the onset of puberty in girls only, and to predispose to earlier initiation of sexual activity (Belsky 2007; Del Giudice and Belsky 2011). Other findings demonstrate that girls with early menarche had greater preferences for infants than girls with late menarche. Early menarche was found to be significantly associated with father absence from home during childhood and adolescence. The implication is that development in these girls accelerates towards reproduction, and that an early interest in infants may help to acquire parenting skills (Maestripieri and Roney 2006).

menarche

the first incidence of menstruation in a female, marking the onset of puberty.

Heterotopy

heterotopy

food consumers such as animals , depending on plants and particularly prey to obtain energy.

This type of developmental reorganisation – **heterotopy**, referring to changes in the spatial arrangement of the developing organism – can be explained by the following example. A typical fish such as a salmon or trout is bilaterally symmetrical in its external morphology, an ancestral trait that is also shared by most land vertebrates. In contrast, flatfish embryos such as turbot or plaice have a unique morphology in terms of left–right asymmetry. Flatfish embryos are bilaterally symmetrical in that the place of their eyes is similar to other fish. They are born with eyes in the normal position but at a certain stage in their development, one eye starts to move across the head, ending up next to the other eye. In the course of their evolution, this anatomy was an adaptive solution because lying on one side on the seafloor and covering oneself with sand, enabled flatfish to capture unsuspecting prey (Arthur 2011). Note that the molecular control of eye asymmetry in flatfish is not yet fully understood.

Flatfish eyes are also an example of convergent evolution in which unrelated species independently arrive at a similar solution to the same problem. Like flatfish, rays have also evolved flat bodies for swimming on the seafloor. But instead of migrating eyes, they have eyes on the upper surface of their bodies that evolved upwards from the sides of their heads (Zimmer 2008).

Heterometry

heterometry

change in the size of the organism's body or body parts. For example, adult humans are only 1.25 times the size of chimps. This may explain an increased brain size of 500 cm² but not the actual size of 1350 cm². So, the increased size of the human brain is a real heterometry.

This type of developmental reorganisation – **heterometry** – refers to situations in which the amount or size of something has changed. Recall from section 8.2 (Evolution of the brain) that in the course of evolution the size of the human brain has increased more than threefold (Passingham 2008). The size of an average adult human brain is about 1,350 cm² whereas the size of an average adult chimpanzee brain is about 400 cm². This increase should be controlled for the confounding role of body size. If body size increases, we may expect that the size of body organs also increases. Humans are indeed larger than chimps but not that much. The difference in average weight between adult humans and chimps is such that humans are only 1.25 times the size of chimps. This may explain an increased brain size of 500 cm^2 but not the actual size of 1,350 cm^2. In other words, the increased size of the human brain is not a side-effect of larger body size but a real heterometry (Arthur 2011).

Understanding of the developmental basis of the increased brain size in the human species is in its infancy. One handicap is, for example, that all brain sizes refer to adults and not to juveniles. The available information on juvenile brains in fossil humans is very limited. In order to understand how brains evolved through development, it is necessary to analyse in different species the developmental stages of the brain, from baby to adult.

Heterotypy

heterotypy
origin of new phenotypes. For example, birds' feathers are a novelty as they did not directly evolve from reptilian scales. Similarly, play is a novel trait in mammals and birds, not or rarely to be found in reptiles.

This is a type of developmental reorganisation – **heterotypy** – in which evolution produces novel phenotypes through development. We discuss, first, some sorts of novelty and then, briefly, a classic question in evolutionary developmental biology: how did birds' feathers originate? The origin of feathers is not a natural topic for evolutionary psychologists, but the example is instructive for how evo-devo explanation works. Then, we move on to the novelty of play.

Different sorts of novelty

We have seen above that 'developmental bias' is the tendency to constrain or expand the way embryos develop into adults. The origin of novel phenotypes is a true case in which the developmental trajectory is reorganised. In standard evolutionary theory, novel phenotypes were treated as variants. But evo-devo studies made it clear that one should distinguish between variation and innovation. Evolutionary novelties include morphological structures like skin appendages (e.g. feathers, hair) and unusual behaviours (e.g. play).

Cambrian Explosion
an event in the Cambrian period (542–488 million years ago [mya]) that produced the body plans of animals. Around 35 body plans exist today, out of the original 100 that are recorded in rocks.

Focusing on morphological structures, biologists have identified different sorts of novelty (Pigliucci and Müller 2010). The first one concerns the origin of body plans, an evolutionary event that occurred in the Cambrian period (542–488 mya) and therefore is known as the **Cambrian Explosion** (Box 12.2 The Cambrian Explosion). The second sort of novelty refers to discrete novel elements added to an existing body plan, such as insect wings, avian feathers, turtle carapace (shell), or the light organ of fireflies. The third sort of novelty concerns major change of an existing body plan character like the narwhal tusk or beetle horns.

BOX 12.2 The Cambrian Explosion

The Cambrian Explosion is an event in the Cambrian period (542–488 mya) which produced the different body architectures as we may recognise them today, for instance, in sponges, insects and primates (Raff 1996). Recall from section 8.2 (Evolution of the brain), that body architecture may be symmetrical or asymmetrical. Symmetry reflects the lifestyle of animals. If animals spend their life attached to a rock or on the seabed, they tend to be asymmetrical (e.g. sponges) or radially

symmetrical (e.g. hydras). Animals that are mostly on the move are bilaterally symmetrical (e.g. fishes, mammals). Furthermore, animals may have an exoskeleton (e.g. insects, turtles) or endoskeleton (e.g. primates and other vertebrates). Around 35 body plans exist today, out of the original 100 that are recorded in rocks. The fossil animals, which included the alarming *Anomalocaris* (see Figure 1.5), were first presented to a broader public by Stephen Gould (1991b) in his *Wonderful Life: The Burgess*

Shale and the Nature of History, and by Simon Conway Morris (1999) with his *The Crucible of Creation: The Burgess Shale and the Rise of Animals.*

What did this explosion, or big bang of animal evolution ignite? Many ideas have been proposed as to the causes of the Explosion. One idea refers to oxygen production. Recall from section 10.4 (How culture is incorporated in evolutionary theory) that we discussed niche construction theory. An example of global niche construction is oxygen production by photosynthetic bacteria that contributed to the Earth's 21 per cent oxygen in the atmosphere. It is thought that two trends in the distant past were linked: the explosion of oxygen about 2.5 billion years ago, and then the Cambrian Explosion of animal evolution about 540 mya (see Figure 10.3). Other ideas for explaining how animal body plans originated and evolved came after the discovery

in the late 1970s that most or all animals share a special family of genes, the **Hox genes** which are important for determining body patterns. Early studies of fruitflies revealed that these genes controlled the identity of different body segments along the body axis. Since then, *Hox* genes have been found in all sorts of animals, including vertebrates.

To conclude, both the discovery of fossil animals from the Cambrian Explosion and the discovery of *Hox* genes have stimulated evo-devo studies enormously. The impact of the discovery of *Hox* genes was first presented to a broader public by Sean Carroll (2005) in his *Endless Forms Most Beautiful: The New Science of Evo Devo,* followed by *The Making of the Fittest: DNA and the Ultimate Forensic Record of Evolution* (2006), and *Remarkable Creatures: Epic Adventures in the Search for the Origin of Species* (2009).

How did feathers evolve through development?

Hox genes

set of regulatory genes that determine body patterns. These genes were discovered in the late 1970s. Regulatory genes are remarkably stable across species, suggesting deep links of homology among multi-cellular organisms.

We now focus on the second sort of novelty – defined as a new element such as feathers added to the body structure that has no homologous counterpart in the ancestral species. Powered flight emerged independently three times in the history of vertebrate animals: in (extinct) pterosaurs, bats and birds. In ground-up theories it is thought that birds' flight evolved through a series of steps: running, leaping, jumping from heights and finally flying. In trees-down theories it is believed that flight began as gliding between trees and then gradually changed into flying with wing strokes (Chatterjee 1997; Shipman 1998).

Flight involved many changes in the anatomy and physiology of birds such as hollow bones, air sacs, and the new feature of feathers. While bats use a broad surface of their skin as parachutes or airfoils, birds are unique in that the major part of their flight surface consists of feathers. Feather-like structures have been found on fossils of a group of dinosaurs that includes birds which suggests that the initial function of feathers was not for flight but probably for insulation and other functions such as camouflage or sexual display (Prum and Brush 2003; Carroll et al. 2005; Xing Xu 2006). As only highly evolved feathers – that is, asymmetrical feathers with a closed vane – are considered useful for flying, they have apparently been co-opted (recruited) for their new aerodynamic function.

How did these amazing structures evolve through development? It has long been thought that feathers emerged as a modification of reptilian scales. However, feathers grow from pits or follicles of the skin and no intermediate stage between the two has been found. Research findings show that avian feathers have no clear homologous structures in ancestral animals, indicating that they are genuine novelties. What is more, biologists found new evidence that developmental processes enable a view on how feathers evolved in the distant past.

Richard Prum and Alan Brush (e.g. 2002, 2003) produced evidence of how feathers evolved through a series of developmental stages, each marked by a novelty as a mechanism of growth. Advances at one stage provided the basis for the next novelty. The authors' theory is based on a new appreciation of what precisely feathers are and how they develop in modern birds. Although feathers show a wide variety and serve many functions, most of them fall into two types: plumulaceous, or downy, feathers with the property of lightweight thermal insulation, and pennaceous feathers with their tightly closed vanes and capacity to create aerodynamic surfaces of the wings and tail. New fossil discoveries also provided additional insights into how dinosaurs evolved feathers at each hypothesised stage. The authors suggest that each stage evolved in a particular group of dinosaurs, using similarities between primitive feather predictions and the shapes of fossil appendages.

12.4 Why mammals play

Novelties in evolution may refer to discrete novel elements added to an existing body plan like feathers, but also to unusual behaviours such as play. Play appears to be idle behaviour, unable to improve the fitness of animals, and therefore likely to be weeded out by natural selection. But play – which is thought to have originated in mammals and birds that emerged between 200 to 150 mya – still exists, making it an intriguing phenomenon that demands explanation. Before we examine the origin of play with the help of the surplus resource theory, we first need to know what play precisely is. Recall that we have already touched on this question in Chapter 8 (Box 8.2 Is play necessary for survival?). We recap the main points and then discuss the surplus resource theory.

What is play?

Nucleus Accumbens (NAcc)

brain structure in the dopaminergic system, involved in the rewarding actions of athletic and intellectual accomplishment, play, aesthetic enjoyment, orgasm, and many drugs of abuse.

We recognise play when we see it or play ourselves, but it is not easy to capture play in scientific terms. Among the characteristics that may be typical for play are: pleasurable, stimulation-seeking, exuberant, energy-consuming, self-motivated, awkward, immature, exaggerated, spontaneous, precocious, juvenile, non-serious, free of adult-imposed rules, non-goal directed.

You may recall from Box 8.2 (Is play necessary for survival?) that Gordon Burghardt (2005, 2010) proposed an influential list of five criteria for defining behaviour as playful. We now recapitulate and discuss the criteria.

BOX 12.3 Play and pleasure of the brain

Does pleasure have an adaptive function? Contemporary neuroscientists say yes (e.g. Kringelbach and Berridge 2010). They argue that pleasure responses are so conspicuous in the life of humans and other animals, and its neural mechanisms are so well developed in the brain that the capacity for pleasure may be thought to be a naturally selected trait. A vast literature demonstrates that the activity of dopaminergic neurons in a brain area known as the **Nucleus Accumbens (NAcc)**, plays an essential role in mediating the pleasure we derive, for example, from juice and tasty food. But dopamine also motivates us to engage in social interactions (Watson et al. 2010). The best evidence comes from studies of social bonding in small rodents, called voles. These animals are monogamous, forming strong pair-bonds for which the release of dopamine is critical. Similar findings apply to the social reward circuitry in primate brains. Malfunction of these circuits is associated with social anxiety and autism.

Social play – also known as rough-and-tumble play – is the earliest form of play between peers in mammalian species. Human children, like all young mammals, are often engaged in running, chasing one another, climbing and play fighting. The capacity to engage in playing socially is an important indicator of healthy development. Lack or deprivation of social play indicates neuropsychiatric disorders like autism, schizophrenia or attentional deficit hyperactivity disorder (ADHD). Playing in the sense of having fun is rewarding in itself, but also essential for the development of social skills (Trezza et al. 2010).

Empirical studies support the idea that playing with another individual is fun. However, this is only likely when the other individual reciprocates the initiative. Studies further show that the dopaminergic brain system is involved in social play. You may recall from section 11.4 (Explaining the adaptive function of mental illness) that this system has different pathways. One of them is the mesolimbic dopamine pathway, running from the ventral tegmental area to the nucleus accumbens or, 'pleasure centre' of the brain (see Figure 11.3 Four dopamine pathways in the brain). This pathway is involved in motivational drive, including the motivation to play, while locally secreted substances in the Nucleus Accumbens are involved in the pleasure of play (Vanderschuren 2010). Play is one of the natural ways to trigger mesolimbic dopamine neurons to release dopamine. Other natural ways include intellectual accomplishment, aesthetic enjoyment and orgasm (Stahl 2004).

The first criterion is that the performance of the behaviour is not fully functional in the form or context in which it is expressed. Play may have some immediate function but does not contribute to survival and reproductive fitness. For example, when young animals are running around without being chased by a predator, it is not fully functional. The immediate function may, for instance, be that the exercise improves the oxygen-carrying capacity of the blood.

The second criterion for defining play is that the behaviour is spontaneous, voluntary, pleasurable, rewarding, or done for its own sake (Box 12.3 Play and pleasure of the brain). Play is thus intrinsically worthwhile, not done for extrinsic rewards. Only one of the overlapping terms needs to apply. Burghardt (2010) notes that the self-rewarding property of play may also apply to other kinds of behaviour such as mating or maternal care. But combined with the first criterion – incompletely functional in the context in which it appears – one can eliminate such behaviours.

The third criterion is that play differs from serious behaviour because it is incomplete, exaggerated, awkward or precocious. For example, play is not complete when young animals engage in nipping behaviour without really biting and hurting their playmates; it is exaggerated when youngsters chase one another far longer than in serious situations; it is awkward when the animals make mistakes; and it is precocious when behaviour patterns appear earlier in development than when the behaviour is performed seriously (e.g. fighting a rival, chasing a prey, mounting a sexual partner).

The fourth criterion is that the behaviour is performed repeatedly during a predictable period in the animal's life. One aspect related to repetition is that the animal may rehearse an action, as in object play, until it has mastered this action ('mastery play').

The fifth criterion for defining play is that the behaviour is initiated when an animal is adequately fed, healthy and free from stress. Animals will not play when they are threatened by predators, experience harsh climatic conditions, or are subject to intense social competition for food, shelter or mates.

In behavioural biology and psychology, forms of play have been divided into three categories: locomotor play, social play and object play. Locomotor play refers to play involving motor actions such as dancing, running, leaping, chasing, bouncing, rolling, hanging upside down, and so forth. Social play may refer to play-fighting or, rough-and-tumble play, hide-and-seek, peek-a-boo, fantasy, or pretend play such as 'playing doctor', and the like. Object play refers to play with sticks, stones, toys, dolls, and so on.

The surplus resource theory

Historically, play has mostly been attributed to mammals. Why? Evolutionary neuroscientist Paul MacLean (1990: 16) suggested the following answer:

> In the evolutionary transition from reptiles to mammals, three cardinal behavioural developments were (1) nursing in conjunction with maternal care, (2) audio-vocal communication for maintaining maternal–offspring contact, and (3) play.

Indeed, it makes sense to associate the origin of play with parental care because it allows offspring to be free of worries.

You may recall from section 7.4 (The neural basis of emotions) that MacLean advanced a theory that the brain consists of three gross layers – a reptilian, palaeo-mammalian and neo-mamalian brain – that evolved successively in reptiles, mammals and primates (see Figure 7.4 Paul MacLean's triune brain). MacLean derived play from parental care and supposed that it evolved along with what he called the mammalian, or emotional brain, thus making play a distinctive attribute of mammals (Burghardt 2001). MacLean, however, overlooked the frequent play in birds. Mammals and birds share extended parental care which frees the young from the demands of survival, allowing them to play. Play and parental care evolved independently in birds and mammals, and may have promoted their family and social life as well as their vocal communication (Conway Morris 2003).

Why is play not found in reptiles? Mammals descended from reptiles about 200 mya. In his study on the origins of play, Burghardt (1984) reviews evolutionary theories of play. An influential theory is the 'surplus resource theory', advanced by polymath and propagandist of Darwin's evolution theory, Herbert Spencer (1820–1903). In his *Principles of Psychology* (1899), one chapter deals with aesthetic sentiments. Before discussing this topic, Spencer poses the question of where the impulse to play comes from, as he believes that play is the precursor of aesthetics and art. Spencer states that

> inferior kinds of animals have in common the trait that all their forces are expended in fulfilling functions essential to the maintenance of life . . . But as we descend to animals of high types . . . we begin to find that time and strength are not wholly absorbed in providing for immediate needs. Better nutrition, gained by superiority, occasionally yields a surplus of vigour . . . Thus it happens that in the more-evolved creatures, there often recurs an energy somewhat in excess of immediate needs. (1899: 694, 695).

Spencer was concerned with an excess of nervous psychic energy which could be discharged in play. In later discussions, this excess or surplus has been differently referred to as hyperactivity, stored metabolic reserves, or excessive drive. The modern version of the surplus resource theory considers three factors that may help to explain why play is abundant in mammals (and birds) and rare or absent in reptiles (Burghardt 1998, 2001, 2005; Barber 1991).

KEY FIGURE Gordon Burghardt

Gordon Burghardt is professor of Evolutionary biology at the University of Chicago. His research interests are focused on chemoreception in snakes, predatory behaviour, heritability of learned behaviour, and evolution of playfulness.

Selected works

Iguanas of the World: Their Behaviour, Ecology and Conservation (1982) edited with Stanley Rand

The Genesis of Animal Play: Testing the Limits (2005)

Photo source: Gordon Burghardt

ectotherm

an animal whose body temperature is maintained by absorbing heat from the surrounding environment (e.g. reptiles). Such animals employ ectothermy.

endotherm

an animal whose body heat is generated through its own metabolic activities (e.g. mammals, birds). Such animals employ endothermy.

According to Gordon Burghardt's account (2005), the first factor refers to physiological contrasts between reptiles and mammals. Reptiles have a lower metabolic rate than mammals and are, therefore, constrained from performing vigorous, energetically expensive behaviours that are not immediately beneficial. 'Metabolic rate' is a measure of the energy used by an animal in a given time period, measured by oxygen consumption or heat production. Reptiles have about 10 per cent of the metabolic rate of a comparably sized mammal. In addition, reptiles are **ectotherms**, or animals that maintain their body temperature by absorbing heat from the surrounding environment. For example, reptiles need to bask in the sun before they are able to come into action. Ectothermy allows only a low-energy lifestyle. In contrast, mammals (and birds) are **endotherms**, or animals that can generate and maintain heat within their body independently of the environmental temperature. Endothermy allows rapid onset of vigorous activities such as pursuit of prey and play.

The second factor relevant to the occurrence of play concerns developmental contrasts between reptiles and mammals. Most neonatal reptiles, except crocodilians, are not cared for by their parents. Reptiles are born with highly functional sensory and motor systems, and must provide their own resources, avoid predators, and grow rapidly on their own. Most behaviours, necessary for survival, are functional at birth. In short, young reptiles look like and behave like miniature adults. Young mammals, on the other hand, enter the world with incomplete sensory and motor systems. Neonates have food, heat, shelter and protection provided by their parents. Mammals have a long juvenile period in which they develop and practise motor, feeding, social and anti-predator skills.

The third factor in the origin of play is psychological. Compared with young reptiles that are ready for survival at birth, mammals are born in boring, or stimulus-deprived environments and, therefore, most likely to engage in behaviour to relieve sensory deprivation and to increase arousal. If young mammals are free from the demands of survival and living in protected environments such as nests and burrows, one would expect them to show vigorous, play-like behaviour as a means to get rid of excess energy.

Thus, according to the surplus resource theory, high energy levels, sufficient extra nutrition, freedom from predation, and sensory deprivation made play-like behaviour possible. In effect, play-like behaviour was originally a byproduct of evolutionary events such as the emergence of parental care – providing animals with food and protecting them against predators – and endothermy – permitting them to use fast-acting muscles and nerves, and lead highly active lives, even at night when solar energy is absent. Once play-like behaviour occurred – when well-fed animals had a surplus of energy and needed to release it through vigorous activity – it could take another role in the maintenance and refinement of physiological and behavioural capacities during the development of individuals. Finally, play could have gained a new role in enhancing behavioural flexibility and generating new behaviours and innovations.

Burghardt (2005, 2011) labelled these three types of play in evolution as primary, secondary and tertiary. Primary play is play-like behaviour that results from non-play factors such as lack of stimulation, immature behaviour, excess metabolic energy, impulsivity and curiosity. This play-like behaviour is the first stage in the evolution of play and may be found in invertebrates as well as vertebrates. Secondary play is mainly found in mammals and birds, and has assumed an important role in helping to maintain physiological, perceptual and behavioural functions. Tertiary play is important for developing and maintaining physiological, social and cognitive skills (see Figure 12.4).

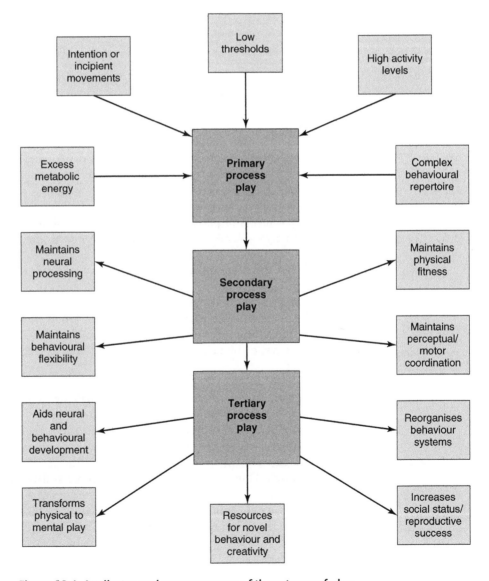

Figure 12.4 Attributes and consequences of three types of play
Source: Burghardt (2010)

To conclude, the modern surplus resource theory makes clear that play can be viewed as both a product and cause of evolutionary change. That is, play emerged as a byproduct of previous evolutionary events like parental care and endothermy, and became, later on, a source of enhanced physiological, behavioural and cognitive functions.

12.5 How play evolved through development

In section 12.2 (The rise of evo-devo) we pointed out that – in contrast to what in standard evolutionary theory is assumed – the production of variant phenotypes on which natural selection acts, is not entirely random but rather biased. For, evolution is channelled through development that may constrain or expand the way embryos develop into adults. This tendency is known as 'developmental bias' (Arthur 2004, 2011). So, the direction of evolutionary change may not only be determined by natural selection but rather by the interaction between natural selection and developmental bias. In the case of feathers, we have seen how these novel structures evolved through a series of developmental stages. In this section we examine how play in rats evolved through development.

Play fighting

Evidence of how play evolves through a series of developmental stages can be found in laboratory studies of play fighting rats. In a recent synthesis of their research findings, Sergio and Vivien Pellis (2009) provide insightful answers to many questions. One of these questions is: what are the most likely building blocks that represent the precursors of play? This question should lead us to know how immature, play-like behaviour develops into genuine play. We focus, first, on what is meant by play fighting in rats.

Recall that in behavioural biology and psychology, forms of play are divided into three categories: locomotor play, social play and object play. Play fighting in mammals differs from real fighting in that it is much more varied and incorporates elements like role reversal and self-handicapping (by larger/stronger partners) that are absent in true fighting (Fry 2005). In human children it also incorporates elements of make-believe, or fantasy as in using pretend guns or adopting roles of 'police' and 'suspect'.

Play fighting in rats is a kind of social play which involves one animal (the attacker), trying to touch the nape of the other's neck, while the recipient (the defender) uses various manoeuvres to avoid this contact. The roles of attacker and defender can alternate. Trying to touch the target and avoiding being touched is what makes play fighting pleasurable. If young rats are socially isolated for a day and deprived of play, they show increased levels of play fighting when reunited. Thus play is rewarding and some resistance to bodily contact makes it even more enjoyable. Play fighting in rats appears in the animal's behavioural repertoire at seventeen to nineteen days after birth. Its frequency shows a gradual increase, reaching a peak between thirty to forty days when they play an hour each day. Around puberty (sixty days), the frequency of play has decreased to a few minutes a day.

Social play has an important function in the juvenile period of rats (and other rodents as well as primates) because play fighting affects how rats cope with situations that require the use of social and cognitive skills. Pellis and Pellis (2009) point out that social isolation and, therefore, lack of opportunity to engage in play fighting, leads to emotional impairment. That is, by failing to fine-tune their emotional responses to the situation, individuals are unable to use their motor, social or cognitive skills effectively. The experiences that the animal acquires from playing with multiple partners may be necessary for taking into account the partner's identity when it decides how to respond.

Play fighting appears to have multiple functions. An immediate function is that play, at all ages, serves as a behavioural tool for rats to regulate how they respond to stress situations, and learn, for instance, how to avoid emotional overreactions. A delayed function of play fighting experience is allowing juveniles to become adults that are better able to cope with the unexpected events in life (Spinka et al. 2001). As animals actively seek and create unexpected situations in play, this experience reduces the fear of novel situations. In effect, it is the prefrontal cortex that dampens the activity of the amygdala – the brain structure known to be implicated in fear – thus preventing emotional overreactions (Pellis et al. 2010).

How did play fighting evolve through development?

Pellis and Pellis (2009) use a stage model that is consistent with Burghardt's model with its primary, secondary and tertiary types of play. In their account, play fighting in juvenile rats starts when the animals perform precocious sexual behaviour that occurs before its performers are capable of reproduction. The authors presume four hypothetical stages in the transformation of immature sexual behaviour into true play fighting:

- In the first stage – labelled 'incipient play' – components of sexual behaviour, particularly precopulatory elements, are expressed in a precocious manner during the first stage of the developmental trajectory.

- In the second stage, precocious sexual behaviour becomes a frequent component of the juvenile period. In this stage – labelled 'rudimentary play fighting' – juvenile interactions show only small differences with adult sexual interactions. The increased frequency of juvenile play is supposed to facilitate sexual development.

- In the third stage, some components of precopulatory sexual behaviour are elaborated during the juvenile period, increasing the differences from adult sexual behaviour. As the playful interactions differ from sexual interactions, the behaviour in this stage is labelled 'true play fighting'.

- In the fourth stage, play fighting is modified to a more exaggerated degree and co-opted (recruited) in novel, non-sexual domains of juvenile and adult life. Because play, in this stage, has become functionally uncoupled from sex, it is labelled 'emancipated play fighting'. Emancipated play fighting is retained in adulthood and used as a means to test and manipulate other individuals.

Primate mothers, unlike rodent mothers, actively play with their offspring. The remarkable thing is that mother–infant play occurs at an earlier stage than when infants play with their peers. This observation led Pellis and Pellis (2009) to pose two questions. What do primate infants gain from this play? And what is the origin of mother–infant play? To answer the first question, the authors suggest that mother–infant play seems to provide important experiences for fine-tuning the appropriate emotional responses to unexpected events. What is gained in a safe context from gentle maternal play can further be worked upon in the rough play between peers. In this view, mother–infant play, as it occurs in primates, inserts a new stage in the developmental trajectory of play, providing infants with a head start in life.

An answer to the second question would be that primates began as nocturnal and solitary living animals. You may recall from section 6.3 (The social evolution of primates) that early primates foraged solitarily and lived in social networks, characterised by sharing sleeping places and regular social interactions. Some primates alive today – e.g. lorises and pottos of Asia and Africa – have maintained this lifestyle. When mothers go foraging and 'park' their baby in a safe location, the infant has no opportunity to play with other infants. Mother–infant play is, then, a substitute for peer–peer play. When primates adopted a more social lifestyle with female kin-bonded groups, infants would have the opportunity to play also with peers.

Playing and schooling

Childhood allows youngsters to play abundantly. In our complex society, children are at the same time expected to acquire skills and knowledge, which equates to schooling with its connotation of discipline. What makes schooling and playing incompatible? What happens if children are deprived of rough-and-tumble play, or play fighting?

You may recall from section 10.5 (Cumulative cultural evolution) that human cultural traditions differ from animal traditions. An important difference is that in human culture successive improvements over generations tend to accumulate. This cumulative process as it occurs in science and technology, is also known as the ratchet effect with the implication that we don't need to reinvent the wheel (Tomasello 1999). Each generation starts with the knowledge of the previous one, thus allowing a rapid expansion of knowledge over time. This ratcheting accelerated with the advent of agriculture about 10,000 years ago when the nomadic lifestyle of hunter-gatherers made way for the sedentary lifestyle. However, we did not abandon nomadic life completely – witness the daily home–work travels, and recurrent holiday treks.

As we said before, learning on the job how to make a living required years of training but as the ratchet advanced, the expanding culture required instruction 'out of context' (Bjorklund and Bering 2002). For example, children readily acquire concepts of numeracy (i.e. the ability to determine correctly small sets of items), counting small sets of items, and simple arithmetic. But cultural inventions like reading, mathematics, technology and science, are rarely learned without instruction. In other words, we cannot assume that all children are intrinsically motivated to learn out-of-context skills or abstract knowledge domains. Schooling in the sense of spending most of the days in classrooms, sitting in chairs and listening to what teachers are saying, may then be at odds with young children's urge to play.

It has, therefore, been suggested that high rates of children's physical play have led to many wrongly diagnosed cases of **attentional deficit hyperactivity disorder** (**ADHD**). The overall percentage of diagnosed kids ranges from 8 to 16 per cent depending on perceived degree of severity. In 2008 more than ten million American

Attention Deficit Hyperactivity Disorder (ADHD)
mental disorder characterised by the three core symptoms of inattention, hyperactivity and impulsiveness.

children were being chronically medicated with drugs to reduce hyperactivity. These drugs have the unintended effect of making young brains sensitive to new drugs. Evolutionary neuroscientist Jaak Panksepp (1998a, 2008) argues that most of ADHD reflects a cultural problem rather than a biological disease. One can easily imagine that impulsive individuals with rapidly shifting attentional responses would have been excellent hunters. A trait such as distractability, for example, may be useful when it comes to efficiently monitoring a shifting environment.

Somehow, educational systems seem unable to make room for physical play. They need to know, however, that the urge to play, particularly rough-and-tumble play, is a homologous trait that children share with all other young mammals (Panksepp 2008). This urge stimulates the mammalian brain to learn about the world as well as from unexpected experiences with other individuals. The urge to play helps to construct a fully developed social brain, engaging not only deep layers of the brain but also higher neocortical areas to generate new scenarios about how to make fun.

Instead of chemically reducing the urge to play by using drugs, a daily portion of physical play may diminish ADHD symptoms in children that would otherwise wind up in the clinical world. Schools might object that allowing ADHD children to engage in more rough-and-tumble play will make them more unruly. But Panksepp (1998b) argues that this play is a well-regulated brain process as young animals, including human children, need only a couple of hours of energetic play each day.

12.6 Summary

- Egg-to-adult development is important for the evolution of organisms. As evolution cannot change one kind of adult organism directly into another, it can only achieve this by changing over generations the developmental trajectory. Thus evolution is channelled through development, constraining or expanding the way embryos develop into adults.

- In the nineteenth century, much attention centred on the idea that individual development recapitulates the evolution of species. This revolutionary blending of evolutionary and developmental themes has been corrected on essential points. The rediscovery of Mendelian genetics in 1900 separated embryology from evolutionary biology because embryos were considered merely vehicles, carrying genes from one generation to another. The interest in evolutionary developmental studies was rekindled in the late 1970s and is still going on.

- Four types of reorganising developmental trajectories can be distinguished: (1) changes in the timing of developmental events (heterochrony); (2) changes in the placement of the organism's body parts (heterotopy); (3) changes in the size of the organism's body or body parts (heterometry); and (4) the origin of new phenotypes (heterotypy).

- A new phenotype is the playful animal. According to the surplus resource theory, play originated in mammals and birds as a byproduct of parental care as well as the capacity to generate heat within the body independently of the environmental temperature. Once play-like behaviour evolved into genuine play, it could take roles in fine-tuning physiological and behavioural capacities of individuals.

● Laboratory studies demonstrate that play fighting in juvenile rats starts when they perform precocious sexual behaviour that occurs before they are capable of reproduction. It is thought that the transformation of immature sexual behaviour into true play fighting passes through different stages. This form of play is retained in adulthood and used as a means to test and manipulate other individuals.

Study questions

1. Why is it incorrect to assume that the production of different phenotypes is random?

2. How has the idea of recapitulation been corrected?

3. What evidence indicates heterochrony (i.e. change in the timing of important developmental events) in humans?

4. Why can play be viewed as both a product and cause of evolutionary change?

5. Why do primate mothers, unlike rodent mothers, actively play with their off-spring?

Suggested reading

The rise of evo-devo

Geary, D. and Bjorklund, D. (2000). Evolutionary developmental psychology. *Child Development, 71,* 57–65.

Lickliter, R. and Honeycut, H. (2003). Developmental dynamics: Toward a biologically plausible evolutionary psychology. *Psychological Bulletin, 129,* 819–835 (comments and reply 836–872).

Love, A. and Raff, R. (2003). Knowing your ancestors: themes in the history of evo-devo. *Evolution & Development, 5,* 327–330.

Maestripieri, D. and Roney, J. (2006). Evolutionary developmental psychology: Contributions from comparative research with nonhuman primates. *Developmental Review, 26,* 120–137.

Robert, J. (2008). Taking old ideas seriously: Evolution, development, and human behaviour. *New Ideas in Psychology, 26,* 367–404.

Types of developmental reorganisation

Hochberg, Z. (2009). Evo-devo of child growth II: human life history and transition between its phases. *European Journal of Endocrinology, 160,* 135–141.

Prum, R. and Brush, A. (2003). Which came first, the feather or the bird? *Scientific American, 288 (3),* 62–69.

Why mammals play

Burghardt, G. (2010). The comparative reach of play and brain. *American Journal of Play, 2,* 338–356.

Sandseter, W. and Kennair, L. (2011). Children's risk play from an evolutionary perspective: The anti-phobic effects of thrilling experiences. *Evolutionary Psychology, 9,* 257–284.

Spinka, M., Newberry, R. and Bekoff, M. (2001). Mammalian play: Training for the unexpected. *The Quarterly Review of Biology, 76*, 141–168.

Trezza, V., Baarendse, P. and Vanderschuren, L. (2010). The pleasures of play: pharmacological insights into social reward mechanisms. *Trends in Pharmacological Sciences, 31*, 463–469.

Vanderschuren, L. (2010). How the brain makes play fun. *American Journal of Play, 2*, 315–337.

How play evolved through development

Bjorklund, D. and Bering, J. (2002). The evolved child: Applying evolutionary developmental psychology to modern schooling. *Learning and Individual Differences, 12*, 347–373.

Jarvis, P. (2006). 'Rough and tumble' play: Lessons in life. *Evolutionary Psychology, 4*, 330–346.

Panksepp, J. (1998b). Attention deficit hyperactivity disorders, psychostimulants, and intolerance of childhood playfulness: A tragedy in the making? *Current Directions in Psychological Science, 7*, 91–98.

Panksepp, J. (2010). Play, ADHD, and the construction of the social brain: Should the first class each day be recess? *American Journal of Play, 1*, 57–81.

Pellegrini, A., Dupuis, D. and Smith, P. (2007). Play in evolution and development. *Developmental Review, 27*, 261–276.

Pellis, S., Pellis, V. and Bell, H. (2010). The function of play in the development of the social brain. *American Journal of Play, 2*, 278–296.

Proyer, R. (2011). Being playful and smart? The relations of playfulness with psychometric and self-estimated intelligence and academic performance. *Learning and Individual Differences, 21*, 463–467.

Reference books

Arthur, W. (2011). *Evolution: A Developmental Approach.* Oxford: Wiley-Blackwell.

Bjorklund, D. and Pellegrini, A. (2002). *The Origins of Human Nature: Evolutionary Developmental Psychology.* Washington, DC: American Psychological Association.

Burghardt, G. (2005). *The Genesis of Animal Play: Testing the Limits.* Cambridge. MA: The MIT Press.

Ellis, B. and Bjorklund, D. (Eds) (2005). *Origins of the Social Mind: Evolutionary Psychology and Child Development.* New York: The Guilford Press.

Gilbert, S. (2010). *Developmental Biology, 9th Edition,* Sunderland, MA: Sinauer Associates, Inc., Publishers.

Hall, B. and Olson, W. (2003). *Keywords and Concepts in Evolutionary Developmental Biology.* Cambridge, MA: The MIT Press.

Hochberg, Z. (2012). *Evo-Devo of Child Growth: Treatise on Child Growth and Human Evolution.* Hoboken, NJ: Wiley-Blackwell.

Pellegrini, A. (Ed.) (2011). *The Oxford Handbook of the Development of Play.* Oxford: Oxford University Press.

Pellis, S. and Pellis, V. (2009). *The Playful Brain: Venturing to the Limits of Neuroscience.* Oxford: One World Publications.

Glossary

adaptation: any structural, behavioural, or cognitive feature of an organism that improves its survival and reproduction in its local environment.

adaptationism: the assumption that any trait of interest is biological in origin and that it must have evolved to solve a particular environmental problem.

adaptive problem: a problem recurrently faced by our ancestors which had an impact on their reproductive success.

adrenarche: the onset of pre-pubertal development marked by the secretion of adrenal androgens (hormones) in the bloodstream at about 6 years of age. Adrenal puberty is a peculiar feature of human development, absent in most other mammalian species. It has only been documented in chimpanzees and gorillas which also undergo a prolonged juvenile phase before reproduction. See also **gonadarche**.

affinity: relationship by marriage (or adoption) rather than genetic kinship. Affinity is common in humans but unknown in other **primates**.

alloparental care: a form of assistance in care for offspring by any member of the group, other than the genetic parent(s), who helps rear the young (e.g. sisters, older siblings, aunts, grandmothers).

altruism: an action which does not benefit the actor, but only the beneficiary.

amygdala: an almond-shaped structure – part of the **limbic system** – located in the medial part of the temporal lobe of the brain, involved in **emotion**.

analogy: similar characteristic resulting from common selective pressures. For example, bats, birds and (extinct) pterosaurs, developed independently the capacity to fly. Compare **homology**.

anisogamy: fusion of **gametes** that differ in size and/or motility.

anomaly: anything that is irregular or deviates from the norm.

anterior cingulate cortex (ACC): an area in the brain where visceral, attentional and emotional information are integrated for the regulation of emotions. This area is thought to monitor conflicts between the actual state of the organism and new information that may have emotional or motivational consequences. When such conflicts are discovered, information about the conflict passes from the ACC to the **prefrontal cortex** (PFC) where differing response options are resolved.

anthropocentrism: the tendency to place ourselves at the centre of evolution.

arcuate nucleus (ARC): a small region at the base of the brain that plays a central role in energy regulation.

Attention Deficit Hyperactivity Disorder (ADHD): **mental disorder** characterised by the three core symptoms of inattention, hyperactivity and impulsiveness.

autotrophs: Food producers such as plants, making their own food from raw materials by photosynthesis. Opposite of **heterotrophs**.

biased cultural transmission: condition in which people preferentially adopt some cultural variants (e.g. certain behaviours, beliefs) rather than others. A bias may be based on content, frequency or model. See also **culture, inheritance**.

bipedalism: ability to walk and run on two feet in an upright position, as in humans and birds. The most important adaptation to erect posture and bipedalism in humans was a positional change of the *foramen magnum*. Great apes and bears also engage in short periods of bipedal locomotion when carrying food or looking for food. See *foramen magnum*.

body mass index (BMI): a measure of weight, scaled for height (body weight in kilograms divided by height in metres squared).

body-to-body transmission: umbrella term for the many processes through which developmentally acquired or learned characteristics are reconstructed in successive generations. Also known, in a broad sense, as **epigenetic inheritance**.

brainstem: the lower part of the brain that becomes the spinal cord.

Broca's area: Region of the left frontal lobe which is believed to take part in the production of language (BAs 44 and 45).

Brodmann's map: map of the cerebral cortex devised by Korbinian Brodmann. It is based on cytoarchitectonic structure, and anatomical areas are identified by number (e.g. Brodmann area [BA] 44).

Cambrian Explosion: an event in the Cambrian period (542–488 million years ago [mya]) that produced the body plans of animals. Around 35 body plans exist today, out of the original 100 that are recorded in rocks.

caudolateral nidopallium: a brain area in birds that is structurally different but functionally equivalent to the mammalian prefrontal cortex. See **analogy** and **convergent evolution**.

Cenozoic: the geological period spanning 65 millions of years ago to the present when the first **primates** appeared.

cerebellum: the 'small brain' behind the **cerebrum** that helps regulate posture, balance and coordination.

cerebral cortex: the layer of grey matter that covers the outside of the brain. It consists mainly of the **neocortex**.

cerebrum: the major part of the brain, excluding the **cerebellum** and the **brainstem**.

character: any distinguishable characteristic, feature, trait or property of an organism that enables it to survive and reproduce in its local environment.

cladogram: branching diagram of relationships between organisms by listing shared derived characters at the branching points.

cognition: all forms of knowing and awareness, such as perceiving, conceiving, remembering, reasoning, judging, imagining and problem-solving.

cognitive capacity: the skill of, or aptitude for perception, concept formation, memory, understanding, awareness, reasoning, judgement, intuition and language.

communication: the transfer of information from sender to receiver by verbal or non-verbal means.

computationalism: the idea that the human mind is an information-processing system that resembles a computer made out of organic components rather than silicon chips.

convergent evolution: evolutionary change in two or more unrelated species that results in the independent development of similar adaptations to similar environmental conditions. See **analogy**.

cooperation: association between individuals which provides larger benefits than they could expect if acting alone.

corvids (*Corvidae*): a family of black, black and white, or brightly coloured birds with large heavy bills which include rooks, crows, magpies, ravens and jays.

creativity: the cognitive capacity to generate new and valuable ideas. This capacity is thought to be not a single capacity, like intelligence, but one that consists of different ingredients, in particular: intrinsic motivation, intelligence, thinking style, personality and expertise.

culture: information that is capable of affecting individuals' behaviour which they acquire from other individuals through teaching, imitation and other forms of **social learning**.

cultural change: an evolutionary process in which favourable cultural variants are selected and socially transmitted. See also **biased cultural transmission, inheritance** and **ratchet effect**.

cumulative cultural evolution: cultural change that requires creation of inventions and faithful social transmission to prevent new generations having to re-invent the wheel. See also **ratchet effect**.

depression/depressive illness: **mental disorder** with core symptoms like depressed mood, disturbed sleep, reduced libido, feelings of worthlessness, anhedonia (i.e. significant diminished enjoyment of previously pleasurable activities), recurrent thoughts of suicide.

designer fallacy: mistaken idea that if living things are very complicated, they could only be the product of an intelligent designer, not evolution.

development: the progressive series of changes in structure, function, and behaviour patterns that occur over the lifespan of an organism. See also **ontogeny**.

developmental bias: the tendency to constrain or expand the way embryos develop into adults.

dispersal: the tendency of an organism to move away, either from its birth site (natal dispersal) or breeding site (breeding dispersal). Opposite of **philopatry**.

DNA: deoxyribonucleid acid is the hereditary material – the substance of genes – in all organisms.

dominance: in **ethology** referring to a superior position in a rank order or social hierarchy. Dominance is anything but static as lower-ranking animals continually test the ability of higher-ranking animals to maintain their position.

dopamine: a **neurotransmitter** that has an important role in motor behaviour and also involved in mental processes such as reward-driven learning.

dopaminergic system: a brain system that regulates the amount of **dopamine** influencing many neurons. This system consists of different pathways that are involved in physiological, motor, motivational and cognitive functions.

dorsolateral prefrontal cortex: a brain region, involved in the rational side of decision-making such as reasoning and planning. It helps **primates** to make alternative scenarios of how to deal with objects (e.g. how to extract seeds from hard-shelled food) or with members of the same species (e.g. how to avoid conflict with a rival).

ecological inheritance: if organisms modify the environment and some of the associated selection pressures, each new generation inherits the changed environment and its modified selection pressures from the previous generation. See **niche construction**.

ectotherm: an animal whose body temperature is maintained by absorbing heat from the surrounding environment (e.g. reptiles). Such animals employ ectothermy. Opposite of **endotherm**.

emotion: a relatively brief episode of coordinated brain, autonomic, and behavioural changes that facilitate a response to an external or internal event of significance for the organism.

emulation: the ability to comprehend the goal of a model and engage in similar behaviour to achieve that goal, without necessarily replicating the specific action of the model. Compare **imitation**.

encephalisation: enlargement of the brain, relative to body size, over the course of evolution.

encephalisation quotient (EQ): the ratio between the actual brain size relative to the expected brain size of an average animal of the same body weight.

endotherm: an animal whose body heat is generated through its own metabolic activities (e.g. mammals, birds). Such animals employ endothermy. Opposite of **ectotherm**. See also **metabolism**.

epigenetic inheritance: in a broad sense, a type of inheritance that bypasses the germ line and includes body-to-body information transfer between generations of individuals. It can take place through developmental interactions between mother and offspring, social learning, or symbolic communication. Also known as **body-to-body transmission**.

ethology: a branch of biology dedicated to the study of behaviour and behavioural traditions.

eukaryotes: organisms with a cell nucleus, and organelles such as mitochondria with their own genome. Compare **prokaryotes**.

eusociality: true sociality, referring to colonial systems (e.g. ants, bees) in which only one female is reproductive while the other animals gather food and care for the young.

evo-devo: Shorthand for evolutionary developmental biology.

evolution: (1) the change in appearance, or gene frequencies, of populations and species over generations; (2) the origins and extinctions of species.

female kin-bonded species: species in which males leave their native group at sexual maturity. Opposite of **male kin-bonded species**.

fitness: the reproductive success of an organism relative to another which is determined by **natural selection**.

foramen magnum: the large opening in the inferior part of the occipital bone of the skull through which the spinal cord, accessory vessels and vertebral arteries enter the skull to connect with the brain. See also **bipedalism**.

frontopolar cortex: the most anterior part of the **prefrontal cortex**, involved in prospective thinking.

fusiform brain area: brain area in the temporal lobe, involved in face recognition.

gamete: reproductive cell. In anisogamous organisms an egg or sperm cell. Gametes produced by different sexes fuse to form zygotes. See also **somatic cell**, **anisogamy**.

gaze: the orientation of the eyes within the face which can be used by others to interpret where an individual is looking. Gaze direction is an effective way of communicating the location of hidden objects and is functionally similar to pointing. Gaze following is widely considered as a crucial step towards understanding another's mental states such as intentions, thoughts or desires. Apes and monkeys are more sensitive to head direction than to gaze direction.

gene pool: the sum total of all genes in an interbreeding population at a particular time that can be described by the frequencies of different **genes** it contains.

gene–culture coevolution: theory that human populations share learned traditions that are expressed in cultural practices, and transmitted socially between individuals in the form of cultural **inheritance**. The theory presumes that human cultural practices modify natural selection processes in human environments, so that cultural transmission affects some selected human genes.

genes: particulate units of **inheritance** that are passed from parents to offspring.

genetic determinism: the doctrine that animal behaviour and mental activity are largely, or completely, controlled by the genetic constitution of the individual.

genetic monogamy: male–female pair reproducing exclusively with one another. All offspring produced are from the pair.

genetic recombination: the production of offspring with combinations of traits that differ from those found in either parent.

genome: the total genetic material within the cell of an organism.

genomics: the branch of genetics concerned with the study of genomes.

genotype: the hidden genetic constitution of an organism.

geological timescale: a scheme spanning the entire history of the Earth, from roughly 4.6 billion years ago to the present. It divides the history into named units (eras, periods, epochs) and is marked by first events such as the emergence of new life forms.

germ line: the germ cells that contribute cells to the next generation of individuals. Other cells of the individual constitute the soma, or all somatic cells. See also **Weismann barrier.**

gestation: the development of the embryo and foetus in the uterus until birth.

gestures: movements of the limbs, head and body used to communicate with conspecifics.

gonadarche: the earliest gonadal changes of **puberty** in which the ovaries of girls and the testes of boys begin to grow and increase the production of the sex stereoids, especially oestradiol and testosterone. Gonads are the organs (testes, ovaries) that make gametes, or reproductive cells. Gonadarche indicates true central puberty while **adrenarche** is an independent maturational process only loosely associated with complete puberty.

gonads: collective term for ovaries and testes.

great apes: the gorillas, common chimpanzees and bonobos of Africa and the orangutans of Southeast Asia. These species are referred to as great apes because they are the largest apes. See **lesser apes, hominids.**

grey matter: the darker tissues of the brain, made up of densely packed cell bodies, as seen in the cerebral **cortex.**

grooming: care of the hair covering and skin by mammals; the mammalian equivalent of preening in birds. An animal's attention to its own body, or 'autogrooming', should be distinguished from 'allogrooming/social grooming' which refers to picking parasites or dirt from the fur as a reward through activation of endogenous **opioids** in the recipient.

Hamilton's rule: a formula named after William Hamilton (1936–2000) which demonstrates that individuals should be altruistic towards relatives, provided that the benefits exceed the costs as valued by the degree of genetic relatedness between actor and recipient.

heritability: the proportion of phenotypic variation that can be attributed to genetic differences between individuals.

heterochrony: change in the timing of developmental events. For example, the time when organisms reach sexual maturity may accelerate under certain conditions.

heterometry: change in the size of the organism's body or body parts. For example, adult humans are only 1.25 times the size of chimps. This may explain an increased brain size of 500 cm^2 but not the actual size of 1,350 cm^2. So, the increased size of the human brain is a real heterometry.

heterotopy: change in the placement of the organism's body parts. For example, flatfish embryos are bilaterally symmetrical in that the position of their eyes is similar to 'normal' fish. But at a certain stage in their development, one eye starts to move across the head, ending up next to the other eye.

heterotrophs: food consumers such as animals, depending on plants and particularly prey to obtain energy. Opposite of **autotrophs.**

heterotypy: origin of new phenotypes. For example, birds' feathers are a novelty as they did not directly evolve from reptilian scales. Similarly, **play** is a novel trait in mammals and birds, not or rarely to be found in reptiles.

hominids: the humans and great apes (chimpanzees, gorillas, orangutans).

hominins: living humans (*H. sapiens*) and the fossil species most closely related to us (e.g. *Australopithecus*, *H. erectus*).

homology: similar character resulting from common ancestry. For example, humans and chimpanzees have forward-projecting eyes and grasping hands due to descent from a common ancestor. Compare **analogy.**

Hox **genes:** set of regulatory genes that determines body patterns. These genes were discovered in the late 1970s, first found in fruit flies and later on in other animals. Regulatory genes are remarkably stable across species, suggesting deep links of **homology** among multi-cellular organisms.

hyperdopaminergic disorder: **mental disorder** associated with abundance of dopamine (e.g. autism, obsessive-compulsive disorder, mania and schizophrenia).

hyperthermia: failing function of thermoregulation when the body produces or absorbs more heat than it can dissipate.

hypodopaminergic disorder: **mental disorder** associated with deprivation of dopamine (e.g. Parkinson's disease, **phenylketonuria**).

hypomania: a milder version of **mania** in which people feel creative, energetic and happy.

hypothalamus: area in the forebrain involved in the control of many autonomic processes (breathing, circulation, temperature, metabolism, sexual function) and in the release of many hormones.

imagination: the cognitive capacity to produce alternative scenarios and situations that are not currently available to perception but formed in the mind.

imitation: any form of learning in which individuals can learn a new behaviour by copying the behaviour of another individual, either of its own or another species, and incorporating it into its own action pattern, vocal repertoire or practical know-how. Compare **emulation**.

inbreeding: breeding between two close genetic relatives. The fitness of offspring is sometimes reduced by inbreeding depression.

inbreeding depression: the phenomenon that descendants of individuals who mated with close relatives tend to have lower fitness due, for example, to lowered genetic variety.

incest: sexual activity or relationship between first-degree relatives (e.g. brother–sister, parent–child), associated with very high risks of abnormality in offspring.

inclusive fitness: a measure that combines (a) an individual's direct genetic contribution to future generations through its own offspring, with (b) the indirect contribution made by aiding the reproduction of relatives. See also **fitness**.

infanticide: the killing of young by conspecifics (members of the same species). This practice occurs mainly in two situations. In adverse environmental circumstances the perpetrators may be the parents, a situation which has been most often reported in birds of prey. In non-human primates, infanticide may create breeding opportunities for males that have limited sexual access to fertile females. Infants are attacked only by strange adult males, never by males who might be their fathers.

inheritance: the transmission of genetic information from one generation (parents) to another (offspring). See also **epigenetic inheritance** and **ecological inheritance**.

insightful learning: a cognitive form of learning involving the mental rearrangement or restructuring of the elements in a problem to achieve an understanding of a problem and arrive at a solution.

insula: a small brain area between the temporal and frontal lobes, receiving homoeostatic and emotional information that originates within the body, as well as olfactory and gustatory information (smell and taste).

intersexual selection: a form of **sexual selection** driven by female choice of suitable mating partners.

intrasexual selection: a form of **sexual selection** driven by competition within the same sex for suitable mating partners.

invertebrates: animals that lack an internal skeleton. All animals other than fish, amphibians, reptiles, birds and mammals are invertebrates. Approximately 95 per cent of all animals are invertebrates. Compare **vertebrates**.

isogamy: fusion of gametes that do not differ in size and/or motility. Opposite of **anisogamy**.

lactation: the synthesis and secretion of milk by a mother's mammary glands.

lactose intolerance: incapacity to digest milk sugar resulting in bloating, gas and diarrhoea.

language: a system for expressing or communicating thoughts and feelings through **speech** sounds or written symbols.

latent inhibition: the capacity to screen from conscious awareness stimuli previously experienced as irrelevant. Reductions in latent inhibition have been generally associated with the tendency towards psychosis. However, 'failure' to screen out previously irrelevant stimuli might also hypothetically contribute to **creativity**, particularly in combination with high IQ.

larynx: the muscular and cartilaginous structure at the top of the trachea (windpipe) and below the tongue that contains the vocal cords.

lek: communal mating areas for birds such as peacocks, bowerbirds and wild turkeys within which males hold small territories, used solely for courtship and copulation. Females are attracted to a lek by the displays of the males and then choose mating partners from among them. See **sexual selection**.

lesser apes: the gibbons and siamangs of Southeast Asia. These species are referred to as lesser apes because they are the smallest apes. Compare **great apes**.

life-history theory: a branch of evolutionary biology, dealing with trade-offs in the allocation of time and resources over the lifespan of an organism.

limbic system: a loosely defined, widespread group of brain nuclei that innervate one another, forming a network that is involved in emotions, memory formation, drive and motivation. It includes parts of the **cerebral cortex**, and subcortical structures like **amygdala** and hippocampus.

lineage: line of descent of a population from its ancestral population. When the members of a population breed and produce the next generation, we can imagine a series of populations over time. Each population of a species is ancestral to the descendant population in the next generation. So a lineage is a series of ancestor–descendant populations, and evolution is then change between generations within a population lineage.

local enhancement: a form of **social learning** in which the activities of some individuals direct the attention of other individuals towards a particular part of the environment.

male kin-bonded species: species in which females leave their native group at sexual maturity. Opposite of **female kin-bonded species.**

mania: mental state characterised by overactivity, increased cognitive activity ranging from enhanced creativity to overoptimistic ideation, and inflated self-esteem.

mating intelligence: construct referring to the capacity to understand the beliefs and desires of opposite-sex partners as well as same-sex rivals. See also **sexual selection.**

menarche: the first incidence of menstruation in a female, marking the onset of puberty.

menopause: progressive failure of the female reproductive organs, usually between 45 and 55 years.

mental disorder: a set of symptoms indicating that a cognitive or emotional capacity (a) fails to perform its naturally selected function, and (b) causes significant harm to the individual and its environment, judged by the standards of present culture.

metabolism: the totality of enzyme-mediated biochemical pathways occurring within the body, both anabolic (build up) and catabolic (break down).

mind–body problem: ancient issue of how to account for and describe the relationship between mental and physical processes.

Miocene: a geological period, extending from around 23–5 mya.

mitochondria: intracellular organelles, derived from bacterial ancestors with their genomes which are the energy factories of the cell.

mitochondrial genome: an energy-generating organel in each cell, containing 37 genes. See also **nuclear genome.**

modern synthesis: integration of population genetics, systematic biology and palaeobiology in evolutionary biology in the 1940s.

modularity: the notion that the brain/mind is composed of a number of modules that can solve specific problems. An example is the module for face recognition.

monogamy: one-male, one-female mating system in which each sex has a single mate for life. See also **genetic, social** and **serial monogamy.**

monotremes: egg-laying mammals comprising the duck-billed platypus and the echidnas, or spiny ant-eaters.

mosaic evolution: the evolution of different parts of an organism at different rates. For example, many aspects of the human **phenotype** have evolved relatively slowly since we diverged from our primate ancestors. A notable example is our nervous system which gave us a huge selective advantage. An example within the human brain is the disproportionate increase of the prefrontal cortex.

mutation: any permanent change in the genetic material of an organism that is not the result of the recombination of the male and female **genome.** Mutation is mostly the result of exposure to radiation or chemicals.

mutualism: a form of **cooperation** between members of different species – interspecific mutualism – or between unrelated members of one species – conspecific mutualism – that provides immediate benefits for the partners involved. See **reciprocity.**

nativism: (1) the doctrine that the mind has certain innate structures and that mental and behavioural traits are largely determined by hereditary rather than environmental factors; (2) the theory that babies are born with a fundamental knowledge of the world (e.g. gravity, motion).

natural selection: the causal mechanism that accounts for the evolutionary change in populations of organisms; or, the process by which the forms of organisms in a population that are best adapted to the environment increase in frequency relative to those less well adapted forms over a number of generations.

nature–nurture controversy: the dispute over the relative contributions of hereditary and constitutional factors (nature) and environmental factors (nurture) to the development of the individual.

negative emotion: emotion associated with diverse forms of threat, or obstruction of a goal, including anger, fright-anxiety, guilt-shame, sadness, envy-jealousy and disgust. Opposite of **positive emotion.** See also **negativity bias.**

negativity bias: in emotions such as fear and anger, a heightened sensitivity to information about things that may have a negative impact on survival and reproduction.

neocortex: the part of the **cerebral cortex** that most recently evolved, and the source of our cognitive, linguistic and cultural capacities. It modulates the expression of emotions that originate from the **limbic system** and affords considerable flexibility and **creativity** in thinking and planning.

neophobia: a persistent and irrational fear of change or of anything new, unfamiliar or strange.

neuromodulation: the action of endogenous substances or neuromodulators – **dopamine, serotonin** and **opioids** – on neurons that are released in certain brain areas and involved at all levels of behaviour from reflexes to cognitions. For example, in primates serotonin has a role in controlling **negative emotion** or mood, and opioids play a role in regulating friendly interactions with conspecifics.

neurotransmitter: a chemical substance that communicates between one neuron to another or between a neuron and a muscle cell. For example, **serotonin** and **dopamine**. See also **neuromodulation**.

niche construction: the practice of countless organisms to modify their local environments by consuming resources, constructing nests, holes, burrows, paths, webs, thus providing protection for their offspring. The human capacity for niche construction (and destruction) has been further amplified by culture as innovation and technology has had an enormous impact on the environment.

nuclear genome: the total genetic material within the cell containing about 25,000 genes. See also **mitochondrial genome**.

Nucleus Accumbens (NAcc): brain structure in the **dopaminergic system**, involved in the rewarding actions of athletic and intellectual accomplishment, **play**, aesthetic enjoyment, orgasm, and many drugs of abuse.

obesity: nutritional disorder developing chronically when energy intake exceeds energy expenditure.

ontogeny: the process of development from fertilised egg to adult. See also **phylogeny** and **recapitulation**.

opioids: a class of natural chemical that has similar properties to morphine and heroine, and which modulates behaviour, for example in reducing reactions to tissue damage, and regulating friendly interactions with conspecifics. See **neuromodulation**.

orbitofrontal cortex: brain region above the orbits, or eyesockets, which responds to external stimuli that are likely to be rewarding or otherwise significant. It is involved in learning the emotional and motivational value of stimuli, such as food, drink and sex.

oviparity: laying eggs in which the embryos have developed little. Birds and many invertebrates are oviparous.

oxygenation: the process by which concentrations of oxygen increase within a tissue.

Palaeolithic: a period distinguished by the development of the first stone tools. This period extends from 2.5 mya to the introduction of agriculture around 10,000 years ago.

parental investment: any investment by a parent in an individual offspring that increases the offspring's chance to survive but imposes a cost in terms of the parent's ability to invest in other offspring.

phenotype: the observable – morphological and behavioural – characteristics of an organism as a result of the interaction between its genotype and the environment. See also **genotype**.

phenylketonuria: a mental disorder associated with a metabolic imbalance leading to progressive mental retardation.

philopatry: the tendency of individuals to return to or stay in the home area (e.g. male birds and female mammals tend to be more philopatric than the opposite sex). The opposite of **dispersal**.

phonation: the production of voiced sounds by means of vibrations of the vocal cords.

phylogeny: the genealogical history of a group of organisms, represented by its hypothesised ancestor–descendant relationships. See also **cladogram**, **ontogeny**.

play: a kind of behaviour mainly to be found in mammals and birds. Criteria to define and recognise play imply that it (1) is incompletely functional in the context in which it appears; (2) is spontaneous, pleasurable, rewarding or voluntary; (3) differs from other more serious behaviours in form (e.g. exaggerated) or timing (e.g. occurring early in life); (4) is repeated, but not in an abnormal and stereotypic form (e.g. distressed rocking); and (5) is initiated in the absence of stress.

Pleistocene: the geological epoch spanning 1.6 million to 10,000 years ago, characterised by repeated cycles of glaciation and warming.

polyandry: one-female, multi-male mating system in which multiple males mate with a single female.

polygynamy: mating system in which the home range of one male overlaps those of several females.

polygynandry: multi-male, multi-female mating system in which both sexes have a variable number of mates.

polygyny: one-male, multi-female mating system in which multiple females mate with a single male.

pons: a key link between the **cerebellum** and the **brainstem**.

positive emotion: emotion associated with diverse forms of goal attainment or the movement towards it, including happiness/joy, love/affection, pride and relief. Opposite of **negative emotion**.

prefrontal cortex (PFC): the most forward part of the frontal lobe of each cerebral hemisphere, involved in high order functions in cognition such as judgement, prediction, planning, moderating correct social behaviour, and integrating information from outside the body with that from within (e.g. the **limbic system**).

primates: term referring to prosimians (lemurs, tarsiers, lorises), monkeys, apes and humans which have in common a set of derived morphological characteristics (traits) that include binocular vision, shortened snout, grasping hands and feet, and considerably larger brains relative to their body size than other mammals.

prokaryotes: single-celled organisms lacking a nucleus and organelles. Compare **eukaryotes**.

puberty: the physiological and mental transition from juvenility to adolescence, lasting about four years and involving the development of the secondary sexual characteristics and adolescent growth spurt. See also **gonadarche**.

quadrupedalism: having a four footed means of locomotion. See also **bipedalism**.

ratchet effect: human cultural traditions that are faithfully transmitted to new generations, serving as a ratchet to prevent having to 're-invent the wheel'. See also **cumulative cultural evolution**.

recapitulation: the idea that development of the individual (**ontogeny**) repeats the evolution of species (**phylogeny**).

reciprocity: a form of cooperation in which benefits are deferred. Compare **mutualism**.

reflex: an automatic, unlearned, relatively fixed response to stimuli that does not require conscious effort and that often involves a faster response than might be possible if a conscious evaluation of the input was required.

regulatory gene: a kind of gene that turns another gene or group of genes on or off. See also *hox* **genes**.

replicator: the mechanism that copies the DNA sequence of the parent and passes it to the offspring.

ritualisation: the process by which an action or behaviour takes on a new, communicative function. For example, the facial expression of disgust originated from the rejection of bad-tasting food to protect the body. Or, courtship feeding of mates is taken from feeding young, signalling the readiness to breed.

savannas: usually semi-arid regions covered with grasses and occasional scattered trees.

scala naturae: mistaken idea that all animals can be arranged in a hierarchy according to their degree of perfection (also known as ladder of perfection, *Great Chain of Being*).

sclera: the tough external layer of the vertebrate eye.

selection pressures: forces that over a long evolutionary time and in a consistent manner shape the organism's traits which cause it to be successful in survival and reproduction.

serial monogamy: pairs that mate and raise offspring cooperatively, but then choose to mate with new partners.

serotonin: a neurotransmitter in the brain and other parts of the central nervous system that has roles in bioregulatory processes like emotion, mood, appetite, sleep and pain.

sex-role reversal: a form of animal behaviour in which each sex behaves in a manner typical of the other sex.

sexual dimorphism: males and females have different **phenotypes**.

sexual monogamy: an exclusive sexual relationship between a male and a female.

sexual selection: the component or subset of **natural selection** that is associated with mating success.

sign language: any system of communication based on hand signals, especially one used by deaf people. There are many such systems, and like natural languages they tend to be mutually unintelligible. See also **language**.

social emotion: kind of **emotion** that requires an evaluation of other individuals as well as some degree of self-consciousness. If evaluation implies that individuals may succeed or fail to meet social norms, this may lead to pairs of emotions such as pride–shame and envy–pity. See also **positive emotion, negative emotion**.

social learning: a change of behaviour that is the result of social interactions with other individuals, usually of the same species.

social monogamy: one-male, one-female's social living arrangement (e.g. shared use of a territory, shared care of offspring).

sociality: sustained **cooperation** between individuals that goes beyond parental care and the continued association of mated pairs.

somatic cell: any body cell of multi-cellular organism other than **gamete**.

speciation: the process by which new species originate and thereafter remain separate.

species: the largest natural population of organisms that can potentially interbreed to produce fertile offspring.

speech: a sound production system which is specialised in complex articulated **vocalisations**. Articulation implies tight coordination between the various organs and muscles that play a role in speech, including the vocal tract, lips, jaw, tongue and soft palate. See also **language**.

symbolism: the capacity to represent objects, people, events or concepts by arbitrary but meaningful symbols and use them in cultural practices. See also **language**.

syntax: the set of rules that describes how words and phrases in a language are arranged into grammatical sentences, or the branch of linguistics that studies such rules.

temperament: the biological foundation of personality, present early in life and including characteristics such as energy level, emotional responsiveness and willingness to explore. Studies of animals, ranging from fish to primates, have documented differences in temperament, particularly along the shy–bold continuum.

terrestrial: referring to animals that spend most of their time on the ground rather than in the air, water or trees.

thalamus: large paired masses of **grey matter** lying between the **brainstem** and the **cerebrum**, the key relay station for sensory information flowing into the brain.

Theory of Mind: the ability to understand another individual's mental states such as knowledge, intentions, desires, goals, beliefs; also known as 'mind-reading' or 'mentalising'. It is called a theory because we have no direct evidence to support our assumption that others have mental states.

variation: phenotypic and/or genotypic differences between individuals of a population.

vertebrates: animals that possess a spinal cord protected by a segmented vertebral column of cartilage and/or bone. Compare **invertebrates**.

viviparity: reproduction in animals such as mammals whose embryos develop within the female parent.

vocalisation: sound produced by the passage of air, causing vibration of membranes in the respiratory tract, such as the vocal cords in the syrinx of birds and the **larynx** of mammals. Apart from human **speech**, the most complex vocalisations are the songs of songbirds, whales and some primates (howler monkeys and gibbons).

waist–hip ratio (WHR): a measure of the circumference of the waist relative to that of the hips.

weaning: the process of reducing an offspring's dependence on its mother or parents, particularly with respect to feeding.

Weismann barrier: the principle named after August Weismann (1834–1914) that hereditary information moves only from reproductive cells to somatic cells, and not vice versa. Thus, it rules out any possibility of the inheritance of acquired characteristics.

References

A

Adolphs, R. (2009). The social brain: Neural basis of social knowledge. *Annual Review of Psychology, 60,* 693–716.

Adriaens, P. and DeBlock, A (Eds) (2001). *Maladapting Minds: Philosophy, Psychiatry and Evolutionary Theory.* Oxford: Oxford University Press. (see p. 314)

Aiello, L. & Wheeler, P. (1995). The expensive hypothesis: The brain and the digestive system in human and primate evolution. *Current Anthropology, 36,* 199–221.

Aiello, L. & Key, C. (2002). Energetic consequences of being *Homo erectus* female. *American Journal of Biology, 14,* 551–565.

Alexander R. (1990). *How did Humans Evolve? Reflections on the Uniquely Unique Species,* Ann Harbor: Museum of Zoology. The University of Michigan.

Allen, C. & Bekoff, M. (1997). *Species of Mind: The Philosophy and Biology of Cognitive Ethology,* Cambridge, Mass.: The MIT Press.

Alessi, G. (1992). Models of proximate and ultimate causation in psychology. *American Psychologist, 47,* 1359–1370.

Allen, N. & Badcock, P. (2006). Darwinian models of depression: A review of evolutionary accounts of mood and mood disorders. *Progress in Neuro-Psychopharmacology & Biological Psychiatry, 30,* 815–826.

Allman, J. (1999). *Evolving Brains.* New York: Scientific American Library.

Amabile, T. (1996). *Creativity in Context.* Boulder, Col.: Westview Press.

American Psychiatric Association (2000). *Diagnostic and Statistic Manual of Mental Disorders, Fourth Edition, Text Revision.* Washington, DC: American Psychiatric Association.

Anderson, J. (2005). *Cognitive Psychology and Its Implications.* New York: Worth Publishers.

Anderson, K., Kaplan, H. & Lancaster, J. (2007). Confidence of paternity, divorce, and investment in children by Albuquerque men. *Evolution and Human Behavior, 28,* 1–10.

Andersson, M. (1994). *Sexual Selection.* Princeton, N.J.: Princeton University Press.

Andreasen, N. (1987). Creativity and mental illness: Prevalence rates in writers and their first degree relatives. *American Journal of Psychiatry, 144,* 1288–1292.

Andreasen, N. (2001). *Brave New Brain: Conquering Mental Illness in the Era of the Genome.* Oxford: Oxford University Press.

Andreasen, N. (2005). *The Creating Brain: The Neuroscience of Genius.* New York: Dana Press.

Andrews, P. (2006). Parent-offspring conflict and cost-benefit analysis in adolescent suicidal behavior. *Human Nature, 17,* 190–211.

APA (2000). *Diagnostic and Statistical Manual of Mental Disorders, Fourth Edition, Text Revision.* Washington, DC: American Psychiatric Association.

Apicella, C. & Marlowe, F. (2004). Perceived mate fidelity and paternal resemblance predict men's investment in children. *Evolution and Human Behavior, 25,* 371–378.

Apostolou, M. (2007). Sexual selection under parental choice: the role of parents in the evolution of human mating. *Evolution and Human Behavior, 28,* 403–409.

Apostolou, M. (2008). Sexual selection under parental choice in agropastoral societies. *Evolution and Human Behavior, 31,* 39–47.

Apostolou, M. (2010). Parental choice: What parents want in a son-in-law and a daughter-in-law across 67 pre-industrial societies. *British Journal of Psychology, 101,* 695–704.

Apperley, I. (2011). *Mindreaders: The Cognitive Basis of 'Theory of Mind'.* Hove: Psychology Press.

Arbib, M. & Fellous, J. (2004). Emotions: From brain to robot. *Trends in Cognitive Sciences, 8,* 554–561.

Arbib, M., Liebal, K. & Pika, S. (2008). Primate vocalization, gesture, and the evolution of language. *Current Anthropology, 49,* 1053–1076.

Arnqvist, G. & Rowe, L. (2005). *Sexual Conflict.* Princeton: Princeton University Press.

Arthur, W. (2004). *Biased Embryos and Evolution.* Cambridge: Cambridge University Press.

Arthur, W. (2011). *Evolution: A Developmental Approach*. Oxford: Wiley-Blackwell.

Ashworth, T. (1980). *Trench Warfare, 1914–1918: The Live and Let Live System*. New York: Holmes & Meier.

Aunger, R. (2002). *The Electric Meme: A New Theory of How We Think*. New York: The Free Press.

Aunger, R. (2007). Major transitions in 'big' history. *Technological Forecasting & Social Change, 74,* 1137–1163.

Aureli, F. & Whiten, A. (2003). Emotions and behavioral flexibility. In D. Maestripieri (Ed.), *Primate Psychology* (pp. 289–323). Cambridge, Mass.: Harvard University Press.

Avital, E. & Lamb, J, (200). *Animal Traditions: Behavioral Inheritance in Evolution*. Cambridge: Cambridge University Press.

Axelrod, R. (1984). *The Evolution of Co-operation*. London: Penguin Books.

Axelrod, R. & Hamilton, W. (1981). The evolution of cooperation. *Science, 211,* 1390–1396.

B

Baars, B. & Gage, N. (2010). *Cognition, Brain, and Consciousness*. Amsterdam: Academic Press.

Bailey, D. & Geary, D. (2009). Hominid brain evolution: Testing climatic, ecological, and social competition models. *Human Nature, 20,* 67–79.

Barash, D. & Lipton, J. (2009). *How Women Got Their Curves and Other Just-So Stories,* New York: Columbia University Press.

Barber, N. (1991). Play and energy regulation in mammals. *The Quarterly Review of Biology, 66,* 129–147.

Barham, L. (2002). Systematic pigment use in the Middle Pleistocene of South-Central Africa. *Current Anthropology, 43,* 181–190.

Barkow, J., Cosmides, L. & Tooby, J. (Eds) (1992). *The Adapted Mind: Evolutionary Psychology and the Generation of Culture*. New York: Oxford University Press.

Barkow, J. (1992). Beneath new culture is old psychology: Gossip and social stratification. In J. Barkow, L. Cosmides & J. Tooby (Eds) *The Adapted Mind: Evolutionary Psychology and the Generation of Culture* (pp. 627–637). New York: Oxford University Press.

Barlow, D. (2002). *Anxiety and its Disorders: The Nature and Treatment of Anxiety and Panic*. New York: The Guilford Press.

Barnes, J. (Ed.) (1995). *The Complete Works of Aristotle, Volume one*. Princeton: Princeton University Press.

Barnes, B. & Dupré, J. (2008). *Genomes and What to Make of Them*. Chicago: The University of Chicago Press.

Barnett, J. et al. (2006). Cognitive reserve in neuropsychiatry. *Psychological Medicine, 36,* 1053–1964.

Baron-Cohen, S. (1995). *Mindblindness: An Essay on Autism and Theory of Mind*. London: The MIT Press.

Baron-Cohen, S. (Ed.) (1997). *The Maladaptive Mind: Classical Readings in Evolutionary Psychopathology*. Erlbaum: Taylor & Francis (see p. 314).

Baron-Cohen, S. (2005). The empathizing system: A revision of the 1996 model of the mind reading system. In B. Ellis & D. Bjorklund (Eds), *Origins of the Social Mind: Evolutionary Psychology and Child Development* (pp. 468–492). New York: The Guilford Press.

Barret, H. (2008). Evolved cognitive mechanisms and human behavior. In C. Crawford & D. Krebs (Eds), *Foundations of Evolutionary Psychology* (pp. 173–189). New York: Lawrence Erlbaum.

Barrett, L., Dunbar, R. & Lycett, J. (2002). *Human Evolutionary Psychology*. New York: Palgrave.

Barrett, L., Henzi, P. & Dunbar, R. (2003). Primate cognition: from 'what now?' to 'what if'? *Trends in Cognitive Sciences, 7,* 494–497.

Barton, R. (2006). Primate brain evolution: Integrating comparative neurophysiological, and ethological data. *Evolutionary Anthropology, 15,* 224–236.

Barton, R. (2007). Mosaic evolution of brain structure in mammals. In J. Kaas & L. Krubitzer (Eds), *Evolution of Nervous Systems, Vol. 3* (pp. 97–102). Amsterdam: Elsevier.

Basalla, G. (1988). *The Evolution of Technology*. Cambridge: Cambridge University Press.

Basu, S. et al. (2009). Recordkeeping alters economic history by promoting reciprocity. *Proceedings of the National Academy of Sciences of the USA, 106,* 1009–1014.

Bateman, A. (1948). Intra-sexual selection in *Drosophila*. *Heredity, 2,* 349–368.

Beatty. J. (1994). The proximate/ultimate distinction in the multiple careers of Ernst Mayr. *Biology and Philosophy, 9,* 333–356.

Bekoff, M. (2007). *The Emotional life of Animals*. Novato, Cal.: New World Library.

Bekoff, M. & Pierce, J. (2009). *Wild Justice: The Moral Lives of Animals*. Chicago: The University of Chicago Press.

Bell, G. (1982). *The Masterpiece of Nature: The Evolution and Genetics of Sexuality*. Berkeley: University of California Press.

Bell, M. at al. (Eds) (2010). *Evolution Since Darwin: The First 150 Years.* Sunderland, Mass.: Sinauer.

Benton, D. (2004). Role of parents in the determination of the food preferences of children and the development of obesity. *International Journal of Obesity, 28, 858–869.*

Belski, J. (2007). Childhood experiences and reproductive strategies. In R. Dunbar & L. Barrett (Eds), *Oxford Handbook of Evolutionary Psychology* (pp. 237–253). Oxford: Oxford University Press,.

Ben-David, J.(1991). Social factors in the origins of a new science: the case of psychology. In G. Freudenthal (Ed.), *Scientific Growth: Essays on the Social Organization and Ethos of Science* (pp 49–70). Berkeley: University Press.

Bennett, M. & Hacker, P. (2003). *Philosophical Foundations of Neuroscience.* Oxford: Blackwell Publishing.

Bentley, R. et al. (2007). Regular rates of popular culture change reflect random copying. *Evolution and Human Behavior, 28, 151–158.*

Bereczkei, T. & Dunbar, R. (1997). Female biased reproductive strategies in a Hungarian Gypsy population, *Proceedings of the Royal Society of London B, 264, 17–22.*

Bereczkei, T. & Dunbar, R. (2002). Helping-at-the-nest and sex-biased parental investment in a Hungarian Gypsy population, *Current Anthropology, 43, 804–809.*

Berra, T. (2009). *Charles Darwin: The Concise Story of an Extraordinary Man.* Baltimore: The Johns Hopkins University Press.

Berra, T., Alvarez, G. & Ceballos, F. (2010). Was the Darwin/Wedgwood dynasty adversely affected by consanguinity? *Bioscience, 60, 376–383.*

Beyin, A. (2011). Upper Pleistocene human dispersals out of Africa: A review of the current state of the debate. *International Journal of Evolutionary Biology,* published online, Vol. 2011, Article ID 615094, 17 pages.

Bingham, P. (1999). Human uniqueness: a general theory. *Quarterly Review of Biology, 74, 133–169.*

Bingham, P. (2000). Human evolution and human history: A complete theory. *Evolutionary Anthropology, 9, 248–257.*

Bittles, A. (2004). Genetic aspects of inbreeding and incest. In A. Wolf & W. Durham (Eds). *Inbreeding, Incest, and the Incest Taboo* (pp. 38–60). Stanford, Cal.: Stanford University Press.

Bjorklund, D. (1997). The role of immaturity in human development. *Psychological Bulletin, 122, 153–169.*

Bjorklund, D. & Pellegrini, A. (2000). Child development and evolutionary psychology, *Child Development, 71, 1687–1708.*

Bjorklund, D. & Pellegrini, A. (2002). *The Origins of Human Nature: Evolutionary Developmental Psychology.* Washington, DC: American Psychological Association.

Bjorklund, D. & Bering. J. (2002). The evolved child: Applying evolutionary developmental psychology to modern schooling. *Learning and Individual Differences, 12, 347–373.*

Blackmore, S. (1999). *The Meme Machine.* Oxford: Oxford University Press.

Boden, M. (1992). *The Creative Mind: Myths and Mechanism*s. Oxford: Oxford University Press.

Boehm, C. (1993). Egalitarian behavior, society and reverse dominance hierarchy. *Current Anthropology, 34, 227–254.*

Boehm, C. (2001). *Hierarchy in the Forest: The Evolution of Egalitarian Behavior.*Cambridge, Mass.: Harvard University Press.

Boesch, C. & Boesch-Ackermann, H. (2000). *The Chimpanzees of the Taï Forest: Behavioral Ecology and Evolution.* Oxford: Oxford University Press.

Boesch, C., Boesch-Ackermann, H. & Vigilant, L. (2006). Cooperative hunting in chimpanzees: kinship or mutualism? In P. Kappeler & C. van Schaik (Eds), *Cooperation in Primates and Humans: Mechanisms and Evolution* (pp. 139–150). Berlin: Springer.

Boesch, C. & Tomasello, M. (1998). Chimpanzee and human cultures, *Current Anthropology, 39, 591–614.*

Boesch, C. (2005). Joint cooperative hunting among wild chimpanzees: Taking natural observations seriously. *Behavioral and Brain Sciences, 28, 692–693.*

Bolhuis, J. & Macphail, E. (2001). A critique of the neuroecology of learning and memory. *Trends in Cognitive Sciences, 5, 426–433.*

Bolhuis, J. & Verhulst, S. (2009). *Tinbergen's Legacy: Function and Mechanism in Behavioral Biology.* Cambridge: Cambridge University Press.

Bolhuis, J. et al. (2011). Darwin in mind: New opportunities for evolutionary psychology. *Plos Biology, 9 (7), 1–8.*

Bondurianski, R. (2001). The evolution of male mate choice in insects: a synthesis of ideas and evidence. *Biological Review, 76, 305–339.*

Bonner, J. (1980). *The Evolution of Culture in Animals.* Princeton: Princeton University Press.

Boorman, S, & Levitt, P. (1980). *The Genetics of Altruism.* New York: Academic Press.

Bourke, A. (2011). *Principles of Social Evolution.* Oxford: Oxford University Press.

Bouzouggar, A,. et al. (2007). 82,000-year-old shell beads from North Africa and implications for the origins of modern human behavior. *Proceedings of the National Academy of the United States of America, 104,* 9964–9969.

Bowlby, J. (1981). *Attachment and Loss, Vol. I Attachment, Harmondsworth: Penguin Books*

Bowlby, J. (1985). *Attachment and Los, Vol. III Loss: Sadness and Depression.* Harmondsworth: Penguin Books.

Bowlby, J. (1991) *Attachment and Loss, Vol. II Separation: Anxiety and Anger.* Harmondsworth: Penguin Books.

Boyd, R., Gintis, H., Bowles, S. and Richerson, P. (2003). The evolution of altruistic punishment. *Proceedings of the National Academy of the United States of America, 100,* 3331–3335, (see p. 174).

Boyd, R. & Silk, J. (2003). *How Humans Evolved.* New York: W.W. Norton & Company.

Boyd, R. & Richerson, P. (1985). *Culture and the Evolutionary Process.* Chicago: University of Chicago Press.

Boyd, R. & Richerson, P. (1996). Why culture is common, but cultural evolution is rare. *Proceedings of the British Academy, 88,* 77–93.

Boyd, R. & Richerson, P. (2005). *The Origin and Evolution of Cultures.* Oxford: Oxford University Press.

Bradley, B. (2008). Reconstructing phylogenies and phenotypes: a molecular view of human evolution, *Journal of Anatomy, 212,* 337–353.

Brain, R. (1979). *The Decorated Body,* London: Hutchinson & Co.

Breland, K. & Breland, M. (1961). The misbehavior of organisms. *American Psychologist, 16,* 681–684.

Brodmann, K. (1909, tr. 2006). *Brodmann's Localization in the Cerebral Cortex,* translated and edited by Laurence Garey. New York: Springer.

Brotherton, P. & Komers, P. (2003). Mate guarding and the evolution of social monogamy. In Reichard, U. & Boesch, C. (Eds), *Monogamy: Mating Strategies and Partnerships in Birds, Humans and Other Mammals* (pp. 42–58). Cambridge: Cambridge University Press.

Brown, D. (1991). *Human Universals.* New York: McGraw-Hill, Inc.

Brown, J. (1995). *Charles Darwin: Voyaging. Volume I.* Princeton: Princeton University Press.

Brown, J. (2002). *Charles Darwin: The Power of Place, Volume II.* New York: Alfred Knopf.

Brown, J. (2007). *Darwin's Origin of Species: A Biography.* New York: Atlantic Monthly Press.

Brown, S. (2000). The 'musilanguage' model of music evolution. In N. Wallin et al. (Eds), *The Origins of Music* pp. (271–300). Cambridge, Mass.: The MIT Press.

Brown, T. (2007). *Genomes 3,* New York: Garland Science.

Brüne, M. (2008). *Textbook of Evolutionary Psychiatry: The Origins of Psychopathology.* Oxford: Oxford University Press.

Brusca, R. & Brusca, G. (2002). *Invertebrates.* Sunderland, Mass.: Sinauer.

Buck, R. (1999). The biological affects: a typology. *Psychological Review, 106,* 301–336.

Budd, G. (2001). Ecology of nontrilobite arthropods and lobopods in the Cambrium. In A. Zhuravlev & R. Riding (Eds), *The Ecology of the Cambrian Radiation* (pp. 404–427). New York: Columbia University Press.

Buller, D. (2005). *Adapting Minds: Evolutionary Psychology and the Persistent Quest.* Cambridge, Mass.: The MIT Press.

Bulmer, M. & Parker, G. (2002). The evolution of anisogamy: a game-theoretical approach. *Proceedings of the Royal Society of London B, 269,* 2381–2388.

Buonomano, D. (2007). The biology of time across different scales. *Nature Chemical Biology, 3,* 594–597.

Burgdorf, J. & Panksepp, J. (2006). The neurobiology of positive emotions. *Neuroscience and Biobehavioral Reviews, 30,* 173–187.

Burghardt, G. (1984). On the origins of play. In Peter Smith (Ed.), *Play in Animals and Humans* (pp. 5–41). Oxford: Basil Blackwell.

Burghardt, G. (1998). The evolutionary origins of play revisited: lessons from turtles. In M. Bekoff & J. Byers (Eds), *Animal Play: Evolutionary, Comparative, and Ecological Perspoectives* (pp. 1–26). Cambridge: Cambridge University Press.

Burghardt, G. (2001). Play: Attributes and neural substrates. In E. Bass (Ed.), *Handbook of Behavioral Neurobiology, Vol. 13, Developmental Psychobiology* (pp. 317–356). New York: Kluwer.

Burghardt, G. (2005). *The Genesis of Animal Play: Testing the Limits.* Cambridge. Mass.: The MIT Press.

Burghardt, G. (2010). The comparative reach of play and brain. *American Journal of Play, 2,* 338–356.

Burghardt, G. (2011). Defining and recognizing play. In Anthony Pellegrini (Ed.), *The Oxford Handbook of the Development of Play* (pp. 9–18). Oxford: Oxford University Press.

Burkhardt, F., Smith, S. (Eds) (1987). *The Correspondence of Charles Darwin*, Vol. II 1837–1843, Appendix IV. Cambridge: Cambridge University Press.

Burrows, A. (2008). The facial expression musculature in primates and its evolutionary significance. *BioEssays, 30*, 212–225.

Buss, D. (1989). Sex differences in human mate preferences: Evolutionary hypotheses tested in 37 cultures. *Behavioral and Brain Sciences, 12*, 1–49.

Buss, D. (Ed.) (2007). *The Handbook of Evolutionary Psychology*. Hoboken, N.J.: John Wiley & Sons, Inc.

Buss, David (2012). *Evolutionary Psychology: The New Science of the Mind. Fourth Edition*. Boston: Pearson & Allyn and Bacon.

Buss, D. (2009). The great struggles of life: Darwin and the emergence of evolutionary psychology. *American Psychologist, 64*, 140–148.

Buss, D. & Dedden, A. (1990). Derogation of competitors. *Journal of Social Psychology and Personal Relationships, 7*, 395–422.

Buss, D. & Haselton, M. (1989). Adaptations, exaptations, and spandrels. *American Psychologist, 53*, 533–548.

Buss, D. & Shackelford, T. (2008). Attractive women want it all: Good genes, economic investment, parenting proclivities, and emotional commitment. *Evolutionary Psychology, 6*, 134–146.

Buss, D. & Hawley, P. (Eds). (2011). *The Evolution of Personality and Individual Differences*, Oxford: Oxford University Press.

Butler, A. & Hodos, W. (2005). *Comparative Vertebrate Neuroanatomy: Evolution and Adaptation*. Hoboken, N.J.: Wiley-Interscience.

Buunk, A., Park, J. and Dubbs, S. (2008). Parent-offspring conflict in mate preferences. *Review of General Psychology, 12*, 47–62.

Byrne, R. (1995). *The Thinking Ape: Evolutionary Origins of Intelligence*. Oxford: Oxford University Press.

Byrne, R. (1988). *Machiavellian Intelligence I: Social Expertise and the Evolution of Intellect in Monkeys, Apes, and Humans*. Oxford: Clarendon Press.

Byrne, R. (1997). The technical intelligence hypothesis: an additional evolutionary stimulus to intelligence? In A. Whiten & R. Byrne (Eds), *Machiavellian Intelligence II: Extensions and Evaluations* (pp. 289–311). Cambridge: Cambridge University Press.

Byrne, R. (2000). Evolution of primate cognition. *Cognitive Science, 24*, 543–570.

Byrne, R. (2003). Novelty in deceit. In S. Reader & K. Laland (Eds), *Animal Innovation* (pp. 237–259). Oxford: Oxford University Press.

Byrne, R. (2004). The manual skills and cognition that lie behind hominid tool use. In A. Russon & D. Begun (Eds), *The Evolution of Thought: Evolutionary Origins of Great Ape Intelligence* (pp. 31–44). Cambridge: Cambridge University Press.

Byrne, R. (2007). Animal cognition: Bring me my spear. *Current Biology, 17*, R164–165.

Byrne, R. & Bates, L. (2010). Primate social cognition: Uniquely primate, uniquely social, or just unique? *Neuron, 65*, 815–830.

C

Cabanac, M. (1999). Emotion and phylogeny. *Journal of Consciousness Studies, 6*, 176–190.

Cacioppo, J. & Gardner, W. (1999). Emotion. *Annual Review of Psychology, 50*, 191–214.

Cachel, S. (2006). *Primate and Human Evolution*. Cambridge: Cambridge University Press.

Caldwell, C. & Millen, A. (2008a). Studying cumulative cultural evolution in the laboratory. *Philosophical Transactions of the Royal Society B, 363*, 3529–3539.

Caldwell, C. & Millen, A. (2008b). Experimental models for testing hypotheses about cumulative cultural evolution. *Evolution and Human Behavior, 29*, 165–171.

Caldwell, C. & Millen, A. (2009). Social learning mechanisms and cumulative cultural evolution. *Psychological Science, 20*, 1478–1483.

Caldwell, C. & Millen, A. (2010). Human cumulative culture in the laboratory: Effects of (micro) population size, *Learning & Behavior, 38*, 310–318.

Call, J. (2008). How apes use gestures: The issue of flexibility. In D. Oller & U. Griebel (Eds), *Evolution of Communicative Flexibility: Complexity, Creativity, and Adaptability in Human and Animal Communication* (pp. 235–252). Cambridge, Mass.: The MIT Press.

Call, J. and Tomasello, M. (Eds), (2007). The gestural repertoire of chimpanzees (*Pan troglodytes*), in *The Gestural Communication of Apes and Monkeys*, edited by Call, J. and Tomasello, M. Mahwah, N.J.: Lawrence Erlbaum, pp. 17–39.

Call, J. & Tomasello, M. (2008). Does the chimpanzee have a theory of mind? 30 years later. *Trends in Cognitive Science, 12*, 187–192.

Callebaut, W. (2005). The ubiquity of modularity, in W. Callebaut, D. Rasskin-Gutman (Eds). *Modularity: Understanding the Development and Evolution of Natural Complex Systems*, (pp. 3–28). Cambridge, Mass.: Massachusetts Institute of Technology.

Campbell, A. (2004). Female competition: Causes, constraints, content, and contexts, *The Journal of Sex Research*, 41: 16–26.

Campbell, Neil et al. (2008). *Biology*, Eight Edition, San Francisco: Pearson.

Candolle, A. de (1873). *Histoire des sciences et des savants depuis deux siècles*, Geneva: Georg.

Carey, N. (2011). *The Epigenetics Revolution: How Modern Biology is Rewriting Our Understanding of Genetics, Disease, and Inheritance*. London: Icon Books.

Carey, F. & Whitaker, M. (2010). Examining the acceptance of and resistance to evolutionary psychology. *Evolutionary Psychology, 8*, 284–296.

Carroll, S. (2001). Chance and necessity: the evolution of morphological complexity and diversity. *Nature, 409*, 1102–1109.

Carroll, S. (2003). Genetics and the making of *Human sapiens*, *Nature, 422*, 849–857.

Carroll, S. et al. (2005). *From DNA to Diversity: Molecular Genetics and the Evolution of Animal Design*. Oxford: Blackwell Publishing.

Carroll, S. (2005). *Endless Forms Most Beautiful: The New Science of Evo Devo*. New York: W.W. Norton & Company.

Caroll, S. (2006). *The Making of the Fittest: DNA and the Ultimate Forensic Record of Evolution*. New York: W.W. Norton & Company.

Caroll, S. (2009). *Remarkable Creatures: Epic Adventures in the Search for the Origin of Species*. London: Quercus.

Carson, S. et al. (2003). Decreased latent inhibition is associated with increased creative achievement in high-functioning individuals. *Journal of Personality and Social Psychology, 85*, 499–506.

Carson, S. (2011). Creativity and psychopathology: A shared vulnerability model. *Canadian Journal of Psychiatry, 56*, 144–153.

Carter, R. (2009). *The Brain Book*. London: Dorling Kindersley.

Cartmill, M. & Smith, F. (2009). *The Human Lineage*. Hoboken, N.J.: Wiley & Sons.

Catchpole, C. & Slater, P. (2008). *Birdsong: Biological Themes and Variations*. Cambridge: Cambridge University Press.

Cavalli-Sforza, L. & Feldman, M. (1981). *Cultural Transmission and Evolution: A Quantitative Approach*. Princeton: Princeton University Press.

Chapais, B. (2008). *Primeval Kinship: How Pair-Bonding Gave Birth to Human Society*. Cambridge, Mass.: Harvard University Press.

Chapais, B. (2010). The deep structure of human society: Primate origins and evolution, in P. Kappeler, J. Silk (Eds), *Mind the Gap* (pp. 19–51). Berlin: Springer Verlag.

Chase, I. et al. (2002). Individual differences versus social dynamics in the formation of animal dominance hierarchies. *Proceedings of the National Academy of the United States of America, 99*, 5744–5749.

Chater, N., Reali, F. and Christiansen, M. (2009). Restrictions on biological adaptations in language evolution. *Proceedings of the National Academy of the United States of America, 106*, 1015–1020, (see p. 250).

Chatterjee, S. (1997). *The Rise of Birds: 225 Million Years of Evolution*. Baltimore: The Johns Hopkins University Press.

Chen, C. et al. (1999). Population migration and the variation of dopamine D4 receptor (DRD4) allele frequencies around the globe. *Evolution and Human Behavior, 20*, 309–324.

Cheney, D. & Seyfarth, R. (1999). Mechanisms underlying the vocalizations of nonhuman primates. In M. Hauser & Konish, M. (Eds), *The Design of Communication* (pp. 629–644). Cambridge, Mass.: The MIT Press.

Cheney, D. & Seyfarth, R. (2007). *Baboon Metaphysics: The Evolution of a Social Mind*. Chicago: The University of Chicago Press.

Cheney, D. & Seyfarth, R. (2010). Primate communication and human language. In P. Kappeler & J. Silk (Eds), *Mind the Gap: Tracing the Origins of Human Universals* (pp. 283–298). New York: Springer.

Cheney, K., Bshary, R. & Grutter, A. (2008). Cleaner fish cause predators to reduce aggression toward bystanders at cleaning stations. *Behavioral Ecology, 19*, 1063–1067.

Cheng, J. et al. (2010). Pride, personality, and the evolutionary foundations of human social status. *Evolution and Human Behavior, 31*, 334–347.

Chisholm, J. (1999). Attachment and time preference: Relations between early stress and sexual behavior in a sample of American university women. *Human Nature, 10*, 51–83.

Christian, D. (2004). *Maps of Time: An Introduction to Big History*. Berkeley: University of California Press.

Christiansen, M. & Kirby, S. (2003). Language evolution: the hardest problem in science? In M. Christiansen & S. Kirby (Eds), *Language Evolution* (pp. 1–15). Oxford: Oxford University Press.

Clarke, D. (1968). *Analytical Archeology*, London: Methuen.

Cloninger, C. (1994). Temperament and personality. *Current Opinion in Neurobiology, 4,* 266–273.

Cloninger, R. et al. (1993). A Psychobiological model of temperament and character. *Archives of General Psychiatry, 50,* 975–990.

Clutton-Brock, T. (1991). *The Evolution of Parental Care.* Princeton, N.J.: Princeton University Press.

Clutton-Brock, T. (2009). Cooperation between non-kin in animal societies. *Nature, 462,* 51–57.

Clutton-Brock, T., Albon, S. & Guiness, F. (1986). Great expectations: dominance, breeding success, and offspring in red deer. *Animal Behavior, 34,* 460–471.

Clutton-Brock, T. & Parker, G. (1995). Punishment in animal societies. *Nature, 373,* 209–216.

Clutton-Brock T. et al. (1999). Selfish sentinels in cooperative mammals, *Science, 284,* 1640–1644.

Cohn, M. et al. (2009). Happiness unpacked: Positive emotions increase life satisfaction by building resilience. *Emotion, 9,* 361–368.

Confer, J. et al. (2010). Evolutionary psychology: Controversies, questions, prospects, and limitations. *American Psychologist, 65,* 110–126.

Conway Morris, S. (1999). *The Crucible of Creation: The Burgess Shale and the Rise of Animals.* Oxford: Oxford University Press.

Conway Morris, S. (2003). *Life's Solution: Inevitable Humans in a Lonely Universe.* Cambridge: Cambridge University Press.

Coolidge, F. & Wynn, T. (2005). Working memory, its executive functions, and the emergence of modern thinking. *Cambridge Archeological Journal, 15,* 5–26.

Corballis, M. (2002). *From Hand to Mouth.* Princeton: Princeton University Press.

Corballis, M. (2003). Recursion as the key to the human mind. In K. Sterelny & J. Fitness (Eds), *From Mating to Mentality: Evaluating Evolutionary Psychology* (pp. 155–171). New York: Psychology Press.

Corballis, M. (2009). Language as gesture. *Human Movement Science, 28,* 556–565.

Corballis, M. (2010). Mirror neurons and the evolution of language. *Brain & Language, 112,* 25–35.

Cornwell, E. (2005). Introductory psychology texts as a view of sociobiology/evolutionary psychology's role in psychology. *Evolutionary Psychology, 3,* 355–374.

Cosmides, L. (1989). The logic of social exchange: Has natural selection shaped how humans reason? Studies with the Wason selection task. *Cognition, 31,* 187–276.

Cosmides, L. and Tooby, J. (1992). Cognitive adaptations for social exchange. In J. Barkow, L. Cosmides and J. Tooby (Eds) *The Adapted Mind: Evolutionary Psychology and the Generation of Culture* (pp. 163–220). New York: Oxford University Press.

Cosmides, L. & Tooby, J. (2005). Neurocognitive adaptations designed for social exchange. In D. Buss (Ed.) *The Handbook of Evolutionary Psychology* (pp. 584–627). Hoboken, N.J.: John Wiley & Sons, Inc.

Covas, R. and Griesser, M. (2007). Life history and the evolution of family living in birds. *Proceedings of the Royal Society of London B, 274,* 1349–1357.

Crawford, C. & Krebs, D. (Eds) (2008). *Foundations of Evolutionary Psychology.* New York: Lawrence Erlbaum associates.

Cronin, H. (1991). *The Ant and the Peacock: Altruism and Sexual Selection From Darwin to Today.* Cambridge: Cambridge University Press.

Czajkowski, N. et al. (2011). The structure of genetic and environmental risk factors for phobias in women. *Psychological Medicine, 41,* 1987–1995.

D

Dakin, R. and Montgomerie, R. (2011). Peahens prefer peacocks displaying more eyespots, but rarely. *Animal Behaviour, 82,* 21–28 (see p. 92).

Dalgleish, T. (2004). The emotional brain. *Nature Reviews Neuroscience, 5,* 582–589.

Daly, M. & Wilson. M. (1982). Whom are newborn babies said to resemble? *Ethology and Sociobiology, 3,* 69–78.

Daly, M. & Wilson. M. (1984). A sociobiological analysis of human infanticide. In G. Hausfater, Sarah Hrdy (Eds), *Infanticide: Comparative and Evolutionary Perspectives* (pp. 487–502). New Brunswick: Aldine Transaction.

Daly, M. & Wilson, M. (1988a). Evolutionary social psychology and family homicide. *Science, 242,* 519–524.

Daly, M. & Wilson, M. (1988b). *Homicide.* New Brunswick, N.J.: Transaction Publishers.

Daly, M. & Wilson, M. (1998). *The Truth about Cinderella: A Darwinian View of Parental Love.* New Haven: Yale University Press.

Danchienne, E., Giraldeay, L. & Cézilly, F. (Eds). (2008). *Behavioral Ecology.* Oxford: Oxford University Press.

Danchin, É. et al. (2004). Public information: From nosy neighbors to cultural information. *Science, 305,* 487–491.

Danielsbacka, M. et al. (2011). Grandparental child care in Europe: Evidence for preferential investment in more certain kin. *Evolutionary Psychology, 9*, 3–24.

Darwin, C. (1859). *On the Origin of Species.* London: John Murray.

Darwin, C. (1868). *The Variation of Animals and Plants under Domestication, Vol. 2.* London: John Murray.

Darwin, C. (1871). *Descent of Man and Selection in Relation to Sex.* London: John Murray.

Darwin, C. (1872). *The Expression of Emotions in Man and Animals.* London: John Murray.

Darwin, C. (2002). *Autobiographies,* edited by Michael Neve and Sharon Messenger. London: Penguin Books.

Davidson R. (2003). Seven sins in the study of emotions: Correctives from affective neuroscience. *Brain and Cognition, 52*, 129–132.

Davidson, R., Scherer, K. & Goldsmith, H. (Eds) (2009). *Handbook of Affective Sciences.* Oxford: Oxford University Press.

Davis, N. & Daly, M. (1997). Evolutionary theory and the human family. *The Quarterly Journal of Biology, 72*, 407–435.

Dawkins, R. (1976, 1989). *The Selfish Gene.* Oxford: Oxford University Press.

Dawkins, R. (1982). *The Extended Phenotype: The Long Reach of the Gene.* Oxford: Oxford University Press (see p. 271).

Dawkins, R. (2004). *The Ancestor's Tale: A Pilgrimage to the Dawn of Life.* London: Weidenfeld & Nicolson.

Dawkins, R. (2009). *The Greatest Show on Earth: The Evidence for Evolution.* London: Transworld Publishers.

Deacon, T. (1997). *The Symbolic Species: The Co-evolution of Language and the Brain.* New York: W.W. Norton & Company.

Deacon, T. (2010). A role for relaxed selection in the evolution of the language capacity. *Proceedings of the National Academy of the United States of America, 107*, 5000–5006.

De Block, A. (2008). Why mental disorders are just mental dysfunctions (and nothing more): Some Darwinian argument. *Studies in History and Philosophy of Biological and Biomedical Sciences, 35*, 338–346 (see p. 313).

Decety, J. et al. (2004). The neural basis of cooperation and competition: an fMRI investigation. *NeuroImage, 23*, 744–751.

Del Giudice, M. (2009). Sex, attachment, and the development of reproductive strategies. *Behavioral and Brain Sciences, 32*, 1–67.

Del Giudice, M. & Belsky, J. (2011). The development of life history strategies: Toward a multistage theory. In D. Buss & P. Hawley (Eds), *The Evolution of Personality and Individual Differences* (pp. 154–176). Oxford: Oxford University Press.

Delsemme, A. (1998). *Our Cosmic Origins: From the Big Bang to the Emergence of Life and Intelligence.* Cambridge: Cambridge University Press.

Denton, D. (2005). *The Primordial Emotions: The Dawning of Consciousness.* Oxford: Oxford University Press.

Denton, D. et al. (2009). The role of primordial emotions in the evolutionary origin of consciousness. *Consciousness and Cognition, 18*, 500–514.

Desmond, A. & Moore, J. (1992). *Darwin.* London: Penguin Books.

Desmond, A., Moore, J. & Brown, J. (2007). *Charles Darwin.* Oxford: Oxford University Press.

d'Errico, F. et al. (2005). *Nassarius kraussianus* shell beads from Blombos Cave: evidence for symbolic behavior in the Middle Stone Age. *Journal of Human Evolution, 48*, 3–24.

de Waal, F. (1982). *Chimpanzee Politics; Sex and Power among Apes.* Baltimore: John Hopkins University Press.

de Waal, F. & Bonnie, K. (2009). In tune with others: The social side of primate culture. In K. Laland & B. Galef (Eds). *The Question of Animal Culture* (pp. 19–40). Cambridge, Mass.: Harvard University Press.

de Waal, F. & Ferrari, P. (Eds) (2012). *The Primate Mind: Built to Connect with Other Minds.* Cambridge, Mass.: Harvard University Press.

Dewsbury, D. (1999). The proximate and the ultimate: past, present, and future. *Behavioural Processes, 46*, 189–199.

Diamond, J. (1994). The evolution of human creativity, In J. Cambell & J. Schopf (Eds), *Creative Evolution?!* (pp. 75–84). Boston: Jones and Bartlett Publishers.

Diamond, J. (1997). *Guns, Germs, and Steel: A Short History of Everybody for the Last 13.000 Years.* London: Jonathan Cape.

Diller, K. & Cann, R. (2012). Genetic influences on language evolution: An evaluation of the evidence. In M. Tallerman & K. Gibson (Eds). *The Oxford Handbook of Language Evolution* (pp. 168–175). Oxford: Oxford University Press.

Dinstein, I. et al. (2008). A mirror up to nature. *Current Biology, 18*, R13–R18.

Distin, K. (2005) *The Selfish Meme: A Critical Reassessment.* Cambridge: Cambridge University Press.

Distin, K. (2011). *Cultural Evolution*. Cambridge: Cambridge University Press (see pp. xxiii, 285).

Dixon, D. et al. (2001). *Cassell's Atlas of Evolution: The Earth, Its Landscape, and Life Forms*. London: Cassell & Co.

Dixon, T. (2003). *From Passions to Emotions: The Creation of a Secular Psychological Category*. Cambridge: Cambridge University Press.

Dixson, A. (1998). *Primate Sexuality: Comparative Studies of the Prosimians, Monkeys, Apes, and Human Beings*. Oxford: Oxford University Press.

Dixson, A. (2009). *Sexual Selection and the Origins of Human Mating Systems*. Oxford: Oxford University Press.

Donald, M. (1991). *Origins of the Modern Mind: Three Stages in the Evolution of Culture and Cognition*. Cambridge, Mass.: Harvard University Press.

Donald, M. (1993). Précis of *Origins of the modern mind: Three stages in the evolution of culture and cognition. Behavioral and Brain Sciences, 16*, 737–791.

Doolittle, W. (1999). Phylogenetic classification and the universal tree of life. *Science, 284*, 2124–2128.

Doolittle, W. (2000). Uprooting the tree of life. *Scientific American. 282* (2), 72–77.

Dorus, S. et al. (2004). Accelerated evolution of nervous system genes in the origin of *Homo sapiens. Cell, 119*, 1027–1040.

Dunbar, R. (1992). Neocortex size as a constraint on group size in primates. *Journal of Human Evolution*, 22: 469–493.

Dunbar, R. (1993). Coevolution of neocortical size, group size and language in humans. *Behavioral and Brain Sciences, 16*, 681–735.

Dunbar, R. (1996). *Grooming, Gossip, and the Evolution of Language*. London: Faber and Faber.

Dunbar, R. (1998). The social brain hypothesis. *Evolutionary Anthropology, 6*, 178–190.

Dunbar, R.(2007). Brain and cognition in evolutionary perspective. In S. Platek, J. Keenan & T. Shackelford (Eds). *Evolutionary Cognitive Neuroscience* (pp. 211–246). Cambridge, Mass.: The MIT Press.

Dunbar, R. (2008). Mind the gap; or why humans are not just great apes. *Proceedings of the British Academy, 154*, 403–423.

Dunbar, R. (2009). Why only humans have language. In R. Botha, C. Knight (Eds), *Prehistory of Language* (pp. 12–35). Oxford: Oxford University Press.

Dunbar, R. (2010). Brain and behavior in primate evolution. In P. Kappeler, J. Silk (Eds), *Mind the Gap: Tracing the Origins of Human Universals* (pp. 315–330). Heidelberg: Springer.

Dunbar, R. & Barrett, L. (Eds) (2007). *Oxford Handbook of Evolutionary Psychology*. Oxford: Oxford University Press (see p. 33).

Dunbar, R. & Shultz, S. (2007). Evolution in the social brain. *Science, 317*, 1344–1347.

Dunn, M., Brinton, S. & Clark, L. (2010). Universal sex differences in online advertisers age preferences: comparing data from 14 cultures and 2 religious groups. *Evolution and Human Behavior, 31*, 383–393.

Durante, K. & Haselton, M. (2008). Changes in women's choice of dress across the ovulatory cycle: Naturalistic and laboratory task-based evidence. *Personality and Social Psychology Bulletin, 34*, 1451–1460.

Durham, W. (1991). *Coevolution: Genes, Culture and Human Diversity*. Stanford: Stanford University Press.

E

Edlund, J. & Sagarin, B. (2010). Mate value and mate preferences: An investigation into decisions made with and without constraints. *Personality and Individual Differences, 49*, 835–839.

Ekman, P. & Friesen, W. (1971). Constants across cultures in the face and emotion. *Journal of Personality and Social Psychology, 17*, 124–129.

Ekman, P. (1980). *The Face of Man: Expressions of Universal Emotions in a New Guinea Village*. New York: Garland STPM Press.

Ekman, P. & Friesen, W. (1978). *Facial Action Coding System*. Palo Alto: Consulting Psychologists Press.

Ekman, P. (1992). An argument for basic emotions, *Cognition and Emotion. 6*, 169–200.

Ekman, P. (2003). *Emotions Revealed: Understanding Faces and Feelings*. London: Weidenfeld & Nicolson.

Eldredge, N. (2005). *Darwin: Discovering the Tree of Life*. New York: W.W. Norton & Company.

Ellis, B. (2004). Timing of pubertal maturation in girls: An integrated life history approach. *Psychological Bulletin, 130*, 920–958.

Ellis, B. & Bjorklund, D. (Eds) (2005). *Origins of the Social Mind: Evolutionary Psychology and Child Development*. New York: The Guilford Press (see p. 337).

Ellis, B. & Essex, M. (2007). Family environments, adrenarche, and sexual maturation : A longitudinal test of a life history model. *Child Development, 78*, 1799–1817.

Elton, S. (2008). The environmental context of human evolutionary history in Eurasia and Africa. *Journal of Anatomy, 212*, 377–393.

Emery, N. (2000). The eyes have it: the neuroethology, function and evolution of social gaze. *Neuroscience and Biobehavioral Reviews, 24*, 581–604.

Emery, N. (2006). Cognitive ornithology: The evolution of avian intelligence. *Philosophical Transactions of the Royal Society B, 361*, 23–43.

Emery, N. & Clayton, N. (2004). The mentality of crows: Convergent evolution of intelligence in corvids and apes. *Science, 306*, 1903–1907.

Emery, N. & Clayton, N. (2005). Evolution of the avian brain and intelligence. *Current Biology, 15*, R946–R950.

Emery, N. & Clayton, N. (2009). Comparative social cognition. *Annual Review of Psychology, 60*, 87–113.

Emlen, S. (1995). An evolutionary theory of the family. *Proceedings of the National Academy of the United States of America, 92*, 8092–8099.

Emlen, S. (1997). The evolutionary study of human family systems. *Social Science Information, 36*, 563–589.

Emlen, S. & Oring, L. (1977). Ecology, sexual selection, and the evolution of mating systems. *Science, 197*, 215–223.

Enard, W. et al. (2002). Molecular evolution of *FOXP2*, a gene involved in speech and language. *Nature, 418*, 869–872.

Enard, W. & Pääbo, S. (2004). Comparative primate genomics. *Annual Review of Genomics and Human Genetics, 5*, 351–378.

Enggist-Dueblin, P. & Pfister, U. (2002). Cultural transmission of vocalizations in ravens, *Corvus corax*. *Animal Behaviour, 64*, 831–841.

Ennatah, S. et al. (2011). Independent introduction of two lactase-persistence alleles into human populations reflects different history of adaptation to milk culture. *The American Journal of Human Genetics, 82*, 57–72.

Enquist, M. & Ghirlanda, S. (2007). Evolution of social learning does not explain the origin of human cumulative culture. *Journal of Theoretical Biology, 129*, 129–135.

Ereshefsky, M. (2009). Defining 'health' and 'disease'. *Studies in History and Philosophy of Biological and Biomedical Science, 40*, 221–227.

Ermer, E., Guerin, S. & Cosmides, L. (2006). Theory of mind 'broad and narrow': Reasoning about social exchange engages to ToM areas, precautionary reasoning does not. *Social Neuroscience, 1*, 196–219.

Evans, J. (2005). Deductive reasoning. In K. Holyaok & R. Morrison (Eds), *The Cambridge Handbook of Thinking and Reasoning* (pp. 169–84). Cambridge: Cambridge University Press.

F

Fadiga, L., Craighero, L. Buccino, G. & Rizzolattis, G. (2002). Speech listening specifically modulates excitability of tongue muscles: A TMS study. *European Journal of Neuroscience, 15*, 399–402 (see p. 272).

Fagan, B. (1999). *World Prehistory: A Brief Introduction*. New York: Longman.

Fairbairn, D., Blanckenthorn, W. & Székely, T. (2007). *Evolutionary Studies of Sexual Size Dimorphism*. Oxford: Oxford University Press.

Fairbanks, L. (2001). Individual differences in response to a stranger: Social impulsivity as a dimension of temperament in vervet monkeys. *Journal of Comparative Psychology, 115*, 22–28.

Falk, D. (2004). Prelinguistic evolution in early hominins: whence motherese? *Behavioral and Brain Sciences, 27*, 491–541.

Fehr, E. & Gächter, S. (2002). Altruistic punishment in humans. *Nature, 415*, 137–140.

Fehr, E. & Gächter, S. (2003). The nature of human altruism. *Nature, 425*, 785–791.

Fehr, E. & Gächter, S. (2004). Third-part punishment and social norms. *Evolution and Human Behavior, 25*, 63–87.

Fellous, J. (1999). Neuromodulatory basis of emotion. *Neuroscientist, 5*, 283–294.

Ferrari, P. et al. (2003). Mirror neurons responding to the observation of ingestive and communicative mouth actions in the monkey ventral premotor cortex. *European Journal of Neuroscience, 17*, 1703–1714.

Fisher, H. (1993). *Anatomy of Love: The Natural History of Monogamy, Adultery and Divorce*. New York: Simon & Schuster.

Fitch, W. (2005). The evolution of language: a comparative review. *Biology and Philosophy, 20*, 193–230.

Fitch, W. (2006). The biology and evolution of music: A comparative perspective. *Cognition, 100*, 173–215.

Fitch, W. (2010). *The Evolution of Language*. Cambridge: Cambridge University Press.

Fitch, W. et al. (2010). Social cognition and the evolution of language: Constructing cognitive phylogenies. *Neuron, 65*, 795–814.

Fitzgerald, C. & Whitaker, M. (2010). Examining the acceptance of and resistance to evolutionary psychology. *Evolutionary Psychology, 8*, 284–296.

Flaherty, A. (2005). Frontotemporal and dopaminergic control of idea generation and creative drive. *The Journal of Comparative Neurology, 493*, 147–153.

Fleagle, J. (1999). *Primate Adaptation and Evolution*. San Diego: Academic Press.

Flier, J. & Maratos-Flier, E. (2007). What fuels fat. *Scientific American, 297 (3)*, 46–55.

Flinn, M., Geary, D. & Ward, C. (2005). Ecological dominance, social competition and coalitionary arms races: Why humans evolved extraordinary intelligence. *Evolution and Human Behavior, 26*, 10–46.

Fodor, J. (1983). *The Modularity of Mind: An Essay on Faculty Psychology*. Cambridge, Mass.: The MIT Press.

Fodor, J. (1985). Précis of *The Modularity of Mind, Behavioral and Brain Sciences, 8*, 1–42.

Fodor, J. (1998). *In Critical Condition: Polemical Essays on Cognition and the Philosophy of Mind*. Cambridge, Mass.: The MIT Press.

Fodor, J. (2000). *The Mind Doesn't Work That Way: The Scope and Limits of Computational Psychology*. Cambridge, Mass.: The MIT Press.

Foley, R. (1998). *Humans before Humanity*. Oxford: Blackwell.

Foley, R. (1996). An evolutionary and chronological framework for human social behavior. *Proceedings of the British Academy, 88*, 95–117.

Foley, R. (1999). Pattern and process in hominid evolution. In J. Bintliff (Ed.), *Structure and Contingency: Evolutionary Processes in Life and Human Society* (pp. 31–42). London: Leicester University Press.

Foley, R. (2001). Evolutionary perspectives on the origin of human social institutions. In W. Runciman (Ed.). *The Origin of Human Social Institutions* (pp. 171–195). Oxford: Oxford University Press.

Foley, R. & Lahr, M. (1997). Mode 3 technologies and the evolution of modern humans. *Cambridge Archeological Journal, 7 (1)* 3–36 (see p. 77).

Ford, H. (1922). *My Life and Work: An Autobiography of Henry Ford*. London: William Heinemann Ltd.

Forbes, S. (2005). *A Natural History of Families*. Princeton: Princeton University Press.

Fox, E. et al. (2000). Facial expressions of emotions: Are angry faces detected more efficiently? *Cognition and Emotion, 14*, 61–92.

Fragaszy, D. & Perry, S. (2008). Towards a biology of traditions. In D. Fragaszy & S. Perry (Eds), *The Biology of Traditions: Models and Evidence* (pp. 1–32). Cambridge: Cambridge University Press.

Francis, R. (2004). *Why Men Won't Ask for Directions: The Seductions of Sociobiology*. Princeton: Princeton University Press.

Fredrickson, B. (1998). What good are positive emotions? *Review of General Psychology, 2*, 300–319.

Freeberg, T. (2006). Social complexity can drive vocal complexity: Group size influences vocal information in Carolina chickadees. *Psychological Science, 17*, 557–561.

Fridlund, A. (1994). *Human Facial Expression: An Evolutionary Perspective*. New York: The Academic Press.

Fry, D. (2005). Rough-and-tumble social play in humans. In A. Pellegrini & P. Smith (Eds), *The Nature of Play: Great Apes and Humans* (pp. 54–85). New York: The Guilford Press.

Furnham, A. (2009). Sex differences in mate selection preferences. *Personality and Individual Differences, 47*, 262–267.

Fuster, J. (2001). The prefrontal cortex-an update: Time is of the essence. *Neuron, 30*, 319–333.

G

Galef, B. (2009). Culture in animals? in K. Laland & B. Galef (Eds), *The Question of Animal Culture* (pp. 222–246). Cambridge, Mass.: Harvard University Press.

Gallese V. et al. (1996). Action recognition in the premotor cortex. *Brain, 119*, 593–609.

Galton, F. (1869). *Hereditary Genius: An Inquiry into its Laws and Consequences*. London: Macmillan

Galton, F. (1874). *English Men of Science: Their Nature and Nurture*. London: Macmillan.

Gamble, C. (1998). Paleolithic society and the release from proximity: a network approach to intimate relations. *World Archeology, 29*, 426–449.

Gangestad, S. & Simpson, J. (2007). Introduction, in S. Gangestad, J. Simpson (Eds), *The Evolution of Mind: Fundamental Questions and Controversies* (pp.1–21). New York: The Guilford Press.

Gangestad, S., Thornhill, R. & Garver-Apgar, C. (2010). Fertility in the cycle predicts women's interest in sexual opportunism. *Evolution and Human Behavior, 31*, 400–411.

Garland, E. et al. (2010). Upwards spirals of positive emotions counter downwards spirals of negativity: Insights from the broaden-and-build theory and affective neuroscience on the treatment of emotion dysfunctions and deficits in psychopathology. *Clinical Psychology Review, 30*, 849–864.

Garstang, W. (1922). The theory of recapitulation: A critical re-statement of the biogenetic law. *Zoological Journal of the Linnean Society, 35*, 81–101.

Gartner, J. (2005). *The Hypomanic Edge: The Link Between (a Little) Craziness and (a Lot of) Success.* New York: Simon and Schuster.

Gaulin, S. & McBurney, D. (2004). *Evolutionary Psychology.* NJ: Pearson Education. Upper Saddle River.

Geary, D. (2000). Evolution and proximate expression of paternal investment. *Psychological Bulletin, 126, 55–77.*

Geary, D. (2005a). Evolution of paternal investment, in D. Buss (Ed.), *The Handbook of Evolutionary Psychology* (pp. 483–505). Hoboken, N.J.: John Wiley & Sons, Inc.

Geary, D. (2005b). *The Origin of Mind: Evolution of Brain, Cognition and General Intelligence.* Washington: American Psychological Association.

Geary, D. (2009). The evolution of general fluid intelligence, In S. Platek *&* T. Shackelford (Eds), *Foundations in Evolutionary Cognitive Neuroscience* (pp. 22–56). Cambridge: Cambridge University Press.

Geary, D. (2010). *Male, Female: The Evolution of Human Sex Differences.* Washington: American Psychological Association.

Geary, D. & Bjorklund, D. (2000). Evolutionary developmental psychology. *Child Development,* 71, 57–65 (see p. 336).

Geary, D. & Flinn, M. (2001). Evolution of human parental behavior and the human family. *Parenting: Science and Practice, 1, 5–61.*

Geher, G. & Miller, G. (Eds) (2007). *Mating Intelligence: Sex, Relationships, and the Mind's Reproductive System.* New York: Psychology Press.

Gentilucci, M. & Corballis, M. (2006). From manual gesture to speech: A gradual transition. *Neuroscience and Biobehavioral Reviews, 30, 949–960.*

Gentner, T. et al. (2006). Recursive syntactic pattern learning by songbirds. *Nature, 440,* 1204–1207.

Gibson, G. (2009). *It Takes a Genome: How a Clash Between Our Genes and Modern Life Is Making Us Sick.* Upper Saddle River. N.J.: Pearson Education.

Gibson, K., Rumbaugh, D. & Beran, M. (2001). Bigger is better: brain size in relationship to cognition. In D. Falk & K Gibson (Eds), *Evolutionary Anatomy of the Primate Cerebral Cortex* (pp. 79–97). Cambridge: Cambridge University Press.

Giddens, A. (1984). *The Constitution of Society.* Berkeley: University of California Press.

Giedion, S. (1969). *Mechanization Takes Command: A contribution to anonymous history.* New York: W.W. Norton & Comp.

Gilbert, P. (1992). *Depression: The Evolution of Powerlessness.* Hove: Psychology Press.

Gilbert, S. (2010). *Developmental Biology, 9th Edition.* Sunderland, Mass.: Sinauer Associates, Inc., Publishers.

Gissis, S. & Jablonka, E. (Eds) (2011). *Transformations of Lamarckism: From Subtle Fluids to Molecular Biology.* Cambridge, Mass.: The MIT Press.

Gleitman, L. & Papafragou, A. (2005). Language and thought. In K. Holyoak & R. Morris (Eds), *The Cambridge Handbook of Thinking and Reasoning* (pp. 633–661). Cambridge: Cambridge University Press.

Gluckman, P. & Hanson, M. (2006). *Mismatch: The Lifestyle Diseases Timebomb.* Oxford: Oxford University Press.

Gluckman, P., Beedle, A. & Hanson, M. (2009). *Principles of Evolutionary Medicine.* Oxford: Oxford University Press.

Gosling, S., & Austin Harley, B. (2009). Animal models of personality and cross-species comparisons. In P. Corr & G. Matthews (Eds), *The Cambridge Handbook of Personality Psychology* (pp. 275–286). Cambridge: Cambridge University Press.

Gottschall, J. (2007). Greater emphasis on female attractiveness in *Homo sapiens:* A revised solution to an old evolutionary riddle. *Evolutionary Psychology, 5,* 347–357.

Gould, J. & Gould, C. (1997). *Sexual Selection: Mate Choice and Courtship in Nature.* New York: Scientific American Library.

Gould, J. & Gould, C. (2007). *Animal Architects: Building and the Evolution of Intelligence.* New York: Basic Books.

Gould, S. (1977). *Ontogeny and Phylogeny.* Cambridge, Mass.: The Belknap Press of the Harvard University Press.

Gould, S. (1991a). Exaptation: A crucial tool for an evolutionary psychology. *Journal of Social Issues, 47,* 43–65.

Gould, S. (1991b). *Wonderful Life; The Burgess Shale and the Nature of History.* London: Penguin Books.

Gould, S. (1997). Sociobiology: The art of storytelling. *New Scientist, 80,* 530–533.

Grant, K., Estes, G. (2009). *Darwin in Galápagos: Footsteps to a New World.* Princeton: Princeton University Press.

Grant, V. (1998). *Maternal Personality, Evolution and the Sex Ratio: Do mothers control the sex of the infant?* London: Routledge.

Grant, V. (2003). The maternal dominance hypothesis: questioning Trivers and Willard. *Evolutionary Psychology, 1,* 96–107.

Grant, V. (2007). Could maternal testosterone levels govern mammalian sex ratio deviations? *Journal of Theoretical Biology, 246,* 708–719.

Gray, P. & Anderson, K. (2010). *Fatherhood: Evolution and Human Paternal Behavior.* Cambridge, Mass.: Harvard University Press.

Greenfield, S. (1996). *The Human Mind Explained.* New York: Henry Holt and Company.

Griebel, U. & Oller, D. (2008). Evolutionary forces favoring communicative flexibility. In D. Oller & U. Griebel (Eds), *Evolution of Communicative Flexibility: Complexity, Creativity, and Adaptability in Human and Animal Communication* (pp. 9–40). Cambridge, Mass.: The MIT Press.

Griffin, A. & West, S. (2003). Kin discrimination and the benefit of helping in cooperatively breeding vertebrates. *Science, 302,* 634–636.

Griffiths, P. (1997). *What Emotions Really Are: The Problem of Psychological Categories.* Chicago: The University of Chicago Press.

Griffiths, P. (1999). Modularity, and the psychoevolutionary theory of emotion, in *Mind and Cognition,* (ed.) W. Lycan, Oxford: Blackwell, pp. 516–529.

Grutter, A. (1999). Cleaner fish really clean. *Nature, 398,* 672–673.

Gundling, T. (2005). *First in Line: Tracing Our Ape Ancestry.* New Haven: Yale University Press.

Güntürkün, O. (2005). The avian 'prefrontal cortex' and cognition. *Current opinion in Neurobiology, 15,* 686–693.

Guthrie, R. (2005). *The Nature of Paleolithic Art.* Chicago: The University of Chicago Press.

H

Haeckel, E. (1866). *Generelle Morphologie der Organismen, 2 volumes.* Berlin: Georg Reimer.

Hagen, E. (1999). The functions of postpartum depression. *Evolution and Human Behavior, 20,* 325–539.

Hall, B. (1999). *Evolutionary Developmental Biology.* Dordrecht: Kluwer Academic Publishers.

Hall, B. & Olson, W. (2003). *Keywords and Concepts in Evolutionary Developmental Biology.* Cambridge, Mass.: The MIT Press.

Hall, B. & Hallgrimsson, B. (2008). *Strickberger's Evolution: The Integration of Genes, Organisms, and Populations.* Boston: Jones and Bartlett Publishers.

Hamilton, W. (1964). The genetical evolution of social behavior. I and II. *Journal of Theoretical Behavior, 7,* 1–52.

Hamilton, W. (1990). Sexual reproduction as an adaptation to resist parasites (A Review). *Proceedings of the National Academy of Sciences of the USA, 87,* 3566–3573.

Hammerschidt, K. & Fischer, J. (2008). Constraints in primate vocal production. In D. Oller & U. Griebe (Eds), *Evolution of Communicative Flexibility: Complexity, Creativity, and Adaptability in Human and Animal Communication* (pp. 93–119). Cambridge, Mass.: The MIT Press.

Hammerstein, P. (Ed.) (2003). *Genetic and Cultural Evolution of Cooperation.* Cambridge, Mass.: The MIT Press.

Hansen, C. & Hansen, R. (1988). Finding the face in the crowd: An anger superiority effect. *Journal of Personality and Social Psychology, 54,* 917–924.

Hapgood, P. & Franklin, N. (2008). The revolution that didn't arrive: A review of Pleistocene Sahul. *Journal of Human Evolution, 55,* 187–222.

Hare, B. et al. (2000). Chimpanzees know what conspecifics do and do not see. *Animal Behaviour, 59,* 771–785.

Hare, B. et al. (2001). Do chimpanzees know what conspecifics know? *Animal Behaviour, 61,* 139–151.

Hare, B. & Tomasello, M. (2004). Chimpanzees are more skilful in competitive than in cooperative tasks. *Animal Behaviour, 68,* 571–581.

Harrington, A. (1991). Beyond phrenology: Localization theory in the modern era. In P. Corsi (Ed.), *The Enchanted Loom: Chapters in the History of Neuroscience* (pp. 207–215). New York: Oxford University Press.

Harris, C. (2011). Menstrual cycle and facial preferences reconsidered. *Sex Roles, 64,* 669–681.

Harris, G. et al. (2007). Children killed by genetic parents versus stepparents. *Evolution and Human Behavior, 28,* 85–95.

Harris. J. (1999). *The Nurture Assumption: Why children turn out of the way they do.* London: Bloomsbury.

Hart, B. & Hart, L. (1992). Reciprocal allogrooming in impala. *Animal Behaviour, 44,* 1073–1083.

Haselton, M. et al. (2007). Ovulatory shifts in human female ornamentation: Near ovulation, women dress to impress. *Hormones and Behavior, 51,* 40–45.

Hauser, M. (1992). Costs of deception: Cheaters are punished in rhesus monkeys (*Macaca mulatta*). *Proceedings of the National Academy of Sciences of the USA*, 89: 12137–12139.

Hauser, M. (1996). *The Evolution of Communication.* Cambridge, Mass.: The MIT Press.

Hauser, M., Chomsky, N. & Fitch, W. (2002). The faculty of language: What is it, who has it, and how did it evolve? *Science*, 298, 1569–1579.

Hawkes, K. (1991). Showing off: tests of an hypothesis about men's foraging goals. *Ethology and Sociobiology*, 12, 29–54.

Hawkes, K. (2002). Showing off, handicap signaling, and the evolution of men's work. *Evolutionary Anthropology*, 11, 58–67.

Hawkes, K. et al. (1998). Grandmothering, menopause, and the evolution of human life histories. *Proceedings of the National Academy of Science USA*, 95, 1336–1339.

Headland, T. & Greene, H. (2011). Hunter-gatherers and other primates as prey, predators, and competitors of snakes. *Proceedings of the National Academy of Sciences of the USA*, 108, E1470–E1474.

Healy, S. & Rowe, C. (2007). A critique of comparative studies of brain size. *Proceedings of the Royal Society B*, 274, 453–464.

Heinrich, B. (1995). An experimental investigation of insight in common ravens (*Corvus corax*). *The Auk*, 112, 994–1003.

Heinrich, B. (1999). *Mind of the Raven: Investigations and Adventures with Wolf-Birds.* New York: HarperCollins Publishers.

Heinrich, B. & Bugnyar, T. (2005). Testing problem solving in ravens: String-pulling to reach food. *Ethology*, 111, 962–976.

Heinrich, B. & Bugnyar, T. (2007). Just how smart are ravens? *Scientific American*, 296 (4), 46–53.

Held, L. Jr (2009). *Quirks of Human Anatomy: An Evo-Devo Look at the Human Body.* Cambridge: Cambridge University Press.

Hennig, W. (1966). *Phylogenetic Systematics*, Urbana: University of Illinois Press.

Henrich, J. (2006). Cooperation, punishment, and the evolution of human institutions. *Science*, 312, 60–61.

Henrich, J. et al. (2006). Costly punishment across human societies. *Science*, 312, 1767–1770.

Henrich, J. & McElreath, R. (2003). The evolution of cultural evolution. *Evolutionary Anthropology*, 12, 123–135.

Henrich, J. & McElreath, R. (2007). Dual-inheritance theory: the evolution of human cultural capacities and cultural evolution. In R. Dunbar & L. Barrett (Eds), *Oxford Handbook of Evolutionary Psychology* (pp. 555–570). Oxford: Oxford University Press.

Henrich, J., Boyd, R. & Richerson, P. (2008). Five misunderstandings about cultural evolution. *Human Nature*, 19, 119–137.

Henrich, J., Boyd, R. & Richerson, P. (2012). The puzzle of monogamous marriage. *Philosophical Transactions of the Royal Society B*, 367, 657–669.

Henshilwood, C. et al. (2011). A 100,000-year-old ochre-processing workshop at Blombos cave, South Africa. *Science*, 334, 219–222.

Hickok, G. (2008). Eight problems for the mirror neuron theory of action understanding in monkeys and humans. *Journal of Cognitive Neuroscience*, 21, 1229–1243.

Hill, K. (2010). Experimental studies of animal social learning in the wild: Trying to untangle the mystery of human culture. *Learning & Behavior*, 38, 319–328.

Hill, C. & Ball, H. (1996). Abnormal births and other 'ill omens': The adaptive case for infanticide. *Human Nature*, 4, 381–401.

Hillis, D. (2007). Making evolution relevant and exciting to biology students. *Evolution*, 61, 1261–1264.

Hinde, R. (1997). *Relationships: A Dialectical Perspective,* Hove: Psychology Press.

Hirata, S., Watanabe, K. & Kawai, M. (2008). 'Sweet-potato washing' revisited. In T. Matsuzawa (Ed.), *Primate Origins of Human Cognition and Behavior* (pp. 487–508). Tokyo: Springer.

Hochberg, Z. (2009). Evo-devo of child growth II: human life history and transition between its phases. *European Journal of Endocrinology*, 160, 135–141.

Hochberg, Z. (2012). *Evo-Devo of Child Growth: Treatise on Child Growth and Human Evolution.* Hoboken, N.J.: Wiley-Blackwell.

Hockett, C. (1960). Logical considerations in the study of animal communication. In W. Lanyon & W. Tavolga (Eds), *Animal Sounds and Communication* (pp. 392–430). Washington, D.C.: American Institute of Biological Sciences.

Hockett, C. (1963). The problem of universals in language. In J. Greenberg (Ed.), *Universals of Language* (pp. 1–29). Cambridge, Mass.: The MIT Press.

Hoekstra, R. (2005). Why sex is good, *Nature*, 434, 571–573.

Hoffert, S. & Anderson, K. (2003). Are all dads equal? Biology versus marriage as a basis for paternal investment. *Journal of Marriage and Family*, 65, 213–2342.

Holcomb, H. (2005). Buller does to Evolutionary Psychology what Kitcher did to Sociobiology. *Evolutionary Psychology, 3,* 392–401.

Holyoak, K. & Thagard, P. (1995). *Mental Leaps: Analogy in Creative Thought.* Cambridge, Mass.: The MIT Press.

Horwitz, A. & Wakefield, J. (2007). *The Loss of Sadness: How Psychiatry Transformed Normal Sorrow into Depressive Disorder.* Oxford: Oxford University Press.

Hovers, E. et al. (2003). An early case of color symbolism: Ochre use by modern humans in Qafzeh Cave. *Current Anthropology, 44,* 491–522.

Hrdy, S. (1999). *Mother Nature: Natural Selection and the Female of the Species.* London: Chatto & Windus.

Hrdy, S. (2007). Evolutionary context of human development: The cooperative breeding model. In C. Salmon & T. Shackelford (Eds), *Family Relationships: An Evolutionary View* (pp. 39–68). Oxford: Oxford University Press.

Hrdy, S. (2009). *Mothers and Others: The Evolutionary Origins of Mutual Understanding.* Cambridge, Mass.: The Belknap Press of Harvard University Press.

Hughes, S., Harrison, M. & Gallup Jr, G. (2007). Sex differences in romantic kissing among college students: An evolutionary perspective. *Evolution and Human Behavior, 5,* 612–631.

Hughes, V. (2011). Shades of grief: When does mourning become a mental illness that doctors should treat? *Scientific American, 304* (6), 17–18.

Humphrey, N. (1983). *Consciousness Regained: Chapters in the Development of Mind.* Oxford: Oxford University Press.

Hunt, J. et al. (2009). Male–male competition, female mate-choice and their interaction: determining total sexual selection. *Journal of Evolutionary Biology, 22,* 13–26.

Hunt, G. & Gray, R. (2002). Diversification and cumulative evolution in New Caledonian crow tool manufacture. *Proceedings of the Royal Society of London B, 270,* 867–874.

Hurford, J. (2002). Language beyond our grasp: What mirror neurons can, and cannot, do for the evolution of language. In D. Oller & U. Griebel (Eds), *Evolution of Communication Systems: A Comparative Approach* (pp. 297–313). Cambridge, Mass.: The MIT Press.

Hurford, J. (2007). *The Origins of Meaning: Language in the Light of Evolution.* Oxford: Oxford University Press.

Hurley, S. & Chater, N. (Eds) (2005). *Perspectives on Imitation: From Neuroscience to Social Science.* Two Volumes. Cambridge, MA: The MIT Press (see p. 285).

Huxley, J. (1914). The courtship habits of the Great Crested Grebe (*Podiceps cristatus*); with an addition to the theory of sexual selection. *Proceedings of the Zoological Society of London, 35,* 491–562.

Huxley, J. (2010; orig. 1942). *The Modern Synthesis:* The definitive edition. Cambridge, Mass.: The MIT Press.

Huxley, T. (1863). *Evidence as to Man's Place in Nature.* New York: McGraw-Hill.

I

Immelman, K. & Beer, C. (1992). *A Dictionary of Ethology.* Cambridge, Mass.: Harvard University Press.

Isbell, L. (2006). Snakes as agents of evolutionary change in primate brains. *Journal of Human Evolution, 51,* 1–35.

Itier, R. & Batty, M. (2009). Neural bases of eye and gaze processing: The core of social cognition. *Neuroscience and Biobehavioral Reviews, 33,* 843–863.

J

Jablonka, E. (2011). Lamarckian problematics in biology. In Gissis, S. & Jablonka, E. (Eds) (2011). *Transformations of Lamarckism: From Subtle Fluids to Molecular Biology* (pp. 145–155). Cambridge, Mass.: The MIT Press.

Jablonka, E., Lamb, M. (2005). *Evolution in Four Dimensions: Genetic, Epigenetic, Behavioral, and Symbolic Variation in the History of Life.* Cambridge, Mass.: The MIT Press.

Jablonka, E., Lamb, M. (2006). The evolution of information in the major transitions. *Journal of Theoretical Biology, 239,* 236–246.

Jablonka, E. & Lamb, M. (2007a). The expanded evolutionary synthesis—a response to Godfrey-Smith, Haig, and West-Eberhard. *Biology and Philosophy, 22,* 453–472.

Jablonka, E. & Lamb, M. (2007b). Précis of *Evolution in Four Dimensions. Behavioral and Brain Sciences, 30,* 353–392.

Jablonka, E. & Lamb, M. (2010). Transgenerational epigenetic inheritance. In Pigliucci, M. & Müller, G. (Eds) (2010). *Evolution—The Extended Synthesis* (pp. 137–174). Cambridge, Mass.: The MIT Press.

Jackson, J. (1887). Remarks on evolution and dissolution of the nervous system. In J. Taylor (Ed.), *Selected Writings of John Hughlings Jackson, Vol. 2* (pp. 92–118). London: Hodder & Stoughton.

James, W. (1890). *The Principles of Psychology, Volume One.* New York: Dover Publications.

Jarvis, P. (2006) Rough and tumble play: Lessons in life. *Evolutionary Psychology, 4,* 336–346.

Jasienski, G. et al. (2004). Large breasts and narrow waists indicate high reproductive potential in women. *Proceedings of the Royal Society of London B, 271,* 1213–1217.

Jerison, H. (1973). *Evolution of the Brain and Intelligence*, New York: Academic Press.

Joffe, T. & Dunbar, R. (1997). Visual and socio-cognitive information processing in primate brain evolution. *Proceedings of the Royal Society of London, 264,* 1303–1307 (see p. 25).

Johnson, K. & Fredrickson, B. (2005). 'We all look the same to me'; Positive emotions eliminate the own-race bias in face recognition. *Psychological Science, 16,* 875–881.

Johnson, K. et al. (2010). Smile to see the forest: Facially expressed positive emotions broaden cognition. *Cognition and Emotion, 24,* 299–321.

Juslin, P. & Sloboda, J. (Eds) (2010), *Handbook of Music and Emotion: Theory, Research, and Applications.* Oxford: Oxford University Press.

K

Kaas, J. (Ed.) (2007). *Evolution of Nervous Systems: A Comprehensive Reference, Four Volumes.* Amsterdam: Academic Press.

Kanwisher, N., McDermoth, J. & Chun, M. (1997). The fusiform face area: A module in human extrastriate cortex specialized for face perception. *The Journal of Neuroscience, 17,* 4302–4311.

Kanwisher, N., Yovel, G. (2006). The fusiform face area: a cortical region specialized for the perception of faces. *Philosophical Transactions of the Royal Society B, 361,* 2109–2128.

Kaplan, H. & Gangestad, S. (2005). Life history theory and evolutionary psychology. In D. Buss (Ed.), *The Handbook of Evolutionary Psychology* (pp. 68–95). Hoboken, N.J.: John Wiley & Sons, Inc.

Karanth, K. et al. (2005). Ancient DNA from giant extinct lemurs confirms single origin of Malagasy primates. *Proceedings of the National Academy of Sciences of the USA, 102,* 5090–5095.

Kauth, B. (Ed.) (2006). *Handbook of the Evolution of Human Sexuality.* New York: The Haworth Press, Inc.

Keller, M. & Miller, G. (2006). Resolving the paradox of common, harmful, heritable mental disorders: Which evolutionary genetic models work best? *Behavioral and Brain Sciences, 29,* 385–452.

Kendrick, K. et al. (2001). Sheep don't forget a face. *Nature, 414,* 165–166.

Kennedy, G. (2005). From the ape's dilemma to the weanling's dilemma: early weaning and its evolutionary context. *Journal of Human Evolution, 48,* 123–145.

Kenrick, D., Gutierres, S. & Goldberg, L. (1989). Influence of popular erotica on judgments of strangers and mates. *Journal of Experimental Psychology, 25,* 159–167.

Kenward, B. et al. (2005). Tool manufacture by naïve juvenile crows. *Nature, 433,* 121.

Key, C. & Aiello, L. (1999). The evolution of social organization. In R. Dunbar, C. Knight & Power, C. (Eds), *The Evolution of Culture* (pp. 15–33). Edinburgh: Edinburgh University Press.

Keysers, C. & Gazzola, V. (2009). Expanding the mirror: vicarious activity for actions, emotions, and sensations. *Current Opinion in Neurobiology, 19,* 666–671.

Keysers, C. & Gazzola, V. (2010). Social Neuroscience: Mirror neurons recorded in humans, *Current Biology, 20,* R353–R354.

King, J. et al. (1999). Perception of personality traits and semantic learning in evolved hominids. In M. Corballis & S. Lea. (Eds), *The Descent of Mind: Psychological Perspectives on Hominid Evolution* (pp. 98–115). Oxford: Oxford University Press.

Kinney, D. & Richards, R. (2007). Artistic creativity and affective disorders: Are they connected? In C. Martindale et al. (Eds), *Evolutionary and Neurocognitive Approaches to Aesthetics, Creativity and the Arts* (pp. 225–237). New York: Baywood Publishing Company.

Kirby, S., Cornish, H. & Smith, K. (2008). Cumulative cultural evolution in the laboratory: An experimental approach to the origins of structure in human language. *Proceedings of the National Academy of Sciences of the USA, 31,* 10681–10686.

Klein, R. (2009). *The Human Career: Human Biological and Cultural Origins.* Chicago: The University of Chicago Press.

Klein, R. & Blake, E. (2002). *The Dawn of Human Culture.* New York: John Wiley & Sons.

Klein, J, & Takahata, N. (2002). *Where Do We Come From? The Molecular Evidence for Human Descent.* Berlin: Springer Verlag.

Kleinginna, P. & Kleinginna A. (1981). A categorized list of emotion definitions, with suggestions for a consensual definition. *Motivation and Emotion, 5,* 345–379.

Knight, C. et al. (1995). The human symbolic revolution: A Darwinian account.*Cambridge Archeological Journal, 51,* 75–114.

Kohler, C. et al. (2004). Differences in facial expression of four universal emotions. *Psychiatry Research, 128,* 235–244.

Köhler, W. (1957, orig. 1925). *The Mentality of Apes.* London: Penguin Books.

Konner, M. (2010). *The Evolution of Childhood: Relationships, Emotion, Mind.* Cambridge, Mass.: The Belknap Press of Harvard University Press.

Korb, J. (2010). Social insects, major evolutionary transitions and multilevel selection, in Peter Kappeler (Ed.), *Animal Behaviour: Evolution and Mechanisms,* pp. 179–211. Berlin: Springer.

Krause, J. & Ruxton, G. (2008). *Living in Groups.* Oxford: Oxford University Press.

Krause, J. et al. (2007). The derived *FOXP2* variant of modern humans was shared with Neanderthals. *Current Biology, 17,* 1908–1912.

Kriegel, U. (2009). Intentionality. In T. Bayne et al. (Eds), *The Oxford Companion to Consciousness* (pp. 382–385). Oxford: Oxford University Press,

Kringelbach, M. & Berridge, K. (Eds) (2010). *Pleasures of the Brain,* Oxford: Oxford University Press.

Kroeber, A. & Kluckhohn, C. (1952). *Culture: A Critical Review of Concepts and Definitions.* New York: Random House.

Kudo, H., & Dunbar, R. (2001). Neocortex size and social network size in primates. *Animal Behaviour, 62,* 711–722.

Kurzban, R. (2002). Essay Review. Alas poor evolutionary psychology: Unfair accused, unjustly condemned. *Human Nature Review, 2,* 99–109.

Kusch, M. (1995). *Psychologism: A Case Study in the Sociology of Knowledge.* London: Routledge.

Kutschera, U. & Niklas, K. (2004). The modern theory of biological evolution: an expanded synthesis. *Naturwissenschaften, 91,* 255–276.

L

Lacey, E. & Sherman, P. (2005). Redefining eusociality: concepts, goals, and levels of analysis. *Annales Zoologic Fennici, 42,* 573–577.

Laland, D. (2004). Social learning strategies. *Learning and Behavior, 32,* 4–14 (see p. 284).

Laland, K. Odling-Smee, J. & Feldman, M. (2000). Niche construction, biological evolution, and cultural change. *Behavioral and Brain Sciences, 23,* 131–175.

Laland, K, & Brown, G. (2002). *Sense and Nonsense: Evolutionary Perspectives on Human Behavior.* Oxford: Oxford University Press.

Laland, K. & Galef, B. (2009). Introduction. In K. Laland and B. Galef (Eds), *The Question of Animal Culture* (pp. 1–18). Cambridge, Mass.: Harvard University Press.

Laland, K. et al. (2010). How culture shaped the human genome: bringing genetics and the human sciences together. *Nature Reviews/Genetics, 11,* 137–148.

Laland, K et al. (2011). Cause and effect in biology revisited: Is Mayr's proximate-ultimate dichotomy still useful? *Science, 334,* 1512–1516.

Lamarck, J. (1809, trans. 1914, 2011). *Zoological Philosophy: An Exposition with Regard to the Natural History of Animals.* Cambridge: Cambridge University Press.

Lane, N. (2009). *Life Ascending: The Ten Great Inventions of Evolution.* London: Profile Books.

Lassek, W. & Gaulin, S. (2008). Waist-hip ratio and cognitive ability: is gluteofemoral fat a priviliged store of neurodevelopmental resources? *Evolution and Human Behavior, 29,* 26–34.

Laurin, M. (2010). *How Vertebrates Left the Water.* Berkeley: University of California Press.

Lazarus, R. (1991). *Emotion and Adaptation.* New York: Oxford University Press.

Leahey, T. (2000). *A History of Psychology: Main Currents of Psychological Thought.* Upper Saddle River, N.J.: Prentice Hall.

Lecointre, G. & Le Guyader, H. (2006). *The Tree of Life : A Phylogenetic Classification.* Cambridge, Mass.: The Belknap Press of Harvard University Press.

LeDoux, J. (1996). *The Emotional Brain: The Mysterious Underpinnings of Emotional Life.* New York: Simon & Schuster.

Lee, P. (1994). Social structure and evolution. In P. Slater & T. Halliday (Eds), *Behaviour and Evolution* (pp. 266–303). Cambridge: Cambridge University Press.

Lee, P. (2003). Innovation as a behavioral response to environmental challenges: A cost and benefit approach. In S. Reader & K. Laland (Eds), *Animal Innovation* (pp. 261–277). Oxford: Oxford University Press.

Lehman, J. et al. (2007). Group size, grooming and social cohesion in primates. *Animal Behaviour, 74,* 1617–1629.

Leroi-Gourhan, A. (1971). *Prähistorische Kunst: Die Ursprünge der Kunst in Europa.* Freiburg im Breisgau: Verlag Herder.

Levenson, R., Ekman, P., Heider, K. & Friesen, W. (1992). Emotion and autonomic nervous system activity in the Minang-Kaban of West Sumatra. *Journal of Personality and Social Psychology 62,* 972–988.

Leroi-Gourhan, A. (1993). *Gestures and Speech*. Cambridge., Mass.: The MIT Press.

Leung, T., King, K. & Wolinska, J. (2012). Escape from the Red Queen: an overlooked scenario in coevolutionary studies. *Oikus*, 121, 641–645.

Levinson, S. (2006). Introduction: The evolution of culture in a microcosm. In S. Levinson & P. Jaisson (Eds), *Evolution and Culture* (pp 1–41). Cambridge, Mass.: The MIT Press.

Levinton, J. (2009). *Marine Biology: Function, Biodiversity, Ecology*. New York: Oxford University.

Levy, F. (2012). Mirror neurons, birdsong and human language: an hypothesis. *Frontiers of Psychiatry*, 2, 1–7 (see p. 259).

Lewin, R. & Foley, R. (2004). *Principles of Human Evolution*. Oxford: Blackwell Publishing.

Lewis, M. (2010). The emergence of human emotions. In M. Lewis, J. Havilland-Jones & L. Barrett (Eds), *Handbook of Emotions* (pp. 304–319), *Third Edition*. New York: The Guilford Press.

Lewontin, R., Rose, S. & Kamin, L. (1984). *Not in Our Genes: Biology, Ideology, and Human Nature*. Harmondsworth: Penguin Books.

Li, N. et al. (2002). The necessities and luxuries of mate preferences: Testing the tradeoffs. *Journal of Personality and Social Psychology*, 82: 947–955.

Lichtneckert, R. & Reichert, H. (2007). Origin and evolution of the first nervous systems. In G. Striedter & J. Rubinstein (Eds), *Evolution of Nervous Systems*, *Vol. 1* (pp. 289–315). Amsterdam: Elsevier.

Lickliter, R. & Honeycut, H. (2003). Developmental dynamics: Toward a Biologically plausible evolutionary psychology. *Psychological Bulletin*, 129, 819–835 (comments and reply 836–872).

Lieberman, D., Tooby, J. & Cosmides, L. (2007). The architecture of human kin recognition. *Nature*, 445, 727–731.

Lieberman, D. (2009). Rethinking the Taiwanese minor marriages data: evidence the mind uses multiple kinship cues to regulate inbreeding avoidance. *Evolution and Human Behavior*, 30, 153–160.

Lipsey, R. et al. (2005). *Economic Transformations: General Purpose Technologies and Long Term Economic Growth*. Oxford: Oxford University Press.

Liqun, L. (2011). Is there a sensitive period in human incest avoidance? *Evolutionary Psychology*, 9, 285–295.

Little, A. et al. (2011). Facial attractiveness: evolutionary based research. *Philosophical Transactions of the Royal Society B*, 366, 1638–1659.

Locke, J. (2006). Parental selection of vocal behavior: Crying, cooing, babbling, and the evolution of language. *Human Nature*, 17, 155–168.

Lorenz, K. (1991). *Here Am I--Where Are You? The Behavior of the Greylag Goose*. New York: Harcourt Brace Jovanovich, Publishers.

Love, A. & Raff, R. (2003). Knowing your ancestors: themes in the history of evo-devo. *Evolution & Development*, 5, 327–330.

Lovejoy, A. (1964). *The Great Chain of Being: The History of an Idea*. Cambridge, MA: Harvard University Press.

Lovejoy, D. (2009). *Neuroendocrinology: An Integrated Approach*. Chichester: Wiley & Sons.

Ludwig, A. (1995). *The Price of Greatness: Resolving the Creativity and Madness Controversy*. New York: The Guilford Press.

Lumsden, C. & Wilson, E. (1981). *Genes, Mind, and Culture: The Coevolutionary Process*. Cambridge, Mass.: Harvard University Process.

Lycett, S. (2010). The importance of history in definitions of *culture*: Implications from phylogenetic approaches to the study of social learning in chimpanzees. *Learning & Behavior*, 38, 252–264.

M

Maccoby, E. (1998). *The Two Sexes: Growing up Apart and Coming Together*. Cambridge, Mass.: The Belknap Press of the Harvard University Press.

MacLean, P. (1949). Psychosomatic disease and the 'visceral brain': Recent developments bearing on the Papez theory of emotion. *Psychosomatic Medicine*, 11, 338–353.

MacLean, P. (1990). *The Triune Brain in Evolution: Role of Paleocerebral Functions*. New York: Plenum Press.

MacNeilage, P. (1998). The frame/content theory of evolution of speech production. *Behavioral and Brain Sciences*, 21, 499–546.

MacNeilage, P. (2008). *The Origin of Speech*. Oxford: Oxford University Press.

Maestripieri, D. (2002). Parent-offspring conflict in primates. *International Journal of Primatology*, 23, 923–951.

Maestripieri, D. & Poney J. (2006). Evolutionary developmental psychology: contributions from comparative research with nonhuman primates. *Developmental Review*, 26, 120–137 (see p. 324).

Marks, I. & Nesse, R. (1994). Fear and fitness: An evolutionary analysis of anxiety disorders. *Ethology and Sociobiology, 15,* 247–261.

Marler, P. (2000). Origins of music and speech: Insights from animals. In N. Wallin (Ed.), *The Origins of Music* (pp. 31–63). Cambridge, Mass.: The MIT Press.

Marlowe, F. (2009). Hadza cooperation: second-party punishment, Yes: third-party punishment, No. *Human Nature, 20,* 417–430 (see p. 173).

Marlowe, F. et al. (2008). More 'altruistic' punishment in larger societies. *Proceedings of the Royal Society B, 275,* 587–590.

Marx, J. (2004). Remembrance of winter past. *Science, 303,* 1607.

Maynard Smith, J. & Harper, D. (2003). *Animal Signals.* Oxford: Oxford University Press.

Maynard Smith, J. & Szathmáry, E. (1995). *The Major Transitions in Evolution.* Oxford: W.H. Freeman and Company.

Maynard Smith, J. & Szathmáry, E. (1999). *The Origins of Life: From the Birth of Life to the Origins of Language.* Oxford: Oxford University Press.

Mayr, E. (1961). Cause and effect in biology. *Science, 134,* 1501–1506.

Mayr, E. (1985). *The Growth of Biological Thought: Diversity, Evolution, and Inheritance.* Cambridge, Mass.: The Belknap Press of Harvard University Press.

Mayr, E. (1997). *This is Biology: The Science of the Living World.* Cambridge, Mass.: The Belknap Press of the Harvard University Press.

Martin, R. (1990). *Primate Origins and Evolution: A Phylogenetic Reconstruction.* Princeton, N.J.: Princeton University Press.

Martinez-Garcia, F., Novejarque, A. & Lanuza, E. (2007). Evolution of the amygdala in vertebrates. In J. Kaas & T. Bullock (Eds), *Evolution of Nervous Systems, Volume 2* (pp. 255–334). Amsterdam: Elsevier.

McBrearty, S.(2007). Down with the revolution. In P. Mellars et al. (Eds), *Rethinking the human revolution* (pp. 133–151), Cambridge, UK: McDonald Institute for Archeological Research.

McBrearty, S. & Brooks, A. (2000). The revolution that wasn't: a new interpretation of the origin of modern human behavior. *Journal of Human Evolution, 39,* 453–563.

McComb, K. & Semple, S. (2005). Coevolution of vocal communication and sociality in primates. *Biological Letters, 1,* 381–385.

McClelland, D. (1961). *The Achieving Society.* Princeton, N.J.: Van Nostrand.

McClelland, D. (1988). *Human Motivation.* Cambridge: Cambridge University Press.

McGrew, W. (1998). Culture in nonhuman primates? *Annual Review of Anthropology 27,* 301–320 (see p. 284).

McGuire, M. & Troisi A. (1998). *Darwinian Psychiatry.* New York: Oxford University Press.

McLain, D. et al. (2000). Ascription of resemblance of newborns by parents and nonrelatives. *Evolution and Human Behavior, 21,* 11–23.

McNally, R. (2001). On Wakefield's harmful dysfunction analysis of mental disorder. *Behavioral Research and Therapy, 39,* 309–314.

McNally, R. (2011). *What is Mental Illness?* Cambridge, Mass.: The Belknap Press of Harvard University Presss.

McNamara, A. (2011). Can we measure memes? *Frontiers in Evolutionary Neuroscience, 3,* 1–7.

McNamara, A. et al. (2008). Neural dynamics of learning sound-action associations. *PloS One, 3 (12),* 1–10.

McNeill, J. & McNeill, W. (2003). *The Human Web: A Bird's-Eye View of World History.* New York: W.W. Norton & Company.

McShea, D. (1996). Metazoan complexity and evolution: is there a trend? *Evolution: International Journal of Organic Evolution, 50,* 477–492.

McShea, D. (2001). The hierarchical structure of organisms: a scale and documentation of a trend in the maximum. *Paleobiology, 27,* 405–423.

Mellars, P. & Stringer, C. (Eds) (1989). *The Human Revolution: Behavioral and Biological Perspectives on the Origins of Modern Humans,* Edinburgh: Edinburgh University Press.

Merkelbach, H. & De Jong, P. (1997). Evolutionary models of phobias. In G. Davey (Ed.), *Phobias: A Handbook of Theory, Research, and Treatment* (pp. 323–347). Chichester, UK: Wiley.

Meston, C. & Buss,. D. (2009). *Why Women Have Sex: Understanding Sexual Motivation from Adventure to Revenge (and Everything in Between).* London: The Bodley Head.

Mesoudi, A., Whiten, A. & Laland, K. (2004). Is human cultural evolution Darwinian? Evidence reviewed from the perspective of *The Origin of Species. Evolution, 58,* 1–11.

Mesoudi, A. (2008). An experimental simulation of the 'copy-successful-individuals' cultural learning strategy": adaptive landscapes, producer-scrounger dynamics, and informational access costs. *Evolution and Human Behavior, 29,* 350–363.

Mesoudi, A., Whiten, A. & Laland, K. (2006). Towards a unified science of cultural evolution. *Behavioral and Brain Sciences, 29,* 329–383.

Mesoudi, A. (2011). *Cultural Evolution: How Darwinian Theory Can Explain Human Culture and Synthesize the Social Sciences.* Chicago: University of Chicago Press.

Meyer, J. et al. (2003). Dysfunctional attitudes and 5-HT2 receptors during depression and self-harm. *American Journal of Psychiatry, 160,* 90–96.

Miller, G. (2002). *The Mating Mind: How Sexual Choice Shaped the Evolution of Human Nature.* New York: Doubleday.

Miller, G. & Todd, P. (1998). Mate choice turns cognitive. *Trends in Cognitive Sciences, 2,* 190–198.

Mitchell, M. (2009). *Complexity: A Guided Tour.* Oxford: Oxford University Press.

Mithen, S. (1998). *The Prehistory of the Mind: A Search for the Origins of Art, Religion, and Science.* London: Thames & Hudson.

Mithen, S. (2005). *The Singing Neanderthals: The Origins of Music, Language, Mind and Body.* London: Weidenfeld & Nicolson.

Mithen, S. (2007). Seven steps in the evolution of the human imagination. In I. Roth (Ed.), *Imaginative Minds* (pp. 3–29). Oxford: Oxford University Press.

Mithen, S. (2009). Holistic communication and the co-evolution of language and music: resurrecting an old idea. In R. Botha & C. Knight (Eds), *The Prehistory of Language* (pp. 58–76). Oxford: Oxford University Press.

Mlodinow, L. (2003). *Some Time with Feynman.* London: Penguin Books.

Møller, A. (2008). Sex and sexual selection, In C. Crawford & D. Krebs (Eds) *Foundations of Evolutionary Psychology* (pp. 71–90). New York: Lawrence Erlbaum associates.

Moore, K. & Persaud, T. (2008). *The Developing Human: Clinically Oriented Embryology, Eighth Edition.* Philadelphia: Elsevier.

Mosser, A. & Packer, C. (2009). Group territoriality and the benefits of sociality in the African lion, *Panthera leo. Animal Behaviour, 78,* 359–370.

Mukamel, R. et al. (2010). Single-neuron responses in humans during execution and observation of actions. *Current Biology, 20,* 750–756.

Müller, A. & Soligo, C. (2005). Primate sociality in evolutionary context. *Journal of Physical Anthropology, 128,* 399–414.

Müller, A., Soligo, C. & Thalmann, U. (2007). New views on the origin of primate social organization. In M. Ravosa & M. Dagosto (Eds), *Primate Origins: Adaptations and Evolution* (pp. 677–701). New York: Springer.

Murphy, D. (2005). Can evolution explain insanity? *Biology and Philosophy, 20,* 745–766.

Murphy, D. (2006). *Psychiatry in the Scientific Image.* Cambridge, Mass.: The MIT Press.

N

Nasar, S. (1998). *A Beautiful Mind: A Life of Mathematical Genius and Nobel Laureate John Nash.* New York: Simon and Schuster.

Nedelcu, A. & Michod, R. (2006) The evolutionary origin of an altruistic gene. *Molecular Biology and Evolution, 23* (8), 1460–1464 (see p. 165).

Nee, S. (2005). The great chain of being. *Nature, 435,* 429.

Nesse, R. (2000). Is depression an adaptation? *Archives of General Psychiatry, 57,* 14–20.

Nesse, R. (2005). Natural selection and the regulation of defenses. A signal detection analysis of the smoke detector principle. *Evolution and Human Behavior, 26,* 88–105.

Nesse, R. & Ellsworth, P. (2009). Evolution, emotions, and emotional disorders. *American Psychologist, 64,* 129–139.

Nesse, R. & Jackson, E. (2011). Evolutionary foundations for psychiatric diagnosis: making DSM-V valid. In P. Adriaens & A. de Block (Eds), *Maladapting Minds: Philosophy, Psychiatry, and Evolutionary Theory* (pp. 173–197). Oxford: Oxford University Press.

Nettle, D. (2001). *Strong Imagination: Madness, Creativity and Human Nature.* Oxford: Oxford University Press.

Nettle, D. (2002). Women's height, reproductive success and the evolution of sexual dimorphism in modern humans. *Proceedings of the Royal Society of London B, 269,* 1919–1923.

Nettle, D. (2004). Evolutionary origins of depression: a review and reformulation. *Journal of Affective Disorders, 81,* 91–102.

Nettle, D. (2006a). Schizotypy and mental health amongst poets, visual artists, and mathematicians. *Journal of Research in Personality, 40,* 876–890.

Nettle, D. (2006b). Reconciling the mutation-selection balance model with the schizotypy-creativity connection. *Behavioral and Brain Sciences, 29,* 418.

Nettle, D. (2009). *Evolution and Genetics for Psychology.* Oxford: Oxford University Press.

Nicolson, N. (1987). Infants, mothers, and other females. In B. Smuts et al. (Eds), *Primate Societies* (pp. 330–342). Chicago: The University of Chicago Press.

Nilsson, D & Pelger, S. (1994). A pessimistic estimate of the time required for an eye. *Proceedings of the Royal Society of London B, 256,* 53–58.

Noble, D. (2006). *The Music of Life: Biology beyond Genes.* Oxford: Oxford University Press.

Northcutt, R. (2001). Evolution of the nervous system: Changing views of brain evolution. *Brain Research Bulletin, 55,* 663–674.

Novak, M., Tarnita, C. & Wilson, E. (2010). The evolution of eusociality. *Nature, 466,* 1057–1062.

O

O'Brien, M. & Shennan, S. (Eds) (2010). *Innovation in Cultural Systems: Contributions from Evolutionary Anthropology.* Cambridge, Mass.: The MIT Press.

Odling-Smee, F. et al. (2003). *Niche Construction: The Neglected Process in Evolution.* Princeton: Princeton University Press.

O'Gorman, R., Wilson, D. & Miller, R. (2005). Altruistic punishing and helping differ in sensitivity to relatedness, friendship, and future interactions. *Evolution and Human Behavior, 26,* 375–387.

Öhmann, A. & Mineka, S. (2001). Fears, phobias, and preparedness: Toward an evolved module of fear and fear learning. *Psychological Review, 108,* 483–522.

Öhman, A. & Mineka, S. (2003). The malicious serpent: Snakes as a prototypical stimulus for an evolved module of fear. *Current Directions in Psychological Science, 12,* 5–9.

Öhmann, A. (2009). Human fear conditioning and the amygdala. In P. Whalen & E. Phelps (Eds), *The Human Amygdala* (pp. 118–154). New York: The Guilford Press.

O'Malley, M & Dupré, J. (2005). Fundamental issues in systems biology. *BioEssays, 27,* 1270–1276.

Oppenheimer, S, (2003). *Out of Eden: The peopling of the world.* London: Constable.

Orth, U. et al. (2010). Tracking the trajectory of shame, guilt, and pride across the life span. *Journal of Personality and Social Psychology, 99,* 1061–1071.

Otto, S. (2009). The evolutionary enigma of sex. *The American Naturalist, 174,* S1–S14.

P

Packer, C., Scheel, C. & Pusey, A. (1990). Why lions form groups: Food is not enough. *American Naturalist, 136,* 1–19.

Pagel, M. (2009). Natural selection 150 years on. *Nature, 457,* 808–811.

Paley, W. (orig. 1802; 2006). *Natural Theology or Evidence of the Existence and Attributes of the Deity, collected from the appearances of nature.* Oxford: Oxford University Press.

Palmer, D. & Barrett, P. (2009). *Evolution: The Story of Life.* London: Octopus Publishing Group.

Palombit, R. (1999). Infanticide and the evolution of pair bonds in nonhuman primates. *Evolutionary Anthropology, 7,* 117–129.

Panksepp, J. (1998a). *Affective Neuroscience: The Foundation of Animal and Human Emotions.* New York: Oxford University Press.

Panksepp, J. (1998b). Attention deficit hyperactivity disorders, psychostimulants, and intolerance of childhood playfulness: A tragedy in the making? *Current Directions in Psychological Science, 7,* 91–98.

Panksepp, J. (2000). The riddle of laughter: Neural and psychoevolutionary underpinnings of joy. *Current Directions in Psychological Science, 9,* 183–186.

Panksepp, J. & Panksepp, J. (2000). The seven sins of evolutionary psychology. *Evolution and Cognition, 6,* 108–131.

Panksepp, J. & Panksepp, J. (2001). A continuing critique of evolutionary psychology. *Evolution and Cognition, 7,* 56–80.

Panksepp, J. et al. (2002). Comparative approaches in evolutionary psychology: Molecular neuroscience meets the mind. *Neuroendocrinology Letters Special Issue Suppl. 4, 23,* 105–115

Panksepp, J. (2003). At the interface of the affective, behavioral, and cognitive neurosciences: Decoding the emotional feelings of the brain. *Brain and Cognition, 52,* 4–14.

Panksepp, J. (2006). Emotional endotypes in evolutionary psychiatry. *Progress in Neuro-Psychopharmacology & Biological Psychiatry, 30,* 774–784.

Panksepp, J. (2007). The neuroevolutionary and neuroaffective psychobiology of the prosocial brain, in R. Dunbar, L. Barrett (Eds), *Oxford Handbook of Evolutionary Psychology* (pp. 145–162). Oxford: Oxford University Press.

Panksepp, J. (2010). Play, ADHD, and the construction of the social brain: Should the first class each day be recess? *American Journal of Play, 1,* 57–81.

Panksepp, J. & Northoff, G. (2009). The trans-species core SELF: The emergence of active cultural and neuro-ecological agents through self-related processing within subcortical-cortical midline networks. *Consciousness and Cognition, 18,* 193–215.

Papini, M. (2008). *Comparative Psychology: Evolution and Development of Behavior.* New York: Psychology Press.

Parker, A. (2003). *In the Blink of an Eye: The Cause of the Most Dramatic Event in the History of Life.* London: The Free Press.

Parker, G., Royle, N. & Hartley, I. (2002). Intrafamilial conflict and parental investment: A synthesis. *Philosophical Transactions of the Royal Society London B, 357,* 295–307.

Parker, G. et al. (2010). Is context everything to the definition of clinical depression? A test of the Horwitz and Wakefield hypothesis, *Journal of Affective Disorders, 136,* 1034–1038.

Parr, L., Cohen, M. & de Waal, F. (2005). Influence of social context on the use of blended and graded facial displays in chimpanzees. *International Journal of Primatology, 26,* 73–103.

Parr, L., Waller, L. & Fugate, J. (2005). Emotional communication in primates: implications for neurobiology, *Current Opinion in Neurobiology, 15,* 716–720.

Parr, L. & Waller, B. (2007). The evolution of human emotions. In J. Kaas & T. Bullock (Eds), *Evolution of Nervous Systems, Vol. 2,* (pp. 447–472). Amsterdam: Elsevier.

Parr, L. et al. (2007). Classifying chimpanzee facial expressions using muscle action. *Emotion, 7,* 172–181.

Parr, L. (2010). Understanding the expression and classification of chimpanzee facial expressions. In E. Lonsdorf et al. (Eds), *The Mind of the Chimpanzee* (pp. 52–59). Chicago: The University of Chicago Press.

Passingham, R. (2008). *What is Special about the Human Brain?* Oxford: Oxford University Press.

Pasternak, C. (Ed.) (2007). *What Makes Us Human?* Oxford: OneWorld Publications (see p. 75).

Pawlowski, B., Dunbar, R. & Lipowicz, A. (2000). Tall men have more reproductive success. *Nature, 403,* 156.

Peirce, C. (1978, orig. 1931). *Collected Papers of Charles Sanders Peirce, Vol. II,* edited by Charles Hartshorne and Paul Weiss, Cambridge, Mass.: Harvard University Press.

Pelligrini, A. (Ed.) (2011). *The Oxford Handbook of the Development of Play.* Oxford: Oxford University Press (see p. 337).

Pellegrini, A., Dupuis, D. & Smith, P. (2007). Play in evolution and development. *Developmental Review, 27,* 261–276.

Pellis, S. & Pellis, V. (2009). *The Playful Brain: Venturing to the Limits of Neuroscience.* Oxford: OneWorld Publications.

Pellis, S., Pellis, V. & Bell, H. (2010). The function of play in the development of the social brain. *American Journal of Play, 2,* 278–296.

Pennington, B. (2002). *The Development of Psychopathology: Nature and Nurture.* New York: The Guilford Press.

Penton-Voak, I. (1999). Menstrual cycle alters face perception. *Nature, 399,* 741–742.

Perelman, P. et al. (2011). A molecular phylogeny of living primates. *PLoS Genetics, 7,* 1–17.

Perilloux, C., Fleischman, D. & Buss, D. (2011). Meet the parents: Parent-offspring convergence and divergence in mate preferences. *Personality and Individual Differences, 50,* 253–258.

Petkov, C. et al. (2008). A voice region in the monkey brain. *Nature Neuroscience, 11,* 367–374.

Petkov, C. Logothetis, N. & Obleser, J. (2009). Where are the human speech and voice regions, and do other animals have anything like them? *The Neuroscientist, 15,* 419–429.

Petrides, M, Cadoret, G. & Mackey, S. (2005). Orofacial somatomotor responses in the macaque monkey homologue of Broca's areas, *Nature, 435,* 1235–1238.

Petrie, M., Halliday, T. & Sanders, C. (1991). Peahens prefer peacocks with elaborate trains. *Animal Behaviour, 41,* 323–331.

Pfeiffer, J. (1982). *The Creative Explosion: An Inquiry into the Origin of Art and Religion.* New York: Harper & Row.

Piersma, T. & Gils, J. van (2011). *The Flexible Phenotype: A Body-Centered Integration of Ecology, Physiology, and Behaviour.* Oxford: Oxford University Press.

Pigliucci, M. & Kaplan, J. (2006). *Making Sense of Evolutionary Biology: The Conceptual Foundations of Evolutionary Biology.* Chicago: The University of Chicago Press.

Pigliucci, M. & Müller, G. (Eds) (2010). *Evolution—The Extended Synthesis.* Cambridge, Mass.: The MIT Press.

Pika, S. (2008). Gestures of apes and pre-linguistic human children: Similar or different? *First Language, 28* (2), 116–140.

Pinel, J. (2003). *Biopsychology, Fifth Edition.* Boston: Alleyn & Bacon (see p. 27).

Pinker, S. (1994). *The Language Instinct.* New York: William Morrow.

Platek, S., Keenan, J. & Shackleford, T. (Eds). (2007). *Evolutionary Cognitive Neuroscience.* London: The MIT Press.

Platek, S. & Shackleford, T. (Eds) (2009). *Foundations in Evolutionary Cognitive Neuroscience.* Cambridge: Cambridge University Press.

Platek, S., Hasicic, A. & Krill, A. (2011). Boldly going where no brain has gone: Futures of evolutionary cognitive neuroscience. *Futures, 43,* 771–776.

Plotkin, H. (1994). *Darwin Machines and the Nature of Knowledge: Concerning Adaptations, Instinct and the Evolution of Intelligence.* London: Penguin Books.

Plotkin, H. (2000). Culture and psychological mechanisms. In R. Aunger (Ed.), *Darwinizing Culture: The Status of Memetics as a Science* (pp. 69–82). Oxford: Oxford University Press.

Plotkin, H. (2002). *The Imagined World Made Real: Towards a Natural Science of Culture.* London: Allen Lane The Penguin Press.

Plotkin, H. (2004). *Evolutionary Thought in Psychology: A Brief History.* Oxford: Blackwell Publishing.

Plotkin, H. (2010). *Evolutionary Worlds Without End.* Oxford: Oxford University Press.

Plutchik, R. (1994). *The Psychology and Biology of Emotion,* New York: HarperCollins.

Pollard, K. (2009). What makes us human? *Scientific American, 300* (5), 32–37.

Pollick, A. & de Waal, F. (2007). Ape gestures and language evolution. *Proceedings of the National Academy of Sciences of the USA, 104,* 8184–8189.

Post, F. (1994). Creativity and Psychopathology: A study of world-famous men. *British Journal of Psychiatry,* 165, 22–34 (see p. 314).

Potts, R. (1996). *Humanity's Descent: The Consequences of Ecological Instability.* New York: Avon Books.

Potts, R. (2004a). Paleoenvironmental basis of cognitive evolution in great apes. *American Journal of Primatology, 62,* 209–228.

Potts, R. (2004b). Paleoenvironments and the adaptability in great apes. In A. Russon & D. Begun (Eds), *The Evolution of Thought: Evolutionary Origins of Great Ape Intelligence* (pp. 237–259). Cambridge: Cambridge University Press.

Povinelli, D. & O'Neill, D. (2000). Do chimpanzees use their gestures to instruct each other? In S. Baron-Cohen et al.(Eds), *Understanding Other Minds: Perspectives from Developmental Cognitive Neuroscience* (p. 459–487). Oxford: Oxford University Press.

Power, M. & Schulkin, J. (2009). *The Evolution of Obesity.* Baltimore: The John Hopkins Press.

Premack, D. & Hauser, M. (2006). Why animals do not have culture. In S. Levinson & P. Jaisson (Eds), *Evolution and Culture* (pp. 275–278). Cambridge, Mass.: The MIT Press.

Preuss, T. (2007). Primate brain evolution in phylogenetic context. In J. Kaas & Preuss, T. (Eds), *Evolution of Nervous Systems, Vol. 4, Primates* (pp. 1–34). Amsterdam: Elsevier.

Previc, F. (1999). Dopamine and the origins of human intelligence. *Brain and Cognition, 41,* 299–350.

Previc, F. (2009). *The Dopaminergic Mind in Human Evolution and History.* Cambridge: Cambridge University Press.

Price, M., Cosmides, L. & Tooby, J. (2002). Punitive sentiment as an anti-free rider psychological device. *Evolution and Human Behavior, 23,* 203–231.

Prokosch, M. et al. (2009). Intelligence and mate choice: intelligent men are always appealing, *Evolution and Human Behavior,* 30: 11–20.

Prothero, D. (2007). *Evolution: What the Fossils Say and Why It Matters.* New York: Columbia University Press.

Provine, R. (2000). *Laughter: A Scientific Investigation.* New York: Penguin Books.

Proyer, R. (2011). Being playful and smart? The relations of playfulness with psychometric and self-estimated intelligence and academic performance. *Learning and Individual Differences, 21,* 463–467.

Prum, R. & Brush, A. (2002). The evolutionary origin and diversification of feathers. *The Quarterly Review of Biology, 77,* 261–295.

Prum, R. & Brush, A. (2003). Which came first, the feather or the bird? *Scientific American, 288 (3),* 62–69.

Pusey, A. (1987). Sex-biased dispersal and inbreeding in birds and mammals. *Trends in Ecology and Evolution, 2,* 295–299.

Pusey, A. (2004). Inbreeding avoidance in primates. In A. Wolf & W. Durham (Eds), *Inbreeding, Incest, and the Incest Taboo* (pp. 61–75). Stanford, Cal.: Stanford University Press.

Purves, D. et al. (2008). *Cognitive Neuroscience.* Sunderland, Mass.: Sinauer Associates.

Pusey, A. & Wolf, M. (1996). Inbreeding avoidance in animals. *Trends in Ecology and Evolution, 11,* 201–206.

Puts, D. (2006). Dominance and the evolution of sexual dimorphism in human voice pitch. *Evolution and Human Behavior, 27,* 283–296.

Puts, D. (2010). Beauty and the beast: mechanisms of sexual selection in humans. *Evolution and Human Behavior, 31,* 157–175.

Q

Quartz, S. (2003). Toward a developmental evolutionary psychology: Genes, development, and the evolution of the human cognitive architecture. In S. Scher & F. Rauscher (Eds), *Evolutionary Psychology: Alternative Approaches* (pp. 185–210). Boston: Kluwer Academic Publishers.

R

Raff, R. (1996). *The Shape of Life: Genes, Development, and the Evolution of Animal Form*. Chicago: The University of Chicago Press.

Raichle, M. (2009). A brief history of human brain mapping. *Trends in Neurosciences, 32*, 118–126.

Ramsey, G., Bastian, M. & van Schaik, C. (2007). Animal innovation defined and operationalized. *Behavioral and Brain Sciences, 30*, 393–437.

Reader, S. & Laland, K. (2002). Social intelligence, innovation, and enhanced brain size in primates. *Proceedings of the National Academy of Sciences of the USA, 99*, 4436–4441.

Reader, S. & Laland, K. (Eds) (2003). *Animal Innovation*. Oxford: Oxford University Press.

Reader, S. & Laland, K. (2010). Experimental identification of social learning in wild animals. *Learning & Behavior, 38*, 265–283.

Reece, J., Urry, L., Cain, M. et al. (Eds) (2011). *Campbell Biology, Ninth Edition*. San Francisco: Pearson Education (see p. 33).

Reichard, U. & Boesch, C. (Eds) (2003). *Monogamy: Mating Strategies and Partnerships in Birds, Humans and Other Mammals*. Cambridge: Cambridge University Press.

Redmond, I. (2008). *Primates of the World*. London: New Holland Publishers.

Rendell, L. & Whitehead, H. (2001). Culture in whales and dolphins. *Behavioral and Brain Sciences, 24*, 309–382.

Reznick, D. (2010). *The Origin Then and Now: An Interpretive Guide to the Origin of Species*, Princeton: Oxford University Press.

Rhodes, G. (2006). The evolutionary psychology of facial beauty. *Annual Review of Psychology, 57*, 199–226.

Richards, G. (2002). *Putting Psychology in its Place: A Critical Historical Review*. Hove: Routledge.

Richards, R. (1987). *Darwin and the Emergence of Evolutionary Theories of Minds and Behavior*. Chicago: The University of Chicago Press.

Richards, R. (1992). *The Meaning of Evolution: The Morphological Construction and Ideological Reconstruction of Darwin's Theory*. Chicago: The University of Chicago Press.

Richards, R. & Kinney, D. (1990). Mood swings and creativity. *Creativity Research Journal, 3*, 202–217.

Richardson, R. (2007). *Evolutionary Psychology as Maladapted Psychology*. Cambridge, Mass.: The MIT Press.

Richerson, P., Boyd, R. & Henrich J. (2010). Gene-culture coevolution in the age of genomics. *Proceedings of the National Academy of Sciences of the USA, 107*, 8985–8992.

Richerson, P. & Boyd, R. (2010). The Darwinian theory of human cultural evolution and gene-culture coevolution. In M. Bell et al. (Eds), *Evolution Since Darwin; The First 150 Years* (pp. 561–588). Sunderland, Mass.: Sinauer.

Richerson, P. & Boyd, R. (2005). *Not by Genes Alone: How Culture Transformed Human Evolution*. Chicago: The University of Chicago Press.

Richmond, B. & Jungers, W. (2008). *Orrorin Tugenensis* femoral morphology and the evolution of hominin bipedalism. *Science, 319*, 1662–1665.

Ridley, M. (2005). *Evolution, Third Edition*. Oxford: Blackwell Publishing.

Rilling, J. et al. (2002). A neural basis for social cooperation. *Neuron, 35*, 395–405.

Ridley, M. (1994). *The Red Queen: Sex and the Evolution of Human Nature*. London: Penguin Books.

Rizzolatti, G. & Sinigaglia, C. (2008). *Mirrors in the Brain: How Our Minds Share Actions and Emotions*. Oxford: Oxford University Press.

Rizzolatti, G. & Arbib, M. (1998). Language within our grasp. *Trends in Neurosciences, 21*, 188–194.

Robert, J. (2008). Taking old ideas seriously: Evolution, development, and human behavior. *New Ideas in Psychology, 26*, 367–404.

Roberts, A. (2011). *Evolution: The Human History*. London: Dorling Kindersley.

Roberts, S., Miner, E. & Shackelford, T. (2010). The future of applied evolutionary psychology for human partnerships. *Review of General Psychology, 14*, 318–329.

Rodseth, L. et al. (1991). The human community as a primate society. *Current Anthropology, 32*, 221–254.

Romanes, G. (2006) [1882] *Animal Intelligence*. London: Kegan Paul.

Romanes, G. [1883] *Mental Evolution in Animals*. London: Kegan Paul (see p. 20).

Roney, J. (2009). The role of sex hormones in the initiation of human mating relationships. In P. Ellison & P. Gray (Eds), *Endocrinology of Social Relationships* (pp. 246–269). Cambridge, Mass.: Harvard University Press.

Roney, J. & Simmons, Z. (2008). Women's estradiol predicts preference for facial cues for men's testosterone. *Hormones and Behavior, 53*, 14–19.

Roney, J., Simmons, Z. & Gray, P. (2011). Changes in estradiol predict within-women shifts in attraction to facial cues of men's testosterone. *Psychoneuroendocrinology, 36*, 742–749.

Ross, C. & MacLarnon, A. (2000). The evolution of non-maternal care in anthropoid primates: A test of the hypotheses. *Folia Primatologica, 71*, 93–113.

Rossano, M. (2003). *Evolutionary Psychology: The Science of Human Behavior and Evolution.* New York: John Wiley & Sons.

Rossano, M. (2010). Making friends, making tools, and making symbols, *Current Anthropology, 51*, S89–S98.

Rozin, P. (2009). Introduction: evolutionary and cultural perspectives on affect. In R. Davidson, K. Scherer & H. Hill Goldsmith (Eds), *Handbook of Affective Sciences* (pp. 839–850). Oxford: Oxford University Press.

Rowe, N. (1996). *The Pictorial Guide to Living Primates.* Charlestown: Pogonias Press.

Rowell, T., Hinde, R. & Spencer-Booth, Y. (1964). 'Aunt'-infant interaction in captive rhesus monkeys. *Animal Behaviour, 12*, 219–226.

Royle, N., Hartley, I., & Parker, G. (2004). Parental investment and family dynamics: Interactions between theory and empirical results. *Population Ecology, 46*, 231–241.

Rozin, P. (1996).Towards a psychology of food and eating: From motivation to module to marker, morality, meaning, and metaphor. *Current Directions in Psychological Science, 5*, 18–24.

Runco, M. (2007). *Creativity: Theories and Themes.* Amsterdam: Academic Press.

Russell, J. (1994). Is there universal recognition of emotion from facial expression? A review of the cross-cultural studies, *Psychological Bulletin, 115*, 102–141.

Ryle, G. (1963). *The Concept of Mind.* Harmondsworth: Penguin Books.

S

Saad, G. (2011). Futures of evolutionary psychology. *Futures, 43*, 725–728 (see p. 32).

Sahlins, M. (1977). *The Use and Abuse of Biology: An Anthropological Critique of Sociobiology.* London: Tavistock Publications.

Salmon, C. (2008). Parent-offspring conflict. In C. Salmon & T. Shackelford (Eds) *Family Relationships: An Evolutionary Perspective* (pp. 145–161). Oxford: Oxford University Press.

Salmon, C. & Shackelford. T. (Eds) (2008). *Family Relationships: An Evolutionary Perspective.* Oxford: Oxford University Press.

Sandseter, W. & Kennair, L. (2011). Children's risk play from an evolutionary perspective: The anti-phobic effects of thrilling experiences. *Evolutionary Psychology, 9*(2), 257–284 (see p. 336).

Santos, A. et al. (2010). Just another face in the crowd: Evidence for decreased detection of angry faces in children with Williams syndrome. *Neuropsychologia, 48*, 1071–1078.

Sarmat, H. & Netsky, M. (2002). When does a ganglion become a brain? Evolutionary origin of the central nervous system. *Seminars in Pediatric Neurology, 9*, 240–253.

Savage-Rumbaugh, S. et al. (1998). *Apes, Language, and the Human Mind.* Oxford: Oxford University Press.

Sawyer, G. & Deak, V. (2007). *The Last Human Ancestor: A Guide to Twenty-Two Species of Extinct Humans.* New Haven: Yale University Press.

Scherer, K. (1994). Emotion serves to decouple stimulus and response. In P. Ekman & R. Davidson (Eds). *The Nature of Emotion: Fundamental Questions* (pp. 127–130). New York: Oxford University.

Scherer, K. (2000). Emotion. In M. Hewstone & W. Straube (Eds), *Introduction to Social Psychology: A European Perspective* (pp. 151–195). Oxford: Blackwell.

Schiller, P. (1957). Innate motor action as a basis of learning. In C. Schiller (Ed.), *Instinctive Behavior: The Development of a Modern Concept* (pp. 264–287). New York: International Universities Press.

Schmandt-Besserat, D. (1992). *Before Writing: Volume 1, From Counting to Cuneiform.* Austin: University of Texas Press.

Schmidt, K. & Cohn, J. (2001). Human facial expressions as adaptations: Evolutionary questions in facial expression research. *American Journal of Physical Anthropology, 22*, 3–24.

Schmidt-Rhaesa, A. (2007). *The Evolution of Organ Systems.* Oxford: Oxford University Press.

Schoenwolf G. et al.(2009). *Larsen's Human Embryology.* Philadelphia: Elsevier Churchill Livingstone.

Schug, J. et al. (2010). Emotional expressivity as a signal of cooperation. *Evolution and Human Behavior, 31*, 87–94.

Schulkin, J., Thompson, B, & Rosen, J. (2003). Demythologizing the emotions: Adaptation, cognition, and visceral representations of emotion in the nervous system. *Brain and Cognition, 52*, 15–23.

Schwartz, J. (2008). *In Pursuit of the Gene: From Darwin to DNA*. Cambridge, MA: Harvard University Press.

Scott-Philips, T. & Kirby, S. (2010). Language evolution in the laboratory. *Trends in Cognitive Sciences, 14*, 411–417.

Scrimshaw, S. (1984). Infanticide in human populations: Societal and individual concerns. In G. Hausfater & S. Hrdy (Eds), *Infanticide: Comparative and Evolutionary Perspectives* (pp. 439–462). New Brunswick: Aldine Transaction.

Sear, R., Lawson, D. & Dickins, T. (2007). Synthesis in the human evolutionary behavioral sciences. *Journal of Evolutionary Psychology, 5*, 3–28.

Sear, R. & Mace, R. (2008). Who keeps children alive? A review of the effects of kin on child survival. *Evolution and Human Behavior, 29*, 1–18.

Sear, R. & Mace, R. (2009). Family matters: Kin, demography and child health in a rural Gambian population. In G. Bentley & R. Mace (Eds), *Substitute Parents: Biological and Social Perspectives on Alloparenting across Human Societies* (pp. 50–76). New York: Berghahn Books.

Searle, J. (1995). *Making the Social World: The Structure of Human Civilization*. Oxford: Oxford University Press.

Seed, A., Emery, N. & Clayton, N. (2009). Intelligence in corvids and apes: A case of convergent evolution? *Ethology, 115*, 401–420.

Segerstråle, U. (2000). *Defenders of the Truth: The Battle for Science in the Sociobiology Debate and Beyond*. Oxford: Oxford University Press.

Seligman, M. (1970). On the generality of the laws of learning. *Psychological Review, 77*, 406–418.

Seligman, M. (1971). Phobias and preparedness. *Behaviour Therapy, 2*, 307–320.

Semendeferi, K. et al. (2001). Prefrontal cortex in humans and apes: A comparative study of area 10. *American Journal of Physical Anthropology, 114*, 224–241.

Senju, A. & Hasegawa, T. (2005). Direct gaze captures visuospatial attention. *Visual Cognition, 12*, 127–144.

Seyfarth, R. & Cheney, D. (2003). Signalers and receivers in animal communication. *Annual Review of Psychology, 54*, 145–173.

Seyfarth, R. & Cheney, D. (2010). Production, usage, and comprehension in animal vocalizations. *Brain & Language, 115*, 92–100.

Shallice, T. & Cooper, R. (2011). *The Organization of Mind*. Oxford: Oxford University Press.

Shepherd, S. (2010). Following gaze: gaze-following behavior as a window into social cognition. *Frontiers in Integrative Neuroscience, 4*, 1–13.

Shettleworth, S. (2009). The evolution of comparative cognition: Is the snark still a boojum? *Behavioral Processes, 80*, 210–217.

Shettleworth, S. (2010). *Cognition, Evolution, and Behavior*. Oxford: Oxford University Press.

Shipman, P. (1998). *Taking Wing: Archeopterix and the Evolution of Bird Flight*. London: Phoenix.

Shubin, N. (2008). *Your Inner Fish: A journey into the 3.5 billion-year history of the human body*. New York: Pantheon Books.

Shultz, S. & Dunbar, R. (2007). The evolution of the social brain: anthropoid primates contrast with other vertebrates. *Proceedings of the Royal Society London B, 274*, 2429–2436.

Shultz, S., Opie, C. & Atkinson, Q. (2011). Stepwise evolution of stable sociality in primates. *Nature, 479*, 219–222.

Shuster, S. & Wade, M. (2003). *Mating Systems and Strategies*. Princeton: Princeton University Press.

Sibley, C. & Ahlquist, J. (1984). The phylogeny of hominoid primates, as indicated by DNA-DNA hybridization. *Journal of Molecular Evolution, 20*, 2–15.

Simeonova, K., Chang, K. & Ketter, T. (2005). Creativity in familial disorder. *Journal of Psychiatric Research, 39*, 623–631.

Simonton, D. (2003). Scientific creativity as constrained stochastic behavior: The integration of product, person, and process perspectives. *Psychological Bulletin, 129*, 475–494.

Singh, D. (1995). Female judgment of male attractiveness and desirability for relationships: Role of waist-hip ratio and financial status. *Journal of Personality and Social Psychology, 69*, 1089–1101.

Singh, D. (2002). Female mate value at a glance: Relationship of waist-hip ratio to health, fecundity and attractiveness. *Neuroendocrinology Letters, 23*, 81–91.

Singh, D. (2006). Universal allure of the hourglass figure: An evolutionary theory of female physical attractiveness. *Clinical and Plastic Surgery, 33*, 359–370.

Singh, D. et al. (2010). Cross-cultural consensus for waist-hip ratio and women's attractiveness. *Evolution and Human Behavior, 31*, 176–181.

Slocombe, K. & Zuberbühler, K. (2005). Functionally referential communication in a chimpanzee. *Current Biology, 15*, 1779–1784.

Sloman, L., Gilbert, P. & Hasey, G. (2003). Evolved mechanisms in depression: the role and interaction of attachment and social rank in depression. *Journal of Affective Disorders. 74*, 107–121 (see p. 314).

Smaers, J. et al. (2011). Primate prefrontal cortex evolution: Human Brains are the extreme of a lateralized ape trend. *Brain, Behavior and Evolution, 77, 67–78.*

Smith, E. & Winterhalten, B. (Eds) (1992). *Evolutionary Ecology and Human Behavior.* New Brunswick: Aldine Transaction.

Smith, E., Borgerhoff, M. & Huill, K. (2001). Controversies in the evolutionary social sciences: A guide for the perplexed. *Trends in Ecology and Evolution,* 16, 120–135 (see p. 32).

Snyder, J. et al. (2011). Trade-offs in a dangerous world: women's fear of crime predicts preferences for aggressive and formidable mates. *Evolution and Human Behavior, 32,* 127–137.

Sober, E. (1993). *The Nature of Selection: Evolutionary Theory in Philosophical Focus.* Chicago: The University of Chicago Press.

Sober, E. & Wilson, D. (1998). *Unto Others: The Evolution and Psychology of Unselfish Behavior.* Cambridge, Mass.: Harvard University Press.

Solomon, N. & Hayes, L. (2009). The biological basis of alloparental behavior in mammals. In G. Bentley & R. Mace (Eds), *Substitute Parents: Biological and Social Perspectives on Alloparenting in Human Societies* (pp. 13–49). New York: Berghahn Books.

Spencer, H. (1899). *The Principles of Psychology, Vol. II.* Osnabrück: Otto Zeller.

Spinka, M., Newberry, R. & Bekoff, M. (2001). Mammalian play: training for the unexpected. *The Quarterly Review of Biology,* 76, 141–168.

Spoor, J. & Kelly, J. (2004). The evolutionary significance of affect in groups: communication and group bonding. *Group Processes & Intergroup Relations,* 7, 398–412.

Sprecher, S., Sullivan, Q. & Hatfield, E. (1994). Mate selection preferences: Gender differences examined in a national sample. *Journal of Personality and Social Psychology,* 66, 1074–1080.

Stahl, S. (2004). *Essential Psychopharmacology: Neuroscientific Basis and Practical Applications, Second Edition.* Cambridge: Cambridge University Press.

Stamenov, M. (2002). Some features that make mirror neurons and human language faculty unique. In M. Stemenov & V. Gallese (Eds), *Mirror Neurons and the Evolution of Brain and Language* (pp. 249–271). Amsterdam: John Benjamins Publishing Company.

Stearns, S. & Hoekstra, R. (2005). *Evolution: an introduction.* Oxford: Oxford University Press.

Sternberg, R. & Lubart, T. (1995a). *Defying the Crowd: Cultivating Creativity in a Culture of Conformity.* New York: The Free Press.

Sternberg, R. & Lubart, T. (1995b). An investment approach to creativity: Theory and data. In S. Smith et al. (Eds), *The Creative Cognition Approach* (pp. 271–302). Cambridge, Mass.: The MIT Press.

Sternberg, R. & O'Hara, L. (1999). Creativity and intelligence. In: R. Sternberg (Ed.), *Handbook of Creativity* (pp. 251–272). Cambridge: Cambridge University Press.

Stevens, J. & Hauser, M. (2004). Why be nice? Psychological constraints on the evolution of cooperation. *Trends in Cognitive Sciences, 8,* 60–65.

Stone, L. , Lurquin, P. with Cavalli-Sforza, L. (2007). *Genes, Culture, and Human Evolution.* Oxford: Blackwell Publishing.

Strachan, T. & Read, A. (2004). *Human Molecular Genetics 3.* London: Garland Science.

Strassmann, B. (2011). Cooperation and competition in a cliff-dwelling people. *Proceedings of the National Academy of the United States of America, 108,* 10894–10901.

Striedter, G. (2005). *Principles of Brain Evolution.* Sunderland, Mass.: Sinauer Ass., Inc.

Striedter, G. (2006). Précis of *Principles of Brain Evolution. Behavioral and Brain Science*s, 29, 1–36.

Striedter, G. (2007). A history of ideas in evolutionary neuroscience. In G. Striedter & J. Rubinstein (Eds), *Evolution of Nervous Systems, Volume 1* (pp. 1–15). Amsterdam: Academic Press.

Stringer, C. (2011). *The Origin of Our Species.* London: Allen Lane.

Sugiyama, Y. (1997). Social tradition and the use of tool composites by wild chimpanzees. *Evolutionary Anthropology, 6,* 23–27.

Sussman, R. & Garber, P. (2004). Rethinking sociality: Cooperation and aggression among primates. In R. Sussman & A. Chapman (Eds). *The Origins and Nature of Sociality* (pp. 161–190). New York: Aldine de Gruyter.

Sussman, R., Garber, R. & Cheverud, J. (2005). Importance of cooperation and affiliation in the evolution of primate sociality. *American Journal of Physical Anthropology,* 128, 84–97.

Swami, V. et al. (2008). Factors influencing preferences for height: A replication and extension. *Personality and Individual Differences, 45,* 395–400.

Symons, D. (1995). Beauty is in the adaptations of the beholder: The evolutionary psychology of female sexual attractiveness. In P. Abramson & S. Pinkerton (Eds), *Sexual Nature/Sexual Culture* (pp. 80–118). Chicago: The University of Chicago Press.

Számado, S. & Szathmáry, E. (2006). Selective scenarios for the emergence of natural language. *Trends in Ecology and Evolution, 21,* 555–561.

Szasz, T. (1987). *Insanity.* New York: Wiley.

T

Takahashi, M., Arita, H., Hiraiwa-Hasegawa, M. & Hasagawa T. (2000). Peahens do not prefer peacocks with more elaborate trains. *Animal Behaviour, 75,* 1209–1219 (see p. 92).

Tallerman,, M. & Gibson, K. (Eds) (2012). *The Oxford Handbook of Language Evolution.* Oxford: Oxford University Press.

Tate, A. et al. (2006). Behavioral and neurophysiological evidence for face identity and face emotion processing in animals, *Philosophical Transactions of the Royal Society of London B, 361:* 2155–2172.

Tattersall, I. (2006). Origin of the Malagasy strepsirhine primates. In L. Gould & M. Sauther (pp. 3–17), *Lemurs: Ecology and Adaptation.* New York: Springer.

Taylor, J. (2009). *Not a chimp: The hunt to find the genes that make us human.* Oxford: Oxford University Press.

Taylor, T. (2010). *The Artificial Ape: How Technology Changed The Course of Human Evolution.* New York: Palgrave Macmillan.

Teffer, K. & Semendeferi, K. (2012). Human prefrontal cortex: Evolution, development and pathology. In M. Hufman & D. Falk (Eds) *Evolution of the Primate Brain: From Neuron to Behavior.* Amsterdam: Elsevier Science (see p. 214).

Thain, M. (2009). *Penguin Dictionary of Human Biology.* London: Penguin Books.

Thain. M. & Hickman, M. (2001). *The Penguin Dictionary of Biology.* London: Penguin Books.

Thambirajah, M. (2005). *Psychological Basis of Psychiatry.* Edinburgh: Elsevier.

Thompson, R. (1994). Behaviorism and neuroscience. *Psychological Review, 101,* 259–265.

Thornhill, R. & Gangestadt, S. (2008). *The Evolutionary Biology of Female Sexuality.* Oxford: Oxford University Press.

Tinbergen, N. (1963). On aims and methods of ethology. *Zeitschrift für Tierpsychologie, 20,* 410–429.

Tinbergen, N. (1951). *The Study of Instinct.* London: Oxford University Press.

Toates, F. (2011). *Biological Psychology, Third Edition.* Harlow England: Pearson.

Tomasello, M. (1999). *The Cultural Origins of Human Cognition.* Cambridge, Mass.: Harvard University Press.

Tomasello, M. (2005). *Constructing Language: A Usage-Based Theory of Language Acquisition.* Cambridge, Mass.: Harvard University Press.

Tomasello, M. (2008). *Origins of Human Communication.* Cambridge, Mass.: The MIT Press.

Tomasello, M. (2009a). *Why We Cooperate.* Cambridge, Mass.: The MIT Press.

Tomasello, M. (2009b). The question of chimpanzee culture, plus postscript. In K. Laland & B. Galef (Eds), *The Question of Animal Culture* (pp. 198–221). Cambridge, Mass.: Harvard University Press.

Tomasello, M. et al. (2003). Chimpanzees understand psychological states–the question is which ones and to what extent. *Trends in Cognitive Sciences, 7,* 153–156.

Tomasello, M. et al. (2005). Understanding and sharing intentions: The origins of cultural cognition. *Behavioral and Brain Sciences, 28,* 675–735.

Tomasello, M. et al. (2007). Reliance on head versus eyes in the gaze following of great apes and human infants: the cooperative eye hypothesis. *Journal of Human Evolution, 52,* 314–320.

Tomasello, M. & Call, J. (2007). Introduction: Intentional communication in nonhuman primates. In J. Call & M. Tomasello, (Eds), *The Gestural Communication of Apes and Monkeys* (pp.1–15). Mahwah, N.J.: Lawrence Erlbaum.

Tooby, J. & Cosmides, L. (1990). The past explains the present: Emotional adaptations and the structure of ancestral environments. *Ethology and Sociobiology, 11,* 375–424.

Tooby, J. & Cosmides, L. (1992). The psychological foundations of culture. In J. Barkow, L. Cosmides & J. Tooby (Eds), *The Adapted Mind: Evolutionary Psychology and the Generation of Culture* (pp. 19–136). New York: Oxford University Press.

Tooby, J. & Cosmides, L. (2005). Conceptual foundations of evolutionary psychology, in D. Buss (Ed.). *The Handbook of Evolutionary Psychology* (pp. 5–67). Hoboken, N.J.: John Wiley & Sons, Inc.

Tooby, J. & Cosmides, L. (2008). The evolutionary psychology of the emotions and their relationship to internal regulatory variables. In M. Lewis, J. Havilland-Jones & L. F. Barrett (Eds) *Handbook of Emotions Third Edition* pp.114–137. New York: The Guilford Press (see p. 176).

Tracy, J. & Robins, R. (2004a). Show your pride. Evidence for a discrete emotion expression. *Psychological Science, 15*, 194–197.

Tracy, J. & Robins, R.(2004b). Putting the self into self-conscious emotions: A theoretical model. *Psychological Inquiry, 15*, 103–125.

Tracy, J. & Robins, R. (2006). Appraisal antecedents of shame and guilt: Support for a theoretical model. *Personality and Social Psychology, 32*, 1339–1351.

Tracy, J., Robins, R. & Tangney, J. (Eds) (2007). *The Self-Conscious Emotions: Theory and Research*. New York: The Guilford Press.

Tracy, J. & Robins, R. (2007a). The nature of pride, In J. Tracy, R. Robins & J. Tangney (Eds), *The Self-Conscious Emotions: Theory and Research* (pp. 263–282). New York: The Guilford Press.

Tracy, J. & Robins, R. (2007b). The self in self-conscious emotions. In J. Tracy, R. Robins & J. Tangney (Eds), *The Self-Conscious Emotions: Theory and Research* (pp. 3–20). New York: The Guilford Press

Tracy, J. & Matsumoto, D. (2008). The spontaneous expression of pride and shame: Evidence for biologically innate nonverbal displays. *Proceedings of the National Academy of Sciences of the USA, 105*, 11655–11660.

Trezza, V., Baarendse, P. & Vanderschuren, L. (2011). The pleasures of play: pharmacological insights into social reward mechanisms. *Trends in Pharmacological Sciences, 31*, 463–469.

Trivers, R. (1971). The evolution of reciprocal altruism. *The Quarterly Review of Biology, 46*, 35–57.

Trivers, R. (1972). Parental investment and sexual selection. In B. Campbell (Ed.), *Sexual Selection and the Descent of Man* (pp. 136–179). London: Heinemann.

Trivers, R. & Willard, D. (1973). Natural selection of parental ability to vary the sex ratio of offspring. *Science, 179*, 90–92.

Trivers, R. (1974). Parent-offspring conflict. *American Zoologist, 14*, 249–264.

Trivers, R. (1985). *Social Evolution*. Reading, Mass.: The Benjamin/Cummings Publishing Company.

Trivers, R. (2002). *Natural Selection and Social Theory: Selected Papers of Robert Trivers*. Oxford: Oxford University Press.

Troisi, A. (2008). Psychopathology and mental illness. In C. Crawford & D. Krebs (Eds), *Foundations of Evolutionary Psychology* (pp. 453–474). New York: Lawrence Erlbaum associates.

Tudge, C. (1996). *The Time Before History: 5 Million Years of Human Impact*. New York: Scribner.

Tudge, C. (2000). *The Variety of Life: A Survey and Celebration of all the Creatures that Have Ever Evolved*. Oxford: Oxford University Press.

Tudge, C. (2005). *The Secret Life of Trees: How They Live and Why They Matter*. London: Penguin Books.

Turner, A. & Antón, M. (2004). *Evolving Eden: An Illustrated Guide to the Evolution of the African Large-Mammal Fauna*. New York: Columbia University Press.

Turner, J. (1997). The evolution of emotions: The nonverbal basis of human social organization. In U. Segerstrale & P. Molnár (Eds), *Nonverbal Communication: Where Nature Meets Culture* (pp. 211–223). Mahwah, NJ: Lawrence Erlbaum.

Turner, J. (2000). *On the Origin of Human Emotions: A Sociological Inquiry into the Evolution of Human Affect*. Stanford, CA: Stanford University Press.

Turner, J. (2003). *Human Institutions: A Theory of Societal Evolution*. Lanham: Rowman & Littlefield Publishers.

Turner, J. (2007). *Human Emotions: A Sociological Theory*. London: Routledge.

Turella, L. et al. (2009). Mirror neurons in humans: Consisting or confounding evidence? *Brain & Language, 108*, 10–21.

Tylor, E. (1871). *Primitive Culture*. London: Murray.

U

Uttal, W. (2001). *The New Phrenology: The Limits of Localizing Cognitive Processes in the Brain*. Cambridge, Mass.: The MIT Press.

Uttal, W. (2009). *Distributed Neural Systems: Beyond the New Phrenology*. Cornwall-on-Hudson, N.Y.: Sloan Publishing.

Uttal, W. (2011). *Mind and Brain: A Critical Appraisal of Cognitive Neuroscience*. Cambridge, Mass.: The MIT Press.

V

Valentine, E. (1997). *Conceptual Issues in Psychology*. London: Routledge.

Valentine, J., Collins, A. & Meyer, C. (1994). Morphological complexity increases in metazoans. *Paleobiology, 20*, 131–142.

VandenBos, G. (Ed.) (2007). *APA Dictionary of Psychology*. Washington, DC: American Psychological Association.

Vanderschuren, L. (2010). How the brain makes play fun. *American Journal of Play, 2*, 315–337.

Vanhaeren, M. et al. (2006). Middle Paleolithic shell beads in Israel and Algeria. *Science, 312*, 1785–1788.

Van Hooff, J. (1972). A comparative approach to the phylogeny of laughter and smiling, in R. Hinde (Ed.), *Non-Verbal Communication* (pp. 209–241). Cambridge: Cambridge University Press.

Van Hooff, J. & Preuschoft, S. (2003). Laughter and smiling: The intertwining of nature and culture. In F. de Waal & P. Tyack (Eds), *Animal Social Complexity: Intelligence, Culture, and Individualized Societies* (pp. 260–287). Cambridge, Mass.: Harvard University Press.

Van der Post, D. & Hogeweg, P. (2009). Cultural inheritance and diversification of diet in variable environments. *Animal Behaviour, 78,* 155–166.

Varga, S. (2011). Defining mental disorder: Exploring the 'natural function' approach. *Philosophy, Ethics, and Humanities in Medicine, 6,* 1–10.

Vargha-Khadem, F. et al, (1995). Praxic and nonverbal cognitive deficits in a large family with a genetically transmitted speech and language disorder. *Proceedings of the National Academy of Sciences of the United States of America, 92,* 930–933.

Vargha-Khadem, F. et al., (2005). FOXP2 and the neuroanatomy of speech and language. *Nature Reviews Neuroscience, 6,* 131–138.

Vermeij, G. (2004). *Nature: An Economic History,* Princeton: Princeton University Press.

Vick, S., Waller, B. & Parr, L. (2007). A cross-species comparison of facial morphology and movement in humans and chimpanzees using the facial action coding system. *Journal of Nonverbal Behavior, 31,* 1–20 (see p. 203).

Visalberghi, E. (2009). Distribution of potential suitable hammers and transport of hammer tools and nuts by wild capuchin monkeys. *Primates, 50,* 95–104.

Von Staden, H. (1989). *The Art of Medicine in Early Alexandria.* Cambridge: Cambridge University Press.

Von Staden, H. (1992). The discovery of the body: Human dissection and its cultural contexts in ancient Greece. *The Yale Journal of Biology and Medicine, 65,* 223–241.

W

Wakefield, J. (1992a). The concept of mental disorder: On the boundary between biological facts and social values. *American Psychologist, 47,* 373–388.

Wakefield, J. (1992b). Disorder as harmful dysfunction: A conceptual critique of *DSM-III-R's* definition of mental disorder. *Psychological Review, 99,* 232–247.

Wakefield, J. (2001). Evolutionary history versus current causal role in the definition of disorder: reply to McNally. *Behavioral Research and Therapy, 39,* 347–366.

Wakefield, J. (2005). Biological function and dysfunction. In D. Buss (Ed.), *The Handbook of Evolutionary Psychology* (pp. 878–902). Hoboken, N.J.: John Wiley & Sons, Inc.

Wakefield, J. Horwitz, A. & Schmitz, M. (2005). Are we overpathologizing the socially anxious? Social phobia from a harmful, dysfunction perspective. *Canadian Journal of Psychiatry, 50,* 317–319 (see p.313).

Waller, B. & Dunbar, R. (2005). Differential behavioral effects of silent bared teeth display and relaxed open mouth display in chimpanzees (*Pan Troglodytes*). *Ethology, 111,* 129–142.

Waller, B. et al. (2008). Selection for universal facial emotion. *Emotion, 8,* 435–439.

Ward, J. (2010). *The Student's Guide to Cognitive Neuroscience.* Hove and New York: Psychology Press.

Ward, J. (2012). *The Student's Guide to Social Neuroscience.* Hove and New York: Psychology Press.

Wason, P. (1966). Reasoning. In Foss, B. (Ed.), *New Horizons in Reasoning* (pp. 135–151). Harmondsworth: Penguin Books.

Watson, J. (1924). *Behaviorism.* Chicago: University of Chicago Press.

Watson, K. et al. (2010). Neuroethology of pleasure. In M. Kringelbach & K. Berridge (Eds), *Pleasures of the Brain* (pp. 85–95). Oxford: Oxford University Press.

Watts, I. (1999). The origin of symbolic culture. In R. Dunbar et al. (Eds), *The Evolution of Human Culture* (pp. 113–146). Edinburgh: Edinburgh University Press.

Waynforth, D. (2010). Evolution, obesity, and why children so often choose the unhealthy eating option. *Medical Hypothesis, 74,* 934–936.

Waynforth, D. & Dunbar, R. (1995). Conditional mate choice strategies in humans: Evidence from 'lonely hearts' advertisements. *Behaviour: An International Journal of Behavioural Biology, 132,* 755–779 (see p. 112).

Webster, G. (2007a). What's in a name? Is 'Evolutionary psychology' eclipsing 'sociobiology' in the scientific literature? *Evolutionary Psychology, 5,* 683–695.

Webster, G. (2007b). Evolutionary theory in cognitive neuroscience: A 20-year quantitative review of publication trends. *Evolutionary Psychology, 5,* 520–530.

Webster, G., Jonason, P. & Orozco, T. (2009). Hot topics in evolutionary psychology: Analysis of title words and citation counts in *Evolution and Human Behavior, 1979–2008). Evolutionary Psychology, 7,* 348–362.

Weinfeld, N. et al. (1999). The nature of individual differences in infant-caregiver attachment: Conceptual and empirical aspects of security. In J. Cassidy & P. Shaver (Eds), *Handbook of Attachment: Theory, Research and Clinical Applications* (pp. 78–101). New York: Guilford Press.

Weisberg, R. (2006). Modes of expertise in creative thinking: evidence from case studies. In K. Anders Ericsson et al. (Eds), *The Cambridge Handbook of Expertise and Expert Performance* (pp. 761–787). Cambridge: Cambridge University Press.

Weisemann, A. (1893). *The Gene Plasm: A Theory of Heredity*, New York: Scribner (see p. 11).

Weisfeld, G, et al. (2003). Possible olfaction-based mechanisms in human kin recognition and inbreeding avoidance. *Journal of Experimental Child Psychology, 85*, 279–295.

West, S., Griffin, A. & Gardner, A. (2007). Evolutionary explanations for cooperation. *Current Biology, 17*, R661–R672.

West, S., El Mouden, C. & Gardner, A. (2011). Sixteen common misconceptions about the evolution of cooperation in humans. *Evolution and Human Behavior, 32*, 231–262.

Westermarck, E. (1891). *The History of Human Marriage*. London: MacMillan.

White, D., Dill, L. & Crawford, C. (2007). A common, conceptual framework for behavioral ecology and evolutionary psychology. *Evolutionary Psychology, 5*, 275–288.

White, R. (2003). *Prehistoric Art: The Symbolic Journey of Mankind*. New York: Harry N. Abrams.

Whiten, A. & Byrne, R. (1988). Tactical deception in primates. *Behavioral and Brain Sciences, 11*, 233–273.

Whiten, A. et al. (1999). Cultures in chimpanzees, *Nature, 399*, 682–685.

Whiten, A. et al. (2001). Charting cultural variation in chimpanzees. *Behaviour, 138*, 1481–1516.

Whiten, A. et al. (2003). Cultural panthropology. *Evolutionary Anthropology, 12*, 92–105.

Whiten, Andrew et al. (2004). How do apes ape? *Learning and Behaviour, 32*, 36–52.

Whiten, A. (2005). The second inheritance system of chimpanzees and humans. *Nature, 437*, 52–55.

Whiten, A. (2009). The identification and differentiation of culture in chimpanzees and other animals: from history to diffusion experiments. In K. Laland & B. Galef (Eds), *The Question of Animal Culture* (pp. 99–124). Cambridge, Mass.: Harvard University Press.

Whiten, A. et al. (2011). Culture evolves. *Philosophical Transactions of the Royal Society B, 366*, 938–948.

Whiten, A. et al. (Eds) (2012). *Culture Evolves*. Oxford: Oxford University Press.

Whitehead, H. & Richerson, P. (2009). The evolution of conformist social learning can cause populations collapse in realistically variable environments. *Evolution and Human Behavior, 30*, 261–273.

Whybrow, P. (2005). *American Mania: When More Is Not Enough*. New York: W.W. Norton & Company.

Wickens, A. (2009). *Introduction to Biopsychology*. Harlow England: Pearson.

Wilkinson, D. (2000). Running with the Red Queen: Reflections on 'sex versus non-sex versus parasite'. *Oikos, 91*, 589–596.

Wilkinson, G. (1984). Reciprocal food sharing in the vampire bat. *Nature, 308*, 181–184.

Wilkinson, G. (1988) Reciprocal altruism in bats and other mammals. *Ethology and Sociobiology, 9*, 85–100.

Williams, G. (1966). *Adaptation and Natural Selection: A Critique of some Current Evolutionary Thought*. Princeton: Princeton University Press.

Wilmer, J. et al. (2010). Human face recognition ability is specific and highly heritable. *Proceedings of the National Academy of Sciences of the United States of America, 107*, 5238–5241.

Wilson, E. (1975, 2000). *Sociobiology: The New Synthesis*. Cambridge, Mass.: The Belknap Press of Harvard University Press.

Wilson, E. (1992). *The Diversity of Life*. London: Penguin Books.

Wilson, E. (1998). *Consilience: The Unity of Knowledge*, New York: Alfred Knopf.

Wilson, E. & Hölldobler, B. (2005). Eusociality: Origin and consequences. *Proceedings of the National Academy of Sciences of the USA, 192*, 13367–13371.

Wilson, E. (2006). *The Creation: An Appeal to Save Life on Earth*. New York: W. W. Norton & Company.

Wilson, M., Daly, M. & Daniele, A. (1995). Familicide: The killing of spouses and children, *Aggressive Behavior, 21*, 275–291.

Wishaw, I. (2003). Did a change in sensory control of skilled movements stimulate the evolution of the primate frontal cortex? *Behavioral Brain Research, 146*, 31–41.

Wolf, A. (1995). *Sexual attraction and Childhood Association: A Chinese Brief for Edward Westermarck*. Stanford, Cal.: Stanford University Press.

Wolf, A. (2004). Explaining the Westermarck effect. In A. Wolf & W. Durham (Eds), *Inbreeding, Incest, and the Incest Taboo* (pp. 76–92). Stanford, Cal.: Stanford University Press.

Wolf, A. & Durham, W. (Eds) (2004). *Inbreeding, Incest, and the Incest Taboo*. Stanford, Cal.: Stanford University Press.

Wood, B. & Harrison, T. (2011). The evolutionary context of the first hominins. *Nature, 470*, 347–352.

Wrangham, R. (1980). An ecological model of female-bonded primate groups. *Behaviour, 75*, 262–300.

Wrangham, R. (1993). The evolution of sexuality in chimpanzees and bonobo's. *Human Nature, 4*, 47–79.

Wrangham, R. (2009). *Catching Fire: How Cooking made Us Human*. London: Profile Books Ltd.

Wrangham, R. & Carmody, R. (2010). Human adaptation to the control of fire. *Evolutionary Anthropology, 19*, 187–199.

Wrangham, R. et al. (1998). Dietary response of chimpanzees and cercopithecines to seasonal variation in fruit abundance. I. Antifeedants. *International Journal of Primatology, 19*, 49–970.

Wynne-Edwards, V. (1962). *Animal Dispersion in Relation to Social Behavior*. Edinburgh: Oliver and Boyd.

X

Xu, X. (2006). Scales, feathers and dinosaurs. *Nature, 440*, 287–288.

Y

Ybarra, O. et al. (2008). Mental exercising through simple socializing: Social Interaction promotes general cognitive functioning. *Personality and Social Psychology Bulletin, 34*, 248–259.

Yoder, A. (2007). Lemurs: Quick guide. *Science, 17*, 866–868.

Z

Zeifman, D. (2001). An ethological analysis of human infant crying: Answering Tinbergen's questions. *Developmental Psychobiology, 39*, 265–285

Zhou, W. et al. (2005). Discrete hierarchical organization of social group sizes. *Proceedings of the Royal Society London B, 272*, 439–444.

Zimmer, C. (2008). The evolution of extraordinary eyes: The cases of flatfishes and stalk-eyed flies. *Evolution: Education and Outreach, 1*, 487–492.

Index

adaptation 13–14, 24, 37, 52, 109, 200, 216, 229, 289, **338**

adaptationism 22, 24, **338**

adrenarche 128, 137, **338**

affinity 157–8, **338**

agriculture 277, 278–9, 311–12, 334

allogrooming 161

alloparental care 132–4, 151, 152, **338**

altruism 37, 39, 132–3, 136, 161, 165, **338**

amygdala 28, 29, 178, 187, 190, 191, 194, 333, **338**

analogies 14, 26, 51–2, **338**

anger 176, 178, 183, 187, 190, 195, 196, 197, 198, 200, 201, 294

anisogamy 90–1, **338**

anterior cingulate cortex (ACC) 190, 213, 214, **338**

anthropocentrism 26, 59–60, 64, 66, 75, **338**

apes 4, 24, 56, 59, 66, 74, 80, 83, 133, 135, 138, 139, 200, 227, 228, 236, 248, 253, 264
    classification 67–8
    cognitive capacities in 216–17, 218–19, 220, 221
    great *see separate entry*
    social life 150, 155, 156, 157, 195, 199, 200

asexual reproduction 50, 89, 90, 160

attention deficit hyperactivity disorder (ADHD) 334–5, **338**

baboons 72, 97, 98, 121, 139, 149, 150, 218, 246, 247, 254, 256, 310

behaviourism 18–21, 27

biology 6–17, 273, 274

bipedalism 4, 75, 77, 303–4, 321, **338**

bipolar disorder 305, 306

birds 7, 29, 66, 89, 91, 92, 93, 96, 220, 300
    adaptation in Galápagos finches 13–14
    alloparental care 133
    analogies 15, 51, 52, **338**
    biparental care 128
    birdsong 235, 238, 239, 240–1, 245, 246, 249–51, 256–7
    brain size 212
    corvids, cognitive capacities in 216–18, 219–20, 221

culture 262, 263, 264, 265, 268
    family living 125, 126, 127, 128, 329
    fear 178, 180
    feathers 326–7
    geological timescale 56, 58
    monogamy 96, 105, 135
    parrots 52, 216, 220, 249, 264, 300
    plants 72
    play 219, 220, 316, 327, 329, 330, 331
    predators 152
    ravens *see separate entry*
    selection pressures for cognition 222
    sociality 150, 160

body mass index (BMI) 40, 109, **338**

bonobo Kanzi 83, 245

brain and cognition 4, 21, 26, 27, 39, 52, 157, 201, 206, 309, 335
    cognitive capacities in apes and corvids 216–21
    cognitive origin of language 83–4, 251–7
    cooperation, cognitive capacities for 165–72
    dopamine *see separate entry*
    emotions 176, 177, 178, 187–94, 213, 300, 305, 329
    group size and neocortex size 255
    human brain, distinctiveness of 211–14, 324–5
    human brain size, reasons for increased 215, 246
    maturation of brain 47, 48
    memes 270–3
    mental gap between man and ape 227, 228
    metabolism 40, **343**
    need for 206–7, 209
    omega-3 fatty acids 132
    primate evolution 72, 74, 179, 212
    selection pressures for great ape cognition 221–5
    serotonin 194, 290, 310–11, **345**
    social cognition in chimpanzees and humans 226–30
    weaning 130, **346**
    see also amygdala; Broca's area; neocortex; prefrontal cortex; thalamus

brainstem 188, 309, **338**
Broca's area 243–4, 245, 246, **338**

Cambrian explosion 58, 274, 325–6, **339**
Cenozoic 24, 58, 72–4, **339**
cheating 165, 167, 170–2
childhood 12, 141, 241, 241–2, 277, 296–7,
    311, 316, 317, 322, 323, 328, 330, 332
    emotions 195–6, 311
    language 228, 247, 249, 252, 253, 257
    playing and schooling 334–5
    reproduction in later life: effect of 126–8,
        137, 324
    see also fathers, mothers and others
chimpanzees 46, 60, 65, 66, 68, 75, 100, 121,
    130, 134–5, 197, 296, 317
    brain and cognition 26, 212, 213, 214, 217,
        218–19, 220, 221, 226–30, 303, 324–5
    communication 241, 242–3, 248, 252, 253,
        256
    culture 262, 263, 264, 265, 267, 281, 282
    dominance 150, 197, 310, **339**
    facial expressions 176, 184–7
    mutualism 163, 164, **343**
    polygynandry 98, **344**
    social cognition in humans and 226–30
    social life 150, 152, 157, 167–70, 197, 199,
        310
    tool-making/use 79, 217, 221
    weaning 130, 131, 132, **346**
cognition see brain and cognition
communication see language
complexity 26, 48–51, 159, 224–5, 227
    group size 152, 156, 212, 227, 255–7
    levels of social 150–1, 158
convergent evolution 216–17, **339**
cooperation see social life
corvids 216–18, 219–20, 221, **339**
    see also crows; jays; ravens
crayfish 209–11
creativity 282, 302–8, **339**
crows 216, 217, 281
culture 12, 16, 170, 206, 207, 262, 273–4, 294,
    297, **339**
    beauty and body adornment 105, 106, 109
    facial expressions 182–3, 185, 297
    grades of 265–7
    humans and other animals 263–5, 267, 281
    inbreeding avoidance 120
    infanticide 139, **342**
    inheritance 268–73
    language and 239–40, 257
    meaning of 262–8

niche construction theory 274–6, 278–9,
    280, 326, **344**
problems and solutions in evolution 43,
    44, 47–8, 52
ratchet effect 265, 280–2, 334, **345**
shame 197
unbiased and biased transmission 269–70
see also gene–culture coevolution

Darwin, Charles 3, 7–9, 12, 13, 18, 26, 56,
    60–1, 89, 91–2, 93, 103, 104, 119–20,
    132, 176, 179–82, 184, 249–50, 317
depression 289, 294–5, 296, 297, 305, 306,
    310–11, **339**
designer fallacy 6–7, **339**
development see evo-devo
diseases 39, 40, 46–7, 90, 94, 109, 191
disgust 37, 178, 185, 187, 190–1, 195
dispersal 121, 126, 157, 199, **339**
divorce 136, 137, 297
DNA 13, 44, 75, 270, 319, 321, **339**
dolphins 26, 50, 52, 75, 216, 220, 239, 300
dominance 150, 164, 165, 197, 200, 218, 247,
    249, 254, 310–11, **339**
dopamine 194, 290, **339**
    dopaminergic system 300, 305, 307, 327,
        328, **339**
    theory of mental illness 289, 297, 298–304

ecological inheritance 274–5, 279, **340**
ecology and social evolution 153–6, 157, 199
egalitarian societies 37, 39, 101
embryonic development, human 317–19, 321,
    322
emotions 3–4, 37, 75, 176, 294–7, **340**
    Darwin and expression of 176, 179–82, 184
    definition 177
    emergence of social 195–201, 222, 311
    fear see separate entry
    function of positive 201
    music and language 250
    negativity bias in 178, **343**
    neural basis of 187–94, 213, 300, 305, 329
    primates, facial expressions in 184–7
    reason for evolution of 176–83
    universality of facial expressions 28,
        182–3, 297
encephalisation 72, 212, **340**
eusociality 51, 52, 133, 160, 165, **340**
evo-devo 12, 18, 27, **340**
    mammals: why they play 327–32
    play evolved through development 332–5
    rise of 316–22

types of developmental reorganisation 322–7
eyes 30, 52, 72, 212, 214, 309, 324
  forward-projecting 69, 70, 72

face recognition 22–3, 24, 170, 201
facial expressions 25, 176, 178, 179–82, 182–3, 191, 198, 227, 272
  language 245, 250
  primates 184–7
  universality of 28, 182–3, 297
false beliefs 227, 229–30, 252
  fixed 293, 304
fathers, mothers and others 38, 119, 301, 317, 329, 333–4
  alloparental care 132–4, 151, 152, **338**
  birth spacing 38, 39, 130, 138
  definition of family 125
  definition of parental care 130
  female care is rule 128
  great ape problem 130–2
  inbreeding avoidance 37, 39, 119–24, 165
  language and bonding 239
  origin of human family 125–8, 323–4
  parent-offspring conflict 131, 137, 138–44
  parental investment *see separate entry*
  paternal child care 134–8, 157
fear 4, 27–30, 37, 176, 195, 196, 197
  amygdala 28, 190, 194, 333, **338**
  anger arouses 200
  facial expression 183, 187
  mental illness 294
  narrows attention 201
  negativity bias 178, **343**
  origin of 29
  phobias 29, 37, 39, 289, 292, 308–10
female kin-bonding 157, 165, 195, 199–200, 222, 334, **340**
females *see* males and females
fitness 24, 48, 90, 95, 134, 200, 216, 316, 327, **340**
  African lions 153
  communication and language 239
  inbreeding depression 119, **342**
  inclusive 132–3, 134, 138–9, 159, 161, **342**
  infant vocalisations 239
  mate choice of children 142
  mental illness 289, 292, 297
foraging 38, 132, 142, 149, 153, 199, 263, 264, 298, 334
  brain and cognition 179, 217, 222, 224, 225
  group size 152
  learning by association 20

mate choice 94
origin of language and 257
primate grasping hands and feet 72
social evolution of primates 155–6, 157
free riding 164

game theory 161–2
gaze following 227, 228–9, 252, 253
gene pool 45, 216, 269, 278, **340**
genes 11, 13, 245–6, 319, 321, 322, 326
  horizontal gene transfer 11, 14–15
genetic determinism 21, 46, **340**
gene–culture coevolution 24–5, 38–9, 42, 43, 48, 276–80, 311–12, **340**
genome 43, 44–7, 48, 159, 160, 206, 269, 278, **340**
genomics 45–6, **340**
geological timescale 24, 56–8, **341**
gestural origin of language 240–6
gibbons 68, 96, 97, 101, 105, 156, 157, 246
grandmothers 133–4, 137, 139
grasping limbs 69, 70, 72, 74
great apes 68, 125, 130–2, 134, 199, **341**
  chimpanzees *see separate entry*
  cognition: selection pressures 221–5
  gestural communication 241–3
  mating systems in African apes 98, 100
grooming 150, 159, 160, 161, 163, 164, 184, 194, 249, 263, 265, **341**
  language as substitute for 254–7

Hamilton's rule *see* inclusive fitness
history of evolutionary psychology 3–6
  biology 6–17, 273, 274
  neuroscience 20–1, 25–30, 274
  psychology 17–25, 274
homicide 139, 141
hominids 68, 75–6, 195, **341**
  great apes *see separate entry*
hominins 68, 77, 257, **341**
homologies 14, 26, 51, 185–7, 243–4, 272, 322, 335, **341**
human behavioural ecology 24, 37–8, 39
  obesity 41–2, 43, **344**
hunter-gatherer societies 37, 38, 42, 83, 100, 101, 105, 108, 278, 301
  alloparental care 133
  father's death and child mortality 137
  marriage types 142
  Pleistocene epoch 24, **344**
  snakes 309
  social bonding 254
  weaning 132, **346**

hypertension 40, 311
hypomania 306, **341**
hypothalamus 191, **341**

imagination 218–20, 222, 264, 268, 301, **341**
imitation 227, 239, 244, 263, 264, 265, 268, 269–70, **342**
    memes 270–3
    ratcheting 282
inbreeding 37, 39, 119–24, 165, **342**
inbreeding depression 119, 121, **342**
inclusive fitness 132–3, 134, 138–9, 159, 161, **342**
industrialisation 279
infanticide 136, 139–40, 141, 142, 152, **342**
inheritance 10, 11–13, 142, 181, **342**
    cultural 268–73
    epigenetic 12, 301, **340**
    genes *see separate entry*
innovation *see* creativity
intrasexual and intersexual selection 92–3, 95, 238–9, **342**
invertebrates 29, 104, 149, 207, 209–11, 281, 331, **342**

jays 125, 150, 216, 217–18, 221

kinship 121, 156–8, 247, 254
kissing 136

lactose tolerance 277, 311–12
Lamarck, Jean-Baptiste 11, 60, 181
language 12, 21, 39, 75, 80, 83, 227, 235, 263, 265, **342**
    animal communication 237–8
    baby talk hypothesis 257
    cognitive origin of 83–4, 251–7
    components of human communication 240–1
    dopamine 302
    gaze following 228
    generalisations 240
    gestural origin of 240–6
    grooming replaced by 254–7
    need for 254
    origin of flexible communication 82, 235–40, 268
    social functions of 254–7
    vocal origin of 246–51
larynx 248, 254, **342**
laughter 184–5, 187, 251
learning 29, 38, 47, 48, 269, 310
    by association 19, 27, 218

social *see separate entry*
    vocal 241, 245, 247, 249–51
    see also gene–culture coevolution
lemurs 24, 67, 97, 121, 153, 155–6
    female kin-bonding 157, 199
life-history theory 126–8, 137, 323–4, **342**
limbic system 188–9, 190, **342**
lineage 60–1, 64, **342**
lions 150, 152–3, 163, 168, 184, 220

macaque monkeys 38–9, 98, 101, 131, 243–4, 247, 272, 282
male-kin bonding 157, 165, 195, 199–200, **343**
males and females 37, 89, 309
    anomaly of women's attractiveness 103–4
    female preferences 109–14
    male preferences 105–9
    mating systems in human evolution 96–102, 135–6, 157, 254
    parental investment: sex-bias 140–1
    sexual reproduction *see separate entry*
    sexual selection *see separate entry*
    shift to monogamous mating 104–5
mammals 58, 59, 67, 69, 70, 72, 91, 114, 309, 325
    allogrooming 161
    alloparental care 133
    brain and cognition 212, 213, 216, 220, 222, 300
    communication 239, 252
    core-self 196
    culture 264
    facial expression 184
    family groups 125
    maternal dominance 141
    parental care 128
    play 220, 316, 327–32, 335
    social life 150, 155–6
mania 305–6, **343**
manipulation and cooperation 164
marriage 142, 157, 165, 169
mass media 106, 311
mate preferences: parents and offspring 142–4
mating competition, forms of 93–4
mating intelligence 114, **343**
mating systems in human evolution 96–102, 104, 135–6, 157, 254
memory 227, 240, 290, 302, 304, 307, 308
    decay 167, 170
    foraging 224
menopause 134, **343**

mental illness 289
  byproduct theory 289, 297, 303–8
  defining 289–93
  distinguishing normal responses from 289,
    293–7
  dopamine theory 289, 297, 298–304
  mismatch theory 289, 297, 308–12
metabolism 40, 330, **343**
migration out of Africa 298–9, 301
Miocene 24, 74, 157, 199–200, 222, 224, 225,
  343
mirror nuerons 243–6, 272
mitochondria 15, 51, 61, 159, 160, **343**
mitochondrial genome 44, 159, 160, **343**
modularity 22–3, 37, 39, 170, **343**
  obesity 40–1, 42, 43, **344**
monogamy 96, 97, 125, 254, **343**
  different forms of 105, 136
  emergence of 98–101
  paternal care 135–6
  serial 97, 105, **345**
  shift to 104–5
mosaic evolution 212, **343**
music 12, 250–1, 269, 272
mutation 9, 16, 245–6, **343**
mutualism 160, 163–4, 165, **343**

natural selection 7, 9–11, 13–15, 18, 27, 77,
  216, 274, 280, **343**
  brain structures 212
  communication 237, 238, 247
  Darwin's theory of sexual selection
    91–2
  emotions 176, 178, 181, 182
  evo-devo 316–17, **340**
  human cultural practices 277, 311
  inbreeding avoidance 121, 123
  inclusive fitness 133, **342**
  mental illness 289, 294, 297, 303–4
  parental investment: sex-bias 140–1
  sex and recombination 90
  sexual selection see separate entry
neocortex 23, 25, 189, 200, 212, 213–14, 227,
  255, 335, **343**
nervous system 43, 44, 47, 48, 206, 269
  from diffuse to central 207–11
neuromodulation 193–4, **343**
neuroscience 20–1, 24–30, 215, 272–3, 274,
  309
niche construction theory 274–6, 278–9, 280,
  326, **344**
nuclear genome 44, 61, **344**
numerical discrimination 166–7

obesity 40–3, 308, 311, **344**
obsessive-compulsive disorder (OCD) 305
opiods 194, **344**
ornamentation 89, 91–2, 103, 103–9, 113
ovulatory shift hypothesis 112–14
own-race bias (ORB) 201

parent-offspring conflict 131, 137, 138–44
parental investment 95–6, 104, 110, 113, 121,
  126–7, 137, 138–9, **344**
  definition of 130
  factors affecting 139–42
  nursing 131, 138, 141
parenting see fathers, mothers and others
parrots 52, 216, 220, 249, 264, 300
paternity certainty 135–6
peacocks 89, 91, 92, 94
phenotypes 22, 27, 121, 316–17, 321, **344**
philopatry 121, **344**
phobias 29, 37, 39, 289, 292, 308–10
phylogenomics 45–6
phylogeny 66, 69, 72–4, 75–6, 98, 239, **344**
  social evolution and 156
  see also tree of life
plants 35, 43, 59, 72, 89, 96, 206
play 219–20, 237, 241, 242, 256, 303, 316,
  344
  evolved through development 332–5
  mammals: why they 327–32
polyandry 93, 98, **344**
polygynandry 97–8, **344**
polygyny 96, 97, 98, 100, 101–2, 105, 125,
  139, **344**
predation 24, 36, 91, 96, 238, 241, 246, 299,
  318, 330
  brain and cognition 207, 211, 216,
    222, 228
  central nervous systems 43, 211
  chimpanzees 163
  creative capacities 39
  eyes 29, 30, 49, 72
  group living 152, 155, 156, 160, 223
  limbic system 188
  mate choice 94
  mutualism 163, **343**
  origin of fear 29
  paternity certainty 136
  projectile throwing 101
  savannah 200, **345**
  tools as weapons 37
prefrontal cortex (PFC) 190, 191, 194,
  212–14, 300, 302, 333, **344**
pride 178, 195, 196, 197, 198, 201, 311

primates 24, 47, 56, 58, 59–60, 125, 296, 298, 299, 325, **344**
  alloparental care 132, 133, **338**
  apes *see separate entry*
  brain and cognition 72, 74, 206, 212, 213–14, 220, 226, 227, 228
  classification of 66–8
  communication: non-human 235, 241–3, 246–8, 251, 253, 254, 255–6
  culture: non-human 263, 264
  defining characters of 68–70
  differences between males and females 91
  emotions 4, 176, 179, 184–7
  female preferences 109
  group size and neocortex size 255
  human characteristics 4, 74–84, 305–6
  inbreeding avoidance 121
  infanticide 136, 139, **342**
  main stages in evolution 72–4
  mating systems in 97–8, 99, 100, 101, 104, 135–6, 156
  mother–infant play 333–4
  origin of 70–2
  origin of term 66
  personality: non-human 303
  reproductive problem of great apes 130–2
  social learning: non-human 38–9
  social life 70, 149, 150, 152, 153–9, 163, 164, 165, 179, 199, 334
  tree of life 65–6
prisoner dilemmas 162
problems and solutions in evolution 35
  complexity, levels of 48–51, 159
  gene-culture coevolution 38–9, 42, 43, 48, **340**
  genome, nervous system and culture as solutions 43–8
  human behavioural ecology 37–8, 39, 41–2, 43
  meaning of problem 35–6
  modular evolutionary psychology 37, 39, 40–1, 42, 43
  obesity 40–3, **344**
  replaying tape of life 51–2
prospective thinking 221
puberty 128, 137–8, 323, 324, 332, **345**
punishment and cooperation 161, 164, 165

ravens 26, 52, 79, 150, 163, 206, 217, 219–20, 221
recapitulation 18, 317–18, **345**
reciprocity 160–3, 167, **345**
recordkeeping 167, 170–1

recursion 240–1, 282
Red Queen hypothesis 90
reflex 178–9, 194, **345**
religions 164
ritualisation 185, 237–8, 242, 249, **345**

sadness 177, 178, 182, 183, 184, 187, 195, 289, 295–7
savannahs 4, 24, 72, 77, 200, **345**
schizophrenia 289, 291, 304, 305, 307, 308, 328
selection pressures 14, 29, 39, 40, 42, 47, 51, 52, 101, **345**
  African lions 153
  brain structures 212
  communication 238–40, 253, 254, 255, 256, 257
  corvids and apes 216
  dairy farming 312
  fixed signals 238
  gene–culture coevolution 277
  great ape cognition 221–5
  mind-readers 227
  niche construction theory 274
self-consciousness 195–6
serotonin 194, 290, 310–11, **345**
sex-bias 121, 140–1, 157, 199
sex-role reversal 92–3, 104, **345**
sexual dimorphism 91, 101–2, 106, **345**
sexual reproduction 45, 50–1, 269
  origin of 89–91, 160
sexual selection 91–6, 97, 104, 106, 109–10, 212, 238–9, **345**
shame 37, 195, 196, 197, 198, 311
sign language 243–4, 245, **345**
social bonding and language 254–7
social cognition 226–30, 235, 254
social cohesion 239
social competition 39, 222
social emotions 195–201, 222, 311, **345**
social intelligence 114
  social brain and 226–7
social learning 12, 15, 38–9, 48, 222, 227, 263, 265, 271–2, 281, **345**
  facial expressions 183
  farming and denser settlement 279
  forms of 264
  imitation *see separate entry*
  obesity 42, **344**
social life 23, 37, 47, 70, 75, 149, 216, 227, 317
  cognitive capacities for cooperation 165–72

complexity, levels of social 150–1, 158
complexity, trends towards increasing 48–51, 159
cooperation solutions 158–65
costs and benefits 151–3
defining sociality 149–50
emergence of social emotions 195–201
fossil evidence 83
group size 25, 152, 156, 212, 227, 255–7
primates, social evolution of 153–8, 165, 179, 199, 334
social monogamy 105, 136, **345**
   see also monogamy
sociobiology 22, 38, 274, 280
speech evolution: frame/content theory 249
starlings, European (*Sturnus vulgarus*) 239, 240–1
stepchildren 141
suicide 141
   attempts 138
symbolism 75, 79–84, 236, 264, 268–9, **345**
symmetry, body 208, 324, 325
syntax 240, 247–8, 251, 253, 254, 268, **345**

temperament 177, 299, 303, **346**
temporal discounting 166
thalamus 28, 212, **346**
   arcuate nucleus (ARC) 41, **338**
theory of mind 171, 172, 227, 282, **346**
   components of 251–2
   language 235, 240, 247–8, 251–4
tool-making/use 215, 216, 217, 221, 222, 263, 264, 265, 281, 282

advanced 75, 77–9, 80, 81
hammer and knife 265, 266
language 254
tools-turned-into-weapons 37, 101
traditional human societies 37, 38, 39, 42, 83, 100, 101, 105, 108
   emotional expressions 182
   father's death and child mortality 137
   marriage types 142
   persistence hunting 301
   snakes 309
   weaning 132, **346**
tree of life 15, 56, 59–66
   see also phylogeny

unrelated individuals and cooperation 151, 159, 160–4, 165
   cognitive capacities 165–72

vampire bats 161
vertebrates 26, 27, 46, 52, 56, 133, 184, 191, 207, 208, 228, 240, 252, 316, 318, 321, 324, 325, 326, 331, **346**
vocalisation 245, 253, 254, 255, 256–7, 301, 329, **346**
   tradition/imitation 263, 264, 265, 268
   vocal origin of language 246–51

waist–hip ratio (WHR) 106–9, **346**
weaning 130–2, 133, 138, **346**
Weismann barrier 11–12, 44–5, 319, **346**
whales 52, 211, 239, 246, 263